Download Forms on Nolo.com

You can download the forms in this book at:

www.nolo.com/back-of-book/CTEN.html

We'll also post updates whenever there's an important change to the law affecting this book—as well as articles and other related materials.

More Resources from Nolo.com

Legal Forms, Books, & Software

Hundreds of do-it-yourself products—all written in plain English, approved, and updated by our in-house legal editors.

Legal Articles

Get informed with thousands of free articles on everyday legal topics. Our articles are accurate, up to date, and reader friendly.

Find a Lawyer

Want to talk to a lawyer? Use Nolo to find a lawyer who can help you with your case.

NOLO
LAW for ALL

NOLO **The Trusted Name**
(but don't take our word for it)

"In Nolo you can trust."
THE NEW YORK TIMES

"Nolo is always there in a jam as the nation's premier publisher of do-it-yourself legal books."
NEWSWEEK

"Nolo publications…guide people simply through the how, when, where and why of the law."
THE WASHINGTON POST

"[Nolo's]…material is developed by experienced attorneys who have a knack for making complicated material accessible."
LIBRARY JOURNAL

"When it comes to self-help legal stuff, nobody does a better job than Nolo…"
USA TODAY

"The most prominent U.S. publisher of self-help legal aids."
TIME MAGAZINE

"Nolo is a pioneer in both consumer and business self-help books and software."
LOS ANGELES TIMES

22nd Edition

California Tenants' Rights

Attorneys Janet Portman & J. Scott Weaver

TWENTY-SECOND EDITION	JUNE 2020
Editor	JANET PORTMAN
Book Design	SUSAN PUTNEY
Cover Design	SUSAN PUTNEY
Proofreading	IRENE BARNARD
Index	RICHARD GENOVA
Printing	BANG PRINTING

ISBN: 978-1-4133-2750-2 (pbk)
ISBN: 978-1-4133-2751-9 (ebook)

Please note

We know that accurate, plain-English legal information can help you solve many of your own legal problems. But this text is not a substitute for personalized advice from a knowledgeable lawyer. If you want the help of a trained professional—and we'll always point out situations in which we think that's a good idea—consult an attorney licensed to practice in California.

About the Authors

Janet Portman, an attorney and Nolo's Executive Editor, received undergraduate and graduate degrees from Stanford and a law degree from Santa Clara University. She is an expert on landlord-tenant law and the coauthor of *Every Landlord's Legal Guide, Every Tenant's Legal Guide, Every Landlord's Guide to Finding Great Tenants, Renters' Rights,* and *Negotiate the Best Lease for Your Business.*

J. Scott Weaver, an attorney and coauthor of *California Tenants' Rights,* has been a San Francisco tenant and housing activist for over 40 years. He's spent the last 30 years exclusively representing San Francisco Bay Area tenants. Scott has litigated several hundred tenant cases involving eviction, wrongful eviction, and habitability issues (including mold, asbestos, and bedbugs), and has brought tenant class action lawsuits. He has taught landlord-tenant law at various legal education seminars.

Table of Contents

Appendixes

California Tenants' Rights: Your Legal Companion

What do you do when your landlord refuses to fix the leaky roof, reneges on a promised parking space, or threatens you with eviction? You might be merely annoyed by the discomfort or inconvenience, or intimidated by the fear of losing your home, but in any case you're probably unsure of your rights under the law. This book is the answer.

Tenant Rights and Responsibilities

California tenants enjoy some of the most innovative and thoughtful landlord-tenant protections in the country, but to take advantage of them, you need to know what they are. Here you'll learn the bottom line on your rights as a renter, including privacy, adequate notice of rent increases and terminations, repairs, fair housing, antiretaliation protection, security deposits, and more.

Armed with the information in this book, you can confidently negotiate with your landlord when you sign a lease or rental agreement, knowing what's what in the way of permissible lease terms. Later, as your tenancy continues, you'll know what you can legally expect from the landlord—and how to enforce your rights if you need to.

You'll learn about your responsibilities, too. For example, if your landlord won't perform important repairs, you have the right to withhold rent payments —but only if you're current on the rent.

Eviction Defense in California

The second half of this book is devoted to eviction defense, which will help you if you've been handed a termination notice and have to decide— quickly—what to do next. Should you fight the termination, and risk eviction, or just move out? It's not always an easy decision.

Even if you win, the toll on your time, energy, and wallet will be significant. And winning is never a sure thing, even if you're sure you have a solid legal defense and can prove it. All bets are off once you turn your fate over to a judge or jury. If you lose, you'll have an eviction on your record, which might make it very hard to rent another place to live. It's not illegal for landlords to flatly refuse to rent to people who have lost an eviction lawsuit, and many do just that.

If you do decide to fight the eviction, we'll guide you through the court process. We provide samples of the official forms, explain how to fill them out, and tell you where to file them.

Rent Control

If you live in one of the many California cities that offer tenants the benefits of rent control or eviction defense (or both), you're lucky. If you don't live in one of these cities, you might still be covered by the 2019 Tenant Protection Act—statewide rent control and eviction protection. You'll find helpful summaries of these laws, along with information on how to find local ordinances online (they change frequently) and how to contact the agencies in charge of enforcing them.

Legal Forms, Letters, and Checklists for California Tenants

This book includes dozens of forms, sample letters, notices, and checklists to help you through the entire rental process, from move-in to move- out. Each form is easy to customize for your particular situation. We provide clear instructions and filled- in samples in the text, and you'll find copies in Appendix C; they are also available for download on the Nolo website on a special companion page for this book (see below for details).

Many of the forms in this book were prepared by Nolo attorney-authors. We also include (where appropriate) some official California court forms (used in evictions), published by the Judicial Council of California.

! CAUTION

Who shouldn't use this book? Do not use this book for the following types of rentals:

Commercial property. Legal rules and practices are different for commercial rentals.

Space or a unit in a mobile home park or marina. Unique rules often apply. For details, see the California Department of Housing and Community Development publication, *2019 California Mobilehome Residency Law*, available at www.hcd.ca.gov.

A live/work unit (such as a loft). While you will be subject to most state laws governing residential units, additional requirements imposed by building codes might also apply. Check with your local building inspector's office for the rules governing live/work units.

Government subsidized housing. If you are a tenant in government-subsidized or -owned housing, such as "Section 8" or project-based properties, your lease will contain terms required by the government, which neither you nor your landlord can change.

Condominiums. Tenants who lease a home in a condominium complex are generally on the same legal footing as those who rent single-family homes, which means this book will apply to them. However, condo tenants are also subject to the condominium's operating rules and regulations (known as "CC&Rs"), which may impose obligations or restrictions on tenants and landlords in addition to those found under state, local, and federal law.

Guide to Abbreviations Used in This Book

We use these standard abbreviations throughout this book for important statutes and court cases covering tenants' rights under California and federal law. There may be times when you will want to refer to the complete statute or case. (See Chapter 18 for advice on how to find a specific statute or case and do legal research.)

California Codes

B&P	Business and Professions
CC	Civil
CCP	Civil Procedure
UHC	Uniform Housing Code
H&S	Health and Safety
CCR	California Code of Regulations

Federal Laws

U.S.C.	United States Code
C.F.R.	Code of Federal Regulations

Cases

Cal.App.	California Court of Appeal
Cal.Rptr.	California Court of Appeal and California Supreme Court
Cal.	California Supreme Court
N.J. Spr.	New Jersey Superior Court Reports
A. or A.2d	Atlantic Reporter
S.E. or S.E.2d	South Eastern Reporter
F. Supp.	United States District Court
F.2d	United States Court of Appeal
U.S.	United States Supreme Court

Opinions

Ops. Cal. Atty. Gen.	California Attorney General Opinions

Get Updates, Forms, and More at This Book's Companion Page on Nolo.com

You can download the eviction and other forms (as well as the sample letters) in this book at:

www.nolo.com/back-of-book/CTEN.html

When there are important changes to the information in this book, we'll post updates on this same dedicated page (what we call the book's companion page). See Appendix B for a complete list of forms on Nolo.com, and for advice on downloading forms from the Nolo website.

Looking for a Place and Renting It

Looking for a house or apartment to rent is often a frustrating and time-consuming task. Because it is human nature to become harried and frazzled under pressure, many people make mistakes at this stage that later turn out to be costly, both in time and money. Try to stay cool.

Get Organized and Set Your Rental Priorities

Before you start looking for a place, make a list of your housing needs and priorities, including:

- price range
- location and neighborhood features
- rooms and other interior features
- security
- pets
- parking, and
- transportation, including your commute.

Organize Your Records

It is extremely important that you keep good records. Get a large manila envelope or file folder in which to keep all papers having to do with your rental transaction. Misplacing and losing papers (deposit agreements, leases, rent receipts, and so on) is a common mistake to avoid. Your landlord is in business and has probably learned how not to make such basic mistakes, so you should do the same. Set up a safe place in which to save your papers, receipts, canceled checks, and anything else that you think might possibly be important later.

Once you have a list of your priorities, it's time to start looking. Craigslist and other online resources will usually be your best bet, but also get leads from people you know who live or work near where you want to live. Walk the neighborhoods that interest you and look for "Apartment for Rent" signs. Other good resources include local real estate offices, property management firms that handle rentals in the area, and college housing offices or alumni.

Learn About Leases and Rental Agreements

Before you start looking for a place, you should know a little about rental agreements. First—the most important rule—don't sign any papers until you understand what's in them, or you might regret it later!

Landlords rent their properties using one of these methods:

- a written lease
- a written rental agreement, or
- an oral lease or rental agreement.

An oral lease or rental agreement is made without anything being written down—you just talk over what the deal is and agree to it. The other two, the written lease and the written rental agreement, have all the terms you agree to written down on paper, which you and the landlord sign. Let's look at each in some detail.

Oral Agreements

An oral agreement is just as valid (enforceable by a court) as a written one, as long as it is for a period of one year or less. The landlord agrees to let you move in, and you agree to pay a certain amount of rent on some schedule, like weekly, every other week, or every month. Your payment of rent can be evidence of an agreement to rent, so it's best not to pay in cash (you'll want a canceled check or electronic trail that shows you paid the rent).

If you pay rent monthly, your agreement will be presumed to be month to month. If you pay weekly, then it is week to week. Most oral agreements are month to month and require a 30-day notice for either party to terminate. But after you have lived there for more than a year, the landlord must give a 60-day notice to terminate your tenancy (see Chapter 14 for more on terminations). However, if you live in a city that has rent control, the ordinance limits how much a landlord can increase rents. Limits on the law might also restrict a landlord's ability to evict. (See Appendix A.)

If you live in an area where a state of emergency has been declared due to a natural disaster or man-made disaster, you might have some protection from rent increases greater than 10%. (See Chapter 3 for a fuller explanation.)

An oral agreement has some advantages: It is relatively informal, and you aren't subjected to the long list of terms and rules contained in most written leases and rental contracts. But as time goes by and circumstances change, people's memories can change, too. Then, if a disagreement arises, both sides end up in front of a judge who has to decide whose recollection of the agreement to believe. For this reason, even if you make an oral agreement, it is wise to get some of the landlord's promises in writing. For example, if your landlord promises to make specific repairs, allow you to have a pet, or do anything else that you want to make sure the landlord remembers, write it down and have the landlord date and sign it.

If a landlord will not put agreements in writing, the next best thing to document the promise is to write a confirmation letter or email. An example is: "Dear Mr. Jones, It was a pleasure meeting with you today. Thank you for accepting me as a tenant and agreeing to install a washing machine in the laundry room before I move in next month. I am excited about moving into this house." Email is perfectly acceptable and has advantages because it will be automatically dated. If you have the right email address for the landlord, he won't be able to give you the "I didn't get it" excuse.

Now, suppose the washing machine never shows up, and you want to sue for a reduction in rent, arguing that you're paying for a rental with a washing machine, but have not received it. If Mr. Jones did not dispute your version of the agreement (by writing back, for example), your letter can

be introduced in court as proof that the promise was indeed made, and was part of the reason you rented the place. (See Chapter 7 on how to get the landlord to follow through on promised repairs and improvements.)

Written Leases and Rental Agreements

A written lease and rental agreement are basically the same except for one important difference: The lease fixes all the terms of the agreement for a given period of time—most commonly, one year. When you rent under a lease, your rent cannot be raised until the lease runs out, nor can you be told to move unless you break the terms of the lease or the law. You, too, are expected to perform your obligations under the lease (including rent payments) until it runs out.

A written rental agreement—often called a "month-to-month" agreement—has everything written down, just like the lease, but the time period of your tenancy is not fixed to a period beyond one month. The agreement self-renews every month until you or the landlord terminate it. This means that you can move out or your landlord can order you to move out on 30 days' notice (if you've lived there for more than a year, the landlord must give you 60 days' notice). And if you're renting under a government-subsidized program, you're entitled to 90 days' notice before the landlord can terminate your tenancy.

For rent increases, 30 days' notice is required, but if your landlord raises the rent more than 10% of the lowest rent charged within the previous 12 months, the landlord must give you 60 days' notice. (See "Rent Increase Notices" in Chapter 3 for a full explanation of these rules.) Some communities have rent control that limits how much a landlord can increase a tenant's rent. Many rent control jurisdictions (and some that don't have rent control) have imposed "just cause for eviction" protections that allow eviction for certain specified reasons only. (See Appendix A for a list of cities with "just-cause" eviction provisions.) And as of 2020, statewide rent control will cover many previously unprotected tenants (see Chapter 3).

If you live in an area where a state of emergency has been declared due to a natural disaster or manmade disaster, you might get relief from rent increases greater than 10%. (See Chapter 3 for a fuller explanation.) These rules regarding rent increases and terminations continue to apply when the rental property is sold mid-lease or mid–rental agreement. The new owner simply steps into the shoes of the old owner, bound by the agreements that come with the property. The new landlord must provide you with information on how to contact the new owner, as well as the address where you should send the rent.

Be careful! Because leases and rental agreements look so much alike, a form can look like a lease and sound like a lease, and even cover a year's period, but contain a provision that rent can be raised or that the agreement can be terminated on 30 days' notice (or 60 days for tenants who have been in the rental for a year or more, and 90 days for subsidized tenancies). These rent increase and termination provisions control: the form is really only a written rental agreement.

Read the rental document carefully! It is crucial that you read the entire lease or rental agreement and understand it before you sign it. You will be bound to these terms for as long as you live in the unit. If the main document refers to another document, such as "house rules," make sure you read these, too. If there is any part of the written document that you don't understand, get advice— but not from the people who want you to sign it. If you want your rights protected, you will have to see to it yourself.

Legally, a written agreement can be typed or written down in longhand on any kind of paper, in any words, so long as the terms are legible. However, as a practical matter, nearly all landlords use standard printed forms that they buy in stationery stores or get from landlord associations. These forms have been prepared by lawyers or real estate associations, and they are usually as favorable as possible to the landlord. We will discuss some of the most common provisions below.

If the lease offered to you by the prospective landlord is not satisfactory, it is legal and simple to change it if both parties can agree on the changes. All you do is cross out unwanted portions, write in desired changes, and have all parties who are going to sign the document initial the changes. Make sure that you sign the lease at the same time as the landlord, and that you get a copy then and there. This assures both sides that no changes can be made after only one party has signed.

FORM

You'll find copies of the California-specific fixed-term lease and rental agreement forms in Appendix C, and the companion page for this book on the Nolo website includes downloadable copies (see Appendix B for the link to the companion page). If your landlord doesn't have a written rental agreement, or proposes using a substandard one, use one of our forms instead. They are fair to both landlord and tenant. The only clause that is different in the month-to-month rental agreement is the term of the tenancy (Clause 4). *The California Landlord's Law Book: Rights & Responsibilities*, by Nils Rosenquest and Janet Portman (Nolo), includes these forms, with complete instructions. Online versions of California leases and rental agreements are also available at www.nolo.com.

Foreign Language Note on California Leases and Rental Agreements

If a written lease or month-to-month rental agreement is negotiated primarily in Spanish, Chinese, Tagalog, Vietnamese, or Korean, the landlord must give the tenant a written translation of the lease or rental agreement before it is signed. The only exception is if the tenant provides his or her own interpreter, who can fluently read and write English and the foreign language, and who is not a minor. (CC § 1632.)

Which Is Better, a Lease or a Month-to-Month Rental Agreement?

If you have a lease for a substantial term, like a year or more, you are assured that the landlord cannot end your tenancy or raise the rent so long as you pay your rent on time and meet your other obligations under the lease and the law. This kind of security is extremely valuable where housing is hard to find and rents are rising.

If your unit is covered by the state or a local rent control and eviction control ordinance, your need for the protection that a lease provides is lessened.

Nevertheless, such laws do allow some rent increases, and they usually allow the landlord to evict in order to move himself or a relative into the place. A lease will normally protect you against these dangers.

Of course, if you expect to be moving in a very short time, you may prefer a month-to-month rental agreement, so that you can leave simply by giving 30 days' notice. But don't be too sure that a month-to-month tenancy is what you want. If you're in a tight rental market, it is usually not difficult to "break" a lease if you have to. We discuss this possibility in Chapter 12. Basically, the rule is that if you have a lease and move out before the term is up, the landlord can sue you for the rent until the lease runs out, but must make a reasonable effort to find another tenant. Once a new tenant moves in, your responsibility for the rent ends.

If you prefer a lease, but are worried about some specific event that might force you to leave the area, consider simply providing for that event in the lease. If your boss might transfer you to Phoenix, put a provision in your lease saying something like this: "Tenant can terminate this lease upon 30 days' written notice, provided that, with such notice, Tenant also gives Landlord written proof from Tenant's employer, saying that Tenant is being transferred to a specified location that is more than one hundred miles from Tenant's current workplace."

The written rental agreement is often preferred by landlords. It gives them the right to raise the rent as often as they wish (unless there is a local rent regulation ordinance) and to get rid of tenants that they don't like. In most cases, from a tenant's point of view, the written rental agreement does not have the advantages of a lease.

The Relationship Between State Law, Local Law, and Rental Agreements

As a general rule, a landlord and tenant are free to agree to just about anything, although market conditions and common practices often affect what the parties agree to. However, landlords and tenants are required to comply with both state and local laws. (For instance, rent control laws limit rent increases and grounds for eviction.) Similarly, state laws place a number of requirements on the landlord (for instance maintaining habitable premises, returning security deposits, etc.). If a provision of a rental agreement conflicts with either state or local law, then it is invalid. Landlords often put provisions in a rental agreement that are not valid, even if you sign the agreement.

Illegal Units

An "illegal unit" is one that was constructed without the proper permits, or it violates planning codes. For instance, a property that is zoned single family usually cannot have two units on it. Even when zoning rules permit a second unit, that unit must be constructed using proper permits, and if it was not, it is an illegal unit—one that should never have existed in the first place.

Illegal units are often referred to as "in-law units" or "granny units." However, not all in-law units or granny units are illegal—landowners can properly build and obtain permits for units that they call by those names. And even an illegal unit can become legal after the fact: State law authorizes local government to adopt ordinances that legalize these units (often called "accessory dwelling units").

As an example of post-construction permitting, in December 2017 the city of Santa Rosa responded to the loss of housing caused by the October 2017 fires by passing an ordinance that, among other things, offered amnesty to illegal units constructed without permits (though instances of code noncompliance could still result in penalties). (Santa Rosa City Code §§ 20-22.030 and following.)

Illegal units are often found in basements of homes and apartment buildings, garages, converted commercial spaces, and rear yard sheds and work-spaces. Some cities have tens of thousands of these units, and they constitute a large part of their housing supply.

Learning Whether Your Unit is Illegal

To find out whether your unit is illegal, you will need to look at records found at your planning or building departments. Much of this information is online.

- The Planning Department will list the zoning for your building. Zoning will tell you whether one unit, two units, four units, and so on are permitted on the property; and whether the units can be used for residential, commercial, or industrial purposes.
- The Building Department will have the permit history for your building, starting from the date the building was constructed. Check to see how many units were included in the permit. Also, the department should issue a "Certificate of Occupancy" or "Permit of Occupancy" for each building constructed.

Should You Rent an Illegal Unit?

While they may not have the proper permits, many illegal units are perfectly adequate living spaces. If you think the unit might be illegal, pay extra close attention to the condition of the unit. For instance, test the hot and cold water on all plumbing fixtures, make sure there are enough electrical outlets to meet your needs, and test the heating system.

There are, however, some risks involved in renting an illegal unit. For example, a nosy neighbor could call the building inspector and the building inspector might determine that the unit is illegal. The inspector might then require the landlord to legalize or to demolish the unit. The landlord would then have to evict you.

So, as an extra precaution, you might want to contact the previous tenant and ask about the condition of the unit and whether the neighbors seemed to accept the unit being there.

Also, as unfair as it might sound, a landlord who wants to get rid of you could use the unit's illegality as a reason for eviction. Remember, it is unlawful for the landlord to rent the unit to you in the first place: Because the thing shouldn't even be there, it cannot lawfully be rented. In an eviction proceeding the landlord could argue that he has a right to evict you because the unit is illegal (this might not work in a city with rent control or just cause for eviction). (*North 7th Street Associates v. Constante*, 7 Cal.App. 5th, Supp. 1 (2016).)

On the other hand, the landlord too could face problems if the illegal nature of the unit comes to light in court. Tenants in an eviction proceeding could argue that they should not be required to pay rent. Tenants can also sue the landlord for recovery of all rents that were illegally collected for the unit. Tenants who lived in illegal units have also successfully sued their landlords for fraud, misrepresentation, and wrongful eviction.

One final word of caution: If the illegal unit you're renting has substantial code noncompliance, that could translate to uncomfortable or even dangerous living conditions for you. If you complain and the landlord won't fix things, you'll be tempted to use one of the tenant remedies (rent withholding or repair-and-deduct) that are designed to force landlords to comply with legal standards. But think ahead: If you avail yourself of one of these remedies (each of which involves your paying less rent than the monthly sum), and the landlord terminates the lease for nonpayment of rent and files an eviction lawsuit against you, you may find yourself out of a place to live when the illegal nature of the rental comes to the court's attention. In short, choosing to live in an illegal rental that has serious deficiencies can result in an unpleasant choice between putting up with substandard conditions and risking losing your home.

Multiple Tenancies in One Unit

It is becoming more and more common for landlords to rent separately to multiple, unrelated tenants living in the same unit, with a separate rental agreement (oral or written) for each tenant. These are often called "rooming house" arrangements and occur in single-family homes, apartments, or flats. Tenants have their own rooms and access to common areas such as the kitchen, hallway, living room, and so on. Tenants pay their own rent directly to the landlord. When one tenant moves out the landlord replaces that tenant with someone whom the landlord chooses.

Under this arrangement, if another tenant does not pay his or her rent, that has no direct impact on you—that problem is between that tenant and the landlord. By comparison, if you and the nonpaying tenant had signed the same rental agreement, you would be equally responsible for any rental shortfall. (See Chapter 2, "Sharing a Home.")

Living in a rooming house situation has its disadvantages. As with any situation where tenants share a unit, everybody has to get along. However, in a rooming house arrangement, you have much less power in dealing with a tenant you don't get along with and whom you don't share a rental agreement with. Instead, you must rely on the landlord to take some action. More importantly, if one of the tenants leaves, the landlord fills the vacancy and may not care much about how compatible you and that new tenant might be.

Finally, a rooming house arrangement could be illegal because, technically, each tenancy could be considered a separate unit. For instance, a property built as a single-family home is supposed to have only one unit (unless there is a legalized "granny unit"). With three or four separate tenancies, and three or four separate units, the setup could be considered a violation of building and zoning laws. (see "Illegal Units," above.)

Typical Provisions in Leases and Rental Agreements

Your lease or rental agreement might be as short as one page or longer than ten. It could be typed or handwritten, easy to understand, or full of legalese. Most landlords use preprinted forms they buy in stationery stores, order from a landlords' association, or find in a software program.

Most leases and rental agreements are prepared by real estate associations and have standard provisions. You'll often see them as numbered paragraphs. Unfortunately, the provisions are often dressed up in fancy legal language and complicated sentences. This section describes the plain meanings for the most common terms you'll find in a lease.

Before getting started on the list below, under-stand that landlords don't have complete freedom to write clauses any way they wish. Some issues (such as the maximum security deposit a landlord can charge) are regulated by federal, state, or local law, though this doesn't stop landlords from deviating from the rule, through ignorance or intentionally. Other issues (such as the parking policy) are up for grabs.

Finally, be willing to refuse to sign an agreement that contains terms that you don't believe you can comply with.

Be Sure to Put Oral Promises in Writing

In most cases, your written agreement will take precedence over any oral promises that your landlord made before signing the agreement. It is therefore important that any oral promises be included in the rental agreement. For instance, if the landlord said that the rent included a parking space, make sure the parking space is included in the description of the premises (discussed below).

Many agreements have blank lines at the end for "Additional Provisions." Make sure any promises not in the agreement are included here.

Names and Addresses of Landlord and Tenants

The tenant may be referred to as the "lessee" and the landlord as the "lessor." They may also be called the "parties" to the agreement. If a property manager or company is authorized to receive notices and legal papers on the landlord's behalf, that name and address should be in the agreement. If you can, get an email address as well.

Learning the Name of the Owner and Manager (If Any)

State law (CC §§ 1962 and 1962.5) provides that the rental document must state the name, phone number, and address of both the manager and the owner (or person authorized by the owner to receive notices, demands, and papers announcing lawsuits against the owner). The document must also state when, where, and to whom rent is to be paid; and the form of payment, such as check, money order, or cash. Even if every other aspect of the lease or rental agreement is reflected in an oral agreement, the landlord must *write down* the above information and give it to the tenant.

Instead of putting this information in each rental agreement, the owner may choose to post notices containing the same information in the building. A notice must be posted in at least two easy-to-see places (including all elevators).

The owner must keep this information current. An owner who fails to follow this law may not evict for nonpayment of any rent that comes due during any period of noncompliance (see Chapter 14 for details). Also, the person who rented the dwelling for the owner automatically becomes his or her agent for receiving notices, demands, and notification of lawsuits (such as a summons).

Landlords typically want all adults who will live on the premises, including both members of a couple, to sign the lease or rental agreement.

Doing this makes everyone who signs responsible for complying with the terms of the lease, including payment of rent. To remind tenants of this rule, many leases and rental agreements state that all tenants are "jointly and severally" liable for paying rent, reimbursing the landlord for property damage, and abiding by terms of the agreement. This means that the misdeeds of one tenant (such as keeping a pet in violation of a no-pets policy) will allow the landlord to evict all of you.

Chapter 2 provides details on the legal responsibilities of tenants and cotenants and related issues such as adding a new roommate. "Families With Children and Overcrowding" in Chapter 4, discusses occupancy limits that may restrict who lives in the rental unit.

Rental Property Address, Parking, Storage, and Other Details

The property address is often called "the premises." Your lease or rental agreement should also include details on any furnishings, parking space, storage areas, or other extras that you have agreed to.

Term of the Tenancy

The term is the length of the rental. The document should include the beginning date and whether it's a month-to-month tenancy or a lease. If it's a lease, the ending (termination) date should also be specified. Leases often have a term of one year. Sometimes a lease will say that after the year, the tenancy becomes month to month. Rent control ordinances with eviction protection also allow a tenant to remain in the premises after the term has expired. The important differences between leases and rental agreements are discussed above. Chapter 14 explains how tenancies end.

Rent

Leases and rental agreements should specify the amount of rent due each month, and must state when and where it's due, acceptable forms of payment (such as cash, check, electronic funds transfer) and late fees. Chapter 3 covers rent rules in detail.

The Date Rent Is Due

Leases and rental agreements must state the day of the month that rent is due, usually the first day of the month. It's important to pay rent on time because "habitual late payment" of rent can be a reason for eviction, even in cities with eviction protection. Many agreements will say "Rent is due on or before the first day of each month and, if not paid by the fifth day of the month, the landlord may impose a late charge of $X.xx." This five-day period is usually referred to as a "grace period," giving many people the mistaken belief that rent is due on the fifth of the month, not the first. They accordingly pay on or before the fifth of the month. Although they might have avoided the late fee, they are technically late with the rent and face the risk of eviction for "habitual late payment."

Deposits and Fees

Expect to see details on the dollar amount of a security deposit and/or last month's rent. Chapter 13 explains state laws that govern the size, use, and return of security deposits and why it's important to know your landlord's cleaning and maintenance requirements.

Utilities

The landlord should state who pays for what utilities. Normally, landlords of multiple-unit properties pay for garbage and for water. Landlords of single-unit properties, such as a rental house, often pay for water if there is a yard. Tenants usually pay for other services, such as phone, gas, and electricity. If tenants will share gas or electric meters (where, for example, a tenant's meter also services a common area, or where one meter measures more than one rental's use), the rental document must disclose this, and how charges will be allocated. (CC § 1940.9.)

Inspect Before You Sign

Always inspect the rental unit before you sign a lease or rental agreement. Think (and look) carefully before signing off on a clause that states that the rental is in fine shape. Check to make sure that the electrical outlets and plumbing fixtures are working properly. Look for damage, signs of leaks, dirt, mildew, pest or rodent problems, and obvious wear and tear. A sample Checklist form is at the end of this chapter. Write down (be as specific as possible) both serious problems, such as a broken heater or leaking roof, and minor flaws such as a stained kitchen counter, dirty drapes, or faded paint. Back up your written statement with photographs. (See "How to Check a Place Over," below, for specific advice.)

As much as possible, try to get your landlord to fix problems before you move in. Write down any agreement in a letter of understanding as described in "Get All Promises in Writing," below.

Keeping tabs on the condition of the rental at move-in is an excellent way to protect yourself when it comes time to move out and get your security deposit returned. Without good proof of the condition of the premises at the start of the tenancy, your landlord may keep all or part of your deposit, claiming you left the place filthy or damaged it—for example, stained the rug, cracked the bathroom mirror, or left behind a broken garbage disposal. Your initial inspection (and photos) will establish that the problems existed at the start of the tenancy and are not your fault. Chapter 13 discusses how to avoid disputes over security deposits at move-out time.

Condition of the Rental Unit

Most leases and rental agreements include a clause in which you agree that the premises are in habitable (livable) condition and you promise to alert the landlord to any defective or dangerous condition. Chapters 6 and 7 cover tenants' important rights and responsibilities regarding repair and maintenance. If it's already obvious that the premises are not habitable, beware. Although signing a lease with such a clause will not prevent you from legitimately asking for repairs, this is no way to begin your tenancy. (See the sidebar above, "Inspect Before You Sign.")

Tenant's Repair and Maintenance Responsibilities

A carefully written lease or rental agreement will include a statement that makes you responsible for keeping the rental premises clean and in good condition and obligates you to reimburse the landlord for the cost of repairing damage caused by your abuse or neglect. Many leases and rental agreements also tell you what you can't do in the way of repairs—such as painting walls or adding built-in bookshelves—without the landlord's written permission. Chapters 5 and 6 cover the rights and responsibilities of landlords and tenants regarding repairs and maintenance, and your options if your landlord fails to provide habitable housing.

Your lease or rental agreement may require you to carry renters' insurance to cover damage and other losses to the rental. (See Chapter 16 for details.)

When and How Landlords May Enter Your Rental Unit

California law specifies when landlords may legally enter rented premises—for example, to deal with an emergency or to make repairs—and the amount of notice required. (CC § 1954.) Chapter 5 gives the specifics concerning the landlord's right to enter rental property and tenant privacy rights. So no matter what this provision says, the landlord can legally enter only for those reasons allowed under Civil Code Section 1954. There is probably no need to negotiate over this provision, because the landlord is limited by state law.

Extended Absences

Some leases and rental agreements require you to notify the landlord in advance if you will be away from the premises for a certain number of consecutive days (often seven or more). Such clauses may give the landlord the right to enter the rental unit during your absence to maintain the property as necessary and to inspect for damage and needed repairs. You'll most often see this type of clause if you live in a cold-weather place where, in case of extremely cold temperatures, landlords want to drain the pipes to guard against breakage.

Limits on Your Behavior

Most form leases and rental agreements contain a clause forbidding you from using the premises or adjacent areas, such as the sidewalk in front of the building, in such a way as to violate any law or ordinance, including laws prohibiting the use, possession, or sale of illegal drugs. These clauses also prohibit you from intentionally damaging the property or creating a nuisance by annoying or disturbing other tenants or nearby residents—for example, by continuously making loud noise. Leases and rental agreements may prohibit smoking, in individual units as well as in common areas. Landlords often impose "house rules" that govern noise, proper trash removal, and so on.

Restrictions on Use of the Property

Rental agreements and leases often include language that limits your use of the rental property and who may stay there. (For example, no plants on wood floors or bikes in the hallway). These restrictions may also be in a separate set of "house rules." Basically, landlords can set any kind of restriction they want, as long as they are not discriminatory or retaliatory or otherwise violate state law. For instance, they cannot prohibit home day care operations (see "Family Day Care Homes," below). Landlords are allowed to restrict or even prohibit smoking in part of or even all of the premises. (CC § 1947.5.) Other common restrictions involving pets, home businesses (other than day care), sublets, and guests are discussed below.

Opening Landlords' Doors to Pets

The San Francisco Society for the Prevention of Cruelty to Animals (SPCA) offers pet-owning tenants helpful materials on how to negotiate with a landlord. The SPCA also offers landlords:

- checklists to help screen pet-owning tenants
- model policies for tenants with dogs or cats
- model agreements to add to standard leases and rental agreements, and
- free mediation if landlords and tenants have problems after moving in.

For more information, contact the San Francisco SPCA at 201 Alabama, San Francisco, CA 94103, 415-554-3000, or check their website at www. sfspca.org.

No Pets

Your landlord has the right to prohibit all pets, or to restrict the types allowed—for example, forbidding dogs or cats, but allowing birds. However, a landlord may not prohibit "service" or "comfort" animals used by people with a physical or mental disability, as provided by the fair housing laws. However, you'll need to follow specific procedures if you wish to request a service or comfort animal. (For more information, see Chapter 4, "Discrimination.") Many landlords spell out pet rules—for example, that tenants will keep the yard free of all animal waste or that dogs will always be on leash.

Landlords may not charge a nonrefundable pet fee. (See the discussions of deposits in Chapter 13.)

No Home Businesses

Landlords may prohibit you from running a business from your home, by including a clause specifying that the premises are "for residential purposes only." The concern here is generally about increased traffic and liability exposure if one of your customers or business associates is hurt on the premises. Obviously, working at home on your computer is not likely to bother your landlord, and might not even be noticed.

If you want to run a day care operation in your rented home, your landlord cannot flatly prohibit it. (H&S § 1597.40.) You must be licensed, and part of that process will involve an on-site inspection, to determine whether the physical space comports with minimum requirements under state law. (See "Family Day Care Homes," below.)

No Assignments or Sublets Without Landlord Permission

Most careful landlords will not let you turn your rental over to another tenant (called "assignment"), let someone live there for a limited time while you're away (called a "sublet"), or let you rent an extra bedroom to another occupant, with you as the "landlord" (also called a sublet), without their written consent. (See Chapter 12 for more on the subject.)

Limits on Guest Stays

It's common for landlords to limit overnight guests, such as allowing a guest for no more than ten days in any six-month period, with written approval required for longer stays. Landlords do this to keep long-term guests from gaining the status of full-fledged tenants who have not been screened or approved and who have not signed the lease or rental agreement.

Prohibitions Against Short-Term Rentals (Airbnb)

Short-term rental websites and services such as Airbnb have become very popular in California, particularly in tourist destination cities such as San Francisco and Santa Monica. Landlords universally hate the practice—from their point of view, the tenant has simply turned the rental into a hotel, making money off the landlord's property and introducing added wear and tear, annoyance from neighbors, and the risk that unscreened occupants will cause trouble. Arguably, a general "no subletting or assigning without permission" clause would cover and prohibit the situation, but to be sure, landlords have begun inserting clauses in their rental agreements and leases that specifically address the practice and forbid it, warning that a breach can lead to eviction. In some cities, such as San Francisco, it is unlawful for a tenant to rent using Airbnb (or similar platforms) without the written permission of the landlord.

Such a clause is probably legal and enforceable, even in cities whose own ordinances attempt to govern the practice (no such ordinance *requires* landlords to allow short-term renting). If you see such a clause in your lease, or if the law requires your landlord's consent, think twice before listing your rental. Landlords can easily find out if you are using the premises for such a business, and may use this as a reason to evict.

Forbidding Signs on the Property

Many lease agreements have provisions that prohibit putting signs in windows or the outside of your unit. These provisions are generally legal, but Civil Code Section 1940.4 creates an exception that allows tenants to display political signs regarding initiatives, elections to public office, and matters that will be voted on by a legislative body, public commission, board, or other elected public body. The signs must be less than six square feet in size. Civil Code Section 1940.4 does not apply if it violates the rules of a condominium association, cooperative housing development, or planned unit development. The tenant posting the sign must comply with any local ordinance that has time limits on when the signs can be posted. In the absence of any legislated limits, landlords may require that the signs be removed within a "reasonable" time period after being posted. A "reasonable" time period is presumed to begin at least 90 days before the election and end 15 days after it. Remember, Section 1940.4 applies only to political signs, and a landlord is otherwise allowed to restrict posting signs around the property.

Disclosures Required by Law

In addition to disclosures described here (under "Utilities" and "Megan's Law Database"), California requires landlords to make the following disclosures, either in the rental document or elsewhere:

- **Location near a former military base.** Landlords must tell you if the property is within a mile of an abandoned or closed military base in which ammunition or explosives were stored. (CC § 1940.7.)
- **Periodic and other pest control.** Landlords who have periodic pest control must inform tenants about the frequency of treatments. (CC § 1940.8.)
- **Intentions to demolish the rental.** If the landlord has applied for a demolition permit, it must inform tenants. (CC § 1940.6(a)(1)(D).)
- **Lead paint.** All landlords must give tenants the federal form, "Disclosure of Information on Lead-Based Paint or Lead-Based Paint Hazards," and inform tenants of the known presence of lead paint. (See Chapter 10 for details).
- **Mold.** Landlords who know of the presence of mold in a rental must inform tenants. (H&S § 26147.) (See Chapter 10 for more on mold.)
- **Bedbugs.** Landlords are required to provide tenants with information regarding bedbugs, including how to identify them and the procedures for reporting bedbugs to the management. (CC § 1954.603.)

Family Day Care Homes

Under state law (H&S § 1597.40), a landlord may not forbid a tenant's use of rental premises as a licensed family day care home. If you obtain a state license to run a family day care home, you may do so legally—regardless of whether your lease or rental agreement prohibits the operation of a business on the premises or limits the number of occupants. Local zoning and occupancy limits also don't apply to a state-licensed family day care home. If you want to run a family day care home, you must notify your landlord in writing of your intent, after having first obtained a state license, 30 days in advance of starting the child care operation.

Megan's Law Database

Every written lease or rental agreement must include a specific paragraph that tells tenants about the statewide database containing the names of registered sexual offenders. Members of the public may view the state's Department of Justice website to see whether a certain individual is on the list (www.meganslaw.ca.gov).

Attorney Fees and Court Costs in a Lawsuit

If you and the landlord get involved in a lawsuit (such as an eviction lawsuit) arising out of the lease or rental agreement, each side will usually pay its own attorney fees. This rule is subject to two exceptions: Some California statutes provide for attorney fees to the prevailing party in a lawsuit for certain violations of the law (that is, the loser pays the winner's fees and costs). For example, statutes covering lawsuits for discrimination, retaliatory eviction, or rent control violations specify that the prevailing (winning) party can recover fees and/or costs.

The second exception arises when a term in a lease agreement states that the winning party in any litigation related to the lease can recover fees and costs from the loser. In that case, if you win, then the landlord pays your fees; and if the landlord wins, you pay his.

You might encounter a lease that states that a losing *tenant* will pay a winning landlord's fees and costs (but not the other way around). Fortunately for tenants, California law will not countenance this one-sided provision. The judge will interpret this provision to require payment of attorney fees to the prevailing (winning) party, no matter who that is. (CC § 1717(a).) Therefore, if you win, then you get your fees paid by the landlord.

Grounds for Termination of Tenancy

You'll often see a general clause stating that any violation of the lease or rental agreement by you, or by your guests, is grounds for terminating the tenancy according to the procedures established by state or local laws. Chapters 14 and 15 cover the legal rules regarding termination and evictions.

Owner Move-In Clause

If the rental is subject to The Tenant Protection Act of 2019 (the "TPA," a law that established rent control and just cause eviction state-wide, with a few exceptions), the landlord may place a clause in the lease that allows for termination with 60 days' notice if the landlord (or a specified relative) intends to move into the rental. The relatives include the landlord's spouse, domestic partner, children, grandchildren, parents, or grandparents. Be sure you understand the import of this clause: The lease will terminate before the date it normally would if the landlord (or relative) "decides to occupy" the rental as a residence. (See Chapters 3 and 14 for more information on the TPA.) (CC §1946.2(b)(2)(A)(ii).)

Invalid Lease Provisions

The legislature has determined that certain provisions found in leases and rental agreements are "unconscionable" or unacceptable. Civil Code Section 1953 invalidates them (this means that a judge will not enforce them). In practice, a landlord's attempt to get you to "waive" (give up) or modify your rights will be fruitless. These rights include:

- the timely and accurate return of security deposit
- the reasons for the landlord's entry to your home, and the notice that must be given
- your right to sue the landlord for negligent or intentional actions
- your right to receive notice of specified events, or to a hearing that may be required by law
- your procedural rights in litigation regarding the tenancy
- rights to have the landlord exercise due care to prevent personal injury, and
- rights to habitable housing and to be free of retaliatory eviction.

Because lease clauses waiving these rights are not enforceable, you might be better off focusing your efforts in getting your landlord to modify other provisions of the agreement. Below are typical examples of unenforceable provisions.

Provision That the Landlord Is Not Responsible for Damage and Injuries

This provision says that if the landlord is negligent in maintaining the place and you, your family, or guests are injured, or your property is damaged (for example, if someone falls down broken stairs), the landlord is not responsible for paying for your losses. This is called an "exculpatory" provision. Under state law, such a provision is invalid. (CC § 1953.) Chapter 9 discusses landlord liability for tenant injuries.

Provision Making Tenant Responsible for Repairs

This provision requires you, the tenant, to repair or maintain the premises. Unless this is based on a legitimate reduction in rent, this type of provision is usually illegal. (CC § 1942.1.) In any event, this provision does not relieve the landlord of the legal obligation to see that the place complies with the housing codes and the duty to maintain a fit and habitable rental. (See Chapter 6 for more information.)

Provision Waiving Your Self-Help Repair Rights

California tenants have the right, in certain circumstances, to make necessary repairs and deduct the cost from the rent; (this remedy is known as "repair and deduct," and is explained in detail in Chapter 6). A lease provision that purports to waive these rights will not be enforced by a judge.

Waiver of Rent Control Laws

Cities that have rent control ordinances specifically forbid lease or rental agreement provisions by which a tenant gives up or waives any rights granted by the rent control ordinance, such as rent ceilings or just cause eviction rules. A landlord who attempts to circumvent a rent control rule may be fined or even face criminal prosecution. Appendix A contains a detailed chart on rent control rules, and Chapter 3 provides an overview of the subject.

Waiver of Right to Legal Notice

This provision says the landlord can sue to evict you or can raise the rent or change the terms of the lease without giving notice (such as a three-day notice to pay your rent or vacate) required by law. It is not valid. (CC § 1953.)

Right to Inspect

Many forms have a provision that gives the landlord the right to come into your place to inspect it, or for other purposes. Under state law, the landlord's right to enter the dwelling is limited to certain reasons, and any attempt to add to these reasons in the lease or rental agreement is void. (CC §§ 1953 and 1954.) We discuss your rights to privacy in detail in Chapter 5.

Right of Reentry Provision

This provision permits the landlord to come in and throw you out if you don't pay the rent, without giving you legal notice or going to court. It is not valid. (CC § 1953(a)(4).)

Waiver of Jury Trial

One variation on this provision says that you waive your right to a trial by jury in any eviction lawsuit brought by the landlord. It is not valid. (CC § 1953.) Similarly, a lease clause in which the tenant agrees that any lawsuit concerning the lease or its implementation will be tried before a judge without a jury is void. (*Grafton Partners LP v. Superior Court (PricewaterhouseCoopers LLP)*, 36 Cal.4th 944 (2005).)

Keep in mind that you and the landlord may still decide, once litigation has begun, that you will submit the case to a judge and not a jury. But an advance waiver of the right to a jury trial is not a legal option in California. Rental agreement provisions requiring the parties to arbitrate a dispute with a "neutral" third party are void under Civil Code Section 1953(a)(4). (*Jaramillo v. JH Real Estate Partners, Inc.,* 111 Cal.App.4th 394 (2003).)

Waiver of Right to Appeal

This provision prevents you from appealing a court decision in any eviction lawsuit. It is not valid. (CC § 1953.)

Provision Setting Notice Period

This provision sets the amount of time the landlord must give you before a notice of termination or rent raise or change in terms takes effect. Under CC Section 1946.1, this type of notice is not legally valid. If you are a month-to-month tenant, the law requires that the landlord give you at least 30 days' notice (60 days for a termination notice in the case of a tenant who has rented for a year or more). (See "Rent Increase Notices" in Chapter 3 for exceptions.)

Cash Rent

Your lease or rental agreement may not demand that you pay the rent solely in cash or by electronic funds transfer. (CC § 1947.3.) Landlords may demand cash rent only after you've given them a check that bounces, or a money order or cashier's check whose issuer has been told to stop payment. Even then, the demand for cash rent may last only three months. If you see a provision such as this, you might want to raise the issue. You might, however, decide that it is more convenient for you to pay rent by electronic means.

Provisions That Might Be Invalid Depending on the Circumstances

The landlord's lease might contain provisions that are invalid due to the makeup of the resident mix or the manner in which monetary consequences are calculated.

Late Charges

This provision requires the tenant to pay a "late charge" if the rent is paid late. The charge may be set as a percentage of the rent (such as 4%), a flat charge (such as $10), or a flat charge per day (such as $5 each day the rent is late). (See "Late Fees" in Chapter 3.) This provision is valid if the amount is a reasonable estimate of the amount the lateness of your payment will cost the landlord— that is, the administrative cost of processing the late payment and the loss of interest on your rent. However, if the charge is so high as to penalize you for being late, the charge is probably a "penalty" provision, which is invalid. If the late charge seems suspiciously high to you (for example, a $100 charge on an $800 rent payment late by a few days), ask the landlord to justify it or lower it.

Rules on Number of Occupants

Landlords in California are free to advertise their rentals as appropriate for specific numbers of residents, but they do not have complete *carte blanche*. They may not fill their units to the point that they've created overcrowding. And at the other end of the spectrum, they cannot adopt policies that have the effect of discriminating against families. Let's look at each of these situations.

- **Overcrowding (minimum square foot requirements).** The Uniform Housing Code (the UHC) is part of California's state housing law and is intended to prevent the unhealthy and dangerous results of overcrowding. (H&S § 17922(a)(1).) The UHC addresses the question of occupancy in terms of the size of the rental's bedrooms. A room that the landlord has "designed or intended" to be used as a bedroom (CC § 1941.2(a)(5)) must be at least 70 square feet for one person, plus an additional 50 square feet for each additional occupant; so, for two people, 120 square feet; and three people, 170 square feet. (UHC § 503.) Cities are free to adopt their own occupancy specifications, and some (notably San Francisco) have allowed for more occupants per bedroom. In some rent control jurisdictions, tenants are allowed to add relatives and roommates up to a certain limit.

- **Discrimination against families.** Many landlords, hoping for reduced wear and tear, would like to rent to adults only, and the fewer, the better. They set "occupancy standards" that require specific numbers of bedrooms per occupant, which makes it difficult for families to rent. For example, insisting on only two occupants per bedroom rules out a one-bedroom unit for a couple with a child; similarly, a two-bedroom would be out of reach for a couple with three kids. Such policies are almost always illegal—in most cases, landlords must apply an occupancy policy of "two per bedroom plus one."

With these understandings in mind, look for an occupancy clause in your lease. If it's a one-bedroom and the lease forbids more than two occupants, it's likely an unenforceable clause. If it's a two-bedroom that specifies that no more than five residents may live there, it's likely to pass legal muster.

A provision forbidding any overnight guests of the opposite sex of the tenant, for example, is illegal. (CC § 51. See also *Atkisson v. Kern County Housing Authority,* 59 Cal.App.3d 89 (1976).) So would a provision saying, "No overnight guests under 12 years of age." (CC § 51. See also *Marina Point, Ltd. v. Wolfson,* 30 Cal.3d 721 (1982) and "Families With Children and Overcrowding" in Chapter 4.)

A landlord must also be reasonable if you become disabled and need an additional person in your home to take care of you, when that person would put you above the occupancy limit. In legalese, the landlord must make a "reasonable accommodation" for you, and vary his policy. For example, suppose you've had surgery and are incapacitated for a period of time; or you become unable to care for yourself due to age or infirmity. You must, however, request the "reasonable accommodation" before allowing the guest or occupant to stay for any period beyond what is allowed in the lease agreement. (See Chapter 4, "Discrimination," for more on requesting reasonable accommodations.)

Some agreements require the tenant to give the landlord prior notice of overnight guests, or to obtain the landlord's prior consent. These provisions are probably valid, though a provision regarding consent would probably be read to mean that the landlord could not arbitrarily or unreasonably withhold consent. These provisions can be annoying, however, as they allow the landlord to nose into the tenant's private affairs. You might ask the landlord to write in something like, "This restriction shall apply only to overnight guests who stay more than five nights in any 30-day period."

Requiring the Tenant to Give Notice on a Specific Day

A tenant is required to give only 30 days' notice to inform the landlord the tenant is moving out (terminating the tenancy). Some landlords want month-to-month tenants to give tenancy termination notices on a specific day of the month, typically the last day. Under this scheme, a termination notice delivered on any other day won't take effect until the last day of the month, which means that a tenant who gives a 30-day notice on, say, the tenth, will in effect be giving 50 days' notice (because the landlord won't recognize it until the 30th of that month). The tenant can, of course, vacate at any time, but the landlord will argue that it is entitled to rent for the entire 50-day period. Typically, the landlord will deduct the unpaid rent from the security deposit.

State law requires that a tenant give only 30 days' notice to end a tenancy, no more. (CC § 1946.1.) Therefore, any provision requiring notice on the first of the month should be unenforceable, and (in the example just above), the landlord should not be able to deduct rent for the extra 20 days.

Provision Restricting Water-Filled Furniture

If the building where you rent was built after 1973, it is not legal for a landlord to ban water-filled furniture. A landlord may, however, require you to have $100,000 of liability insurance to cover potential damage and meet other requirements specified by law. (Chapter 15 discusses renters' insurance.) For property built before 1973, a landlord may legally refuse to allow waterbeds. (CC § 1940.5.)

Penalty and Liquidated Damages Provision

Occasionally, a lease includes a "penalty" or "liquidated damages" clause. These provisions are not necessarily labeled "penalty" or "liquidated damages," but they nevertheless may have the effect of a penalty—one that bears no relation to the damage a landlord would actually suffer if the tenant breached the agreement. For instance, a clause may say that if you move out before the expiration of the lease, you have

to pay a specified sum and/or forfeit your deposit. This is probably a penalty and unlawful under California Code Section 1671(d).

If you think that sounds unfair, you're right. As is discussed in Chapter 12, if you move out before your lease expires, you are legally responsible to pay the landlord only for the actual losses you cause. The landlord is legally obligated to minimize those losses by trying to find a new tenant to replace you as soon as possible. Why should the landlord, who didn't lose any money when you moved out, get a windfall?

Courts don't look kindly on liquidated damages, either. If the amount of liquidated damages far exceeds the landlord's actual damages, a judge will probably rule that you don't have to pay them. Of course, it takes time and trouble to go to court to get your money (the security deposit) back, so it's better to get a clause like this crossed out of the lease before you sign it.

Holding Deposits and Credit-Check Fees

Almost every landlord requires the tenant to give a substantial security deposit, sometimes including "last month's rent." The laws concerning how much can be charged and when and how deposits must be accounted for are discussed in Chapter 13. Here we will discuss some other fees and deposits that are occasionally required.

Holding Deposit

Some landlords request a deposit to "hold" the unit for you until your credit is checked, deposits and rent paid, and a formal agreement made. This is often called a "holding" or "bond" deposit.

Be sure you understand from the outset what will happen to the deposit if you decide to back out of the deal, or the landlord decides not to accept you, or you end up signing an agreement.

- **You back out or the landlord decides not to rent to you.** Your landlord is probably entitled to keep an amount reasonably related to his loss. His costs could include, for example, more advertising expenses and prorated rent during the time the property was held vacant, and the value of his time spent processing your application. If you sue a landlord who keeps a larger amount, a judge would likely find that the landlord is imposing an unlawful penalty.
- **You end up becoming a tenant at this property.** The holding deposit should be applied to your security deposit or first month's rent payment.

To avoid misunderstandings, get these scenarios and consequences in writing at the time you give the landlord your deposit.

Credit-Check and Screening Fees

Landlords often charge a fee to check the credit and background of prospective tenants. But state law limits credit-check or application fees and specifies what landlords must do when accepting these types of screening fees from prospective tenants. Under California Code Section 1950.6, landlords can charge only "actual out-of-pocket" costs of obtaining a credit or similar tenant "screening" report, plus "the reasonable value of time spent" obtaining a credit report or checking personal references and background information on a prospective tenant.

The maximum screening fee a landlord can charge is set by law. (CC § 1950.6.) The maximum ($49.12 as of 2018) is adjusted by the state annually in December, based on the Consumer Price Index. To determine the current allowable charge, Google "California tenant application screening fee," and look for a link to the California Apartment Association among the list of results. This organization is likely to list the current figure.

Upon an applicant's request, a landlord must provide a copy of any consumer credit report that the landlord obtained on the individual. California

Code Section 1950.6 also requires that the landlord give or mail applicants a receipt itemizing their credit-check and screening fees. If a landlord ends up spending less than the fee charged the applicant (for the credit report and time), the landlord must refund the difference. (This may be the entire screening fee if the landlord never got a credit report or checked references on an applicant.)

Finally, landlords cannot charge any screening or credit-check fee if they don't have a vacancy and are simply putting someone on a waiting list (unless the applicant agrees to this in writing).

To avoid disputes over credit-check fees and the amount of time a landlord takes to check your credit and background, it is wise to sign a brief agreement with a landlord, authorizing the landlord to check your credit information, such as the one shown below.

Landlord-Tenant Agreement Regarding Tenant's Credit Information

---

Credit Information

Tenant authorizes Landlord to verify all credit information for the purpose of renting the premises at _____.

Landlord shall not release such information for any other purpose without the express written approval of the Tenant.

If Landlord does not agree to sign lease within _____ days of receiving a deposit from Tenant for the purpose of reserving the premises, the total application fee of $_____ shall be refunded to Tenant, less the amount actually spent to verify credit or background information.

Tenant may withdraw from the agreement and receive a refund of the total application fee (less an amount used to verify credit information) up until such time as Landlord signs the lease.

_____
Landlord

_____
Tenant

Rental Applications and Credit Reports

You will probably be required to fill out a written rental application by the landlord or manager, and pay a credit-check fee (discussed above).

Rental Applications

The rental application will likely ask you for information regarding your employment, income, and credit history (including any bankruptcies), housing history (including evictions), as well as any criminal convictions (recent advice from HUD counsels landlords against asking about arrest history, however). It's legal to ask for your Social Security number, driver's license number, or other identifying information (such as an Individual Taxpayer Identification Number, or ITIN). Under California state law, it is illegal, however, for landlords to ask for proof of an applicant's right to be in the United States under U.S. immigration laws.

Landlords may also ask you for some references from your current and previous landlords, and others such as your employer. Make sure that all of your references are people who know you well and who have positive impressions of you. Enthusiastic employment references are a good choice.

Credit Reports

The most important part of the rental application is the credit check. If you have a poor credit record, be armed with information about yourself, showing that you will pay your rent despite what your credit record shows.

Several companies, called tenant-screening agencies, collect and sell credit and other information about tenants—for example, whether they pay their rent on time or have ever been evicted. These reports go way beyond the information contained in a credit report.

California tenants have considerable protections with respect to reporting eviction lawsuits that they win (or that the landlord wins after 60 days). With some exceptions (noted below), the court clerks must hide, or "mask," eviction case records unless the landlord prevailed (obtains a judgment) within 60 days of filing the eviction complaint. And if the landlord obtains a judgment more than 60 days after the filing of the complaint, the records will be unmasked only upon order of the court.

The law provides for specified exceptions to these rules. Court records of the case will be made available to:

- the parties to the case and their lawyers
- a person (such as a journalist) who provides the court clerk with the names of at least one plaintiff and one defendant, and the address of the premises
- a resident of the premises who gives the clerk the name of one of the parties or the case number, and who shows proof of residency, and
- a person who has an order from a court, issued upon a showing of good cause.

These exceptions are designed to allow interested parties, including the press and other residents of the rental property (neighbors), to have access to the court records. (CCP §§ 1161.2 and 1167.)

Investigative Reports

If asked to, screening companies will also gather and sell "investigative reports" about a person's character, general reputation, personal characteristics, or mode of living.

Many landlords routinely request screening and credit reports on prospective tenants from these agencies. If a landlord rejects, or charges higher rent, to someone because of negative information in a credit or screening report, the landlord must so notify the tenant and give the person the name and address of the agency that reported the negative information. The landlord must also tell applicants that they have a right to obtain a copy of the file from the agency that reported the negative information, as long as they request the file within 60 days. (CC § 1785.20.) Landlords must also tell you that the credit reporting agency did not make the rejection decision and cannot explain it; and that if you dispute the information in the report, you can provide a consumer statement for your file that sets forth your position.

Almost all background or investigative checks are considered "investigative consumer reports" under the federal Fair Credit Reporting Act. (15 U.S.C. §§ 1681 and following.) A landlord who requests a background check on a prospective tenant must:

- tell the applicant within three days of requesting the report that the report may be made; and that it will concern the applicant's character, reputation, personal characteristics, and criminal history, and
- tell the applicant that more information about the nature and scope of the report will be provided upon written request. The landlord must provide this additional information within five days of being asked by the applicant.

Free Credit Report

If you'd like to see a copy of your credit report, it's simple and cheap. The Federal Trade Commission (FTC) approved a rule that allows consumers to receive a free copy of their credit report every 12 months. Go to www.annualcreditreport. com. Because your credit report is so important, you should always check it before you start your housing search. This will give you the opportunity to correct or clear up any mistakes such as out-of-date or just plain wrong information.

TIP

If the landlord or manager checks your credit, you should be aware that the check will probably result in an "inquiry" in your credit record. An inquiry is an indication in your credit record that someone has asked for your credit record. Many inquiries within a short period of time may raise doubts about your creditworthiness later—a creditor may think you were shopping around and looking to borrow a lot. You may need to explain that the inquiries were from landlords, and you were merely shopping and bargaining for the best rental.

How Landlords Must Handle Your Credit Information

Landlords must take steps to safeguard and eventually destroy credit reports and any information they have that's derived from these reports. This "Disposal Rule" comes from the Federal Trade Commission (FTC), which issues rules that implement the Fair and Accurate Credit Transaction Act of 2003, 69 Fed. Reg. 68690 (the "FACT Act"). The rule applies to all businesses, even one-person landlords. You might want to ask your prospective landlords whether they follow the practices described below.

Safe Retention

Landlords should keep these reports in a secure location, in order to minimize the chance that someone will use the information for illegal purposes, including identity theft. Good practices include storing these reports, and any other documents that include information taken from them, in a locked cabinet. Only known and trusted people should have access, and only on a need-to-know basis. Reports stored on a computer, a phone or other device, or information derived from them, must also be kept secure.

Destroying Unneeded Reports Routinely

The FACT Act requires landlords to dispose of credit reports and any information taken from them when they no longer need them. Landlords may think they need these reports long after they've rejected or accepted an applicant—the reports may be essential in refuting a fair employment or housing claim. Under federal law, such claims must be filed within two years of the claimed discrimination. Landlords whose states gives plaintiffs extra time to sue may keep the records at least two years and longer.

Landlords should destroy old records using an effective destruction method. The Disposal Rule requires landlords to choose a level of document destruction that is reasonable in the context of their business. For example, a landlord with a few rentals would do just fine with an inexpensive shredder, but a multiproperty owner might want to contract with a shredding service. Computer files must also be erased, by deleting not only the directory, but the text as well.

Remedies When Landlords Willfully Disregard the Disposal Rule

The Disposal Rule comes with teeth for those who willfully disregard it—landlords who know about the law and how to comply, but deliberately refuse to do so. You can sue for your actual damages (say, the cost of covering a portion of a credit card's unauthorized use), or damages per violation of between $100 and $1,000, plus your attorney fees and costs of suit, plus punitive damages. The FTC and state counterparts can also enforce the FACT Act and impose fines.

Permissible Reasons for Rejecting Tenants

Federal and state antidiscrimination laws (covered in Chapter 4) limit what landlords can say and do in the tenant selection process. Basically, a landlord is legally free to choose among prospective tenants as long as all tenants are evaluated more or less equally. That said, a landlord is entitled to reject you for legitimate business reasons, such as your poor credit history, which leads the landlord to believe that you will be unable to pay the rent; negative references from previous landlords indicating problems, such as property damage or consistent late rent payments; criminal convictions that reasonably indicate that you pose a threat to persons or property; and previous eviction lawsuits.

How to Check a Place Over

If you see a place that you think you will like, take a walk around the neighborhood. Check out stores, schools, and bus stops. Walk around the building you are interested in renting and try to meet some of the neighbors. (If you can, talk to the tenants who are moving out.) Ask them how they have gotten along with the landlord. Make sure that you can feel at home in all respects. Take an especially close look at the condition of the unit you may rent. Look for dirt and damage, and carefully check all doors, windows, screens, stoves, furnaces, hot water heaters, and any other appliances. Make lists of any defects you find—later you can negotiate with the landlord for improvements and repairs. At the very least, be sure to get the landlord to sign an acknowledgment of the existing conditions, so she can't blame you later for causing them (and deducting from your security deposit accordingly). The best way to do this is by completing the Landlord-Tenant Checklist, discussed below.

A Checklist of Things to Inspect

A sample checklist of things you should look for when inspecting a place is shown at the end of this chapter, and you can download it from this book's companion page on Nolo.com. The checklist includes the requirements in the State Housing

Law. (See Chapter 6.) While checking some items on this list may seem obvious almost to the point of being simple-minded, the unhappy truth is that many people do not check a rental unit thoroughly before moving in and have all sorts of trouble getting repairs made later. So please slow down and look carefully (and then look again) before you sign on the dotted line.

Check the STRUCTURE
(Floors, Walls, Ceiling, Foundation)

The structure of the place must be weatherproof, waterproof, and rodent proof.

"Weatherproof" means there must be no holes, cracks, or broken plaster. Check to see if all the walls are flush (that they meet directly, with no space in between). See if any floorboards are warped. Does wall plaster fall off when you touch it?

"Waterproof" means no water should leak in. If you see dark round spots on the ceilings or dark streaks on the walls, rainwater might have been leaking through.

"Rodent proof" means no cracks and holes that rats and mice could use.

Check the PLUMBING

The landlord must provide hot and cold running water connected to your community's water system and also to its sewage system (unless you have a septic system).

All plumbing must be in good condition, free of rust and leaks. Sometimes the condition of the plumbing is hard to discover, but you can run these tests to see if there might be problems.

- Flush the toilet. Does it take too long to flush? Does it leak on the floor? Is the water discolored? If so, the pipes may be rusty or unclean.
- If the water is connected, fill a sink with hot and cold water. Turn the faucets on all the way, and listen for vibrating or knocking sounds in the pipes. See if the water in the sink is discolored. Drain the sink, and see if it takes too long for the water to run out.

Check the BATHROOM

The State Housing Law requires that every apartment and house have at least one working toilet, washbasin, and bathtub (or shower) in it. The toilet and bathtub (or shower) must be in a room that gives privacy to the occupant and is ventilated. All of these facilities must be installed and maintained in a safe and sanitary condition.

Check the KITCHEN

The State Housing Law requires that every apartment and house have a kitchen. The kitchen must have a kitchen sink, which cannot be made of wood or other absorbent material.

Check the HOT WATER

You must have both hot and cold running water (although you can be required to pay the water and gas bills). "Hot" water means a temperature of not less than 110 degrees F.

Check the HEAT

The landlord must provide adequate heating facilities. Unvented fuel-burning heaters are not permitted.

Check the LIGHT AND VENTILATION

All rooms you live in must have natural light through windows or skylights, which must have an area not less than one-tenth of the floor area of the room, with a minimum of ten square feet.

Hallways and stairs in the building must be lighted at all times.

Proper ventilation is an important safeguard against mold. Make sure you can open the windows, and look for working fans in the bathroom and above the stove.

Check for Signs of INSECTS, VERMIN, AND RODENTS

The landlord must provide facilities that prevent insect and rodent infestation and, if there is infestation, provide for extermination services.

These pests can be hard to notice. Remember, however, that they are very shy and stay out of sight. Therefore, if you see any fresh signs of them, they are probably very numerous and will bother you later on. Also, these pests travel from house to house. If your neighbors have them, they will probably get to you.

Check for rodent trails and excrement. Rats and mice travel the same path day after day and leave a gray coloring along the floor and baseboards. Look at the kitchen carefully, for rodents go there for food supplies. Check in closets and cupboards and behind appliances for cockroaches.

Check for possible breeding grounds for pests, such as nearby stagnant water or garages and basements with piles of litter or old couches.

Check the WIRING AND ELECTRICITY

Loose or exposed wiring can be dangerous, leading to shock or fires. The landlord must provide safe and proper wiring.

If electrical power is available in the area, the rental must be connected to it. Every room you live in must have at least two outlets (or one outlet and one light fixture). Every bathroom must have at least one light fixture. Be sure to check to make sure they all work properly.

Check for FIRE SAFETY

The landlord must provide safe exits leading to a street or hallway. Hallways, stairways, and exits must be free from litter. State law requires landlords to provide information on emergency procedures in case of fire to tenants in multistory rental properties. (H&S § 13220.) Storage rooms, garages, and basements must not contain combustible materials. State law requires that all multiple-unit dwellings offered for rental be equipped with smoke detectors, and that the landlord provide replacement batteries. (H&S § 13113.7.)

Check for CARBON MONOXIDE DETECTORS

Health and Safety Code Sections 17916 and 17926.1 require carbon monoxide detectors in all dwelling units. (See the "Carbon Monoxide" section of Chapter 10 for details on carbon monoxide concerns in rentals.)

Check for Adequate TRASH AND GARAGE RECEPTACLES

The landlord must provide adequate garbage and trash storage and removal facilities. Garbage cans must have tight-fitting covers.

Check the General CLEANLINESS OF THE AREA

Landlords must keep those parts of the building that they control (hallways, stairs, yards, basement, driveway, and so on) in a clean, sanitary, and safe condition.

Check the LOCKS

Landlords must install deadbolts on swinging main entry doors, common area doors, and gates and certain windows. (See Chapter 11 for details.) (CC § 1941.3.)

Check for EARTHQUAKE SAFETY

A building's earthquake resistance is a very important consideration in deciding where you want to rent, yet few people even think about it. Because the law does not provide specific protection for tenants living in unsafe buildings, you must be a wise shopper and ask the following specific questions about the building and its surroundings.

How Safe Is the Land Under the Building?

Proximity to a major fault is not the only factor you should consider when scoping out a place to rent. Be aware that:

- An unstable hillside is susceptible to landslides if an earthquake hits. The danger depends on the soil condition—rock is better than unconsolidated dirt. Flat, solid ground is best.
- The worst place for a building is on landfill. Fill is common along many California bays and rivers, including San Francisco Bay. In a quake with a lot of vigorous shaking, older fill and bay mud may liquefy.

Don't rent a place that is downstream from a dam. Some dams could fail (leak or even break) in an extremely strong earthquake.

How Safe Is the Building Itself?

Ask the building's manager or owner these questions:

- Does the building have a steel or wood frame? Is it built from steel-reinforced concrete, or is it a concrete shear wall building that is not irregularly shaped or does not have a "soft story"? These are usually safe buildings. Pay particular attention to buildings that have a ground-level garage. Solid shear walls that normally support that portion of the building during an earthquake are often removed to make way for garage doors or windows. The result is a building that is more likely to collapse onto that first floor in a major earthquake. Ask the manager or owner whether the walls of the garage (especially the front and back walls) have been strengthened with plywood sheathing. If they haven't been strengthened, know that you are taking a risk when you rent there.
- Is the building bolted to the foundation? If not, it can be shaken off of its foundation and severely damaged.
- Does the building have a lateral bracing system? If not, it will not be able to withstand the lateral forces of an earthquake.
- Is there plywood sheathing built around sliding glass doors, bay windows, or picture windows to decrease the risk of breakage?
- Does the building have a tile roof? Tile roofs are very heavy and may collapse during an earthquake. However, if the building is in a high-risk area for wildfires, tile roofs are highly recommended because they are fire-resistant.
- Are all water heaters properly strapped and fitted with a flexible gas supply line, so that they can't fall over and cause a fire or explosion triggered from a gas leak? State law requires existing water heaters to be braced, anchored, or strapped. (H&S §§ 19210–19217.)

- Where is the main gas shutoff, so that you may shut the gas off during an emergency? If the main gas line to the building is not shut off after a major earthquake, there is a high risk of fire or explosions due to leaking gas.
- Does the manager or owner have an earthquake preparedness plan to ensure that all tenants know how to safely exit the building and how to shut off any utilities if necessary?

(!) CAUTION

Beware of brick! Unreinforced brick buildings have the worst record in terms of durability during an earthquake. Some buildings that are not made of brick have a brick or stone veneer attached to the outside walls for aesthetic purposes. This veneer might be nice to look at, but unreinforced veneer is very susceptible to earthquake damage. Your building may not collapse in a major earthquake because it has a brick veneer, but anyone standing next to the building during an earthquake could be injured by bricks or stones falling off of the building.

Check Out the Landlord and Building

Your prospective landlord will probably check you out pretty thoroughly (asking for references and getting a credit report). Turnaround is fair play. Start by asking other residents, especially the person whose unit you're considering renting, about the pluses and minuses of living in the building and how the landlord handles things like repairs. If possible, talk with people in the neighborhood about the reputation of the building or the landlord. Finally, you may find useful information through public records or by doing Internet searches. For instance, you can do an online search of the County Superior Court to see if your landlord has been involved in any lawsuits, and what those lawsuits involved.

RESOURCE

For more information on earthquake safety. Check the California Seismic Safety Commission website (www.seismic.ca.gov) for information, such as the *Homeowner's Guide to Earthquake Safety* (http://ssc. ca.gov/forms_pubs/hog.html). Your city or town may also have neighborhood earthquake preparedness groups and lots of useful local information.

What If the Place Does Not Meet the Above Standards?

If the rental has serious problems, you should not rent it if you can possibly avoid it. A landlord who would even show you such a place probably won't or can't make the needed repairs. If the landlord promises to fix it up, be careful. First, ask other tenants how good the landlord is at keeping promises.

Second, get these promises in writing and make sure the landlord signs it, as illustrated in "Get All Promises in Writing," below. Be sure the agreement includes dates on which certain repairs will be completed. Also, try to include a statement that you will not have to pay your rent if the landlord fails to meet the completion dates. A landlord who doesn't want to agree to these things probably isn't taking his obligation to repair very seriously.

How to Bargain for the Best Deal

Once you decide that you would like to rent a particular place, negotiate the terms of the rental with the landlord or manager. Often you will be presented with a "take it or leave it" rental document, where the landlord is not open to making changes. Many

times, however, landlords will be open to reasonable changes. Whether it's the rent that you are trying to change, improvements you would like, or particular terms in the contract, it never hurts to try.

How good a deal you can get from a landlord depends on how badly you are needed. If there are very few places available at the asking rent and a lot of people are looking, the landlord might tell you to take the deal (rent, security deposit, and form lease) or forget the whole thing. Even an attempt to bargain could make the landlord reluctant to rent to you.

If you are in an area where there are lots of places for rent and not too many people looking, you will have more bargaining power. The landlord wants to rent the place soon (to get the rent) and might be afraid of losing you to another landlord.

If you can, try to talk to the last tenant who lived in the place. That person might give you some very valuable information on how to deal with the landlord, what is wrong with the place, and generally what it is like to live there. Other tenants or neighbors in the area might also be helpful on this.

Get All Promises in Writing

Tenants often move into an apartment that has not been properly cleaned, or that needs painting or repairs. The landlord may say that the tenant can deduct money from the rent in exchange for cleaning, painting, or repairs. Whatever promises the landlord makes, you should be aware that it is very common for this sort of vague, oral agreement to lead to misunderstanding, bitterness, and financial loss. The time to protect yourself is at the beginning. This could be your only chance to do so.

Sample Addendum to Lease or Rental Agreement

January 1, 20xx

Landlord Smith Realty and Tenant Patricia Parker make the following agreement, which is hereby added to the lease (or rental agreement) they entered into on _____ (date):

Patricia Parker agrees to buy paint and painting supplies not to exceed a cost of $225 and to paint apartment #4 at 1500 Acorn Street, Cloverdale, California, on or before February 1, 20xx and to forward all receipts for painting supplies and paint to Smith Realty.

Smith Realty agrees to reduce the payment due February 1, 20xx by $225 in consideration for the painting to be done by Patricia Parker; and in addition to allow Patricia Parker to deduct the actual cost of paint and painting supplies (not to exceed $120) from the rent payment due February 1, 20xx.

The premises are being rented with the following defects:

- dent in oven door
- gouge over fireplace in wall

These defects will be fixed by Smith Realty by _____ (date).

Smith Realty Company

By: B. C. Smith

Patricia Parker

If a landlord promises to clean, paint, build a deck, install a fence, or reimburse you for material and work, or if there are any other kinds of promises you want to depend upon, get them in writing and include a date for completing the work. Asking for a promise in writing need not cause you tension or embarrassment. Just tell the landlord, politely, that you have made a simple list of what has been agreed to, and you want to go over it for clarification. If the landlord agrees that the list is accurate, include a line saying that this list is made a part of the written lease or rental agreement, and have the landlord date and sign it. Prepare two copies, one for the landlord and one for your own file. (See "Sample Addendum to Lease or Rental Agreement," above.) Or, you could include the list on the lease itself, if it has a lease clause that covers "Additional terms."

If the landlord won't paint, clean, or make repairs, be sure to list the faults as particularly and completely as you can (on the lease itself if possible), and ask the landlord to sign and date the list. Otherwise, when you move out the landlord may claim that you caused the damage and refuse to refund all, or a part, of your deposit.

If the landlord doesn't want to sign your list, get a few of the most responsible of your friends to take a look at it and write a simple dated note of what they saw. Take photos on your phone and date-stamp them. All notes and links to pictures should go into your file with your other records.

The Landlord-Tenant Checklist

Another good self-protection device for both landlord and tenant involves taking an inventory of the condition of the premises at the time you move in, when the landlord conducts the pre–move-out inspections, and then again when you move out. This means no more than making a brief written record of the condition of each room and having it signed by you and your landlord. Not only does the inventory give both of you an accurate record of the condition of the unit, but the act of making it provides a framework for communication and the resolution of potential disputes about security deposits when you move out. (See "Avoiding Deposit Problems" in Chapter 13.) We include a sample landlord-tenant checklist below.

FORM

You'll find the Landlord/Tenant Checklist in Appendix C, and on this book's companion page on the Nolo website (see Appendix B for the link to the forms in this book). You can edit the form to fit your particular rental.

When filling out your checklist, mark "OK" in the space next to items that are in satisfactory condition (in the Condition on Arrival column). Make a note—as specific as possible—next to items that are not working or are in bad or filthy condition. Thus, you might state next to the "Stove and Refrigerator" listing: "generally good, but crack in freezer door." Be sure to note things like worn rugs, chipped enamel, holes in screens, and dirty cabinets, and inventory all furnishings.

Be sure you check the box at the bottom of the third page of the checklist, acknowledging that you tested the smoke detector and fire extinguisher in the landlord's presence and found them to be in working order.

Cosigning Leases

A cosigner (also referred to as a guarantor or a surety) is someone who signs a rental agreement to guarantee that the cosigner will pay the rent for the premises or for damages to the property if the tenant fails to do so. The cosigner will be asked to sign a separate agreement or will sign the lease agreement itself. Cosigners must assume that they will be liable in the event of nonpayment of rent or damage to the property.

However, there may be exceptions to this general rule. A cosigner could argue that the agreement between the cosigner and the landlord is so vague that it is not enforceable—against the tenant or the cosigner. Also, if a landlord and tenant change the terms of their rental agreement—or even renew it—without the signed approval of the cosigner, the cosigner is no longer responsible. (CC § 2819; *Wexler v. McLucas,* 48 Cal.App.3d Supp. 9 (1975).)

Many tenants and landlords allow the tenant to stay on, paying rent, after the lease has expired. The tenant has become a month-to-month tenant, and both parties are subject to the terms and conditions of the original lease. When this happens, a cosigner may revoke (cancel) the guarantee. (CC § 2815.)

Landlords must take extra steps to get money out of a cosigner when the landlord sues a tenant for eviction and includes a request for back rent. The cosigner can't be sued in the eviction lawsuit. The cosigner must be sued separately, either in a regular civil lawsuit or in small claims court.

TIP

Cosigners and applicants with a disability. If you are an applicant with a disability, as that term is defined by law, and you have insufficient income for the rental (but are otherwise a suitable tenant), federal law requires landlords to accommodate you by considering a cosigner whom you have offered. This is true even when the landlord does not usually accept cosigners. If the proposed cosigner would be acceptable to any reasonable landlord in this situation, the landlord risks a fair housing claim if the cosigner is rejected.

Landlord/Tenant Checklist
General Condition of Rental Unit and Premises

1834 Fell Street
Street Address

Apt. 5
Unit Number

San Francisco
City

	Condition on Arrival	Condition on Initial Move-Out Inspection	Condition on Departure	Actual or Estimated Cost of Cleaning, Repair/Replacement
Living Room				
Floors & Floor Coverings	OK			
Drapes & Window Coverings	OK			
Walls & Ceilings	OK			
Light Fixtures	OK			
Windows, Screens, & Doors	back door scratched			
Front Door & Locks	OK			
Smoke Detector	OK			
Fireplace	N/A			
Other				
Kitchen				
Floors & Floor Coverings	cigarette burn hole in carpet			
Walls & Ceilings	OK			
Light Fixtures	OK			
Cabinets	OK			
Counters	discolored			
Stove/Oven	OK			
Refrigerator	OK			
Dishwasher	OK			
Garbage Disposal	N/A			
Sink & Plumbing	OK			
Smoke Detector	OK			
Other				

	Condition on Arrival	Condition on Initial Move-Out Inspection	Condition on Departure	Actual or Estimated Cost of Cleaning, Repair/Replacement
Dining Room				
Floors & Floor Coverings	OK			
Walls & Ceilings	crack in ceiling			
Light Fixtures	OK			
Windows, Screens, & Doors	OK			
Smoke Detector	OK			
Other				
Bathroom				
Floors & Floor Coverings	OK			
Walls & Ceilings	OK			
Windows, Screens, & Doors	OK			
Light Fixtures	OK			
Bathtub/Shower	tub chipped			
Sinks & Counters	OK			
Toilet	OK			
Other				
Other				
Bedroom				
Floors & Floor Coverings	OK			
Windows, Screens, & Doors	OK			
Walls & Ceilings	OK			
Light Fixtures	dented			
Smoke Detector	OK			
Other				
Other				
Other				

Other Areas	Condition on Arrival	Condition on Initial Move-Out Inspection	Condition on Departure	Actual or Estimated Cost of Cleaning, Repair/Replacement
Heating System				
Air-Conditioning				
Lawn/Garden				
Stairs & Hallway				
Patio, Terrace, Deck, etc.				
Basement				
Parking Area				
Other				
Other				
Other				
Other				
Other				

☒ Tenants acknowledge that all smoke detectors were tested in their presence and found to be in working order, and that the testing procedure was explained to them. Tenants agree to promptly notify Landlord in writing should any smoke detector appear to be malfunctioning or inoperable. Tenants will not refuse Landlord access for the purpose of inspecting, maintaining, repairing, or installing legally required smoke detectors.

Notes: _____

	Condition on Arrival	Condition on Initial Move-Out Inspection	Condition on Departure	Actual or Estimated Cost of Cleaning, Repair/Replacement
Living Room				
Coffee Table	two scratches on top			
End Tables	N/A			
Lamps	OK			
Chairs	OK			
Sofa	OK			
Other				
Other				
Kitchen				
Broiler Pan	N/A			
Ice Trays	OK			
Other				
Other				
Dining Room				
Chairs	OK			
Stools	N/A			
Table	leg bent slightly			
Other				
Other				
Bathroom				
Mirrors	OK			
Shower Curtain	OK			
Hamper	N/A			
Other				

	Condition on Arrival	Condition on Initial Move-Out Inspection	Condition on Departure	Actual or Estimated Cost of Cleaning, Repair/Replacement
Bedroom				
Beds (single)	OK			
Beds (double)	N/A			
Chairs	OK			
Chests	N/A			
Dressing Tables	OK			
Lamps	OK			
Mirrors	OK			
Night Tables	N/A			
Other	N/A			
Other				
Other Area				
Bookcases				
Desks				
Pictures				
Other	hallway picture frame chipped			
Other				

Use this space to provide any additional explanation:

Landlord/Tenant Checklist completed on moving in on _____May 1_____, 20_XX_ and _____

_____Ira Eppler_____ Landlord/Manager   _____Chloe Gustafson_____ Tenant

_____ Tenant

_____ Tenant

Landlord/Tenant Checklist completed at Initial Move-Out Inspection on _____, 20_____ and _____

_____ Landlord/Manager   _____ Tenant

_____ Tenant

_____ Tenant

Landlord/Tenant Checklist completed on moving out on _____, 20_____ and _____

_____ Landlord/Manager   _____ Tenant

_____ Tenant

_____ Tenant

Know Your Manager

Many medium-to-large apartment complexes have managers. (State law requires a resident manager in any multiunit property of 16 units or more. (CCR Title 25, § 42.) Some owners use management corporations, who specialize in managing lots of rental units and who get paid a percentage (usually between 5% and 10%) of the rental income. Such companies tend to be sticklers for rules and procedures, but are usually less emotionally involved than owners, and are often more rational at arriving at businesslike compromises.

Often, however, the owner will simply give a resident free or reduced rent to be a "resident manager" and to look after the property on a part-time basis. This can be either good or bad as far as you are concerned, depending on the personality of the manager and whether the manager has any real authority (or ability) to take care of problems. Just as there are all sorts of landlords, there is an equal variety of managers.

In dealing with a manager on a day-to-day basis, not only is it important to notice who he is and how best to deal with him, it is also important to notice his relationship to the owner. If you can, find out how long the manager has been working for the owner. For instance, a manager who has been around for many years would know about the building and its tenants and would presumably be reliable and have a working relationship with the landlord.

Remember, the owner and the manager may have very different interests. Some owners, for example, may want the property to yield a maximum amount of profit with a minimal amount of trouble, while others may be investing for long-term real property appreciation and be willing to be relatively generous to tenants in the meantime (these owners realize that low tenant turnover is the key to making money). Similarly, some managers might want to do as little work as possible for their free rent, while others, especially those who are in the business, may want to do a bang-up job in hopes that word will spread and they will get other jobs.

A landlord is legally responsible for the quality of the job done (or not done) by the manager or management company. Should you be in a situation in which the premises are not being kept clean or in good repair, or if the manager is obnoxious or invading your privacy, you will probably want to deal directly with the owner. In any case, where communications are sticky or broken down, you should send duplicate copies of letters and other communications to the owner as well as to the manager.

Sharing a Home

Lots of unmarried people rent a place together. Whether it involves sharing a bed or not, sharing a home can have all sorts of legal ramifications. So you need to be mindful of both the legal relationship with the landlord and the legal relationships among the people you are living with.

TIP

Be clear about the practical issues, too. Before you move in with roommates, even your closest friends, make sure you're compatible on key issues such as neatness and cleaning standards, financial responsibility, food sharing, privacy, noise, smoking, and overnight guests. The Sample Agreement Between Roommates, below, covers some key issues, such as moving out; you may want to add others.

The Legal Obligations of Roommates to the Landlord

If two people—let's call them James and Helen —together enter into a single lease or rental agreement (written or oral), they are each legally responsible to the landlord for all rent and all damages to the apartment—except "normal wear and tear." It makes no difference who—or whose friends—caused the damage, or who left without paying the rent. Let's look at several common situations.

EXAMPLE 1: James and Helen both sign a written rental agreement providing for a total monthly rent of $1,500 for a flat. They agree between themselves to pay one-half each. After three months, James refuses to pay his half of the rent (or moves out with no notice to Helen and the landlord). In either situation, Helen is legally obligated to pay all the rent, as far as the landlord is concerned. James, of course, is equally liable, but if he is unreachable or out of work, the landlord will almost surely come after Helen for the whole amount. Since James and Helen have rented under a month-to-month written

rental agreement, Helen can cut her losses by giving the landlord a 30-day written notice of intention to move. She can do this even if James is lying around the place, refusing to pay or get out.

If Helen ends up paying the landlord all of the rent due (more than her agreed share), she has a right to recover half of that from James. If James does not voluntarily pay, Helen can sue James in small claims court.

RESOURCE

See *Everybody's Guide to Small Claims Court in California*, by Cara O'Neill (Nolo), for more information on how to use small claims court.

EXAMPLE 2: The same fact situation as Example 1, except that this time there is a lease for one year. Again, both partners are independently liable for the whole rent. If one refuses to pay, the other is still liable, unless a third person can be found to take over the lease, in which case both partners are off the hook from the day that a new tenant takes over. As we discuss in Chapter 12, because of housing shortages in many parts of the state, it is often easy for a tenant to get out of a lease at little or no cost, simply by finding an acceptable new tenant and steering him or her to the landlord. A Craigslist ad will usually do it. The landlord has an obligation to limit his damages (called "mitigation of damages" in legal lingo) by renting to a suitable new tenant as soon as possible. Should the landlord fail to do this, he limits his legal right to collect all the damages from the original tenants.

EXAMPLE 3: Tom, Dick, and Harry each rent rooms in a flat and have access to the kitchen and other common areas. They each have separate rental agreements and pay rent separately to the landlord. Tom loses his job and cannot pay rent. Dick and Harry are not responsible for Tom's rent, so the landlord has to go after Tom directly. If Tom moves out, the landlord is the one who selects Tom's replacement. An arrangement like this is often referred to as a "rooming house" arrangement.

Sample Agreement Between Roommates

Agreement

Helen Mattson and James Kennedy, upon renting an apartment at 1500 Redwood Street, #4, Philo, California, agree as follows:

1. Helen and James are each obligated to pay one-half of the rent and one-half of the utilities, including the basic monthly cable bill. Rent shall be paid on the first of each month.

2. If either Helen or James wants to move out, the one moving will give the other person 30 days' notice and will pay his/her share of the rent for the entire 30-day period even if he/she moves out sooner. If both Helen and James wish to move, they will be jointly responsible for giving the landlord 30 days' notice.

3. No third persons will be invited to stay overnight in the apartment without the mutual agreement of both Helen and James.

4. If we have a dispute that we are not able to resolve, we agree to mediate that dispute with [*fill in, with a group such as a Community Board or a named mutual friend*].

5. If both Helen and James want to keep the apartment but do not wish to live together, they will have a third party flip a coin to see who gets to stay. The loser will move out within 30 days and will pay all of his/her obligations for rent, utilities, and any damage to the apartment.

[*Here is an alternative for number 5.*]

5. If both Helen and James want to keep the apartment but no longer wish to live together, the apartment will be retained by the person who needs it most. Need will be determined by taking into consideration the relative financial condition of each party, proximity to work, the needs of minor children, if any, and [*list any other factors important to you*]. If Helen and James can't decide this issue by themselves or with the help of a mutually agreed-upon mediator, the determination will be made by a third party (the arbitrator). If it is not possible for Helen and James to agree on an arbitrator, the arbitrator will be chosen by [*fill in name*]. The arbitrator will be paid by the person who gets to keep the apartment. The determination will be made within ten days after either party informs the other that he or she wishes to separate, and after the arbitrator has listened to each person present his or her case. The arbitration award will be conclusive on the parties, and will be prepared in such a way that a formal judgment can be entered thereon in any court having jurisdiction over the dispute if either party so desires. After the determination is made, the person who is to leave will have an additional ten days to do so. The person who leaves is obligated for all rent, utilities, and any damage costs for 30 days from the day of the original determination to separate.

July 1, 20XX	*Helen Mattson*
Date	Helen Mattson
July 1, 20XX	*James Kennedy*
Date	James Kennedy

Your Responsibility for Rent If You Move Out and Your Roommate Stays

If you are on a month-to-month tenancy, you should give written notice to both the landlord and your cotenant that you are terminating your tenancy at the premises, even if your roommate is going to stay. This should end your obligations to the landlord and you shouldn't be liable for your room-mate's rent. (*Schmidt v. Felix,* 157 Cal.App.2d 642 (1958), *Kavin v. Frye,* 204 Cal.App.4th 35 (2012).)

But be aware that you may still be on the hook, if you signed a "guarantee" of the lease. Look carefully at the lease. Do you see language like, "Tenants shall be jointly and severally liable until the tenancy has terminated"? When just one tenant leaves, the tenancy has not terminated. Or, do you see "tenants shall be liable for all rent until all keys are turned in"? Again, your departure is not the same as "all keys ... turned in." With language like this, you will have to do a bit more to get out from under what is essentially a guarantee of the rent, even when you're no longer living there.

The obligation to "guarantee" your roommate's continued payment of rent must be explicit and unambiguous. (CC §§ 2787, 2799.) If you agreed to be "jointly and severally" liable for the rent (by signing a lease with promises like those above), you may have effectively guaranteed your roommate's rent. If you think that there is a chance that you have "guaranteed" the rent, you can write a simple letter to the landlord telling him that you are "revoking" (cancelling) any guarantee that you would be responsible for your roommate's rental obligations. (CC § 2815).

If you are on a fixed-term lease, you will be legally responsible to the landlord for rent up to the end of the lease. Unfortunately, there is not much you can do to avoid this except to help the cotenant find a suitable replacement and get consent from the landlord for that replacement. (When the premises are rerented, your obligation ends.) At some point before the end of the lease, you should give a written notification that your obligations to the landlord will terminate on the termination date. Now, suppose your roommate remains after the termination of the lease, as a month-to-month tenant? To avoid continued responsibility for rent for any period after the expiration of the lease, follow the process outlined above: First, determine whether there is a guarantee; and second, if there is one, send a letter to the landlord revoking any such guarantee.

Having a Friend Move In

Perhaps just as common as two or more people renting a home together is for one person to move into a place already rented and occupied by another. This is often simple and smooth when the landlord is cooperative, but can involve some tricky legal questions if the landlord raises objections.

In some situations, where the landlord is not in the area or is not likely to make waves, it might be tempting to simply have the second person move in and worry about the consequences later. But you have to assume there will be a "later" and that the consequences could be eviction if you have a rental or lease agreement that prohibits assignment or subletting without the consent of the landlord (most written agreements do). Even if there is no prohibition against subletting it is better to inform the landlord of the replacement.

Cities with rent control and/or just cause for eviction often have special rules regarding adding or replacing roommates. They are listed in Appendix A along with contact information, including Web addresses.

! CAUTION

Your tenancy may be at stake. Under state law, a written rental agreement may be terminated on 30 days' notice (60 days if the tenant has lived there for one year or more, and 90 days for government-subsidized tenancies) without the necessity of the landlord giving a reason. Thus, a landlord who wants to get rid of you can normally do so without too much trouble if you don't have a lease. So it pays to be reasonable when moving roommates in and out. Remember, if you live in a city with eviction controls ("just cause eviction protection"), the ordinance will provide you with some additional protections.

Sample Letter or Email When a New Roommate Moves In

1500 Redwood Street #4
Philo, California 00000

June 27, 20xx

Smith Realty
10 Ocean Street
Elk, California 00000

I live at the above address, and regularly pay rent to your office.

As of July 1, 20xx, there will be a second person living in my apartment. As set forth in my lease, I enclose the increased rent due, which now comes to a total of $1,500. I will continue to make payments in this amount as long as two people occupy the apartment.

Should you wish to sign a new lease specifically to cover two people, please let me know. My friend, Helen Mattson, is regularly employed and has an excellent credit rating.

Very truly yours,

James Kennedy

James Kennedy

The Legal Relationship Between the Person Moving In and the Landlord

If Helen moves into James's apartment without being added to the rental agreement or lease, what is the relationship between Helen and James's landlord? Is Helen obligated to pay rent if James fails to pay? What if James moves out, but Helen wants to remain? If James ruins the paint or breaks the furniture, does Helen have any obligation to pay for the damage?

Here, Helen's agreement is with James only. Many landlords prefer to deal with only one tenant and, in this case, James is the one. If Helen doesn't pay the rent to James, it's James's problem as far as the landlord is concerned, who will still look to James for full payment. If Helen pays the rent to James and James doesn't pay the landlord, Helen (along with James) could be evicted for nonpayment of rent. If Helen moves out and doesn't get her deposit back from James, she has to sue James, not the landlord. If James moves out, Helen has no relationship with the landlord and can be evicted.

Helen can attempt to gain tenancy status as a cotenant of James. This would give her the full rights and obligations of a tenant. This can be done in any of the following ways:

- Sign a new lease, rental agreement, or addendum to a rental agreement that names both James and Helen as tenants.
- Notify the landlord in writing of Helen's presence in the apartment. (This would be especially important to do in a rent control jurisdiction, as long as you don't have the risk of "illegally subletting" the unit). Again, this could take the form of a confirmation letter like the ones we have described previously. Helen could then argue later that the landlord effectively consented to her occupancy by continuing to accept rent with the knowledge that she was living there. This could be especially important in rent control cities. (*Parkmerced Co. v. San Francisco Rent Stabilization & Arbitration Board*, 215 Cal.App.3d 490 (1989).)

- In the same vein, Helen could pay rent directly to the landlord, and the landlord's continued acceptance of rent could create a tenancy. (*Parkmerced Co. v. San Francisco Rent Stabilization & Arbitration Board*, 215 Cal.App.3d 490 (1989).)

If the situation arises that James will be moving out before Helen, but Helen wants to stay, the legal relationship between Helen and the landlord should be clarified if it hasn't yet been. It's in everybody's interest that the discussion take place as soon as possible. (See the Sample Letter or Email below.) Cities with rent control may have special rules regarding roommates, so check with your local rent board is this situation arises.

Sample Letter or Email When One Tenant Moves Out and the Other Remains (Lease)

1500 Redwood Street #4
Philo, California 00000

June 27, 20xx

Smith Realty
10 Ocean Street
Elk, California 00000

I live at the above address under a lease that expires on October 30, 20xx. A change in my job makes it necessary that I leave the last day of July. As you know, for the last six months my friend, Helen Mattson, has been sharing this apartment. Helen wishes to remain and enter into a new lease with you for the remainder of the original lease term. She is employed, has a stable income, and will, of course, continue to be a responsible tenant.

We will soon be contacting your office to work out the details of the transfer. If you have any concerns about this proposal, please give us a call.

Very truly yours,

James Kennedy
James Kennedy

 RENT CONTROL

If Helen has attained the status of a tenant, the landlord will probably not be able to raise the rent after James leaves, except as otherwise permitted by the local rent control ordinance. If, on the other hand, Helen has not become a tenant, she will be considered a "new tenant," and the rent can be raised as much as the landlord wants. Check your rent control ordinance, or ask the rent board, to learn whether you are protected.

Sample Letter or Email When One Tenant Moves Out and the Other Remains (Rental Agreement)

1500 Redwood Street #4
Philo, California 00000

June 27, 20xx

Smith Realty
10 Ocean Street
Elk, California 00000

I live at the above address and regularly pay rent to your office. On July 31, 20xx, I will be moving out. As you know, my friend, Helen Mattson, also resides here. She wishes to remain and will continue to pay rent to your office on the first of each month.

Very truly yours,

James Kennedy
James Kennedy

The Legal Relationship Between the Person Moving In and the Person Already There

Unless the person moving in has established a legal relationship with the landlord (that is, the new person has followed one of the steps outlined in the previous section), the person already there becomes the landlord of the person moving in. This relationship is legally described as one between a "sublandlord" (that's the original tenant) and a "subtenant." Commonly, the sublandlord is also known as the "master tenant." If the tenancy is covered by statewide rent control, the master tenant cannot charge a subtenant any more than the total rent that the master tenant pays the landlord. (See CC § 1947.12(c), and the statewide rent control discussion in Chapter 3.) Many local rent control ordinances have similar provisions.

Because the master tenant is the subtenant's landlord, the master tenant can raise the rent or even evict the subtenant by giving proper legal notice. This is true even when the landlord did not know about the subtenant (but keep in mind, as explained above, that if the lease contains a "no sublet without consent" clause, the landlord could in turn evict the tenant/sublandlord for violating this clause).

Some rent control jurisdictions address evictions and how much rent the master tenant can charge in a master tenant-subtenant situation. For example, in San Francisco the subtenant's rent must be no more than a stated portion, or percent, of the master tenant's own rent. (See Topic # 154, Limits on Rent Charged by Master Tenants, on the San Francisco Rent Board website, https://sfrb.org.)

Resolving Disputes Among Residents

In either a cotenant-cotenant situation or a master tenant-subtenant situation, disputes between residents may arise. A relationship that is all sunshine and roses at the start often becomes unhappy over time. When feelings change, memories blur as to promises made in happier times, and the nicest people become paranoid and nasty. We suggest that before memories blur (preferably at the time that the living arrangement is set up), both people make a little note as to their mutual understandings, either as part of a comprehensive living together arrangement or in a separate agreement (see the "Sample Agreement Between Roommates," above).

If you don't have an agreement already in place and get into a serious dispute with your friend involving your shared home, you will have to do the best you can to muddle through to a fair solution. Here are a few ideas to guide your thinking:

- If only one of you has signed the agreement with the landlord and that person pays all the rent, then that person probably should have the first claim on the apartment, especially if that person occupied the apartment first. The other should be given a reasonable period of time to find another place, especially if he or she has been contributing to the rent and/ or has been living in the home for any considerable period of time.

- If you both signed a lease or rental agreement and/or both regularly pay rent to the landlord, your rights to the apartment are probably legally equal, even if one of you got there first. Try to talk out your situation, letting the person stay who genuinely needs the place the most. Some people find it helpful to set up an informal mediation proceeding with a third person helping the parties arrive at their own solution. If this doesn't work, you may wish to locate a neutral third-party arbitrator to hear the facts and make a decision. If you do this, make sure that the arbitrator is not a close friend, as the person who loses is likely to have hard feelings. Lean over backwards to be fair about adjusting money details concerning such things as last month's rent and security deposits. Allow the person moving out a reasonable period of time to find another place. *We have found that the best compromises are made when both people feel that they have gone more than halfway.*

- Each person has the right to his or her belongings. This is true even if they are behind in their share of the rent. Never lock up the other person's property.

It is generally illegal to deny a person access to his or her home, and doing so could result in a lawsuit where you would face liability for actual damages, statutory damages, and attorney fees. (CC § 789.3.) If, however, you or one of your cotenants has filed a certain type of injunction against another tenant, the landlord has 24 hours to change the locks upon your written request. If the landlord fails to do so, the tenant can change the locks. (See the discussion below for specifics.)

Victims of Harassment, Domestic Violence, Sexual Assault, Stalking, or Elder or Dependent Adult Abuse

Occasionally, cotenant relationships result in violence, abuse, or other forms of harassment. If the harassment rises to a severe level, the law allows you to go to court and ask for a "Restraining Order." The California Judicial Council provides some information about restraining orders. For further information go to www.courts.ca.gov/1044.htm and to www.courts.ca.gov/selfhelp-domestic violence.htm (for information related to domestic violence restraining orders) and to www.courts.ca.gov/selfhelp-elder.htm (for information related to elder and dependent adult abuse). If you cannot download forms, then your local court should also have information about obtaining a restraining order. Note also that courts have their own rules about how these requests are reviewed by a judge, so be sure to follow their procedures.

If you get a restraining order *against a cotenant or subtenant* forbidding him (or her) from contacting you ("no contact" orders) and the order is not more than 180 days old, you can demand in writing that the landlord change the locks within 24 hours. If the landlord does not, you have the right to change the locks yourself if you do it in a workmanlike manner. If you do end up changing the locks, you are required to notify the landlord within 24 hours and provide him with a key. (CC § 1941.6.)

Sometimes the target of a "non contact" order is someone other than a cotenant or subtenant. If you get a restraining order forbidding contact against someone who is not a tenant in your apartment (such as a guest or a neighbor), you can have the locks changed as specified above if you act within 180 days of getting the order. Alternatively, if you file a police report against a non-tenant alleging domestic violence, sexual abuse, or stalking, you may likewise have the locks changed as outlined above. (CC § 1941.5.)

California gives tenants in these situations some protection from landlord retaliation. A landlord cannot terminate or fail to renew a tenancy based on a household member's status as a victim of domestic violence, sexual abuse, stalking, elder or dependent abuse, or human trafficking. (CCP § 1161.3.) A landlord may terminate a tenancy on that basis if one of the two situations below exists:

- the tenant allows the abuser to visit the property and the landlord has given a three-day notice of violation, which the tenant has failed to cure, or
- the landlord reasonably believes that the abuser poses a physical threat to the tenant or other tenants or a threat to their quiet enjoyment, the landlord has given a three-day notice of violation, and the tenant has failed to correct the violation. (CCP § 1161.3(b).)

 RESOURCE

A number of California cities and counties have free or low-cost landlord-tenant mediation and arbitration services. In addition, the nonprofit Community Board program offers excellent mediation services in many San Francisco neighborhoods.

Guests

What about overnight guests—particularly those who stay over often? What relationship, if any, do these people have with the landlord? More important, is the landlord entitled to any legal recourse if you have a "regular" guest? The answer to this question often depends on what it says in a lease or written rental agreement or written house rules. (See Chapter 1.) Many restrict the right to have overnight guests to a certain number of days per year, and/or require notification if a guest will stay more than a few days. While these sorts of lease provisions aren't always strictly enforced, they are valid and can be grounds for a landlord evicting a tenant. Even in rent control areas that require just cause for eviction, a tenant who violates guest rules may be evicted. Under the terms of many ordinances, the tenant must first be given a written notice to correct the violation before the landlord goes to court.

Landlords do not want someone's status as a "guest" to suddenly change to that of a "subtenant." Easing this fear should be a first line of defense should a dispute arise. Indicators of whether a person is a guest or subtenant include whether the person:

- is paying any rent (normally, guests do not)
- has another residence where they keep most of their belongings
- has sole use of an area of the apartment (sole use of a bedroom, for example, suggests a permanent stay; sharing with another resident, without more, connotes guest status), and
- for those enjoying sole use and even those who are sharing a space with someone else, whether the landlord knew of the newcomer, approved of him or her being there, and accepted rent after that.

An additional landlord concern is the fear that additional occupants cause utility charges to increase and cause greater "wear and tear" on the building. Again, we suggest having a straightforward discussion about the guest or guests in question before the fact. Such discussions should be confirmed in writing in case the dispute turns into an eviction lawsuit. Keep in mind that the guest provision in your lease or rental agreement is probably valid, and if the landlord requires you to strictly adhere to it, you should comply in order to avoid eviction.

All About Rent

Today most tenants pay 35% or more of their incomes on rent—sometimes many thousands of dollars a month. This money obviously means a lot to you, so you should understand your rights regarding when and how to pay, how much to pay, limits on late rent and returned check fees, and whether and by how much the landlord can increase the rent.

How Much Can the Landlord Charge?

Historically, landlords have been allowed to charge as much rent as the market will bear (that is, the amount a willing renter and a willing landlord will agree to). The market rent bears little or no relationship to the landlord's actual expenses, but is determined by the number of people looking for rentals, how much they can afford, and the number of rentals available. Historically, landlords have been allowed to increase rents by any amount as long as the increase is not motivated by discrimination (discussed in Chapter 4) or in retaliation for the tenant's exercising a legal right.

Several sets of laws now limit the landlord's ability to raise the rent. They are:

- Local Rent Control Laws, which exist in many cities (see our rent control chart in Appendix A).
- Statewide rent control, effective January 1, 2020, which covers an estimated 4.6 million households.
- Protections against price-gouging, where there has been a natural disaster.
- Restrictions imposed under government-funded housing assistance programs, such as Section 8.

These rent restrictions are discussed later in this chapter.

When Is Rent Due?

Under state law, rent is due at the end of the term of the tenancy—for example, at the end of the month, in a month-to-month tenancy—unless the lease or rental agreement provides otherwise. (CC § 1947.) Almost every lease and rental agreement require payment at the beginning of the term. Thus, rent for use of the place in March would be due on March 1.

If the rent due date falls on a weekend or holiday, your rent is still due on that date, unless your lease or rental agreement specifies otherwise (many landlords will give you until the next business day). (*Gans v. Smull*, 111 Cal.App.4th 985 (2003).)

If you fail to pay your rent on the date it is due, the landlord may not throw you out or sue to evict you the next day. The landlord must first serve you with a written three-day notice demanding that you pay the rent or vacate. If the third day falls on a Saturday, Sunday, or holiday, you get until the next business day to pay the rent. (CCP § 12a.) If, at the end of the three days (or more, if extended by a Saturday, Sunday, or holiday), you have neither moved out nor paid the rent, the landlord can file an eviction lawsuit against you. (See Chapter 14 for details on three-day notices.)

Form of Rent Payment

Your lease or rental agreement should specify what form of payment the landlord will accept, such as cash, personal check, money order, or electronic transfer. For a new tenancy, cash cannot be the only option. A landlord cannot demand that rent be paid only in cash, unless you have previously given the landlord a bounced check or have issued a stop payment on a rent check—and the landlord gave you written notice to that effect. In that event, the landlord's demand for cash only may last no longer than three months. (CC § 1947.3.) The landlord may also not demand that you pay rent via online payment or electronic funds transfer, unless the landlord gives you an alternative form of payment other than cash.

Renters' Tax Credit

California gives qualified low-income renters a nonrefundable tax credit against their "net tax" that can be claimed on their state income tax return. (Cal. Rev. & Tax. Code § 17053.5.) Eligible renters are those who, filing singly or jointly, have an adjusted gross yearly income that's less than specified amounts. The California Franchise Tax Board (FTB) adjusts the minimum income amounts yearly. For tax year 2019, the amounts are:

- $42,932 or less if your filing status is single; or if you are married or a member of a registered domestic partnership but filing separately, and
- $85,864 or less if you are married or a member of a registered domestic partnership and filing jointly, the head of a household, or a qualified widow or widower.

To learn of the minimum income amounts for subsequent years, visit the FTB website at www.ftb.ca.gov and type "renter's tax credit" into the search box on the home page.

To claim the credits, taxpayers must satisfy the following requirements:

- For at least half the year, you paid rent for property in California that was also your principal residence, and that property was not exempt from property tax (such as church property).
- You did not live with another person for more than half the year (such as a parent) who claimed you as a dependent.
- You were not a minor living with and under the care of a parent, foster parent, or legal guardian.
- You or your spouse or registered domestic partner was not granted a homeowner's property tax exemption during the tax year (however, you may still claim the credit if your spouse or registered domestic partner did claim a homeowner's exemption, but you maintained a separate residence for the entire year).

TIP

Document your rent payment. Sometimes misunderstandings arise over whether the rent has been paid and, if so, how much. Payment by check or electronic transfer of funds is the best way to document your history of rent payment, because you have quick access to your record of payments. Payments made by money order, however, can take weeks, sometimes months, to trace. Therefore, if you are paying your rent by money order or cash, it is especially important to get a receipt from your landlord. The law entitles you to a written receipt upon your payment of rent. (CC § 1479, CCP § 2075.)

Payment By a Third Party

Tenants might arrange to have their rent paid by a parent, guardian, charity, or directly by the government. Landlords must accept these payments from current tenants as long as the third party states in writing that he or she is not a current tenant of the property, and that the landlord's acceptance of the payment will not create a new tenancy with the third party. Notably, this law does not require the landlord enter into a contract with a federal, state, or local housing assistance program, including the federal housing assistance voucher programs under Section 8 of the United States Housing Act of 1937 (42 U.S.C. § 1437f). (CC § 1947.3.)

The landlord's obligation to accept payments from the third parties listed above does not apply to applicants, because the law speaks only of tenants, not applicants or prospective tenants. An applicant who wants to offer another source for rent payments must offer a lease guarantor, whom the landlord may screen for creditworthiness. If the landlord decides to accept the guarantor, the guarantor becomes contractually obligated to pay your rent if you do not. By contrast, if you get a charity check, the nonprofit or charity isn't contractually agreeing to pay your rent. It's simply a gift (though the charity will probably ask the landlord to agree in writing that you won't be evicted for nonpayment after the charity or nonprofit pays any rent due).

If you would like to have a third party pay your rent, you can use our form, Statement of Third Party Paying Rent, to satisfy this requirement. Landlords may require a separate form for each rent payment, or the landlord and the third party can agree that one form will suffice for multiple payments.

FORM

You'll find a copy of the Statement of Third Party Paying Rent in Appendix C, and the Nolo website includes a downloadable copy. (See Appendix B for the link to the forms in this book.)

Late Fees and Returned Check Charges

A fairly common landlord practice is to charge a fee to tenants who are late with their rent, or who bounce a check. Some cities with rent control ordinances regulate the amount of late fee charges. Check any rent control ordinance applicable to your rental. Most California cities and unincorporated areas, however, do not regulate what you can be charged for late fees.

Late Fees

Late charges must be reasonably related to the amount of money it costs the landlord to deal with your lateness. (CC § 1671(d).) Provisions in rental agreements and lease clauses that provide for unreasonably high late charges are not enforceable. (*Orozco v. Casimiro*, 212 Cal.App.4th Supp. 7 (2004).) In one case, a judge invalidated a $50.00 late fee because the landlord could not prove that the charge was "reasonably related" to the losses caused by the late payment. (*Del Monte Properties & Investments, Inc. v. Dolan*, 22 Cal.App.5th Supp. 20 (2018).)

While there are no statutory guidelines as to how much a landlord can reasonably charge as a late fee, here are some guidelines that will help you decide if the amount is excessive:

- A reasonable late charge might be a flat charge of no more than $25 to $100, depending on the amount of rent. It is common for a landlord to give a tenant a grace period of from one to five days, but there is no law that requires this. A late charge that is out of proportion to the rent (say $100 for being one day late with rent on an $800 per month apartment) would probably not be upheld in court.
- If your landlord imposes a late charge that increases with each additional day of lateness, it should be moderate and have an upper limit. For example, $20 for the first day rent is late, plus $10 for each additional day, with a maximum late charge of 4% to 6% of the rental amount, might be acceptable to a judge, unless the property carries a high rent, in which case somewhat higher amounts might be allowed.

Some landlords try to disguise excessive late charges as a "discount" for early payment of rent. One landlord we know concluded he couldn't get away with charging a $100 late charge on a late $850 rent payment, so instead he designed a rental agreement calling for a rent of $950 with a $100 discount if the rent was not more than three days late. Ingenious as this sounds, it is unlikely to stand up in court, unless the discount for timely payments is very modest. This is because the effect of giving a relatively large discount is the same as charging an excessive late fee, and a judge is likely to see it as such and throw it out.

Returned Check Charges

Landlords who accept checks as rent payment may legally charge an extra fee if a tenant's rent check bounces. As with late fees, bounced check charges must be reasonable—generally, no more than the amount the landlord's bank charges for a returned check (such as $15 to $25) per returned item, plus a few dollars for the landlord's trouble. State law sets a limit of $25 for the first bounced check and $35 for subsequent checks. (CC § 1719.)

Partial Rent Payments

On occasion, you may be short of money to pay your full rent on time. The best way to deal with this is to discuss the problem with your landlord and try to get the landlord to accept a partial payment. Except in the unusual situation where your lease or rental agreement gives you the right to make partial payments, the landlord is under no obligation to accept part of the rent on the due date along with your promise to catch up later.

Unfortunately, there is normally nothing to stop the landlord from accepting a partial rent payment on one day and serving you with a three-day notice to pay the rest of the rent or quit the next. However, if you can get your landlord to specifically agree in writing that you can have a longer time to pay, the landlord is bound by this agreement. Here is a sample.

Sample Agreement for Partial Rent Payments

John Lewis, Landlord, and Betty Wong, Tenant, agree as follows:

1. That Betty Wong has paid one-half of her $1,000 rent for Apartment #2 at 11 Billy St., Fair Oaks, CA, on March 1, 20xx, which is the date the rent for the month of March is due.

2. That John Lewis agrees to accept all the remainder of the rent on or before March 15, 20xx and to hold off on any legal proceeding premised on this instance of late rent to evict Betty Wong until after that date.

March 1, 20xx	*John Lewis*
Date	John Lewis, Landlord

March 1, 20xx	*Betty Wong*
Date	Betty Wong, Tenant

TIP

Use the memo line on your rent check to record the month for which you are paying your rent. (For instance, write "Rent for February 2015" if you are paying rent for that month.) This is especially important if you are making a partial payment. In that case you might want to write "First of two installments of rent for April 2015."

Rent Increases

Rent may not be increased during a fixed-term lease unless the lease allows it. If you rent month to month, the landlord can increase your rent with a properly delivered 30- or 90-day notice (see below).

A rent increase is invalid if the landlord imposed it in order to retaliate against you because you exercised any of your legal rights, such as complaining about the condition of the building or organizing a tenants' union. (CC § 1942.5).

A rent increase is invalid if the landlord imposed it in order to discriminate against you on the basis of race, national origin, sex, children, or any other prohibited reason mentioned in Chapter 4.

As discussed later in this chapter, the amount of rent charged may be subject to local rent control, statewide rent control, or government housing assistance (such as Section 8). Additionally, if the governor has declared a natural disaster, landlords may not raise rents above a specified amount.

Other than these restrictions, there is nothing in state law to prevent the landlord from doubling or even tripling the rent. Again, you are legally protected against such acts only if you are lucky enough to live in a city or county that has a local rent control ordinance.

Rent Increase Notices

Most of the time, a landlord may raise the rent on a month-to-month tenancy by "serving" a written notice on the tenant saying that the rent will be increased in 30 days (or more). (If the tenant has a *lease,* no rent increase is appropriate until the lease ends.) Local rent control laws, of course, limit the increase to the amount set by the rent control board. (See Appendix A.) A new statewide rent control law will help those who do not have the advantage of a local rent law. Also, if your area is under a state of emergency, state law limits the amount a landlord can increase your rent. (See below).

30-Day or 90-Day Notice?

In certain situations, you're entitled to 90, not 30, days' notice of a rent increase. If the total of all the rent increases over the past 12 months (including the current raise) is equal to or less than 10% of the lowest rent charged to you during that time, 30 days' notice will suffice. But if the total increase is more than 10% of any monthly rent charged during the previous 12 months, you are entitled to a 90-day notice. In either event, the notice period is extended five (5) days if it is sent to you by mail. Follow these steps to know which notice period applies to the rent increase you've received.

Step 1. Calculate when the new rent will take effect under a 30-day notice. For now, assume a 30-day period is all that's needed. Determine when the new rent will kick in by looking at your rent increase notice (see the discussion below for information on how your landlord must deliver the notice).

Step 2. Check your rent rate history. Count back 12 months from the effective date of the increase (you got that date in Step 1, above). Look at the rent you were charged for each of those 12 months, and choose the lowest rent.

Step 3. Calculate 10% of the lowest rent charged. Multiply the lowest rent charged (you identified that figure in Step 2) times 0.1 to get your "10% Figure" (this will be a dollar amount).

Step 4. Compare the new rent to the lowest rent plus the 10% figure. Now add the lowest rent charged during the last 12 months and the "10% figure" calculated in Step 3. If the new rent is more than the sum of the lowest rent and the "10% figure," then a 90-day notice is required.

It's important to understand what happens if your landlord gives you a 30-day notice when a 90-day notice is what's called for. We think that the notice is defective—it's as if the landlord never gave you notice at all, so you do not have to pay the added rent. Nor do you have to pay the added rent in 90 days—it's not up to you to add the needed time to a defective notice. The landlord will have to start over and give you a new notice with the proper, 90-day period specified.

The examples below illustrate how to calculate the 10% figure. As you'll see, the tricky situations arise when landlords raise the rent frequently within any 12-month period.

RENT CONTROL

Rent control. Normally, increases in rent control situations will be well below the 10% threshold, because either the increase is tied to inflation (which has historically been 3% or less for many years), or because a local rent board regulates them yearly (and no board is likely to approve an increase that high!). However, if your landlord has banked prior increases or has permission to impose a capital expenditures increase, the total may well exceed 10% of the lowest rent charged in the previous 12 months. In those situations, the landlord would have to use a 90-day notice. Appendix A contains details on local rent control ordinances.

EXAMPLE 1: Len rents a house to Tom for $2,000 a month. Len wants to raise the rent $200, to $2,200, effective February 1. Tom looks back at how much rent he has been charged for the 12 months preceding Feb. 1. The rent was $2,000 for each of those months. Tom does the math and figures out that 10% of $2,000 is $200. Since the increase isn't *more* than 10% of the lowest rent charged in the 12 months preceding the February 1 target date, Len can properly use a 30-day notice. Assuming Len has served the notice correctly, Tom must pay the new rent on February 1.

EXAMPLE 2: Sally decided to raise Spencer's rent by $200 from $1,300 to $1,500. On May 1, she gave him a 30-day notice. Spencer knew that he would be entitled to 90 days' notice if the increase (combined with any others he'd had over the past 12 months) was over 10% of the lowest rent charged during those 12 months. Sally didn't know the law.

Spencer's rent had been a steady $1,300 from June 1 of the preceding year to now. He knew that any increase over $130 (that's 10% of $1,300) required a 90-day notice. He reasoned that Sally's notice was simply ineffective, and when June 1 arrived, he gave Sally a rent check for $1,300.

Sally looked at the amount and demanded the new rent, then listened incredulously as Spencer explained the law. She argued that he should just "tack on" 30 days to her notice, making the rent increase effective July 1. Spencer refused, and Sally wisely decided to start over by delivering a proper 90-day notice on June 1. Spencer won't have to pay the new rent until August 1—if Sally had done it right from the start, the increase would have kicked in on July 1.

Effect of Sale of Premises on Tenants' Rights

If your landlord sells the house or apartment building where you rent, your rights as a tenant remain the same. If you have a month-to-month agreement, the new landlord must give you 30 days' notice in order to raise your rent (90 days in some situations), change other terms of your tenancy, or have you move out (90 days if you've lived there for more than one year). There may be further restrictions in communities with rent control laws requiring the landlord to show "just cause" to evict. (See Chapter 3 for the law on rent increases and details on rent control, and Chapter 14 for information on evictions.)

If you have a lease, the new landlord cannot evict you (unless you violate a term of the lease) or change the terms of your agreement until the lease runs out. (Landlord bankruptcy is an exception to this.) For example, the new landlord cannot make you give away your dog if your lease does not prohibit pets.

If the property was sold at a foreclosure sale, California law (CCP § 1161b(b)) requires the new owner to honor the lease in most cases, and to give 90 days' notice to terminate a month-to-month tenancy. Again, this is subject to the just cause eviction rules in many cities with rent control—and in a few cities (Glendale and San Diego) without it.

How Rent Increase Notices Must Be Served

Questions often arise over the way landlords must tell you about a rent increase, which is understandable because the law has changed. In the past, landlords had to serve you personally or, if that wasn't possible, serve a responsible member of your household (followed by mailing a copy to you); this is called "substituted service." As a last resort, a landlord could post the increase on the door (and mail a copy also).

Now, however, landlords can serve a rent increase notice by ordinary first-class mail addressed to you at the premises—without having to try to serve you personally first. Of course, a landlord can still serve a rent increase by personal service or substituted service, explained above.

If you receive a notice by mail only, the date that the notice takes effect is extended by five days. This means getting 35 days' notice for a 10%-or-less increase and 65 days' notice for an over-10% increase. (CC § 827(b)(1)(B)(2) & (3); CCP § 1013.)

Be very sure to understand that if your landlord wants to change other terms of the tenancy besides the rent, such as the amount of the security deposit or a pets rule, the landlord must use personal or substituted service. *Mail service is available only for rent changes.*

Responding to Improper Notice of a Rent Increase

If your landlord has delivered the bad news in the wrong way—using a 30-day notice when a 90-day was required, or failing to add time for mailed notices—you have a choice. You can stand on your rights and refuse to pay—hoping that this will buy you some time while the landlord goes back to square one and does it right. However, there is always the chance that the landlord will persist with the improper notice and proceed with a three-day notice to pay rent or quit, which is the first step in an eviction lawsuit.

If you get a three-day notice to pay rent or quit, you have to think long and hard whether it's worth it to go to court and prove your point in this arena. Even if you win, you'll spend time and money proving your point. Especially if the amount of the increase is in keeping with market rents and you have a good relationship with the landlord, you may want to simply pay the increase within the three days.

Responding to Improper Notice of Other Tenancy Changes

State laws allow landlords to change other terms of a tenancy besides increasing rent by giving a 30-day notice. (CC § 827.) For instance, they may change or establish "house rules" (regarding noise or other behavior issues); or they may introduce a "no pets" policy. A landlord cannot impose these terms to discriminate against you or to retaliate for your assertion of a legal right. However, if you are in a rent control jurisdiction and the changes lessen the value of your tenancy, you could petition for a "reduction in services" (discussed below). Finally, some of these changes can be just plain unfair. For instance, a notice prohibiting pets after you have already gotten a pet with the landlord's permission might not be enforced by a judge, under the doctrine of "waiver and estoppel," discussed in Chapter 14.

Rent Control and Eviction Protection

Rent control is a local and state-wide phenomenon, established through the legislative process, local initiative process, or by the act of a city council or a county board of supervisors. State law regulates some specifics of the various rent control ordinances. The Costa-Hawkins Rental Housing Act restricts cities' power to impose rent control on single-family homes and condominium units, and also requires cities to allow landlords to raise rents after certain types of vacancies occur. (CC §§ 1954.50–1954.53.)

Rent control ordinances generally control more than how much rent a landlord may charge. Many cities' ordinances also govern how and under what circumstances a landlord may terminate a tenancy, even one from month to month, by requiring the landlord to have "just cause" to evict. The statewide law also controls both rent hikes and eviction.

Before we describe how rent control works, a few words of caution:

- Cities change their rent control laws frequently, and court decisions and voter referenda affect them. You should read the material here only to get a broad idea of rent control. It is absolutely necessary that you also contact your city or county to find out whether rent control presently exists and, if it does, to get a copy of current ordinances and any regulations interpreting it. The Rent Control Chart in Appendix A gives you all the necessary contact information.

- California's statewide law, the Tenant Protection Act, does not apply to every rental that's not already covered by local ordinances. Only qualified properties and tenancies will get its protections of limited rent hikes and eviction protection. In some situations, tenants might get rent protection but not eviction protection, and vice versa. To make matters more murky, the law is very poorly written and we expect legal battles over some very basic questions. See "Statewide Rent Control," below, for more information.

In order to summarize how each ordinance works, we have prepared a Rent Control Chart (in Appendix A) that outlines the major points of each ordinance. Here are brief explanations of key terms we use in the chart and the discussion below. Later, we'll address the Tenant Protection Act of 2019 (the "TPA").

Legal Framework for Rent Control

Most ordinances set up a governing body to execute the law—usually called a "rent board."

The rent board then writes "rules and regulations" that are more detailed instructions about how the law applies on a day-to-day basis. If you are in a rent control city, it is a good idea to familiarize yourself with both the ordinance and the rules and regulations. Appendix A has contact information and Web addresses for cities with rent control and "just cause for eviction" laws.

Exceptions

No city's rent control ordinance covers all rental housing within the city. Single family homes and condominium units are generally exempt (excluded) from rent control protections, as is new construction. San Francisco, for example, exempts all rental units built after June 1979, whereas Los Angeles exempts those built after October 1978.

Registration

Many cities require the owners of rent controlled properties to register the properties with the agency that administers the rent control ordinance. This allows the rent board to keep track of the city's rental units, as well as to obtain operating funds from the registration fees.

These cities forbid landlords who fail to register their properties from raising rent. In fact, cities may require a landlord to refund past rent increases if the increases were made during a period in which the landlord failed to register property. However, the courts have ruled that it is unconstitutional for rent control ordinances requiring registration to allow tenants to withhold rents just because the property isn't registered. (*Floystrup v. Berkeley Rent Stabilization Board,* 219 Cal.App.3d 1309 (1990).)

Some cities impose administrative penalties or fines on landlords who fail to register property. However, these penalties do not apply in cases where the landlord's failure to register was not in bad faith and was quickly corrected (that is, the landlord registered the property) in response to a notice from the city. (CC § 1947.7.) To make things easier for landlords who make honest mistakes, state law requires cities to allow landlords any rent increases, which would have been allowed had the property been registered, to be phased in over future years if the following conditions are met:

- The landlord's original failure to register the property was unintentional and not in bad faith.
- The landlord has since registered the property as required by the city and paid all back registration fees.
- The landlord has paid back to the tenant any rents collected in excess of the lawful rate during the time the property wasn't properly registered.

Some rent control ordinances require, as part of the registration process, that the landlord provide the name and address of current tenants. Additional information concerning a tenant may be requested. Under state law, rent control agencies are directed to treat this information as confidential. (CC § 1947.7.)

Rent Formula and Individual Adjustments

Formulas for allowing rent increases vary from city to city. All cities allow periodic (usually yearly) across-the-board increases. The amount of the increase may be set by the rent control board, or the ordinance may allow periodic increases of either a fixed percentage or a percentage tied to a local or national consumer price index. In most cities, landlords (and sometimes tenants) may petition the board for higher (or lower) rents based on certain criteria.

By state law, landlords can raise rents to any level after a tenant voluntarily vacates or is evicted because the tenant violated a term of the rental agreement. (CC § 1954.53(a)(1).) However, once the property is rerented, a city's rent control ordinance will once again apply and will limit rent increases for the new tenants in that residence. The only exception is where the ordinance provides that the property is no longer subject to rent control, as is the case in Hayward, Palm Springs, and Thousand Oaks.

Decreases in Services as Illegal Rent Increases

If for some reason you're not getting all the use out of your apartment that you had or were promised when you moved in, the rent board may determine that your rent should be lowered until your service—including repair and maintenance—is restored. You can also request "retroactive rent abatement," which asks for a reimbursement for rent overpayment during the time when the services were not provided. Examples of such "services" include lack of heat, removal of a storage area, ineffective pest control, or a leaking roof.

Capital Expenditures

In most rent control situations, landlords may ask their rent boards for permission to raise rents above the yearly allotment if they can prove that they have had to spend significant amounts on capital improvements to the property. "Capital improvements" means work that adds significant value to the property, appreciably prolongs its useful life, or adapts it to new uses. It is major work done to the structure of the building, such as replacing the roof, redoing the wiring, repairing a foundation, and seismic upgrading. Capital improvements do not include routine repair and maintenance.

Unfortunately, it's often difficult to know for sure whether a particular piece of work will qualify as a capital improvement. Rent control boards across the state do not consistently use the same criteria when evaluating a landlord's request. But some cases are pretty clear—we know of an Oakland landlord who gave his tenants bottles of champagne to thank them for their patience while construction was done on their building—and then argued to the rent board that his capital expenditures included not only the cost of the construction work, but also the cost of the champagne!

Eviction Protection (Just Cause for Eviction)

Rent control limits how much a landlord can charge a tenant, but when a unit becomes vacant, in most instances there is no limit as to how much a landlord can charge. Because this would encourage landlords to create vacancies, most rent control laws have "just cause" eviction protections. These provisions allow landlords to evict, but only for certain specified reasons, such as nonpayment of rent, violation of the lease, or owner move-in. In situations where the tenant is not at fault (for instance owner-move-in evictions), some cities require the landlord to make relocation payments to the tenant as part of the eviction. "Just cause" for eviction provisions vary from city to city, and some rent control jurisdictions have no such protections against eviction—in other words, a landlord can evict for "any reason or no reason at all." In all jurisdictions, however, a landlord is not allowed to evict in order to retaliate against a tenant or to discriminate (see Chapters 4 and 14).

Rent Control Board Hearings

Almost all cities with rent control provide for a hearing procedure to deal with certain types of complaints and requests for rent adjustments. In cities with weak rent control, a tenant's protest of a rent increase higher than that allowed by the applicable rent increase formula will result in a hearing at which the landlord must justify the increase. In other rent control cities, the landlord must request a hearing in order to increase rent above the formula amount. Finally, a few cities allow tenants to initiate hearings to decrease rents on the basis of the landlord's alleged neglect or lack of maintenance on the property or removal of services.

In the first two types of hearings, whether initiated by a tenant who protests a rent increase over the formula amount in a weak rent control city, or by a landlord in a city that requires landlords to first obtain permission before exceeding the formula increase, the landlord must demonstrate at the hearing that a rent increase higher than that normally allowed is needed in order to obtain a fair return on the owner's investment. This most often means establishing that taxes, maintenance costs, utility charges, or other business expenses, as well as the amortized cost of any capital improvements, make it difficult to obtain a fair return on one's investment, given the existing level of rent.

Initiating the Hearing

A hearing is normally initiated by the filing of a petition or application with the rent board. In describing this process, let's assume that a landlord is filing a petition in a rent control city that requires landlords to obtain permission before raising rents above the formula increase allowed. You, the tenant, wish to protest the increase. Remember, this process is approximately reversed in weak rent control cities, which require the tenant to protest such an increase.

In some cities, a landlord can file two types of petitions seeking an above-formula rent increase. If a landlord seeks an increase on account of recent capital improvements the landlord has made, the landlord will file a "petition for certification" of such improvements. If the owner seeks a rent increase on other grounds, the landlord files a "petition for arbitration."

Preparing for the Hearing

As a general rule, you will greatly increase your chances of winning if you appear at the hearing fully prepared. The hearing officer will be much better disposed to listen to your concerns if you are thoroughly familiar with the issues and make your presentation in an organized way. As part of your preparation, try to find out how much time you will be allowed to present your case.

While this may be the only case that you have at the time, keep in mind that the Hearing Officer or Administrative Law Judge who will hear your case has many cases to consider and many sides to hear from. This means that your presentation should be direct and focused on the essential issues. It should answer these questions:

1. **What parts of the rent control ordinance apply to your case?** Here, you'll need to have studied the ordinance and any regulations, and have citations to them at your fingertips.

2. **What do you need to prove your claim that the rent increase is too high or that your rent should be lowered?** Be sure you understand what you want the hearing officer to conclude at the end of the hearing.

3. **What evidence do you have to prove these allegations?** Evidence can consist of oral testimony by you, your landlord, or other witnesses; written statements ("sworn declarations") about what a witness heard; and other documents, government records, text messages, emails, photos, or videos.

A helpful first step is to prepare a written outline that responds to the three questions above. Try to be specific about the evidence that you will want to present and where it fits in to what you need to prove. That will give you time to gather it all up and put it into a nice logical package for your presentation at the hearing.

You should also be prepared to produce a witness who is familiar with any items that you think might be contested. If for some reason your witness cannot appear in person, you may present a sworn written statement or "declaration" from that person. The statement should be as specific as possible. At the end, the words "I declare under penalty of perjury under the laws of California that the foregoing is true and correct" should appear, followed by the date and the person's signature.

Before the date set for your hearing, go and watch someone else's hearing. (Most cities' hearings are open to the public, and even if they are sometimes closed, you can almost always arrange to attend as an observer if you call ahead.) Seeing another hearing may even make the difference between winning and losing at yours. This is

because both your confidence and your capabilities will grow as you understand what the hearing officers are interested in and how they conduct the hearing. By watching a hearing, you will learn that while they are relatively informal, all follow some procedural rules. It is a great help to know what these are so you can swim with the current, not against it.

You are permitted to have an attorney or any other person, such as an employee or volunteer from a local tenants' rights group, represent you at a rent adjustment hearing. (Many landlords are represented at such hearings by their apartment managers or management companies.) Hiring someone to speak for you is probably not necessary. If you do a careful job in preparing your case, you will probably do as well alone as with a lawyer or other representative. One good alternative is for a group of tenants in your building to chip in and consult with an attorney or someone else thoroughly familiar with rent board hearings to discuss strategy. After the lawyer provides you with advice and information, you can handle the hearing yourself.

Keep all documents in one place and be sure to take them all to the hearing. This should include the petition, statements, photographs, relevant correspondence, and any notes that you have kept. Some cases involve a lot of documents, while others involve only a few.

> ! CAUTION
> **Try very hard not to get wrapped up in extensive details.** Doing so detracts from the truly important facts that you are trying to prove. You can't afford to squander your time—rent board hearings last only a couple of hours. Use that time wisely.

It is helpful to have an outline that highlights your arguments as well a list of your documents. You can use these as checklists to make sure you don't forget to say something or to present certain documents. You might want to have a script for your presentation. Be sure to make at least three copies of each document that you want to introduce into evidence: one copy for the hearing officer, one for the landlord, and one for yourself (the original will be kept by the court clerk). Put the documents into logical order so that you are not fumbling through them when you make your case.

The Actual Hearing

Once you've prepared for the hearing, it's time to make your case. Here's how to be most effective.

Before the Hearing Begins

Arrive at the hearing room at least a few minutes before it is set to begin. Check in with the clerk or other official. Ask to see the file that contains the papers relevant to the application (either yours or the landlord's, depending on the type of ordinance). Review this material to see if there are any comments by office workers, rent board investigators, your landlord, or other tenants. Read the comments very closely, and prepare to answer questions from the hearing officer on any of these points.

As you sit in the hearing room, you will probably see a long table, with the hearing officer seated at the head. In a few cities, the hearing is held before several members of the rent board, and they may sit more formally on a dais or raised platform. In any event, you, the landlord, your representatives (if any), and any witnesses will be asked to sit at a table or come to the front of the room. A clerk or other employee may make summary notes of testimony given at the hearing. Or, in some cities, hearings are tape recorded. If, under the procedure followed in your city, no record is kept, you have the right to have the proceedings transcribed or tape recorded, though at your own expense.

The Hearing Officer's Role

The hearing officer (who may be a city employee or volunteer mediator or arbitrator) or chairperson of the rent board will introduce herself or himself and the other people in the room. If you have witnesses, tell the hearing officer. The hearing officer, or sometimes an employee of the rent board, will usually summarize the issues involved in the hearing. At some point, you will be sworn to tell the truth; it is perjury to lie at the hearing. When these preliminaries are complete, you and your landlord will have an opportunity to present your cases.

A rent adjustment hearing is not like a court hearing. There are no formal rules of evidence. Hearing officers will usually allow you to bring in any information that may be important, though in a court of law it might not be admissible. Relax and just be yourself.

Making Your Case

Present your points clearly, but in a nonargumentative way. Sometimes an outline on a 3" x 5" card will help you to focus. Don't get carried away with unnecessary details. You probably won't be given much time, so be prepared and get to the point quickly. The hearing officer may ask you questions to help you explain your position. Make sure you present all documentary evidence and witnesses necessary to back up your case. Later, the hearing officer will give the landlord or her representative a chance to present her case and to ask you questions. Answer the questions quietly. It is always counterproductive to get into an argument. Even if you feel the landlord is lying or misleading, don't interrupt. You will be given time later to rebut the testimony. Direct all your argument to the hearing officer, not to the landlord or her representative.

When your witnesses are given the opportunity to testify, the normal procedure is simply to let them have their say. You may ask questions if the witness forgets something important, but remember, this is not a court and you don't want to come on like a lawyer. Very likely, the hearing officer will also ask your witnesses questions. The landlord has the right to ask the witnesses questions as well.

In rare instances, you may get a hearing officer or rent board chairperson who dominates the hearing or seems to be hostile to you, or perhaps to tenants in general. If so, you will want to stand up for your rights, without needlessly confronting the hearing officer. Obviously, this can be tricky, but if you know your legal rights and put them forth in a polite but direct way, you should do fine. If you feel that the hearing officer is simply not listening to you, politely insist on your right to complete your statement and question your witnesses.

Just before the hearing ends, the hearing officer should ask if you have any final comments to make. Don't repeat what you have already said, but make sure all your points have been covered and heard.

Handling Surprises

As any attorney with experience will tell you, it's very common for issues to come up mid-hearing that you did not anticipate. When this happens, it's wise to ask to take a break. You may, for instance, learn for the first time that a particular document or a particular witness is important to the case. If this happens, you may want to ask the hearing officer to "leave the record open" for, let's say, a week so that you can find and offer that witness, or submit that document or witness statement. In other words, you'll be asking the hearing officer to delay considering the matter until you can present the evidence in question.

The hearing officer is not likely to grant your request unless you can show why you did not have the evidence in question at the hearing (perhaps the landlord's statement was unexpected), and why the evidence is important to your case. In other words, you need to give the hearing officer a preview of what that person or document will say, and why it's important to the case. Lawyers call this preview an "offer of proof."

You can make your offer of proof like this: Suppose the landlord testifies unexpectedly that you refused to let him in to make a plumbing repair when, in fact, you have a witness who will testify that the landlord was allowed entry into the unit but bungled the repair. You will want to provide a statement from the witness that describes what the witness saw—it will be up to you to convince the officer that the events described constituted a bungled repair. In your offer of proof you could say, "Your honor, the landlord's statement is completely false, I can provide a statement from Tommy Friend

that will say that I did let the landlord in, that he spent five minutes trying to remove the pipe fitting but was unsuccessful, that the landlord left the corroded and leaking pipe in place." You might also want to explain why you did not anticipate that the landlord would testify that you didn't let him in. Hearing officers are not required to leave the record open, but if it would lead to a fairer determination, they often do.

The End of the Hearing

At the end of the hearing, the hearing officer will usually tell you when you can expect the decision. A written decision will usually be mailed to you within a few days or weeks of the hearing. Some cities, however, do not issue written decisions; the hearing officer just announces the decision at the end of the hearing.

The Decision

Depending on the city and the hearing procedure, you might end up with a written decision and an explanation of why it was so decided.

In most cities, if a landlord's application for an increase was heard by a hearing officer, you have the right to appeal to the full rent board if the increase is allowed and you still feel it is improper. Your landlord has this same right if you prevail. If you make an appeal, you must file within a certain time and state your reason for the appeal. You may or may not have the opportunity to appear in person before the rent board.

The rent board will probably take the findings of the hearing officer at face value and limit its role to deciding whether the hearing officer applied the law to these facts correctly. On the other hand, the rent boards of some cities (including Los Angeles) will allow the entire hearing to be held again. (This is sometimes called a "de novo" hearing.) In addition, the board will not usually consider any facts you raise in your statement that you could have brought up at the earlier hearing, but didn't. If you discover a new piece of information after the original hearing, however, the board might consider it.

If it's your landlord who is appealing and you are satisfied with the earlier decision, you will want to emphasize the thoroughness and integrity of the earlier procedure and be ready to present detailed information only if it seems to be needed.

The rent board will generally have more discretion to make a decision than does a single hearing officer. If your case is unique, the board may consider the consequences of establishing a new legal rule or interpretation.

If you again lose your decision before the board, or if your city permits only one hearing in the first place, you may be able to take your case to court, if you are convinced that the rent board or hearing board failed to follow either the law or their own procedures. However, if the hearing officer or board has broad discretion to decide issues such as the one you presented, you are unlikely to get the decision overturned in court. Speak to an attorney about this as soon as possible, as there is a time limit (usually 30 days) for filing an appeal. To appeal a rent board decision, you must have a transcript of the hearing to give to the court.

What to Do If the Landlord Violates Rent Control Rules

Take the following steps if you suspect your landlord has in any way violated your city's rent control rules.

- Get a copy of your local ordinance—and any regulation interpreting it—and make sure you are right. You may want to call the local rent board to confirm that what the landlord is doing violates the law. Contact any local tenants' rights organization and get the benefit of its advice. To find yours, check the statewide tenants' rights organization, www.tenantstogether.org.
- If you think your landlord may have made a good faith mistake, try to work the problems out informally.
- If that doesn't work, file a formal complaint with your city rent board.

- If the landlord's conduct is extreme, talk to a lawyer. You may have a valid suit based on the intentional infliction of emotional distress, on invasion of privacy, or on some other grounds, including those provided in the ordinance itself.

Statewide Rent Control

So far in this chapter, we've talked about local rent control ordinances and how rent hikes and terminations under these rules differ from non–rent-controlled situations. But now there's a twist: Effective January 1, 2020, most residential tenancies in California will be covered by some form of rent and eviction control. The 2019 Tenant Protection Act ("TPA") places a rent "cap" (which affects rent increases but not initial base rents) and eviction control for the entire state where rent control does not already exist (although many rental situations are not covered, as explained below). Local rent control laws remain unaffected by the new legislation, and tenants covered by those existing rent control laws will generally enjoy greater protections than the new state law provides.

In this chapter, we'll explain the rent control aspect of the TPA, starting most importantly with which tenants and properties are exempt (not covered) by the rent restrictions. Then we explain how to calculate the permissible rent cap, and what to do if you think you've received an illegal rent hike. Later, in Chapter 14, we'll explain the eviction protection/just cause portions of the law.

Tenants Who Are Exempt from Statewide Rent Control

The hardest part of the TPA is figuring out which tenants, and which tenancies, are not covered by its rent control protections (in legalese, these tenancies are "exempt"). To make matters worse, the exemption rules we're about to explain are not exactly the same as the exemption rules for statewide eviction protection (we'll get to those in Chapter 14).

So take a deep breath as we describe the situations where rent caps do not apply. Put another way, if any of the following describes your situation, you do not have the TPA's protection of rent hike caps. Your landlord may increase the rent as much and as frequently as he or she wants (assuming you don't have the benefit of local rent control). Read on to understand the exemptions, and how you might win back the benefit of the TPA's caps. (CC § 1947.12(d).)

- **Properties that are already subject to a local rent control.** Currently, annual increases under local laws are less than the allowable cap under the TPA (5% plus CPI), so these local laws will continue to provide greater protections for those covered by them.
- **Tenancies where none of the tenants have resided in the unit for twelve months or more.**
- **Many, but not all, single-family dwellings (single houses and condominiums) are exempt from the rent limitations.** See more detail below.
- **A duplex in which the owner occupied one of the units at the beginning of the tenancy and has continuously occupied the unit as the owner's principal place of residence.**
- **Multi-family residences whose certificates of occupancy were issued within the previous 15 years.**
- **Specialty housing** such as nonprofit hospitals, religious facilities, licensed care and health facilities, school or college dormitories operated by the school or college, government sponsored subsidized, public, and affordable housing, hotels, and other transient housing properties (but residential hotels are covered by the TPA).

Single-family homes and condominiums

The Legislature made this exemption pretty confusing, piling an exception onto an exemption! Here's how to approach it:

- Assume that your single family home or condo is exempt from rent control—you are not protected from an unlimited rent hike.

- But wait! Ask yourself whether one of the following is true in your case. If either one is true, then in fact your rental *is* covered by the TPA and you have the benefit of rent control. (CC § 1947.12(d)(5).)

Does an "entity" own or co-own the property?
If the owner of the unit is a real estate investment trust (REIT), a corporation, or a limited liability company (LLC) where at least one of the voting "members" (owners) of the LLC is a corporation, your rental is covered by the TPA. You can find out who owns your single-family house or condo (remember, the owner isn't necessarily the person who says they're your landlord) by going to your local Recorder's Office. Follow the instructions below in "Who Owns the Property?" for help on learning the identity of the owner or owners.

Did the landlord give you the required notice?
Landlords of single-family rentals must give tenants the following notice in order to preserve their exemption from the TPA's rent hike caps:

"This property is not subject to the rent limits imposed by Section 1947.12 of the Civil Code and is not subject to the just cause requirements of Section 1946.2 of the Civil Code. This property meets the requirements of Sections 1947.12(c)(5) and 1946.2(e)(7) of the Civil Code and the owner is not any of the following: (1) a real estate investment trust, as defined by Section 856 of the Internal Revenue Code; (2) a corporation; or (3) a limited liability company in which at least one member is a corporation."

The notice must be given to all tenancies in effect before July 1, 2020 and must be included in all rental agreements in effect after July 1, 2020.

To summarize, your single family rental is exempt from the TPA's rent control protections and you do not have the benefit of the TPA's rent caps *unless* your landlord either:

- Is a REIT, a corporation, or an LLC where at least one of the voting members is a corporation, or
- Your landlord failed to give you the required notice concerning the property's exemption.

Who Owns the Property?

After you've found the property owner's name, check for the following:

REITs. A list of real estate investment trusts (REITs) can be found at www.reitnotes.com/list-of-US-SEC-registered-reits-SIC-6798. Type the name of the owner as you know it into the search box. If you get a match, your home is not exempt—you're protected under the TPA against rent hikes that surpass the cap.

Corporations and limited liability companies. These entities are registered with California's Secretary of State. To look them up, go to https://businesssearch.sos.ca.gov and type in the owner's name as you know it. Look for that name in the results page. If it's there, click the name, and on the next page, click the link "SI" or "SI Complete" (SI stands for Statement of Information). Then click the PDF icon for the SI. It will list the members of the LLC. Check to see if one of the members is a corporation. If so, your home is not exempt—you have the rent cap protections of the TPA.

Rent Control Rules

This section is for tenants who are satisfied that the TPA applies to them. Keep in mind that the TPA does not regulate the amount of rent the landlord may charge for new tenancies. The statute permits the landlord to establish the initial rental rate with no maximum; the TPA controls only the future increase amounts. (CC § 1947.12.) Here are the rules:

- The TPA limits increases during a 12-month period to five percent plus the percentage increase in the Consumer Price Index (our shorthand is "CPI plus 5"), during the period of April 1 of the prior year to April 1 of the current year. In no event can the total hike be more than 10% of the lowest charged monthly rent during the twelve months preceding the effective date of the new rent.

The landlord can impose only two increases per year to reach the maximum increase.

- For subtenancies, the rent paid by the master tenant plus the rent paid by the subtenant (or subtenants) cannot exceed the amount of rent the landlord is collecting for the unit (in other words, tenants can't make money by subleasing). Many leases prohibit subleasing without the landlord's consent; the new law is careful to point out that this "no profiteering" rule on subleasing does not mean that tenants have a right to sublease.

Calculating the permissible rent hike

The Legislature didn't make it easy for landlords or tenants to calculate the permissible rent hike.

- **5%.** First, take the lowest rent you paid during the previous twelve months and multiply it times 1.05.
- **CPI increase.** Next, figure out the CPI increase (CC § 1947.12(g)(2)). At the time this book went to press, we found this website, https://californiarentcontrolcalculator.com, which provides a calculator that helps you figure out the allowable CPI increase. Fill in your zip code and rental amount, and the calculator will give you the amount of permissible increase. But remember, the landlord can increase the rent only two times per year, and no more than a combination of 5% plus the CPI increase every 12 months. (CC § 1947(g)(2).) Additional calculators are bound to show up online; try searching for "CPI rent increase calculator California."

EXAMPLE: Tina, who had lived in her apartment for five years, was paying $2,000 rent per month. The landlord increased her rent seven months later by $50, making her rent $2,050. Six months later, he increased her rent by another $100 for a total of $2,150. The most recent cost of living increase was 2.5%. Tina's rent increase was correctly calculated by multiplying the lowest rent she paid ($2,000) by 7.5% (5% plus 2.5% cost of living).

Rent increases between March 15, 2019 and January 1, 2020

The rules governing the maximum rent increase are retroactive to March 15, 2019. For any increase imposed between March 15, 2019, and January 1, 2020, the landlord can either capture the maximum increase or reduce the amount to the maximum permitted increase as of January 1:

- If the increase was less than the maximum permissible amount, the landlord may further increase the rent in no more than two installments to reach the maximum amount.
- If the increase already exceeds the maximum permissible amount, the landlord must reduce the rent to the maximum amount as of January 1, 2020. The landlord does not need to refund the tenant for any prior overpayments.

These rules are a bit hard to understand in the abstract. Let's look at an example, where we explain the effect of the "look-back" rule for rent increases.

On April 1, 2019, Lucinda Landlord raised the rent on Tyrone Tenant for his one-bedroom apartment in Folsom, effective May 1. Tyrone's base rent on April 1, 2019 was $1,500, and as of April 1, 2019, the CPI increased 2.0% over April, 2018, for the region that included Folsom. (CPI is calculated and reported by the U.S. Department of Labor's Bureau of Labor Statistics and covers metropolitan and geographical regions). We know now that under the new law, the most that Lucinda could have legally raised Tyrone's rent was 7% (CPI of 2% + 5% = 7%). This results in a maximum hike of $105, with a new rent of $1,605.

Now let's look at the results under the TPA, with its look-back provision, under two scenarios: one where Lucinda raised the rent below what the new law allows, and one where her increase was above the legal limit.

Rent increase below the limit. Suppose Lucinda raised the rent only 4%, or $60 per month. Under the new law, Lucinda could have increased Tyrone's rent 7%, or $105 per month. So, effective January 1, 2020, Lucinda can increase Tyrone's rent an additional $45 per month to $1,605 per month.

Rent increase above the limit. Now let's suppose that Lucinda raised the rent by 10%, or $150. Ten percent exceeds the maximum permitted rent increase (which is 7%), by 3%. In other words, Tyrone has been paying an additional 3%, or $45 per month extra. Therefore, effective January 1, 2020, Lucinda must reduce Tyrone's rent increase by $45, to the maximum allowed ($105), for a new rent of $1,605 per month. However, even though Tyrone paid more than the maximum during 2019, Lucinda does not have to refund any of the overpayments that Tyrone paid during a period of eight months ($360).

Local Rent Control vs Statewide Rent Control

Most local rent control laws are stronger than the TPA. If you are covered by a local law, your local rent increase limitations would apply. But some people who live in a rent control city are not covered by their local law. They might be exempt under local law, but they could be protected under the TPA. Here are some examples:

1. Roberto lives in a single-family home in Los Angeles that is exempt from the Los Angeles rent ordinance. However, his landlord is a corporation, so statewide rent control applies. The landlord can increase Roberto's rent by only 5% plus the increase in the cost of living per 12-month period.

2. Sylvia lives in a building in San Jose that was constructed in 1996. Under San Jose's law, the building is considered "new construction" and exempt from the ordinance's rent protections. But because the building was built more than 15 years ago, Sylvia can take advantage of the rent protections of the statewide rent control law.

3. Gabriel lives in a three-unit building where the landlord lives in one of the units. This unit is exempt under the Palm Springs Rent Ordinance, but covered by California's rent control law because the statewide law exempts only two-unit buildings.

What to Do If You Receive an Illegal Rent Increase Under the TPA

If you are covered by statewide rent control and receive a rent increase notice greater than 5% plus the cost of living increase, you should not have to pay it. Unfortunately, the TPA does not designate an agency or rent board to oversee its implementation, so it's up to you to protect your rights. If you receive an illegal notice, send your landlord a written notification that the increase violates Civil Code Section 1947.12. Demand that the landlord immediately withdraw the notice and get confirmation in writing that the landlord has done so. In your letter, say that if you receive a notice whose rent increase complies with state law, you agree to pay that amount.

Landlords who will not listen to reason might proceed with a Three-Day Notice to Pay Rent or Quit, which is the first step in an eviction lawsuit. If you get a three-day notice to pay the increased rent or quit, but you don't pay the rent or leave and the landlord files an eviction lawsuit, the judge can decide whether the landlord is entitled to the amount demanded. (See Chapter 15, The Eviction Lawsuit.) Some tenants will take this route and risk the possibility of eviction.

Rather than risk losing your home, you could instead pay the increased rent under protest (accompany your payment with a written statement of why you think the increase is illegal), and then sue the landlord in small claims court for the improperly charged amount. Point out to the judge that under the law, your payment of rent was not a waiver of your right to sue. (CC § 1947.12(i).)

Before you make your decision, check with a local tenants' rights organization to see how courts in your area are enforcing the TPA.

Rent Limitations in Areas Hit By Natural Disaster—Anti-Price Gouging

While only some tenants will enjoy the benefits of statewide or local rent control, all tenants will be protected by the state's anti-price gouging law following the declaration of a natural disaster. California passed the law after a rash of devastating wildfires caused shortages of housing and other basic consumer goods. Some unscrupulous landlords and merchants had taken advantage of these shortages by increasing rents and prices of housing and other basic human needs, such as food, gas, and medicine. This law is far from perfect, but it does offer some relief in a time when Californians are recovering from the devastation of a fire, earthquake, or other natural disaster.

Basics of the Anti-Price Gouging Law

The Anti-Price Gouging Law (Penal Code § 396) makes it a crime to increase rents or costs of goods by more than 10% for 30 days after a state of emergency due to manmade or natural disaster has been declared. The state of emergency can be extended by the president, governor, or authorized local official for successive 30-day periods. Of course, if you are also covered by a local rent control law or the TPA, the rent hike protections they provide will probably be much better, and you won't need the anti-price gouging shield.

Finding out whether a state of emergency has been declared

If you think the anti-price gouging law should apply to you, you'll need to determine whether a state of emergency has been declared and, if so, whether it is still in effect. At the time of this writing, a state of emergency exists in the following counties and the Anti-Price Gouging Law will be in effect until December 31, 2020: Butte, Los Angeles, Mendocino, Napa, Santa Barbara, Sonoma, and Ventura Counties.

In the event that future natural disasters prompt additional declarations, here's how to learn whether your geographic area is covered:

- The California Office of Emergency Services is required to have up-to-date information on its website: www.caloes.ca.gov/cal-oes-divisions/legal-affairs/price-gouging.
- Tenants Together, a statewide tenant advocacy organization, has disaster and other helpful information on its website at www.tenantstogether.org/resources/price-gouging-ban-areas-affected-states-emergency.
- Your local or state representative should also have relevant information. Also keep in mind that a state of emergency may be extended by local, state, or federal officials, so you might want to impress on your representative the need to have it extended.

What to do if you receive a rent increase that violates the anti-price gouging law

Keep in mind that the anti-price gouging law is effective only for 30 days following the declaration of the state of emergency (unless it's been extended during that time). During a state of emergency, the landlord can raise your rent by only 10%. If your landlord tries to raise it by more than that, you should write a letter or email and explain that the law allows only a 10% increase while the state of emergency is in effect. Keep in mind that after the state of emergency expires, the landlord can increase the rent by any amount.

Government-Funded Housing Assistance Programs

Tenants who participate in any of the numerous local, state, and federal housing assistance programs will also be protected to some extent from excessive rent hikes. These programs include Section 8 and other voucher programs; local, state, and federal affordable housing projects; and inclusionary housing programs. Follow these steps if you think you're in such a rental and have received an illegal rent hike:

- **Learn the name of your assistance program.** Review your lease agreement and any of the documents that came with it. (If you cannot find these documents, ask your building manager for a copy of your lease.) Government programs often have long and complex agreements, but you should at least be able to determine the exact name of the program you are in, as well as the governmental agency responsible for monitoring it.
- **Contact the government agency responsible for your program.** Agencies usually have a person or team of people who make sure the program is implemented according to the law. Explain your questions and concerns.
- **If you are not satisfied, contact your local, state, or U.S. representative.** The elected representative whom you contact will be a local, state, or federal representative, according to the program you're in. These representatives are attuned to the issues their constituents are facing. They have staff who help people who are having trouble with bureaucratic red tape.
- **Get some legal help.** You might also want to contact your local Legal Aid Society. Get their contact information by looking online for "Legal Aid Society of (your county)."

Discrimination

There was a time when landlords could refuse to rent to just about anyone they didn't like. All sorts of groups—including African Americans, Asians, Chicanos, women, unmarried couples, gays, families with children, and many more—were routinely subjected to discrimination. Fortunately, our state and federal legislatures have taken steps to end these abuses.

Today it is illegal for a landlord to refuse to rent to you or engage in any other kind of discrimination on the basis of your membership in any one of several "protected" groups. In addition, a refusal to rent to you that is not closely related to the legitimate business needs of the landlord might also be illegal.

Relevant state laws include Civil Code Sections 51–55 and Government Code Sections 12927 and 12955–12988. These laws prohibit discrimination on the following grounds:

- race
- religion
- ethnic background and national origin
- immigration status
- sex, sexual orientation, and gender identity
- marital status
- source of income
- physical and mental disability
- families with children (unless the rental units are specifically designated for older citizens, as is the case with retirement communities)
- military or veterans status, or
- association with any of these groups.

The above list includes not just actual membership in the listed groups, but perceived membership. Perceived membership means, for example, that the landlord thinks you're undocumented, or a member of a particular religion, even though you really are not.

In addition, the California Supreme Court has held that state law forbids landlords from discriminating on the basis of one's personal characteristic or trait. (*Harris v. Capitol Growth Investors XIV*, 52 Cal.3d 1142 (1991).)

Forbidden Types of Discrimination

State law, and in some cases federal law, absolutely forbids discrimination on the following grounds, regardless of a landlord's claim of a legitimate business need:

Race, color: This is forbidden by California's Unruh Civil Rights Act (CC §§ 51–53), the Fair Employment and Housing Act (GC §§ 12955–12988), the U.S. Civil Rights Act of 1866 (42 U.S.C. § 1982—see *Jones v. Mayer Co.*, 329 U.S. 409 (1968)), and the Federal Fair Housing Act of 1968 (42 U.S.C. §§ 3601–3619).

Religion: This is forbidden by all the laws listed above, except the Civil Rights Act of 1866.

Ethnic background and national origin: Same as Religion, above.

Immigration status. A landlord may not discriminate based on an applicant's or tenant's citizenship (usually, lack thereof), immigration status, or perceived immigration status (see below for more on immigration).

Sex (including sexual harassment—see below): Same as Religion, above.

Marital status (including discrimination against couples because they are unmarried): This is forbidden under California law by both the Unruh and Fair Employment and Housing Acts. (*Smith v. Fair Employment & Housing Commission*, 12 Cal.4th 1143, 51 Cal.Rptr.2d 700 (1996); *Hess v. Fair Employment and Housing Comm.*, 138 Cal. App.3d 232 (1982); and *Atkisson v. Kern County Housing Authority*, 59 Cal.App.3d 89 (1976).)

Age: This is expressly forbidden by state law. (CC § 51.2.) In federal law, discrimination on the basis of age—including against children and discrimination against the elderly, sometimes called "reverse discrimination"—is considered a part of discrimination on the basis of familial status.

Families with children: Discrimination against families with children is forbidden by the federal Fair Housing Amendments Act of 1988 (42 U.S.C. § 3604) and by the Unruh Civil Rights Act, except in housing reserved exclusively for senior citizens. (CC § 51.3 defines senior citizen housing as that reserved for persons 62 years of age or older, or a complex of 150 or more units (35 in non-metropolitan areas) for persons older than 55 years. Under federal law, housing for older persons is housing solely occupied by persons 62 or older, or housing intended for people over 55 that is, in fact, 80% occupied by people 55 or older (42 U.S.C. § 3607).)

Disability: Under the federal Fair Housing Act and the state's Unruh and Fair Employment and Housing Acts, it is illegal for a landlord to refuse to rent to a person with a physical or mental disability (including hearing, mobility, and visual impairments, chronic alcoholism, chronic mental illness, AIDS, and mental retardation); or to offer different terms to applicants with disabilities. The landlord must permit the tenant to make reasonable modifications to the premises if necessary for the tenant to fully and safely use the premises. When reasonable, the landlord may, however, require the tenant to restore the interior of the premises at the end of the tenancy. In addition, a landlord must rent to an otherwise qualified disabled person with a properly trained and documented service or comfort (emotional support) animal, even if the landlord otherwise bans pets. For more on the rights of disabled tenants, see "Disabled Renters' Housing Rights" on the Nolo website at www.nolo.com/legal-encyclopedia/disabled-renters-housing-rights-30121.html.

A landlord may not take action against a tenant for frequently seeking emergency medical assistance or assistance from law enforcement. (CC § 1946.8, CCP § 1161.3.)

Sexual orientation: This includes homosexuality. Discrimination on this basis is forbidden by the Unruh Civil Rights Act. (*Hubert v. Williams,* 133 Cal.App.3d Supp. 1 (1982).) In addition, a number of California cities specifically ban discrimination for this reason.

Gender identity: Landlords may not discriminate against tenants who have changed, or are in the process of changing their gender, through hormone treatment, surgery, or both. In practical terms, if a tenant's or applicant's dress and mannerisms don't match the landlord's expectations for someone with that person's stated gender identity, the landlord cannot refuse to rent (or otherwise discriminate) on that basis. (GC § 12920.)

Smoking: Discrimination against tenants on the basis that they are smokers is perfectly legal. Civil Code Section 1947.5 allows landlords to prohibit smoking in all or part of the premises, including all or part of any common areas in a multiunit building. Landlords may also forbid the use of vaping devices. California courts have refused to give nonsmokers protection against discrimination (in a restaurant context). (*King v. Hofer,* 42 Cal.4th 678 (1996).)

Animals: Although it is generally legal to refuse to rent to people with pets, it is illegal to do so in the case of service or comfort animals for tenants with physical or mental disabilities. (CC § 54.1(b)(5).) If you rent a condominium, you may keep one pet under specified conditions per state law. (CC § 1360.5.)

Public assistance or source of income: Discrimination against people on public assistance is forbidden by the Unruh Civil Rights Act and the Fair Housing and Employment Act (GC § 12955.). (59 Ops. Cal. Atty. Gen. 223 (1976).) However, refusing to rent to persons under a certain income level, if applied across the board, is not illegal. (*Harris v. Capital Growth Investors XIV,* 52 Cal.3d 1142 (1991).)

As of January 1, 2020, landlords cannot discriminate against tenants whose rent is paid to the landlord on behalf of a tenant (for instance, Section 8 vouchers). Previously, some local laws offered this protection. (*City and County of San Francisco v. Post,* 22 Cal.App.5th 121 (2018).)

Immigration status: Landlords may not ask tenants, prospective tenants, or occupants or prospective occupants about their citizenship or immigration status; or require them to produce documents proving legal status. The law provides for an exception; the landlord may inquire if the landlord participates in a federal government program that provides for rent limitations or assistance to a qualified tenant. Landlords cannot terminate or evict a tenant based on that tenant's immigration status (real or perceived), or that of someone with whom the tenant associates. They also may not disclose or threaten to disclose to any third party (including law enforcement) the immigration status or perceived immigration status of any tenant, prospective tenant, occupant or prospective occupant. Again, an exception exists in the event that the landlord reveals such information in order to comply with any legal obligation under federal law, including a subpoena, warrant, or order issued by a court. (CC §§ 1940.3, 1940.35.) They may, however, ask a tenant whom they intend to pay as a resident manager to fill out IRS Form I-9, which will result in the landlord being shown identifying documents or visas that establish the tenant/manager's right to work in this country.

Military or Veteran Status. As of January 1, 2020, landlords may not discriminate against persons because of their military or veteran status.

Perceived characteristics. The law protects you when the landlord *thinks* you're a member of a protected group, but you are not. Let's say you are a straight white man, but the landlord thinks you are homosexual and discriminates against you on that basis. The fact that you are not a member of a protected group would not prevent you from suing the landlord for unlawful discrimination. (CC § 51(e)(6).)

"Persons associated with." The law also protects tenants who are not members of a protected class, but who associate with members of a protected group. Suppose, for instance, that a white tenant has African American friends who visit his apartment. It is illegal for the landlord to discriminate against the tenant because of the race, color, and so on of the people with whom the tenant associates. (CC § 51(e)(6), *Winchell v. English*, 62 Cal.App.3d 25 (1976).)

Other unlawful discrimination: After reading the above list outlining the types of discrimination forbidden by California and federal law, you might

assume that it is legal for a landlord to discriminate for other reasons—for instance, discrimination against men with beards or long hair. California's Unruh Civil Rights Act has been construed by various California appellate courts to forbid all forms of "arbitrary" discrimination that bear no relationship to a landlord's legitimate business concerns. So, even though the Unruh Act contains only the words "sex, race, color, religion, ancestry, or national origin" to describe types of discrimination that are illegal, the courts have ruled that these categories are just examples of types of arbitrary and illegal discrimination. On this basis, the California Supreme Court has ruled that landlords can't discriminate against families with children, and has stated that discrimination on the basis of one's personal characteristic or trait is also illegal. (*Harris v. Capital Growth Investors XIV*, 52 Cal.3d 1142 (1991).)

Information on Fair Housing Laws

For information on the rules and regulations of the Fair Housing Act, contact a local office of the U.S. Department of Housing and Urban Development (HUD). Find your local office at www.hud.gov. For information on state fair housing laws, contact the Department of Fair Employment and Housing (DFEH) at 800-884-1684 or check the DFEH website at www.dfeh.ca.gov. You'll also find good online information at www.housing.org, a website maintained by the nonprofit Project Sentinel. For information on local housing discrimination laws, contact your local city manager's or mayor's office.

What Constitutes Discrimination?

Although the most common forms of illegal discrimination in rental housing consist of refusing to rent to prospective tenants for an arbitrary reason, or offering to rent to one person on tougher terms than are offered to others with no good reason for making the distinction, these aren't the only ways a landlord can be legally liable for unlawful discrimination. A landlord's termination of, or attempt to terminate a tenancy for a discriminatory reason; harassment; or discrimination in providing services such as the use of pool or meeting room facilities or other common areas is illegal. These actions can provide the discriminated-against tenant with a defense to an eviction lawsuit as well as a basis for suing the landlord for damages. (See "What to Do About Discrimination," below.)

A landlord also has a duty to take reasonable steps to prevent other tenants from harassing a tenant for discriminatory reasons. For instance, a tenant who is harassed by other tenants at the common swimming pool because he is African American could expect the landlord to act—and hold the landlord legally responsible—in the absence of a reasonable response. One court held a landlord liable for harassment of a lesbian by other tenants in a retirement home complex. (*Wetzel v. Glen St. Andrew Living Community, LLC* 7th Circuit, Case No. 17-1322 (2018).)

In addition, a landlord's failure to "reasonably accommodate" a person's disability may also constitute an act of discrimination. This issue often arises when a person requires a service or support animal, or access for a home care worker (see discussion below).

> **EXAMPLE 1:** Bill Lee rents apartments in his six-unit apartment building without regard to racial or other unlawful criteria. His tenants include an African-American family and a single Latin-American woman with children. When Constance Block buys the building from Bill, she immediately gives only these two tenants 30-day notices. Unless Constance can come up with a valid nondiscriminatory reason for evicting these tenants, they can fight the eviction on the basis of unlawful discrimination. They can also sue Constance for damages in state or federal court.

> **EXAMPLE 2:** Now, let's assume that Constance, having lost both the eviction lawsuits and the tenants'

suits for damages against her, still tries to discriminate by adopting a less blatant strategy. One way she does this is by adopting an inconsistent policy of responding to late rent payments. When her Caucasian tenants without children are late with the rent, she doesn't give them a three-day notice to pay rent or quit until after a five-day "grace period," while nonwhite tenants receive their three-day notices the day after the rent is due. In addition, when nonwhite tenants request repairs or raise other issues about the condition of the premises, the speed of Constance's response mimics a turtle's walk after waking from a snooze in the sun. These more subtle (or not so subtle, depending on the situation) means of discrimination are also illegal, and Constance's tenants have grounds to sue her, as well as to defend any eviction lawsuit she brings against them.

Legal Reasons to Discriminate

The fact that all forms of arbitrary discrimination in rental housing are illegal does not mean that every time you are turned down for an apartment, you are being discriminated against for an illegal reason. The landlord might have discriminated against you for a legal reason. What are legal reasons that justify a landlord in discriminating against a prospective tenant? There is no list set out in a statute, but if a landlord discriminates against prospective tenants because they have characteristics that would tend to make them poor tenants, the landlord is on solid legal ground. These characteristics include a bad credit history, credit references that don't check out, negative references from past landlords, a past history of not paying rent or of using residential premises to run an illegal business (for example, drugs or prostitution), status as a sex offender or felon, and anything else that honestly and directly relates to the quality of being a good tenant. A landlord can refuse to rent to a tenant, for example, on the basis of income, by requiring the tenant's income to be at least three times the amount of rent. (*Harris v. Capital Growth Investors XIV,* 52 Cal.3d 1142 (1991).)

If a landlord relies on a credit report to take any action that negatively affects a tenant's (or prospective tenant's) interest, the tenant has a right to a copy of the report. (CC § 1787.2.)

Note that the law allows for a couple of specific exceptions to the rules described above. Educational institutions are allowed to set aside housing for married couples and for male and female students. (GC § 12955(a)(2).) In addition, landlords can establish "senior" communities where at least 80% of the residents are age 55 or older; and can establish "seniors only" communities where all residents (including adult children and spouses) are age 62 or older (excluding caregivers and employees). (CC §§ 51.2–51.4.)

Rentals to Single Boarders in Single-Family Homes

You might have seen an advertisement like this, in a newsletter or supermarket notice board: "Widow seeks single, older Christian lady to share her home as a boarder ...." Based on what you know about illegal housing discrimination, you might be wondering how this type of advertisement escapes prosecution. Isn't the ad above a perfect example of marital, age, religious, and sexual discrimination?

The answer is, yes. But the reality of the situation is that few spurned boarders, and certainly fewer government agencies, are interested in suing one-person landlords and forcing them to accept a housemate not of their choosing. And state housing law does, in any event, make housing preferences like the example above perfectly legal as long as there is:

- only one boarder, and
- the landlord has used no discriminatory advertising. (GC §§ 12955(c) & (d) and § 12927(c).)

The ban against discriminatory advertising means that the owner must not make any discriminatory notices, statements, or advertisements. However, how a one-person landlord would be able to communicate her preferences for her boarder without making any "notices, statements, or advertisements" is beyond our understanding.

In order to clarify the law, the legislature amended the state Fair Employment and Housing Law to provide that advertisements for a boarder of a certain sex to share the same dwelling unit will not be considered a discriminatory act. (GC § 12927(2)(B).) In other words, the widow would be on solid ground if she mentions in a print or online ad only her desire for a female roommate. Her stated preferences for an older, single Christian would still, theoretically, constitute housing discrimination.

Occasional Rentals

Consider the owner who rents out his home while on a temporary job assignment in another state, or the family that occasionally takes an extended summer vacation and rents out their home. What about the teacher who rents out her home during every summer—an occasional *but regular* rental situation? And how about the landlord who owns a vacation rental—one that the family uses regularly, but that is also regularly rented to weekenders and others on vacation? Are tenants who rent from these landlords entitled to the protection of the fair housing laws?

Unfortunately, the answers to these questions are not very clear. On the one hand, the Unruh Act applies only to "business establishments," which would seem to exclude the sporadic or one-time rental, but possibly not the infrequent-but-regular rental. However, the California Supreme Court has been mandated to apply Unruh "in the broadest sense reasonably possible," which might mean that tenants who rent in these situations would be covered by the fair housing laws. (*Burks v. Poppy Construction Company*, 57 Cal.2d 463, 20 Cal. Rptr. 609 (1962).) Moreover, the Fair Employment and Housing Act applies generally to "owners," and is not restricted to business establishments.

Small-scale landlords are subject to the fair housing laws. Regularly renting out a single apartment or house, or even half of an owner-occupied duplex, does constitute the operation of a business to which the Unruh Act applies.

Do Antidiscrimination Laws Cover Owner-Occupied Rentals?

An owner-occupant of a duplex, triplex, or larger complex is governed by civil rights laws in the renting of the other unit(s) in the building, even though the owner lives in one of the other units. In this situation, the owner-occupant is renting out property for use as a separate household, where kitchen or bathroom facilities aren't shared with the tenant. (See *Swann v. Burkett*, 209 Cal. App.2d 685 (1962) and 58 Ops. Cal. Atty. Gen. 608 (1975).) The State Fair Employment and Housing Act also applies, but the federal Fair Housing Acts do not.

Families With Children and Overcrowding

The fact that discrimination against families with children is illegal does not mean a landlord must rent you a one-bedroom apartment if you have a family of five. In other words, it is legal to establish reasonable space-to-people ratios. But it is not legal to use "overcrowding" as a euphemism justifying discrimination against a family with children, if a landlord would rent to the same number of adults.

A few landlords, realizing they are no longer able to enforce a blanket policy of excluding children, try to adopt criteria that for all practical purposes forbid children, under the guise of preventing overcrowding. A common but illegal policy is to allow only one person per bedroom, with a married or living-together couple counting as one person. This standard would result in renting a two-bedroom unit to a husband and wife and their one child, but would allow a landlord to exclude a family with two children. One court has ruled against a landlord who did not permit more than four persons to occupy three-bedroom apartments. (*Zakaria v. Lincoln Property Co.*, 229 Cal.Rptr. 669 (1986).) Another court held that a rule precluding a two-child family from occupying a two-bedroom apartment violated a local ordinance similar to state

law. (*Smith v. Ring Brothers Management Corp.*, 183 Cal.App.3d 649, 228 Cal.Rptr. 525 (1986).)

The Fair Employment and Housing Commission is the enforcement arm of the California Department of Fair Employment and Housing (DFEH). The DFEH (one of the places a tenant can complain about discrimination) will investigate a complaint for possible filing with the Commission based on a "two-plus-one" rule: If a landlord's policy is more restrictive than two persons per bedroom plus one additional occupant, it is suspect. Thus, a family might have a case if the landlord insists on two or fewer people in a one-bedroom unit, four or fewer in a two-bedroom unit, six or fewer in a three-bedroom unit, and so on. However, landlords who draw the line at three people to a one-bedroom, five to a two-bedroom, and seven to a three-bedroom unit are probably within their rights.

The "two per bedroom plus one more" rule of thumb is not, however, absolute. A landlord might be able to justify a lower occupancy policy for a particular rental if he can point to "legitimate business reasons." This is hard to do—while the inability of the infrastructure to support more tenants (perhaps the septic system or plumbing has a limited capacity) might justify a lower occupancy policy, a landlord's desire to ensure a quiet, uncrowded environment for upscale older tenants will not. If your landlord's occupancy policy limits the number of tenants for any reason other than health, safety, and legitimate business needs, it might be illegal discrimination against families.

Look at the history of a landlord's rental policies. If the landlord used to disallow children before someone complained or sued about this, and only then adopted strict occupancy limits, it is likely that the landlord still intends to keep out children, and a court might well find the new policy illegal.

Often a child will be born after tenants have already resided in a place for some time. Is your landlord entitled to evict you if the birth of the new child would result in a seriously overcrowded situation? Legally, perhaps, especially if your lease or rental agreement makes it clear that the property can be occupied only by a set number of people, and the baby is one too many. However, if you face this situation and feel the landlord is in fact using the crowding issue as an excuse to get you out, carefully research the landlord's rental policies on other apartments. For example, if you find situations in which the landlord is allowing four adults to occupy a unit the same size as yours, and the landlord moves to evict you because the birth of your second child means your unit is now occupied by four people, you clearly have a good case.

Your landlord has the right, however, to insist on a reasonable increase in rent after a child is born if your lease or rental agreement specifically limits occupancy to a defined number of people—unless you're in a rent control city such as San Francisco, which prohibits landlords from charging extra rent for a newborn child.

How to Tell If a Landlord Is Discriminating

Discrimination can take place during the application process, and later during a tenant's rental term. Here are some tips on how to spot discrimination in either situation.

Discrimination in Renting the Apartment

Occasionally apartment house managers—and even landlords themselves—will tell you that they will not rent to African Americans, Spanish-surnamed people, Asians, and so on. This does not happen that often, because these people are learning that they can be penalized for discriminating.

Today, most landlords who wish to discriminate try to be subtle about it. When you phone to see if a place is still available, the landlord might say it has been filled if he hears a Southern or Spanish accent. If he says it is vacant, then when you come to look at it he sees that you are African American,

he might say it has just been rented. Or, he might say he requires a large security deposit which he "forgot to put in the ad." Or he might say that the ad misprinted the rent, which is really much higher. Many variations on these themes can be played.

If you suspect that the landlord is discriminating against you, it is important that you do some things to check it out. For example, if you think the landlord is asking for a high rent or security deposit just to get rid of you, ask other tenants what they pay. The best way to check is to run a "test." Many areas have governmental agencies (such as a Human Rights Commission) or nonprofit organizations (such as Project Sentinel in Northern California) who are trained to "test" to see if a residential landlord is discriminating.

If such resources are unavailable in your area, have someone who would not normally face discrimination (for example, a white male without kids) revisit the place soon after you do and ask if it is available and, if so, on what terms. If the response is better, the landlord was probably discriminating against you. Be sure that your friend's references, type of job, and lifestyle are similar to yours, so the landlord cannot later say he took your friend and turned you down because of these differences.

Discrimination During Your Tenancy

Anti-discrimination laws apply equally once a tenant has rented a unit. For instance, a landlord cannot discriminate because you have a child, or invite friends over who are African American, or become disabled and require a reasonable accommodation. Again, it comes down to proof. Is the landlord taking certain action for a discriminatory reason or for a legitimate business reason? Sometimes it is obvious, sometimes not. Look at how reasonable the landlord's actions seem, how other tenants are treated in comparison to how you are treated, and what the landlord has said and done in the past with respect to protected groups.

Disability and Requesting Reasonable Accommodations

In addition to protections against harassment, eviction, and refusal to rent, a landlord's failure to "reasonably accommodate" a person with a disability who has requested a change in policies or practices; or who has requested physical changes to the tenant's unit or common areas, is a form of discrimination. (GC § 12927(c)(1); CC § 54.1(b)(3)(B)).)

"Disability" is very broadly defined. Disability includes any physical or mental impairment that substantially limits one or more major life activities. "Major life activities" include such things as caring for oneself, walking, seeing, hearing, breathing, learning, and working. (CC § 1761(g); GC § 12926.) The most common examples of requests from tenants with disabilities are requests for service or support animals (when there is a "no pets" policy), asking to have a live-in caregiver (when there is a "no guests" policy), and asking for physical modifications to a rental unit. In most cases, a landlord must modify its "no pets" policy to allow a support animal to live with a person suffering chronic depression and bipolar disorder. (*Auburn Woods I Homeowners Assn. v. Fair Employment and Housing Commission,* 121 Cal. App.4th 1578 (2004).) Likewise, a tenant who is either temporarily disabled (for instance, recovering from hip surgery) or permanently not able to care for himself may generally expect the landlord to modify its "no guests" policy. Under Government Code Section 12927(c)(1), a tenant may, at his own expense, make "reasonable" modifications to the unit in order to have an equal opportunity to fully enjoy the unit. However, a landlord may condition approval of these modifications on the tenant agreeing to restore the unit to its original condition before the modification (absent normal wear and tear).

It's important to understand that not every disability requires an accommodation, and not every requested accommodation is reasonable to address a particular disability. For example, someone with severely impaired vision may not need a ground-floor apartment at all; another person with the same impairment might. And a reasonable accommodation is one that not only specifically addresses the tenant's particular disability, but is not so extreme as to seriously affect the landlord's ability to do business. The tenant needs to establish how the requested accommodation addresses the disability, and must be prepared to show that the request is doable from the landlord's point of view. (For example, it might not be reasonable for a tenant who uses a wheelchair to ask the landlord to install an elevator in a multistory building. The accommodation—the elevator—addresses the disability, but the request would probably be deemed unreasonable.)

If you feel you are entitled to an accommodation, your first step is to make a written request to your landlord, asking that the landlord provide the accommodation based on your disability. The letter should state that you have a legally recognized disability, and describe how the accommodation (such as a service dog) would address that disability. For instance, a service dog would provide assistance by helping you walk and remain stable. Landlords are entitled to some substantiation of both your status as a person with a disability (unless it's obvious), and that the specific accommodation you've asked for will enable you to live safely and comfortably in the rental. Ask a medical professional who has personal knowledge of you to provide a letter along the lines described above.

Emotional Support and Comfort Animals

Landlords are increasingly asked by applicants and tenants with a legal disability to allow that person to live with a "support animal" or "comfort animal." Legally speaking, these are animals commonly kept in households (such as a dog, cat, small bird, rabbit, hamster, gerbil, other rodent, fish, turtle, or other small, domesticated animal that is traditionally kept in the home for pleasure rather than for commercial purposes). The animal must have been trained to provide therapeutic emotional support. Importantly, reptiles (other than turtles), barnyard animals, monkeys, kangaroos, and other non-domesticated animals are not common household animals (though they can sometimes qualify as helpers, see below).

If asked by your landlord, you'll need to show that the animal has been trained to deliver the assistance you require as a result of your disability. Landlords may ask for confirmation from a health care professional that the animal does work, performs tasks, provides assistance, or provides therapeutic emotional support that is related to your disability.

In rare situations, animals that are not commonly kept in households can qualify as assistance animals. For example, a health care professional might certify that a trained capuchin monkey, who can retrieve items from a refrigerator and serve them to the tenant, is unique and provides substantial support not possible from a dog. In these rare instances, the health care professional should inform the landlord of:

- the date of your last consultation
- any unique circumstances justifying your need for the particular animal(s), and
- whether the provider has reliable information about this specific animal or whether the provider specifically recommended this type of animal.

For more on these rules, see the HUD guidance memo, *FHEO Notice 2020-01* (type the memo's name into the search box on www.hud.gov).

The landlord is required to respond promptly and, if necessary, engage in an "interactive process" to address your request. If the landlord grants your request, then the two of you should write and sign a statement memorializing your understanding. If the landlord does not agree, it's time to explore the options discussed below. Be aware that if, after the denial of your request, you decide (for example) to get a dog anyway, you could face an eviction. You might feel that you are on solid ground, but be sure to discuss this option with an attorney experienced in this area of law before you take this step.

What to Do About Discrimination

There are several legal responses to the problems raised by discrimination. Regardless of what you do, if you really want to live in the place, you must act fast or the landlord will rent it to someone else before you can stop it.

Complain to the California Department of Fair Employment and Housing

The State of California Department of Fair Employment and Housing (DFEH) takes complaints on discrimination in rental housing. It has the power to order hefty damages for a tenant who has been discriminated against.

If you believe that you have been discriminated against, you can contact the office nearest you or call DFEH at 800-884-1684. You can also visit the DFEH online at www.dfeh.ca.gov, where you will also find phone numbers and addresses of regional offices. You will be asked to fill out a complaint form, and an investigator will be assigned to your case. You must file your complaint within 60 days of the date of the violation or the date when you first learned of the violation. The investigator will contact you and the landlord and try to work the problem out through compromise and conciliation. If this fails, the Department may conduct hearings and maybe take the matter to court. You can also consult a private attorney and consider suing.

> TIP
>
> **Check out Project Sentinel.** This Northern California nonprofit association provides an excellent source of online information at www.housing.org. Project Sentinel also offers a free mediation service for landlords and tenants and has the authority to investigate reports of housing discrimination.

Complain to the U.S. Department of Housing and Urban Development

You can also lodge a complaint with the U.S. Department of Housing and Urban Development (HUD) if the discrimination is based on race, religion, national origin, sex, family status, or disability. Search for "Housing Discrimination" under the "Topic Areas" on www.hud.gov, or call 800-347-3739. HUD has most of the same powers as does the state DFEH but must give the state agency the opportunity (30 days) to act on the case first. The HUD equal opportunity office for California is located at 450 Golden Gate Ave., San Francisco, CA 94102, 415-489-6400.

Sue the Discriminating Landlord

You might also want to consider seeing a lawyer and suing the landlord. If you have been discriminated against because of sex, race, religion, physical disability, national origin, age, or familial status, you can sue in state or federal court. Discrimination claims on the basis of marital status and all "personal trait" discrimination claims can be brought only in state court. If you can prove your case, you will almost certainly be eligible to recover money damages.

Legal Penalties for Discrimination

State and federal courts and housing agencies that find that discrimination has taken place have the power (depending on the agency) to order the landlord to rent a particular unit to you, or to pay you for "actual" or "compensatory" damages, including any higher rent you had to pay as a result of being turned down; and damages for humiliation and emotional distress. Under California's Unruh Civil Rights Act, for example, you may be awarded triple actual damages in a lawsuit for a violation of discrimination laws, and at least $4,000 must be awarded when tenants go to court and win. If you win, you will also be awarded attorney fees.

For more information on complaint procedures and penalties, contact the DFEH or HUD (contact information above).

Many, if not most, attorneys have had little experience with discrimination lawsuits. This is particularly true of lawsuits brought in federal court. Rather than try to find an attorney at random, you would be wise to check with an organization in your area dedicated to civil rights and fighting discrimination. They will undoubtedly be able to direct you to an experienced attorney.

Sexual Harassment by Landlords or Managers

Sexual harassment includes "sexual advances, solicitations, sexual requests, demands for sexual compliance, ... or other visual, or physical conduct of a sexual nature or of a hostile nature based on gender that were unwelcome and pervasive or severe." (CC § 51.9.)

Sexual harassment by a landlord or manager is illegal under state and federal laws prohibiting discrimination on the basis of sex: California's Unruh Civil Rights Act, the Fair Employment and Housing Act, and the Federal Fair Housing Act of 1968. Harassment that involves a violation of a tenant's privacy rights is illegal under state law. (CC § 1954.)

It's against the law for a landlord or manager to retaliate against tenants for having exercised their rights to be free from sex discrimination, including sexual harassment. Retaliation includes increasing rent, giving a termination notice, or even threatening to do so. (See Chapter 14 for advice on defending yourself against retaliatory eviction.)

Here are some things you can do to stop sexual harassment and protect your rights as a tenant. These are also crucial steps to take if you later decide to take formal action against the harassment.

Document the Harassment

Write down what the landlord or manager said or did to you, and the place and dates of the incidents. Keep copies of any sexually explicit material or threatening letters, texts, or emails the landlord or manager sent you. Note names of any witnesses and talk with other tenants to find out whether they have been harassed.

Tell the Harasser to Stop

The first step is to deal directly with the harassment when it occurs—whether it's to reject repeated requests for a date or express your distaste for sexually explicit comments or physical contact. Ask the harasser to agree to stop. As always, follow up with a letter or email, in which you recount the incident(s), describe the conversation between you, and summarize any agreement that you reached.

Report the Incidents

If the sexual harassment continues, whether by the owner or employees or agents, it is imperative that you write a written complaint to the landlord. Do so in a letter or an email. Your account of events, and any response the landlord might make, can become very important evidence should you take stronger steps, or if the landlord retaliates against you. Remember, it is unlawful for the landlord (or the manager) to increase rent, evict, or otherwise take negative acts against you because you have made this complaint—and unless you have written evidence of your complaint, you will have a hard time raising a retaliation defense.

If you feel the situation is serious or bound to escalate, say that you will take action against the harassment if it doesn't stop at once. Include a citation to the state and federal laws prohibiting discrimination on the basis of sex (see above). If other tenants have been harassed, ask them to send a joint letter. Keep copies of all correspondence.

Complain to a Fair Housing Agency

"What to Do About Discrimination," above, provides more information on how the Department of Fair Employment and Housing can help, although, as we note, there are limits to their assistance.

File a Civil Harassment Complaint

If the landlord or manager is harassing because of your sex, sexual orientation, or for some other discriminatory reason, you have the option of going to court to get a "Civil Harassment Restraining Order." This order could prevent (restrain) the landlord or manager from contacting you or coming within a certain number of feet of your home. These kinds of orders are often obtained without the assistance of an attorney. The California Judicial Council provides some information about restraining orders as well as easy to use forms. For further information go to www.courts.ca.gov/1044.htm.

Each court has its own rules about how these requests are reviewed by a judge, so be sure to familiarize yourself with the procedures.

File a Lawsuit

If the harassment continues or if you're threatened with retaliatory eviction, you might also want to consult with an attorney about filing a civil lawsuit. If you have told the landlord about the resident manager's harassment and he has not taken reasonable steps to stop it, the landlord could be liable as well. Both the landlord and harassing manager might be liable for the damages and penalties discussed above.

Tenant's Right to Privacy

Section 1954 of the Civil Code establishes the circumstances under which a landlord can enter a tenant's home, and Section 1953(a)(1) provides that these circumstances cannot be expanded, or the tenant's privacy rights waived or modified, by any lease or rental agreement provision.

No matter what your lease says, your landlord may legally enter your residence only for certain specified instances. Landlords may not abuse their rights to enter or use entry as a way of harassing the tenant. Any provision of a lease or rental agreement that attempts to waive (give up) your privacy rights is not valid and will not be enforced by a judge. (CC § 1953(a).) The specified permitted reasons to enter are:

1. to deal with an emergency
2. when you give permission for the landlord to enter
3. to read a utility meter
4. to maintain a carbon monoxide detector
5. to inspect a waterbed installation in order to make sure it complies with state law
6. to make needed or agreed-upon repairs (or assess the need for them)
7. to install, inspect, repair, or read a water sub meter or to repair a condition causing abnormally high water usage (CC § 1954.211)
8. to inspect for weather protection, elevated porches and decks, and certain structural components to the property
9. to show the property to prospective new tenants or purchasers, and
10. when you give permission for an initial final inspection, after you've given notice that you're moving out (or your lease is about to end).

In most instances (emergencies and tenant permission excepted), a landlord can enter only during "normal business hours" and then only after "reasonable notice," presumed to be 24 hours. (For reason number 8 above, a landlord must give you 48 hours' notice.) In addition, the landlord must give you written notice in many situations, as explained in "Entries That Require Written Notice," below.

Permissible Reasons to Enter

Because your right to privacy is so important, let's examine Section 1954 of the Civil Code carefully to make sure you thoroughly understand the details of how your right to privacy works.

Entry in Case of an Emergency

Under Civil Code Section 1954, your landlord or manager can enter the property without giving advance notice in order to respond to a true emergency that threatens injury or property damage if not corrected immediately. For example, a fire or a gas or serious water leak is a true emergency that, if not corrected, will result in damage, injury, or even loss of life. On the other hand, a landlord's urge to repair an important but non–life- or property-threatening defect, like a stopped-up drain, isn't a true emergency that allows entry without proper notice.

To facilitate a landlord's right of entry, the landlord and manager are entitled to have a key to the premises, including keys to any locks you might add. No notice, oral or written, is required for entry in case of an emergency.

Entry With the Permission of the Tenant

If landlords want to enter your unit for any reason that is not described above, they will need your permission to do so. For instance, a landlord might want to enter to "inspect" the unit. The law permits this in only certain instances (see below), but there could be reasons that you would agree to it anyway. If it's convenient to the tenant, the tenant may also agree to an entry without requiring the landlord to give notice. For example, if your landlord (whom you feel is well motivated) wants to fix a maintenance problem that needs regular attending to—for example, a fussy heater or temperamental plumbing—you might want to work out a detailed agreement with the landlord allowing entry in specified circumstances. Be sure to confirm any agreement by writing either a letter or an email.

Entries That Require Written Notice

Except in an emergency or by agreement with the tenant, the landlord is required to give "reasonable notice" of the landlord's or landlord's agent's intention to enter the unit. The notice must state the date, approximate time, and purpose of the entry. The time of entry must be during "normal business hours," usually between 9:00 a.m. to 5:00 p.m. Monday through Friday. In many circumstances, a notice stating that the landlord is going to enter "between 9:00 a.m. and 5:00 p.m." will not satisfy the "approximate time" requirement.

If the entry is in order to show the property to prospective purchasers, a few different rules about proper notice and time of entry apply (see below). As a general rule, 24 hours' notice is considered "reasonable notice." Because the rule is not absolute, less than 24 hours might be considered reasonable in some situations, where others could require more than 24 hours' notice.

Entry to Make Repairs

The law allows a landlord (or the landlord's repair-person) to enter a unit after giving written notice, in order to make "necessary or agreed upon" repairs, decorations, alterations, or improvements. Landlords may not, however, enter in order to make extensive alterations that unreasonably interfere with the tenant's right to possession. It's legal for the tenant and landlord to agree to entries *without* notice in order to make repairs, as long as the actual entry to repair is no more than one week after the agreement. Of course, if you do come to an agreement such as this, be sure to send a letter or email that states the terms of that agreement. (CC § 1954(d)(3).)

If possible, try to work with your landlord if the necessary or agreed upon repairs will take large chunks of time (sometimes days), especially if they require the tenant's preparation in advance. For example, repairing a plumbing leak behind the wall may take several days to complete. Agreeing to a schedule to accomplish this work will benefit both the landlord and the tenant.

Entry to Inspect

As a general matter, a landlord is not entitled to enter a unit for the vague purpose of inspection. However, the landlord may give notice to inspect in the following circumstances:

- to install, inspect, repair, or read a utility meter that is in the unit, or repair a condition that causes abnormally high water use. (CC § 1954.211.)
- to inspect and maintain a carbon monoxide detector (H & S §§ 17926, 17926.1.)
- to inspect a waterbed, both at the point of installation and periodically afterward (CC § 1940.5(f))
- for buildings that contain three units or more, to inspect or repair conditions relating to weather protection, exterior porches or decks, or structural components (Health and Safety Code § 17973)
- to allow inspection for bedbugs by a pest control operator (CC § 1954.604), and
- when the tenant is going to be moving out, to inspect, with the tenant's permission, in order to do a "pre–move-out" inspection. (CC § 1950.5(f).) The landlord must give 48 hours' notice. In most situations, it's to your advantage to agree to the inspection, because addressing what the landlord finds (if reasonable) will probably help you to get your security deposit back. (See Chapter 13, Security Deposits and Last Month's Rent.)

Your lease or rental agreement might include a clause that states that you agree to an annual or semiannual inspection by the landlord. Technically, this type of preapproval is invalid because it waives a right under California Code Section 1954, which California Code Section 1953 does not allow. But think twice before refusing your landlord access in order to assess the need for repairs: If the landlord is conscientious about keeping the property in good shape, this might be the only way to find out whether certain aspects of the property need attention. You might not notice details of wear that the landlord, familiar with the building, will spot. Of course, if the entry is a ruse to bother or harass you, pipe up.

While not technically allowed, a landlord might ask the unit in order to evaluate potential repair issues. If the landlord is sincere about this intention, it is to your advantage to consent to such an inspection.

Entry to Show Property

Your landlord may enter your property to show it to prospective tenants (toward the end of a tenancy) and to prospective purchasers when the property is on the market, as long as the landlord complies with the "business hours" and "reasonable notice" provisions discussed below.

Generally, normal business hours are considered 9:00 a.m. to 5:00 p.m., Monday to Friday. Some landlords (and their selling agents) contend that for showing a property, "normal business hours" includes evenings and weekend open houses. The court in *Dromy v. Lukovsky,* 219 Cal.App.4th 278 (2013) seemed to say that weekend open houses were "normal business hours" in this context, but was also careful to protect the tenant's privacy rights by limiting the number of open houses to two per month. In any event, landlords and tenants can reach understandings on their own, as explained just below.

Unfortunately, problems often occur when an overeager real estate salesperson shows up on your doorstep without warning or calls on very short notice and asks to be let in to show the place to a possible buyer. In this situation, you are within your rights to say politely but firmly, "I'm busy right now—try again in a few days after we've set a time convenient for all of us." Naturally, this type of misunderstanding is not conducive to your peace of mind, especially if you fear that the landlord or real estate person might use a passkey to enter when you are not home.

There are several ways to deal with this situation:

- You can stand on your rights and notify your landlord to follow the law or you will sue for invasion of privacy (see "What to Do About a Landlord's Improper Entry," below).

- You can work out a compromise with the landlord or agent, agreeing to entry on certain specified days and times. For instance, Tuesday afternoons between noon and 2:00 p.m., or Thursday evenings between 7:00 p.m. and 9:00 p.m., plus one or two Sunday open houses per month, as agreed in advance. This way you both have firm schedules to work from.

- You can try to work out a compromise with your landlord by which you agree to allow the unit to be shown on shorter-than-24-hour notice in exchange for a reduction in the rent or other benefit. For example, you might agree in advance that a four-hour notice period is reasonable for up to eight house showings a month, in exchange for having your rent reduced $400 per month. This kind of tradeoff is perfectly logical—your rent pays for your right to treat your home like your castle, and any diminution of this right should be accompanied by a decrease in your rent.

If you believe that someone is entering your unit without your knowledge and want to prove that it's happening, use a webcam attached to your computer. These cost as little as $20 and, if properly positioned, can catch the culprit in the act. If your computer is not in a convenient location for this purpose, try a wide-angle lens security camera, which you can get for $20–$60 each.

CAUTION

Under no circumstances should you allow your landlord to place a key-holding "lock box" on the door. This is a metal box that attaches to the front door and contains the key to that door. It can be opened by a master key held by area real estate salespeople. Because a lock box allows a salesperson to enter in disregard of the 24-hour notice requirement, it should not be used—period.

Written and Oral Notice

Except in cases of emergency entry, when you are present and agree to an entry, or when you have abandoned the premises or otherwise moved out, the landlord must give you written notice of any intent to enter, including the day and approximate time, and the purpose. (Because the statute specifies "the date" that the landlord intends to enter, landlords cannot legally give you a range of dates, as in "between June 4 and June 8." (CC § 1954(d)(1).) The landlord may do this by delivering it personally to you, by leaving it with a responsible person at your home, or by leaving it on, under, or near the usual entry door. The landlord can also mail it to you, within six days of the planned entry.

Special rules apply when the landlord wants to enter to show your home to a prospective purchaser. If the landlord has advised you in writing of his intent to sell the premises within four months of his intended entry, and has told you that he or his real estate agent might be contacting you for the purpose of showing your rental, his oral notice (in person or by phone) will be sufficient. If delivered 24 hours before the intended entry, this oral notice will be presumed reasonable. The landlord or his agent must leave you a note stating that they were in your unit. (CC § 1954(d)(2).)

Finally, landlords and tenants can dispense with the written notice requirement if they agree that the landlord may enter without notice to make specified repairs or supply services, as long as the entry is no more than within one week after the agreement. For example, on Sunday you and your landlord could agree that she'll fix your dishwasher by the end of the week, and you might agree that she won't need to give you written notice of the precise day and time. That's valid as long as the landlord does the work by the next Sunday. If she doesn't get to it, she'll need to give written notice as explained earlier. (CC § 1954(d)(3).)

What to Do About a Landlord's Improper Entry

When you rent a home, the landlord is giving you exclusive possession of the premises. State law requires that the landlord protect your "quiet enjoyment and possession" of the premises from all intruders (including the landlord). (CC § 1927.)

Unfortunately, some landlords do not follow these basic rules. Suppose your landlord violates your right to privacy—what can you do about it?

As you have probably figured out by now, it is one thing to have a right, and quite another thing to get the benefits of it. This is especially true for tenants who do not have a lease and have not lived in the rental long enough to qualify for just cause eviction protections. In this situation, if you set about aggressively demanding your rights, you might end up with a notice to vacate—and while you might ultimately prevail by showing that the landlord has acted illegally in retaliation, you'll have expended a lot of time, energy, and money proving your point. It is also generally true that you can rarely accomplish good results with hard words. This doesn't mean that you shouldn't be firm or determined, but rather, try not to be offensive.

Here is a step-by-step approach that usually works in dealing with a landlord who is violating your right to privacy:

Step 1: Talk to the landlord (or manager) about your concerns in a friendly but firm way. If you come to an understanding, follow up with a note to confirm it.

Step 2: If this doesn't work, or if your landlord doesn't follow the agreement that you have worked out, it's time for a tougher letter. A sample letter or email is shown below.

Step 3: If, despite this letter or email, the invasions of your privacy continue, document them and either see a lawyer or take your landlord to small claims court. If the landlord's actions are extreme or outrageous (for instance, he enters the apartment frequently and starts yelling), you might want to consider a Civil Harassment Restraining Order (discussed at the end of Chapter 4).

One challenge with an invasion of privacy lawsuit is that you'll need to show actual harm that will translate into a money award (damages). These damages fall into one or more of three categories:

- Economic (financial damages), such as the value of lost time from work, property damage, cost of security cameras, or the lost value of your tenancy due to the interference (you had to move and your new rental is more expensive)
- Non-economic damages (emotional distress), which could can range from highly unpleasant reactions such as anxiety, worry, and embarrassment, to more severe responses such as sleeplessness, nausea, and headaches, and
- Statutory penalties and punitive damages. If a judge decides that the violation was intended to "influence the tenant to vacate," you would be entitled to statutory damages (amounts specified in the Civil Code) of $2,000 per incident. (CC § 1940.2(b).)

Furthermore, blatant, unlawful entries could be an indication of other conduct that may violate your rights. If this is the case, you might want to consult with an attorney before going to small claims court.

Finally, some people have considered changing the locks to the premises as a solution to the problem of unwanted entries. This is a risky proposition. Most written agreements forbid altering the premises without the landlord's permission and some specifically prohibit changing the locks. If this is the case, you should reconsider this tactic unless you want to face the possibility of a three-day notice to cure or quit and then a possible eviction.

Sample Letter or Email When Landlord Violates Privacy

June 13, 20xx

Roper Real Estate Management Co.
11 Peach Street
San Diego, CA 00000

Dear Mr. Roper:

Several times in the last two months, your employees have entered my apartment without my being home and without notifying me in advance. In no situation was there any emergency involved. This has caused me considerable anxiety and stress, to the point that my peaceful enjoyment of my tenancy has been seriously disrupted.

This letter is to formally notify you that I value my privacy highly and insist that my legal rights to that privacy, as guaranteed to me under Section 1954 of the Civil Code, be respected. Specifically, in nonemergency situations, I would like to have 24 hours' written notice of your intent to enter my home.

I assume this notice will be sufficient to correct this matter. If you want to talk about this, please call me at 121-2121 between the hours of 9:00 a.m. and 5:00 p.m.

Yours truly,

Sally South

Sally South

If your landlord or manager comes onto your property or into your home and harms you in any way, sexually harasses you, threatens you, or damages any of your property, see an attorney. You should also report the matter to the police. Some California police departments have taken the excellent step of setting up special landlord-tenant units. The officers and legal experts in these units have been given special training in landlord-tenant law and are often helpful in handling disputes and setting straight a landlord who has taken illegal measures against a tenant.

Landlords sometimes trespass when the tenant has failed to pay rent. The landlord, faced with the necessity of paying a lot of money to legally get a tenant to move out, resorts to threats or even force. But the landlord's frustration is no justification for illegal acts. (See "Illegal Self-Help Evictions" in Chapter 14.) All threats, intimidation, and any physical attacks on the tenant should be reported to the police. Of course, it is illegal for the landlord to come on the property and do such things as remove windows and doors, turn off the utilities, or change the locks. If this is done, the tenant should see an attorney at once.

Do not overreact when a landlord gets hostile. While a tenant has the right to take reasonable steps to protect himself, his family, and his possessions from harm, the steps must be reasonably related to the threat. The wisest thing to do, whenever you have good reason to fear that you or your property may be harmed, is to call the police.

You should know that a landlord's repeated abuse of a tenant's right to privacy gives a tenant under a lease a legal excuse to break it by moving out, without liability for further rent; and to sue for constructive eviction.

Other Types of Invasions of Privacy

Entering a tenant's home without the tenant's knowledge or consent isn't the only way a landlord can interfere with the tenant's privacy. Here are a few other commonly encountered situations, with advice on how to handle them.

Health, Safety, or Building Inspections

The law concerning when, how, and why your landlord can enter your rented home is, as you have seen, fairly short, simple, and tenant-friendly. But the rules are different when it comes to entry by state or local health, safety, or building inspectors.

Neighbor's Complaints to Government Inspectors

If inspectors have credible reasons to suspect that a tenant's rental unit violates housing codes or local standards—for example, a neighbor has complained about noxious smells coming from the tenant's home or about his 20 cats—the authorities will usually knock on the tenant's door and ask for permission to enter. Except in the case of genuine emergency, you have the right to say no.

But your refusal will buy you only a little time in most cases, and you do not want the inspector to be against you before he or she has even seen your unit. Inspectors have ways to get around tenant refusals. A common first step (maybe even before the inspectors stop by the rental unit) is to ask your landlord to let them in. Many landlords will comply, although their legal authority to do so is questionable unless there is a genuine emergency. If inspectors can't reach the landlord (or if the landlord won't cooperate), their next step will probably be to get a search warrant based on the information from the complaining neighbor.

To obtain a warrant, the inspectors must convince a judge that the source of their information—the neighbor—is reliable, and that there is a strong likelihood that public health or safety is at risk. Armed with a search warrant, inspectors have a clear right to insist on entry. If they believe that a tenant will refuse entry, they may bring along police officers, who have the right to do whatever it takes to overcome the tenant's objections.

Random Inspections

Fire, health, and other municipal inspectors some-times randomly inspect apartment buildings even if they don't suspect noncompliance. These inspec-tions are allowed under some local ordinances in California. To find out whether your city has a program of random building inspections, call your city manager or mayor's office.

You have the right to say no to a random building inspection. If you do so, the inspector may request that a judge issue a search warrant, allowing the inspector to enter to check for fire or safety violations. Again, if there is any expectation that you will resist, a police officer will usually accompany the inspector.

An inspector who arrives when you are not home might ask your landlord to open the door on the spot, in violation of California state privacy laws. If the inspector has come with a warrant, the landlord can probably give consent and open the door, since even you, the tenant, couldn't prevent entry. But what if the inspector is there without a warrant? A cautious landlord will ask an inspector without a warrant to enter after they have given you reasonable notice (presumed to be 24 hours) under state law (or after they've obtained a search warrant).

Inspection Fees

Many cities impose fees for inspections, on a per unit or building basis or a sliding scale based on the number of your landlord's holdings. Some fees are imposed only if violations are found. If your ordinance imposes fees regardless of violations, your landlord might pass the inspection cost on to the tenant in the form of a rent hike. It's not illegal to do this, however, rent control (statewide or by city) could severely limit the rent increase.

If your ordinance imposes a fee only when violations are found, your landlord should not pass the cost on to you if the noncompliance is not your fault. For example, if inspectors find that the owner failed to install state-mandated smoke alarms, the owner should pay for the inspection; but if you have allowed garbage to pile up in violation of city health laws, you should pay the inspector's bill.

The Police

Even the police may not enter a tenant's rental unit unless they can show you or your landlord a recently issued search or arrest warrant, signed by a judge or magistrate. The police do not need a search warrant, however, if they need to enter to

- prevent or stop a catastrophe or a serious crime

- apprehend a fleeing criminal suspected of a serious offense, or
- prevent the imminent destruction of evidence of a serious crime.

The landlord cannot use the police to stop a person whom a tenant has invited in for the purpose of providing tenants' rights information or organizing a tenants' association. (CC § 1942.6.) Likewise, a landlord cannot call the police to evict you for hosting or organizing such a meeting or association—even if you are behind in your rent. (See Chapter 14, Overview of Evictions and Tenancy Terminations.)

Putting "For Sale" or "For Rent" Signs on the Property

Occasionally, friction is caused by landlords who put "For Sale" or "For Rent" signs on tenants' homes, such as a "For Sale" sign on the lawn of a rented single-family house. Although a landlord might otherwise be very conscientious about respecting your privacy when it comes to giving 24 hours' notice before showing property to prospective buyers or renters, putting a sale or rental sign on the property is a virtual invitation to prospective buyers or renters to disturb you with unwelcome inquiries. There is little law on the subject of your rights in this situation. However, it is our opinion that because you have rented the unit, including the yard, the landlord has no right to trespass and erect a sign, and if your privacy is completely ruined by repeated inquiries, you may sue for invasion of privacy, just as if the landlord personally had made repeated illegal entries.

Keep in mind that with computerized multiple-listing services, many real estate offices can, and commonly do, sell houses and all sorts of other real estate without ever placing a For Sale sign on the property, except perhaps during the hours when an open house is in progress. If a real estate office puts a sign advertising sale or rental in front of the property you rent, you should at least insist that it clearly indicate a telephone number to call and warn against disturbing the occupant in words like, "Inquire at 555-1357—Do Not Disturb Occupant." If this doesn't do the trick and informal conversations with the landlord do not result in removal of the sign, your best bet is to simply remove it yourself and return it to the landlord, or to write the landlord a firm letter explaining why your privacy is being invaded and asking that the sign be removed. If the violations of your privacy continue, document them and consider suing in small claims court. Of course, you will want to show the judge a copy of the letter.

Landlord Allowing Others to Enter the Premises

Except in the circumstances set out above in "Permissible Reasons to Enter," your landlord has no right to enter your premises. It follows that the landlord also has no right to give others permission to enter. This includes allowing someone to enter who professes to have your permission. For example, landlords are often asked to open the door to people claiming to be the tenant's best friend or long-lost relative. Careful landlords will insist that these stories be backed up by clear permission from you, in writing or by phone at least. If your landlord has given in to an appealing story without checking with you first, he'll be liable if there is property loss or a physical assault.

Giving Information About You to Strangers

Your landlord might be approached by strangers, including creditors, banks, and perhaps even prospective landlords, to provide credit or other information about you. As with letting a stranger into your home, this could cause you considerable anxiety. Basically, your landlord has a legal right to give out normal business information about you as long as it's factual. However, if your landlord spreads false stories about you—for example, says you filed for bankruptcy when this isn't true—and you are damaged as a result (your credit rating is adversely affected or you don't get a job), you have grounds to sue the landlord.

In addition, if a landlord or a manager spreads other types of gossip about you (whether or not true), such as who stayed overnight in your apartment or that you drink too much, you could be in good shape to sue and obtain a substantial recovery, especially if the gossip damages you. This is because spreading this type of information usually has no legitimate purpose and is just plain malicious. If flagrant and damaging, this sort of gossip can be an invasion of privacy for which you might have a valid reason to sue.

Calling or Visiting You at Work

Should a need arise for your landlord to call you at work (say when your Uncle Harry shows up and asks to be let into your apartment), try to be understanding when you take the call, no matter how inconvenient it may be. However, situations justifying a landlord calling you at work are fairly rare. If a landlord calls you to complain about late rent payments or other problems, politely say that you'll discuss it when you're at home. If this doesn't work, follow up with a brief note. If the landlord persists or tries to talk to your boss or other employees about the problem, your privacy is definitely being invaded. Consider going to small claims court or seeing a lawyer.

Unduly Restrictive Rules on Guests

A few landlords, overly concerned about their tenants moving new occupants into the property, go overboard in keeping tabs on the tenants' legitimate guests who stay overnight or for a few days. Often their leases, rental agreements, or rules and regulations will require you to "register" any overnight guest. While your landlord has a legitimate concern about persons who begin as "guests" becoming permanent unauthorized residents of the property (see Chapter 2), it is overkill to require you to inform your landlord of a guest whose stay is only for a day or two. As with other subjects we mention in this chapter, extreme behavior in this area—whether by an owner or a management employee—can be considered an invasion of privacy for which you may have a valid cause of action.

Major Repairs & Maintenance

Everywhere in California, you are legally entitled to rental property that meets basic structural, health, and safety standards and is in good repair. But suppose a landlord comes up short? When landlords fail to take care of important maintenance, you might have the legal right to use the "big sticks" in a tenant's arsenal—the rights to:

- withhold rent
- pay for repairs yourself and deduct the cost from the rent
- sue the landlord, or
- move out without notice.

This chapter describes your right to basic, important things, such as hot water, a floor that will not collapse under your feet, decent heat, and a roof that doesn't leak—in other words, your right to a safe and livable home. It also provides practical advice on how to get a reluctant landlord to perform needed repairs (and how to get them done yourself, using the big sticks mentioned above, if the landlord refuses). Less important maintenance and repair issues—such as unclogging kitchen drains or mowing the front lawn—are covered in the next chapter.

Your Basic Right to Habitable Premises

All landlords are legally required to make the premises habitable when they originally rent a unit, and to maintain it in that condition throughout the tenancy. In legal terminology, this is called "the implied warranty of habitability." The word "implied" means that by offering a residential rental, the landlord is promising you a habitable place to live—even if the lease doesn't say so and the landlord doesn't realize it.

Importantly, you have the right to a habitable rental even if you've willingly moved into a place that's clearly below habitability standards, or even if the lease or rental agreement you've signed states that the landlord doesn't have to provide a habitable unit.

In this chapter, we will be using the words "habitable" and "uninhabitable" frequently. They are often misunderstood and misused. Some think that a unit is "uninhabitable" if you cannot live in it at all. This is incorrect. "Uninhabitable" simply means that the property does not substantially comply with one or more of the state or local code requirements pertaining to premises rented for human occupancy. Conversely, "habitable" means that the unit is in compliance with all these standards—no more. The sections below describe the minimum requirements for habitability. We start with the more general requirements of the Civil Code, progressing to the more specific requirements of the Health and Safety Code and the Uniform Housing Code.

Conditions Covered By the Civil Code

The major California law defining habitable housing is Civil Code Section 1941.1 and Section 1941.3. According to these laws, at a minimum every rental must have:

- effective waterproofing and weather protection of roof and exterior walls, including unbroken windows and doors
- plumbing or gas facilities that conformed to applicable law in effect at the time of installation, maintained in good working order
- a water supply approved under applicable law that is under the control of the tenant, capable of producing hot and cold running water, or a system that is under the control of the landlord, that produces hot and cold running water, furnished to appropriate fixtures, and connected to a sewage disposal system approved under applicable law
- heating facilities that conformed with applicable law at the time of installation, maintained in good working order
- electrical lighting, with wiring and electrical equipment that conformed with applicable law at the time of installation, maintained in good working order

Housing Standards Under State Law

Rental housing standards established by Civil Code Sections 1941.1–.3, the State Housing Law and its implementing regulations, and the Uniform Housing Code (UHC) include:

- A structure that is weatherproof and waterproof; no holes or cracks through which wind, rain, or rodents can enter (CC § 1941.1).
- A plumbing system in good working order (free of rust and leaks), connected to both the local water supply and sewage system or septic tank. The landlord is not responsible for low pressure, contamination, or other failures in the local water supply—his obligation is only to connect a working plumbing system to the water supply (CC § 1941.1).
- A hot water system capable of producing water of at least 110 degrees Fahrenheit (CC § 1941.1 and UHC).
- A heating system that was legal when installed, maintained in good working order (CC § 1941.1), and capable of heating every room to at least 70 degrees F. (UHC).
- An electrical system that was legal when installed, and which is in good working order and without loose or exposed wiring (CC § 1941.1). There must be at least two outlets, or one outlet and one light fixture, in every room but the bathroom (where only one light fixture is required). Common stairs and hallways must be lighted at all times (UHC).
- A lack of insect or rodent infestations, rubbish, or garbage in all areas (CC § 1941.1). With respect to the living areas, the landlord's obligation to the tenant is only to rent out units that are initially free of insects, rodents, and garbage. If the tenant's housekeeping attracts pests, that's not the landlord's responsibility. However, the landlord is obliged to keep all common areas clean and free of rodents, insects, and garbage at all times.
- Enough garbage and trash receptacles in clean condition and good repair to contain tenants' trash and garbage without overflowing before the refuse collectors remove it each week (CC § 1941.1).
- Floors, stairways, and railings kept in good repair (CC § 1941.1).
- The absence or containment of known lead paint hazards (deteriorated lead-based paint, lead-contaminated dust or soil, or lead-based paint disturbed without containment (CC § 1941.1; H&S § 17920.10). See Chapter 10 for more information.)
- Deadbolt locks on certain doors and windows (CC § 1941.3).
- Ground fault circuit interrupters for swimming pools (effective July 1, 1998), and antisuction protections on wading pools, excepting single-family residence rentals (effective January 1, 1998 for new pools and January 1, 2000 for existing pools) (H&S §§ 116049.1 and 116064).

Each rental dwelling must, under both the UHC and the State Housing Law, have the following:

- A working toilet, wash basin, and bathtub or shower. The toilet and bathtub or shower must be in a room that is ventilated and allows for privacy.
- A kitchen with a sink, which cannot be made of an absorbent material such as wood.
- Natural lighting in every room through windows or skylights having an area of at least one-tenth of the room's floor area, with a minimum of 12 square feet (three square feet for bathroom windows). Each window must be openable at least halfway, unless a fan provides for ventilation.
- Safe fire or emergency exits leading to a street or hallway. Stairs, hallways, and exits must be litter free. Storage areas, garages, and basements must be free of combustible materials.
- Every apartment building having 16 or more units must have a resident manager (25 CCR § 42).

Civil Code Section 1941.4 and Public Utilities Code Section 788 require landlords to install a telephone jack and place and maintain inside phone wiring.

Health and Safety Code Section 13113.7 requires smoke detectors in all multiunit dwellings, from duplex on up. Landlords must provide information on emergency procedures in case of fire to tenants in multistory rental properties. (H&S § 13220.)

Health and Safety Code Section 17926.1 requires carbon monoxide detectors in all dwelling units, and Health and Safety Code Section 13220 requires landlords to provide information on emergency procedures in all multistory buildings.

- building, grounds, and appurtenances at the time of the commencement of the lease or rental agreement, and all areas under control of the landlord, kept in every part clean, sanitary, and free from all accumulations of debris, filth, rubbish, garbage, rodents, and vermin
- an adequate number of appropriate receptacles for garbage and rubbish, in clean condition and good repair at the time of the commencement of the lease or rental agreement, with the landlord providing appropriate serviceable receptacles thereafter and being responsible for the clean condition and good repair of the receptacles under the landlord's control
- floors, stairways, and railings maintained in good repair
- deadbolt locks on certain doors and windows (CC § 1941.3) (see Chapter 11 for specifics), and
- no lead paint hazards (deteriorated lead-based paint, lead-contaminated dust or soil, or lead-based paint disturbed without containment). (CC §§ 1941.1 and 1941.3; H&S § 17920.10.)

California Health and Safety Codes

Civil Code Section 1941.1 also requires landlords to comply with the conditions listed in California Health and Safety Code Section 17920.3. That law provides an extensive and detailed list of landlord obligations. For instance, subsection (a) discusses "adequate sanitation" to include such things as proper ventilation and the absence of dampness in the living spaces. Subsection (g) defines "weather protection" to include absence of falling plaster, cracked or dry rotted walls, roofs, or windows and lack of paint. Subsection (c) includes "any nuisance" as a substandard condition. This term is very broadly interpreted, as explained (below).

Health and Safety Code Section 17973 requires landlords of buildings containing three units or more to inspect "exterior elevated elements" before January 1, 2025. Exterior elevated elements include decks, walkways, stairs, railings, porches, and so on, which extend beyond the exterior walls of the building, are at least six feet above the ground, and are made (entirely or in part) of wood. Owners must hire a certified professional, such as licensed architect, structural engineer, or specified classes of licensed contractors.

Although other parts of California law already require a landlord to maintain these features of the property, this section goes a step further and requires the landlord to have a *professional* inspect it.

Uniform Housing Code and Local Codes

Yet another source of law gives meaning to your right to a fit and habitable dwelling. The Uniform Housing Code, an industry code that is adopted by the state legislature and counties and cities (which may increase its requirements and protections), sets minimum standards. Many of them overlap the standards in the State Housing Law, above, but some are unique. If you haven't yet seen in the state statutes the maintenance problem that's bedeviling you, read on. Each rental dwelling must have:

- A working toilet, washbasin, and bathtub or shower. The toilet and bathtub or shower must be in a room that is ventilated and allows for privacy.
- A kitchen with a sink, which cannot be made of an absorbent material such as wood.
- Natural lighting in every room through windows or skylights having an area of at least one-tenth of the room's floor area, with a minimum of 12 square feet (three square feet for bathroom windows). The windows in each room must be able to be opened at least halfway for ventilation, unless a fan provides for ventilation.
- Safe fire or emergency exits leading to a street or hallway. Stairs, hallways, and exits must be litter free. Storage areas, garages, and basements must be free of combustible materials.
- Every apartment building having 16 or more units must have a resident manager. (25 CC § 42.)

Exemptions for Older Buildings

When state agencies adopt a new housing code, or change an old one, it doesn't necessarily mean that all existing buildings have to be upgraded. Especially when it comes to items that would involve major structural changes, lawmakers will often exempt older buildings by writing a "grandfather clause" into the code, exempting all buildings constructed before a certain date. Typically, however, a landlord who later undertakes major renovations or remodeling must comply with the new rules. If you suspect that major work is being planned or done without bringing the building up to code, contact your local housing department. If you fear landlord retaliation, do so anonymously, if possible. (Tenants' protections against retaliatory conduct are discussed in Chapter 14.)

Other new code requirements that are easy and inexpensive to make—for example, installing locks, peepholes, or smoke detectors—must be made regardless of the age of the building.

City or county building or housing codes are different from industry codes. They regulate structural aspects of buildings and usually set specific space and occupancy standards, such as the minimum size of sleeping rooms. They also establish minimum requirements for light and ventilation, sanitation and sewage disposal, heating, water supply (such as how hot the water must be), fire protection, and wiring (such as the number of electrical outlets per room). In addition, housing codes typically make property owners responsible for keeping hallways, lobbies, elevators, and the other parts of the premises the owner controls clean, sanitary, and safe.

Your local building or housing authority, and health or fire department, might have an informational booklet that describes the exact requirements your landlord must meet. In most urban areas,

these local codes are more thorough than the state's general housing law—for example, some cities require landlords to install specific security items, such as peepholes, in exterior doors. However, local laws usually don't explain what you can do if your landlord fails to comply. To find out, you'll need to consult "How to Get Action From Your Landlord: The Light Touch," below.

Fit and Habitable: Court Decisions

State and local legislators and state agencies aren't the only ones who have weighed in on the subject of what constitutes habitable housing. Judges, too, faced with cases in which tenants didn't pay the rent because they felt that the premises were unlivable, have often written decisions that gave tenants extended rights. In fact, the whole notion of an implied warranty of habitability came from a court case, not from the legislature (that case was *Green v. Superior Court*, 10 Cal.3d 616 (1974)).

In evaluating whether a landlord is providing habitable housing, courts may also consider the weather, the terrain, and where the rental property is located. Features or services that might be considered nonessential extras in some parts of the country are legally viewed as absolutely necessary components of habitable housing in others. For example, in areas with severe winters, such as the Sierra, storm windows may be basic equipment.

Finally, keep in mind that the meaning of the term "habitable housing" is not static, and court decisions are made in light of changes in living conditions and technology. For example, courts consider the prevalence of crime in urban areas when determining what constitutes habitable housing; and extensive mold contamination (unrecognized until relatively recently) can make some dwellings unfit. Good locks, security personnel, exterior lighting, and secure common areas are now, in some cities, as important to tenants as are water and heat. (Chapter 11 discusses your rights to adequate security measures.)

What's a Nuisance?

A "nuisance" is defined under Civil Code Section 3479 as "anything which is injurious to health, including, but not limited to the illegal sale of controlled substances, or is indecent or offensive to the senses, or an obstruction to the free use of property, so as to interfere with the comfortable enjoyment of life or property...." This definition would include the presence of mold or other toxic substances, dangerous electrical wiring, drug dealing or other illegal activities, excessive noise or other disturbances, lack of heat or hot water, or foul odors.

The Effect of a Change of Ownership

Whenever there is a new owner, the new owner "steps into the shoes" of the old owner. In other words, the rights and obligations that the original landlord and tenant had before the change in ownership remain in place. The new owner just takes the place, responsibility-wise, of the old owner. Even if the former owner neglected the property, that does not alter the new owner's duty to provide habitable housing. (*Knight v. Hallsthammar,* 29 Cal.3d 46 (1981).) This is true even if the property has been foreclosed by a mortgagor (a bank) or if it has been put into receivership. (*Erlach v. Sierra Asset Servicing, LLC* 226 Cal.App.4th 1281 (2014).)

Your Repair and Maintenance Responsibilities

You now know that you can expect your landlord to provide safe and habitable housing and adhere to norms of cleanliness and behavior under a variety of overlapping and specific legal rules. But your landlord isn't the only one with legal responsibilities. If you don't keep up your end of the bargain, at the least you can expect a deduction from your security deposit when you move out, for needed cleaning or repairs. Most importantly, you cannot claim the landlord breached the implied warranty of habitability if you violated any of the following obligations and that violation "contributed substantially" to the habitability problem. (CC § 1941.2.) State housing law requires you to:

- Keep your rental as clean and sanitary as the condition of the premises permits. For example, you cannot claim that the premises are not sanitary when you have failed to undertake routine cleaning.
- Dispose of all rubbish, garbage, and other waste in a clean and sanitary manner. For instance, if mice or ants invaded your kitchen because you forgot to take out the garbage before you left on a two-week vacation, you would be responsible for paying any necessary extermination costs.
- Properly use and operate all electrical, gas, and plumbing fixtures, and keep them as clean and sanitary as their condition permits. For example, bathtub caulking that has sprouted mold and mildew may render the tub unusable (or at least disgusting), but because proper cleaning could have prevented it, you are responsible. On the other hand, if the bathroom has no fan and the window has been painted shut, the bathroom will be hard to air out; resulting mildew might be your landlord's responsibility.
- Not permit anyone on the premises who, with your permission, willfully or wantonly destroys, defaces, damages, impairs, or removes any part of the structure or dwelling unit or the facilities or equipment—and of course, you yourself must not do any such thing.
- Occupy and use the premises as your home, using it only as it was designed or intended to be used for living, sleeping, cooking, or dining. For example, you can't use the dining room as a machine shop and then complain about the stains in the carpet.

What About Things You Break?

If you cause a serious habitability problem in your unit—for example, you carelessly break the sole toilet—you are responsible. A landlord who finds out about the problem can insist that you pay for the repair. Legally, you can't just decide to live without plumbing for a while to save money. If you drag your feet, the landlord can use your security deposit to pay for it, and if the amount of the deposit isn't enough, sue you besides. Your landlord can't, however, charge you for problems caused by normal wear and tear—for example, a carpet that has worn out from use. (Chapter 13 discusses the difference between normal wear and tear and damage.)

Agreeing to Be Responsible for Repairs

As we've explained, you cannot waive (give up) your rights to habitable premises under Civil Code Section 1941 or 1942. Therefore, you cannot be made responsible for repairing any condition listed in those code sections unless your conduct "substantially contributed" to the condition. (For example, you failed to keep the place clean and you ended up with cockroaches). (CC § 1942.1.)

There is a rare exception to this rule. At the beginning of the tenancy, you and your landlord can agree, *in writing and before you move in*, that you are obligated to improve, repair, and/or maintain all or part of the premises as part of the consideration of the rental amount. In other words, you and the landlord can agree that in exchange for you doing maintenance and repairs, the landlord will charge you less rent. (CC §§ 1942.1, 19453(b).) Landlords rarely attempt to use this provision because:

- The landlord still has the ultimate duty to comply with building, housing, health, and fire codes.

- Such a provision would not relieve the landlord of civil liability for any personal injury or property damage caused by a defective condition—so the landlord could be sued by a third party for the tenant's failure to keep the place safe.
- Most landlords want to be in control of the physical condition of the property.
- Many types of repairs (like roof repairs, major electrical or plumbing repairs, and structural repairs) would require the tenant to go outside the unit itself to fix it. Tenants rarely have the time, inclination, or expertise to embark on such projects.

Major Versus Minor Repairs

The remedies available to tenants who are facing major repairs that the landlord won't address are powerful tools: Rent withholding, repair and deduct, and breaking the lease and moving out, and suing. In addition, if you are in a rent control city, depending on the ordinance, you might be able to get a rent reduction. All are discussed in detail below. These remedies are not, in most situations, appropriate for minor repairs. If you use a "big stick" remedy to address an insignificant problem, you're courting trouble—a termination notice for unpaid rent, for example. So it's important from the get-go to be able to correctly tell the difference between major and minor repairs.

The difference between major repair problems and minor ones is usually the degree of severity. Put another way, how much does the defect affect the livability, use, and enjoyment of the premises? The severity of the problem or problems will depend on their nature and impact on you. The more severe the problem and the more profound its impact, the more justified a tenant will be in using "big stick" remedies such as rent withholding or terminating tenancy without notice. (Although, to be on the safe side, you could still decide on a less aggressive approach.)

Problems that are less severe do not usually warrant withholding rent, but might warrant other remedies described in this chapter and Chapter 7.

When evaluating whether the problem that's bedeviling you is major or minor, consider:

- Does the issue involve your right to something obviously basic, like a roof that does not leak, hot and cold running water, safe electricity, absence of a persistent mouse infestation, or heat in the dead of winter? Or, is the problem more technical, such as a fire extinguisher that does not work or a dripping faucet? The landlord is obligated to fix all these problems, but the steps you would take if they are not fixed would be different.

- How does the problem affect you? A mere inconvenience doesn't constitute a major problem. For example, the roof leak might be in a utility room that you seldom enter or use. While the landlord should fix the problem, you would probably not be justified in withholding the rent or terminating the lease if the landlord doesn't step up.

- Are you facing more than one problem? Often times major and minor habitability concerns may be present in the same unit. So, while the leak in the utility room might not be enough to justify rent withholding, the combination of that problem with electrical outlets that spark, kitchen flooring that has chipped away, the absence of smoke detectors, and an unusable sink in a second bathroom might together support your use of a drastic tenant remedy.

How to Get Action From Your Landlord: The Light Touch

Knowing that you have a legal right to habitable housing and getting it are, obviously, horses of very different colors. A lot depends on the attitude of your landlord—but some depends on your strategy, too. Here are some tips to maximize your chances of getting quick results, short of using the big sticks that we explain in the next section.

Put Repair Requests in Writing

By far the best approach is to put every repair and maintenance request in writing, keeping a copy for your files. You might want to call first, but be sure to follow up with a written request. (Use email if you wish (but avoid texts)—see below.)

Written communications to your landlord are important because they:

- are far more likely to be taken seriously than face-to-face conversations or phone calls, because it's clear to the landlord you're keeping a record of your requests

- are less likely to be forgotten or misunderstood

- satisfy the legal requirement that you give your landlord a reasonable opportunity to fix a problem before you withhold rent or exercise other legal rights (see "What to Do If the Landlord Won't Make Repairs," below), and

- are evidence in case you ever need to prove that the serious problems with your rental were the subject of repeated repair requests.

In your request, be as specific as possible regarding the problem, its effect on you, what you want done, and when. For example, if the thermostat on your heater is always finicky and often doesn't function at all, explain that you have been without heat during the last two days during which the nighttime low was below freezing—don't simply say "the heater needs to be fixed." If the problem poses a health or safety threat, such as a broken front-door lock or loose step, say so and ask for it to be fixed immediately. Competent landlords will respond extra quickly to genuinely dangerous situations, as opposed to those that are merely inconvenient. Finally, be sure to note the date of the request and how many requests, if any, have preceded this one.

If your landlord provides a repair request form, use it. If not, do your own (email is a quick way to notify your landlord, and it provides a paper trail). (See the sample shown below.) Always make a copy of your request and keep it in a safe place in your files.

You might want to offer help that will make it easier for the landlord to get the repairs done. For example, you might want to suggest times that you will be available to let repair people come and evaluate the need and expense of the repair. Although you are not obligated to make these offers, you might decide that it is easier and faster for you to coordinate the visits from repair people.

Instead of sending a handwritten or typed note, you can use email, which offers several advantages over the old-fashioned methods:

- Because you don't have to wait until the landlord gets the letter in the mail, it's the quickest way to communicate.
- A sent email gives you reliable evidence as to when it was sent, because it automatically includes a date stamp.
- An email is less likely to get lost because it will be stored in your email account.
- Assuming that you have the correct email address for your landlord, it is impossible for him to say "I never got it."

Because the use of emails has now become so widespread, courts commonly allow parties to introduce emails as evidence in court. You can legally use this form of communication in almost every instance with your landlord, except to give a document that requires a signature (like a lease agreement) or to legally notify your landlord that you are ending your tenancy. Resist the temptation to communicate by text message, however—texting is much more difficult to reproduce in a manner that will be accepted as evidence by a court.

You can also use the electronic signature service called Docusign for signing leases, but understand that it's a little complicated to use, and

both parties (landlord and tenant) must agree to accept it. Landlords should not insist on it. By far the most common approach is to send the file to the prospective tenant, have the tenant print the signature page, sign it, scan it, send it back via email or fax, and send the original via regular mail. Or, you can agree that the signers will "sign" on the computer, using digital signatures. The landlord will need to sign up with an e-signature program to make this method workable and reliable.

Sample Request for Repair or Maintenance

To: Kay Sera, Landlord,
        Stately View Apartments

From: Will Tripp
        376 Seventh Avenue,
        Apartment No. 45
        Appleville, CA 00000

Re: Roof leak

Date: March 10, 20xx

As I mentioned to you on the phone yesterday, on March 9, 20xx I noticed dark stains on the ceilings of the upstairs bedroom and bath. These stains are moist and appear to be the result of the recent heavy rains. I would very much appreciate it if you would promptly look into the apparent roof leak. If the leak continues, my property may be damaged and two rooms may become unusable. Please call me so that I'll know when to expect you or a repairperson. You can reach me at work during the day (555-1234) or at home at night (555-4546).

Thank you very much for your attention to this problem. I expect to hear from you within the next few days, and expect that the situation will be corrected within a couple of weeks.

Yours truly,

Will Tripp
Will Tripp

CAUTION

In dangerous situations, you must take precautions, too. Once you're aware of a dangerous situation, you must take reasonable steps to avoid injury. Don't continue to use the outlet when you see sparks fly from the wall; don't park in the garage at night if the lights are burned out and there is a safer alternative. If you don't take reasonable care and are injured and sue the landlord, you can expect a judge or jury to hold the landlord only partially responsible. (See Chapter 9.)

Deliver Your Repair Request to the Landlord

If your landlord has an on-site office or a resident manager, deliver your repair request personally. If you send it by U.S. mail rather than by email, consider sending it certified (return receipt requested), or use a delivery service (such as Federal Express) that will give you a receipt establishing delivery. If you fax your request, ask for a call (or a return fax) acknowledging receipt. If your property has an on-site manager, you could notify this person first, either orally or in writing. The landlord is ultimately responsible for getting repairs done, however, and if the resident manager does not respond promptly enough, or if you don't have a resident manager, you need to go to the landlord directly. Again, the easiest and most reliable way to notify the landlord is by email.

If you want to place some extra emphasis on your communication, choose a letter sent by certified mail, or via US Postal Priority Mail, UPS, or Federal Express. These methods will provide you with a receipt that confirms that the letter was sent to the landlord at a particular date. Although taking steps to verify delivery will cost a little more, it has two major advantages over regular mail:

- It will get the landlord's attention and high-light the fact that you are serious about your request.

- The signed receipt is evidence that the landlord did, in fact, receive the letter. You might need this in the event that the landlord fails to make the repair and you decide to do it yourself or withhold rent. If a dispute arises as to your right to use a self-help measure, you'll be able to prove in court that you satisfied the legal requirement of notifying the landlord first.

If your first request doesn't produce results—or at least a call or note from the landlord telling you when repairs will be made—send another. Mention that this is the second (or third) time you have brought the matter to the landlord's attention. If the problem is getting worse, emphasize this development. If the problem is getting worse, emphasize this fact. If you have low hopes for any response and are beginning to think of your next move (a self-help remedy, as described below), you might mention your intent to use such a remedy. And, of course, be sure to keep a record of all repair requests.

Keep Notes on All Conversations

Besides keeping a copy of every written repair request (including emails), keep a record of oral communications, too. If the landlord calls you in response to your repair request, make notes during the conversation or immediately afterward; write down the date and time that the conversation occurred and when you made your notes. These notes could come in handy to refresh your memory and help you reconstruct the history of your case. In most situations, if a dispute ends up in court, and you are unable to remember the details of the conversation, your notes can be introduced to fill the gap. Don't tape-record the phone call—it's illegal unless the other side agrees. (Penal Code § 632.)

You can keep track of other kinds of communications, too. If your dealings with your landlord are accomplished online, print out the message.

Put the Landlord's Promises in Writing

If you and your landlord agree on a plan of action, it's especially wise to write down your understanding of this agreement. Send an email to the landlord describing your understanding, inviting him to reply if he thinks that you have missed or misstated anything. If he doesn't write back, the law presumes that he agreed with your version of the conversation. (See the Sample Letter or Email of Understanding Regarding Repairs, below.)

Sample Letter or Email of Understanding Regarding Repairs

1234 Appian Way, #3
Beach City, CA 00000

September 3, 20xx

Ms. Iona Lott, Landlord
100 Civic Center Drive
Beach City, CA 00000

Dear Ms. Lott,

Thank you for calling me yesterday, September 2, 20xx, regarding my request for repairs, dated August 27, 20xx. In that request, I told you that the hot water in my unit is very hot (123 degrees F. on my thermometer), even though the temperature gauge on the water heater is turned down as far as it can go. I am concerned that my young daughter may be injured by this scalding water, and am anxious that the temperature be lowered as soon as possible.

As I understand it, you agreed to have Ralph, your handyman, come check the problem on Saturday morning, September 6, between 9 and 10 a.m. Ralph will bring along a new thermostat should he need to replace the old one.

Please let me know if your recollection of our conversation and plans differs from mine.

Yours truly,

Howard Hillman

Howard Hillman

What to Do If the Landlord Won't Make Repairs

If your persistent and businesslike requests for repairs are ignored, you can take stronger measures. Your options include:

- calling state or local building or health inspectors
- withholding the rent
- repairing the problem (or having it repaired by a professional) and deducting the cost from your rent
- moving out
- paying the rent and then suing the landlord for the difference between the rent you paid and the value of the defective premises, or
- if you live in a rent control city, you might be able to file a petition for reduction in services (tenants who have only the protections of the statewide rent control and eviction protection laws do not have this option).

FORM

This chapter includes sample letters you can send your landlord when you intend to withhold rent or use the repair-and-deduct remedy. Or you can use the general Notice to Repair form included in Appendix C. The Nolo website includes a downloadable version of the Notice to Repair form (see Appendix B for a link to the forms in this book). You can edit the letter to fit your particular situation.

If the landlord hasn't fixed a serious problem that is a health or safety risk or a substantial inconvenience—rats in the kitchen, for example—you will want to take fast action. But before you use any of these big sticks, make sure that you can answer "Yes" to all of the questions in "Big Stick Prerequisites," below.

TIP
Before doing repairs yourself, withholding rent, or using another "big stick," get proof of how bad the problem was. Take pictures of the problem or ask others to view the problem and write a description. Also consider asking an experienced and impartial contractor or repairperson to examine the situation and give you a written description of the problem and estimate for repair. Be sure the description is signed and dated.

Report Code Violations to Housing Inspectors

A local building, health, or fire department usually gets involved when a tenant complains to a government agency about serious health and safety issues (a change in property ownership or owner financing may also trigger an inspection). The agency inspects the building and, if problems are found, issues a deficiency notice that requires the owner to remedy all violations. A landlord who fails to comply can face civil and criminal penalties—including not being able to evict a tenant of the property for nonpayment of rent. (H&S §§ 17997–17997.5.)

Many of the agencies who conduct these inspections are lax in their enforcement, due to understaffing or for other reasons. It's important for you to establish a good relationship with the inspector from the start. Tell the inspector about the problem or problems and how you are affected, but don't be pushy. Also ask what can be done to fix the problem and how the inspector can help. Inspectors do not like to feel like they are in the middle of a landlord-tenant dispute (even though they are), so focus your conversation on getting the repairs made and not what a bad person the landlord is.

The level of enforcement by housing inspectors varies greatly from city to city and county to county. Larger cities, for instance, have agencies that are dedicated solely to housing inspection. These agencies regularly issue citations to landlords, and follow up on those citations. In other areas, housing inspection is a part-time job, where inspectors cite only the most egregious violations, and employ very little follow-up. If the latter describes your situation, your attempt to pressure the landlord may result in a "clean bill of health" from a very lax inspector. Try to find out how effective the inspectors in your city or county are and whether it's worth your while to contact them.

Also, if your unit is an "illegal unit" such as a "mother-in-law" unit that was not built with permits, or a converted garage or commercial space, you really need to think twice. If the unit is illegal and an inspector comes to visit, the inspector will likely issue a citation ordering the landlord to remove the unit from residential use. In this case, calling the building inspector would end up costing you your home.

If you decide to complain to building, health, or fire inspectors, start with an Internet search of local government agencies, such as building, housing inspection, or health departments Or, call your local supervisor or city council. Also, look for a local tenants' rights group.

You might be wondering whether the landlord can evict you for calling the building inspectors. You're not alone in your worry. This type of landlord behavior is called "retaliation," and is strictly forbidden. Civil Code Section 1942.5 prohibits a landlord from evicting, raising rent, or any other like conduct, in retaliation for the tenants' exercise of their rights under the law. In such a case, a tenant will have a solid defense to an eviction or a rent increase. In addition, the tenant will have the right to sue the landlord for retaliation and can recover actual damages, statutory damages, punitive damages, and attorney fees.

What Does the Notice from the Building Inspector Mean?

If the housing or building inspectors find some violations, they will prepare a notice ordering the landlord to fix the violations, usually called a "Notice of Violation" or "Notice of Abatement."

Big Stick Prerequisites

Before you take drastic action, such as withholding the rent or moving out, be sure you can say "Yes" to each question below:

- **How serious is the problem or problems?** Not every building code violation or annoying defect in your rental home (like your water heater's ability to reach only 107 degrees F, three degrees short of the code-specified 110 degrees) justifies use of a "big stick" against the landlord. In other words, be sure that this is a true habitability problem.

- **Did someone other than you or a guest cause the problem?** If you're at fault, you shouldn't pursue the self-help options.

- **Did you tell the landlord about the problem and give him a reasonable opportunity to get it fixed?** The landlord has 30 days under state law or less if the circumstances warrant prompter attention.

- **Have you consulted with a lawyer or other person knowledgeable about tenants' rights?** Rent withholding could lead to an eviction attempt by your landlord. If that situation should arise, you want to make sure that you are on firm legal

footing, that you understand the time and effort it will take to fight the eviction, and that you have resources available to help you through such a fight.

- **Have you considered the repair and deduct option discussed below?** Repair and deduct is a much safer and effective option if you can use it.

- **Are you willing to risk eviction if a judge or jury decides that you shouldn't have used the "big stick"?** For example, if you withhold rent, the landlord may sue to evict you based on nonpayment of rent. Even if you're sure that your course of action was justified, a judge may decide otherwise. The experience will take time, effort, and money. And if you go through the eviction case and lose, a negative mark on your credit record may cause serious problems for future rentals, loans, and employment.

- **If you move out, can you find a comparable or better unit?** If the building is closed following deficiencies you've reported to inspectors, your landlord must help you with relocation expenses, but it will be a hassle to get the money (and to move). (H&S § 17980.7.)

The inspectors usually post the notice on the outside of the building, and mail a copy to the landlord. The notice might say that the building is "uninhabitable," but that does not mean that you have to move, it just means that the landlord has to fix the defects.

What Happens When the Tenant Is Ordered to Vacate Due to the Landlord's Failure to Repair?

In very extreme cases, where the landlord has repeatedly failed to fix the problems, the building will be "red-tagged" and the tenant will be required to vacate. This happens in one of two ways: In the first instance, the city will file a legal action

to get an order requiring the landlord to fix the problems. If necessary, the judge will order the building vacated so the work can get done. The court order should also direct the landlord to pay the tenant's relocation expenses—the difference between the tenant's rent and the fair market rent of a comparable unit over a period of 120 days. (H & S §§ 17980.6, 17980.7.)

Instead of going to court first, a local agency will sometimes require the tenant to vacate. In this situation, the tenant is also entitled to relocation expenses. (H & S § 17975 and following.)

Except in the case of illegal units, it is very rare that the defects are so severe that the tenant will be required to vacate.

Withhold the Rent

If problems are serious and other attempts to repair them have failed, you may be able to stop paying any rent to the landlord until the repairs are made. Before you can properly withhold the rent, be sure that you can say "Yes" to the questions in "Big Stick Prerequisites," above.

When you withhold rent, you simply stop paying rent until the landlord fixes the problem (at least two cities, however, have established escrow programs for tenants who withhold rent, as described in Step 1, below). The theory is that the landlord will be powerfully motivated to do the repair when the rent has stopped coming in. Once the rental is habitable, you begin paying rent. You will also owe the landlord a portion of the withheld rent, which reflects the value of the rental in its unfit condition (see "Paying the Landlord for the Value of the Unfit Rental," below, for methods of computing the proper amount).

> **CAUTION**
>
> **Be sure you're ready to risk your tenancy.** We can't say it enough times: Before withholding rent, be sure your ducks are in order and you are willing to risk an eviction lawsuit. If you can address the problem without incurring that risk (such as by suing in small claims court), you might be better off.

The Rent Withholding Steps

Here are the steps to follow when you've decided to withhold rent.

Step 1: We strongly encourage you to set aside the money that you would otherwise be paying for rent—and not to spend it until the matter is resolved. Under state law, you are not required to set up either a formal "escrow" account, or a separate account, but having a separate account is an easier way to keep track of the money. A separate account might be a better assurance that won't spend the money, and if the case goes to trial, it's a way of showing the other side (and the

judge) that you are withholding the rent because of the habitability problems, rather than for your own financial benefit. In a few cities, including Los Angeles, when landlords haven't complied with repairs ordered by building or health inspectors, the city can impose a rent escrow. Tenants pay rent directly to the city, which can authorize distributions for the purposes of repair only. Check your local ordinances to see if a rent escrow ordinance applies to you.

Step 2: Notify your landlord of your intent to withhold the rent. Hopefully, you've followed our suggestions and sent written repair requests to your landlord. You might have already signaled your intent to withhold the rent if the problem isn't fixed. If you haven't yet, now's the time to give your landlord written notice of the problem and your intent to withhold rent. A sample letter or email is shown below. In your letter, refer to the California case (*Green v. Superior Court*, 10 Cal.3d 616 (1974)) that allows withholding. Send the letter "return receipt requested."

> **FORM**
>
> **In addition to the sample letter or email shown below, you can use the Notice of Rent Withholding form included in Appendix C.** The Nolo website includes a downloadable version of the Notice of Rent Withholding form (see Appendix B for a link to the forms in this book), which you can edit to fit your particular situation.

Step 3: Collect evidence. In case your landlord tries to evict you for nonpayment of rent, you will want to prepare your defense from day one. You'll need to prove that the problem truly is serious and that you complied with the notice requirements of the rent withholding law. Of course, you'll want to keep notices from the building inspectors, copies of all correspondence with the landlord, plus photographs of the problem. Be sure to consider other ways (besides your own testimony) you can convince the judge that the problem was real and serious. For example, if your heater delivers a frigid blast, you'll want an estimate from a heating repairperson that corroborates the fact that the heater doesn't work.

In Superior Court, where evictions are handled, you cannot simply present a repairperson's written description of the problem (as you could in small claims court). For this reason, when choosing your repairperson/witness, pick someone who you think will come to court to testify about the nature of the problem.

Sample Letter or Email Telling the Landlord You Intend to Withhold Rent

58 Coral Shores, #37
Shady Bay, CA 00000
407-555-5632

August 5, 20xx

Mr. Roy Hernandez
3200 Harbor Drive
Shady Bay, CA 12345

Dear Mr. Hernandez:

My family and I are your tenants at the above address. As you know, I called you on August 3, 20xx to report that the front porch has collapsed from dry rot at the top of the stairs, making it impossible to enter the flat except by climbing through a front window. You assured me that you would send a contractor the next day. No one came on August 4.

Under California Civil Code Section 1941.1, you are responsible for keeping the porch in good repair. California law gives tenants the right to withhold rent if your failure to make repairs renders the rental uninhabitable. (*Green v. Superior Court*, 10 Cal.3d. 616 (1974).) The absence of a front entrance makes our house unfit.

By hand-delivering this notice to you today, August 5, I am giving you reasonable notice as required by law. If the porch is not repaired by August 10, I will withhold rent until it is.

Yours truly,

Alicia Sanchez
Alicia Sanchez

Step 4: Repeat your request for repairs. If the landlord hasn't responded satisfactorily to your first letter, give the landlord one last deadline—say, 48 hours or whatever period you feel is reasonable under the circumstances.

> **TIP**
>
> **Refer to Civil Code Section 1942.4.** Tenants who have withheld rent on account of serious repair problems can find themselves sued for eviction on the basis of rent nonpayment. As you consider taking the step to withhold rent, you don't know whether your landlord will react this way. But consider this: If sued, you'll defend yourself by referring to Section 1942.4, which says that a landlord is not entitled to receive rent if all of the following exist: 1) The unit substantially lacks the characteristics required under Civil Code Section 1941.1 or Health and Safety Code Section 17920.3 or 17920.10; 2) a building, health, or housing inspector has cited the building for substantial defects; 3) the landlord has failed to repair them within 35 days; and 4) the tenant did not cause the defect. These requirements need not be met at the outset for rent withholding. However, if the conditions above describe your predicament, your right to withhold rent is reinforced and strengthened.

Your Landlord's Response to Rent Withholding

Your landlord will have several options after learning that you are withholding rent.

- The landlord might proceed with the needed repair and then ask you to pay all or part of the rent. The two of you will need to negotiate how much you should cough up—see "Paying the Landlord for the Value of the Unfit Rental," below.
- The landlord might wait after a couple of months of rent withholding and hope you will take advantage of having lived there rent-free for a while and just move out on your own. Or,

- All too often, landlords will issue a three-day notice to pay rent or quit. If you do not pay the rent, the landlord will proceed with an eviction by filing a "summons and complaint." (See Chapter 15, The Eviction Lawsuit.) You would then need to file an answer and prove that your rent withholding was justified. Even if it was justified, the court will most likely order that you pay a percentage of the rent. You can be evicted if you do not pay that percentage—that's why we strongly recommend that you set it aside.

In Los Angeles and Sacramento, you may be able to deposit the rent you are withholding with the court or with the housing authority. In that situation, your landlord cannot file an eviction action against you based on nonpayment of rent. The landlord can ask for release of some of the withheld rent to pay for repairs. While repairs are being made, you might be told to continue to pay the entire rent to the court or housing authority, or you could be directed to pay some rent to the landlord and the balance to the court or housing authority. When the dwelling is certified as fit by the local housing authorities or the court, any money in the account is returned to the landlord, minus court costs, inspection fees, and any money you get to keep (reflecting the lowered value of the rental while it was substandard).

Paying the Landlord for the Value of the Unfit Rental

Many tenants make the unfortunate mistake of thinking that if they withhold the rent correctly, they won't have to pay anything for the months they endured an unfit rental. This is not so. Unless you've had to move out because of the repair problem, you owe the landlord the reasonable rental value of the rental in its unfit state, during the time you withheld rent. In legalese, this is a retroactive rent "abatement," or reduction.

You may get retroactive rent abatement through a court process (if the landlord has filed for eviction, but you've prevailed because the unit was unfit);

or through negotiation with your landlord (when no court is involved); or through a rent arbitration proceeding, if you live in a rent control city that provides for such a proceeding (see below). Here's how a judge will determine how much the landlord should compensate you for the inconvenience of having lived in a substandard rental unit. If a court is not involved, you can use this same system in negotiating with your landlord.

Percentage reduction. The most sensible approach is to start by asking how much of the unit is affected by the defect, and then to calculate the percentage of the rent attributable to that part. For example, if the roof leaked into the living room of your $900/month apartment, rendering the room unusable, you could reduce the rent by the percentage of the rent attributable to the living room. If the living room is the main living space and the other rooms are too small to live in comfortably, the percentage of loss would be much greater than it would be in more spacious apartments. Obviously, this approach is far from an exact science.

Sometimes, the calculations will be simple—for example, using the fair market value approach, if a broken air conditioner reduces your flat to an oven, its rental value can be determined by consulting ads for non–air-conditioned flats in your area. The percentage reduction method might, in some situations, yield a lower rental value. Choose the method that benefits you and ask the judge to adopt that figure (or negotiate for that figure when dealing directly with your landlord) and to rule that the landlord is entitled only to that amount of rent per month, times the number of months that you endured the substandard conditions. The difference between the full rent and the realistic rent should go to you.

Market value. A less common approach to determine how much rent you owe for a substandard rental is to ask: What's the fair market value of the premises in that condition? For example, if an apartment with a broken heater normally rented for $1,200 per month but was worth only $600 without operable heating, the landlord would be entitled to only $600/month from the withheld rent. Of course, the difficulty with this approach—as with many things in law—is that it is staggeringly unrealistic. An apartment with no heat in winter has no market value, because no one would rent it. As you can see, how much a unit is worth in a defective condition is extremely hard to determine. This method is not appropriate in a rent control or other situation where your rent is below market. In that situation, the percentage reduction method should always be used.

> ⓘ **CAUTION**
>
> **You must pay the reduced rent within five days of winning an eviction lawsuit.** If you don't pay on time, the landlord will win and you'll be evicted. The lesson is clear: When withholding rent, keep it in a safe place (such as an escrow account) so that you can promptly pay the abated rent.

EXAMPLE: When Henry and Sue moved into their apartment, it was neat and well maintained. Soon after, the building was sold to an out-of-state owner, who hired an off-site manager to handle repairs and maintenance. Gradually, the premises began to deteriorate. At the beginning of May, 15 months into their two-year lease, Henry and Sue could count several violations of the building code, including the landlord's failure to maintain the common areas, remove the garbage promptly, and fix a broken water heater.

Henry and Sue sent numerous requests for repairs to their landlord over a two-month period, during which they gritted their teeth and put up with the situation.

In response, Henry and Sue's landlord filed an eviction lawsuit. In their defense, Henry and Sue pointed to the numerous code and habitability violations. The court agreed with the couple, did not allow the eviction, and ordered the following:

- During the time that they lived in these uninhabitable conditions, Henry and Sue were not required to pay full rent. Using the "market value" approach, the court decided that their defective rental was worth half its stated rent. Accordingly, since the landlord owed them a refund for portions of their rent for May and June, Henry and Sue would be paid this amount from the escrow account.
- The balance of the rent in the account would be released to the landlord (less the costs of the escrow and the tenants' attorney fees), but only when the building inspector certified to the court that the building was up to code and fit for human habitation.
- Henry and Sue could continue to pay 50% of the rent until needed repairs were made and certified by the building inspector.

Make Repairs and Deduct the Cost—"Repair and Deduct"

If feasible, a far better option is to use the "repair and deduct" remedy. It is quicker, safer, gets the job done, and you are less likely to find yourself in court. Furthermore, the law explicitly states that a landlord cannot retaliate against you because you have exercised this right. (CC §§ 1942 and 1942.5.) It works like this: If you have tried and failed to get the landlord to fix a serious defect that renders your rental unfit, you can hire a repairperson to fix it (or buy a replacement part and do it yourself) and subtract the cost from the following month's rent. You can't spend more than one month's rent, and can use this remedy only twice in any 12-month period. You cannot use this option if the repair or replacement problem is the result of your failure to use the rental with ordinary care, or if it concerns a matter that you're responsible for (such as maintaining the unit in a clean and sanitary state).

Even if you have several repair problems, you can use this option to take care of just the ones that can easily be fixed or the ones that bother you the most. The landlord is still responsible for getting the other problems fixed.

When to Use Repair and Deduct

Repair and deduct's restrictions on how much you can spend (and how often) make the remedy a poor choice for tenants when it comes to expensive projects such as a major roof repair. Obviously, if you're limited to a twice-a-year expenditure of your monthly rent, you are not going to be able to pay for a $20,000 roof job. Sometimes, however, a number of tenants might pool their dollar limits to accomplish a costly repair. However, as we've explained, a major repair is one that remedies a habitability problem, regardless of its cost. There could be times when a relatively inexpensive job will turn an unfit rental into a habitable one. In these situations, if you're confident that you can competently choose a repairperson or replacement part, you will probably be better off using this remedy instead of withholding the rent. Here's why:

- **It's faster.** Because you'll be doing the work or supervising its completion, you can get going right away (after you've given the landlord time to do it, as explained below). With rent withholding, you'll have to wait for the landlord to do the work. Also,

- **When the job is not costly, it's less risky.** When you use this remedy, you will give your landlord a short rent check. The landlord can serve you a three-day notice to pay or vacate, then file for eviction on that basis, if she feels you've used the remedy improperly. But she'll be less likely to do so if the check she gets is short by only a portion of the monthly rent, instead of not receiving any check at all, which happens with rent withholding.

The Repair and Deduct Steps

Follow these steps when deciding to use the repair and deduct remedy.

Step 1: Notify your landlord in writing of the problem and allow for a reasonable time to fix it. If you've tried gentle persuasion, as suggested above, you've already taken this step. It doesn't hurt to write again, however, and signal your intention to invoke your right to repair and deduct. As ever, be sure to keep copies of your letters, and send them "return receipt" so that the landlord cannot claim later that he didn't receive them.

The big question here is: What's a "reasonable time" for the landlord to take action? Under the statute, 30 days is "presumed" reasonable. This means that if you wait 30 days, the landlord will have the burden of convincing a judge that your subsequent use of the remedy was too hasty. However, in some situations, a shorter time would also be reasonable, and you could act sooner than 30 days if circumstances warrant. For example, no heat in the midst of a cold spell requires a faster response than a finicky heater in the summertime; and a broken front door in an iffy neighborhood is worthy of immediate attention—in some situations, no more than a few hours would be a reasonable time to wait before handling the problem yourself.

Step 2: Collect evidence. In case your landlord tries to evict you for nonpayment of rent, you will want to prepare your defense from day one. See the same advice under Step 3 in "Withhold the Rent," above.

Step 3: Gather bids or collect pricing information. By choosing to use this remedy, you're doing the landlord's job for him. Put yourself in his shoes and approach the job as if the property belonged to you. While you don't have to hire the cheapest laborer or firm in the phone book, you do need to make sure the problem is taken care of, at the same time paying attention to cost. At the same time, the quality of the work needs to be in keeping with the standards that the landlord applies to the rest of the property. For example, if you're looking for a furnace repairperson, it might make sense to use an authorized repair shop if you know that the landlord consistently chooses "safe" repairmen. On the other hand, a handyman might be just fine if the landlord himself does the work (when he does it) or hires handymen himself.

Save your research or bids in a safe place. You may need them should the landlord challenge you on your choice and whether you made a good faith effort to secure the best deal.

Step 4: Attach copies of the bills, receipts, or invoices, plus evidence that you have paid them, to your next rent check, with a letter explaining why the rent is reduced. Do not reduce the rent until you have done the work and paid for it.

Sample Letter or Email Telling the Landlord You Intend to Repair and Deduct

8976 Maple Avenue
Katyville, CA 00000
360-555-6543

January 14, 20xx

Hattie Connifer
200 Capitol Expressway, Suite 300
Katyville, CA 00000

Dear Ms. Connifer:

On January 10, I called your office and spoke to you about a major problem: I have no hot water. As I explained on the phone, on the evening of January 9 the water heater for my flat sprang a leak. Luckily, I was home and was able to divert the water to the outside with a hose, turn off the intake valve, and shut off the pilot.

At the end of our conversation on January 10, you assured me that you would send a repairperson to the flat the next day, January 11. As of today, no one has showed up, and I am enduring my fourth day of no hot water.

Under California law, I am entitled to remedy the problem and deduct the cost from my rent if you do not attend to the problem within 24 hours (California Civil Code §§ 1941–1942.5). I intend to do this if the heater is not replaced within 24 hours after you receive this letter, which I am personally delivering to your office.

Yours truly,

Wanda Wright
Wanda Wright

Stay or Go? Consider the Practicalities

You might find that the choice of whether to declare the tenancy at an end or to move out while repairs are made is up to you. Consider the following issues:

Terminate the lease or rental agreement. You'll want to terminate the rental if you can find new housing of comparable quality and cost. You won't have to live with the uncertainty of when you'll move back to the original dwelling, and it will save you the time and aggravation of an extra household move.

If you decide to terminate the original lease or rental agreement, finalize the decision in writing. Have the landlord write "Terminated" on each page of your lease or rental agreement. Both of you should sign and date each page. Your landlord should refund your security deposit according to normal procedures. (See Chapter 13.)

Leave temporarily without terminating the lease. If your rental is a particularly great deal, the local market is very tight, or the repairs can be accomplished within a reasonable time, you'll want to hang on to your unit. If you are protected by rent control and you have lived in your rental for a significant period of time, you'll probably be loath to move. (Check your rent control ordinance or the statewide law for any special rules dealing with temporary move-outs.) Find a month-to-month rental while the original unit is repaired.

An agreement about moving out should be in writing and specify the repairs to be made, how long they will take, whether the tenant can leave any personal belongings at the property, and what compensation the landlord will provide in exchange for the tenant moving out under these terms (if any). The agreement should also state that the tenant's responsibilities have been suspended from a certain date until the day you move back in. Be sure to include the landlord's promise to notify you promptly as soon as the rental is ready. If the landlord will help you with relocation costs, note them. Both of you should sign and date this document.

Sue the Landlord

A consumer who purchases a product—be it a car, a hair dryer, or a steak dinner—is justified in expecting a minimum level of quality, and is entitled to compensation if the product is seriously flawed. The same goes for tenants. If your rental is not habitable, you can sue the landlord—whether or not you move out. You can use small claims court, which allows claims of up to $10,000, or hire an attorney and file in Superior Court. You can sue whether or not you move out of the property. Your landlord cannot retaliate against you because you have filed a lawsuit.

In your small claims lawsuit, you ask the judge to rule that your unrepaired rental was not worth what you've paid for it. You want to be paid the difference between the monthly rent and the real value of the unit, times the number of months that you've lived with the substandard conditions. In short, you'll ask for a retroactive rent decrease—what we explained as a rent abatement above in "Withhold the Rent." In addition, you can sue your landlord for:

- the value of lost or damaged property—for example, furniture ruined by water leaking through the roof
- compensation for personal injuries—including pain and suffering—caused by the defect (see Chapter 9), and
- your attorney fees and court costs if you had to hire a lawyer to sue the landlord (Chapter 18 discusses attorney fees).

You'll probably want to ask the court for an order directing the landlord to repair the defects, with rent reduced until they are fixed. But in small claims court, judges can only order the landlord to pay you for your losses. In practice, usually the money judgment gets the landlord's attention and repairs follow soon thereafter.

If your rental has significant and longstanding habitability problems, or if there are other aggravating factors (such as retaliation by the landlord), you might be able to convince a lawyer to take your case. In Superior Court, where a case like this would be handled, you could sue for the damages outlined above. In addition, you can sue for "tort" damages, such as discomfort and annoyance, emotional distress, lost earnings, and punitive damages. (*Stoiber v. Honeychuck,* 101 Cal.App.3d 90 (1980).) Furthermore, even if your rental agreement does not provide for attorney fees, some statutes do provide for attorney fees if certain situations apply (for example, CC § 1942.4, where a violation cited by a building, housing, or health inspector has not been corrected for more than 35 days; or CC § 1942.5, concerning retaliation). Time limits (called "statutes of limitations") govern how long you have to file these lawsuits, so you are encouraged to explore this alternative sooner rather than later.

Reduction in Services Petition

Many of the rent control ordinances throughout California allow tenants to file "reduction in services" petitions when the landlord fails to properly maintain the premises in habitable condition (California's statewide law does not have this provision). So instead of going to court to get the "retroactive rent abatement" discussed previously, a tenant need only go to the local rent board and file a petition for a reduction in services.

A reduction in services petition is a much safer route because you are not involved in an eviction lawsuit. Instead, you attend a hearing to determine how much the landlord owes you. The tenant has the burden of showing that the conditions existed, when they started, and when the landlord was notified. The hearing officer will then make a determination as to the amount of reduced rent. (See Appendix A for information about rent control in your area, and contact the rent board for information about how to proceed.)

Move Out When Repairs Haven't Been Done

If your dwelling isn't habitable and hasn't been made so despite your complaints and repair requests, you also have the right to move out. This will discharge you from any further obligations under the rental agreement or lease. (CC § 1942(a).) This drastic measure is justified only when there are truly serious problems, such as the lack of essential services, or unsafe or unhealthy conditions. Chapter 10 explains your right to move out because of environmental toxins.

Your right to move out of a seriously unfit dwelling is borrowed directly from consumer protection laws. Just as the purchaser of a significantly defective car may return the car for a refund, you can consider the housing contract terminated and simply return the rental unit to the landlord if the housing is unlivable.

The law, of course, has a convoluted phrase to describe this simple concept. It's called "constructive eviction," which means that the landlord, by refusing to fix serious health or safety problems, has for all practical purposes "evicted" you. Once you have been constructively evicted (that is, you have a valid reason to move out), you have no further responsibility for rent.

Before moving out, you must give the landlord notice of the problem and a reasonable opportunity to fix it. Refer to Steps 1 and 2 in "The Repair and Deduct Steps," above, for guidance on how to proceed.

If you move out permanently because of habitability problems, you might want to sue the landlord to compensate you for your losses. You can use small claims court or file a civil action in Superior Court. For example, you might be able to recover moving expenses, discomfort and annoyance, and emotional distress. In some instances, you could recover punitive damages. (*Stoiber v. Honeychuck,* 101 Cal.App.3d 90 (1980). Also, if the conditions were substandard during prior months when you did pay the full rent, you may sue to be reimbursed for the difference between the value of the defective dwelling and the rent paid.

In addition, if you are unable to find comparable housing for the same rent and end up paying more rent than you would have under the old lease, you may be able to recover the difference. (See "Sue the Landlord," above.)

Move Out When the Premises Have Been Destroyed

If your home is totally destroyed by fire, natural disaster, or any other reason beyond your control, which obviously renders it unlivable, you have the legal right to consider the lease or rental agreement at an end and to move out without responsibility for future rent. (CC § 1933(4).) You are not, however, entitled to reimbursement for rent payments you've already made. (*Pedro v. Potter,* 197 Cal. 751 (1926).) Some rent control jurisdictions have rules regarding property damaged by fire or natural disaster.

> **TIP**
>
> **If you have renters' insurance, file a claim.** You may get help for resettlement costs and coverage for your lost or destroyed possessions. Coverage may not extend to destruction caused by floods or earthquakes. (Renters' insurance is covered in Chapter 16.)

Partial destruction, however, is another matter. If you must find another place to live because of partial damage to or destruction of the premises— no matter the cause—you and the landlord will face the question of whether to terminate the lease or rental agreement or just suspend it while repairs are made. Your course of action might depend on whether your lease or rental agreement addresses this eventuality (if it doesn't, state law takes over).

Check Your Lease or Rental Agreement

First, check your lease or rental agreement for a clause covering what happens if the premises are partially damaged or destroyed. The rental document might give the landlord the right to terminate your rental or merely suspend it while repairs are made. If the landlord decides to keep the lease or rental agreement alive during repairs, you won't have to pay the landlord rent while you're living elsewhere, but it is unlikely that you'd get rental assistance from the landlord if your replacement housing is more expensive than your regular rent. Or, your landlord can declare the rental to be over (even if you'd rather move out temporarily). If you disagree with the landlord's call, there is probably very little you can do. Contact an attorney if you have a strong reason to return to the premises. Also, if the destruction was due to a fire and the landlord was at least partially at fault, it would be a good idea to contact an attorney to see if a lawsuit is feasible.

Default Rules for Partially Destroyed Rentals

Most residential rental agreements and leases do not include clauses that deal with the partial destruction of the property. If your rental documents are silent on the issue, the fate of your rental will depend on the application of the facts of your situation to state law, which provides that the lease or rental agreement will terminate if:

- the destruction is not the fault of the tenant
- the landlord had reason to believe, when the lease or rental agreement was signed, that the destroyed portion or aspect of the rental premises was a "material inducement" to the tenant (that is, a major reason why the tenant rented the premises), and

- the tenant gives notice to the landlord that the tenant considers the lease to be over because of the destruction of an important aspect of the premises. (CC § 1932(2).)

EXAMPLE: Sandra wanted a rental with a large, fenced yard that would be a safe play area for her three small children. When she saw Alex's duplex, she was delighted at the spacious backyard and told him that it was the perfect answer to her needs. When he offered to show her another duplex that had no yard but a larger interior, she declined and told him that her most important requirement was the yard, and that she would make do with smaller rooms. Sandra signed a year's lease in late fall.

The weather that winter was exceptionally severe, and the rainstorms caused the hill behind Sandra's home to slide, burying the backyard in a foot of mud and crushing the fences. Although the house itself escaped damage, the yard was ruined. Sandra wrote to Alex to tell him that she considered the lease to be over, since the backyard, now unusable, was a major reason for her decision to rent. Sandra moved out and although she did not recover the balance of that month's rent, she was not responsible for any future rent. She got her entire security deposit back when Alex examined the house and determined that there was no damage beyond normal wear and tear.

Minor Repairs & Maintenance

Ask a group of tenants which rental problem is most annoying, and chances are you'd hear, "Repairs!" Most wouldn't be referring to major problems that make a unit unlivable. What really bugs tenants are the day-to-day but nonetheless important problems: leaky faucets, malfunctioning appliances, security devices that don't work, worn carpets, noisy heaters, hot water heaters that produce a pathetic quantity of tepid water, and dozens of other frustrating breakdowns.

Unfortunately, if your landlord refuses to attend to minor repairs, you don't have much legal clout. You can't withhold rent, move out, or use most of the other "big stick" legal weapons discussed in Chapter 6. Even so, there are several proven strategies for getting results.

Minor Repairs: What Are They?

If a landlord balks at making repairs, your first step is to decide whether the problem is major (affecting the habitability of your rental unit) or minor. This distinction is necessary because you have different legal options depending on your conclusion.

Minor repair and maintenance includes:

- small plumbing jobs, like replacing washers and cleaning drains
- system upkeep, like changing heating filters
- structural upkeep, like replacing excessively worn flooring
- small repair jobs like fixing broken light fixtures or replacing the grout around bathtub tile, and
- routine repairs to and maintenance of common areas, such as pools, spas, and laundry rooms.

Don't assume that inexpensive repairs are always minor repairs. Sometimes an extremely important repair costs very little. For example, if the only thing between you and a heated apartment is the replacement of a $45 furnace part, like a thermostat, the repair is "major" because an unheated dwelling is uninhabitable, even though the repair cost is insignificant. And because this is true, if the landlord didn't replace the part promptly, you would probably be entitled to withhold rent or use one of the other "big stick" strategies (in this instance, using the Repair and Deduct remedy is probably the most effective and prudent). By contrast, replacing a living room carpet that is worn but is not a trip hazard, will be very expensive, but will be considered a minor repair if the consequence of not replacing it is less than an unfit dwelling.

Even minor repairs are the landlord's responsibility, especially if they involve those Civil Code, Health and Safety Code, and Uniform Housing Code requirements described in the previous chapter. But landlords are not required to keep the premises looking just like new—ordinary wear and tear does not have to be repaired during your tenancy. (When you move out, however, the cost of dealing with ordinary wear and tear will fall on the landlord and cannot come out of your security deposit.)

The Landlord's Responsibilities

Not every minor problem is your landlord's legal responsibility. If you or one of your guests caused it, carelessly or intentionally, you are responsible for repairing it—or, if your lease or rental agreement prohibits you from doing so, for paying the landlord to do it. But if you had nothing to do with the repair problem and it's not a cosmetic issue, chances go way up that your landlord is responsible, for one of the following reasons:

- A state or local building code requires that the landlord keep the damaged item (for example, a kitchen sink) in good repair.
- A lease or rental agreement provision or advertisement describes or lists particular items, such as hot tubs, trash compactors, and air conditioners. By implication, this makes the landlord responsible for maintaining or repairing them.

Common Misconceptions About Routine Maintenance

Many tenants (and landlords) mistakenly think that every time a rental unit turns over, or a certain number of years have passed, the landlord must paint or clean drapes and carpets, or do some other kind of refurbishing. Unfortunately for tenants, the law almost never mandates cosmetic changes—even badly needed ones. Here are some common misconceptions:

Paint. California landlords are not required to repaint at specified times. Unless the paint creates a habitability problem—for example, it's so thick around a window that the window can't be opened, or flaking lead-based paint poses obvious health risks—the landlord can just let it go. (Lead-based paint creates so many potential problems that we discuss it separately in Chapter 10.)

Drapes and carpets. So long as drapes and carpets are not so damp or full of mildew as to amount to a health hazard, and so long as carpets don't have dangerous holes that could cause someone to trip and fall, your landlord isn't legally required to replace them.

Windows. You're responsible for fixing (or paying to fix) a broken window that you or your guest intentionally or carelessly broke. If a burglar, vandal, or neighborhood child breaks a window, however, the landlord is usually legally responsible for the repair.

Rekeying. Unfortunately, landlords are not legally required to change the locks for new tenants. However, if you tell a landlord in writing that you are worried about renting a unit secured by locks for which previous tenants (and perhaps their friends) have keys, most landlords rekey the locks. (If the landlord knows of your concern but does not respond, and you are attacked or your place is burglarized by someone using an old key, the chances of the landlord being held liable in a lawsuit go way up. (See Chapter 13.) California landlords must, however, at least provide door and window locks. (CC § 1941.1). Chapter 11 gives you the details.

- The landlord made explicit promises when showing you the unit—for example, regarding the security or air-conditioning system.
- The landlord has assumed the obligation to maintain a particular feature, such as a whirlpool bathtub, because the landlord has fixed or maintained it in the past.

Each of these reasons is discussed below. If you're not sure whether a minor repair or maintenance problem is the landlord's responsibility, scan the discussion to find out.

Building Codes

California state law (and some city ordinances) covers structural requirements, such as roofs, flooring, windows, and essential services such as hot water and heat. If your repair problem is also a violation of the building code, you may be facing a habitability problem, as discussed in Chapter 6. But building codes often cover other, less essential details as well. For example, state code requires a minimum number of electrical outlets per room. When a room has too few outlets, it's inconvenient, but probably not unsafe or unhealthy. Likewise, the fact that you may have a faucet that drips probably does not render the dwelling unfit, but the landlord is still legally required to fix the problem.

Promises in the Lease or Rental Agreement

When it comes to legal responsibility for repairs, your own lease or rental agreement is often just as important (or more so) than building codes or state laws. If items such as drapes, washing machines, swimming pools, saunas, parking places, intercoms, or dishwashers come with the rental, then your landlord must continue to provide these amenities and maintain them in good working order. The only exception would be if you agreed in writing to take care of these items when you moved in.

Promises in Ads

If an advertisement for your unit described or listed a feature, such as a cable TV hookup, that significantly affected your decision to move into the particular rental unit, you have the right to hold the landlord to these promises. Even if your written rental agreement says nothing about appliances, if the landlord's ad listed a dishwasher, clothes washer and dryer, garbage disposal, microwave oven, security gates, and Jacuzzi, you have a right to expect that all of them will be repaired by the landlord if they break through no fault of yours.

> **EXAMPLE:** Tina sees Joel's ad for an apartment, which says "heated swimming pool." After Tina moves in, Joel stops heating the pool regularly because his utility costs have risen. Joel has violated his promise to keep the pool heated.

The promise doesn't have to be in words.

> **EXAMPLE:** Tom's real estate agent showed him a glossy color photo of an available apartment, which featured a smiling resident using an intercom to welcome a guest. The apartment Tom rented did not have a working intercom, and he complained to the management, arguing that the advertisement implied that all units were so equipped. The landlord realized that he would have to fix the intercom.

Promises Made Before You Rented the Unit

It's a rare landlord or manager who refrains from even the slightest bit of puffing when showing a rental to a prospective tenant. You're quite likely to hear rosy plans for amenities or services that haven't yet materialized ("We plan to redo this kitchen—you'll love the snappy way that trash compactor will work!").

An oral promise might not be worth much. Most lease agreements have clauses at the end that say that the agreement is the "entire agreement" or that there are no other promises between the landlord and tenant. They also say that the

agreement cannot be modified or amended unless in writing signed by both parties. These clauses are binding in most cases and effectively nullify any prior promises, oral or written, unless you were able to get them included in the agreement. Whenever you hear rosy promises, you would be wise to get them in writing, as part of (or attached to) your lease or rental agreement.

If this advice is coming to you now a bit late, and you don't in fact have anything in writing, don't give up hope. You can write or email the landlord to remind him of his promise and ask that he live up to that promise. If the feature substantially affected your decision to move in, then say so in the letter.

Another option is to look carefully at the Civil Code, Health and Safety Code, and any local building codes and see if any apply to your situation. For instance, you might argue that the garbage disposal is a "plumbing facility" or electrical equipment" that is covered under Civil Code Section 1941.1(a)(2) or (5), or "mechanical equipment" covered under Health and Safety Code Section 17920.3(f).

> **TIP**
>
> **It is always a good idea to have oral agreements and promises in writing.** One way to do this is to write a simple confirmation letter or email. Something like: "Dear Mr. Smith, It was a pleasure talking with you on the telephone this afternoon. During that conversation you agreed to install a washer/dryer in the laundry room before the end of next month. I appreciate your attention to this matter." If the landlord doesn't write back, disputing your assertions, a judge can conclude that the landlord agreed with your version of the conversation.

Implied Promises

Suppose your rental agreement doesn't mention a garbage disposal, and neither does any ad you saw before moving in. And, in fairness, you can't remember your landlord ever pointing it out when showing you the unit. But there is a garbage disposal, and it was working when you moved in. Now the garbage disposal is broken and, despite repeated requests, your landlord hasn't fixed it. Do you have a legal leg to stand on in demanding that your landlord make this minor repair? Yes. Many courts will hold a landlord legally responsible for maintaining all significant aspects of your rental unit. A garbage disposal is an "electrical fixture" that probably falls under the Civil Code Section 1941.1(a)(5).

If you rent a unit that *already has* certain features —light fixtures that work, doors that open and close smoothly, faucets that don't leak, tile that doesn't fall off the wall—many judges reason that the landlord has made an implied contract to keep them in workable order throughout your tenancy.

Another factor that is evidence of an implied contract is the landlord's past conduct. A landlord who has consistently fixed or maintained a particular feature of your rental has made an implied obligation to continue doing so.

> **EXAMPLE:** Tina's apartment has a built-in dishwasher. When she rented the apartment, neither the lease nor the landlord said anything about the dishwasher or who was responsible for repairing it. The dishwasher has broken down a few times and whenever Tina asked Joel to fix it, he did. By doing so, Joel has established a practice that he—not the tenant—is responsible for repairing the dishwasher.

TIP

Check your lease. Landlords who want to avoid responsibility for appliance repairs often insert clauses in their leases or rental agreements stating that the appliances are not maintained by the landlord.

TIP

Using the Landlord-Tenant Checklist at the start of your tenancy will give you a record of appliances and features—and their condition. If something needs repairs, you'll be able to use the checklist as proof of its original condition. (See Chapter 1 for instructions on using the checklist.)

Agreeing to Do Maintenance

Leases and rental agreements usually include a general statement that you are responsible for keeping your rental unit clean, safe, and in good condition, and for reimbursing your landlord for the cost of repairing damage you cause, as explained at length in Chapter 6. Your lease or rental agreement will probably also say that you can't make alterations or repairs, such as painting the walls, installing bookcases, or fixing electrical problems, without your landlord's permission (see Chapter 8).

Landlords who are tired of maintenance and repair jobs may use the lease, rental agreement, or separate contract to give these responsibilities to a tenant. Especially if you rent a single-family home or duplex, you may be asked to agree to mow the lawn, trim the bushes, and do minor plumbing jobs and painting.

Commonly, a landlord proposes a rent reduction in exchange for some work. Or the landlord may offer other perks (a parking space, for example), or will offer an amenity if the tenant will perform the maintenance—for example, a hot tub in exchange for your promise to clean it.

Although usually legal, these arrangements often lead to dissatisfaction—typically, the landlord feels that the tenant has neglected certain tasks, or the tenant feels that there is too much work. If the dispute boils over, the landlord may try to evict the tenant.

When you take on repair duties, here's how to protect yourself and avoid disputes:

- **Sign an agreement that is separate from your rental agreement or lease.** This is especially important if you are a resident manager or plan to do considerable work for your landlord on a continuing basis, such as keeping hallways, elevators, or a laundry room clean, or maintaining the landscaping. Tenants who are also building managers are in this position. Ask your landlord to pay you for your work, rather than give you a rent reduction. That way, if the landlord claims that the job is not done right, the worst that can happen is that you may be fired but your tenancy should not be affected. But if your maintenance duties are tied to a rental agreement and things go wrong, the amount of rent you will have to pay or even your status as a tenant may be uncertain. And if the maintenance jobs are spelled out in a lease clause, the landlord also has the option of terminating the lease on the grounds that your poor performance constitutes a breach of the lease. Be forewarned, however, that many landlords will not want to enter into an employer-employee relationship with you, because becoming an employer has its own set of complications.

- **Clearly write out your responsibilities and the landlord's expectations.** List your tasks and the frequency with which your landlord expects them to be done. Weekly tasks might include, for example, cleaning the laundry room, sweeping and wet mopping the lobby, and mowing the grass between April 1 and November 1.
- **Make sure the agreement is fair.** Ideally, your landlord will pay you a fair hourly rate. If your only choice is a rent reduction, make sure the trade-off is equitable. If you're getting only a $100 rent reduction for work that would cost the landlord $400 if done by a cleaning service, you're being ripped off.
- **Check out Wage Order 5.** Resident managers and other employees whose wages are paid (in full or in part) in the form of a rent reduction may be subject to California Wage Order 5, which limits the amount that a landlord can use a rent reduction to pay a tenant/employee. This rule usually benefits the employee, so it may be worth your while to Google California Wage Order 5.

- **Discuss problems with the landlord and try to work out a mutually satisfactory agreement.** If the landlord has complained about your work, maybe it's because the owner underestimated what's involved in cleaning the hallways and grounds. Your landlord may be willing to pay you more for better results or shorten your list of jobs. If not, cancel the arrangement.

Watch Out for Illegal Retaliation

Landlords who delegate some tasks are not relieved of all repair and maintenance responsibilities. For example, if you and your landlord agree that you will do gardening work in exchange for a rent reduction, and the landlord feels that you are not doing a proper job, the landlord cannot respond by shutting off your water.

CAUTION
Don't perform repairs involving hazardous materials. Any repair involving old paint or insulation (opening up a ceiling or wall cavity, for example) may expose you or others to dangerous levels of toxic materials. For example, sanding a surface for a seemingly innocuous paint job may actually create lead-based paint dust; the quick installation of a smoke alarm could involve disturbing an asbestos-filled ceiling. (See Chapter 10 for more information on environmental hazards.)

Getting the Landlord to Make Minor Repairs

By now you should have a pretty good idea as to whether your landlord is legally responsible for fixing the particular minor problem that is bedeviling you. Your next job is to get the landlord to do it. First, try to get the landlord to cooperate. If you can't, it may be time to take a more demanding approach.

Make a Written Request for Repairs

Chances are you have already asked your landlord or manager to make repairs, only to be put off, ignored, or even told to forget it. Your next step is to write a formal demand letter or email—or, if you have already done it, a second one.

Before you pick up your pen or turn on your computer, take a minute to think about what words will most likely get action. Begin by remembering your landlord's overriding business concerns: to make money, avoid hassles with tenants, and stay out of legal hot water. A request that zeroes in on these issues will likely get the job done.

How to Write a Persuasive Repair Request

Whether this is your first or second formal demand letter, frame your repair request along one or more of the following lines, if possible:

- **It's a small problem now, but has the potential to be a very big deal.** A bathtub faucet that drips badly may be simply annoying now, but devastating later if the washer gives out while you're not home, flooding the tub and ruining the floor and downstairs neighbor's ceiling. When you ask that the faucet be repaired, point out the risk of letting things go.
- **There is a potential for injury.** Landlords hate to be sued. If a potential injury-causing problem is brought to their attention, it's likely that their fear of lawsuits will overcome their lethargy, and you'll finally get results. Say, for instance, you have asked your land-lord to repair the electrical outlet in your kitchen so that you can use your toaster. If you've received no response, try again with a different pitch: Point out that, on occasion, you have observed sparks flying from the wall, and a short in the wiring could cause an injury or fire.
- **There is a security problem that imperils your safety.** Landlords are increasingly aware that they can also be sued for criminal assaults against tenants if the premises aren't reason-

ably secure. (Chapter 11 discusses this topic in detail.) If you can figure out a way to emphasize the security risks of not fixing a problem—for example, a burned-out light-bulb in the garage or a door that doesn't always latch properly—you may motivate the landlord to act promptly.

- **The problem affects other tenants.** If you can point to a disaster-waiting-to-happen that affects more than one tenant, you will greatly increase your chances of some action. For example, accumulated oil puddles in the garage threaten the safety of all tenants and guests, not just you. Faced with the possibility of a small army of potential plaintiffs, each accompanied by an eager attorney, even the most slothful landlord may spring into action.
- **You're willing to try to fix it, but may make the problem worse.** Finally, you might try offering to fix the problem yourself in a way that is likely to elicit a quick "No thanks, I'll call my contractor right away!" This is a bit risky, since your bluff might be called, but even the most dense landlord will think twice when you offer to make an electrical repair with a chisel and masking tape.

See the sample letter below for more ideas on writing a persuasive repair request.

A written demand for repair or maintenance lets your landlord know that you are serious about the issue and are not content to just let it go. In addition, if your dispute ends up in small claims court, the letter or email can be introduced as evidence. Like this sample letter, your demand letter should:

- be neatly typed and use businesslike language.
- concisely and accurately state the important facts (this is important in case your letter ends up before a judge, who will need to be educated about the situation).
- be polite and nonpersonal. Obviously, a personal attack on your landlord may trigger an equally emotional response. Because you are appealing to the landlord's business

interests, you want to encourage the landlord to evaluate the issue soberly, not out of anger.

- state exactly what you want, and why you think it is important.

Always keep a copy of the letter or email for your files, and hand-deliver the letter or send it "return receipt requested."

Sample Letter or Email Asking for Minor Repairs

90 Willow Run, Apartment 3A
Morgantown, California 00000

February 28, 20xx

Mr. Lee Sloan
37 Main Street, Suite 100
Morgantown, California 00000

Dear Mr. Sloan:

I would appreciate it if you could schedule an appointment with me to look at three problems in my apartment that have come up recently.

First, the kitchen sink faucet is dripping, and it's getting worse. I'm concerned that a plate or dish towel might stop up the drain, leading to an overflow. At any rate, the water bill is yours, and I'm sure that you don't want to pay for wasted water.

I've also been having trouble opening the sliding doors on the bedroom closet. The track appears to be coming away from the wall, and the doors wobble and look like they might fall into the room when I open and close the closet.

Finally, it would really be great if you would give some thought to repainting the interior hallways. They looked clean when I moved in a year ago, but now are pretty grimy. I've spoken with the tenants in four of the other six units and they, too, would appreciate a return to your standards of old.

Thanks very much for thinking about my requests. I hope to hear from you soon.

Yours truly,

Chris Jensen

Chris Jensen

Your Options If the Landlord Refuses to Make a Minor Repair

If your letter has not convinced your landlord to fix this minor issue and you do not believe that further coaxing will work, it's time to consider other options. They are:

- seek mediation or arbitration for "reduction in services"
- report code violations to a building inspector
- make the repairs yourself—or using a qualified person
- repair it yourself and deduct the cost of the repair from rent, or
- sue in small claims court.

Few, if any, minor repair problems warrant rent withholding because your tenancy is at risk when habitability issues are not substantial. In weighing these options, consider the nature of the repair (not all repairs warrant calling the building inspector or repairing and deducting), the cost of fixing it yourself and the chances of you getting reimbursed, and the hassle to you. Some may feel that the easiest way to deal with it is to fix the problem themselves and absorb the cost. Others may feel that it "sets a bad precedent" to pay for what the landlord should be responsible for.

As we've explained previously, it is unlawful for a landlord to retaliate (get back at you) for exercising your lawful rights. (CC § 1942.5.) However, be sure you are on solid ground before asserting your rights. For instance, does the repair address a habitability concern described in Civil Code Section 1941.1 or Health and Safety Code Section 17920.3? Are you charging a fair amount for the repair, and did you give your landlord reasonable notice?

Propose Mediation or File a Petition for Arbitration for Reduction in Services

Many community organizations and even some courts offer mediation services. These services try to get parties together to work on a mutually agreeable solution to a problem, and most of these services have experience with landlord/tenant issues. Participation in mediation is totally voluntary, however, and if your landlord does not want to participate, the service will be of little use.

As stated in the previous chapter, many jurisdictions with rent control allow tenants to petition for a reduction in rent due to a reduction in the services provided. If you live in such a city with rent control, you should contact your rent board to see how they can help.

Using either of these remedies involves little or no risk.

Reporting Code Violations

If appealing to your landlord's business sensibilities doesn't work, other strategies are available to pry minor repairs out of your landlord.

If the problem you want fixed constitutes a code violation, such as inadequate electrical outlets or low water pressure, you should find an ally in the building or housing agency in charge of enforcing the code. (Chapter 6 explains how to find and what to expect from these local agencies.) Whether you'll get any action out of the agency will depend on the seriousness of the violation, the workload of the agency, and its ability to enforce its compliance orders. Because by definition your problem is minor, don't expect lots of help if code enforcement officials are already overworked.

Making Repairs Yourself—Or Using a Qualified Repairperson

If your landlord has refused to make a requested repair, and it's the type of repair you think he should make, you may decide to go ahead and make the repair yourself (or use a qualified person). After the repair, you have three options:

1. If the repair is for a condition listed in Civil Code Sections 1941.1 or 1941.3, you may choose to deduct the cost from your rent.

2. You may also decide to seek reimbursement in small claims court—but before you do this, you must write a letter to your landlord, requesting the reimbursement.

3. You may want to just avoid the hassle and absorb the cost yourself.

The first step is to determine whether the landlord is legally responsible for the repair, or you are. Again, if the condition involves the Civil Code, Health and Safety Code, or the Uniform Housing Code requirements described in the previous chapter, it will be the landlord's responsibility to fix it. In either event, you will want to notify the landlord of the problem and that you intend to fix the problem (or have a qualified person fix it). If you decide to do it yourself, be sure it's something you are capable of doing competently. If not, find a qualified person to do the job.

Be careful if the landlord objects to your taking care of the repair yourself or does not give you permission to do it. Depending on the nature of the repair, you could be violating your lease agreement if it has a provision that says that the tenant cannot make "repairs, alterations or improvements" to the premises (sometimes these clauses add, "without the landlord's consent"). (Improvements and alterations are covered in the following chapter.) Note, however, if the repair is of a condition listed in Civil Code Section 1941.1, you have a legal right to repair the problem and deduct the cost from your rent, regardless of the presence of such a lease clause (discussed below).

If you have gone ahead with the repair, consider the choices outlined above.

Repair Yourself, Deduct the Cost of Repair from Your Rent

One option is to deduct the cost of the repair from your rent, as described in the previous chapter. Remember, you can use this remedy only if the defective condition is "substantial" or serious enough such that the landlord should fix it.

Additionally, under Civil Code Section 1942, you can only deduct up to a month's rent, two times in any 12-month period. Details of how to take advantage of this are in Chapter 6, Major Repairs & Maintenance. Civil Code Section 1941.1 lists the types of repairs that are allowed before rent can be deducted.

If you repair and deduct, the landlord may give you a three-day notice to pay rent or quit. If the repair was a type described in Civil Code Section 1941.1, you should be able to successfully fight an eviction. You might also consider paying the rent within the three days to avoid eviction, then sue in small claims court.

Sue in Small Claims Court

Another option is to sue in small claims court. But before you do, write a second demand letter. Like the first letter (see the sample above), your second letter should describe the problems and alert the landlord to the negative consequences (to the landlord, not just to you) that may follow if repairs aren't made. In addition, state that you intend to sue if you don't get results. This may get the landlord's attention and save you a trip to the courthouse.

> **EXAMPLE:** Chris Jensen wrote to her landlord on February 28, requesting repairs as shown in the sample letter above. She got no reply. Ten days later, she sent a second letter that summarized the first and concluded with this paragraph:
>
> "If you are unable to attend to these repairs, I'll need to call in a handyman to repair the faucet and doors, and I will seek reimbursement from you in small claims court if necessary. As for the deterioration of the paint, I believe I am entitled to a reduction in rent, which I will also seek in small claims court. Of course, I sincerely hope that this will not be necessary."

If the second letter doesn't produce results, it's time to proceed with the repair. Most small claims courts prefer (or require) that before filing, the person making the claim first notify the defendant in writing of the exact amount owed and for what, and give them a reasonable time to respond. If you have not yet done this, you will need to send one more letter informing the landlord of the amount you are claiming and the reasons for your demand. If you get no results, then it's time to file the small claims court action. You won't need a lawyer (in fact, in California you can't bring a lawyer to small claims court). Just go to the court and ask for the forms you need to sue someone. To find your court, search online for your county's small claims court. (You may find some of the forms you need online.) In small claims court, you can't get an order from the judge directing your landlord to paint, fix the dishwasher, or repair the intercom. You may, however, be compensated in dollars for living in a rental unit with repair problems. Here's how it works.

When you file your small claims court suit, you'll ask for an amount that reflects the difference between your rent and the value of the unit with repair problems. For example, if you're living with a broken air conditioner, and know that apartments without air conditioners rent for $100 less per month, use that figure (multiplied by the number of months or parts thereof that the unit's been broken) as your measure of damages. In court, your argument will be that you are not getting the benefit of what you're paying rent for—for example, a functioning dishwasher, presentable paint, or a working air conditioner. If you paid for a repair, include that in the same lawsuit.

! CAUTION
Don't stop paying rent. Although fairness dictates that if your rental unit is full of repair problems you ought to pay less rent, it's a mistake to pay your landlord less than the full monthly rent. Rent withholding, as discussed in Chapter 6, is legally appropriate only for major repairs. If you withhold even a portion of the rent because of a minor repair problem, you risk eviction for nonpayment of rent.

Your goal in small claims court is to convince the judge that these problems really make your rental unit worth less money. Use common sense—

don't go running to court for small things. A small claims court judge is not going to adjust your rent because a little grout is missing from your bathroom tile. But if your dishwasher is broken, three faucets leak noisily, and the bathroom door won't close, your chances of winning go way up. You'll need to show the judge that:

- there are several minor defects, not just an isolated one, and
- you've given the landlord plenty of time and notice to fix the problems.

Be sure to bring evidence. Winning in small claims court depends more on what you drag into court with you than on what you say. Examples of key evidence include:

- copies of letters you've written asking for repairs
- your written notes on your landlord's response to your repair requests, including the number of times they were ignored or promised repairs didn't materialize
- witnesses—a family member, for example, who can describe the inoperable air conditioner
- photographs—your pictures of the cracked, flaking plaster, for example
- a copy of the local building or housing code, if the problem is covered there
- your lease or rental agreement, if it lists any of the items that need repair
- your lease or rental agreement, if it prohibits you from making repairs yourself
- a copy of the Landlord-Tenant Checklist, which you should have completed when you moved in and which is signed by you and the landlord, showing that the problem did not exist at the start of your tenancy, and
- ads, brochures, or "For Rent" signs describing features of your rental that are missing or malfunctioning.

EXAMPLE: Judy signed a one-year lease for a studio apartment at $750 a month. When she moved in, the place was in good shape. But six months into her tenancy, the condition of the apartment began to deteriorate. A water leak from the roof stained and buckled several areas of the hardwood floors; the kitchen cabinets, which were apparently badly made, warped, and would not shut; the dishwasher became so noisy the neighbor banged on the wall when it was in use; the soap dish fell off the bathroom wall; and the white entryway rug started to fall apart. Judy asked her landlord to attend to these problems and followed up with several written demand letters. Two months after her original request, Judy wrote a final demand letter.

When the landlord still did nothing, Judy filed suit in small claims court, asking the judge to award her damages (money) representing the difference between her rent and the value of the deteriorated apartment. After considering Judy's evidence, including copies of her demand letter, photographs of the defects, and the testimony of her neighbor, the judge agreed with Judy. The judge figured that the deteriorated apartment would have rented for $150 less a month, and ordered the landlord to pay Judy $450 to make up for the three months she had lived with the defects. Judy's landlord was quick to make repairs after learning this expensive lesson in court.

RESOURCE

Everybody's Guide to Small Claims Court in California, **by Cara O'Neill (Nolo),** has all the details you need to file a small claims court lawsuit. See www.nolo.com for a sample chapter and table of contents for this book.

Finally, if you live in a city that has rent control, you could also look into the possibility of filing a Reduction in Services Petition, which was described in the previous chapter. The basic theory is that if you landlord has not properly maintained your unit, you should have your rent reduced in an amount that will compensate you for the lack of maintenance (or other) services that your landlord was supposed to provide under the rental agreement. If available, this is probably the safest and easiest way to address a repair problem—especially with minor repairs. See Appendix A for information about rent control in your area, and contact the rent board about how to proceed.

Improvements, Alterations, & Satellite Dishes

Your lease or rental agreement probably includes a clause prohibiting you from making any alterations or improvements to your unit without the express, written consent of the landlord. (Often, your landlord will forbid you to undertake repairs, too. This issue is discussed in Chapter 1.) Landlords use these clauses—some of which contain a long list of prohibitions—so that tenants don't change the light fixtures, knock out a wall, install a built-in dishwasher, or even pound in a nail to hang a picture unless the landlord agrees first.

But what if you make an alteration or improvement without getting your landlord's permission—for example, you bolt a closet storage system to the wall? This could be a lease violation that could lead to an eviction. But even if you avoid that, when you leave you're likely to face the question of whether an improvement that is physically attached to the property is the property of the landlord or you. To help you avoid problems, this chapter explains:

- what types of improvements and alterations become the landlord's property
- what you can do, ahead of time, to avoid losing your property
- how to minimize your losses if your landlord insists that the improvement remain on the property, and
- special rules for cable TV access and satellite dishes.

TIP
Tenants with disabilities have rights under federal and state laws to make reasonable modifications to their rental unit. For details on this subject, check out the "Disabled Renters' Housing Rights" article on the Nolo website at www.nolo.com/legal-encyclopedia/disabled-renters-housing-rights-30121.html.

Improvements That Could Become Part of the Property

It's a natural desire to "feather your nest," and tenants do it all the time, by changing plumbing and light fixtures, attaching storage systems, and installing appliances. At move-out, tenants often take these pricey items with them. Discovering altered countertops, holes from hollow-wall bolts, and re-installed fixtures, the landlord demands that the upgrade be returned; and if not returned, that the tenant pay the landlord for the value of the missing upgrade, installed. When does the tenant have to pay up (or, more likely, when can the landlord deduct that amount from the security deposit before returning it)?

The answer takes us into the age-old law of "fixtures," developed centuries ago in England when tenants were farmers, not city-dwellers. Once the farmer planted a seed, sunk a fence post, or built a shed, these items became part of the landlord's property, and were called fixtures. They could not be taken away at the end of the tenancy—and practically speaking, most tenants wouldn't want to do so anyway (who is going to transplant a field of oats?). The rule was simple: Anything "affixed" to the land belonged to the landlord; items not affixed (like a shovel) were the tenant's personal property and could be taken away at the end of the tenancy.

These days, despite the fact that most tenants can quite feasibly remove items they've attached to the property, and have good reason for doing so, some judges stubbornly adhere to the old rule: If the item was attached in any way to the property (screwed, bolted, or otherwise), it belongs to the landlord. But some will follow modern case law, and analyze the question on a case-by-case basis, asking what the parties intended, and whether a particular result would be unjust to either side. Note that the law still says that items affixed to the property belong to the landlord, absent an agreement to the contrary (CC § 600), but the question, now nuanced, is: What does it *mean* to "affix" something to the property? Here are some of the considerations a thoughtful judge will bring to bear:

The foremost question is:

What did the tenant intend would happen at the end of the tenancy? The tenant's intent when bringing the item onto the property is the primary question. The answer depends on the circumstances at the time the item was installed. (*Banks v. Cintworth*, 201 Cal.App.2d 789 (1962).) If it's clear that the item was slated for removal, the tenant gets to take it; but if circumstances show that it's unlikely that the tenant planned to detach it at the end of the tenancy, the item is more likely to be a fixture and will stay put.

Some of the factors that judges consider are:

- **What does the rental agreement say?** A lease that forbids alterations or improvements without the landlord's consent puts the tenant who ignores this clause at an initial disadvantage, at least. Tenants can mitigate this disadvantage by showing, for example, that upon learning of the improvement, the landlord applauded it, which essentially waives the prohibition in the lease.

- **How easy (or difficult) is it to remove?** If the property is easy to remove, it is more likely that the tenant intended it to be his property rather than a "fixture." So, for instance a bookcase that is attached to a wall might be easy to remove, however, a bookcase that is built into the wall would be more difficult and therefore a "fixture."

- **How disruptive, time-consuming, and expensive was the installation?** The more disruptive, expensive, and difficult the installation, the more likely the item will be deemed a fixture. That's because it's unlikely the tenant intended to undo his work upon leaving (even if he

could). For instance, unscrewing a kitchen faucet and installing a new one is usually quick and easy; so too is replacing the original fixture—so the fancy new one is probably the personal property of the tenant. Or, placing a few hollow-wall anchors to secure a bookshelf or a shelving system is minimal work and the holes can be easily patched. But reconstructing a kitchen counter that the tenant rebuilt to accommodate a dishwasher is a major undertaking that most tenants wouldn't do when they leave. The dishwasher that goes into the new space is likely to be considered a fixture. (*Pajaro Valley Bank v. County of Santa Cruz*, 207 Cal.App.2d 621 (1962).)

Fortunately for tenants, the law falls on your side unless there is a clear intention that the property is a fixture. Courts should resolve doubts in favor of the tenant (that is, that the tenant did not intend to incorporate the property to the premises). To find otherwise would result in an unfair forfeiture of the tenant's property and lead to the unjust enrichment of the landlord. (*Pomeroy v. Ball*, 118 Cal. 635 (1887).)

Nevertheless, even when you have a strong case for labeling the item your personal property, there's no guarantee that a court will rule in your favor. As noted, some judges will base their determination solely on whether the property is physically attached to the realty by a screw, bolt, or otherwise. That's why it's best to clarify beforehand, as explained in the following section.

CAUTION

You might have to pay for damage resulting from the removal of your personal property. Suppose you prevail on the closet storage system you installed with hollow wall anchors, and the landlord can neither demand that you leave it in place, nor charge you for the value of the system, when you remove it. But removing it will leave holes. The cost to repair the wall can fairly be taken out of your security deposit.

Improvements That Plug or Screw In

The act of plugging in an appliance doesn't make the appliance a part of the premises. The same is true for simple wiring or pipe attachments to join an appliance to an electrical or water source. For example, a refrigerator or freestanding stove that the tenant brought in remains the property of the tenant. Similarly, portable dishwashers that connect to the kitchen faucet by means of a coupling may be removed.

Improving Your Rental Without Enriching Your Landlord

Your best protection against losing an item you paid for is not to attach it to a wall in your unit. Fortunately, hundreds of items are on the market—bookcases, lighting systems, closet organizers, and even dishwashers—that you can take with you when you leave. To get some good ideas, visit a large hardware store, a home improvement center, or a business devoted to closet organization systems.

If you are determined to attach something to the wall or floor, talk to the landlord first. A reasonable landlord should agree to either pay for the improvement or to let you remove it when you leave.

Decide beforehand which option you prefer. For example, because a custom-made track lighting system won't do you any good if you take it with you, find out whether the landlord will pay for it in the first place. On the other hand, if you want to take the fixture with you, impress upon the landlord your intent to carefully restore the property to its original condition. Keep in mind that if your restoration attempts are less than acceptable, the landlord will be justified in deducting from your security deposit the amount of money necessary to do the job right. And if the deposit is insufficient, the landlord can sue you in small claims court for the excess.

Approach your landlord as one business person dealing with another. If the improvement will remain and you seek reimbursement, point out that it will make the property more attractive. It might even justify a higher rent for the next tenant and thus pay for itself over the long run. Your landlord might agree to reduce your rent a little each month or simply reimburse you all at once.

If you and the landlord reach an understanding, put it in writing, using our Agreement Regarding Tenant Alterations to Rental Unit (see the sample, below). Carefully describe the project and materials, and state whether the landlord will reimburse you or allow you to take the improvement with you.

FORM

You'll find a link to the Agreement Regarding Tenant Alterations to Rental Unit on the companion page for this book on the Nolo website. See Appendix B for the link to the forms in this book. You can edit the form to fit your situation.

TIP

Save all receipts for materials and labor. Whether you will be reimbursed or will take the fixture with you, it is important to keep a good record of the amount of money you spent on the project. That way, there can be no dispute as to what you're owed if you are to be reimbursed. If the landlord changes his mind and doesn't let you remove the improvement at the end of your tenancy, you'll have receipts to back up your small claims lawsuit for the value of the addition.

Cable TV Access

If you're lucky, cable TV may already be in the rental property through coaxial cables that are strung along telephone poles or underground and into the building, with a single plug on the exterior of the structure and with branches to individual units. To sign up for service, you need only call the

Agreement Regarding Tenant Alterations to Rental Unit

Lenny Lander _____ (Landlord)

and _Tom Tenant_____ (Tenant)

agree as follows:

1. Tenant may make the following alterations to the rental unit at: ___54 Alta Way, Anytown, CA 94567_____

    _____

2. Tenant will accomplish the work described in Paragraph 1 by using the following materials and procedures: _____
    _Lumen track lighting system, hard wired_____

    _____ .

3. Tenant will do only the work outlined in Paragraph 1 using only the materials and procedures outlined in Paragraph 2.

4. The alterations carried out by Tenant (check either a or b):

    ☑ a. will become Landlord's property and are not to be removed by Tenant during or at the end of the tenancy

    ☐ b. will be considered Tenant's personal property, and as such may be removed by Tenant at any time up to the end of the tenancy. Tenant promises to return the premises to their original condition upon removing the improvement.

5. Landlord will reimburse Tenant only for the costs checked below:

    ☑ the cost of materials listed in Paragraph 2

    ☐ labor costs at the rate of $ _____ per hour for work done in a workmanlike manner acceptable to Landlord up to _____ hours.

6. After receiving appropriate documentation of the cost of materials and labor, Landlord shall make any payment called for under Paragraph 5 by:

    ☑ lump sum payment, within ____15____ days of receiving documentation of costs, or

    ☐ by reducing Tenant's rent by $ _____ per month for the number of months necessary to cover the total amounts under the terms of this agreement.

7. If under Paragraph 4 of this contract the alterations are Tenant's personal property, Tenant must return the premises to their original condition upon removing the alterations. If Tenant fails to do this, Landlord will deduct the cost to restore the premises to their original condition from Tenant's security deposit. If the security deposit is insufficient to cover the costs of restoration, Landlord may take legal action, if necessary, to collect the balance.

8. If Tenant fails to remove an improvement that is his or her personal property on or before the end of the tenancy, it will be considered the property of Landlord, who may choose to keep the improvement (with no financial liability to Tenant), or remove it and charge Tenant for the costs of removal and restoration. Landlord may deduct any costs of removal and restoration from Tenant's security deposit. If the security deposit is insufficient to cover the costs of removal and restoration, Landlord may take legal action, if necessary, to collect the balance.

9. If Tenant removes an item that is Landlord's property, Tenant will owe Landlord the fair market value of the item removed plus any costs incurred by Landlord to restore the premises to their original condition.

10. If Landlord and Tenant are involved in any legal proceeding arising out of this agreement, the prevailing party shall recover reasonable attorney fees, court costs, and any costs reasonably necessary to collect a judgment.

_Lenny Lander_____   ___January 4, 20xx_____
Signature of Landlord   Date

_Tom Tenant_____   _January 4, 20xx_____
Signature of Tenant   Date

cable provider to activate the existing cable line to your unit. But what happens if the building does not have cable access now? And if the landlord has a contract with one provider, can you insist that he open his lines to another, competing provider?

Providing cable access is a bit more complicated than the situation you face when you ask to install a bookcase or paint a room. The federal government has something to say under the Federal Telecommunications Act of 1996 (47 U.S.C. §§ 151 and following). In this Act, Congress decreed that all Americans should have as much access as possible to information that comes through a cable or over the air on wireless transmissions. The Act makes it very difficult for state and local governments, zoning commissions, home-owners' associations, and landlords to impose restrictions that hamper a person's ability to take advantage of these new types of communications.

Previously Unwired Buildings

Fortunately, most residential rental properties are already wired for cable. In competitive urban markets especially, landlords have figured out that they'll have a hard time attracting tenants if they do not give them the option of paying for cable. However, in the event that the property does not have cable, your landlord is entitled to say "No" to tenants who ask for access. If this is the response you get from your landlord, you may want to consider mounting a satellite dish. (See "Satellite Dishes and Other Antennas," below, for rules governing these devices.)

Buildings With Existing Contracts

Many multifamily buildings are already wired for cable. In the past, landlords have been able to secure attractive deals with the service providers, passing savings on to tenants. Many landlords signed "exclusive" contracts, whereby they promise the cable provider that they will not allow other providers into the building.

In October 2007, the Federal Communications Commission (FCC) ruled that not only are exclusive contracts unenforceable, but exclusive clauses in existing contracts will not be enforced. This means that any exclusive clauses the landlord may now have in its contracts are unenforceable, and the landlord may not enter into any new ones. Landlords do *not*, however, have to let any cable company who asks into their building, nor do they have to allow access to a particular company when asked by tenants. If you would like cable service other than the one currently offered on the property, you'll need to convince your landlord that inviting that company into its property makes good marketing sense. For more information, see the FCC's "Small Entity Compliance Guide" (type this title into the search box at www.fcc.gov).

Satellite Dishes and Other Antennas

Wireless communications have the potential to reach more people with less hardware than any cable system. But there is one, essential piece of equipment: a satellite dish with wires connecting it to the television set or computer.

You may be familiar with the car-sized dishes often seen in backyards or on roofs of houses—the pink flamingo of the modern age. Smaller and cheaper dishes, two feet or less in diameter, are now available. Wires from the dishes can easily be run under a door or through an open window to a TV or computer. Tenants have attached these dishes to interior walls, roofs, windowsills, balconies, and railings. Landlords object, citing their unsightly looks and the potential for liability if one falls and injures someone.

Fortunately, the Federal Communications Commission has provided considerable guidance on residential use of satellite dishes and antennas (Over-the-Air Reception Devices Rule, 47 C.F.R. § 1.4000, further explained in the FCC's Fact Sheet,

"Over-the-Air Reception Devices Rule"). Basically, the FCC prohibits landlords from imposing restrictions that unreasonably impair your ability to install, maintain, or use a dish or other antenna that meets the criteria described below. Here's a brief overview of the FCC rule.

> **RESOURCE**
>
> **For complete details on the FCC's rule on satellite dishes and other antennas,** see www.fcc.gov/guides/installing-consumer-owned-antennas-and-satellite-dishes. The FCC's rule was upheld in *Building Owners and Managers Assn. v. FCC,* 254 F.3d 89 (D.C. Cir.) (2001).

Devices Covered by the FCC Rule

The FCC's rule applies to video antennas, including direct-to-home satellite dishes that are less than one meter (39.37 inches) in diameter, TV antennas, and wireless cable antennas. These pieces of equipment receive video programming signals from direct broadcast satellites, wireless cable providers, and television broadcast stations. Antennas up to 18 inches in diameter that transmit as well as receive fixed wireless telecom signals (not just video) are also included.

There are, however, some exceptions. Antennas used for AM/FM radio, amateur ("ham"), and Citizen's Band ("CB") radio or Digital Audio Radio Services ("DARS") are excluded from the FCC's rule. Landlords may restrict the installation of these types of antennas in the same way that they can restrict any modification or alteration of rented space, as explained in the first section of this chapter.

Permissible Installation of Satellite Dishes and Antennas

You may place dishes or other antennas only in your own, exclusive rented space, such as inside the rental unit or on a balcony, terrace, deck, or patio. The device must be wholly within the rented space (if it overhangs the balcony, the landlord may prohibit that placement). Also, landlords may prohibit you from drilling through exterior walls, even if that wall is also part of your rented space.

The FCC rule specifies that you cannot place a reception device in common areas, such as roofs, hallways, walkways, or the exterior walls of the building. Exterior windows are no different from exterior walls—for this reason, placing a dish or antenna on a window by means of a series of suction cups is impermissible under the FCC rule (obviously, such an installation is also unsafe). Tenants who rent single-family homes, however, may install devices in the home itself or on patios, yards, gardens, or other similar areas.

Restrictions on Installation Techniques

Landlords are free to set restrictions on how the devices are installed, as long as the restrictions are not unreasonably expensive or are imposed for safety reasons or to preserve historic aspects of the structure. Landlords cannot insist that their maintenance personnel (or professional installers) do the work (but landlords may set reasonable guidelines as to how to install the devices, as explained below). Most importantly, if your landlord has not communicated an installation policy, you may go ahead and install the device without asking permission first (of course, do so in a safe manner). (*In re Frankfurt,* 16 FCC Rcd. 2875 (2001).)

Expense

Landlords may not impose a flat fee or charge you additional rent if you want to erect a dish or other antenna. On the other hand, the landlord may be able to insist on certain installation techniques that will add expense—as long as the cost isn't excessive and reception will not be impaired. Examples of acceptable expenses include:

- insisting that an antenna be painted green in order to blend into the landscaping, or
- requiring the use of a universal bracket that future tenants could use, saving wear and tear on the building.

TIP
Rules for mounting satellite dishes or other antennas shouldn't be more restrictive than those that apply to artwork, flags, clotheslines, or similar items. After all, attaching telecommunications items is no more intrusive or invasive than bolting a sundial to the porch, screwing a thermometer to the wall, or nailing a rain gauge to a railing. If your landlord's standards for telecommunications devices are much stricter than guidelines for other improvements or alterations, you may have a good argument that the landlord is violating the FCC rules. (See "How to Handle Disputes About the Use and Placement of Satellite Dishes and Other Antennas," below, for information on how to respond to unreasonable landlord rules.)

Safety Concerns

Landlords can insist that you place and install devices in a way that will minimize the chances of accidents and will not violate safety or fire codes. In fact, the FCC directs landlords to give tenants written notice of safety restrictions, so that tenants will know in advance how to comply. For example, it's not a good idea to place a satellite dish on a fire escape, near a power plant, or near a walkway where passers-by might accidentally hit their heads. Your landlord may also insist on proper installation techniques, such as those explained in the instructions that come with most devices.

Now, suppose that proper installation (attaching a dish to a wall) means that the landlord will have to eventually patch and paint a wall. Can the landlord use this as reason for preventing installation? No—unless there are legitimate reasons for prohibiting the installation, such as a safety concern. When you move out and remove the device, however, your landlord may charge you for the cost of repairing the attachment spot (such as replastering and repainting).

CAUTION
A savvy landlord will require tenants who install antennas or dishes to carry renters' insurance. If the device falls and injures someone, your policy will cover any claim. Whether requiring renters' insurance unreasonably increases the cost to you of receiving over-the-air signals has not been decided by the FCC or the courts.

Preserving the Building's Historical Integrity

Your landlord may argue that the historical integrity of the property will be compromised if an antenna or satellite dish is attached. This isn't an easy claim to make. A landlord can use this argument only if the property is included in (or eligible for) the National Register of Historic Places—the nation's official list of buildings, structures, objects, sites, and districts worthy of preservation for their significance in American history, architecture, archaeology, and culture. For more information on what's required to qualify for the Register and for a database of registered places, see www.nps.gov/subjects/nationalregister/index.htm.

Placement and Orientation of Antennas and Reception Devices

Tenants have the right to place an antenna where they'll receive an "acceptable quality" signal. As long as the tenant's chosen spot is within the exclusive rented space, not on an exterior wall or in a common area as discussed above, the landlord may not set rules on placement—for example, the landlord cannot require that an antenna be placed only in the rear of the rental property if this results in the tenant's receiving a "substantially degraded" signal or no signal at all.

Reception devices that need to maintain line-of-sight contact with a transmitter or view a satellite may not work if they're stuck behind a wall or below the roofline. In particular, a dish must be on a south-facing wall, since satellites are in the southern hemisphere. Faced with a reception problem, you may want to move the device to another location or mount it on a pole, so that it clears the obstructing roof or wall. Tenants who have no other workable exclusive space may want to mount their devices on a mast, in hopes of clearing the obstacle. Depending on the situation, you may have the right to do so. Here are the rules for masts.

- **Single-family rentals.** Tenants may erect a mast that's 12 feet or less above the roofline without asking permission first—and the landlord must allow it if the mast is installed in a safe manner. If the mast is taller than 12 feet, the landlord may require the tenant to obtain permission before erecting it—but if the installation meets reasonable safety requirements, the landlord should allow its use.

- **Multifamily rentals.** Tenants may use a mast as long as it does not extend beyond their exclusive rented space. For example, in a two-story rental, a mast that is attached to the ground-floor patio and extends into the airspace opposite your own second floor would be permissible. On the other hand, a mast attached to a top-story deck, which extends above the roofline or outward over the railing, would not be protected by the FCC's rule—a landlord could prohibit this installation because it extends beyond your exclusive rented space.

Supplying a Central Antenna or Satellite Dish for All Tenants

Faced with the prospect of many dishes and or other antennas adorning an otherwise clean set of balconies, some landlords have installed a central dish or other antenna for use by all.

Landlords may install a central antenna and restrict the use of individual antennas by tenants only if the central device provides:

- **Equal access.** You must be able to get the same programming or fixed wireless service that you could receive with your own antenna.

- **Equal quality.** The signal quality to and from your home via the central antenna must be as good as or better than what you could get using your own device.

- **Equal value.** The costs of using the central device must be the same as or less than the cost of installing, maintaining, and using an individual antenna.

- **Equal readiness.** Landlords can't prohibit individual devices if installation of a central antenna will unreasonably delay your ability to receive programming or fixed wireless services—for example, when the central antenna won't be available for months.

If a landlord has installed a central antenna after tenants have installed their own, the landlord may require removal of the individual antennas, as long as the central device meets the above requirements. Your landlord will have to pay you for the removal of your device and compensate you for the value of the antenna.

How to Handle Disputes About the Use and Placement of Satellite Dishes and Other Antennas

In spite of the FCC's attempts to clarify tenants' rights to reception and landlords' rights to control what happens on their property, there are many possibilities for disagreements. For example, what exactly is "acceptable" reception? If the landlord requires antennas to be painted, at what point is the expense considered "unreasonable?"

Ideally, your landlord will avoid disputes in the first place, by setting reasonable policies. But, if all else fails, here are some tips to help you resolve the problem with a minimum of fuss and expense.

Discussion, Mediation, and Help from the FCC

First, approach the problem the way you would any dispute—talk it out and try to reach an acceptable conclusion. Follow our advice in Chapter 17 for settling disputes on your own—for example, through negotiation or mediation. You'll find the information on the FCC website very helpful (www.fcc.gov/guides/installing-consumer-owned-antennas-and-satellite-dishes). Once you find the document, go to "For More Information."). Your direct broadcast satellite company, multichannel distribution service, TV broadcast station, or fixed wireless company may also be able to suggest alternatives that are safe and acceptable to both you and your landlord.

Get the FCC Involved

If your own attempts don't resolve the problem, you can call the FCC and ask for oral guidance. You may also formally ask the FCC for a written opinion, called a Declaratory Ruling. For information on obtaining oral or written guidance from the FCC, follow the directions as shown on the FCC website at www.fcc.gov (see the link above). Fortunately for tenants, unless the landlord's objections concern safety or historic preservation, the landlord must allow the device to remain pending the FCC's ruling.

Go to Court

When all else fails, you can head for court. If the antenna or satellite dish hasn't been installed yet and you and the landlord are arguing about the reasonableness of the landlord's policies or your plans, you can ask a court to rule on who's right (just as you would when seeking the FCC's opinion). You'll have to go to superior court for a resolution of your dispute, where you'll ask for an order called a "Declaratory Judgment." Similarly, if the antenna or dish *has* been installed and the landlord wants a judge to order it removed, the landlord will have to go to superior court and ask for such an order. Unfortunately, the simpler option of small claims court will not usually be available in these situations, because most small courts handle only disputes that can be settled or decided with money, not requests about whether it's acceptable to do (or not do) a particular task.

Needless to say, being in superior court means that the case will be drawn-out and expensive. You could handle it yourself, but be forewarned—you'll need to be adept at arguing about First Amendment law and Congressional intent, and must be willing to spend long hours preparing your case. In the end, you might decide that it would have been cheaper to follow the Giants on cable TV or your computer.

CHAPTER

9

Injuries on the Premises

If you have been injured on your landlord's property, you may have a good legal claim against your landlord. That doesn't mean you'll have to file a lawsuit—valid claims against landlords are often settled before anyone goes to court. It may well be to your advantage to negotiate with the landlord's insurance adjuster or lawyer yourself, rather than to immediately hire a lawyer, who will typically take 25% to 40% of the recovery. But if you feel your injury is serious, you should at least consult with a lawyer to get a more expert evaluation of your case. That way, you will have a better understanding of both the value of your case and its potential pitfalls.

This chapter explains how to evaluate whether your landlord is liable for your injury, and what to do to maximize your chances of a just settlement or lawsuit verdict. Skip this chapter if you haven't been injured or aren't interested in learning about the issue.

What to Do If You're Injured

What is the best course of action to take if you're injured? If your injury is significant and costly—it has resulted in lost work, doctors' bills, and physical or emotional discomfort—and you think the landlord is at fault, you'll want to consider legal action. But don't go rushing off to the nearest personal injury lawyer just yet. Especially if your injury isn't very severe, you might be better off—at least initially—handling the claim yourself.

But if your injury is severe, see a lawyer right away. Injuries in this category include:

- a long-term or permanently disabling injury, such as the loss of a limb
- an injury that results in medical costs and lost income over $10,000, or
- heavy-duty toxic exposure, such as lead or pesticide poisoning.

This book can't cover all the ins and outs of pursuing a personal injury claim. Here, however, is an outline of the basic steps you should follow.

Get Immediate Medical Attention

The success of an accident claim often depends on what you do in the first hours and days after your injury. Although you might be in pain, angry, or even depressed, attention to these details immediately following the incident will pay off later.

It is essential to get prompt medical attention for your injury, even if you consider it to be of marginal help to your physical recovery. No insurance company, judge, or jury will take your word alone for the extent of your injury, pain and suffering. It might seem obvious to you that a sprained ankle caused immobility, swelling and pain, and made you miss a week's work. Nonetheless, you'll need the confirmation of a physician, and the professional opinion that you didn't suffer a mere soft tissue bruise, when it comes to convincing a skeptical insurance adjuster or jury of your injury's impact.

Moreover, if you intend to hold the landlord financially responsible for your injuries, the law expects you to take whatever steps are possible to lessen the extent of your injuries and speed your recovery. Oddly, the reason has little to do with concern for your physical well-being; rather, the law expects you to take reasonable steps to lessen the accident's financial impact on the landlord. In short, you'll need the verification of a doctor that you were a conscientious patient who did not prolong or ignore your injuries.

> EXAMPLE: May-Ling, a new tenant, slipped on a puddle of oil-slicked rainwater that habitually accumulated at the base of the garage stairs. She fell and badly twisted her back. Thinking that time would heal her wounds, she did not seek medical attention, though she did stay home from work for a week.
>
> She then filed a claim with the landlord's insurance company, seeking compensation for her pain and suffering and lost wages. The insurance adjuster questioned the severity of her injury and suggested that, had she consulted a doctor, she might have

recovered sooner with the aid of muscle-relaxing medication. Unable to verify the extent of her injury and having no way to effectively answer the claim that medical attention might have helped her, May-Ling settled her claim for a disappointing amount.

You will also need to follow the advice of your doctor. Remember, the landlord's insurance company will be allowed to look at your medical records regarding this injury. If they see that you did not follow your doctor's recommendations, that failure could be considered a "failure to mitigate" (lessen) your damages.

> **EXAMPLE:** Let's say May-Ling went to the doctor, who confirmed that she had a back injury and instructed her to go to physical therapy for further treatment. May-Ling thought that physical therapy would give her minimal benefits and was too much of a bother. When it came time to review the case, the insurance adjuster determined that her back problems continued longer because she did not follow her doctor's advice. As a result, the adjuster offered less in the way of a settlement.

Write Everything Down

Resolving injury claims takes months, many times years. During that time, memories fade. Details that you might not have thought were significant later become important. That's why, as soon as possible after the accident, you should jot down everything you can remember about how it happened. Include a complete list of everyone who was present and what they said. For example, suppose you tripped on a loose stair and the manager rushed over and blurted out, "I told Jim [the landlord] we should have replaced that last month!" Be sure to write this down and note the names of anyone who heard the manager say it. Write down the details about how the accident happened: What time of day was it? Were the lights working? Which step did you trip on, and so on.

Take pictures of the scene of the accident from several different angles. Also, you might have bruising, a cast, or scarring later on. Be sure to take photographs of these injuries. Your phone will date and time-stamp the photos; be sure to upload them to a secure location.

Describe the precise nature of your injuries, including pain, the locations on your body where it hurts, as well as associated symptoms like headaches, loss of sleep, or anxiety. Make notes of every economic loss, such as lost wages, missed classes and events, and transportation and medical costs. If you have a conversation regarding the incident with anyone (the landlord, other tenants, an insurance adjuster, or medical personnel), make a written summary of the conversation.

 CAUTION

Assume that anything you write down is going to be used as evidence in court. For this reason, be thoughtful before writing down what happened. Stick to the facts as you know them, write down what you saw, heard, or touched. Do not get into your thoughts or speculation about the events; they are not evidence and could possibly be used against you in cross-examination at trial.

Preserve Evidence

Claims are often won by the production of a persuasive piece of physical evidence: the worn or broken stair that caused the fall, the unattached throw rug that slipped when stepped on, the electrical outlet faceplate that showed burn marks from a short. Remember that physical evidence that is not preserved within a short time can be lost, modified by time or weather, repaired, or destroyed. For example, the landlord, not wanting more accidents, might quickly replace a loose stair that caused you to fall, and throw the old one away.

If preservation of the evidence would involve dismantling the landlord's property, you might have to settle for the next-best alternative, photographs or videos. Don't wait—make your record before repairs are made. And to forestall challenges to the accuracy of your pictures (or a claim they were doctored), have someone else take a second set, and ask that person to be prepared to testify in court that the pictures are a fair and accurate depiction of the scene.

If you are experiencing pain, keep what's known as a "pain diary." Every day (and more often if appropriate), jot down how you feel, what you can and cannot do, and what medication you're taking to help yourself. This log might come in handy if you are asked to document your condition. But again, be thoughtful about what you write down, because this will be used as evidence in court. Probably the worst thing you can do is to overstate or dramatize your injuries.

Obtain Copies of Medical Records and Evidence of Lost Wages

Insurance carriers usually ask for copies of medical records and medical bills in order to substantiate your claim of injury. It is helpful to get copies of relevant medical records in advance.

Often, insurance companies make a broad request for all of your medical records. But most people want their private medical records to remain private. Fortunately, the law doesn't give the insurance company access to everything: The insurance company has the right to records related to the particular injury, and to other, previous conditions concerned with the same part of your body. (*In re Lifschultz*, 2 Cal.3d 415, 431 (1970).) They do not have the right to records pertaining to unrelated conditions. For example, if you already had back problems and reinjured it in the accident, they would be entitled to see records related to that previous injury (see "Pre-Existing Conditions," below). The best practice is for you to make the request to your doctors yourself, asking only for records related to the part of the body affected by the accident. Then, give these records to the insurance company.

If you claim that you lost work because of the injury, try to get a letter from your boss outlining what days you were off work and what your pay rate is.

Pre-Existing Conditions

People might think that if you injure a part of your body that was previously injured, that somehow diminishes the value of the case. This is not the law. A wrongdoer is liable to the extent that he made matters worse for the claimant. A classic example taught in law schools is the hemophiliac who is in an auto accident and bleeds to death from his relatively minor injuries. Is the defendant responsible for his death? Yes, even though most people would not have died in that circumstance.

So, how would an adjuster evaluate a person's pre-existing back pain in light of a new injury? The insurance company wants to make sure it's not being asked to compensate you for an injury that you already had, which has not been aggravated by the accident.

On the other hand, suppose you have a history of back problems. You trip and badly hurt your back such the injury is greater than it would have been for a person without back problems. Your injury is greater and therefore your recovery should be greater.

Contact Witnesses

Having an eyewitness can be an immeasurable help. Witnesses can corroborate your version of events and might even have seen important aspects of the situation that you missed. But you must act very quickly to find and preserve the observations and memories of those who could bolster your case —people's memories fade quickly, and strangers can be very hard to track down later.

Don't tell witnesses not to talk to "the other side." Witnesses have no legal obligation to talk to you, although most will if they feel you have been wronged. Similarly, you have no authority to tell them not to talk to others. Moreover, trying to do so could come back to haunt you via a suggestion that you had something to hide. If a favorable witness tells an insurance adjuster a different story, you can expose the inconsistencies later in court.

If you find people who witnessed the incident, get their names, addresses, and as much information about what they saw as possible. Talk with them about what they saw and write it up. Ask them if they would be willing to review your summary for accuracy; if so, mail them a copy and ask them to correct it, sign it, and return it to you in the stamped envelope you have provided.

Don't overlook the witness who heard or saw another witness. It can often be important to have a witness who can describe what another witness said or did. For example, the manager who blurted out, "I told him we should have fixed that last month" will have every incentive to deny making that statement, because it pins knowledge of the defect on the property owner, his boss. If someone besides you also heard the manager say it, he'll have a tougher time disowning it. Get that person's name and statement.

Evaluate Your Case

Before you go making demands for money from your landlord or an insurance company, you need to know whether you have a legal leg to stand on. That's what most of the rest of this chapter explains. For now, remember that this evaluation step is critical and can't be skipped!

Notify the Landlord and the Insurance Carrier

Once you're convinced that you have a good case, write to the owner of the rental property, stating that you have been injured and need to contact the owner's liability insurance carrier. You should have the owner's name and address on your lease or rental agreement (if you don't, send the letter to wherever you send the monthly rent). If you deal with a manager or management company, you should also notify them.

If a third party is involved, it won't hurt to notify them, too, if there is some basis for thinking that they may have been at least partially responsible. For example, a contractor or subcontractor might have created or contributed to the dangerous situation, or a repairperson might have done a faulty job, causing your injury.

Sample Letter or Email to Landlord Regarding Tenant Injury

Alice Watson
37 Ninth Avenue North
South Fork, CA 00000
401-555-4567

February 28, 20xx

Fernando Diaz
3757 East Seventh Street
South Fork, CA 00000

Dear Mr. Diaz:

On February 25, 20xx, I was injured in a fall on the front steps of the duplex that I rent from you. The middle step splintered and collapsed as I walked down the stairs. Please refer this matter to the carrier of your business liability insurance and have them contact me at the above address.

Thank you for your cooperation.

Yours truly,

Alex Watson

Alex Watson

A sample letter or email is shown above. If your case is substantial, you can expect that the owner will contact the insurer right away. On the other hand, a landlord who suspects that the claim is phony or trivial may hold off notifying the insurance company, fearing a rate increase or policy cancellation. You cannot force the landlord to refer the case or disclose the name of the insurer; all you can do is persevere until your persistence and the threat of a lawsuit become real enough for the landlord to call in the insurance company's help. (Or, your landlord could decide to settle with you without involving his carrier, which might be all right too, as explained below.)

Negotiate, Mediate, or Sue

If you are successful at reaching the landlord's insurance carrier, chances are that you'll negotiate a settlement. You might choose mediation (in which a neutral third party helps both sides reach a settlement) if you feel that the insurance company is interested in settling the matter and will deal with you fairly. (If the result isn't adequate, you can always file a lawsuit.) But if the landlord stonewalls you, refusing to refer your claim to the insurance carrier or a lawyer, you might need to consider a lawsuit. Chapter 18 gives detailed information on negotiating with, mediating with, and suing your landlord if necessary. It also helps you decide whether to take your case to small claims court yourself, saving time and the expense of hiring a lawyer; or whether you are better off in a formal court with a lawyer.

!

CAUTION

Don't wait too long before filing suit. You must file your lawsuit within the time specified by California's "statute of limitations," which is two years from the date of injury for most injuries. However, choosing the proper statute of limitations can get tricky. On this point, you would be wise to consult a lawyer (you needn't hire the lawyer to handle the entire case, however).

RESOURCE

How to Win Your Personal Injury Claim, **by Joseph Matthews (Nolo),** explains personal injury cases and how to work out a fair settlement without going to court.

Everybody's Guide to Small Claims Court in California, by Cara O'Neill (Nolo), provides great advice on small claims court, where you can sue for up to $10,000.

Represent Yourself in Court: How to Prepare & Try a Winning Case, by Paul Bergman and Sara J. Berman (Nolo), will help you prepare and present your case should you end up in court.

Is the Landlord Liable?

It isn't always easy to determine whether the landlord is legally responsible for an injury. Basically, your landlord might be liable if all four of the following conditions are met:

- The landlord had a legal obligation ("duty") to repair or correct a condition existing on the premises.
- The landlord knew or should have known of the condition that caused the injury.
- The landlord failed to take reasonable steps to correct the condition, and
- The landlord's failure was a substantial factor in causing the injury.

Whether the landlord was negligent is usually the most disputed feature of a personal injury action. A landlord is required to exercise "ordinary care or skill" in managing the property. Landlords are negligent when they fail to exercise reasonable care in correcting any unsafe conditions under the landlord's control that the landlord knew about or should have known about.

The Landlord Did Not Exercise Reasonable Care

Figuring out whether the landlord exercised "reasonable care" can be a simple matter or a very complex one. Violating a health and safety law or certain laws that govern other aspects of the landlord-tenant relationship; or failure to make certain repairs (all discussed below), are almost always a failure to exercise reasonable care. That's because the landlord has a legal and/or contractual obligation to keep the premises safe. Likewise, if a landlord intended to harm you (by assaulting you or engaging in sexual harassment), this conduct is clearly unreasonable. Many situations, however, are less than clear and require a broader analysis as to whether the landlord acted "reasonably" under the circumstances.

Evaluating Negligence Cases

If you think your landlord's carelessness caused your injury, you'll need answers to these questions before you can present your claim:

- Did the landlord know, or should he have known, of the defective condition that caused the injury?
- Did the landlord have access to or control over the area or item where you were hurt?
- How likely was it that an accident of this nature would occur?
- How difficult or expensive would it have been for the landlord to correct the condition so as to reduce the chance of injury?
- How serious was the injury that would likely occur because of the condition?
- Did your landlord take reasonable steps to correct the condition that caused the injury?
- Was the condition a substantial factor in causing the injury?

These questions are addressed in detail below.

"Negligence" (or failure to exercise reasonable care) is always determined in light of the unique facts of each situation. For example, it might be reasonable to put adequate lights in a dark, remote stairwell. If your landlord doesn't, and you're hurt because you couldn't see the broken steps and fell, your landlord's failure to install the lights might be negligence. On the other hand, extra lights in a lobby that's already well-lit might or might not be a reasonable expectation.

To determine whether your landlord was negligent and should be held responsible for your injury, you must answer six questions. The insurance adjuster will use these same questions to evaluate your claim, as will a lawyer (if you consult one). If the insurance company isn't forthcoming, you should be able to head to court confidently, where a judge or jury will use the same questions when deciding your case.

Question 1: Did your landlord know or should have known of the defective condition that caused the injury? Typically, a landlord is put on notice of a defect in your living unit by your reporting the condition to him, either in writing or orally. There may be other ways that he "should have known" of the defect in your unit. One example might be his having done a routine inspection of the unit with your permission. Another example might be more indirect. For instance, he may know that the windows in the whole building are likely in need of repair. If glass falls out of one of the windows as you open it, a jury could determine that he should have known about the unsafe conditions. And, as stated before, a landlord has an obligation when renting the premises to perform a reasonable inspection and correct any unsafe conditions. If the unsafe condition existed at the beginning of your tenancy, then he is put on notice of the condition and that should satisfy the "should have known" requirement.

Question 2: Did the landlord have access to or control over the area where you were hurt? It stands to reason that the landlord is not necessarily liable for injuries sustained in areas that he cannot gain access to. As stated previously in Chapter 5, the landlord has the right to enter your unit for the purpose of making repairs. If the defect is in your unit, then the landlord has access to the area where you were hurt. If, for some reason you deny the landlord access to your unit for the purpose of making repairs, you should not be able to then sue for an injury caused by the condition you refused to let the landlord fix.

Access to and control over common areas of the building such as stairways, lobby, parking areas, or utility rooms rarely presents a problem, because these are areas that the landlord has both access to and control over.

The owner also has control over the building's utility systems. If a malfunction causes injury (like boiling water in your sink because of a broken thermostat), he may likewise be held responsible. On the other hand, if you're hurt when your own bookcase falls on you, the landlord won't be held responsible, because he does not control how the bookcase is built, set up, or maintained.

Interestingly, the landlord may be held responsible for injuries that occur on property that he doesn't even own, as long as he makes use of it and takes no steps to fix problems or at least warn you of them. In one case, a tenant sued a landlord when the tenant tripped on a poorly maintained strip of land that actually belonged to the city, because the landlord knew that this adjacent land was regularly used by his tenants. (*Alcaraz v. Vece,* 14 Cal.4th. 1149 (1997).)

For example, common sense would tell anyone that loose handrails or stairs are likely to lead to accidents, but it would be unusual for injuries to result from peeling wallpaper or a thumbtack that's fallen from a bulletin board.

Question 3: How likely was it that an accident of this nature would occur? In legal circles, this issue is often referred to as "foreseeability of harm." The basic concept is that a landlord is held liable for any injury caused by a defective condition if a reasonable person could foresee (anticipate) that it would cause injury. It is not necessary that the injury is of the exact nature that one might foresee, but only that the condition created a risk that someone would be injured.

Question 4: How difficult or expensive would it have been for the landlord to correct the condition and reduce the risk of injury? The chances that your landlord will be held liable are greater if a reasonably priced response could have averted the accident. In other words, could something as simple as warning signs, a bright light, or caution tape have prevented people from tripping over an unexpected step leading to the patio, or would major structural remodeling have been necessary to reduce the likelihood of injury? But if there is a great risk of very serious injury, a landlord will be expected to spend money to avert it. For example, a high-rise deck with rotten support beams must be repaired, regardless of the cost, because there is a great risk of collapse and dreadful injuries to anyone on or under the deck. A landlord who knew about the condition of the deck and failed to repair it would surely be held liable if an accident did occur.

Keep in mind, however, that if the defect was one that the landlord was obligated to fix (such as a problem with the electrical system) and the landlord knew or should have known of the defect, he will be held liable because failing to address it is a habitability and a code violation.

Question 5: Was a serious injury likely to result from the condition? The amount of time and money your landlord is expected to spend on making the premises safe will also depend on the seriousness of the probable injury if he fails to do so. For example, if the umbrella on a poolside table wouldn't open, no one would expect it to cause serious injury. If you're sunburned at the pool as a result, it's not likely that a judge would rule that your landlord had the duty of keeping you from getting burned. But if a major injury is the likely result of a dangerous situation—suppose the pool diving board was broken, making it likely you'd fall on the deck when using it—the owner is expected to take the situation more seriously and fix it faster.

The answers to these five questions should tell you (or an insurance adjuster or judge) whether or not there was a dangerous condition on the landlord's property that the landlord had a legal duty to deal with. Lawyers call this having a "duty of due care."

Let's look at how these first five questions would get answered in a few possible scenarios.

EXAMPLE 1: Mark broke his leg when he tripped on a loose step on the stairway from the lobby to the first floor. Since the step had been loose for several months, chances are the landlord's insurance company would settle a claim like this.

Mark's position is strong because of the answers to the four questions:

1. The landlord was legally responsible for (in control of) the condition of the common stairways.
2. It was highly foreseeable to any reasonable person that someone would slip on a loose step.
3. Securing the step would have been simple and inexpensive.
4. The probable result of leaving the step loose—falling and injuring oneself on the stairs—is a serious matter.

EXAMPLE 2: Lee slipped on a marble that had been dropped in the lobby by another tenant's child just a few minutes earlier. Lee twisted his ankle and lost two weeks' work. Lee will have a tough time establishing that his landlord had a duty to protect him from this injury. Here's what the questions turn up:

1. The landlord does have control over the public sidewalk.
2. The likelihood of injury from something a tenant drops is fairly low.
3. The burden on the landlord to eliminate all possible problems at all times by constantly inspecting or sweeping the lobby is unreasonable.
4. Finally, the seriousness of any likely injury resulting from not checking constantly is open to great debate.

EXAMPLE 3: James suffered a concussion when he hit his head on a dull-colored overhead beam in the apartment garage. When the injury occurred, he was standing on a stool, loading items onto the roof rack of his SUV. Did the landlord have a duty to take precautions in this situation? Probably not, but the answers to the four questions are not so easy.

1. The landlord exercises control over the garage, and certainly has a responsibility to reasonably protect tenants from harm there.
2. The likelihood of injury from a beam is fairly slim, since most people don't stand on stools in the garage, and those who do have the opportunity to see the beam and avoid it.
3. As to eliminating the condition that led to the injury, it's highly unlikely anyone would expect the landlord to rebuild the garage. But it's possible that a judge might think it reasonable to paint the beams a bright color and post warning signs, especially if lots of people put trucks and other large vehicles in the garage.
4. As to the seriousness of probable harm, injury from low beams is likely to be to the head, which is a serious matter.

In short, this situation is too close to call, but if an insurance adjuster or jury considered the case, they might decide that James was partially at fault (for not watching out for the beams) and reduce any award accordingly. (See "If You're at Fault, Too," below.)

If, based on these first five questions, you think the landlord had a legal duty to deal with a condition on the premises that posed a danger to you, keep going. You have two more questions to answer.

Question 6: Did your landlord fail to take reasonable steps to correct the condition? The law won't expect your landlord to undertake Herculean measures to shield you from a condition that poses some risk. Instead, the landlord is required to take only reasonable steps. For example, if you've demonstrated that a stair was in a dangerous condition, you also need to show that the landlord's failure to fix it was unreasonable in the circumstances. Let's take the broken step that Mark (Example 1, above) tripped over. Obviously, leaving it broken for months is unreasonably careless—that is, negligent—under the circumstances.

But what if the step had torn loose only an hour earlier, when another tenant dragged a heavy footlocker up the staircase? Mark's landlord would probably concede that he had a duty to maintain the stairways, but would argue that the manager's daily sweeping and inspection of the stairs that same morning met that burden. In the absence of being notified of the problem, he would probably claim that his inspection routine met his duty of keeping the stairs safe. If a jury agreed, Mark would not be able to establish that the landlord acted unreasonably under the circumstances.

Examples of Injuries From Landlord Negligence

Here are some examples of injuries for which tenants have recovered money damages due to the landlord's negligence:

- Tenant falls down a staircase due to a defective handrail.
- Tenant trips over a hole in the carpet on a common stairway not properly maintained by the landlord.
- Tenant injured and property damaged by fire resulting from an obviously defective heater or wiring.
- Tenant gets sick from pesticide sprayed in common areas and on exterior walls without advance notice.
- Tenant's child is scalded by water from a water heater with a broken thermostat.
- Tenant slips and falls on a puddle of oil-slicked rainwater in the garage.
- Tenant's guest injured when she slips on ultraslick floor wax applied by the landlord's cleaning service.
- Tenant receives electrical burns when attempting to insert the stove's damaged plug into the wall outlet.
- Tenant slips and falls on wet grass cuttings left on a common walkway.

Question 7: Was the condition a substantial factor in causing the injury? This last question establishes the crucial link between the landlord's negligence and your injury. Not every dangerous situation results in an accident. You'll have to prove that the landlord's failure to exercise reasonable care was a substantial factor in causing your injury. A "substantial factor" is one that a reasonable person would consider to have contributed to the harm. The negligence does not have to be the only cause of the harm, but it must be a contributing cause. Sometimes this is self-evident: One minute you're fine, and the next minute you've slipped on a freshly waxed floor and have a broken arm. But it's not always so simple. For example, in the case of the loose stair, the landlord might be able to show that the tenant barely lost his balance because of the loose stair and that he had really injured his ankle during a touch football game he'd just played.

Here's a final example, applying all seven questions to a tenant's injury.

> **EXAMPLE:** Scotty's apartment complex had a pool bordered by a concrete deck. On his way to the pool, Scotty slipped and fell, breaking his arm. The concrete where he fell was slick because the landlord had cleaned the pool and spilled some of the cleaning solution earlier that morning. To assess his chances of collecting against his landlord for his injury, Scotty asked himself these questions:
>
> 1. Did the landlord control the pool area and the cleaning solution? Absolutely. The pool was part of a common area, and the landlord had done the cleaning.
> 2. Was an accident like Scotty's foreseeable? Certainly. It's likely that a barefoot person heading for the pool would slip on slick cement.
> 3. Could the landlord have eliminated the dangerous condition without much effort or money? Of course. All that was necessary was to hose down the deck.
> 4. How serious was the probable injury? Falling on cement presents a high likelihood of broken bones, a serious injury.

Having established that the landlord owed him a duty of care, Scotty considered the rest of his case.

1. Had his landlord also breached this duty? Yes; Scotty was sure a jury would conclude that leaving spilled cleaning solution on the deck was an unreasonable thing to do.

2. Did the spilled cleaning solution cause his fall? This one is easy, because several people saw the accident and others could describe Scotty's robust fitness before the fall. Scotty hadn't himself been careless (see "If You're at Fault, Too," below), so he decided he had a pretty good case.

The Landlord Violated a Health or Safety Law

A landlord can be held liable for failure to exercise reasonable care if the landlord violated a health or safety law. The California legislature has enacted health and safety laws requiring smoke detectors, sprinklers, inside-release security bars on windows, childproof fences around swimming pools, as well as habitability obligations discussed in Chapters 6 and 7. To put real teeth behind these important laws, legislators (and sometimes the courts) have decided that if landlords don't take reasonable steps to comply with certain health or safety statutes, the law will consider them negligent. And if that negligence results in an injury, the landlord is liable for it. You don't need to prove that an accident was forseeable or likely to be serious, nor do you have to show that complying with the law would have been relatively inexpensive. The legal term for this rule is "negligence per se."

EXAMPLE: State law specifies that all rental units must have smoke detectors, but there are none in your unit. A fire started at night while you were sleeping and you were injured. If you can show that had there been detectors, you would have become aware of the fire sooner and would have likely escaped without injury, you will not have to prove that the landlord was responsible for the fire

starting. You only have to prove that the failure to have working smoke detectors was a substantial factor in causing your injuries.

Bear in mind that landlords are expected only to take reasonable steps to comply with safety and health laws that fall within the negligence per se realm. For example, your landlord must supply smoke detectors. If the landlord has supplied one but you have disabled it, your landlord won't be held responsible if you are hurt by a fire that could have been stopped had you left the detector alone.

The landlord's violation of a health or safety law might also indirectly cause an injury. For example, if the landlord lets the furnace deteriorate in violation of local law, and you are injured trying to repair it, the landlord will probably be liable unless your repair efforts are extremely careless themselves.

EXAMPLE: The state housing code requires landlords to provide hot water. In the middle of the winter, your hot water heater has been broken for a week, despite your repeated complaints to the landlord. Finally, to give your sick child a hot bath, you carry pots of steaming water from the stove to the bathtub. Doing this, you spill the hot water and burn yourself seriously.

You sue the landlord for failure to provide hot water as required by state law. If the case goes to court, it will be up to the judge to decide whether the landlord's failure to provide hot water caused your injury. Because a judge could reasonably conclude that your response to the lack of hot water was a forseeable one, your landlord's insurance company might be willing to offer a fair settlement.

The Landlord Didn't Make Certain Repairs

Likewise, landlords can be held liable for failure to make repairs that they were obligated to make. For perfectly sensible reasons, many landlords do not want tenants to undertake even relatively simple tasks like painting, plastering, or unclogging a drain. Your lease or rental agreement may prohibit you from making any repairs or alterations without the owner's consent, or limit what you can do. (Chapter 8 discusses this.)

But in exchange for a landlord's reserving the right to make all these repairs, the law imposes a responsibility. If, after being told about a problem, the landlord doesn't maintain or repair something you aren't allowed to touch, and you are injured as a result, the landlord is probably liable. The legal reason is that the landlord breached the contract (the lease) by not making the repairs. (The landlord might be negligent as well; remember, there is nothing to stop you from presenting multiple reasons why the landlord should be held liable.)

EXAMPLE: The Rules and Regulations attached to Lori's lease state that management will inspect and clean the fan above her stove every six months. Jake, an affable but somewhat scatterbrained graduate student in charge of maintenance at the apartment complex, was supposed to do the fan checks. But deep into his studies and social life, Jake scheduled no inspections for a long time. Lori was injured when the accumulated grease in the fan filter caught fire.

Lori sued the landlord, alleging that his failure to live up to his contractual promise to clean the fan was the cause of her injuries. The jury agreed and awarded her a large sum.

Some other common examples might include:

- **Environmental hazards.** If your lease forbids repainting without the landlord's consent, the landlord is obligated to maintain the painted surfaces. If an old layer of lead paint begins to crack, deteriorate, and enter the air, the landlord will be liable for the health problems that follow. (Chapter 10 covers environmental health hazards such as lead-based paint.)
- **Security breaches.** Landlords typically forbid tenants from installing locks of their own. That means landlords may be liable if their failure to provide secure locks contributes to a crime. (See Chapter 11.)

The Landlord Didn't Keep the Premises Habitable

One of a landlord's basic responsibilities is to keep the rental property in a "habitable" condition.

Failure to maintain a habitable dwelling may make the landlord liable for injuries caused by the substandard conditions. For example, a tenant who is bitten by a rat in a vermin-infested building may argue that the owner's failure to maintain a rat-free building constituted a breach of duty to keep the place habitable, which in turn led to the injury. You must show that the landlord knew of the defect and had a reasonable amount of time to fix it.

Remember that the defect must be serious enough such that an injury from the defect is foreseeable. For example, a large, jagged broken picture window would probably make the premises unfit for habitation, but a torn screen door obviously would not. The tenant who cut herself trying to cover the window with cardboard might sue under negligence and a violation of the implied warranty of habitability, while the tenant who injured herself trying to repair the screen would be limited to a theory of negligence.

EXAMPLE: Jose notified his landlord about the mice that he had seen several times in his kitchen. Despite Jose's repeated complaints, the landlord did nothing to eliminate the problem. When Jose reached into his cupboard for a box of cereal, a mouse bit him. Jose sued his landlord for the medical treatment he required, including extremely painful rabies shots. He alleged that the landlord's failure to eradicate the rodent problem constituted a breach of the implied warranty of habitability, and that this breach was responsible for his injury. The jury agreed and gave Jose a large monetary award.

The injury sustained by Jose in the example above could also justify a claim that the injury resulted from the landlord's negligence. And, if Jose's landlord had failed to take reasonable steps to comply with a state or local statute concerning rodent control, the landlord might automatically be considered negligent. Finally, the owner may also be liable if the lease forbade Jose from making repairs, such as repairing improper sewage connections or changing the way garbage was stored. As you can see, sometimes there are several legal theories that will fit the facts and support your claim for damages.

The Landlord Acted Recklessly

In the legal sense of the word, "recklessness" usually means extreme carelessness regarding an obvious defect or problem. A landlord who is aware of a long-existing and obviously dangerous defect but neglects to correct it may be guilty of recklessness, not just ordinary carelessness.

If your landlord or an employee acted recklessly, your monetary recovery could be significant. This is because a jury has the power to award not only actual damages (which include medical bills, loss of earnings, and pain and suffering) but also extra, "punitive" damages. (See "How Much Money You're Entitled To," below.) Punitive damages are almost never given in simple negligence cases, but are appropriate to punish recklessness and to send a sobering message to others who might behave similarly. But don't count your millions before you have them: In every situation, the line between ordinary negligence and recklessness is wherever the unpredictable jury thinks it should be. The size of the punitive award is likewise up to the jury, and can often be reduced later by a judge or appellate court.

The very unpredictability of punitive damage awards, however, can be to your advantage when negotiating with the landlord. The landlord might settle your claim rather than risk letting an indignant jury award you punitive damages.

EXAMPLE: The handrail along the stairs to the first floor of the apartment house Jack owned had been hanging loose for several months. Jack attempted to fix it two or three times by taping the supports to the wall. The tape did no good, however, and the railing was literally flapping in the breeze. One dark night when Hilda, one of Jack's tenants, reached for the railing, the entire thing came off in her hand, causing her to fall and break her hip.

Hilda sued Jack for her injuries. In her lawsuit, she pointed to the ridiculously ineffective measures that Jack had taken to deal with an obviously dangerous situation, and charged that he had acted with reckless disregard for the safety of his tenants. (Hilda also argued that Jack was negligent because of his unreasonable behavior and because he had violated a local ordinance regarding maintenance of handrails.) The jury agreed with Hilda and awarded her punitive damages.

The Landlord Intentionally Harmed You

Intentional injuries are rare but, unfortunately, they occur more often than you might guess. For example, if a landlord or manager struck and injured you during an argument, obviously that would be an intentional act for which the landlord would be liable.

Less obvious, but no less serious, are emotional or psychological injuries that can, in extreme circumstances, also be inflicted intentionally. Intentional infliction of emotional distress often arises in these situations:

- **Sexual harassment.** Repeated, disturbing attentions of a sexual nature that the harasser refuses to stop, which leave the victim fearful, humiliated, and upset, can form the basis for a claim of intentional harm. The same is true for a single, egregious act. (See Chapter 4.)

  EXAMPLE: Rita's landlord Brad took advantage of every opportunity to make suggestive comments about her looks and social life. When she asked him to stop, he replied that he was "just looking out for her," and he stepped up his unwanted attentions. Rita finally had enough, broke the lease, and moved out. When Brad sued her for unpaid rent, she turned around and sued him for the emotional distress caused by his harassment. To his surprise, Brad was slapped with a multi-thousand dollar judgment, including punitive damages.

- **Assault.** Threatening or menacing someone without actually touching them is an assault, which can be enormously frightening and lead to psychological damage.
- **Repeated invasions of privacy.** Deliberately invading a tenant's privacy—by unauthorized entries, for example—may cause extreme worry and distress. (Chapter 5 covers tenants' privacy rights.)

The Injury Was Caused by a Person Hired by the Landlord

Sometimes an injury can result from the negligence of a third party whom the landlord has hired to do work on the property. For example, a landlord might hire a carpenter to do work on a vacant unit. The carpenter leaves a mess in the hallway, causing you to trip and fall. Here, the landlord was not the direct cause of the injury. Nevertheless, the landlord has a "non-delegable duty" to maintain the premises in a safe condition and he can't shift (delegate) that duty to someone else. The landlord is therefore legally responsible for the injury. (*Srithong v. Total Investment Company*, 23 Cal. App.4th 721 (1994).) Of course, you can also look to the contractor's insurance company for compensation as well; however, many contractors do not carry insurance.

Likewise, if a landlord's agent, such as a resident manager, assaults or sexually harasses a tenant, a landlord can be held liable for the resident manager's actions. (See Chapter 11.)

The Injury Was Caused by a Criminal Act on the Premises

Oftentimes inadequate security or other lapses by the landlord result in allowing criminal conduct by a third party, which causes the tenant injury. This could happen because a parking lot lacks adequate lighting at night, or the front door to an apartment in a high crime area does not have a working lock. A landlord's duties regarding adequate security are discussed in Chapter 6 (Major Repairs & Maintenance) and Chapter 11 (Crime on the Premises).

Previously, landlords had no legal responsibility because the connection between the landlord's failure to exercise care and the criminal act of an unrelated party was considered by the courts as too remote. Modern courts have recognized the connection between the failure to exercise care (such as leaving in place a non-working door lock) and a foreseeable crime (such as a burglary).

How can you determine whether your landlord failed to exercise reasonable care when it comes to security? That involves the same kind of analysis we went through when asking the question for a non-crime injury (see "The Landlord Did Not Exercise Reasonable Care," above). But in a security context, we have to place special emphasis on the foreseeability of the injury and the cost to the landlord to prevent the injury. For instance, in *Vasquez v. Residential Investments, Inc.,* 118 Cal. App.4th 269 (2004), the court held a landlord civilly liable for the murder of one of his tenants when the landlord failed to repair the front door, allowing her boyfriend to enter and later kill her. It reasoned that the cost to repair the front door was minimal while the risk of a criminal intruder was foreseeable. By contrast, *Castenada v. Olsher,* 41 Cal.4th 1205 (2007) refused to hold a landlord liable for a mobile home park tenant injured by gang members. The court stated that there was no evidence that the landlord knew of violent gang confrontations and that the landlord did not have a duty to hire security guards or install brighter lights in the park.

These types of cases are complicated and often hotly contested. (See Chapter 11, Crime on the Premises). Seek legal advice if you find yourself injured because of a criminal act on the premises.

If You're at Fault, Too

If you sue your landlord for negligence, the landlord may turn right around and accuse you of negligence, too. And if you are partially to blame for your injury, the landlord's liability for your losses will be reduced accordingly.

Your Own Carelessness

If you are also guilty of unreasonable carelessness —for example, you were drunk and, as a result, didn't (or couldn't) watch your step when you tripped on a loose tread on a poorly maintained stairway—the landlord's liability will be proportionately reduced.

The legal principle is called "comparative negligence." Basically, this means that if you are partially at fault, you can collect only part of the value of your losses. For example, if a judge or jury ruled that you had suffered $10,000 in damages (such as medical costs or lost earnings) but that you were 20% at fault, you would recover only $8,000. If you're 99% at fault, you'll receive only 1% of your damages from your landlord.

Your Risk-Taking

Carelessness on your part is not the only way that your monetary recovery can be reduced. If you deliberately chose to act in a way that caused or worsened your injury, another doctrine may apply. Called "assumption of risk," it refers to a tenant who knows the danger of a certain action and decides to take the chance anyway.

> **EXAMPLE:** In a hurry to get to work, you take a shortcut to the garage by cutting across an abandoned strip of pavement that you know has an uneven, broken surface. You disregard the sign posted by your landlord: "Danger: Use Front Walkway Only." If you trip and hurt your knee, you'll have a hard time pinning blame on your landlord, because you deliberately chose a dangerous route to the garage.

How Much Money You're Entitled To

If you were injured on your landlord's property and have convinced an insurance adjuster or jury that the landlord is responsible, at least in part, you can ask for monetary compensation, called "compensatory damages." Injured tenants can recover the money they have lost (wages) and spent (doctors' bills), plus compensation for physical pain and suffering, mental anguish, and lost opportunities.

Medical care and related expenses. You can recover for doctors' and physical therapists' bills, including future care. Even if your bills were covered by your own insurance company or medical plan, you can still sue for the amounts—but your insurance company may come after you, via a lien claim, if you recover anything in excess of your copayments or deductibles.

Missed work time. You can sue for lost wages and income while you were unable to work and undergoing treatment for your injuries. You can also recover for expected losses due to continuing care. The fact that you used sick or vacation pay to cover your time off from work is irrelevant. You are entitled to save this pay to use at your discretion at other times. In short, using up vacation or sick pay is considered the same as losing the pay itself.

Pain and other physical suffering. The type of injury you have suffered and its expected duration will affect the amount you can demand for pain and suffering. A certain amount of pain and suffering can be expected from a serious injury. For instance, if you break your arm, physical pain can be expected for a period of time and you won't have to spend a lot of energy proving that you were in pain. But if you are claiming pain beyond what one would normally expect for your type of injury, you are much better off if you have medical documentation to back it up. For instance, if your doctor has prescribed strong antipain medication, you'll have some objective corroboration of your distress. And the longer your recovery period, the greater your pain and suffering.

Permanent physical disability or disfigurement. If your injury has clear long-lasting or permanent effects—such as scars, back or joint stiffness, or a significant reduction in your mobility—the amount of your damages goes way up.

Loss of family, social, career, and educational experiences or opportunities. If you can demonstrate that the injury prevented you from advancing in your job or landing a better one, you can ask for compensation representing the lost income. Of course, it's hard to prove that missing a job interview resulted in income loss (after all, you didn't yet have the job). But the possibility that you might have moved ahead may be enough to convince the insurance company to sweeten their offer.

Emotional damages resulting from any of the above. Emotional distress—including stress, anxiety, worry, fear, embarrassment, depression, and strains on family relationships— can be compensated. Often these reactions have physical manifestations such as nausea, difficulty sleeping, crying, binge eating, and the like. Like pain and suffering, however, it's easier to prove if you have a therapist, physician, or counselor to substantiate your claim. If you have consulted a therapist, physician, or counselor, their evaluations of your reported symptoms can serve as proof of your problems. Be aware, however, that when you choose to sue for mental or emotional injuries, your doctor's notes and files regarding your symptoms and treatment will usually be made available to the other side.

In some cases, injured tenants can collect more than compensatory damages. A judge or jury may award punitive damages if it decides that the landlord acted outrageously, either intentionally or with extreme carelessness (recklessness). Punitive damages are punishments for this conduct.

Environmental Hazards

Because of some relatively recent changes in the law, landlords are expected to deal with some serious environmental health hazards. Simply put, laws now require landlords to take steps to ensure that you and your family aren't sickened by several common hazards, including lead, asbestos, and radon. Recently, the presence of mold has gotten the attention of landlords, tenants, and legislators.

This chapter explains landlords' obligations and offers some suggestions on how to spot problem areas, work with the landlord (or housing authorities), and take steps to protect yourself.

Duty to Disclose Presence of Environmental Hazards

Because materials such as asbestos and lead are so dangerous to health, both the state legislature and Congress have enacted laws and regulations regarding disclosure of these hazards, as well as the proper method for removing them from a building. Many landlords include with their lease packages standard form notifications regarding asbestos, lead, and mold.

- **Asbestos.** A landlord of a property built before 1981 has an obligation to notify tenants of the presence of asbestos-containing materials or presumed asbestos-containing materials if he knows or should know of their presence at the property. (29 C.F.R. 1926.1101(k)(2)(ii)(D).)
- **Lead.** An owner also has an obligation to notify tenants about the presence of lead at the property. (24 C.F.R. part 35.)
- **Mold.** If a landlord knows or has reasonable cause to believe that there are dangerous levels of mold at a property, he is required to notify all prospective and current tenants. (H&S §§ 26147(a), 26148(b).)
- **Bedbugs.** Landlords are required to provide new tenants with specified information about bedbugs, similar in nature to that provided regarding asbestos and lead (CC § 1954.603).

Civil Code Section 1954.602 prohibits landlords from renting a unit that they know has a current bedbug infestation.

Landlords are required to notify you about these hazards before you move in and during the tenancy if new, relevant information comes to light. Renovation also triggers notification. For example, if construction at the property may disturb asbestos or lead-based paint, or if the landlord learns about dangerous levels of mold at the property, tenants must be informed. Likewise, a landlord (or a registered pest control company) is required to notify tenants about the application of pesticides at the property. (CC §§ 1940.8, 1940.85; B&P § 8538.)

Finally, tenants must notify the landlord when they know or should know that asbestos has been disturbed. (H&S § 25359.7(b).) We highly recommend that you notify the landlord whenever you become aware of any environmental hazard.

Asbestos

Exposure to asbestos has long been linked to an increased risk of cancer, particularly for workers in the asbestos manufacturing industry or in construction jobs involving the use of asbestos materials. More recently, the danger of asbestos in homes has also been recognized.

Homes built before the mid-1970s often contain asbestos insulation around heating systems. Many homes had their ceilings sprayed with an asbestos slurry that resulted in a "popcorn" texture. Until 1981, asbestos was also present in other building materials, such as vinyl flooring and tiles. Asbestos that is intact (or covered up) is generally not a problem, and the current wisdom is to leave it in place but monitor it for signs of deterioration. However, asbestos that has begun to break down and enter the air—for example, when it is disturbed during maintenance or renovation work—can become a significant health problem for people who breathe it.

OSHA Regulations

Until quite recently, landlords had no legal obligation to test for the presence of asbestos absent clear evidence that it was likely to be a health hazard. Now, owners of buildings constructed before 1981 must install warning labels, train staff, and notify people who work in areas that might contain asbestos. Unless the owner rules out the presence of asbestos by having a licensed inspector test the property, the law presumes that asbestos is present.

The U.S. Occupational Safety and Health Administration (OSHA) wrote these requirements to protect people who might be working in these buildings. But they also apply to tenants. "Guidance for Controlling Asbestos-containing Materials in Buildings," June, 1985, EPA 560/5-85-024 is a helpful summary of these requirements. California has additional requirements that can be found in Health and Safety Code Section 25915 and following and California Code of Regulations, Title VII, Section 1529. In the process of complying with OSHA's requirements to inform and protect employees or outside contractors, your landlord will learn whether there is asbestos on the property and (based on its type and quantity) what must be done to protect the workers. But when landlords know about the presence of any dangerous defect on the rental property, regardless of the way they learned it, the law requires the landlord to take reasonable steps to make sure that tenants aren't harmed. Inhaling airborne asbestos creates such a significant health risk that the law requires landlords to act with extreme care when dealing with asbestos that has been disturbed.

OSHA regulations cover two classes of materials: those that definitely contain asbestos (such as certain kinds of flooring and ceilings) and those that the law presumes contain asbestos. The second class is extremely inclusive, describing, among other things, any surfacing material that is "sprayed, troweled on, or otherwise applied." Under this definition, virtually every dwelling built before 1980 must be suspected of containing asbestos. Asbestos or asbestos-containing materials are typically found in or on:

- sprayed-on "cottage cheese" ceilings
- acoustic tile ceilings
- vinyl flooring, and
- insulation around heating and hot water pipes.

OSHA and California laws outline the landlord's obligations for testing asbestos, removing it from the premises, notifying tenants of construction that will require protecting workers (and indirectly tenants), cleanup, and disposal.

- **Testing.** Landlords must test for asbestos when undertaking significant repairs.
- **Notification.** Signs must be posted whenever construction work involves disturbance of asbestos-containing materials.
- **Removal.** Workers must be specially trained in the removal of asbestos, and must follow strict procedures for removal. These often include containment of work areas, air monitoring, and regular cleanup.
- **Disposal.** Asbestos-containing materials cannot be dumped in the trash or a dumpster. They must be disposed of in specified "hazardous waste dumps."

Deteriorating Asbestos: An Obvious, Dangerous Defect

Problems with asbestos often arise when neither the landlord nor the tenant realizes that the material is embedded in ceilings and floors. Sometimes, however, the situation is not so subtle. Deteriorating asbestos that is open and obvious is a dangerous defect that your landlord must address pronto. It's no different from a broken front step or an inoperable front door lock. As the owner, the landlord is responsible for fixing conditions that could cause significant injury.

When the Landlord Must Test for Asbestos

Landlords are required to comply with OSHA's asbestos testing and protective rules when they undertake major remodeling or renovation jobs of buildings built before 1981. This also applies when they undertake lesser projects (such as the preparation of an asbestos-containing ceiling or wall for repainting). Even relatively noninvasive custodial work—such as stripping floor tiles containing asbestos—comes within the long reach of OSHA.

OSHA has concluded that buildings built after 1981 are unlikely to contain asbestos, but if your post-1981 building does have asbestos (perhaps the builder or remodeler used recycled building materials), OSHA regulations cover it, too.

Protection From Asbestos

OSHA is very specific regarding the level of training, work techniques, and protective clothing for employees whose work involves disturbing asbestos. But they do not specifically address the measures that a landlord must take to protect tenants from exposure (for example, contractors often use plastic sheeting to contain the dust and fibers). However, the worker protection requirements give very useful clues as to what you can reasonably expect from your landlord in the way of tenant protections. In short, the more your landlord must do to protect workers, the more she must do to warn and protect tenants, too. If she doesn't and you are injured as a result, she risks being found liable. (See Chapter 9.) OSHA and California Laws regulate asbestos testing.

- **Custodial work.** At the low end of the asbestos-disturbing spectrum, workers doing custodial work—for example, stripping the floor tiles in the lobby—must be trained (and supervised by a trained superior) in safe asbestos-handling techniques. Before the work begins, the landlord is required to post at the site where and when asbestos will be disturbed. The landlord should also make sure that tenants, their guests, and children don't come into contact with the debris or are exposed to dust. Conscientious landlords will use written notices to alert tenants, and place cones and caution tape around the area. Even more prudent landlords will "contain" the area by using plastic sheeting.

- **Major repairs, renovations, or remediation.** If the landlord plans renovation or repair work for a pre-1981 building, whether in a common area or in an individual unit, the landlord must test for asbestos. If the tests show that asbestos is present, the landlord must provide more protection, including air monitoring, protective clothing, and medical surveillance of workers. You are entitled to appropriate warnings, and your landlord should minimize your exposure through fastidious work site procedures and isolation of dangerous materials.

EXAMPLE: Sally returned home to her apartment to find that workers were removing the ugly, stained ceiling tile in the lobby and hallways. She learned from the contractor that the project would last four days. Sally was concerned that her young sons, returning home from school in the afternoon and curious about the renovations, would hang around the halls and lobby or at least pass through them as they went in and out to play. Either way, Sally's sons would be exposed to the airborne fibers. Sally wrote a note to the landlord, explaining her concerns.

Sally's landlord recognized the reasonableness of her fears and the potential for injury. He spoke with the contractor, one who had been specially trained and licensed in asbestos removal, and arranged for the work to be done between the hours of 8 a.m. and 3 p.m. He insisted, and the contractor readily agreed, that the old tiles be removed and any asbestos-containing material covered at the end of each work day. Finally, the landlord hired two adults to monitor foot traffic in and around the renovation site, to ensure that no one lingered near the workers or came into contact with the removed materials.

How to Determine If Asbestos Is in Your Rental

You may learn of the presence of asbestos when your landlord tests in preparation for major renovations. Or, it might be obvious to you if, for example, the textured ceiling begins to slough off. Are there other ways to learn that asbestos is present?

You can't identify asbestos just by looking at it. Only someone trained in fiber identification using a special polarized light microscope can tell for sure. State-certified labs throughout California can identify asbestos in building materials. Contact a lab to find out how the sample should be collected and sent for testing. It's not an expensive test and should cost about $35 per sample. There's a list of labs on the Department of Public Health website at www.cdph.ca.gov (look for the Indoor Air Quality Program and choose asbestos). Because any amount of asbestos is potentially harmful, for your own safety you should closely follow the procedures for collecting the samples.

Alerting and Motivating Your Landlord

Many landlords, unfortunately, have no idea about their duty to deal with the risks posed by asbestos. If you live in an older building and suspect that there is asbestos on the premises that is not being managed properly, alert your landlord and see to it that your health is protected. Here are some strategies.

When the asbestos is obvious but intact. Asbestos that is intact—for example, asbestos insulation that is covered with foil or wrapped with tape—probably does not pose a significant health risk to you, since the fibers can't enter the air. It is important, however, that asbestos be monitored for signs of deterioration. For example, if the tape wrapping is tearing or falling away, it is no longer doing its job of containment. If you are worried about whether asbestos-containing materials in your home are dangerous, ask your landlord, in writing, to have the material inspected by a trained professional.

CAUTION

Never disturb asbestos-containing materials. Don't drill holes in walls or ceilings that contain asbestos, or sand asbestos tiles in preparation for a new coat of paint. First, you want to protect your health. Second, intentionally disturbing asbestos will almost certainly reduce, if not defeat, any legal claim you might have if your health is harmed by an asbestos-related problem. The law won't hold your landlord responsible for an injury that you deliberately courted, ignoring a risk you knew about.

When deteriorating asbestos is obvious. Take immediate action if asbestos in your living space has begun to break down or slough off. Asbestos-containing materials that have begun to break down are extremely dangerous. Small particles become airborne and, if inhaled, may become lodged in your lungs. If airborne asbestos is present in your living space, it might make your premises legally uninhabitable. (See Chapter 6 for your legal options, which may include withholding rent. Also, the text below discusses the option of moving out.) Immediate action is required. A sample letter from a tenant concerned about deteriorating asbestos is shown below.

How do I know whether work is being done properly? Asbestos abatement procedures are complicated and can only be done by people who are specially trained and licensed to do it. For instance, workers usually have to wear respirators and special protective clothing, put up plastic containment chambers to keep the asbestos from spreading throughout the unit or building, and post signs warning people in the area that asbestos is being disturbed. If you believe that asbestos removal is being done and you do not see the above safety measures in action, then unlicensed persons are likely doing the work. For the sake of your own health and that of the workers, you need to take immediate action, as explained just below.

TIP

Keep copies of all correspondence regarding asbestos or other environmental health hazards. If your landlord fails to take the right steps and you want to move out or seek other legal remedies, you'll need to be able to prove that you notified the landlord of the problem and waited a reasonable amount of time for a response.

Sample Letter or Email Regarding Deteriorating Asbestos

37 Ninth Avenue North
Central City, California 00000
312-555-4567

February 28, 20xx

Margaret Mears
3757 East Seventh Street
Central City, California 00000

Dear Ms. Mears:

As you know, the ceilings in my apartment are sprayed-on acoustical plaster. I have begun to notice an excessive amount of fine, white dust in the apartment, and I believe it is the result of the breakdown of the plaster. I am quite concerned about this. Because the building was built before 1978, this material is presumed to contain asbestos, unless proven otherwise, and inhaling asbestos can cause serious illness. Please contact me immediately so that you can take a look and arrange for a licensed inspector to examine the ceilings.

Yours truly,

Terry Lu

Terry Lu

When custodial or repair work is done improperly.
When it comes to asbestos removal, the people who suffer most from a landlord's disregard of workplace safety are usually the workers themselves. But improper asbestos removal or disturbance is likely to affect you, too. Fortunately, there is something you can do about it. OSHA wants to hear about violations of workplace safety rules. You can reach OSHA by calling the phone number listed below in "Asbestos Resources." The California Department of Industrial Relations is the state equivalent of OSHA, and you can contact it, too (see "Asbestos Resources" for details, below).

Sample Letter or Email Requesting Reimbursement for Temporary Housing

1289 Central Avenue, Apartment 8
Anytown, CA 00000
713-555-7890

June 13, 20xx

Mr. Frank Brown, Owner
Sunshine Properties
75 Main Street
Anytown, CA 00000

Dear Mr. Brown:

I have just received the notice you sent to all tenants on the first floor, alerting us to your plans to tear out the heating ducts and insulation during the week of July 6. The work will involve removing heating vents inside our apartment and removing the asbestos insulation through the openings. You estimate that the work will take two days for each apartment.

I do not think that it is safe for me and my elderly mother to live in the apartment during this process. I am concerned that we will inhale airborne asbestos fibers that may cause difficulties in breathing. My mother suffers from chronic bronchitis and cannot risk exposure to anything that might worsen the condition. Dr. Jones, who treats my mother, would be happy to corroborate this fact.

I think that the best solution would be for us to move out while this work is being done. The nearby Best California Motel has reasonable rates and would be convenient to our jobs and transportation. Please contact me so that we might discuss this before the renovation work begins. You can call me at home at the above number most nights and weekends.

Finally, because the work involves removing hazardous materials, please provide me with information, including certifications, about the qualified professional who will be overseeing this removal.

Yours truly,

Sharon Rock

Sharon Rock

cc: Dr. Jones

Move Out If Necessary

Sometimes it isn't possible to shield yourself from the effects of deteriorating asbestos, or even your landlord's major repairs or renovations involving asbestos. For example, if the acoustic ceilings in your apartment are being removed, it is unlikely (even if you and your landlord are prepared to take every precaution) that you can avoid inhaling some dangerous airborne fibers. In situations like this, the best alternative might be to move out at least temporarily until the work is completed. (See Chapter 6 for a discussion of moving out because your rental is uninhabitable.) Because the responsibility to repair and maintain the structure is the landlord's, the cost of temporary shelter should be covered by the landlord as long as you can convincingly establish that remaining on the premises would constitute a significant health risk. (See the sample letter or email above.)

If you are able to give valid reasons why you should be temporarily absent while the asbestos removal work is done, and if you have a reasonable landlord who appreciates the potentially serious legal consequences of denying your reasonable request, chances are you'll be able to come to an agreement. (Don't ask to stay at the Ritz, however!)

But what if the landlord stubbornly refuses? Obviously, to protect your health, you'll want to move out anyway. And assuming the asbestos problems really are serious, you should stand a good chance of prevailing in a small claims court lawsuit for the cost of your temporary housing. Be sure to keep a copy of the letter you have sent (preferably by certified mail) to the landlord, a record of the landlord's refusal to pay for temporary accommodations, and all receipts for your expenses.

CAUTION

Protect your possessions. If you decide to move out and leave some of your belongings behind, make sure that they are removed to an area that will not be affected by the work. Asbestos removal often creates dust that could settle anywhere in your unit (that's why proper procedures, including containment, are absolutely essential). Cover or tightly box your belongings.

Remember, disturbing any amount of asbestos is potentially dangerous. Make sure that the asbestos removal and the cleanup afterwards are done properly. If it is not, it may not be safe to move back in. How can you tell? For removal of more than 100 square feet of asbestos-containing materials, certain OSHA requirements kick in.

- The asbestos removal must be supervised by a Certified Asbestos Supervisor or a Certified Asbestos Consultant and Technician. The technician creates the work plan and a safety plan for the removal, and oversees the clean-up afterwards.
- When the work is finished, the technician tests to make sure no asbestos has been left behind.
- A separate company should remove and clean up under the direction of the technician.

The asbestos removal company must be certified by Cal/OSHA. Even projects involving the removal of less than 100 square feet of asbestos-containing material from one site require compliance with the detailed provisions of law (8 CCR § 1529).

If you find that your landlord is trying to cut corners and ignore the requirements of Cal/OSHA, you should think seriously about moving back into a unit that has improperly removed asbestos.

TIP

Come to court prepared with asbestos-related information. If you go to small claims court, be prepared to show test results that confirm the presence of asbestos, along with photos. Be ready to explain the serious dangers of breathing asbestos fibers and why the landlord's work was so invasive that temporarily moving out was your only sensible alternative. (See "Asbestos Resources," below. Also, see Chapter 17 for a discussion of small claims lawsuits.)

Asbestos Resources

For further information on asbestos rules, inspections, and control, contact the nearest office of the U.S. Occupational Safety and Health Administration (OSHA). Find the closest office at www.osha.gov or call 800-321-OSHA (6742). OSHA has lots of information on its website; look for asbestos in the A to Z index at www.osha.gov.

OSHA has also developed interactive computer software for property owners, called "Asbestos Advisor," designed to help identify asbestos and suggest ways to handle it. It may help you, or interested members of any tenants' association in your building, to determine whether asbestos is present and whether your landlord is managing it properly. The "Asbestos Advisor" is available free on OSHA's website, www.osha.gov.

California has a state counterpart to the federal OSHA regulations (the law relevant to landlords is known as California's Asbestos Standards in General Industry (8 CCR § 5208)). Information on state enforcement is on the Department of Industrial Relations website at www.dir.ca.gov/dosh/asbestos.html.

Instead of suing in small claims court, you may be tempted to utilize what the law calls a "repair and deduct" remedy (discussed in Chapter 7) by simply deducting the cost of replacement housing from your rent, or even withholding rent. These are bad ideas, especially if you want to stay in your apartment, or move back in after the work is completed. It's a far better idea to file a straightforward lawsuit asking for reimbursement. Even if you lose the lawsuit, you would not be without a home.

If your landlord refuses to cover temporary housing expenses, you might also want to consider moving out permanently. This option is most appropriate when the risk is great and the length of exposure relatively long. But to justify breaking the lease (and to avoid liability for future rent), you will have to be able to show that airborne asbestos really did make the premises uninhabitable. (See Chapter 6 for a full discussion of breaking the lease due to uninhabitability.) If the landlord is ripping out whole ceilings over a month's time, this argument will be strong. However, it will not amount to much if the landlord is drilling two small holes in the ceiling to install a smoke detector.

Court-Ordered Renovations

In rare instances, local health authorities may sue a landlord who fails to repair code violations in a reasonable time. If a judge rules that the rental property's conditions "substantially endanger the health and safety of residents," and if your landlord must ask you to move in order to make repairs, state law dictates what happens:

- The landlord must provide you with comparable temporary housing nearby (you still pay your original rent to the landlord). If comparable housing isn't possible, the landlord pays the difference between the old rent and your new rent elsewhere, for up to four months.
- The landlord must pay your moving expenses, including packing and unpacking costs.
- The landlord insures your belongings in transit, or pays for the replacement value of property lost, stolen, or damaged in transit.
- The landlord pays your new utility connection charges.
- You must have the first offer to move back in when repairs are completed. (H&S § 17980.7.)

Lead

Exposure to deteriorating lead-based paint and lead water pipes may lead to serious health problems, particularly in children. High exposures in children have been linked to learning difficulties, attention disorders, hyperactivity, and in extreme circumstances, brain damage. Studies show that the effects of lead poisoning can be lifelong, affecting both personality and intelligence. In adults, the effects of lead poisoning can include nerve disorders, high blood pressure, reproductive disorders, and muscle and joint pain.

Lead Inspections

Under California law, landlords are required to maintain premises fee of deteriorated lead-based paint and lead-contaminated soil. Nor should they disturb lead-based paint without proper containment. (H&S § 17920.10.) Somewhat paradoxically, however, inspections for the presence of lead hazards are not required by state or federal law. Still, some landlords voluntarily arrange for an inspection in order to certify on the disclosure form that the property is lead-free and exempt from federal regulations. (See list of exemptions, below.) Also, when a property owner takes out a loan or buys insurance, the bank or insurance company may require a lead inspection.

Professional lead inspectors don't always inspect every unit in large, multifamily properties. Instead, they inspect a sampling of the units and apply their conclusions to the property as a whole. Giving you the results and conclusions of a building-wide evaluation satisfies the law, even if your particular unit was not tested. If, however, your landlord has specific information regarding your unit that is inconsistent with the building-wide evaluation, he or she must disclose it to you.

(For information on arranging a professional lead inspection or using a home testing kit, see "Dealing With Lead on Your Own," below.)

Buildings constructed before 1978 are likely to contain some source of lead: lead-based paint, lead pipes or fixtures, or lead-based solder used on copper pipes. In 1978, the federal government required the reduction of lead in house paint; lead pipes are generally found only in homes built before 1930, and lead-based solder in home plumbing systems was banned in 1988. Pre-1950 housing in poor and urban neighborhoods that has been allowed to deteriorate is by far the greatest source of lead-based paint poisonings.

Discovering (or being told by the landlord) that there is lead on the premises is not necessarily the end of a healthy and safe tenancy. In fact, the mere presence of lead-based paint is not necessarily harmful to health. Lead-based paint is not a health hazard as long as it is intact (which includes being covered by an impermeable layer of a different paint or other substance). The danger arises when old paint becomes loose or chipped, creating lead-based dust or particles that may be inhaled or ingested. The danger posed by lead in the soil depends on its concentration.

Recognizing Lead in Your Home

If your landlord has tested for lead and complied with federal disclosure requirements, you can skip this section. However, most landlords have not tested for lead. There are several clues as to whether there is lead in or around your home, and ways that you (or, ideally, your landlord) can find out for sure.

The easiest and most reliable way to test for lead is to take a sample (for instance, a chip of lead-based paint or soil sample) and mail it to a laboratory that tests for lead. You can easily find a lab by doing an Internet search. Call the lab in advance to find out the correct procedure for obtaining the sample. The lab will mail you the results and let you know whether the paint or soil contains dangerous levels of lead. You can then pass this information on to your landlord.

Paint

Your first step should be to determine the age of the building. If the landlord doesn't know or won't say, go to the local building permit office and ask to see the building's construction permit. If there is no permit on file, you'll have to estimate the structure's age.

As noted above, housing that was built before January 1, 1978, is almost certain to have lead-based paint. But buildings constructed later may have it, too, since the 1978 ban did not include a recall and lead-based paint remained on the shelves.

How Lead Poisoning Occurs

Lead-laden dust caused by the deterioration of exposed lead-based paint is the greatest source of lead poisoning. Falling on windowsills, walls, and floors, this dust makes its way into the human body when it is stirred up, becomes airborne, and is inhaled, or when it is transmitted directly from hand to mouth. Exterior lead-based house paint is also a potential problem because it can slough off walls directly into the soil and be tracked into the house.

Lead dust results from renovations or remodeling —including, unfortunately, those very projects undertaken to rid premises of the lead-based paint. Lead poisoning can also occur from drinking water that contains leached-out lead from lead pipes or from deteriorating lead solder used in copper pipes.

Children between the ages of 18 months and five years are the most likely to be poisoned by lead-based paint. Their poisoning is detected when they become ill or, increasingly, in routine examinations that check for elevated blood levels of lead.

Poisoning most often occurs from continued exposure to deteriorated lead-based paint. If blood levels are high because of this exposure, the levels will go down over time once the cause of the exposure (such as the lead dust) is removed.

Lead Pipes

As lead pipes deteriorate, the amount of lead in the water increases. Pre-1930 construction generally used lead pipes. It's difficult to know for sure whether you have lead pipes until you examine the plumbing. When you look under the sink, you might be able to see the pipe coming out from the wall; if so, look for the tell-tale dark gray color. A plumber should be able to identify the pipes without difficulty. Local water departments will often test the water in your home to see if it contains unsafe levels of lead.

Lead Solder

Lead solder was used to join sections of pipe as recently as 1988. You won't know whether it was used unless you can look at several soldered junctions; even then, you will probably need a plumber to tell you whether the solder was leaded or not.

Imported Vinyl Miniblinds

In 1996, the Consumer Product Safety Commission announced that miniblinds from China, Taiwan, Indonesia, and Mexico are likely to contain lead, which manufacturers add to stabilize the plastic. (American-made blinds may have also contained lead and are now made without lead, and should so state on the package.) As the surface vinyl deteriorates in the sun, lead dust enters the air. Even when landlords know that an apartment has leaded miniblinds, they don't have to tell tenants *unless* they know that the blinds have begun to deteriorate and produce lead dust. Be smart: Ask the landlord to replace old blinds now, before a problem occurs.

Soil

For decades, American cars ran on leaded gasoline —and the effects are still with us. Exhaust from lead-burning cars contains lead, which falls to the ground where it remains, relatively inert, for years. Neighborhoods adjacent to heavily traveled roadways have significant amounts of lead in the soil; the readings drop off dramatically as the distance from the roads increases. If you live near a busy freeway or throughway, assume the worst and take care of yourself. (See "Getting the Landlord to Act," below, for suggestions on self-help.)

During renovation work

As we explained at the outset, lead is a problem when it has begun to deteriorate. Renovation work often includes removing or sanding painted surfaces; and when the paint is lead-based, this can result in lead paint dust, which can be inhaled or ingested.

As with asbestos removal, renovating that includes disturbing lead-based paint requires special training and specified procedures. If you think that renovations in your rented space or the common areas are causing lead particles to become airborne or potentially airborne, you need to act very quickly. Notify the landlord of your concerns, but also notify local officials such as the health department or the building or housing departments. Tell the inspectors that construction work is causing lead-based dust to become airborne.

Federal Protections

Unfortunately, neither federal nor state law requires landlords to test for lead, However, Health and Safety Code Section 17920.10 requires the landlord to remove all "lead hazards." Still, the laws aimed at reducing lead poisoning do give some important benefits to tenants. At the least, if the landlord knows there are lead paint hazards on the premises, you're entitled to know that.

Lead-Based Paint Disclosure

All property owners must inform tenants, before they sign or renew a lease or rental agreement, of any information they possess on lead paint hazard conditions on the property. Owners must also provide the tenant with a pamphlet, "Protect Your Family from Lead in Your Home." This information will help you know what to look for if you think lead might be a problem. If the property has been tested (testing must be done only by state-certified lead inspectors), a copy of the report, or a summary written by the inspector, must be shown to tenants.

With certain exceptions (listed below), every lease and rental agreement must include a disclosure page, even if the landlord has not tested. You can see the federally approved disclosure form "Disclosure of Information on Lead-Based Paint or Lead-Based Paint Hazards" by going to the Environmental Protection Agency's website, www.epa.gov/lead.

If you were a tenant in your current home on December 6, 1996, your landlord must comply with these disclosure requirements according to whether you are a tenant with a lease or are renting month to month.

- **Tenants with leases.** Your landlord need not comply until your lease is up and you renew or stay on as a month-to-month tenant.
- **Month-to-month tenants.** Your landlord should have given you a disclosure statement when you wrote your first rent check dated after December 6, 1996 (September 6, 1996, if the landlord owns five or more units).

Rental Properties Exempt From Federal Regulations

- Housing for which a construction permit was obtained, or on which construction was started, after January 1, 1978. Older buildings that have been completely renovated since 1978 are *not* exempt, even if every painted surface was removed or replaced.
- Housing certified as lead-free by a state-accredited lead inspector. Lead-free means the absence of any lead paint—even paint that has been completely painted over and encapsulated.
- Lofts, efficiencies, studios, and other "zero-bedroom" units, including dormitory housing and rentals in sorority and fraternity houses. University-owned apartments and married student housing are not exempt.
- Short-term vacation rentals.
- A single room rented in a residential home.
- Housing designed for persons with disabilities (as explained in HUD's Fair Housing Accessibility Guidelines, 24 C.F.R., Ch. I, Subchapter A, App. II) *unless* any child less than six years old resides there or is expected to reside there.
- Retirement communities (housing designed for seniors, where one or more tenant is at least 62 years old) *unless* children under the age of six are present or expected to live there.

Information

The landlord must give all tenants the lead hazard information booklet "Protect Your Family From Lead in Your Home," written by the Environmental Protection Agency (EPA). If they choose, landlords may reproduce the booklet in a legal-size, 8½ x 14-inch format, and attach it to the lease. California's pamphlet, "Residential Environmental Hazards A Guide for Homeowners, Homebuyers, Landlords and Tenants," is a legally approved substitute. (You'll find this on the California Department of Public Health website at www.cdph.ca.gov.)

If your landlord has not given you a disclosure form or an EPA booklet, ask for them. If you get no results, notify the EPA. This will probably result in no more than a letter or call from the inspectors, since the EPA will usually not cite landlords unless their noncompliance with the laws is willful, widespread, and continuing. But a landlord who continues to ignore the law may be subject to the penalties described below.

Enforcement and Penalties

HUD and the EPA enforce renters' rights to know about the presence of lead-based paint by using "testers," as they do when looking for illegal discrimination (see Chapter 4). Posing as applicants, testers who get the rental will document whether landlords disclosed lead paint information when they signed the lease or rental agreement. Of course, individual complaints from tenants who have not received the required booklets can trigger an investigation, too.

Landlords who fail to distribute the required information booklet, or who do not give tenants the disclosure statement, may be fined up to $16,000 per violation for willful and continuing noncompliance.

Government testers are also on the lookout for property owners who falsely claim that they have no knowledge of lead-based paint hazards on their property. Here's how it often comes up: A tenant complains to HUD if he becomes ill with lead poisoning after the landlord told him that she knew of no lead-based paint hazards on the premises. If HUD decides to investigate whether, in fact, the landlord knew about the hazard and failed to tell this tenant, their investigators get access to the landlord's records. They comb leasing, maintenance, and repair files—virtually the landlord's entire business records. If HUD finds evidence that the landlord knew (or had reason to know) of lead paint hazards, such as a contract from a painting firm that includes costs for lead paint removal or a loan document indicating the presence of lead paint, the landlord will be hard-pressed to explain why she's checked the box on the disclosure form stating that she has no reports or records regarding the presence of lead-based paint on the property. The tenant, in turn, will have good evidence to use in court.

Federal Rules Covering Renovations

When landlords renovate occupied rental units or common areas in buildings constructed before 1978, EPA regulations require that current tenants receive lead hazard information before the renovation work begins. (40 C.F.R. §§ 745.80–88.)

The obligation to distribute lead information rests with the "renovator." If the landlord hires an outside contractor to perform renovation work, the contractor is the renovator. But if the landlord, property manager, superintendent, or other employees perform the renovation work, the landlord is the renovator and is obliged to give you the required information.

The type of information that the renovator must give you depends on where the renovation is taking place. If the landlord is working on an occupied rental unit, resident tenants must get a copy of the EPA pamphlet "Protect Your Family From Lead in Your Home" (even if you already got one when you moved in). If common areas will be affected, the landlord must distribute a notice to every rental unit in the building.

What Qualifies as a Renovation?

According to EPA regulations, a "renovation" is any change to an occupied rental unit or common area of the building that disturbs painted surfaces. Here are some examples:

- removing or modifying a painted door, wall, baseboard, or ceiling
- scraping or sanding paint, or
- removing a large structure like a wall, partition, or window.

Not every renovation triggers the federal law, though. There are four big exceptions:

Emergency renovations. If a sudden or unexpected event, such as a fire or flood, requires emergency repairs to a rental unit or to the property's common areas, there's no need to distribute lead hazard information to tenants before work begins.

Minor repairs or maintenance. Minor work that affects two square feet or less of a painted surface is also exempt. Minor repairs include routine electrical and plumbing work, so long as no more than six square feet of the wall, ceiling, or other painted surface gets disturbed by the work, or 20 square feet or less on the exterior.

Renovations in lead-free properties. If a licensed inspector has certified that the rental unit or building in which the renovation takes place contains no lead paint, the landlord isn't required to give out the required information.

Common area renovations in buildings with three or fewer units. Tenants in buildings with three or fewer units are not entitled to information about common area renovations.

If your landlord has repainted a rental unit in preparation for your arrival, this won't qualify as a "renovation" unless accompanied by sanding, scraping, or other surface preparation activities that may generate paint dust. Minor "spot" scraping or sanding can qualify for the "minor repairs and maintenance" exception if no more than two square feet of paint is disturbed on any surface to be painted. (EPA Interpretive Guidance, Part I, May 28, 1999.)

Receiving the EPA Pamphlet When Your Rental Is Renovated

Before starting a renovation to an occupied rental unit, the renovator must give the EPA pamphlet "Renovate Right: Important Lead Hazard Information for Families, Child Care Providers, and Schools" to at least one adult occupant of the unit being occupied, preferably the tenant. This requirement applies to all rental properties, including single-family homes and duplexes, unless the property has been certified lead-free by a licensed inspector.

The renovator may mail or hand-deliver the pamphlet to you. If the landlord mails it, he must get a "certificate of mailing" from the post office dated at least seven days before the renovation work begins. You should get the pamphlet 60 days (or fewer) before the work begins (delivering the pamphlet more than 60 days in advance won't satisfy the landlord's obligations under the law).

Notice of Common Area Renovation

If the building has four or more units, the renovator —be it the landlord or his contractor—must notify tenants of all "affected units" about the renovation and tell them how to obtain a free copy of the EPA pamphlet "Protect Your Family From Lead in Your Home." (C.F.R. § 745.84(b)(2).) In most cases, common area renovations will affect all units in the property, meaning that all tenants must be notified about the renovation. But when renovating a "limited use common area" in a large apartment building, such as the 16th floor hallway but no others, the landlord need only notify those units serviced by, or in close proximity to, the limited use common area. The EPA defines large buildings as those having 50 or more units.

To comply, the renovator must deliver a notice to every affected unit describing the nature and location of the renovation work, its location, and the dates the renovator expects to begin and finish work. If the renovator can't provide specific dates, he may use terms like "on or about," "in early June," or "in late July" to describe expected starting and ending dates for the renovation. The notices must be delivered within 60 days before work begins. The notices may be slipped under apartment doors or given to any adult occupant of the rental unit. Landlords may not mail the notices.

Penalties

Failing to give tenants the required information about renovation lead hazards can result in harsh penalties. Renovators who knowingly violate the regulations can get hit with a penalty of up to $25,000 per day for each violation, and willful violations can also result in imprisonment. (40 C.F.R. § 745.87; 15 U.S.C. § 2615.)

RESOURCE

Lead regulations and laws. The Residential Lead-Based Paint Hazard Reduction Act was enacted in 1992 to reduce lead levels. It is commonly referred to as Title X [Ten] (42 U.S.C. § 4852d). The Environmental Protection Agency (EPA) has written regulations that explain how landlords should implement lead hazard reduction (24 C.F.R. Part 35 and 40 C.F.R. Part 745). California has enacted several statutes that target workplaces and schools, and focus on childhood poisoning prevention. (For more information, see "Resources: Lead," below.)

Dealing With Lead on Your Own

You don't need to automatically move out of a rental that contains lead. Remember, only deteriorating lead is the culprit.

If you have seen some deterioration and have confirmed that lead is present by doing the testing suggested above, it might be time to alert your landlord in writing. Your landlord should hire a professional to evaluate the situation and present a "scope of work" to "remediate" the lead. Unfortunately, not all landlords appreciate the dangers that lead may present. If your landlord refuses to take proper steps, you may have to act on your own. If you can afford it, we recommend that you hire a certified

lead inspector or a certified lead risk assessor. That person will assess the presence and extent of lead and recommend appropriate steps to deal with it. You may also ask the inspector about precautions you can take to limit your exposure.

An individual assessment of your home is the best way to determine if there is a problem, the extent of the problem, and what should be done to make your home safe. If you cannot afford such an assessment, here are examples of some precautions recommended by professionals:

- Vacuum thoroughly and regularly, using a "HEPA" ("high energy particle arresting") vacuum that will filter out the fine lead dust. Ask your landlord to provide one.
- Even where a unit has been repainted, the old lead paint layer will eventually be reexposed if the surface gets a lot of wear, such as door and windowsill areas. Wash them with a phosphate-based cleaner or a solution (like "Leadisolve") designed for lead pickup.

CAUTION

Don't disturb lead paint in buildings built before 1978. Do not sand walls, windowsills, doors, or other surfaces—you'll risk releasing lead into the air (possibly even from paint several layers down), creating the very hazards you are attempting to avoid. Only painters who have been trained and equipped to capture and remove lead dust and chips should undertake renovations of this order. If you knowingly disturb lead and suffer an injury, it will be difficult to place legal responsibility on your landlord.

- If your unit has lead pipes or copper pipe with lead solder, draw water out of the pipes by letting the taps run for 60 seconds before using—even if you plan to boil it for tea. Don't use hot water for cooking. Better yet, use bottled water for drinking and cooking.
- If lead is in the soil outside, provide throw rugs at each entrance or ask folks to remove their shoes before entering.

- Consider covering lead-laced soil with sod or an impermeable material.
- If your household has young children (especially those who are still crawling), use extra care to clean floors, especially around windows. Wash children's toys and hands frequently, and clean pacifiers and bottles after they fall on the floor.
- Test your children for lead poisoning. Elevated blood levels in young children can be picked up in a simple blood test. Increasingly, the test is done as part of routine checkups. If you live in a building that you suspect places your child at risk for lead poisoning, you need this information to protect your child. The Centers for Disease Control and Prevention recommend giving children a blood level test at age six months to one year. Do follow-up tests as needed.

CAUTION

If a child's blood level is high, discuss your living situation with your doctor. Include your landlord's response to your requests that he remove the lead-based paint. If you have done lead testing, show those test results to the doctor. Your next step might be to see a lawyer, and if your doctor suggests that you consider moving out, you should definitely find an attorney who can give you some guidance on next steps.

Getting the Landlord to Act

Landlords are required to remove known lead hazards once they become aware of them. H&S § 17920.10.) Getting your landlord to hire qualified contractors to remove the hazard might be difficult. But even the most penurious, callous, or shortsighted landlord might respond to a threat to the bottom line.

Many landlords have learned (sometimes the hard way) that testing for lead and taking measures before tenants get sick is well worth the cost and time. Although landlords aren't liable for lead poisoning unless it can be shown that they knew that lead was present, these days it is increasingly difficult for landlords to plausibly argue that they were ignorant of this well-publicized issue. The cost of testing, risk assessment, and lead management pales in comparison to potential legal liability if, for instance, a child is poisoned by lead-based paint.

Notify the Landlord of Problems

If you discover a lead hazard on the property, tell the landlord at once, in writing. A sample letter or email is shown below.

Sample Letter or Email Regarding Lead Test Results

45 East Avenue North
Central City, CA 00000
816-555-7890

February 28, 20xx

Lester Levine
3757 East Seventh Street
Central City, CA 00000

Dear Mr. Levine:

We recently hired the environmental engineering firm of Checkit & Howe to test our duplex for the presence of lead-based paint. A report of their findings is enclosed. As you can see, there is indeed old, unstable lead paint on most of the windowsills and in the upstairs hall.

We are concerned about the effect that this deteriorating paint will have on the health of our children, aged three months and three years. At a minimum, we would like to discuss a safe and effective response to this problem. Please contact us as soon as possible so that we can arrange a meeting. We're home in the evenings and on weekends.

Yours truly,

Maynard G. and Zelda Krebs
Maynard G. and Zelda Krebs

Encl: Report of Checkit & Howe

Although the goal of your efforts is a safe place to live, not a successful lawsuit, don't lose sight of the fact that your landlord may avoid liability for lead injuries unless you can show that the landlord knew (or should have known) of lead hazards and failed to take reasonable steps to reduce them. In short, if you believe there is a lead risk on your property, you want to make it impossible for the landlord to plausibly deny knowing about it. If you use a kit to test your rental unit or its water supply and find the presence of lead, send the results (certified mail) to the landlord. If your child has elevated blood levels, do the same. Keep these receipts and any other evidence of the landlord's knowledge, such as notes of a conversation in which the landlord acknowledged the presence of pre-1978, chipping paint but refused to buy a HEPA vacuum.

TIP

Educate your landlord. If the landlord isn't aware of the potential liability for lead poisoning, try this tactic: Go to the websites mentioned below in "Resources: Lead" and print the pages or pamphlets that explain the risks to landlords who ignore the writing (and the paint) on the wall.

Involve State, Local, or Federal Inspectors

Under state law and the ordinances of some cities (such as San Francisco), health inspectors have the power to inspect and order cleanups when a tenant complains to their enforcement agencies or reports a child's elevated blood level. (H&S §§ 124160, 124165.) You can also report a lead problem to your local EPA office (for contact information, see "Resources: Lead," below).

Repair and Deduct

The repair and deduct remedy, discussed in Chapter 6, is also available to remove lead hazards as described in Health and Safety Code Section 17920.10. But remember, you can use repair and deduct only twice per year; and the amount you can claim each time can't be more than one month's rent. If removing the lead hazard will cost more than two months' rent, this remedy might not be available to you.

Consider a Lawsuit

Some lead-management measures, such as scrupulous housekeeping, are more time-consuming than expensive. However, money enters the picture when there's so much lead dust that containment is the only reasonable response—for example, sealing lead-based paint by covering it with a durable finish. If actual removal of the painted surfaces is necessary (perhaps the underlying structure is so deteriorated that it must be replaced), considerable expense is in the offing.

Forcing the landlord to deal with lead on the property will involve asking a judge to issue an order that directs that the work be accomplished in a certain way within a certain time. Lawsuits like this cannot be filed in small claims court. These lawsuits are typically complicated affairs that require lawyers. They can be very effective when a group of tenants sue together. (See Chapter 18 for suggestions on finding and working with a lawyer.)

If you spend time and money dealing with lead containment—using special detergents or vacuums, devoting extra time to fastidious housekeeping, putting up with the intrusion of contractors trying to deal with the lead problem—ask your landlord to reduce the rent accordingly. After all, these expenses are necessitated by the dilapidation of the property. If the landlord refuses and you have a lease requiring that you live in the unit for months or years, consider going to small claims court for an order reducing your rent, and ask that you be compensated for past labor and expenses, too. (See Chapter 7 and *Everybody's Guide to Small Claims Court in California,* by Cara O'Neill (Nolo), for help.)

Resources: Lead

Information on the evaluation and control of lead dust, and copies of the "Protect Your Family From Lead in Your Home" pamphlet, may be obtained from the regional offices of the federal EPA or by calling the National Lead Information Center at 800-424-LEAD. Information (including pamphlets on renovation and a parents' guide) is also available from the EPA on its website: www.epa.gov/lead.

The U.S. Occupational Safety and Health Administration (OSHA) has developed interactive software, "Lead in Construction Advisor," that will help you assess the lead problems on your property and design appropriate responses. You can find the program at www.dol.gov.

The U.S. Department of Housing and Urban Development (HUD) issues a pamphlet entitled "Guidance on the Lead-Based Paint Disclosure Rule, Parts I and II," which is available on the HUD website at www.hud.gov.

For a copy of the California Department of Public Health's "Residential Environmental Hazards: A Guide for Homeowners, Homebuyers, Landlords, and Tenants," contact the Department of Public Health at 800-597-LEAD. Their website is www.cdph.ca.gov.

The lead paint renovation rules can be found at 40 C.F.R. Part 745, Federal Register Vol. 63, No. 104, pp. 29908–29921.

Move Out If Necessary

If the risk of lead poisoning is high and cannot be controlled, the smartest move may be moving out. Before making this decision, you should have verification of the existence of the lead (such as lab tests) and its deterioration (good, close-up photos). If you have a child whose blood shows elevated lead, you may want to include a doctor's note on the advisability of moving out. Finally, the advice of an attorney is always recommended when you are considering a step such as this. Here are two scenarios that usually justify a move:

The rental is permeated with lead that you cannot effectively control. If lead constitutes a serious danger to your health—perhaps deteriorating paint has caused a serious lead dust problem, or old lead pipes have contaminated the water supply—you would be justified in breaking the lease and moving out on the grounds that your unit is legally uninhabitable. (See Chapter 6 for more on this topic.) To help counter any possible lawsuit by the landlord against you for future unpaid rent, be sure that you have your evidence in hand, such as a report from an EPA inspector or a state or local health inspector.

Renovations will create a lead problem. If the landlord plans repairs or renovations in an effort to contain a serious lead problem, you may be wise to leave the premises. Even meticulous cleanup procedures cannot eliminate the risk of inhaling lead dust created by renovation. If you live in a rent control city, you may be entitled to relocation expenses, even if the move is temporary. If not, ask your landlord to pay reasonable relocation expenses. If the landlord refuses, consider a lawsuit or small claims court.

Radon

Radon is a naturally occurring radioactive gas that is associated with lung cancer. The U.S. Environmental Protection Agency (EPA) estimates that over one-quarter of American homes have unacceptably high levels of radon. Radon can enter and contaminate a house built on soil and rock containing uranium deposits. It can also enter through water from private wells drilled in uranium-rich soil.

Radon becomes a lethal health threat when it enters from the soil and is trapped in homes that are over-insulated or poorly ventilated. Radon is a smaller risk when it escapes from building materials that have incorporated uranium-filled rocks and soils (like certain types of composite tiles or bricks), or is released into the air from aerated household water that has passed through underground concentrations of uranium. Problems occur most frequently in areas where rocky soil is relatively rich in uranium and in climates where occupants keep their windows tightly shut to maintain heat in the winter and air-conditioning in the summer. If you smoke and your house has high radon levels, your risk of developing lung cancer is especially high.

Fortunately, there are usually simple, inexpensive ways to measure and reduce radon levels in buildings. For example, good ventilation will disperse the gas in most situations. Solutions range from the obvious (open the windows) to the somewhat complex (use fans), but none of them involves tremendous expense.

There are no California or federal laws that require a private landlord to try to detect or get rid of radon. The radon problem has not become the subject of national laws requiring testing or even disclosure. But if you find radon in your rented property, there are still things you can do.

Finding Radon

Radon is invisible and odorless. To test the air in your house, you can buy a do-it-yourself kit (make sure it says "Meets EPA Requirements") or hire a professional. Testing takes at least three days, and sometimes months. Testers should have a certificate issued by the National Environmental Health Association (NEHA) or the National Radon Safety Board (NSRB). (H&S § 106780.)

Testing for radon makes sense if you live in an area that is naturally rich in uranium soil and rock, such as the Sierra region. For information on your county, check at EPA's map of radon zones at www. epa.gov/radon/zonemap.html. Visit your public library and ask how you can find out about your local geology. City planning departments, insurance brokers (who may have experience in dealing with radon-related claims), architects (who ought to understand the local geology), environmental engineers, and neighbors may be fruitful sources.

Solving Radon Problems

If radon is present in significant amounts, it needs to be blown out and kept out of the building.

Getting it out. Once radon has entered the house, it needs to be dispelled with fans and open windows. Because of the increased costs of heating and air-conditioning, and the loss of security when windows are left open, these methods should be only temporary. The only good long-term solution is keeping radon out.

Keeping it out. Sealing cracks and other openings in the foundation is a basic radon reduction technique. Another method is soil suction—sucking the radon out of the soil before it enters the foundation or basement, and venting it into the air above the roof through a pipe. Increasing the air pressure within a house can also work, because radon enters houses when the air pressure inside is less than that of the surrounding soil. Equalizing the pressure in the basement or foundation reduces this pull.

The Landlord's Responsibility

Keeping radon out of your dwelling involves major expenditures and modifications to the building's structure. Obviously, this kind of work is your landlord's responsibility.

If your landlord is unaware of the radon issue, give the landlord a copy of the EPA booklet explaining it. (See "Radon Resources," below.) If you have grounds for concern—you notice radon detection devices in local stores, your neighborhood has several buildings that are vented for radon control or the geology of the area suggests the presence of uranium-rich soils—suggest that your landlord hire a testing firm. As always, if a group of tenants voice their concern, the landlord is more likely to pay attention than if you act alone. Obviously, if you perform a test, send the landlord a certified letter with a copy of the report.

Keep copies of letters, emails, and reports, and write a letter of understanding to the landlord summarizing any oral discussions of the issue. Meticulous business practices like these will impress your landlord with your seriousness and willingness to take legal action if necessary.

Radon Resources

For information on the detection and removal of radon, contact the U.S. Environmental Protection Agency (EPA) Radon Hotline at 800-767-7236 or visit the EPA website (www.epa.gov/radon). You can also download a copy of the booklet "A Radon Guide for Tenants" and other publications, including "A Citizen's Guide to Radon." California's Department of Public Health has lots of information—go to their website at www.cdph.ca.gov and type "radon" into the search box.

Move Out If Necessary

Unacceptably high levels of radon render a home unfit for habitation. If a certified tester has reached that conclusion, you have all that you need to demand that the landlord take prompt steps to remedy the problem. If the landlord fails to address it within a very short time, you can break your lease or month-to-month rental agreement and move out, citing a breach of the implied warranty of habitability (see Chapter 6). Your suspicion alone that radon is present (perhaps because your neighbor has a radon problem) will probably not protect you if the landlord sues you for unpaid rent.

It may be appropriate to move out temporarily if the landlord plans to install pumps or vents, which may take some time. See the discussion above that suggests strategies for recouping expenses of temporary housing.

Carbon Monoxide

Carbon monoxide (CO) is a colorless, odorless, lethal gas. Unlike radon, whose deadly effects work over time, CO can build up and kill within a matter of hours. And, unlike any of the environmental hazards discussed so far, CO cannot be covered up or managed.

When CO is inhaled, it enters the bloodstream and replaces oxygen. Dizziness, nausea, confusion, and tiredness can result; high concentrations bring on unconsciousness, brain damage, and death. It is possible to be poisoned from CO while you sleep, without waking up.

Sources of Carbon Monoxide

Carbon monoxide is a byproduct of fuel combustion; electric appliances cannot produce it. Common home appliances, such as gas dryers, stoves, and ovens; refrigerators, ranges, water heaters or space heaters; oil furnaces, fireplaces, charcoal grills, and wood stoves all produce CO. Automobiles and gas gardening equipment also produce CO. If appliances or fireplaces are not vented properly, CO can build up within a home and poison the occupants. In tight, "energy-efficient" apartments, indoor accumulations are especially dangerous. No state or federal agency has issued guidelines on permissible exposures.

CAUTION

If you smell gas, it's not CO. Carbon monoxide has no smell. Only a CO detector will alert you to its presence. To help identify leaking natural gas, utility companies add a smelly ingredient; when you "smell gas," you are smelling that additive. Because natural gas is so combustible, call the utility company or 911 immediately if you smell it.

Preventing Carbon Monoxide Problems

State law (H&S § 17926.1) requires that landlords install and maintain a carbon monoxide device approved and listed by the State Fire Marshal.

Fortunately, relatively inexpensive devices, similar to smoke detectors, can monitor CO levels and sound an alarm if they get too high. If your landlord has a regular maintenance program, it should prevent the common malfunctions that cause CO buildup. But even the most careful service program cannot rule out unexpected problems like the blocking of a chimney by a bird's nest or the sudden failure of a machine part.

(!) CAUTION

If your CO detector sounds an alarm, leave immediately and do a household head count. Because one of the effects of CO poisoning is confusion and disorientation, get everyone out immediately—then check for signs of poisoning and call the fire department or 911.

Responsibility for Carbon Monoxide

Most CO hazards are caused by a malfunctioning appliance or a clogged vent, flue, or chimney. It follows that the responsibility for preventing a CO buildup depends on who is responsible for the upkeep of the appliance.

Appliances. Appliances that are part of the rental, especially built-in units, are typically the responsibility of the landlord, although you are responsible for intentional or unreasonably careless damage. For example, if the pilot light on the gas stove that came with the rental is improperly calibrated and emits high amounts of CO, the landlord is responsible for fixing it. On the other hand, if you bring in a portable oil space heater that malfunctions, that is your responsibility.

Sample Letter or Email Asking for Check of CO Detector

34 Maple Avenue North, #3
Mountain Town, CA 00000
303-555-1234

February 14, 20xx

Cindy Cerene
1818 East Seventh Street
Mountain Town, CA 00000

Dear Ms. Cerene:

The kitchen in the apartment we rent from you has a gas stove and cook-top, which are about 15 years old, and there is a gas furnace in the hallway. These appliances appear to be working normally, but especially in the winter, when storm windows make the house airtight, I am concerned about the possible buildup of carbon monoxide. I would like you to check the CO detector in the hallway near the bedrooms.

As you know, CO is a deadly gas that can kill within hours. We can't see it or smell it, and it could accumulate and poison us during the night. The only way to protect ourselves (besides your regular maintenance of these appliances) is with a detector. I am concerned that the CO detector is not functioning, so please check it as soon as possible.

Thanks very much for your consideration of this matter.

Yours truly,

Brian O'Rourke
Brian O'Rourke

Vents. Vents, chimneys, and flues are part of the structure, and the landlord typically handles their maintenance. In single-family houses, however, it is not unusual for landlord and tenant to agree to shift maintenance responsibility to the tenant.

If you have or suspect a CO problem that can be traced to the landlord's faulty maintenance, promptly request that the landlord fix it. If you are poisoned because your landlord failed to routinely maintain the appliances or to respond promptly to your repair request, the landlord will have a difficult time avoiding legal responsibility. (See Chapter 9.) You can call your local utility company and ask it to inspect the appliance that you suspect is causing the problem. Tell them your carbon monoxide detector has indicated that there is CO in your unit. They will inspect, and if the appliance is the source of the CO problem, they will shut it down and notify the landlord. If your landlord has not responded adequately, you might want to point out that failure to do so could cause a tragedy—and a lawsuit.

A sample letter or email bringing a CO problem to the landlord's attention is shown above. If you write such a letter, you would be smart to hand-deliver it to your landlord or manager, since the problem needs immediate attention. And in the meantime, don't use the appliance you suspect of causing the problem.

Carbon Monoxide Resources

The EPA website offers useful instructional material, including downloadable educational pamphlets, at www.epa.gov/indoor-air-quality-iaq. Local natural gas utility companies often have consumer information brochures available to their customers. You can also check out the American Gas Association website www.aga.org for consumer pamphlets on carbon monoxide. The Chimney Safety Institute of America, in Plainfield, Illinois (317-837-5362), publishes brochures on carbon monoxide and chimney safety. For more information, visit their website at www.csia.org.

Mold

Molds can be found virtually everywhere. If you go outside, mold will be in the air. If it's wet out, there will be more mold. In other words, we inhale mold spores wherever we go, and our bodies are equipped to deal with it. But as the mold colonies grow, more and more spores are released into the air and, at some point, it can start to become a problem. This happens only when we are exposed to areas with high concentrations of mold, particularly certain strains, usually indoors where mold may grow on sheetrock or wood, or between walls.

As long as the mold spores have warm moisture and a source of nourishment (who knew sheetrock was tasty), mold won't go away on its own. That's why it's important to deal with it as soon as you notice it.

There is considerable debate within the scientific and medical community about which molds, and what situations, pose serious health risks to people in their homes. Unlike lead, for example, where lead levels in blood can be accurately measured (and their effects scientifically predicted), mold is elusive. There is no debate, however, that mold can cause respiratory ailments. This is especially true for vulnerable populations such as people who have asthma or suppressed immune systems (including AIDS or cancer patients receiving chemotherapy). People with allergies, young children, and the elderly are also vulnerable. No matter what the situation, it is important to determine what is causing the mold, make the necessary repairs, and safely remove the mold.

Where Mold Is Found

Mold comes in various colors and shapes. The villains—with names like stachybotrys, penicillium, aspergillus, paecilomyces, and fusarium—are black, white, green, or gray. Some are powdery, others shiny. Some molds look and smell disgusting; others are barely seen—hidden between walls, under floors or carpets and above ceilings, or in less accessible spots such as basements and attics.

Mold often grows on water-soaked materials, such as wall paneling, paint, fabric, ceiling tiles, newspapers, or cardboard boxes. However, all that's really needed is an organic food source, water, and time. Throw in a little warmth and darkness and the organism will grow very quickly, sometimes spreading within 24 hours.

Humidity sets up prime growing conditions for mold. Buildings in naturally humid climates have experienced more mold problems than residences in drier climates. But mold can grow irrespective of the natural climate, as long as moisture is present. Here's how:

- Floods, leaking pipes, windows, or roofs may introduce moisture that will lead to mold growth in any structure—in fact, these are the leading causes of mold.
- Tightly sealed buildings (common with new construction) that are not well ventilated may trap mold-producing moisture inside.
- Overcrowding, poor ventilation, numerous over-watered houseplants, and poor housekeeping may also contribute to the spread of mold.

Unsightly as it may be, not all mold is harmful to your health. It takes an expert to know whether a particular mold is harmful or just annoying. (Even if it's just annoying, it will still need to be dealt with). Your first response to discovering mold shouldn't be to demand that the landlord call in the folks with the white suits and ventilators. Most of the time, proper cleanup and maintenance will remove mold. Better yet, focus on early detection and prevention of mold, as discussed below.

Laws on Mold Affecting Landlords

Unlike other environmental hazards such as lead, landlord responsibilities regarding mold have not been clearly spelled out in building codes, ordinances, statutes, and regulations. The main reason for the lack of standards is that the problem has only recently been acknowledged. California has been at the leading edge in trying to get a handle on the problem, as explained below.

Despite the sparse legal guidance regarding mold, one thing is certain: California law requires landlords to disclose to current and prospective tenants the presence of mold that that the landlord knows, should know, or suspects would affect the tenant's rental. (H&S § 26147.) But as you will see below, knowing mold is present is only the beginning of the journey.

Federal Law

No federal law sets permissible exposure limits or building tolerance standards for mold in residential properties.

State Law

A landlord is responsible for correcting conditions that are causing mold growth. For instance, a landlord is required to provide proper weather protection, so if a leaking roof or leaking windows result in mold growth, the landlord must both fix the leak and clean up the mold. Likewise, a landlord is responsible for conditions, such as lack of ventilation, that cause "dampness in habitable rooms," visible mold growth, or any nuisance (H&S §§ 17920.3(a)(6), (7), (11), (13), and 17920.3(c).) For instance if there is no vent fan or window that can be opened in a shower room, mold growth is likely to result and should be corrected by the landlord.

Landlords are not, however, responsible for mold caused by a tenant's neglect. For example, if the tenant did not use the working vent fan in the bathroom when taking showers, causing moisture and mold to accumulate in the shower stall, the landlord will not be responsible for cleanup. Also, landlords are not responsible for correcting a mold problem until they have received notice of the problem. (CC § 1941.7.)

Even when mold has grown as a result of a roof leak or other problem that a landlord must fix, a landlord would not be required to remove the mold if it's legally considered to be a minor instance of mold. But the difference between a "minor" presence of mold and mold that poses a habitability problem is very unclear. The state of California has not established definitive criteria for determining when mold growth constitutes a danger to the "health, safety, and welfare" of the residents. Instead, it has left it up to local health and building inspectors to make that determination (H&S § 17920.3(a)(13)). Unfortunately, what would be considered "unhealthy" and "unsafe" can differ from county to county and inspector to inspector. Nevertheless, the landlord would be well advised not to be penny wise and pound foolish. A "minor" mold growth can easily turn into a major one.

The California Department of Public Health's *Statement on Building, Dampness, Mold, and Health* has provided some general guidance for determining whether indoor mold poses a significant health risk. They recommend focusing on the extent of the structural problems, instead of determining the specific type of mold involved, or even measuring its concentration or presence: "Available evidence suggests that the more extensive, widespread, or severe the water damage, dampness, visible mold, or mold odor, the greater the health risks, and also that children are more sensitive to dampness and mold than adults." (You can read the entire booklet by entering the title of the report, Statement on Building Dampness, Mold, and Health, in your Internet search engine.)

Local Law

San Francisco has added mold to its list of nuisances, thereby allowing tenants to sue landlords under private and public nuisance laws if they fail to clean up serious outbreaks (San Francisco Health Code § 581).

Landlord Responsibility for Tenant Exposure to Mold

Evaluating the landlord's responsibility for mold problems involves two questions.

1. **Is the landlord responsible for addressing the underlying cause of the mold?** Another way of putting this is, did the water or dampness result from a failure of a part of the building that the landlord is responsible for? For example, landlords control and must maintain roofs, windows, and pipes, so if a leaking roof, window, or pipe introduces moisture that grows mold, the landlord must make repairs. (See Chapter 6, Major Repairs & Maintenance.) But before you can confidently lay the cleanup on the landlord, read on.

2. **Is the landlord responsible for cleaning up the mold?** Usually, the answer is "Yes," provided that 1) The mold was not due to the tenant's neglect, 2) The landlord was notified of the mold, and 3) The mold growth was not "minor."

Most reasonable landlords will follow the California Department of Public Health guidelines, referenced above. Your remedies in the instance where the landlord has not addressed the mold issue are much the same as those described in Chapter 6—rent withholding, repair and deduct, suing the landlord, or moving out.

Landlords often attempt to shift responsibility for a mold problem onto a tenant. This may or may not be justified. If the property does not have adequate ventilation, that is a habitability issue that the landlord is responsible for. (H&S § 17920.3(a).) On the other hand, the tenant would be responsible if he failed to use the working fan in the shower room and mold appeared as a result.

Prevention—The Best Way to Avoid Mold Problems

A smart landlord's efforts should be directed squarely at preventing the conditions that lead to the growth of mold—and you should be the landlord's partner in this effort. This approach requires maintaining the structural integrity of the property (the roof, plumbing, and windows), which is the landlord's job. You, in turn, need to follow some practical steps and promptly report problems that need the landlord's attention.

The following steps are especially important if you live in a humid environment or have spotted mold problems in the past:

- **Check over the premises and note any mold problems; ask the landlord to fix them before you move in.** Fill out the Landlord-Tenant Checklist form in the appendix and follow the advice on inspecting rental property at the start of a tenancy.
- **Understand the risks of poor housekeeping practices and recognize the factors that contribute to the growth of mold.** In particular, be sure you know how to:
  - ventilate the rental unit
  - avoid creating areas of standing water— for example, by emptying saucers under houseplants, and
  - clean vulnerable areas, such as bathrooms, with cleaning solutions that will discourage the growth of mold.

The EPA website, in "Resources: Mold," below, includes lots of practical tips for discouraging the appearance of mold in residential settings.

- **Immediately report specific signs of mold, or conditions that may lead to mold, such as plumbing leaks and weatherproofing problems.**
- **Ask for all repairs and maintenance needed to clean up or reduce mold—for example:**
  - Request exhaust fans in rooms with high humidity (bathrooms, kitchens, and service porches), especially if window ventilation is poor in these areas.
  - Ask for dehumidifiers in chronically damp environments, such as basements and other rooms below grade.
  - Reduce the amount of window condensation by using storm windows, if they're available.

These preventive steps will do more than decrease the chances that mold will begin to grow. If you have asked for them in writing and included the underlying reason for the request, you'll have good evidence to show a judge if a landlord refuses to step forward and your possessions are damaged or you are made ill by the persistence of the problem.

EXAMPLE: The closet in Jay's bedroom begins to sprout mold along the walls and ceiling. Jay asks his landlord, Sam, to address the problem (Jay suspects that the roof is leaking). Sam refuses, and Jay begins to feel sick; his clothes and shoes are also ruined by the mold. When Jay sues Sam for the value of his ruined possessions, and physical pain and suffering, he shows the judge the written requests for repairs that Sam ignored. After showing the judge photos and an impressively moldy pair of shoes, Jay wins his case.

If you think your case is worth more than $10,000, you should probably seek the opinion of an attorney before going to small claims court. By filing in small claims court, you will have to limit your demand to $10,000.

How to Clean Up Mold

Although reports of mold sightings are sometimes alarming, the fact is that most mold is relatively harmless and easily dealt with. Some problems, like those caused by leaks, will not go away until after the landlord has dealt with the cause of the leak. Even then, there may be mold on the interior sheetrock that emits a smell. Sometimes, however, the problem is a minor one. If you think that you have a relatively minor and non-recurring mold problem, you can probably take care of it yourself.

Most of the time, a weak bleach solution (one cup of bleach per gallon of water—do not use undiluted bleach) will remove mold from nonporous materials. You should follow these commonsense steps to clean up mold if the job is small. Use gloves and avoid exposing eyes and lungs to airborne mold dust (if you disturb mold and cause it to enter the air, use masks). Allow for frequent work breaks in areas with plenty of fresh air.

- Clean or remove all infested areas, such as a bathroom or closet wall. Begin work on a small patch and watch to see if you develop adverse health reactions, such as nausea or headaches. If so, stop and contact the landlord, who will need to call in the professionals.

- Don't try removing mold from fabrics such as towels, linens, drapes, carpets, and clothing—you'll have to dispose of these items.
- Contain the workspace by using plastic sheeting and enclosing debris in plastic bags.

(For more information, check out the sites noted in "Resources: Mold," below.)

CAUTION
People with respiratory problems, fragile health, or compromised immune systems should not participate in cleanup activities. If you have health concerns, ask for cleanup assistance. You may want to gently remind your landlord that it's a lot cheaper than responding to a lawsuit.

When the Landlord Won't Address a Serious Mold Problem

Some mold problems are longstanding or have caused substantial damage to the unit—or both. This usually happens when mold has grown inside a wall because of leaks from outside or from interior plumbing; or because of condensation caused by inadequate insulation. These problems can be complicated to address because the water source is not easy to identify, or mold is hidden from view, or the remediation of the mold requires highly specialized skills. Unfortunately, many landlords do not view these problems as serious ones that demand extra attention on their part. Many times, they will cut corners to avoid the extra expense of thorough water detection or proper mold remediation.

It is essential that you continue to notify the landlord of leaks, condensation, visible mold, or a moldy smell, and describe any impact that it may be having on your family's health. If you have done testing and found that the type of mold you have is particularly dangerous (see below), provide the landlord with the test results. Ask your landlord to have an assessment done by a professional mold inspector, one who will prepare a plan to remediate the mold, and ask the landlord for a copy of the inspector's report (however, landlords are not required to give it to you).

Resources: Mold

For information on the detection, removal, and prevention of mold, see the EPA website at www.epa.gov/mold. Publications with the homeowner in mind are available from the California Department of Public Health at www.cdph.ca.gov.

Air testing for mold is costly—often $1,000 or more for a single family home—but it is the best way to determine how much mold you are actually breathing in. If you are having significant physical symptoms, or the mold is having a health impact on your family, then it's probably money well spent. That way you can better determine whether in fact it's the mold that is causing these problems. The tester should, at a minimum, be a certified mold inspector, but preferably an environmental engineer or an industrial hygienist. Of course, the more expertise, the greater the cost, but if you are contemplating a lawsuit, the better expert will probably help your case more. The expert will probably inspect the property to determine the potential causes of the mold and will likely do air testing to see how much mold you are breathing and what kind of mold it is. Your expert will give you an idea of the extent of mold contamination and what it will take to remediate it. You should also ask about what you and your family can do to protect yourselves.

Many people report that when they are out of the environment, let's say for a week's vacation, their physical symptoms improve; and when they come back, they get worse again. This is also a good indicator of how severe the mold problem is. Conversely, if you don't get any better when you are away for a while, that's probably a good indicator that the cause of your symptoms is something other than the mold in your apartment.

Your repair and deduct remedy (discussed in Chapter 6) is probably available if you identify the source of the moisture problem and that problem is one of those enumerated in Civil Code Section 1941.1 or 17920.3 (which it probably is).

In a rent control jurisdiction, you may also be able to file a petition to have your rent reduced due to a reduction in services (maintenance and repair).

Insurance Coverage for Mold Damage

If your possessions have been ruined by mold and must be replaced, ask your landlord to cover the costs of replacing your damaged items. Also contact your renters' insurance agent immediately. Your renters' insurance may cover the cost of replacement (unfortunately, most policies have severe limitations or exclusions for claims related to mold). Do not expect the policy to cover the costs of medical bills, however—you'll need to turn to your own health insurance for that (or, you can sue the landlord).

Bedbugs

Bedbugs live on human blood, and are wingless insects that are about one-quarter inch in length, oval but flattened from top to bottom. They're nearly white (after molting) and range to tan or deep brown or burnt orange (after they've sipped some blood, a dark red mass appears within the insect's body). They seek crevices and dark cracks, commonly hiding during the day and finding their hosts at night. Bedbugs nest in mattresses, bed frames, and adjacent furniture, though they can also infest an entire room or apartment. They easily spread from apartment to apartment via cracks in the walls, heating systems, and other openings.

Relatively scarce during the latter part of the 20th century, bedbug populations have resurged recently in Europe, North America, and Australia, possibly a result of the banning of effective but toxic pesticides such as DDT. Bedbugs do not carry disease-causing germs (perhaps their one saving feature). Bedbugs are expert stowaways, crawling into luggage, clothing, pillows, boxes, and furniture as these items are moved from an infested home or hotel to another location. Secondhand furniture is a common source of infestation.

> ### Required Disclosures Regarding Bedbugs
>
> California requires landlords to make several disclosures regarding bedbugs:
> - Landlords must provide new tenants with specified information about bedbugs, similar to the information regarding asbestos and lead. (CC § 1954.603.)
> - Civil Code Section 1954.602 prohibits landlords from renting a unit that they know has a current bedbug infestation.
> - If a landlord has a contract for periodic pest control service, the landlord must provide new tenants with all notices that any licensed pest control company has given regarding the chemicals that it regularly applies. (CC § 1940.8.)
> - Registered pest control operators are required to provide specified information about any chemicals applied to control pests. (B&P § 8538.)
> - The landlord must give tenants specified information about any chemicals applied to control pests if the application is not done by a licensed pest control operator. (CC § 1940.8.5.)
> - When a unit has been inspected by a pest control operator, landlords must provide the tenant, in writing, with the inspector's findings within two business days of receiving it. When a report confirms an infestation in a common area, all tenants must be given the report. (CC § 1954.605.)

You may not be able to see bedbugs, but you are likely to feel their bites when you wake up in the morning (if they don't wake you up during the night). Their bites are about ⅛ inch in diameter or bigger and often turn into welts, often with visible blood at the top of the mound. Many people report itching from the bites, while others hardly feel them at all. You may also see blood on your sheets, another sign that bedbugs are likely in your unit. For more information on identifying bedbugs, go to the California Department of Public Health website and search for "bedbugs."

Getting rid of bedbugs is more difficult than you might expect, so be prepared to do more than you would normally expect to. The standard procedure is for you to prepare your unit for treatment by a professional pest control company, who will make multiple visits to the property. The company might also employ other measures, depending on the circumstances. Guidelines for the control and prevention of bedbugs can be found at the California Department of Public Health website: www.cdph.ca.gov.

Bedbug problems can get out of control very quickly, so it is important to take immediate action.

How to Deal With an Infestation

You'll learn that bedbugs have infested your home when you experience annoying bites that appear during the night. To minimize the outbreak and attempt to stop the spread of the pests to other rental units, your landlord must take the following steps immediately. You, too, must cooperate by cleaning and decluttering. First, you must notify the landlord that you have been bitten by bedbugs. If you have captured one, show it to the landlord. Otherwise, you can show bite marks, blood on the sheets (or dark brown stains, which are the bugs' excrement), or any other signs that there may be bedbugs. It is unlawful for a landlord to raise your rent or evict you because you have reported that you suspect bedbugs in your unit. (CC § 1942.5.)

You might want to talk with other tenants in the building to ask if they have a similar problem and to give them the information you now have about bedbugs.

After reporting, you will need to cooperate by allowing the landlord's pest control operator access to your unit to inspect it. (CC § 1954.604.) The pest control operator should provide you with its findings. You will also need to follow the pest control operator's instructions about getting rid of the bedbugs. This may include cleaning and decluttering the unit and getting it ready for the pest control operator to "treat" (and possibly retreat) the unit with an insecticide.

If your landlord refuses to effectively deal with the infestation, you may have grounds to move out (because the rental has become uninhabitable). Understand that, unlike some other pest problems, dealing with bedbugs requires building-wide attention, which means that you must have your landlord's active involvement. Moreover, hiring an experienced pest control operator is the only way to deal with a bedbug infestation. A can of Raid is not going to do the job.

Confirm the Infestation

First, you and the landlord must make sure that you're in fact dealing with bedbugs and not some other pest, such as fleas. If you're not sure, submit your catch to a competent entomologist (insect specialist) for evaluation.

It is best to try to capture a critter or two, that way the landlord cannot deny that there is a bedbug problem. Go online and check to see if what you have looks like any of the photos of bedbugs you see on your computer screen. You can often find bedbugs at the underside of your mattress or box spring (especially in corners and under folds). Short of capturing a bedbug, you can show your landlord the bites on your body or the blood on your mattress. Just reporting the bedbug bites should alert your landlord to the problem (if he hasn't already heard it from another tenant).

If the landlord is doing his job properly, he will hire a licensed pest control service to investigate the problem and recommend appropriate action.

Inspection by a Registered Pest Control Operator

In a multiunit building, bedbugs can travel from one unit to another, leading to the nightmare of an entirely infested building. But chances are that one unit is the original source (and it will likely have the highest concentrations of bedbugs).

Pest Control Operators (PCOs) should, at a minimum, carefully inspect all units above, below, and to each side of any unit that has reported bedbugs. They should also check nearby common areas, like hall carpets. The should look at seams and joints of mattresses, bed frames, baseboards, cracks, picture frames, as well as upholstered furniture. Even with careful inspection, actually finding bedbugs is often difficult; you can help by telling the exterminator where you have seen bedbugs and how you think the bedbugs have gotten into your unit. Your landlord should give all tenants proper notice of the inspection beforehand.

After inspection, the PCO should develop a treatment plan for eradicating the bedbugs and preventing them from coming back. If the infestation is significant, the plan should include treatment of affected *and* adjacent units. This involves spraying chemicals in each unit, which will kill the bugs. PCOs usually apply three of these "treatments," approximately two weeks apart. The PCO should give the landlord, and the landlord should give you, the date for each treatment and instructions as to how to get your unit ready for the treatment. It is essential that you follow these instructions.

Declutter, Leave, Exterminate, Vacuum—And Do It Again

Bedbugs thrive in clutter, which simply gives them more hiding places. To effectively deal with the bugs, tenants in infested units must first remove clutter and neaten up. You must remove all items from closets, shelves, and drawers; and wash all bedding and clothing (putting washed items in sealed plastic bags). You need to leave your unit during treatment, and return when the exterminator gives the all clear. Most of the time, tenants can return the same day.

Upon return, you must thoroughly vacuum. Experienced exterminators will recommend a second and even a third treatment, with exhaustive cleaning and clutter-removing in between.

Infested items that can't be treated must be destroyed. Don't simply remove infested items and bring them back! Use extreme care when removing infested belongings and furniture. Bag them in plastic before carting them away—otherwise, you may inadvertently distribute the bugs to the rest of the building.

Bag the Bed

Bedbugs will usually be found in an infested room's bed. The only way to rid a mattress of bedbugs is to enclose it in a large plastic bag that will trap the bedbugs (they will eventually die inside). Use a bag guaranteed to trap bedbugs (some bags will simply deter allergens). See the articles from the California Department of Public Health, above, for more information on bed bags.

Exterminations and Relocation Costs: Who Pays?

Landlords often instinctively blame the tenant for the bedbug problem, but determining the cause of a bedbug problem is very difficult—especially in apartment buildings. For instance, they can enter the unit through walls, under doors, or via a common vacuum cleaner. No matter how the infestation began, the landlord is responsible for eradicating it. If the landlord has evidence that you caused the problem, he may later sue you in small claims court for the cost.

Tenant relocation is seldom an issue. When a unit is treated, the tenant must be out for a matter of several hours and then may return to the unit. If the bedbug problem is uncontrolled and the landlord has refused to deal with it, the tenant may choose to move out and sue for relocation expenses and other losses due to the infestation.

Bedbugs in Multifamily Buildings

In a multiunit building, if the landlord approaches a bedbug problem by "boxing" the building as explained above, it may be able to identify the most infested rental unit. But identifying the source (or most infested) unit is not the same as proving that these tenants caused the problem. For example, suppose management traces the infestation to Unit 2, whose occupant moved into the building a few weeks ago. Serial mapping may show that adjoining Units 1 and 3 became infested after Unit 2 did, thereby suggesting that tenants in Units 1 and 3 were not responsible for their infestations. Suppose the tenant in the source unit (Unit 2) argues that the former occupants introduced the bedbug eggs that conveniently hatched after their departure. How will a landlord disprove this? Perhaps the landlord will discover that the new tenant came from a building that was also infested, but lacking this, the owner will have a hard time laying responsibility on the new resident. And even if the landlord did a thorough inspection of the unit before rerenting, there's no guarantee that they didn't miss some miniscule eggs.

If mapping identifies a source unit that's occupied by a long-term resident, it will be similarly difficult to develop the facts needed to prove that this tenant introduced the bugs. How will the landlord learn about its tenants' habits, purchases, and travels, short of a full-blown lawsuit? And even if management discovers, for example, that these tenants bought a secondhand couch recently, how will they prove it contained bedbugs? Or that bugs came home with them following their recent stay in a hotel, or travel abroad?

In short, because of the practical difficulty of identifying the tenant or guest who introduced the bugs, the landlord often ends up footing the bill for extermination and relocation costs.

Proper Cleaning and Housekeeping for Bedbugs

As you know from reading about your right to privacy, landlords must maintain a delicate balance between insisting that tenants take proper care of their property and respecting their privacy. Landlords can require that rental units be kept in a sanitary condition, but they can't inspect every week to make sure their tenants' housekeeping efforts are adequate.

When it comes to effectively eliminating bedbugs, however, extreme housekeeping is needed. Most tenants are so grateful that their landlord is taking steps to deal with the bugs that they cooperate voluntarily. This is not the time to balk at inspections and regular treatments. Failure to cooperate will not only defeat the eradication efforts, it will destroy any chance you might have at compensation.

Bedbugs in Single-Family Rentals

Tenants of single-family rentals face a simpler picture when it comes to determining who's responsible for an infestation, because there's no issue of boxing the infestation and determining the source. If you are a long-term tenant who reports a problem, chances are it's a result of your activities; but tenants who have just moved in may argue that the former residents introduced the eggs.

Ruined Belongings: Who Pays?

In many cases, bedbugs infest both the rental and its contents—books, clothes, furniture, appliances. One New York landlord reported getting a phone call from his tenant who discovered bedbugs and moved out with only the clothes on his back, leaving everything—everything—behind. This tenant sued the owner for the replacement cost of his belongings, claiming that the landlord's ineffective eradication methods left him no choice. Who pays?

A landlord has a duty at law to maintain the premises free of pests. That includes bedbugs. The landlord is responsible for bedbug infestation if he fails to respond quickly and properly when bedbugs are reported. Landlords often try to shift the blame to their tenants, saying the tenants brought the bedbugs in, but this is almost impossible to prove. If the landlord does not take action, he is on the hook. Nevertheless, tenants also have responsibilities as well, most notably to allow access for inspection and to follow the instructions of the PCO. A tenant's failure in these regards will undermine his claim for damages.

Will Insurance Step Up for Bedbugs?

If you're facing a bedbug problem, you'll want to know whether your landlord's insurance policy or your own renter's policy will help you with the cost of replacing ruined belongings and related expenses. Here's the scoop:

Tenants' claims against the landlord's policy for lost or damaged belongings, medical expenses, and related moving and living expenses. Your landlord's commercial general liability policy will probably cover your claims here, although many policies have exclusions for pests.

Tenants' claims against their renters' insurance policies. If you have renters' insurance, you might get some help here. If you are at fault (you introduced the bugs), the property portion of your policy should cover you, in the same way that it will cover you if you ruined your furniture when accidentally starting a fire in the kitchen. If another tenant caused the infestation, you can still make a claim on your policy (your carrier may turn around and sue the responsible tenant, but that's their problem, not yours). (See Chapter 16 for a discussion of renters' insurance.)

Breaking a Lease for a Bedbug-Infested Rental

Most landlords will not tell prospective tenants about a past bedbug problem. Knowing that a bedbug can remain alive and dormant for over a year, and that eradication attempts are often not 100% effective, many prospects will never consider living in a unit that has experienced a bedbug problem, even when the landlord has done everything possible to deal with the bugs. Some landlords believe that disclosing a rental's bedbug past will make it unrentable, period.

Still, because a landlord is required to disclose whether a PCO has entered into a contract with the landlord to apply pesticides at the property (and give specifics as to the pest targeted and the chemicals used), you should learn of the problem when reading these disclosures. (Because the duty is to disclose to "new tenants," you might not get it until you've signed the lease or rental agreement.) (CC § 1940.8.) A landlord is required to disclose to tenants the findings of any PCO who has inspected any affected units or in common areas of the building. (CC § 1954.605.)

If a landlord knowingly withheld material facts (such as the presence of bedbugs), or has rendered the premises uninhabitable due to a persistent bedbug infestation that has not been successfully addressed (no matter how hard the landlord might have tried), the tenant has a basis for terminating the lease agreement and just moving out. (CC § 1689(b)(1).) Furthermore, you may be able to argue that the landlord committed fraud by withholding material facts about your tenancy. (CC §§ 1592, 1573.)

In addition to breaking the lease, you may be able to file a lawsuit for damages against your landlord. If you live in a building with other units where the tenants were also affected, you may want to go in together on a lawsuit against your landlord. Again, your landlord's liability is not automatic. However, if the landlord did not do a proper job eradicating the bedbugs, or if, before you moved in, the landlord withheld facts about the presence of bedbugs at the building, you may have grounds to sue. You may be entitled to compensation for lost property; out-of-pocket costs, including relocation expenses and medical expenses; and physical, mental, and emotional suffering.

Electromagnetic Fields

Power lines, electrical wiring, and appliances emit low-level electric and magnetic fields. The farther away you are from the source of these fields, the weaker their force.

The controversy surrounding electromagnetic fields (EMFs) concerns whether exposure to them increases a person's chances of getting certain cancers—specifically, childhood leukemia. Although some early research raised the possibility of a link, later scientific studies have discounted it. See, for example, the exhaustive research done by the World Health Organization on the health consequences of EMFs, available at www.who.int/peh-emf/about/en.

Because the landlord cannot insist that the power companies move their transmitters or block the emissions, the landlord is not responsible for EMFs or their effect—if any—on you. If you're worried, your only practical option is to move. If you have a month-to-month rental agreement or the lease is up, you can easily move on without legal repercussions. But what if you decide midlease that the EMFs are intolerable? Legally, you would be justified in breaking a lease or rental agreement only if the property presents a significant threat to your health or safety. (Breaking a lease when the property is unfit is explained at length in Chapter 6.) Given the professional debate regarding the danger from EMFs, it is unclear whether a court would decide that their presence makes the property unlivable.

The National Institute of Environmental Health Sciences has useful resources on EMFs. To find these, simply do a search on their website at www.niehs.nih.gov.

Crime on the Premises

Your landlord has some degree of legal responsibility to provide secure housing. This means the landlord must take reasonable steps to:

- protect tenants from foreseeable criminal activity by other tenants or their guests, or by anyone entering the property by legal or illegal means
- protect tenants from the criminal acts of fellow tenants
- warn tenants about dangerous situations they are aware of but cannot eliminate, and
- protect the neighborhood from their tenants' illegal and noxious activities, such as drug dealing that the landlord knows about (or should know about).

When landlords don't live up to this responsibility, they may be liable for any injuries or losses that befall you as a result. This chapter explores the security measures that you can legally expect from your landlord—and how to insist on them if your landlord doesn't do enough to safeguard tenants.

The Landlord's Basic Duty to Keep You Safe

State law requires landlords to take reasonable precautions to protect tenants from foreseeable harm. You can't expect your landlord to eliminate crime in your city or to provide an army of armed security. On the other hand, the landlord can't just turn over the keys, trusting to the local constable and fate to assure your safety, especially when there are known dangers in or around your rental unit.

State Laws

State and local building and housing codes have specific rules designed to protect tenants. State law requires deadbolt locks on main exterior doors (except for sliding doors), common area doors, and gates and certain windows. (CC § 1941.3.) The law requires the following:

- A deadbolt lock that is at least $^{13}/_{16}$ inch long for each main entry door. A thumb-turn lock in place on July 1, 1998, will satisfy the requirement, but a $^{13}/_{16}$th of an inch deadbolt must be installed when the landlord repairs or replaces the lock. If there are other kinds of locking mechanisms used instead of a deadbolt, they must be inspected and approved by a state or local agency.
- Locks that comply with state or local fire and safety codes in existing doors or gates that connect common areas (such as lobbies, patios, and walkways) to rental units or to areas beyond the property (such as a main front door).
- Window locks on louvered and casement windows. Prefabricated windows with their own opening and locking mechanisms are exempt, as are those that are more than 12 feet above the ground. However, a window that is over 12 feet from the ground but less than six feet from a roof or any other platform must have a lock.

Civil Code Section 1941.1 requires a landlord to maintain unbroken doors and windows, and keep electrical wiring and equipment in good working order and condition. If, for instance, lights are out in the hallway and not replaced, it is the landlord's obligation to replace them. Likewise, a landlord would be required to repair and maintain an existing intercom system. This does not require a landlord to install new lighting, or a new intercom system, but if one is already there, it must be properly maintained.

Health and Safety Code Section 11570 defines a nuisance as any "building or place used for the purpose of unlawfully selling, serving, storing, keeping, manufacturing, or giving away any controlled substance." Landlords are required to keep their properties free of any nuisances, which means removing any such uses from their property.

If you are the victim of domestic violence, sexual assault, or stalking, you may be entitled to additional protections under Civil Code Sections 1940.6 or 1940.7. (See Chapter 2.)

Local Ordinances

Many counties and cities have adopted housing codes designed to minimize the chances of a criminal incident on residential rental property—for example, by requiring peepholes. If your landlord does not comply with specific equipment requirements, you can complain to the agency in charge of enforcing the codes, often a local building or housing authority. (See below.)

If you are injured when a criminal takes advantage of your landlord's violation of a safety law—for example, an intruder enters your apartment building by way of a lock that's been broken for weeks—the landlord may be liable for your injuries.

RESOURCE

To get a copy of your local housing code or ordinance, call your city manager's or mayor's office, or look it up online or at your local public library. You may be able to get information from a local housing agency or local tenants' association. Many counties and cities have posted their ordinances online. Go to www.statelocalgov.net/state-ca.cfm and search for your county or city.

The Landlord's General Responsibility

In addition to complying with local and state laws that require basic security measures, landlords have a general common law duty to act reasonably under the circumstances—or, expressed in legal jargon, to "act with due care." (See Chapter 10 on your landlord's duty to keep you safe from noncriminal harm.) For example, common areas must be kept clean and safe, so that they do not create a risk of accidents. When it comes to security, too, California judges have ruled that landlords must take reasonable precautions to protect tenants from foreseeable criminal assaults and property crimes.

The meaning of "reasonable precautions" depends on the situation. In general, courts will look at the connection between the failure to provide proper security and how likely it was that the tenant would be injured because of the lack of security. For instance, the cost of replacing a broken door is minimal, but, especially in a high crime area, the foreseeability of a burglar gaining entry through the broken door is great. So, fixing the door is a reasonable precaution that the landlord should have undertaken. On the other hand, courts will require greater foreseeability if the cost for protection is greater. For instance, before requiring a landlord to hire security guards, one must show a likelihood greater than the threat of intrusion that a crime would be committed—which is usually accomplished by showing prior criminal acts on the premises.

If you have a security concern, it's important to notify your landlord immediately. That way he can't complain that he didn't know about the problem.

Unfortunately, a landlord's responsibility in this area is not black or white. The questions below should assist you in evaluating your landlord's duty.

Did your landlord control the area where the crime occurred?

Your landlord isn't expected to police the entire world. For example, a lobby, hallway, or other common area is an area of high landlord control. However, the landlord exerts no control over the sidewalk outside the front door.

How likely is it that a crime would occur?

Landlords are duty-bound to respond to the foreseeable, not the improbable. Have there been prior criminal incidents on the rental property? Elsewhere in the neighborhood? A landlord who knows that an offense is likely (because of a rash of break-ins or prior crime on the property) has a heightened legal responsibility to guard against future crime.

How difficult or expensive would it have been for the landlord to reduce the risk of crime?

If relatively cheap or simple measures could significantly lower the risk of crime, it is likely that a court would find that your landlord had a duty to undertake them, especially in an area where criminal activity is high. For instance, would reasonably inexpensive new locks and better lighting discourage thieves? However, if the only solution to the problem is costly, such as structural remodeling or hiring a full-time doorman, a court would be less likely to impose these costs on your landlord unless the danger is very great.

How serious an injury was likely to result from the crime?

Most cases involving serious injuries such as instances of aggravated assault, sexual assault, or homicide, will focus on the duty of the landlord. Where the victim claims that the landlord should have implemented additional security measures, such as hiring security guards, the more he or she will have to show that the property owner knew of the likelihood of such violent criminal activity. In one case, a mobile home park tenant was shot by a stray bullet, fired in a confrontation between rival gangs. The Supreme Court held that the mobile home park owner had no duty to evict gang members, install additional lighting, or hire security guards, even though gang members had been reported harassing other tenants, possibly breaking a car window, and other low-level troublesome behavior. This behavior did not make injury from gun activity likely. (*Castenada v. Olsher*, 41 Cal.4th 1205 (2007).) By contrast, in *Vasquez v. Residential Investments, Inc.*, 118 Cal.App.4th 269 (2004), the court held a landlord liable for the murder of one of his tenants when the landlord failed to repair the front door, allowing the tenant's boyfriend to enter and kill her. It reasoned that the landlord was legally responsible for repairing the door and the cost to repair it was minimal. At the same time, the risk of a criminal intruder was foreseeable.

Let's look at how these questions might be answered in three crime situations.

EXAMPLE 1: Sam was accosted outside the entryway to his duplex by a stranger who was lurking in the tall, overgrown bushes in the front yard next to the sidewalk. There had been many previous assaults in the building. Both the bushes and the lack of exterior floodlights near the entryway prevented Sam from seeing his assailant until it was too late. If Sam filed a claim with the landlord's liability insurance company or sued the landlord, an adjuster or judge would probably conclude that the landlord was bound to take measures to protect Sam's safety, because:

1. The landlord controlled the common areas outside the duplex.
2. It was foreseeable that an assailant would lurk in the bushes and that another assault would occur.
3. The burden of trimming the shrubbery and installing lights was small in comparison to the risk of injury.

EXAMPLE 2: Caroline was assaulted in the house she rented by someone whom she let in, thinking that he was a gas company repairperson. There was a peephole in the front door, as required by local law, which she could have used had she asked to see proof of his identification. When Caroline sued her landlord, the judge tossed the case out. Her case collapsed on question 1: The landlord had no control over Caroline foolishly opening the door to someone whom she could have safely questioned (and excluded) from inside.

EXAMPLE 3: Max was assaulted and robbed in the open parking lot next to his apartment house when he came home from work late one night. The landlord knew that several muggings had recently been reported in the neighborhood, and he knew that his tenants parked there (he even mentioned the "free parking" when showing the rentals). Floodlights lighted the parking lot, but it was not fenced and gated. Here's how the questions might be answered:

1. The landlord didn't own the lot, yet he knowingly benefited from his tenants' use of it. A judge might conclude that he had to take reasonable precautions with respect to the use of the lot (such as warning tenants of the danger).
2. An assault seemed reasonably foreseeable in view of the recent nearby muggings.
3. However, the burden of totally eliminating the danger (fencing the lot) would have been very expensive.

When Max sued, the case turned on whether the landlord's duty of care toward his tenants extended to their use of property that he did not own but benefited from. The judge has not announced his decision.

If, based on these questions, you think the landlord had a legal duty to deal with a condition on the premises that exposed you to the risk of crime, keep going. You have two more questions to answer.

Did your landlord fail to take reasonable steps to prevent a crime?

As ever, "reasonableness" is evaluated within the context of each situation. For example, returning to Sam (Example 1, above), the fact that the landlord let the bushes grow high and didn't replace the lights clearly was unreasonable. But suppose the landlord had cut the bushes back halfway and installed one light. Would that have been enough? It would be up to a jury to decide.

The greater the danger, the more a landlord must do. Past criminal activity on the premises increases your landlord's duty to keep you safe. "Reasonable precautions" in a crime-free neighborhood are not the same as those called for when three apartments in the landlord's building have been burglarized within the past month.

> **EXAMPLE:** Allison rented an apartment in Manor Arms after being shown the building by the resident manager. Nothing was said about recent criminal activity in the building. A month after moving in, Allison was assaulted by a man who stopped her in the hallway, claiming to be a building inspector. Unbeknownst to Allison, similar assaults had occurred in the building in the past six months, and the manager even had a composite drawing of the suspect done by the local police. Allison's assailant was captured and proved to be the person responsible for the earlier crimes.
>
> Allison sued the building owners after their insurance carrier refused to offer her a reasonable settlement. In her lawsuit, Allison claimed that the owners were negligent (unreasonably careless) in failing to warn her of the specific danger posed by

the repeat assailant and in failing to beef up their security (such as hiring a guard service) after the first assault. The jury agreed and awarded Allison a large sum of money.

Landlords cannot eliminate all danger to tenants. In some situations, it may be enough to warn you. Just as caution tape and warning cones alert tenants to a freshly washed floor, you can expect your landlord to warn you about possible criminal problems by using:

- newsletters that remind tenants to be on the alert and use good sense
- letters that communicate specific information, such as a physical description of an assailant who has struck nearby, and
- signs that remind tenants to use the building's safety features, such as a notice posted in the lobby asking tenants to securely lock the front door behind them.

Did your landlord's failure to take reasonable steps to keep you safe contribute to the crime?

You must be able to connect the landlord's failure to provide reasonable security with the criminal incident. It is often very difficult for tenants to convince a jury that the landlord's failure to live up to his or her duty to keep you safe caused (or contributed to) the assault or burglary.

Think of it this way: If you fall because the rotten front step collapsed, you can usually trace the collapse directly to the landlord's failure to maintain the property. Now, suppose you can prove that the front door lock was broken (and had been for weeks) on the night you were assaulted. To hold the landlord liable, you have to be able to show that the assailant got into the building via that unlocked front door. This is where many lawsuits against landlords fall apart—the tenants can't connect the landlord's failure with the criminal's entry. You'd have to show that the landlord's failure to take reasonable measures was a substantial factor in the ability of the criminal to commit the crime.

If the jury decides that the landlord's failure to take reasonable measures was a substantial factor in the commission of the crime, both the landlord and the criminal are jointly and severally liable for all "economic" damages. Thus, the landlord is 100% on the hook for damages such as medical expenses, lost wages, and out-of-pocket expenses. As to "non-economic" damages such as pain, suffering, emotional distress, and psychological injuries, a jury will be required to apportion fault between the landlord and the criminal. For example, jurors might decide that the landlord is 60% at fault and the criminal 40%. In addition to economic damages, the landlord would have to pay 60% of the non-economic damages. Not surprisingly, victims rarely collect the criminal's share.

In Sam's case (Example 1, above), he convinced the jury that, had the bushes been properly trimmed and the area well-lit, he could have seen the assailant or, more likely, the assailant wouldn't have chosen this exposed place to commit a crime. The jury found that the landlord was 70% at fault for Sam's injuries.

The Landlord's Promises

A landlord who promises specific security features —such as a doorman, security patrols, interior cameras, or an alarm system—must either provide them or be liable (at least partially) for any criminal act that they would have prevented. Remember, your lease is a contract, and if it includes a "24-hour security" promise or a commitment to have a doorman on duty at night, you have a right to expect it. Even a landlord's oral descriptions of security bind the landlord if they were a factor that led you to rent the unit. You can often also rely on statements about security in advertisements.

Your landlord won't be liable for failing to provide what was promised, however, unless this failure caused or contributed to the crime. Burned-out lightbulbs in the parking lot won't mean anything if the burglar got in through an unlocked trap door on the roof.

EXAMPLE 1: The manager of Jeff's apartment building gave him a thorough tour of the "highly secure" building before Jeff decided to move in. Jeff was particularly impressed with the security locks on the gates of the high fences at the front and rear of the property. Confident that the interior of the property was accessible only to tenants and their guests, Jeff didn't hesitate to take his kitchen garbage to the dumpsters at the rear of the building late one evening. There he was accosted by an intruder who got in through a rear gate that had a broken lock. Jeff's landlord was held liable because she had failed to maintain the sophisticated, effective locks that had been promised.

EXAMPLE 2: The information packet given to Maria when she moved into her apartment stressed the need to keep careful track of door keys: "If you lose your keys, call the management and the lock will be changed immediately." When Maria lost her purse containing her keys, she immediately called the management company but couldn't reach them because it was after 5 p.m. and there was no after-hours emergency procedure. That evening, Maria was assaulted by someone who got into her apartment by using her lost key.

Maria sued the owner and management company on the grounds that they had completely disregarded their own standard (to change the locks promptly) and so were partially responsible (along with the criminal) for the assailant's entry. The jury agreed and awarded Maria a large sum.

Problems With Other Tenants

Sometimes danger lurks within as well as beyond the gate. And your landlord has a duty to take reasonable steps to protect you if another resident on the property (including a roommate) threatens to harm you or your property.

Your landlord should respond to a troublesome tenant in essentially the same way he would respond to a loose stair or broken front-door lock. A landlord who knows about a problem (or should know about it) is expected to take reasonable steps to prevent foreseeable harm to other tenants. If the landlord fails to do that, and you are injured or robbed by another tenant, you may sue and recover damages.

When the Landlord Must Act

The landlord won't be held liable for another tenant's illegal acts unless the problem tenant had done or threatened similar criminal conduct in the recent past, and the landlord knew about it. In short, you'll need to convince an insurance adjuster, judge, or jury that:

- it was reasonable to expect the landlord to know or learn that the tenant was causing the problem complained about
- once known, the landlord could have taken steps to control or evict the troublemaker, and
- the landlord's failure to take reasonable steps was a substantial factor in causing your injury.

Unless there's a clear history of serious problems with the offending tenant, landlords usually win these cases. On the other hand, tenants sometimes win if they can show that the landlord knew about a resident's tendency toward violence and failed to take reasonable precautions to safeguard the other tenants.

EXAMPLE: Sally complained to her manager that Earl, who lived in another unit, had repeatedly verbally and physically assaulted her. The manager promised to take care of the situation, but did not terminate Earl's tenancy or even warn Earl that he would be evicted if he didn't stop; nor did he place security cameras at the place of the attacks. Earl assaulted Sally again. The judge decided that the management owed Sally a duty to protect her from Earl's foreseeable attack. The jury decided that management breached that duty and that it was the legal cause of Sally's injuries. (Based on *Madhani v. Cooper*, 106 Cal.App.4th 412 (2003).)

TIP

If you fear violence from another tenant, let your landlord know in writing. Not only does this underscore the seriousness of the situation, but it will be irrefutable proof that the landlord was on notice that problems were brewing. When more than one resident complains, the landlord will face more pressure to take action. If there is an altercation later, the landlord cannot plausibly claim ignorance.

CAUTION

Get your facts straight before making accusations. If you believe that certain individuals are breaking the law—or just causing trouble—be certain that you have the facts straight before telling others about them. Otherwise, you might find yourself on the wrong end of a libel or slander lawsuit.

Domestic Violence, Stalking, Sexual Assault, Human Trafficking, and Abuse of Elder or Dependent Adult

Victims of domestic violence, stalking, sexual assault, human trafficking, or abuse of an elder or dependent adult may terminate a fixed-term lease on 30 days' written notice. You must include with the notice a copy of a court-issued restraining order, a police-issued emergency protective order, or a police report documenting the incident. The order or report must have been made within the previous 180 days. (CC § 1946.7.) Only the victim and family members (but not nonfamily roommates) may avoid liability for the rent for the balance of the lease term. If the perpetrator of the incident remains behind, the landlord can give him or her a three-day notice for "nuisance" and proceed with an eviction.

What Your Landlord Must Do

A landlord who knows about the potential for danger from another tenant must take reasonable steps to address the problem, such as alerting other tenants and/or evicting or at least warning the troublemaker.

For example, suppose your neighbor bangs on the walls every time you practice the violin during the afternoon—and the pounding is getting louder. If you've tried to talk things out and been greeted with a raised fist, it's time to alert the landlord. You can reasonably expect the landlord to intervene and attempt to broker a solution—perhaps an adjustment of your practice schedule or some heavy-duty earplugs for the neighbor. If the circumstances are more threatening—for example, your neighbor brandishes a gun—your landlord might be legally expected to call the police, post a security guard, and warn other tenants pending the speedy eviction of the dangerous tenant.

Intervention and eviction of the troublemaker are the usual ways that landlords meet their duty to take care that residents don't harm other residents. But the law doesn't require your landlord to have a crystal ball.

Getting a Restraining Order

If another tenant seriously threatens you and won't leave you alone, and your landlord either won't evict the aggressor or the eviction is taking some time, consider obtaining a Civil Harassment Restraining Order. The procedures for a Civil Harassment Restraining Order are designed for situations like this and can usually be done without the assistance of an attorney. The Clerk of the Court should be able to give you both the Civil Harassment forms and the instructions.

A judge will sign these orders after you demonstrate that you really are in danger—for example, the aggressor has made repeated verbal threats to harm you or your family. The order directs the person to stay away from you. Its principal value is that the police will react faster and more firmly than they might otherwise. To obtain a restraining order, call your local courthouse for information.

After the order is signed by a Judge, you will have to have the order personally served on the threatening party. Then, give a copy to the local police. If you obtain a restraining order, make a copy and give it to your landlord and to the manager, if any. Ask the landlord to alert other on-site personnel, such as security guards and maintenance personnel, of the existence and meaning of the order. A wise landlord will usually consider a restraining order as ample grounds for a swift termination and eviction. If the aggressor returns after he is evicted, request that the landlord order him off the property and call the police.

If you get no cooperation from your landlord and are still fearful, move. Your safety is worth far more than your right to live in a particular rental space. Your landlord might feel that you have broken the lease and might try to keep your security deposit to cover unpaid rent for the balance of the lease or rental agreement, but if you go to court to contest this, your chances of winning are good. You can argue that by failing to evict the troublemaker, the landlord breached the covenants of habitability and quiet enjoyment, which justified your moving out. (See Chapter 6 for information on the warranty of habitability.) If your situation involves domestic violence, you might have specific rights. (See "Domestic Violence, Stalking, Sexual Assault, Human Trafficking, and Abuse of Elder or Dependent Adult," above.)

EXAMPLE: Abbot and his mother rented a duplex from Xavier, who knew that Abbot was emotionally disabled and took regular medication to control his behavior. Unknown to his mother or Xavier, Abbot began skipping his medication and eventually attacked Larry, the other tenant in the duplex, with a baseball bat. Xavier was not held liable, since it would have been illegal to refuse to rent to Abbot, a disabled person, under the Federal Fair Housing Amendments Act. Xavier did not know that Abbot had discontinued his medication, nor would it have been reasonable to expect Xavier to monitor Abbot's dosages. If Xavier had known that Abbot was off his medication, however, he would have been duty-bound to speak to Abbot and his mother, and possibly warn the other resident.

Illegal Activity on the Property and Nearby

Illegal activities on the premises create problems for law-abiding tenants and enormous financial risks and penalties for landlords. Law-abiding tenants move out, and may also sue if they are hurt or annoyed by drug dealers or other criminals. Landlords face trouble from other quarters—they can be fined for tolerating a legal nuisance, face criminal charges, and even lose their property.

(See "Activities That Are Always Considered Nuisances," below, for a list of illegal nuisances in California.)

Government Lawsuits Against the Landlord

The legal meaning of "nuisance" bears only a little resemblance to its meaning in everyday life.

California has vigorous nuisance abatement laws, which allow the government, and sometimes the neighbors, to sue to stop these sorts of problems. (CC §§ 3479, 3491.) Using public nuisance abatement laws against crime-tolerant landlords is increasingly common in large cities with pervasive drug problems.

In extreme cases, where the conduct giving rise to the nuisance complaint is illegal (drug dealing or prostitution, for example), landlords themselves face civil fines or criminal punishment for tolerating the behavior.

Activities That Are Always Considered Nuisances

A "nuisance" is broadly defined as anything that is injurious to health, offensive to the senses, or unreasonably interferes with the free use and enjoyment of life or property. (CC § 3479.) Because of this broad language, knowing what is and is not a nuisance is often not clear. But certain acts are automatically deemed nuisances. They include:
- illegal gambling, lewdness, or prostitution (Penal Code §§ 11225 and following)
- use, storage, manufacture, or sale of illegal drugs (H&S §§ 11570 and following; and CC §§ 3479, 3486)
- criminal street gang activities (Penal Code § 186.22a)
- holding dogfighting or cockfighting competition (CC § 3482.8), and
- unlawful distribution of weapons and/or ammunition. (CC § 3485.)

Seizure of the Landlord's Property

It's rare, but the government sometimes seizes property because of the illegal activities of one or more tenants. A successful forfeiture proceeding is absolutely devastating from the landlord's point of view. The landlord loses not only the property, but also all the rent money that the landlord received from the drug-dealing tenants.

Few tenants want to live in government-run housing that starts off as a drug den. But a landlord who hears the word "forfeiture" will probably be highly motivated to get rid of the offending tenants. If your building is plagued by drug dealing or other illegal activities, start by involving your local district attorney, city attorney, or county counsel.

Small Claims Lawsuits Filed by Neighbors

Overworked and understaffed police and health departments are often unable to make a real dent in problem-plagued neighborhoods.

Determined tenants and neighbors have stepped into the breach, bringing their own lawsuits seeking the elimination of the offensive behavior. Basically, tenants and neighbors sue a landlord for failing to take steps to clean up the property, and seek:

- monetary compensation for each of them for having put up with the situation. Each neighbor generally sues for the maximum allowed in state small claims court ($10,000), and the landlord often pays the maximum to *each neighbor*, and
- an order from the judge directing the landlord to evict the troublemakers, install security, and repair the premises.

Small (But Sometimes Mighty) Claims Court

The private enforcement of public nuisance laws has been creatively and successfully pursued in small claims courts in California, where groups of affected neighbors have brought multiple lawsuits targeted at drug houses. This approach makes sense whenever a landlord is confronted by a large group of tenants all suing for the small claims maximum dollar amount, thus motivating the landlord to clean up the property.

In one case in Berkeley, California, a group of 75 neighbors filed separate actions in small claims court against the owner of a known drug house in the neighborhood. Each plaintiff asked for $5,000 (the limit at the time) for "mental and emotional distress," plus court costs. The cases were heard as one case. The judge ruled in the plaintiffs' favor and awarded a total of $218,325, plus court costs. This sent a very clear message to this particular defendant, and to landlords everywhere who thought that they did not have to do anything about illegal activities in their property. (*Lew v. Superior Court*, 20 Cal.App.4th 869 (1993).)

Getting Results From the Landlord

Here are some suggestions on how to encourage your landlord to fulfill the responsibility to provide a safe place to live.

Evaluate the Situation

Before approaching your landlord with requests for improved security, collect hard evidence concerning the building's vulnerability to crime. The best way to evaluate the safety of your rented home is to conduct a security inspection of the rental property. Your goal is to answer two questions:

- If I (or a family member, roommate, or guest) were here alone at night, would I feel safe?
- If I were an assailant or a thief, how difficult would it be to get into the building or individual rental unit?

Analyze the Building

Start by circulating a letter to other residents, explaining your concerns and suggestions for improved security on the property, and solicit their comments. Call a meeting to discuss the results and plan your next moves.

You'll learn the most about your building's vulnerability if several tenants walk or drive around the rental property at different times of the day and night—you might see something at 11 p.m. that you wouldn't notice at 11 a.m. A reasonably safe and secure single-family home, duplex, or multiunit rental will have strong locks on windows and doors, solid exterior doors, good interior and exterior lighting, trees and shrubs trimmed, and other features that will hinder unwanted intrusions. To see how your rental unit, building, and grounds measure up, consult the list of Important Security Features, below.

You may also want to get a security evaluation and advice from your renters' insurance agent. Because insurance companies are potentially liable for large settlements or awards, they are concerned with reducing crime on rental property. So talk to your insurance company and, even more important, encourage your landlord to talk to hers about equipment and safety systems that can prevent break-ins and assaults.

Involve Other Tenants

If you are a renter in a multiunit building, work with other tenants on security issues. Here's why:

- **Landlords respond to armies more readily than to individuals.** Once you get other tenants involved, your chances of getting the landlord to implement anticrime measures greatly increase. The consequences of rent withholding, complaints to the police, or small claims actions are much greater if done by a group than by a sole tenant. (These tactics are discussed below.)
- **Involving others reduces the chances of retaliation.** You are protected against landlord retaliation (such as terminations, rent hikes, and withdrawal of services) for exercising your rights to voice your opinions to the landlord, complain to enforcement agencies, and organize collectively. (See Chapter 14 for a thorough explanation of antiretaliation laws.) But if your landlord does retaliate, you'll have to fight it, which will involve time and effort. Acting as a group may make it less tempting for your landlord to retaliate—few landlords want instantly empty buildings or, worse, buildings full of angry residents.
- **You'll learn more about security problems.** For example, maybe the upstairs neighbor, who is home during the day, can tell you that the 24-hour security guard really lounges in the manager's office all afternoon, watching the soaps.
- **Involving others increases your safety.** Once you and your neighbors realize that you are all in the same boat, it is more likely that you will look out for each other.

Resources: Organize Against Drug Dealers

Contact your local police department to find out if they have a "Safe Streets Now!" program in place. This approach to public nuisances (targeting everything from drug dealing to abandoned, unhealthy buildings) empowers neighbors to deal with the problem without directly confronting dealers or even the property's owner. Here's how it works:

Under the auspices of the local police department, neighbors, police, city staff, and community-based organization representatives come together to put pressure on the landlord who is hosting the nuisance. The program consists of these steps:

- The neighbors identify the property creating the public nuisance.
- Neighbors take notes on what's happening, recording their findings in a log and gathering other evidence (such as photos).
- Neighbors phone in or otherwise relay each incident to the police.
- Neighbors write a "demand letter" to the property owner, demanding that the owner rid the property of the problem and promising to take the owner to small claims court if the nuisance isn't corrected promptly. Each neighbor will sue for $10,000 in damages (the maximum allowed in small claims court). Landlords quickly get the picture: Suddenly they're facing many thousands of dollars in damages. This usually gets their attention.

In the majority of cases, landlords voluntarily remove the problem tenants or loiterers from their properties after receiving the demand letter, and the cases never make it to court.

Safe Streets Now! programs are already set up in several California cities. If your town doesn't have one, there's no reason it can't start one—contact another city that has one for guidance (type "Safe Streets Now" into your Internet search engine and scan the results for California cities).

Consider the Neighborhood

The extent of your vulnerability depends on not only the security systems in your building, but also the surrounding neighborhood. Many police departments keep records of reports of criminal activity in city neighborhoods. This can be a gold mine of information that you can pass on to your landlord. Also, neighborhood associations sometimes have information about criminal activities in the surrounding area. Then, armed with what you have learned, you are in a good position to suggest ways both your landlord and other tenants can keep the rental property safe.

If there has been little or no crime in your area, you have less to worry about and less legal reason to expect your landlord to equip the property with extensive security devices.

Request Improvements

Once you and other tenants have gathered information about your vulnerability to crime and what can be done to reduce your risk, you'll be ready to take specific steps to make your lives safer.

It's quite likely that you know more about the security needs of the rental units and building (and landlords' legal responsibilities) than the owner, especially if the owner is an absentee landlord. To improve security in your rental, you may first have to educate your landlord about:

- **Statutory security requirements.** Because state and often local ordinances or laws require specific security devices, such as deadbolts, peepholes, or window locks, start by asking your landlord to comply with the law. (See "The Landlord's Basic Duty to Keep You Safe," at the beginning of this chapter.) Put your request in writing. (Of course, keep copies of all correspondence.) Attach a copy of the ordinance or statute to your request. If you get no response, submit a second request. Then, if there is still no compliance, consider your options, which include the right to install the locks using the repair and

deduct or rent withholding remedies. (See "Protecting Yourself," below.)

- **Promised security measures that are missing or malfunctioning.** If the landlord has promised security beyond the basics dictated by law—such as an advertisement promising garage parking or security personnel—you have a legal right to expect that the landlord deliver; see above. Send a written reminder to the landlord and attach a copy of the advertisement or lease provision that backs up your request.

- **Security required by the surroundings and circumstances.** Your own assessment of the property and the neighborhood might lead you to conclude that the landlord is shirking his duty to protect tenants. But if you do not have a clear-cut ordinance or statute to point to, you will have to do some extra work motivating the landlord. Use the information you've gathered to convince the landlord that, given the area's crime problems, more effective security measures are required—and that if security isn't improved, the landlord could be legally liable for injuries that result. Try to give concrete suggestions, such as better lighting, trimming shrubs, self-closing doors, and so on.

Oral requests sometimes get results, but more often they are ignored. Putting security requests in writing and having them signed by as many tenants as possible is a far better way to get results. Most landlords understand that when tenants have a written record of their complaints about personal safety issues—especially when the landlord has not kept promises to provide security systems—and nothing is done, the chances of a successful lawsuit go way up.

So write a letter even if you think it's hopeless, even if your landlord is notoriously stingy or impossibly stubborn. By creating a paper trail, you have provided the landlord with a considerably increased incentive to take action. Your letter should:

- remind the landlord that he or she has control of the problem

- set out the foreseeable consequence (an assault) of not dealing with the property's obvious lack of security
- propose that the solution is relatively easy, and
- suggest that the consequences—a burglary or assault—are serious.

A sample letter or email alerting the landlord to dangerous conditions is shown below.

Meet With the Landlord

If your written requests don't produce results, invite your landlord to meet with you (and other tenants, if possible) to discuss your concerns. You may want to involve a local mediation service, which has the advantage of giving you a skillful and neutral moderator. You'll be especially glad for the presence of the mediator if your landlord arrives with an attorney. If you or other tenants end up in court over your landlord's failure to keep the premises safe, the refusal to discuss the situation with you will hardly help the landlord's case. (Chapter 18 gives suggestions on finding and working with a mediator.)

Get Help From the Government

If gentle (or even concerted) persuasion fails to get desired security improvements, call in the reinforcements. Depending on what the exact problem is and where you live, contact either building or health inspectors or local law enforcement agencies, who have the power to order the landlord to comply with the law. For example, if the landlord refuses to oust drug-dealing tenants, contact the local district attorney (and ask about a Safe Streets Now! program—see "Resources: Organize Against Drug Dealers," above). This alone may result in the landlord taking the desired actions.

Withhold Rent or Repair and Deduct

If your rented home becomes truly dangerous, it may be legally considered uninhabitable—which means

that you might be justified in withholding rent. And if you're dealing with broken or missing locks, in violation of state law, withholding is definitely an option. A safer option would be to repair the lock yourself and deduct the cost from your rent. (CC §§ 1941.3, 1942.) (Chapter 6 explains rent withholding and repair and deduct in detail.)

Sample Letter or Email Alerting the Landlord to Dangerous Conditions

789 Westmoreland Avenue, #5
Central City, CA 00000
555-123-4567

January 3, 20xx

Mr. Wesley Smith, Landlord
123 East Street
Central City, CA 00000

Dear Mr. Smith:

As tenants of the Westmoreland Avenue building, we are concerned that there is a dangerous condition on the property that deserves your prompt attention.

As you know, the large sliding doors on the bottom floor (in the lobby) are secured by turn locks that can be easily forced open. On occasion we have seen a dowel placed in the track to prevent the doors from being opened, but lately the dowels have often been missing. Several times, the doors have even been left open all night.

We are worried that an intruder will have an easy time of getting into the building. There have been several burglaries in the neighborhood within the past two months. The situation would be greatly helped if you could send a glass repairperson to replace the locks with much stronger ones. Needless to say, a burglary or assault is a worrisome prospect.

Thank you for your prompt consideration of this matter.

[*signed by as many tenants as possible*]

Because this is a relatively drastic step, we suggest you think carefully if you withhold rent. Doing so might trigger an eviction lawsuit for nonpayment of rent, putting you at risk of losing your home. Here are some guidelines that must be met by any claim that a unit is uninhabitable because of high crime danger.

- **Make sure the problem is truly serious now, not merely annoying or a potential problem.** For example, having to walk past dope dealers on your way through the front hall is unavoidable, frightening, and loaded with potential for violence. On the other hand, unverified stories regarding prostitution in your neighborhood or even in your building are less compelling.

- **Don't act until you've given the landlord notice of the problem and time to respond.** In general, as discussed in Chapter 6, you must tell the landlord about it and allow time to respond, either by fixing the problem or approaching the legal authorities (police or district attorney), who are better equipped to deal with it. For example, if drug dealers have moved in next door, you must alert the landlord and allow time to begin eviction procedures; if gangs have invaded your neighborhood, you must complain to the landlord and give the police time to act.

- **Make sure the landlord has a legal obligation to provide the security requested.** For instance, the landlord has a statutory duty to provide working locks and other safety features. But withholding rent because the landlord has not hired security guards or taken more extraordinary measures is extremely risky, and you face a serious risk of being evicted if you do this.

Break the Lease

If your rented home is legally considered uninhabitable, you might be justified in moving out, for the same reasons you may be able to withhold rent.

You may also be justified in breaking the lease and moving out if the promised security was an important factor in your decision to rent your place, and the landlord failed to follow through on that promise. This remedy is explained in Chapter 6 in connection with repairs or maintenance that have been promised but not delivered.

> **EXAMPLE:** Wendy, a flight attendant, rented her apartment in Safe Harbor after reading its advertisement in the local newspaper that promised "Security personnel on duty at all times." (Around the clock security service was important because the neighborhood was known for its incidents of assaults and burglaries.) When she was shown around the property, Wendy told the manager that she often came home late at night. She was assured that there was a 24-hour guard service. However, after coming home several nights in the early morning hours and discovering that there were no security guards on duty, Wendy confronted the management and was told that financial constraints had made it necessary to cut back on the guards' hours. Wendy wrote the landlord a letter asking that the guard service be restored. When it wasn't, she promptly moved out.
>
> Safe Harbor kept Wendy's entire security deposit (one month's rent), claiming that her departure violated the lease and that management had been unable to find a replacement tenant for four weeks. Wendy sued Safe Harbor for the return of her entire deposit, arguing that in fact it was Safe Harbor who had broken the lease by failing to provide security as promised. The judge decided that the promise of 24-hour security was an important part of Safe Harbor's obligations and that its failure to deliver constituted a breach of the lease, which excused Wendy from her obligation to stay and pay rent. And the judge ordered Safe Harbor to refund Wendy a portion of the rent she had already paid, on the grounds that she had paid for an apartment with a guard but had not received it.

You may be able to break a lease and move with little or no financial consequence. Your landlord will have a duty to make reasonable efforts to rerent your unit and apply the new rent to what you owe on the balance of your lease. (This duty is discussed in detail in Chapter 12.) If the rental market is tight and your rental is reasonably attractive and competitively priced, your landlord may have little excuse for not rerenting quickly. Of course, if the dangerous conditions that prompted your early departure are noticed by prospective tenants (who reject the rental for that reason), the landlord may have a hard time rerenting. Fortunately for you, the harder it is for the landlord to rerent, the stronger your case that the rental was unacceptably unsafe, justifying your breaking the lease. In short, you win either way.

Sue in Small Claims Court

A much less risky option would be to sue the landlord in small claims court. Small claims court would allow you to get three types of damages:

- compensation for your out-of-pocket costs (including any costs you have incurred in making repairs yourself—let's say, to fix a broken lock)
- compensation for the reduced rental value of the property due to the criminal activity (measured as the monthly rent minus the value of your crime-prone unit), and
- damages for mental and emotional distress, including anxiety, fear for safety, and discomfort and annoyance. (*Lew v. Superior Court*, 20 Cal.App.4th 869 (1993).)

If you can get other tenants in the building to file their own separate lawsuits at the same time, you may be able to have the matters heard as one before the same judge. (The legal term for this is "consolidation of cases.")

Small claims court lawsuits, particularly those involving consolidated cases, can send a powerful message to your landlord, especially if you win. If the landlord loses and does not take action, he risks getting sued by you and other tenants in the building, over and over again.

Important Security Features

- Exterior lighting directed at entranceways and walkways that is activated by motion or a timer, and not dependent on the memory of managers or tenants to turn it on. Many security experts regard the absence or failure of exterior lights as the single most common failing that facilitates break-ins and crime.
- Good, strong interior lights in hallways, stairwells, doorways, and parking garages.
- Sturdy deadbolt door locks on individual rental units and solid window and patio door locks, as well as peepholes (with a wide-angle lens for viewing) at the front door of each unit (see above for the locks required by law). All exterior doors should be solid and have deadbolt locks. Solid metal window bars or grills over ground-floor windows are often a good idea in higher-crime neighborhoods, but landlords may not be able to install them due to restrictions of local fire codes. All grills or bars should have a release mechanism allowing the tenant to open them from inside (local codes frequently require these grills to open from the inside).
- Intercom and buzzer systems that allow you to control the opening of the front door from the safety of your apartment.
- Neat and compact landscaping that does not obscure entryways or afford easy hiding places adjacent to doorways or windows.
- In some areas, a 24-hour doorman is essential and may do more to reduce crime outside the building than anything else.
- Driveways, garages, and underground parking that are well-lit and secure from unauthorized entries. Fences and automatic gates may be a virtual necessity in some areas.
- Elevators that require a passkey for entry. If this won't solve the problem, you may even want to request the landlord to install closed circuit monitoring. Obviously this is expensive, since it requires someone to watch the monitor, but it may be worth suggesting if your building has fairly high rents or is in a particularly crime-prone area.

Because a landlord's responsibility for crime on the premises (or potential crime on the premises) is not always a cut-and-dried issue, you should be prepared well ahead of time to make your argument. Do not assume that the judge will be up to speed on the nuances of this area of law. Review the legal points raised in this chapter. You may want to make a copy of the *Lew v. Superior Court* case cited above, because it covers a number of the legal issues. Also, provide crime statistics for your neighborhood, reports of crime in your building, and photographs and diagrams of the areas of the building where criminals may be likely to enter. Nolo's *Everybody's Guide to Small Claims Court* and *Everybody's Guide to Small Claims Court in California* provide more detail about how the small claims court process works.

Protecting Yourself

Faced with an unsafe living situation, your only option may be to pursue self-help remedies such as installing your own security protections or moving out.

Use Good Judgment

If you live in a dangerous building or high-crime neighborhood, your first thought must be to watch out for yourself. Just as defensive driving techniques may do more to keep you safe than confronting dangerous drivers or equipping your car with every imaginable safety device, you'll want to rely primarily on your own good judgment and willingness to change your habits.

If you have identified vulnerable aspects of your building or rental unit, chances are that others have, too. If you were a burglar or mugger, how would you strike? Avoid dangerous situations— for example:

- Don't use an isolated parking lot late at night.
- Consider curtailing your evening's activities. No late-night movie is worth the risk of an assault.
- Use a fan for air circulation instead of opening easily accessible windows at night.

Install Your Own Security Protections

In some situations, you may be able to take matters into your own hands, at least as regards your own rented space. Although your lease may prohibit you from making alterations or repairs without the landlord's permission (see Chapter 8), you can use self-help methods of rent withholding and repair and deduct if you need to supply the door and window locks mandated by state law (CC § 1941.3). Be sure to follow the steps described in Chapter 6 for notifying the landlord first, and document your costs. And because your landlord has the right to enter in an emergency, you have to give the landlord keys to any locks you install.

You may be able to install effective security devices that do not require permanent installation and thus won't risk violating your landlord's ban on alterations. For example, consider using a motion-activated alarm that you hang from a door. Your local hardware store will have other items.

Consider Moving

Sad to say, often your most effective response to a dangerous rental situation is to move. Many tenants on a tight budget believe they can't afford any better alternatives. While understandable, this view is often wrong. Look around your area for places where low rents don't mean high crime. Although sometimes well-kept secrets, these neighborhoods often exist. Or consider the possibility of getting a roommate or sharing a house so you can afford to live in a better part of town.

If you have a month-to-month rental agreement, you can usually move out with 30 days' notice. Breaking a lease may be a little more difficult, unless you're moving out because your rental is uninhabitable or your landlord failed to follow through with promised security measures, as discussed in "Getting Results From the Landlord," above.

Breaking a Lease, Subleasing, and Other Leasing Problems

A lease lasts for a fixed term, typically one As a general rule, neither you nor your landlord may unilaterally end the tenancy before the year is up, unless you have violated the terms of the lease or the landlord has failed to meet a responsibility, such as to provide a habitable place to live. Here's an overview of special issues that arise when a tenant rents under a fixed-term lease, as opposed to a month-to-month rental agreement.

What Happens When the Lease Runs Out

Often a tenant wishes to stay in a dwelling after a lease term expires. If you are in this situation, read your lease carefully, as it might have a provision covering what happens at the end of the lease term. In the absence of a lease provision, state law provides that if a lease runs out and the landlord thereafter accepts rent, the tenant becomes a month-to-month tenant under the same terms outlined in the old lease. (CC § 1945.) All the terms of the original lease, with the exception of the period-of-occupancy clause, are still binding and become, in effect, an oral month-to-month agreement. This means that in the case of an expired one-year lease that becomes month to month, the landlord can terminate the tenancy with a 60-day notice, and the tenant can terminate with a 30-day notice. The rent can be increased after a 30- or 60-day notice, depending on how high the increase is.

Sometimes a lease will contain a provision calling for automatic renewal if the tenant stays beyond the end of the lease term. This would mean that if a tenant held over one day after a one-year lease expired, he would have renewed the lease for another year. This provision is legal only if the renewal or extension provision is printed in at least eight-point boldface type, immediately above the place where the tenant signs the lease. If a renewal provision is not set forth in this way, the tenant may legally disregard it. (CC § 1945.5.)

If your rental is subject to local or statewide just cause for eviction laws, your landlord cannot refuse to renew your lease just because it has ended. You may stay unless the landlord has a valid reason for not continuing the tenancy. The landlord may insist that you sign a lease that is substantially similar to your old one. If you're not given such a lease and don't move out, you'll become a month-to-month tenant, subject to the same rental terms as before. (See Appendix A for more details on local eviction protection laws, and Chapter 14 for more information on statewide eviction protection.)

Subleases and Assignments

A subtenant is a person to whom a tenant subleases all or part of the property. The tenant in this situation is known as a "master tenant." Subleases can occur where the tenant moves out temporarily—for example, for a couple of months in the summer—and rents the entire dwelling to someone else; or where the tenant rents one or more rooms while continuing to live there. (See Chapter 2 for a discussion of adding a roommate.)

Typically, a subtenant does not have a separate agreement with the landlord. The subtenant's right of occupancy depends on:

- the continuing existence of the tenancy between the landlord and the tenant, and
- whatever implied, oral, or written rental agreement the subtenant has with the tenant, who functions as the subtenant's landlord.

But what about the tenant who has no intention of returning, such as a tenant with a year lease who stays six months and sublets to someone else for the remaining six months of the lease term? Technically, this is not a sublet, but an "assignment," under which the tenant has legally transferred all rights to the property to someone else. We distinguish the term "assignment" from "sublet" in part because lawyers often do, and to explain why most lease and rental agreement forms forbid both assignments and sublets without the landlord's consent.

There is one important technical difference between an assignment and sublease: Where an assignment is involved, the new tenant (the "assignee") is responsible to the landlord for everything the original tenant was liable for—even without an agreement between that person and the landlord. (CC § 822.) (The previous occupant (assignor) remains liable to the landlord also, unless the landlord agrees otherwise in writing.) This is different from the situation in which a tenant sublets to a second tenant who is responsible to the first tenant, not the landlord.

Tenants normally face the need to sublease or assign their tenancies in the following situations:

- You have a lease or a rental agreement and want to leave for some set period of time and then return and get your home back (see "Subleasing and Returning Later," below).
- You have a lease and want to leave permanently before it ends (see "How to Break a Lease," below).
- You want to bring in a roommate (see Chapter 2).

Most leases and rental agreements have provisions that prohibit subletting and assignment without the consent of the landlord. If you violate these provisions, you could face an eviction. Therefore, it is important that you read your lease or rental agreement before you take any steps toward assigning or subletting. That means, in most instances, that you have to ask your landlord ahead of time for permission to sublet. (For more on subleasing, see Chapter 2, Sharing a Home.)

RENT CONTROL

Many local rent control laws have additional rules regarding subleasing and assignment. Some of these rules can override the provisions in your rental agreement. It is a good idea to contact your rent board and familiarize yourself with any rules on this subject before you ask your landlord for permission to have a subtenant.

Subleasing and Returning Later

Most leases and rental agreements require the landlord's consent in advance for subletting. If you sublet without consent, the landlord will have a valid reason to terminate the lease. Your landlord can't unreasonably refuse to give consent if you do ask beforehand. (*Kendall v. Pestana,* 40 Cal.3d 488 (1986).)

If a tenant sublets on the sly when a lease or rental agreement prohibits it, the landlord may be able to evict both the original tenant and the subtenant. In addition, you can't sublease what you don't have a right to. So if you have a month-to-month tenancy, you can sublet on that basis, but you can't give someone a one-year sublease. If you have a one-year lease, you can't sublease beyond that period—though in practice many landlords continue to accept monthly rent after a fixed-term lease expires. Legally, that converts the fixed-term tenancy to a month-to-month one.

Whenever you let anyone move into your place for a while, it is important to have a written agreement, incorporating your lease or rental agreement, which sets out all the terms of the arrangement. We include here an example of a possible sublease arrangement, with the warning that it will have to be modified to suit your individual circumstances. Also, your landlord may require your subtenant to sign a separate agreement clarifying what the subtenant's rights are with respect to the landlord.

How to Break a Lease

If you want to move out before your lease expires, you may not have too much of a problem. In areas of California that are popular, the same shortage of housing that gives the landlord an advantage at the time of the original rental also makes it possible for a tenant to get out of a lease fairly easily.

Tenants who are in the military or are victims of domestic violence may have the legal right to move out early (see "Tenants Who May Break a Lease," below). Tenants may also have the right to break a lease and move out early due to defective conditions in the rental premises, as discussed in Chapter 6 (CC § 1942).

Circumstances that are beyond the landlord's control sometimes make it necessary to break a lease and move. For example, tenants might get a new job in a new locale, or need to move in order to care for a family member. In these instances, the two pertinent Civil Code provisions are Civil Code Sections 1951.2 and 1951.4, discussed below.

General Rules

When you sign a lease, you promise to pay rent for a specified period of time (like one year). Simply moving out does not get you off the hook as far as paying for the whole lease term is concerned. You have made a contract and are legally bound to fulfill it. This means that you are obligated to pay rent for the full lease term, whether or not you continue to occupy the dwelling. (CC § 1951.2.) If you do not pay, your landlord can sue you, get a judgment, and try to collect the money by doing such things as attaching your wages.

But the law requires landlords to take all reasonable steps to keep losses to a minimum—a concept known as mitigation of damages. (CC § 1951.2.) This means that when a tenant leaves in the middle of the lease term, the landlord must take reasonable efforts to rent the premises to another tenant as soon as reasonably possible.

If the landlord rerents the property quickly and doesn't lose any rent, the former tenant doesn't owe the landlord anything. However, in areas where the market is soft, the tenant could end up paying for several months. The tenant could also end up paying for the difference between the old, high rent and the new, lower market rate rent.

Tenants Who May Break a Lease

Two groups of tenants have special rights to break a lease without responsibility for future rent:

- **Tenants who enter active military service.** The Servicemembers Civil Relief Act (50 App. U.S.C.A. §§ 501 and following) allows tenants who enter active military service (or are called up to the National Guard for more than one month at a time) *after* signing a lease, to break the lease with 30 days' written notice.

- **Victims of domestic violence, stalking, or sexual assault.** These tenants may break a lease on 30 days' written notice, which includes a copy of a court-issued restraining order against the perpetrator, a police-ordered "emergency protective order," or a police report documenting the incident. (CC § 1946.7.) Only the victim and family members (not nonfamily roommates) may avoid liability for the rent for the balance of the lease term. If the perpetrator of the incident remains behind, he or she can be evicted under a "nuisance" theory, starting with the landlord giving that person a three-day notice to vacate (see Chapter 14 for details). (CCP § 1161 (4).)

EXAMPLE: Susan Wong rented an apartment from Stephan Leness in January for a term of one year, at the monthly rent of $1,000. Everything went well until September, when Susan had to move to be closer to her invalid mother. Under the general rule, Susan is theoretically liable to Stephan for $3,000—the rent for October, November, and December. However, if Stephan mitigated these damages by taking out an ad and rerenting on October 15, Susan would owe much less. If the new tenant paid $500 for the last half of October and $1,000 in November and December, Stephan must credit the total $2,500 he got from the new tenant against Susan's $3,000 liability. This leaves Susan liable for only $500, plus Stephan's advertising costs of $20, for a total of $520 (which could be deducted from her security deposit).

To summarize, a fixed-term tenant who leaves before the end of the lease is responsible for:

- the remaining rent due under the lease, plus any reasonable advertising expenses incurred in finding a new tenant, minus
- any rent the landlord can collect from a new tenant between the time the original tenant leaves and the end of the lease term.

These sums may be taken from the security deposit (the balance, assuming no deductions for excessive wear and tear or damage, goes back to the tenant according to the provisions explained in Chapter 13).

Sample Sublease Agreement

Sublease Agreement

This is an agreement between Leon Hernandez of 1500 Acorn Street #4, Cloverdale, California, and Joan Ehrman, now residing at 77 Wheat Avenue, Berkeley, California.

1. In consideration of $600 per month payable on the first day of each month, Leon Hernandez agrees to sublease apartment #4 at 1500 Acorn Street, Cloverdale, California, to Joan Ehrman from August 1, 20xx to December 30, 20xx.

2. Leon Hernandez hereby acknowledges receipt of $2,400, which represents payment of the first and last months' rent and a $1,200 security deposit. The security deposit will be returned to Joan Ehrman on December 30, 20xx if the premises are completely clean and have suffered no damage.

3. A copy of the agreement between Smith Realty and Leon Hernandez is stapled to this agreement and is incorporated as if set out in full. Joan Ehrman specifically covenants and agrees to adhere to all the rules and regulations set out in Sections 1-10 of this lease.

Leon Hernandez   9/30/20xx
Leon Hernandez   Date

Joan Ehrman   9/30/xx
Joan Ehrman   Date

CAUTION

If your lease contains a liquidated damages clause—requiring you to pay the landlord a certain amount of money as damages for breaking the lease—a court probably won't make you pay it if the amount of liquidated damages far exceeds the amount the landlord actually lost. You will have to compensate the landlord only for his actual losses. (See "Penalty and Liquidated Damages Provision" in Chapter 1 for more on liquidated damages clauses.)

CAUTION

A lease can provide that the tenant who breaks a lease without a legal justification *will* be liable for rent through the end of the lease. If the landlord follows the rules set out in Civil Code Section 1951.4, the landlord will not be required to minimize damages—the landlord can instead demand the balance of the full rent through the end of the lease, but only if the unit is kept vacant for the balance of the term (entry for maintenance not included). For this rule to apply, the lease has to allow assignment or subletting (subject to the landlord not unreasonably withholding consent). The lease itself must include a clause that is substantially like this: "The lessor has the remedy described in California Civil Code Section 1951.4 (lessor may continue lease in effect after lessee's breach and abandonment and recover rent as it becomes due, if lessee has right to sublet or assign, subject only to reasonable limitations)." This clause must be in eight-point type and placed immediately before the signature line on the lease. In this instance, you might want to take the initiative and find an assignee or subtenant to propose to the landlord. The landlord would need a good reason to refuse the proposed assignee or subtenant.

Self-Protection When Breaking a Lease

If you have a provision in your rental agreement that allows for assignment or subletting, you might want to consider finding and proposing an assignee or subtenant even before you move out or notify the landlord of your plans. Put yourself in the landlord's shoes by posting an online ad for your unit (clearly identifying the opportunity as a sublet or assignment). Of course, you cannot represent to any potential renter that you have authority to make a deal. The most you can do is deliver a potential renter to the landlord, and hope that your proposed tenant meets the landlord's screening criteria. Doing the landlord's work for him could possibly save you the advertising and costs that the landlord will charge you. (Bold tenants whose leases lack the right to assign or sublet might still want to look for and propose a replacement tenant. Who knows—your landlord might be happy to avoid the re-rental work and move in the person you've found right away.)

If you do not have the right to sublet or assign and are sure your landlord would not appreciate your DIY efforts, or you just cannot do the work involved in finding a new tenant, go ahead and notify your landlord in writing as soon as you know that you are going to move out before the end of a lease term. The more notice you give the landlord, the better your chances are that he will find another tenant.

Sample Agreement Regarding Cancellation of Lease

Agreement Regarding Cancellation of Lease

This agreement is between Leon Hernandez of 1500 Acorn Street #4, Cloverdale, California, and Smith Realty Co., of 10 Jones Street, Cloverdale, California, and by its owner, B. R. Smith.

In consideration of the amount of $150, Smith Realty Co. hereby agrees to cancel the lease of Leon Hernandez on Apt. #4 at 1500 Acorn Street, Cloverdale, California, as of October 31, 20xx. The $150 payment is hereby acknowledged to be made this date by subtracting it from Leon Hernandez's $1,200 security deposit.

B. R. Smith	*9/30/20xx*
B. R. Smith	Date
Leon Hernandez	*9/30/xx*
Leon Hernandez	Date

After sending the landlord your written notice, it is wise to stop by and have a talk. The landlord may have another tenant ready to move in and not be concerned by your moving out. In some cases, the landlord may demand an amount of money to compensate him for rerenting the place. If the amount is small, it may be easier to agree to pay rather than to become involved in a dispute. If your landlord has a deposit, you might even offer a part of it (or all of it) in full settlement of all possible damage claims arising from your leaving in the middle of the lease term. As noted above, since the landlord has a duty to try and rerent the place (mitigate damages), and since this is often reasonably easy to do, you should not agree to pay much in the way of damages. Get any agreement you make in writing. A sample agreement is shown above.

Sample Letter or Email to Landlord Suggesting Potential Tenants

1500 Acorn Street #4
Cloverdale, California
October 1, 20xx

Smith Realty Co.
10 Jones Street
Cloverdale, California

As I told you on September 15, 20xx, I plan to move out of this apartment on October 31, 20xx. Because I wish to keep damages to a minimum, I am giving you the names, addresses, and phone numbers of four people who have expressed an interest in renting this apartment on or about November 1, 20xx at the same rent that I pay. I assume that you will find one of these potential tenants to be suitable, unless of course you have already arranged to rent the apartment.

(include list of names, addresses, and phone numbers)

Very truly yours,
Leon Hernandez
Leon Hernandez

If it is not possible to deal rationally with your landlord, or if you can't get a written release, you should take steps to protect yourself. You may want to prepare yourself for an eventual small claims court fight, so remember to get everything in writing so that you can present it to court, if necessary. Don't let your landlord scare you into paying a lot of money. Simply post an advertisement on Craigslist or in your local paper to lease your dwelling at the same rent that you are paying. When people call, show them the place, but tell them that any lease arrangement must be worked out with your landlord. Also request that the potential tenants contact the landlord directly. To protect yourself, keep a list of all tenants who appear suitable and who express an interest in moving in. Include information on your list that shows that the potential tenants are responsible— for example, include something about their job or family. Write a letter or email to your landlord with a list of the names (see the sample, above), and keep a copy for your file. The landlord has a right to approve or disapprove of whomever you suggest as a tenant, but may not be unreasonable about it; landlords must keep their losses to a minimum (mitigate damages) as discussed above. Also, when you move out, be sure the unit is clean and ready to rent to the next tenant, so that your landlord has no basis to claim that it was not in rentable condition and that you are responsible for rent during the time it took to get it cleaned.

💡 **TIP**

Protect yourself from possible liability for the rent. As explained, you are responsible for the rental payment for the entire term of the lease. If you sublet the unit with the landlord's permission, you will still be liable if the new tenant fails to pay up. But what if the lease expires and the sublessee stays on a month-to-month basis and is later short on the rent? Could the landlord go after you? The answer is: Possibly. To protect yourself, keep tabs on when the original lease will expire. Write a letter as soon as it expires, stating that you are "revoking"

any guarantee that would hold you responsible for the subtenant's rental obligations. (CC § 2815.) See "Your Responsibility for Rent If You Move Out and Your Roommate Stays," in Chapter 2.

Possible Legal Action

If you move out and break a lease, the landlord may keep your deposit or sue you for the lost rent and the expense of getting a new tenant. This is not likely if the landlord has gotten a new tenant to move in almost immediately after you've moved out, because in such a situation there would be little or no damages. However, occasionally it takes the landlord a little time or expense (for advertising) to get a new tenant. This is especially likely in a resort area (off season) or near a university in the summer. In this case, a landlord may pocket the deposit or sue in small claims or superior court.

If you are sued, you will receive legal documents setting out the landlord's claim. Read them carefully to see if the amount the landlord asks for is fair. As explained above, if you take the proper steps to protect yourself, the landlord should be entitled to little or nothing. In unusual situations, however, the landlord may be entitled to some recovery. For example, if a tenant with a year's lease at a $1,200 per month rental moved out in midyear and no new tenant could be found who would pay more than $1,150 per month, then the landlord would likely recover damages. In this case, the old tenant would be liable for the $50 a month difference between what he paid and what the new tenant paid, multiplied by the number of months left on the lease at the time he moved out. A tenant might also be liable for damages if it took the landlord some period of time, such as a month, to find a new tenant. In this case, the first tenant would be liable for the month's rent (if the landlord had made diligent efforts to find a new tenant).

Landlords often simply keep the entire deposit— it's a lot easier than going to court. In that event, you'll have to go to small claims court to sue to get it back. Use the same approach you'd adopt if the landlord had gone to court first.

If you are sued in small claims court for an amount that seems excessive, simply tell the judge your side of the case and bring with you any witnesses and written documentation that would help tell your story. If you are sued in superior court, you may want to see a lawyer, especially if there is a lot of money involved. (See Chapter 18.)

Belongings You Leave Behind

If you leave belongings on the premises when you move out, you must ask the landlord for them, in writing, within 18 days. Your request must describe the property and must give the landlord your mailing address. Within five days of receiving your request, the landlord may demand, in writing, that you pay reasonable costs for storage. You must pay the charges and pick up the property within 72 hours of receiving the landlord's demand.

If the landlord doesn't comply with your request, you can sue for your actual damages and, if the landlord acted in bad faith, for another $250 in damages. (CC § 1965.)

The landlord may notify you, in writing, that the property is still there. The notice should describe the property and tell you where the property can be claimed, how long you have to claim it, and that you may have to pay reasonable costs for storage. The landlord must give you at least 15 days (18 days, if the notice is mailed) to claim the property.

If the property is worth less than $700, the landlord is free to dispose of it. If it is worth more than that, the landlord must sell it at a public sale, subtract costs of sale and storage, and turn the rest over to the county. You have a year to claim the net profit from the sale. (CC §§ 1983, 1988.)

Landlords Must Notify Tenants of Right to Reclaim Abandoned Property

All 30-day and 60-day notices, and all subsidized housing 90-day termination of tenancy notices, must contain the following statement about state law allowing former tenants to reclaim abandoned property after having vacated the rental premises. (CC §§ 1946, 1946.1.)

> **NOTICE:** State law permits former tenants to reclaim abandoned personal property left at the former address of the tenant, subject to certain conditions. You may or may not be able to reclaim property without incurring additional costs, depending on the cost of storing the property and the length of time before it is reclaimed. In general, these costs will be lower the sooner you contact your former landlord after being notified that property belonging to you was left behind after you moved out.

A Tenant's Death: Consequences for Cotenants and the Landlord's Duties

When a tenant dies, family members and cotenants will naturally be concerned about what happens to the lease or rental agreement—is it still in effect? When does it terminate? What happens to the security deposit and the tenant's belongings in the rental? And, if the deceased tenant had a cotenant or subtenant, those people will also wonder about their status. If the tenant had time remaining on a lease, can the next of kin take over? The sections below address these issues, written with the understanding that the tenant's next of kin and/or roommates are likely the ones needing the information.

Death of a Tenant With No Cotenants: Requests for the Tenant's Property

When a tenant who has no cotenants dies, the tenancy is terminated and the premises immediately reverts to the landlord. The landlord is legally required to take reasonable precautions to preserve a deceased tenant's property. When a tenant who lives alone passes away, the landlord's first response should be to secure the premises after the body has been removed. The best way to do this is to change the locks, so that people with copies of existing keys cannot get in.

It's very common for landlords to be approached by a friend or relative of a recently deceased tenant, asking for items such as the tenant's address book (to notify friends and family of the death), or clothing needed for the funeral. These are reasonable requests, but when landlords allow a visitor to enter the rental, they run the risk that the person will take valuable items, and that the executor or administrator of the tenant's estate or next of kin will sue the landlord for allowing it to happen. On the other hand, most landlords won't want to supervise a grieving family member's visit to the rental. In practice, landlords and would-be visitors work it out, ideally when the visitor has a provable, close relationship to the tenant and lives locally.

Family members or others may also want access to the rental in the weeks after the tenant's death. At this point, careful landlords will not allow access unless the visitor can prove that they have a legal right to have it. The proof that the visitor can bring with him when approaching the landlord depends on how the estate will be settled. Here are the possibilities.

Estates That Are in Probate

If the deceased tenant's estate has begun the probate process in court (a proceeding that divvies up the assets and pays bills), the judge will have appointed a personal representative of the estate.

This person is called the executor if the deceased person named one in a will; if there was no will, the court appoints an administrator. The personal representative is not necessarily the next of kin, and is the only person who has the right to take possession of the deceased tenant's property.

The personal representative's authority comes from documents called Letters Testamentary (for executors) or Letters of Administration (for administrators), which are signed by a judge. These documents look official and have a court seal, and any personal representative should have a set of originals. If you are the representative seeking access, make an appointment to see the landlord and bring the originals with you. Make a copy that you can leave with the landlord.

Small Estates That Will Avoid Formal Probate

Estates that are worth less than $150,000 (excluding certain assets) will not go through probate, nor will probate be involved if the tenant used a probate-avoiding living trust (see below). Because there's no court proceeding for a small estate, you (the visitor) won't have any letters to show the landlord.

If the deceased had a will, the named executor will distribute the assets according to the will's terms. If the deceased died without a will, the person or persons who are entitled to the property, as determined by California's laws of intestate succession, are entitled to the property. (Prob. Code §§ 6400–6414.) In either situation, the claimants must fill out and have notarized an affidavit that attests to their right to obtain the property. The claimants show this affidavit to banks, storage unit owners, and so on—and to landlords. Importantly, claimants must wait 40 days after the person dies before claiming the personal property.

As explained, the most official-looking document that small estate claimants have will be their own sworn statement that they are entitled to the property. If you are the claimant, come to the landlord's property with the original affidavit and a copy to leave with the landlord. But because the affidavit was prepared without court oversight, landlords may worry that they have no way of verifying that the visitor is entitled to the property inside the tenant's unit. You can address that worry to some extent by offering to sign an agreement, promising to reimburse the landlord for any monetary losses the landlord might suffer as a result of your actions. For example, if the tenant's estate later claimed that you removed cash and jewelry, and a court held the landlord partially responsible because of allowing you to enter, you would be legally bound to pay any damages that the landlord was ordered to pay to the estate.

The indemnification agreement shown below accomplishes this task. The indemnification agreement asks you to state why you are entitled to access. The landlord should ask for identification, and to see a copy of the tenant's will if you claim to be the executor. Hopefully, by using this form you will satisfy the landlord that you are someone who has made a credible case for the right to enter the tenant's rental. Below, you'll see a filled-out sample of the Indemnification of Landlord form.

CAUTION

Very savvy landlords may still balk. Keep in mind that the tenant's estate is not bound by your agreement with the landlord, which means it can still look to the landlord to make good on any losses caused by your removal of property. In theory, the landlord can then look to you for reimbursement, relying on the agreement you signed and suing you if necessary. But the indemnification agreement is only as good as your ability to pay off any judgment against you. So if someone takes valuables and disappears, or has few assets (is "judgment proof," in legalese), the landlord will have a hard time collecting. A landlord who understands all of this might not find your proffered indemnification agreement very impressive.

Handling a Small Estate

Executors of small estates, or next of kin in situations where there is no will, can handle the transfer process themselves, though they may need help along the way (particularly when faced with intestate succession complexities). *How to Probate an Estate in California*, by Julia Nissley and Lisa Fialco (Nolo) explains the basics. See also the Judicial Branch of California's informative summary, "Affidavit for Transfer of Personal Property Worth $150,000 or Less," on their website, www.courts.ca.gov (search for the article title on the home page).

FORM

You'll find a tear-out copy of the Declaration Re: Small Estate of Less Than $150,000 in Appendix C and a downloadable version on the Nolo website. This form does not need to be filed in court. See Appendix B for the link to the forms in this book.

Estates That Avoid Probate Through the Use of Living Trusts

A living trust is a probate-avoiding tool that allows a deceased's property to be distributed without going to probate court. The trust names a "successor trustee," who assumes control of the deceased's property when the deceased dies. The successor trustee gathers all of the property, both tangible and intangible, and distributes it to the beneficiaries as specified in the trust.

Although the successor trustee doesn't have to go to court and obtain official letters, he or she will have the next best thing: A copy of the trust document itself, which was prepared by the deceased and signed in the presence of a notary. The trustee should bring this to the property and show it to the landlord, directing attention to the clause that

Sample Declaration Re Small Estate of Less Than $150,000

‾ DO NOT FILE WITH THE COURT ‾

DECLARATION RE SMALL ESTATE OF LESS THAN $150,000
CALIFORNIA PROBATE CODE SECTIONS 13100-13115

I, William Mead _____ , state as follows:

1. Eric Mead _____ (name of decedent), died on

   June 1, 20xx _____ (date of death) in Pine Grove, CA _____ (place of death).

2. At least 40 days have elapsed since the death of the decedent, as shown in a certified copy of the decedent's death certificate, attached to this declaration.

3. ☒ No proceeding is now being   **OR**   ☐ The decedent's Personal
   or has been conducted in   Representative has consented in
   California for administration of   writing to the payment, transfer, or
   the decedent's estate.   delivery to me of the property
                                       described in this declaration.

4. The current gross fair market value of the decedent's real and personal property in California, excluding the property described in Probate Code Section 13050, does not exceed $150,000.

5. The following property is to be paid, transferred or delivered to me according to Probate Code Section 13100: [*describe the property to be transferred*]

   _____

   Eric's clothing, furniture, and all personal effects _____

   _____

6. The successor(s) of the decedent, as defined in California Probate Code Section 13006, is/are:

   _____

   myself (Mr. Mead's son) _____

   _____

7. I am:

   ☒ the successor(s) of the   **OR**   ☐ authorized under Section 13051 of the
   decedent (as defined in Section   California Probate Code to act on behalf of
   13006 of the California Probate   the successor of the decedent (as defined in
   Code) with respect to the   Section 13006 of the California Probate
   decedent's interest in the   Code) with respect to the decedent's interest
   described property.   in the described property.

8. No other person has a superior right to the interest of the decedent in the described property.

9. I request that the above-described property be paid, delivered or transferred to me.

I declare under penalty of perjury under the laws of the State of California that the foregoing is true and correct.

Date July 27, 20xx Sign Name *William Mead* _____ Print Name William Mead

Date _____ Sign Name _____ Print Name _____

Sample Indemnification of Landlord

Indemnification of Landlord

This indemnification agreement is between _____Jay Smith_____, Landlord/Manager of the rental property at ___4 Colorado St, Anytown, CA 90000___ and _____Mary Jones_____ [Visitor]. This agreement concerns Visitor's access to the Rental Premises rented by _____Suki Lee_____ [Deceased Tenant].

No executor or administrator has been appointed to represent the estate of Deceased Tenant. Visitor is Deceased Tenant's _____daughter_____ (for example, daughter, friend), and is taking responsibility, in the absence of a court-appointed personal representative, to gather and dispose of Deceased Tenant's property according to California law.

[Check if applicable]

☐ Visitor is Deceased Tenant's executor.

Visitor accepts responsibility for any liability to Deceased Tenant's estate or third parties resulting from Visitor's removal of property from the Rental Premises.

In the event of any third-party claim, demand, suit, action, or proceeding [Claim] against Landlord based upon Visitor's removal or use of property, Landlord will have the right to select counsel to defend itself. If the third-party claim results in an enforceable judgment or is settled, Visitor will indemnify and hold harmless Landlord and any successors or assigns. Visitor will cooperate fully in the defense of any such Claim. Landlord may settle any such Claim against it or waive any appeal of any judgment of a trial court or arbitrator against it. If a Claim is successfully defended, Visitor's indemnity will be limited to fifty percent (50%) of the cost of defense.

Suki Lee
Visitor's signature

June 1, 20XX
Date

Suki Lee
Print name

Jay Smith
Landlord or Manager's signature

June 1, 20XX
Date

Jay Smith
Print name

Visitor's contact information: Home
45 7th Street
Street

Oak Hill, CA 90000
City, state, zip

123-456-7890
Phone

slee@coldmail.com
Cell

Visitor's contact information: Work
1002 Main Street
Street

Oak Hill, CA 90000
City, state, zip

123-678-9011
Phone

123-890-1234
Cell

Other ID (such as a driver's license): ___CA DL# R0231456___ names the successor trustee. For added assurance, you might offer the indemnification agreement, described above. You could also copy and leave with the landlord the "Certification of Trust"—a short document that accompanies a trust made in California (other states may call this document an "abstract of trust" or a "memorandum of trust"). It establishes the existence of the trust without revealing any of the details as to who gets what.

Keep in mind that even if you are the named beneficiary for a particular item under the terms of the trust, you do not have the right to enter to take it—that task belongs solely to the successor trustee, who should distribute it to you as directed by the terms of the trust.

⊘ CAUTION

Do not use the indemnification agreement if you want to take property that you claim belongs to you. It's one thing to ask to remove the tenant's property; it's another matter altogether to ask to remove property that you claim belongs to you. California law does provide a method that such persons can use (Prob. Code §§ 13100 and 13101), but it's not available until 40 days after the tenant's death, and you must show up with a signed affidavit (sworn statement) attesting, among other things, to your right to the property. So, if you want the return of the tools that you loaned to your now-deceased friend, you'll have to do a bit of work. Obtaining property in this way is fully described in *How to Probate an Estate in California*, by Julia Nissley and Lisa Fialco (Nolo).

📄 FORM

You'll find a tear-out copy of the Indemnification of Landlord form in Appendix C and on the Nolo website. See Appendix B for the link to the forms in this book.

Death of a Tenant With Cotenants or Subtenants: Requests for the Tenant's Property

You might be the cotenant of someone who has died (each of you signed the same lease or rental agreement), or the resident subtenant (you rented directly from the tenant). In either case, you are now living among the deceased's tenant's belongings, and could face the same requests from family or kin that the landlord would encounter if the tenant had lived alone (see above). Begin by understanding that relatives and friends of your deceased roommate have no immediate right to his or her belongings; you do not have to admit anyone to your home unless you want to (law enforcement situations excepted, of course).

Although you have no specific responsibility for preserving the tenant's belongings, you could face civil liability to the estate if you let someone in who removes the deceased's property and absconds with it. For that reason, read the three scenarios described just above and put yourself in the landlord's shoes, asking for the same proof as if you were, indeed, the landlord. Be sure to use your common sense: If the deceased's brother asks for clothing for the funeral, and you feel comfortable monitoring his activity while in the rental, you're unlikely to encounter problems.

⊘ CAUTION

Protect yourself from claims that you have taken the deceased's property. The last thing you want is a claim by the estate that you helped yourself to your deceased roommate's valuables. If you are concerned about this eventuality, consider asking a third party to do an inventory of the tenant's belongings as soon as possible (you might ask the landlord).

If you are, instead, the executor, administrator, successor trustee, or beneficiary in a small estate situation, come armed with the documents explained in those sections.

What Happens to the Lease or Rental Agreement?

The landlord and the tenant's estate (or next of kin), and possibly any cotenants or subtenants, will need to confront the question of what happens to the tenant's rental agreement or lease now that the tenant is dead—and in particular, whether the landlord is entitled to rent past the date of the tenant's death; and in a cotenancy situation, whether remaining cotenants can demand rent from the estate (if so, for how long). Occasionally, relatives or friends may want to take over the tenant's unit. Do they have the right to do so? The answers depend on whether the tenant lived alone or with cotenants, and rented under a rental agreement or a lease.

Single Tenants With Month-to-Month Rental Agreements

A deceased tenant's month-to-month rental agreement and responsibility for rent will end 30 days after the date the tenant last paid rent. For example, if rent was last paid on October 1 for the period October 1 to 31, then the tenancy expires on October 31st. It does not matter whether the tenant died on the 2nd of the month or the 30th of the month—as of 12:01 a.m. on November 1, the rental agreement is over and so is any obligation to pay rent.

This rule will not prevent the landlord, however, from being compensated by the estate if the tenant's belongings remain on the property after the next rent due date, as noted above. This often happens while the legalities of who is entitled to what are being sorted out and is sure to happen if the tenant dies right before the next rent payment was due. When the tenant's belongings remain in

the unit, the landlord is dealing with a "holdover tenant" situation, and is entitled to rent for those days. Landlords can deduct this amount from the security deposit, or (when the deposit is insufficient) make a claim to the estate for prorated rent through the date the property remained on the premises (this is how the landlord would ask for unpaid back rent, too).

If the security deposit cannot cover the holdover rent and there's a probate proceeding, the landlord will file a creditor's claim form (available from the court clerk) with the probate clerk of the superior court. The landlord has four months in which to file the claim, beginning when the court officially appoints the estate's executor. If the estate doesn't go through probate (many small estates do not), the landlord can bill the next of kin.

In practice, landlords will avoid keeping a deceased tenant's belongings in a rental, expecting to bill the estate for rent. Instead, they will want to get the rental on the market as soon as possible, and that means emptying the unit of the tenant's property. But the landlord can't just throw the property away or sell it. The landlord must follow the procedures outlined in the section above ("Belongings You Leave Behind"), as if the tenant had moved out and abandoned the property. Any proceeds and claims should be directed at the estate.

Because the tenancy will legally end as of the next rent due date, the landlord is not obliged to accept a substitute tenant proposed by the deceased tenant's family or friends. If someone would like to move in, the landlord should treat that person just as it would any other applicant, by evaluating the applicant's creditworthiness and rental history with the same care the landlord uses with any applicant.

Cotenants and Subtenants With Month-to-Month Rental Agreements

When a cotenant dies, the remaining tenants retain their monthly rental agreement—it is not automatically terminated by law, as it is when a sole tenant dies. But the remaining cotenants must come up with the full rent as soon as the next rent due date, and in practice, this means quickly finding a new roommate whom the landlord will accept as a new tenant.

Until a new cotenant joins the tenancy as a cotenant, the remaining cotenants must cover the entire rent. Because the deceased's obligation to pay rent ended the day before rent was next due, the remaining tenants cannot look to the estate to pay the deceased's share while they look for a new roommate.

If there is a subtenant who paid rent to the deceased (as opposed to the landlord), the subtenant's rights will end at the same time as the deceased tenant's monthly agreement ends—the day before the date that rent is next due. Unless the subtenant makes a new arrangement with the landlord, or the landlord accepts rent from the subtenant, the subtenant will have to move at the end of the period for which rent was paid. An exception may exist if a rent control ordinance addresses the situation. (See Appendix A for further information.)

Single Tenants With Leases

Unlike the result described above for month-to-month tenants, when a tenant with a lease dies, the lease is not terminated. Instead, the landlord treats the situation as he would if the tenant had broken the lease by moving away midterm, without a legal justification. In other words, the tenant (now, the estate or next of kin) remains responsible for the rent through the end of the lease term, but the landlord must use reasonable efforts to find a replacement tenant (the landlord's duty to mitigate damages is explained in detail earlier in this chapter). (*Joost v. Castel*, 33 Cal. App. 2d 138 (1939); CC § 1934.) When the landlord begins receiving rent from the next tenant (or when the landlord could have received rent, had the landlord used reasonable efforts to find a replacement), the estate's responsibility for rent ends.

Cotenants With Leases

Finally, when one member of a cotenancy dies, the remaining tenants are not treated as if they have moved out mid-lease. Instead, as happens when a cotenant moves out without dying, those who remain must shoulder the entire rent themselves if they hope to avoid termination for nonpayment of rent. Typically, they find a replacement whom they present to the landlord. Once the landlord accepts that replacement, by adding the new person to the lease or otherwise treating the newcomer as a tenant (by accepting rent from the new resident, for example), the new assortment of cotenants can work out among themselves how they will divide up responsibility for the rent.

What Happens to the Deceased Tenant's Security Deposit?

Security deposits can involve hefty sums—many thousands of dollars might be sitting in the landlord's bank account. What happens to the deceased tenant's deposit? It depends on whether the tenant was renting solo, or was in a cotenancy situation. These situations are covered below.

Solo Tenants With Rental Agreements or Leases

As explained above, the tenancy will terminate at the end of the period for which rent was last paid (for deceased tenants who rented month to month), or when the landlord rerents the unit (lease holding tenants). At that time, landlords must handle the deposit as they would normally, deducting for damage and unpaid rent, and sending the balance, if any, to the estate.

If the deposit is inadequate to cover deductions for unpaid rent and damage, the landlord can make a claim to the deceased tenant's estate for any unpaid rent through the date the property remained on the premises. If the estate is in probate, the landlord will submit a filled-out creditor's claim form (available from the court clerk) to the probate clerk of the superior court. The landlord has four months in which to file the claim, beginning when the court officially appoints the estate's executor. If the estate doesn't go through probate (many small estates do not), the landlord will probably bill the next of kin.

Cotenants With Rental Agreements or Leases

By contrast to the result just above, the fate of the deposit of a deceased cotenant is quite murky. The estate, of course, would like the landlord to return the deceased tenant's share of the deposit as of the date the monthly rental agreement terminated (the last day for which rent was paid) or when responsibility for the rent under a lease ended. The remaining cotenants, on the other hand, might want the deposit to stay put, ready to cover any damage that the landlord charges for when the last of them moves out (particularly if they believe that existing damage was caused by their deceased roommate). And landlords would just as soon do nothing—their interest is in keeping the deposit topped-off and firmly in their bank account, returning it to whatever tenants are on the scene when the tenancy ends. Remember, landlords generally don't care how cotenants divided up the deposit (or how they allocate the rent). As long as the sums are paid in full, they're happy and it's up to the roommates to share the responsibility in a way that they can agree upon.

The safest course for both the remaining tenants and the estate (and any new roommate) would be to have the landlord conduct an inspection when the estate's obligation for rent ends, as if the entire tenancy were ending. But the landlord is under no legal obligation to do so—that's because the tenancy is not ending, and final inspections are required only when, in fact, the tenancy is about to end. So you'll need your landlord's cooperation if you want an interim inspection.

With an interim inspection held soon after the deceased tenant's death, any damage can be assessed, the deposit used as needed, and the balance "returned" to the cotenants. The remaining cotenants could sort out among themselves who was responsible for the deductions. In theory, if the deceased tenant did not contribute to the deductions, the estate would be entitled to his or her full share of the deposit. But if the landlord deducts only for damage caused by the deceased tenant, for example, that amount would be subtracted from the deceased tenant's share and the remaining tenants would return only the balance to the estate.

> **EXAMPLE:** Tom, Dick, and Harry were cotenants who each contributed $1,000 toward the $3,000 security deposit. Tom died suddenly and Dick and Harry decided to remain in the rental. They asked their landlord, Len, to conduct a "final inspection," as if they were vacating. Len decided to deduct for repairing holes in the wall of Tom's bedroom, which would require $500 worth of work. Len sent a check for $2,500 to Dick (who had written the original check, having collected shares from Tom and Harry), who sent $500 to Tom's estate.
>
> Because they were remaining, Dick and Harry had to immediately pay the $3,000 deposit themselves (essentially, they and Len simply traded checks). When they found Rex, a new roommate whom the landlord accepted as a tenant, Rex contributed his $1,000 to the $3,000 deposit, by writing $500 checks to Dick and Harry.
>
> The advantage of the process just described is that when the deceased tenant's share of the deposit is insufficient to cover that tenant's damage, the other cotenants can protect their shares by making a claim on the estate right away. For example, suppose the damage caused by Tom required $1,500 worth of repairs. With proper documentation, Dick and Harry could make a claim on Tom's estate for the $500 not covered by Tom's share. This system is also fair for any new roommate—Rex, who took over Tom's bedroom, will not end up being charged with damage that occurred before he moved in.

Security Deposits and Last Month's Rent

Almost all landlords require their tenants to put up some money before moving in. This payment might be called a "security deposit," "cleaning fee," "last month's rent," or something else. Whatever you name it, the law considers any advance payment a "security deposit," whether it is called a "deposit," a "pet deposit," or a "fee." The only exception to this rule is a fee to check your credit, which should be no more than the landlord's actual costs associated with the credit check up to an amount specified by law. (the allowable fee in 2019 was $50.94). (CC § 1950.6)

Because security deposits constitute a big investment on your part, and because deposits have historically been a major source of friction between landlord and tenant, it is essential that you understand the legal rules in this area. State law regarding security deposit can be found at Civil Code Section 1950.5.

Amount of Deposit

State law provides that the total of all deposits and fees required by the landlord—for security, cleaning, last month's rent, and so on—may not exceed an amount equal to two months' rent, if the premises are unfurnished. If the premises are furnished, the limit is an amount equal to three months' rent ("furnished" usually means the inclusion of all basic furniture).

If you are a military servicemember, the landlord can charge no more than one month's deposit for an unfurnished unit and two months' rent for a furnished unit. "Servicemembers" include persons on active duty, reserve duty, or who are in the National Guard.

If you have a waterbed, the maximum allowed deposit increases by half a month's rent—to 2.5 times the monthly rent for unfurnished property and three-and-a-half times the monthly rent for furnished property. (CC § 1950.5(c).)

If you have asked for alterations, the landlord may charge you for them as long as they were not needed as a result of damage left behind by a prior tenant (the landlord should have deducted from that tenant's security deposit to cover them.) (CC § 1950.5(c).) Be aware that some landlords improperly try to introduce all sorts of extra or nonrefundable fees under this "alterations" exception to the basic deposit rules.

If the landlord uses some of your security deposit during your tenancy (for example, because you broke something and didn't fix it or pay for it), the landlord may require you to replenish the security deposit.

Nonrefundable Deposits

No lease or rental agreement may call any deposit "nonrefundable." Nor may a landlord escape this rule by demanding a "cleaning" or "security" or "pet" fee instead of using the word "deposit." Under the law, the security deposit rules we discuss here apply to any "payment, fee, deposit or charge" that's intended to cover damage and unpaid rent. (CC § 1950.5.) Landlords may not charge initiation fees—these are considered part of the security deposit. (CC § 1950.5(b).)

Be sure to understand that landlords may impose a fee amounting to their actual costs associated with use of a screening service, credit service, and the actual time spent by the landlord doing so, but in no event can it be more than $50.94 (as of 2019), (which may increase yearly, according to the Consumer Price Index) to cover expenses associated with a credit check. (CC § 1950.6.)

What the Deposit May Be Used For

State law says that the deposit may be used by the landlord "in only those amounts as may be reasonably necessary" to do the following four things *only*:

1. to cover unpaid rent
2. to repair damage to the premises caused by the tenant (except for "ordinary wear and tear")
3. to clean the premises, if necessary, to the level of cleanliness that existed when the tenancy began, and
4. if the rental agreement allows it, to pay for the tenant's failure to restore or replace the landlord's personal property. (CC § 1950.5(e).)

Admittedly, the second and third reasons can be hard to apply. Just how clean was the unit when you moved in? As noted below, using the Landlord-Tenant Checklist at the beginning of your tenancy is a good way to document the unit's condition. And, where does "normal wear and tear" stop and "damage" begin? At the very least, a tenant is not responsible for damage or wear and tear done to the premises by an earlier tenant. (CC § 1950.5(e).)

> **TIP**
>
> **Document the condition of your unit before you move in.** This can be done in any number of ways. First, you can use the Landlord-Tenant checklist provided in Appendix C. Even if the landlord does not do the walk-through with you, you can do it yourself and send the landlord a copy. Second, you can take photos or videos to document the conditions (be sure they are date-stamped). Sometimes you do not notice certain conditions until after you've moved into the unit. When you do, be sure to notify the landlord, either by letter or email.

Landlord's Duty to Return Deposits

Within 21 days after you move out—whether voluntarily after giving 30 days' written notice, by abandonment, or by eviction—the landlord must do one of two things:

1. Return all of your deposit via first-class mail (or electronic transfer to your bank account if you agree in writing), or

2. Give you personally or by first-class mail (or by email, if you agree in writing) an "itemized statement" in writing, saying why the landlord is retaining part or all of the deposit, including receipts for work done and items purchased, if the amount is $125 or more, and return any remaining part to you.

Pre–Move-Out Inspection

Tenants have the right under Civil Code Section 1950.5(f) to have the landlord do a pre–move-out inspection of their unit. The purpose of this is to determine what, if any, property damage or uncleanliness the landlord intends to charge for. The tenant then has the right to repair the property damage and clean before moving out. The landlord is not required to follow these rules in situations where the tenant has received a three-day notice for nonpayment of rent, breach of the lease, nuisance, or waste. And, the landlord can deduct for damage or necessary cleaning that couldn't be seen due to the presence of the tenant's possessions in the rental (or that appeared after the landlord did the inspection). (See Chapter 14, Overview of Evictions and Tenancy Terminations.)

You'll have an opportunity to remedy the problems before the final inspection. Here's how this works: Within a reasonable time after either you or the landlord notify the other of the end of your tenancy, the landlord must tell you in writing of your right to be present at an initial inspection, which must take place (if you request it) no sooner than two weeks before the end of the tenancy. You and the landlord should schedule the inspection at a mutually convenient time, and the landlord must give you 48 hours' notice of the inspection if you haven't agreed upon a time but you still want the inspection. (The two of you can forgo the 48 hours' notice if you both agree.)

Based upon the inspection, the landlord must give you an itemized statement of intended deductions, plus a copy of Civil Code Sections 1950.5(b) (1) through 1950.5(b)(4) and 1950.5(d). If you're not present at the inspection, the landlord should leave the list in the unit. You can remedy the problems as long as you don't violate any "no alterations" clause in your lease or rental agreement—for example, you can certainly do more cleaning, but if there's a deduction for damage that will require major work (such as repairing sheetrock or electrical items), you might need to ask permission first.

Move Out Inspection

The landlord will inspect when you leave, and must give you another itemized statement of deductions within 21 days after you've vacated. The landlord must also include copies of receipts for work (labor and materials) to clean the rental unit or replace or repair damaged items if the total charges exceed $125. If the landlord or an employee of the landlord did the work, the statement must include the time spent and the reasonable hourly rate charged. Landlords who cannot complete the work within the three-week period, or who do not have the necessary receipts, may deduct a good faith estimate of the charges, but must supply the receipts within 14 days of receiving them. You can waive your rights under these new provisions in writing, but you may rescind (take back) that waiver if you do so within 14 days after receiving the itemized statement of deductions. (CC § 1950.5(g).) If your efforts to fix or clean don't measure up, the landlord can still charge you. If you disagree, you'll be in the same position as anyone fighting a security deposit deduction—you'll argue that it's "clean enough" and the landlord will argue otherwise. The landlord can also charge you for damage or uncleanliness that crops up after the initial inspection. (CC § 1950.5.)

Security Deposit Problems

If a landlord fails to return your security deposit within the 21 days or doesn't otherwise follow the legal steps for itemization and return, you won't necessarily get the entire deposit back. That's because a landlord can argue in court that, despite his failure to follow correct procedures, you do owe back rent or have damaged the premises. He can ask the judge to "set off" these amounts against the security deposit. To defeat the landlord's claim of set-off, you'll have to convince the judge that the landlord waited too long to bring these charges up, or that it would be fundamentally unfair to allow him a "second chance" to dip into your security deposit. (*Granberry v. Islay Investments,* 38 Cal. Rptr.2d 650, 9 Cal.4th 738 (1995).)

If the landlord's illegal use or tardy return of your deposit was done in "bad faith," however, a judge may not only not disallow a set-off, but may impose a penalty of up to twice the security deposit as well (you get the penalty). To show "bad faith," you will have to convince the judge that the landlord acted unreasonably under the circumstances. That is a higher bar than alleging mere negligence (such as the landlord forgetting to mail the check) or ignorance of the law (showing that the landlord didn't know about the three-week deadline). Bad faith might include, for example, repeated failures to refund the deposit despite your documented attempts to get some action (accompanying your requests with a citation to the law, as shown in the sample letter/email below, will make it hard for the landlord to claim ignorance). Landlords who knowingly break the law, especially those who do so repeatedly, come much closer to acting in "bad faith."

> **TIP**
> **When two or more cotenants rent under the same rental agreement or lease,** the landlord does not have to return or account for any of the deposit until all of the tenants leave. If you move out early, however, your landlord might voluntarily work out an appropriate agreement and return your share of the security deposit. If not, you should try to work things out with the remaining tenants (or a new roommate, if there is one).

Effect of Sale of Premises on Security Deposits

A landlord who sells the building is supposed to do one of two things: return the deposit to the tenant, or transfer it to the new owner. (CC § 1950.5(i).)

It's been known to happen, however, that the landlord does neither but walks off with the money. The tenant often never knows of this. In fact, the tenant usually doesn't even know the building was sold until sometime later. But the new owner cannot require the tenant to replace any security deposit kept by the old landlord. (CC § 1950.5(j).)

The law requires the new owner to get all security deposits from the old landlord. Whether or not the new owner does so, that person becomes responsible for returning the security deposit to the tenant at the end of the tenancy, just as if the new owner were the old landlord. (CC § 1950.5(j).)

Effect of Foreclosure on Security Deposits

If the property you're renting is foreclosed, the foreclosing bank or purchaser must honor existing agreements, and give you 90 days' notice if they want to terminate your tenancy. If you are on a fixed-term lease, it should remain in effect, except in those situations that are discussed in "Your Rights if Your Building is Foreclosed Upon," in Chapter 14.

Unfortunately, defaulting owners often disappear without returning the security deposit. And banks, eager to get remaining tenants off the property so that they can sell vacant homes, often offer tenants "cash for keys" to leave peaceably but the cash being offered seldom provides for the additional return of the deposit. Do not accept a "cash for keys" offer until after you have talked with an attorney or a tenants' rights organization.

Legally, the new owner, bank or otherwise, is subject to the same deposit rules as described just above, when the rental property is voluntarily sold (these rules apply when rental property is sold "whether by sale, assignment, death, appointment of receiver *or otherwise.*" (CC § 1950.5(h), italics added.) If your rental was foreclosed and is now owned by a bank or an investor, these new owners must account for and return the deposit as required by law, regardless of whether the defaulting owner turned the deposit over to the deed or mortgage holder before the foreclosure. If the new owners fail to do so, your recourse is to go to small claims court, as described later in this chapter.

May the Landlord Increase the Security Deposit?

Tenants often ask if it's legal for a landlord to raise their security deposits after they move in. It depends.

If you have a fixed-term lease (for example, a lease for a year) and the deposit is currently less than the legal limit, the landlord may not raise the security deposit during that year unless the lease allows this.

If you have a rental agreement and the security deposit and other fees already add up to the legal limit, the security deposit may not be increased.

If neither of these two situations describes you and you are a month-to-month tenant, then the landlord may force you to pay an additional security deposit—if it's done right. (The new total may not exceed the legal limit.) To legally raise a deposit, landlords must give you at least 30 days' written notice of the increase, and they must have it properly "served" on you. This means that they must try to have it handed to you at your residence or place of work; a notice served by mail alone is not legal unless you voluntarily go along with it. (CC § 827; CCP § 1162.) (See "Rent Increase Notices" in Chapter 3 regarding the law on how the landlord may change terms of a tenancy.)

Avoiding Deposit Problems

Problems involving security deposits often arise like this:

- The tenant moves out.
- The landlord keeps all or part of the deposit on the grounds of damage or lack of cleaning.
- The tenant says that the place was left in good condition.

If tenant and landlord can't reach a compromise, the tenant will probably sue the landlord for the money withheld, leaving it up to the judge to decide who is telling the truth. For both sides, this is a pretty risky, messy, and time-consuming way of handling things.

The best way to try to prevent this from happening is to arrange to meet with the landlord or manager before you've moved your belongings out and after you've cleaned up. Be sure to take advantage of your right to a pre–move-out inspection, as explained above. Tour the apartment together and check for any damage, dirt, and so on. Then remedy any uncleanliness or repairs that the landlord has noted.

Your landlord should schedule a final inspection. Assuming you made out a list of damage already there when you moved in (see "The Landlord-Tenant Checklist" in Chapter 1), pull it out now and check it against the present condition of the place. Hopefully any cleaning or repairs you've done since the pre–move-out inspection will be acknowledged. Try to work out any disputes on the spot and ask the landlord to give you the security deposit before you leave. Be reasonable, and be willing to compromise. It is better to give up a few dollars for some questionable damage than to have to sue for the whole deposit later.

If you cannot get the landlord to meet with you when you leave, then make your own tour. Bring at least one witness (a person who helped clean often would make a very convincing witness), take some photos, and keep all your receipts for cleaning and repair materials, so you will be ready to prove your case if you later have to sue in small claims court in order to get your deposit back. (Remember, after you're out, it is usually too late to come back to take pictures.)

When the Landlord Won't Return Your Deposit

Let's assume that 21 days have passed since the day you moved out and you have received neither your deposit nor an itemization of what it was used for. It's time to take action. We suggest the following step-by-step approach.

Step 1. Make a Formal Demand

If you feel that your landlord has improperly kept your deposit, the first thing you should do is ask for it in writing. Here is a sample demand letter or email.

Sample Letter or Email Demanding Security Deposit

1504 Oak Street #2
Cloverdale, CA 00000
November 21, 20xx

Smith Realty Co.
10 Jones Street 00000
Cloverdale, CA

As you know, until October 31, 20xx, I resided in Apartment #4 at 1500 Acorn Street and regularly paid my rent to your office. When I moved out, I left the unit cleaner than it was when I moved in.

As of today, I have received neither my $1,200 security deposit nor any accounting from you for that money. Please be aware that I know about my rights under California Civil Code Sec. 1950.5, and that if I do not receive my money within the next week, I will regard the retention of these deposits as showing bad faith on your part and shall sue you not only for the $1,200 in deposits, but also for twice that amount, as allowed by Sec. 1950.5 of the Civil Code.

May I hear from you promptly?

Very truly yours,
Leon Hernandez
Leon Hernandez

Step 2. Consider Compromise

If the landlord offers to meet you or offers a compromise settlement, try to meet the landlord halfway, but don't go overboard. After all, a law requiring that your deposits be returned if you leave a rental property in the same level of cleanliness it had when you moved in and undamaged but for reasonable wear and tear is there to protect you. You might suggest that the dispute be mediated.

Many cities, counties, and nonprofit organizations such as San Francisco's Community Boards, offer tenant-landlord mediation services designed to help you and the landlord arrive at a mutually satisfactory settlement.

Step 3. Sue in Small Claims Court

If the formal demand doesn't work and there is no reasonable prospect of compromise, consider suing the landlord in small claims court. Many courts have programs to assist people who file in small claims court. Though you cannot bring a lawyer to small claims court, you might ask an attorney to help you prepare the case.

And if the landlord has acted in bad faith in keeping your security deposit, the landlord may be liable for up to twice the amount of the deposit in statutory damages. (CC § 1950.5(1).)

The rules governing small claims proceedings are contained in the Code of Civil Procedure, beginning with Section 116. The cost for filing papers and serving the landlord will be modest. The best source of information on how to prepare and present a small claims court case and collect money if you win is *Everybody's Guide to Small Claims Court in California,* by Cara O'Neill (Nolo), which devotes a chapter to tenant-landlord cases, including how to prepare and present a deposit case. You might also want to contact a tenants' rights organization.

To sue your landlord in small claims court, go to your local courthouse (there may be more than one, so call first or go online to make sure you go to the right place) and find the clerk of the small claims court. The clerk is required by law to help you fill out the papers necessary to sue your landlord.

Investigate Your Landlord

If you suspect that your landlord has a practice of holding onto security deposits, consider investigating whether his previous activities have landed him in court, sued by prior tenants. Most courts provide online access to court filings. If the information is not available online, you will have to go to the courthouse to get the information.

Court filings are organized both by name and by case number. Type in the landlord's name to see what, if any, lawsuits have been filed against him. If you can, look at the complaint to see what the case was about, and get the names of the person (the plaintiff) suing the landlord and/or the plaintiff's attorney. It might also prove fruitful to track down any former tenants of your unit or of units in the building, to ask about particulars of their cases.

If you find that your landlord is a frequent defendant, chances are that he's known among the judges as such, which is a good thing for you. But whether, and to what extent, you can get evidence of his past transgressions before the judge in your case is hard to say. Experienced lawyers have ways of getting such evidence before the court—and in trying to keep it out.

On the court form, state how much you are claiming the landlord owes you. This amount cannot exceed $10,000. You figure the amount you want to claim by asking for the total deposit, less anything that should reasonably be withheld for unpaid rent, damage, or dirty conditions. Add up to twice the amount of the deposit in "punitive damages" if you believe the landlord's failure to return your deposit (or reasonably itemize expenses) constitutes bad faith. If this adds up to more than $10,000, then you either have to waive the excess over $10,000 or else not use the small claims court. If you have to decide between suing in small claims court or in regular court (for an amount more than $10,000), consider that you may not easily win the full punitive damages.

If your rental agreement is oral, you must file your lawsuit against the landlord within two years after the 21 days (for the landlord to return your deposit) run out. (CCP § 339.5.) If you have a written lease, you have four years in which to file. (CCP §§ 337(1), 337.2, 343.) However, whether the agreement is written or oral, we advise you not to wait, but to file promptly. Judges are just not very sympathetic to old disputes.

After you file the form with the small claims clerk, the clerk will normally send a copy of it to the landlord by certified mail, with an order to appear in court for a trial on the suit at a certain date and time. To find out that date and time, ask the clerk. That date must be not less than 20 nor more than 70 days after the date of the order to appear. (CCP § 116.330.) If the landlord does not sign for the certified mail notice, you will have to arrange for a new court date and arrange to have the papers served by personal service.

Small claims court trials are very informal. No lawyers are present, and there are no formal rules of evidence. There is no jury. When you come to court for your hearing, bring the file or envelope with your records. All papers or pictures that you believe help your case should be included, such as a copy of your lease or rental agreement. Also bring with you all witnesses who have first-hand information about the facts in dispute, especially any people who helped in the cleanup. If you do not have any experience with a court, visit the courthouse a day or two before and watch a few cases. You will see that it is a very simple procedure.

TIP

If you cannot speak English and cannot find a volunteer interpreter or afford to hire an interpreter, the court will probably be able to arrange for a volunteer for you. Have a friend call the clerk about this in advance.

On the day your case is to be heard, get to the court a little early and check for your courtroom (referred to as a "department"). Tell the clerk or bailiff that you are present and sit down and wait until your case is called. When your turn comes, stand at the large table at the front of the room and tell the judge clearly what is in dispute. Remember, judges hear many cases every day, and they will not be particularly excited by yours. If you are long-winded, they might stop listening and start thinking about what's for lunch.

Start your presentation with the problem (for example, "Lester Landlord has failed to return to me $1,000 in security deposits in the six weeks since I moved out of his house at 222 Spring Street"), and then present the directly relevant facts that explain why you should win (for example, "The house was clean and undamaged, and my rent was paid in full"). Again, be brief and to the point—don't ramble. You may show pictures and documents to the judge. When you are done with your oral presentation, tell the judge you have witnesses who want to testify.

The landlord will also have a chance to tell his side. You can expect it to be very different from yours, but stay cool! When he is done, you may ask him questions if you feel that he has not told the truth or if he has left some things out. But often asking the landlord a lot of vague questions just gives him more opportunity to tell his side of the case. It is especially important not to argue with the landlord or any of his witnesses—just get your facts out and back them up with convincing evidence.

In a case where a landlord has not returned your cleaning deposit after you have moved out and asked for it, you might present your case something like this:

"Good morning, Your Honor. My name is Susan Smit and I now live at 2330 Jones Street. From January 1, 2007 until July 1, 2013, I lived at 1500 Williams Street in a building owned by the Jefferson Realty Company. When I moved out, the Realty Company refused to refund my $1,200 cleaning deposit even though I left the place spotless. I carefully cleaned the rugs, washed and waxed the kitchen and bathroom floors, washed the inside of the cupboards, and washed the windows. Your Honor, I want to show you some pictures that were taken of my apartment the day I moved out. *(If you completed a checklist of the condition of the premises, you will want to show it to the judge at this time.)* These were taken by Mrs. Edna Jackson, who is here today and will testify. Your Honor, I don't have much else to say, except that in addition to the amount of my deposit, I am asking for the full $2,400 in statutory damages (twice the amount of my deposit) allowed by law. I am entitled to these damages because I repeatedly asked Jefferson for my deposit and cited the law involved. I believe the landlord has acted in bad faith and had no reason at all to withhold my deposits."

Appealing a Small Claims Court Judgment

The person who brings the small claims action (the "Claimant" or "Plaintiff") does not have the right to appeal a judgment from a small claims court judge. On the other hand, the "Respondent" or "Defendant" (usually the landlord) does have the right to appeal. A judge in the superior court hears the case as if it were a completely new trial—each side presents its evidence as if the small claims case never happened. Unlike the small claims proceedings, each side is allowed to bring an attorney to the hearing. If you have an attorney fee provision in your rental agreement and the landlord appeals the small claims court decision, you should be awarded your costs and attorney fees if you win. Likewise, landlords will be entitled to attorney fees from you if they win. (CC § 1717).

If your landlord failed to alert you to your right to a pre–move-out inspection and is now deducting for cleanliness issues or damages, you will be at an advantage if you can plausibly argue that, had you been afforded the opportunity to remedy these issues, you could (and would) have done so. For example, suppose you're being charged for failing to wax the kitchen floor (which was otherwise clean). You can argue that, had you known of this requirement, it would have been easy for you to comply, and that the landlord should not be allowed to charge you for a task you would have done. Unfortunately, the landlord's failure to follow the pre–move-out inspection procedure does not result in your automatic win when you sue for your deposit.

In most courts, your witnesses do not take the witness stand, but remain at the table in front of the judge and simply explain what they know about the dispute. Typical testimony might go like this:

"Good morning, Your Honor. My name is Mrs. Edna Jackson and I live at 1498 Williams Street. On July 1, 2013, when the plaintiff moved out, I helped her move and clean up. The place was very clean when we finished. And just to show how clean it was, I took the pictures that you were just shown. I'm sure those are the pictures I took because I signed and dated them on the back after they were developed."

Step 4. Call the District Attorney

If your landlord has a habit of refusing to return security deposits to tenants, your local district attorney might bring a civil action for fines and an injunction requiring the landlord to return the deposit. (CC § 1950.5(m).)

Rent Withholding as a Way to Get Deposits Back in Advance

Suppose, after you move in, you learn from other tenants that your landlord has a tendency to cheat tenants out of their security deposits—perhaps by inventing or exaggerating a need for repairs or cleaning after they move out. When you decide to leave, you fear the same sort of trouble and you'd rather not deal with the risk and hassle of suing the landlord in small claims court.

There is a way to handle this problem that many tenants use: A month or two before you leave, tell the landlord that you are not making your usual rent payment, and that she should keep your deposit and apply it to the rent.

Your letter or email might look like the sample below.

Sample Letter or Email Requesting Landlord to Apply Deposit to Last Month's Rent

1500 Acorn Street #4
Cloverdale, CA 00000

September 15, 20xx

Smith Realty Co.
10 Jones Street
Cloverdale, CA 00000

Dear Sirs:

As you know, I occupy Apartment #4 at 1500 Acorn Street and regularly pay rent to your office once a month.

Please take note that this is a formal written notice of my intention to vacate Apartment #4 on October 31, 20xx.

In speaking to other tenants in this area, I have learned that from time to time the return of cleaning deposits has been the subject of dispute between you and your tenants. Accordingly, I have decided on the following course of action: Instead of sending you the normal $1,200 rent payment today, I am sending you $400 and ask that you apply the $800 cleaning deposit to my last month's rent.

I will leave the apartment spotless and undamaged so that you will suffer no damage whatsoever. If you should doubt this or want to discuss the matter further, please give me a call and come over. I think that you will be satisfied that I am dealing with you honestly and in good faith and that the apartment, which is clean and in perfect repair now, will be in the same condition when I leave.

Very truly yours,

Leon Hernandez

Leon Hernandez

This type of "rent withholding" is not legal. You have no legal right to compel the landlord to apply your deposit to unpaid rent while you are still living there, and if you do not pay your rent on time, the landlord can serve you with a three-day notice (ordering you to pay the rent or get out in three days). If you do not comply with such a notice, however, it is very unlikely that the landlord will follow it up with a suit to evict you for nonpayment of rent. (The landlord cannot simply lock you out.) It would probably take at least a few weeks to bring a case to trial, and the landlord knows you plan to leave soon, anyway.

Nevertheless, we do not recommend that you use this rent withholding device against a landlord unless you are pretty sure that you're dealing with someone who cheats on security deposits. The fair landlord has a legitimate right and need to get the rent on time and to keep the security deposit until it's clear that the tenant has left the place in good shape. And if you need a good reference from a landlord whom you've manipulated in this way, forget it.

Interest on Security Deposits

As a matter of fairness, landlords should pay you interest on your security deposit. It is your money—not theirs—and they are merely holding it for you. They should put it into some type of interest-bearing account and pay the interest to you. Unfortunately, no state law says that landlords must pay interest on security deposits, though several local ordinances do. Form leases and rental agreements customarily used by landlords do not typically require them to pay interest on your security deposit.

Last Month's Rent

Many landlords require some payment for "last month's rent." The legal effect of such a requirement should depend largely upon the exact language used in the lease or rental agreement.

If the lease or rental agreement says "security for last month's rent," or has a heading called "Security" and then lists "last month's rent" as one of the items on the list, then you have not actually paid the last month's rent, but just provided security for it. So, if the landlord legally raises the rent before you move out, you must pay the difference between the final rent and your security for last month's rent. For example, suppose when you moved in the monthly rent was $1,300, and the rental agreement said, "Security: … last month's rent: $1,300." After two years, the rent has been raised to $1,500, and the tenant leaves. The tenant owes the landlord the $200 difference for the last month's rent.

If, however, the lease or rental agreement does not say that the payment is for security, but simply says "last month's rent: $1,300," then, in our opinion, the tenant has paid the last month's rent—well in advance of the last month. This money is not a security payment—it's an advance payment of the last month's rent. The landlord does not hold it as a trustee for the tenant, and a rent increase later on will not affect the amount of the last month's rent, which the tenant has already paid. So, in the above example, the tenant would not owe an additional $200 to the landlord.

Despite this commonsense approach, some judges are inclined to rule that the tenant must pay the extra $200. If the rental agreement is unclear as to whether this payment is intended as security, point out to the judge that because the landlord provided the form agreement, by law any ambiguities should be resolved against the writer (the landlord). (CC § 1654.)

When Your Landlord Demands More Money

If your landlord claims, after you have moved out, that your security deposit is not sufficient to cover cleaning or repair costs or unpaid rent, your landlord may:

- negotiate with you directly to collect the amount in dispute
- hire a collection agency to try to collect from you, or
- sue you in small claims court.

Negotiating

Your landlord will likely send you an itemized statement with a balance due at the bottom within 21 days after you move out. If you believe your landlord has a legitimate beef, you might want to negotiate at this point. You might be able to negotiate a payment arrangement that is agreeable to you and to your landlord if you are having financial difficulties. If you wait until your landlord has expended more time and energy trying to collect from you, your landlord might not be as willing to accommodate your needs.

Hiring a Collection Agency

Your landlord might hire a collection agency to try to collect from you. If you are contacted by a collection agency, don't panic. You still have rights despite the seriousness of the debt or what the collection agency tells you in its effort to intimidate you. For a detailed discussion of what to do when the bill collector calls, see *Solve Your Money Troubles: Strategies to Get Out of Debt and Stay That Way*, by Amy Loftsgordon and Cara O'Neill (Nolo).

Small Claims Court

Finally, your landlord could try to sue you in small claims court.

If that happens, you will first receive a copy of the landlord's Claim of Plaintiff form, which sets forth the reasons your former landlord is suing you and for how much. The form should also specify a hearing date. You are entitled to receive service of the Claim of Plaintiff form at least 15 days before the date of the court hearing if you are served within the county in which the courthouse is located. If you are served in a county other than the one where the hearing is to take place, you must be served at least 20 days before the hearing date. (CCP § 116.340(b).)

If you believe you have a claim against the landlord, you can file a "counterclaim" with the court. (CCP § 116.360.) You are required to serve your counterclaim no less than five days before the hearing. If you believe that your claim against the landlord is worth more than $10,000, then you may file an action in superior court and request that the landlord's small claims matter be transferred to the higher court. (CCP § 116.390.)

You do not need to file any papers to defend a case in small claims court. You just show up on the date and at the time indicated, ready to tell your side of the story. Take as many of the following items of evidence as possible:

- Two copies of the Landlord-Tenant Checklist, which you should have filled out with the landlord when you first moved in and again when you moved out. (See Chapter 1.)

This evidence is especially important if the Checklist shows that the premises were dirty or damaged when you moved in or that the premises were clean and undamaged when you moved out.

- Photos or a video of the premises before you moved in.
- Photos or videos or notes of the condition of the unit at the pre–move-out inspection.
- Photos or a video of the premises on the day that you moved out, which show that they were clean and undamaged.
- Receipts for professional cleaning of items such as carpets or drapes, or for any repairs that you paid for before moving out.
- One or two witnesses who were familiar with your residence and are willing to testify that the place was clean and undamaged when you moved out. People who helped you clean up or move out are particularly helpful.

Overview of Evictions and Tenancy Terminations

The next two chapters discuss the process that a landlord has to go through in order to legally evict you from your home. This is the only way a landlord can legally get you out. For instance, the landlord cannot just tell you to move, throw your belongings on the street, change the locks, cut off your utilities, or harass you out. A landlord who does any of these things could face serious legal consequences.

A legal eviction has two phases. The first, covered in this chapter, discusses how a tenancy legally terminates (ends) and some (but not all) of the protections that you might have. It's only after a tenancy is properly terminated that a landlord can proceed with the second phase, which is an eviction lawsuit. While these two phases can take a month or several months to complete, we suggest that you acquaint yourself with your rights and remedies as soon as you get a hint that your landlord might be trying to get you out.

Illegal Self-Help Evictions

The most basic thing a tenant should know is that California law clearly states that when landlords wish to evict a tenant, they must first go to court, giving the tenant prior notice of the court proceedings. Civil Code Section 789.3 was enacted specifically to address some self-help eviction practices. We'll look at these practices next.

Utility Cutoffs

Any landlord who causes any utility service (including water, heat, light, electricity, gas, telephone, elevator, or refrigeration) to be cut off with intent to terminate a tenant's occupancy is liable to the tenant for certain damages. (CC § 789.3.) This law applies whether the utilities are paid for by the landlord or the tenant, and whether the landlord cuts off the utilities directly or indirectly—for example, by not paying the utility bill.

The tenant may sue the landlord and recover the following amounts:

- actual losses, including such things as meat spoiling in the refrigerator after the electricity is turned off or motel bills if the tenant has to find a temporary place to live
- statutory damages of up to $100 for each day or part thereof that a utility was turned off (but not less than $250 in statutory damages for each separate violation)
- a reasonable attorney fee, and
- a court order compelling the landlord to turn on the utilities.

You can bring your suit in small claims court (for up to $10,000) or sue in superior court, if you want to sue for more money.

Tenants can also sue for mental anguish if the landlord's acts were especially outrageous. For example, a jury awarded 23 tenants of a San Francisco residential hotel $1.48 million from their landlord. The landlord had cut off water, entered tenants' rooms without notice, and threatened the tenants, most of whom were elderly or disabled. (*Balmoral Hotel Tenants Association v. Lee,* 226 Cal. App.3d 686, 276 Cal.Rptr. 640 (1990).)

Threatened Shut-Offs by Utility Companies

Many tenants, in both single-family and multifamily rentals, have their utilities paid for by the landlord (of course, they pay for them indirectly, in the form of rent). If the landlord doesn't pay those utility bills, as a means to pressure you to leave or for any other reason, the utility company is legally allowed to terminate the utility service. However, the utility must provide you with written notice (either in the mail or by posting) that they will be doing so. (Gov't Code § 6037.2; Pub. Util. Code §§ 777, 777.1, 10009b, 12833(b), and 16481(b).) If you receive such a notice, you have very little time before the shut-off notice takes effect (anywhere from 7 to 15 days). Your first order of business is to immediately contact the landlord in writing and demand that he pay the utility bill.

If the landlord does not pay the bill, you can become the customer responsible for the future bills. You must be "creditworthy" in the eyes of the utility company. To establish creditworthiness, you can show the utility company previous utility bills that you paid at other properties, or proof of prompt rental payments to your landlord. The manner in which you set up the account depends on whether the rental is metered separately.

- If your unit is metered separately, you can initiate contact with the utility company and have the bill put in your name. If your unit has more than one occupant, the utility company can require all of you to be on the bill; however, one tenant can agree to be responsible for the entire bill.

- If service is not separately metered, each tenant can make an agreement to be responsible for paying the utilities. Again, one (or more) tenants can agree to be responsible to pay the entire bill if other tenants cannot or will not make an agreement with the utility company.

EXAMPLE: Stephan, Kevin, and Klay each live in separate units in a three-unit building that has only one electric meter. The landlord has left town and the electric company has given a termination notice. Stephan and Kevin have agreed to be responsible for payment if Klay will also agree. They figure that each will pay ⅓ the total bill. (They know that if one of them does not pay the bill, the others will have to make up for the difference.) If Klay agrees, and everybody's credit is good enough, the utility company has to put the bill in their names. Unfortunately, Klay has bad credit and his finances are uncertain. Klay does not want to make an agreement with the utility company, but promises to pay his ⅓ share if he can. In this case, the utility can refuse to put the service in just Stephan and Kevin's name unless Stephan and Kevin agree to be responsible for the whole bill.

So much for future utility charges. What about those in arrears? If you live in a single-family home,

the utility cannot charge you the delinquent amount that the landlord owes. In multi-unit buildings, utilities often will not charge the tenants for the delinquent charges, only charges in the future.

Now that you're going to be paying for the utility directly, don't forget that your monthly rental cost already covers those utilities. Now, you're paying for them twice. Consequently, you have the right to deduct the cost of the utility service that you are directly paying for. This right is in addition to your rights under Civil Code Section 1942 (the repair and deduct statute), and you are not limited to deduct only twice in a 12-month period. (Gov't. Code § 6037.2; Pub. Util. Code §§ 777, 777.1, 10009b, 12833(b), and 16481(b); H&S § 116916)). You also have the right to sue the landlord under the above statutes and under Civil Code Section 789.3, and to receive your actual damages and attorney fees.

Lockouts

If the landlord changes your locks, removes outside doors or windows, or removes your personal property from your home with the intention of terminating your tenancy, the landlord is in violation of state law. (CC § 789.3.) The damages are the same as set out above for utility cutoffs. You can sue for damages in small claims court, but if you want quick action to get back into your home, see a lawyer, because this law allows you to collect attorney fees.

You might also call the police or district attorney, because these acts are crimes (trespass, malicious mischief, and forcible entry). Even if the police won't arrest the landlord, they might persuade the landlord to let you in. Ask the police to write a report on the incident; it might help you in a later lawsuit against the landlord.

Tenants who live in residential hotels (apartment buildings that are called hotels) for more than 30 days are also protected against lockouts. (CCP § 1159; CC § 1940.)

Requiring Residential Hotel Tenants to Check Out

A large number of Californians reside in "residential hotel" or "SRO" hotel units. These units are often a single room with a sink, no kitchen facilities, and shared bathrooms down the hall. These tenants are usually very low income and are often prey to unscrupulous landlords whose goal is to squeeze every penny out of their tenants. Because they normally reside in their units for more than 30 days, these tenants are usually protected by local rent control and eviction control ordinances and have just cause protections. They now fall under the state rent and eviction control laws.

In order to evade these protections, landlords of these hotels had previously required the tenant to "check out" for a day or two and then "reregister." As short-term tenants, the residents wouldn't be able to take advantage of laws that would otherwise protect them (such as habitability and eviction protections). Civil Code Section 1940.1 specifically forbids this practice. Any landlord violating this section faces civil liability.

Overview of Eviction Procedure

As we've explained, the legal process for eviction begins with terminating the tenancy. The landlord can begin formal eviction proceedings in court only after the tenant has refused to move, after the landlord has properly terminated the tenancy. This court action is called an "unlawful detainer" (that is, the tenant is unlawfully detaining, or remaining, on the premises after termination of tenancy). The court process is a "summary," or very quick, proceeding. Even though tenants have all substantive and procedural rights in these actions, they move very quickly through the court.

Tenancy terminations can happen in one of four ways:

- You have a fixed-term lease that has expired and the lease has not been renewed. However, if you are covered by a state or local "just cause for eviction" law, then this may not be true. (CC § 1946.2.)
- You have received a three-day notice because of a lease violation.
- You receive a 30-, 60-, or 90-day notice terminating your tenancy, or
- You have given the landlord a 30-day notice stating that you are moving out.

In this chapter, we explain some, but not all of the legal requirements related to the proper termination of a tenancy.

The Summons and Complaint

If you have not moved out when the notice period runs out, the landlord may file a Complaint–Unlawful Detainer against you in court. Filing a Complaint begins a lawsuit. The landlord will then have a copy of the Complaint served on you, together with another document called a Summons–Unlawful Detainer. The Summons will tell you that you have five days to file a formal written response with the court.

Your Response

If you don't respond to the court, in proper written form and within the time allowed, the landlord may ask the court for a default judgment against you. That means you lose without a trial.

If you choose to respond, you have several options (all described in Chapter 15):

- If the Summons was not properly served on you, consider filing a Motion to Quash Service of Summons.
- If the Complaint is not in proper technical form or does not properly allege the landlord's right to evict you, consider filing a Demurrer.
- You may simply file an "Answer," which is a written response that denies allegations of

the complaint and also raises defenses such as violation of the rent control ordinance, retaliation, or discrimination. An Answer might be your first response, or a response that you would make if you lose a Motion to Quash or Demurrer. Tenants usually file a Demand for Jury Trial along with their Answer.

- Settlement can happen at any time during the legal proceeding, sometimes even after a trial. Courts often schedule meetings for the purpose of settlement, but you or your representative can talk with the other side about resolving the case at any time.

Trial

After you file your Answer, the landlord will ask the court to set a trial date. Tenants usually request a jury trial at the time they file their answer. The court will usually set the trial within 21 days of the request, although the parties can agree to change the date to a more mutually convenient one. During that period, the landlord and tenant may conduct written discovery, make pretrial motions, and often discuss settlement. If the case is not decided by a pretrial motion, or does not settle, you will have to appear at trial on the date the court sets it. Even then, cases often settle "on the courthouse steps." Otherwise, it will be decided by a judge or a jury (if you requested a jury).

Actual Eviction

If you lose the trial, the landlord will get a "writ of possession" that the sheriff (or marshal) will serve on you. This will give you five days to leave. If you are not out on the fifth day, the sheriff or marshal will physically throw you out, unless a court grants a temporary stay of the eviction to give you more time to move.

Other remedies may be available if you lose, which will be covered later in this chapter and in Chapter 15.

Termination of Tenancy

In most instances, a landlord will begin the process of termination of tenancy by giving a three-day notice, or a 30-, 60-, or 90-day notice. (The usual exception to the need for a notice is in a situation when a fixed-term lease has expired). Legal requirements for these notices are very technical, so we are going to spend some time explaining them. Why? Because when the landlord doesn't follow them, you might have an opportunity to challenge the validity of the notice in court.

One very important principle applies to all notice requirements in eviction cases: Because the landlord is trying to evict you from your home, and because the law gives the landlord special privileges in eviction cases (a quicker lawsuit), the landlord must strictly comply with all of the law's notice requirements. (*Kwok v. Bergren*, 130 Cal.App.3d 596, 599 (1982).) If the landlord makes even a small mistake in a required notice, or doesn't serve it properly, the eviction itself might be invalid and the landlord may have to start the process over.

Notice to End a Fixed-Term Lease

When a fixed-term lease expires, you are supposed to move out right away, unless your city has a rent control ordinance that requires the landlord to have just cause to evict you. As of January 1, 2020, many units will be covered by statewide just cause for eviction protections (see discussion below). If you don't move, the landlord may file an eviction lawsuit immediately, without first serving any notice on you.

If you live in a city with a rent control or other ordinance requiring just cause for eviction, or if you are covered by statewide just cause for eviction protections, expiration of the lease does not by itself justify an eviction. You are entitled to remain unless you are evicted for one of the reasons listed in the ordinance or the state law.

If the landlord wants to evict you during the term of your lease for your breach of the lease (such as nonpayment of rent), the landlord will have to serve a notice on you before suing to evict. The notice is normally a three-day notice.

The Three-Day Notice Because of Nonpayment of Rent or Other Tenant Violation

The landlord can serve you with a three-day notice if you or another tenant have violated the terms of your lease or rental agreement. There are basically three types, discussed below.

Three-Day Notice to Pay Rent or Quit

If you fail to pay your rent on time, the landlord must serve a written three-day notice on you before suing to evict you on that ground. The notice must tell you to pay the rent or move in three days. The notice must state the amount of rent you must pay to avoid eviction, and this amount may not be more than what you actually owe in rent. (The three-day notice can ask for less than what you owe, but not more.) For example, late charges, check-bounce, or other fees of any kind; or interest or utility charges are not, in most cases, "rent" for the purpose of a three-day notice to pay rent or quit. The notice may not ask for rent that was due more than one year ago (a very rare occurrence).

All notices to pay rent or quit are required to include the precise sum due, the name, address, and telephone number of the person to whom payment is to be made, and, if payment may be made personally, the days and hours that the person receiving the rent is available to receive the rent. If the person is not available to receive it in person, it can be mailed no later than day three to the address in the notice; or, if there is no address, to the address where rent is normally paid. (Consider getting a certificate of mailing from the Post Office to document when the rent was sent.)

Once the payment is mailed, you have satisfied the demand of the notice to pay rent or quit. If you usually pay rent by electronic transfer, payment may be made in that manner as well. The notice may also allow payment by electronic transfer by providing the name and address of the bank and the account number to which the rent may be deposited. (*Sleep v. EZ Mateo*, 15 Cal.App.5th Supp. 1, 9 (2017)) (CCP § 1161(2).) Some judges also require landlords to include the dates for which the rent is due.

Because rent is almost always due at the beginning of a month, the landlord is entitled to request the total rent for the period for that month, less any partial payments you have made. Thus, if your $850 rent is due on the first of the month, the landlord has the right to ask you in a three-day notice for the entire $850 on the second day of the month. (CCP § 1161(2); *Werner v. Sargeant*, 121 Cal.App.2d 833 (1953).)

The method of calculating the three days changed as of September 1, 2019. Saturdays, Sundays, and holidays are no longer counted in the three-day period. (CCP § 1161(2).)

> **EXAMPLE:** Anthony received a three-day notice on a Thursday. Friday is day one, Saturday and Sunday are not counted, Monday is day two, and Tuesday is day three. He has until the close of business Tuesday to pay the rent.

If you pay the entire amount stated in the three-day notice before the end of the three days (plus any extension for Saturday, Sunday, or a holiday), the demand of the notice is satisfied , and you don't have to leave. (CCP § 1161(2).) After three days, the landlord may refuse your money and proceed with the eviction.

A landlord who accepts the rent after the three-day period, however, waives the right to evict for the late payment. (*EDC Associates Ltd. v. Gutierrez*, 153 Cal.App.3d 169 (1984).) A landlord does not have to accept partial payments of rent, but if he cashes your check for partial payment and still wants to evict you for not paying the whole rent, the landlord must prepare a new three-day notice stating the now-lower, past-due rent amount.

Sometimes landlords make mistakes in their notices. For example, they might state an incorrect amount of rent due or give the wrong name, address, or telephone number of the person who should receive the rent. If you think they have made a mistake, you might want to go ahead and pay the correct amount of rent due in order to avoid the inconvenience of going to court (if you can afford to).

Three-Day Notice to Perform Covenant (Correct Violation) or Quit

If you are accused of violating a provision of your lease or rental agreement, the three-day notice must tell you to stop the conduct if it's curable. For example, suppose the landlord believes that you have a dog in violation of a lease provision that prohibits pets. The notice must say in effect, "Either get rid of the dog in three days or move out in three days." In all cases, the violation of the lease or rental agreement must be substantial, not minor, in order to justify evicting you from your home. (*McNeece v. Wood*, 204 Cal.280, 285 (1928); CCP § 1161(3).) As with notices for nonpayment of rent, Saturdays, Sundays, and holidays are not counted when calculating the three days.

Unconditional Three-Day Notice to Quit

For certain violations, the landlord does not have to give you a chance to correct the violation. A landlord can serve you with a three-day notice to vacate if the landlord believes that you are committing "waste" (that is, damaging the premises), creating a "nuisance" on the premises (for example, dumping garbage in the backyard or seriously and repeatedly disturbing other tenants or neighbors), or using it for an illegal purpose (such as to sell illegal drugs). In these situations, the notice need not give you the alternative of stopping your misbehavior. (CCP § 1161(4).)

The landlord can also give you this kind of three-day notice if you sublet the premises, contrary to a lease or rental agreement provision prohibiting sublets. However, subletting in a city with eviction protection might not necessarily justify an unconditional quit notice. If "illegal subletting" is not a "just cause" for eviction, the landlord would then call it a violation of the lease agreement and would have to provide the opportunity to cure. Likewise, under statewide just cause for eviction controls, the landlord must give you a chance to cure a subletting breach.

Under a new state law, a landlord cannot evict you for making frequent calls for police or emergency assistance. (CC § 1946.8, CCP § 1161.3). Frequent calls for help arise most often in situations of domestic violence, or when an occupant has a physical or mental condition that requires frequent emergency help.

Unlike a notice to pay rent or quit and a notice to perform covenant or quit, the time for counting the three days for unconditional notices has not changed. Saturdays, Sundays and holidays all count. So if you are served with an unconditional notice on a Friday, day three is Monday. If you are not out by Monday at 11:59 pm, the landlord can go to court and file an unlawful detainer on Tuesday.

How a Three-Day Notice Must Be Served on You and Your Timeline for Responding

If you do not respond to the three-day notice (by either paying the rent, curing the violation, or moving), the landlord can proceed with a formal court action to have you evicted. For instance, in the case of a three-day notice to pay rent or quit, you must pay the rent or leave before the three days expire. So it's important to know exactly which day is the last day to respond to it.

First, to be effective, the three-day notice must be properly served on you. If there is more than one tenant on a written lease or rental agreement, it is legally sufficient for a landlord to serve just one. (*University of Southern California v. Weiss,* 208 Cal.App.2d 759, 769, 25 Cal.Rptr. 475 (1962).) However, what about subtenants—residents to whom you've rented space? If the notice is based on either nonpayment of rent or to perform covenant or quit, the landlord must serve all known subtenants. (*Briggs v. Electronic Memories and Magnetics Corporation,* 53 Cal.App.3d 604, 612 (1975); *Kwok v. Bergren,* 130 Cal.App.3d 596, 600 (1982); *Four Seas Investment Corp. v. International Hotel Tenants Association,* 81 Cal. App.3d 604, 612 (1978). These courts reasoned that the subtenants should have the opportunity to cure any nonpayment or breach of the lease. It would seem that this rule should also apply to cotenants, however no court has so ruled.

The landlord (or landlord's agent) must try to find you and hand the notice to you. If the server tries to find you at home and at work but can't, the server may hand it to "a person of suitable age and discretion" at your home or work and also mail a copy to you. If there's no one suitable at your home or work to leave it with, then—and only then—may the server serve it on you by the "nail and mail" method. This involves posting a copy in a conspicuous place on your premises, such as the front door, and mailing another to you. (CCP § 1162.)

Landlords are often sloppy about following these procedures. It is common, for example, for a landlord to make one attempt to find the tenant at home, and no attempt to find the tenant at work, and then simply nail the notice to the tenant's door and mail a copy. This is not proper service.

Sloppy landlords often fall back on a legal doctrine that states that if the tenant actually receives the notice, it doesn't matter that it wasn't served properly. The theory is that actual receipt of the notice "cures" any defect in service. (*University of Southern California v. Weiss,* 208 Cal.App.2d 759 (1962).) If the case later goes to court, the landlord can prove you received the notice by calling you to the witness stand and asking you.

For this reason, it is usually unwise for a tenant who actually received the notice to rely on a landlord's faulty service of notice as a defense.

Counting the Three Days After Service

You have three full days to comply with the demands in a three-day notice. In the case of a three-day notice to pay rent or quit or a three-day notice to perform covenant or quit, you do not count Saturdays, Sundays, or holidays when computing the time to comply. If you do comply, then the landlord may not sue to evict you.

If you receive an unconditional notice, you have to be out in the three days or the landlord can sue to evict you. For the unconditional notice, Saturdays, Sundays, and holidays *are* counted.

The date of service is the date you were handed the notice, if you were personally served. If the landlord left the notice with someone else at your home (or office), or posted a copy on the premises and mailed another copy, the date of service is the date the landlord took that action. It doesn't matter that you didn't actually receive the notice until later. (*Walters v. Meyers,* 226 Cal.App.3d. Supp. 15 (1990).)

To count the three days, do the following:
- Ignore the date of service and start counting on the next day.
- If you were served personally, count three days. You must comply with the notice before the end of the third day.
- If you were served by "nail and mail," count three days. (There may be lingering confusion about whether to add an additional five days to account for time in the mail. Not so—you are not entitled to an additional five days. (*Losornio v. Motta,* 67 Cal.App.4th 110 (1998).)
- In the case of a three-day notice to pay rent or quit, or a three-day notice to perform covenant or quit, Saturdays, Sundays, and holidays are not counted in computing the three days.

EXAMPLE 1: You are served with a three-day notice to pay rent or quit on Wednesday. To count the three days, do not count Wednesday; begin with Thursday (day one). Friday is day two. Saturday and Sunday are not counted so Monday is day three. You have until the end of the day on Monday to pay the rent or move out. If the landlord files an eviction lawsuit before Tuesday, it should be thrown out of court if you raise the issue. (See *LaManna v. Vognar*, 17 Cal.App.4th Supp. 1 (1993).) Tenants should raise this issue by filing a Demurrer—see the Demurrer section, in Chapter 15.

EXAMPLE 2: You're served with an unconditional three-day notice on Friday. Saturday is the first day, Sunday is the second day, and Monday is the third day. Neither of the weekend days extends the three-day period. (But if that Monday happens to be a holiday—like Presidents' Day, Martin Luther King's birthday, Memorial birthday, Labor Day, or any other court holiday—the three-day period is extended to Tuesday.)

The 30-, 60-, or 90-Day Notice to Terminate a Month-to-Month Tenancy

A landlord can serve you with a 30-, 60-, or 90-day notice for "any reason or no reason at all," as long as it isn't an unlawful reason (such as to discriminate or to retaliate against you for exercising a legal right). This rule has four exceptions:

- You are covered by statewide "just cause" for eviction protections (see below)
- You live in a city that has "just cause" for eviction protections (see Appendix A for rent control and eviction protection cities and rules)
- You have a fixed-term lease that has not expired, and
- Your landlord accepts payments from a Section 8 or other similar government subsidy program.

To terminate a month-to-month tenancy for reasons that are not "for cause" (the landlord is terminating for reasons other than rent nonpayment, lease violations, or uncurable violations), the landlord must serve you with a notice of termination of tenancy. It simply says that you are to get out in 30 or 60 days (or more). (Tenants who have resided continuously in the rental for a year or more are entitled to 60 days' notice; if less than one tear, only 30 days' notice is required.) The notice need not state why the landlord wants you out (but remember, if you are covered under statewide rent control or a local rent control ordinance requires that the notice state just cause to evict, the landlord must list it).

If your landlord receives rent or other payments from the Department of Housing & Urban Development (HUD) or a local or state program (most of which operate as "housing authorities") on your behalf, you are entitled to 90 days' notice, not 30 or 60. (CC § 1954.535; *Wasatch Property Management. v. DeGrate*, 35 Cal.4th 111 (2005).) In addition, the landlord must state the reason for termination on the 90-day notice. And if you are a Section 8 tenant, your landlord cannot give you a 90-day notice until your initial rental term has elapsed. During the 90-day period prior to termination, the landlord cannot increase the rent or otherwise require any subsidized tenant to pay more than he or she paid under the subsidy.

A 30- or 60-day notice is not required if the landlord does not want to renew a fixed-term lease. However, both statewide and local rent control laws require "just cause" to evict, and mere expiration of a lease is not one of the reasons allowed for eviction. The landlord may evict only if the tenant refuses to sign a similar lease or extension whose terms, including rent, are legal under local and state law.

The tenant is entitled to stay until the end of the lease term, but no longer. However, many landlords use a 30- or 60-day notice near the end of a lease term as a practical way to remind the tenant that the lease is about to expire and will not be renewed.

If your property has been sold at a foreclosure sale (at a "trustee sale"), the new owner must serve you with a 90-day notice to terminate your tenancy. If you are covered by statewide "just cause" protections or live in a city or county with "just cause" for eviction protections—such as a rent control jurisdiction—the new owner can evict only for certain specified reasons. (*Gross v. Superior Court,* 171 Cal.App. 3d 265 (1985).) Your rights after foreclosure sale are discussed in greater detail later in this chapter.

Any 30-, 60-, or 90-day notice served by the landlord must contain the following language:

> State law permits former tenants to reclaim abandoned personal property left at the former address of the tenant, subject to certain conditions. You may or may not be able to reclaim property without incurring additional costs, depending on the cost of storing the property and the length of time before it is reclaimed. In general, these costs will be lower the sooner you contact your former landlord after being notified that property belonging to you was left behind after you moved out.

Tenant's 30-Day Notice to Terminate Tenancy

When tenants decide to move, they need only give a 30-day notice that they are moving. The tenant may not rescind (cancel) this notice without the landlord also agreeing that you can stay, so be sure you intend to move out before giving such a notice. After the 30 days have expired (and after the tenant moves) the tenant is no longer required to pay rent. The notice must be in writing, state clearly that the tenant will be moving, and be signed by the tenant. This notice is required if the tenant wishes to get the security deposit back and does not want to get stuck owing rent after the thirty days. The notice may be served on the landlord personally, or by leaving a copy with a person over 18 years of age at the office or residence of the landlord and mailing the notice; or by certified or registered mail. The notice may be served by certified or registered mail on the landlord's agent who receives rental payments. (CC § 1946, CCP § 1162.)

How a 30- or 60-, or 90-Day Notice Must Be Served on You

Here are some key points about 30-, 60-, or 90-day notices:

- A 30-, 60-, or 90-day notice may be served on any day of the month. It need not be served on the first day, the "rent day," or any other day—unless the rental agreement requires it to be served on a certain day.
- It may be served in the same manner as the three-day notice (see above), *or* by certified or registered mail. (CC § 1946.)
- If the last day falls on a Saturday, Sunday, or holiday, you have all day Monday to move if you want to.

○ **CAUTION**

Don't rely on an extra five days if you were served by certified mail or "nail and mail." There is some authority for this theory—under California Civil Procedure Section 1013, litigants get an additional five days when they're served by nonpersonal service with papers in an ongoing lawsuit. But terminating a tenancy is not part of a lawsuit—the lawsuit (the unlawful detainer case) begins later, and only if the tenant doesn't comply. (*Losornio v. Motta,* 67 Cal.App.4th 110 (1998).) So don't rely on this theory.

EXAMPLE: You have a month-to-month tenancy, pay rent on the first, and have lived there for six months. If your landlord serves you with a 30-day notice on June 15, you are supposed to vacate on July 15. But if July 15 falls on a weekend or holiday, the next business day is "moving day."

Withdrawal of a 30-, 60-, or 90-Day Notice

The notice can be withdrawn only if the landlord and tenant agree to nullify it. However, now and then a landlord will accept rent covering a period beyond the 30, 60, or 90 days. When this happens, the legal effect is the withdrawal of the termination. (*EDC Associates v. Gutierrez,* 153 Cal. App.3d 167 (1984).)

> **EXAMPLE:** The landlord serves you with a 30-day notice on June 10, requiring you to move on July 10. Your rent is $1,000 a month, due on the first. On July 1, you pay the usual $1,000 rent. If the landlord accepts it, she has accepted rent for the whole month of July, including the part beyond July 10. By doing so, she has probably impliedly withdrawn the notice.

Statewide "Just Cause for Eviction" Laws

Effective January 1, 2020, many California tenants will be covered by controls on rents (see Chapter 3) and limitations on evictions. Under "just cause for eviction" principles, landlords may terminate and evict only for a reason that is specifically allowed by law. Under "just cause," it is no longer the case that a landlord can evict for "any reason or no reason at all." (CC § 1946.2.)

This law, called The Tenant Protection Act ("TPA"), is new and many of its provisions are open to interpretation. We cannot anticipate how courts will interpret some of these provisions or whether the legislature will make amendments to clarify some of the language in the new law. We will post updates on this book's companion page as needed.

Who Is Covered by Statewide Eviction Protections?

Unless a unit is specifically exempted (excluded) from the law, "just cause for eviction" applies to all California tenancies where either: 1) all the tenants have resided in the unit for at least 12 continuous months, or 2) where a tenant has resided in the unit for at least 24 continuous months. (CC § 1946.2(a)). If you fall into either of these categories then your next step is to see if any of the exemptions below apply. If an exemption applies, you do not have statewide eviction protection. (CC § 1946.2(e); all references below are to the Civil Code).

Units covered by local "just cause for eviction" laws are not covered by the new state law.

Under the TPA, local "just cause" for eviction protections in effect on or before September 1, 2019, remain in full force and effect. (CC § 1946.2(g)(1).) Most cities with rent control also have "just cause" protections, other cities have "just cause for eviction" protections but no rent control.

For cities that pass an eviction protection ordinance after September 1, 2019, those ordinances must be at least as protective as the TPA. (CC § 1946.2(g)(1)(B).) Most local eviction protection laws are stronger than the state law, so this exemption is to your advantage. If you are in a rent control city, but your unit is not covered by your local law, then state law might apply (see examples below).

Units where the tenant shares a bathroom or kitchen with the owner who occupies the unit as a principal residence are exempt. (CC § 1946.2(e)(4).)

Single-family owner-occupied residences. For this exemption to apply, the owner-occupant can rent up to two bedrooms in the property, counting the bedroom in any accessory ("mother-in-law") unit. (CC § 1946.2(3)(5).).

Most single-family homes and condominiums. Most, but not all, single-family homes and condominiums are exempt under the state law. (CC § 1946.2(e)(8).) Tenants are often unaware that their building is a condominium. A condominium is any unit that can be sold separately from any other unit in the building.

In condominium buildings, each unit is also taxed separately. The local Tax Assessor's Office and Recorder's Office will have information to tell you if your unit is a condominium. This exemption does not apply if either one of the following is true:

- The owner of the unit is a real estate investment trust (REIT), a corporation, or a limited liability company (LLC) where at least one of the "members" (owners) of the LLC is a corporation (see Chapter 3 for information on finding out who owns your building), or
- The landlord has not given the following written notice :
  "This property is not subject to the rent limits imposed by Section 1947.12 of the Civil Code and is not subject to the just cause requirements of Section 1946.2 of the Civil Code. This property meets the requirements of Sections 1947.12(c)(5) and 1946.2(e)(8) of the Civil Code and the owner is not any of the following: (1) a real estate investment trust, as defined by Section 856 of the Internal Revenue Code; (2) a corporation; or (3) a limited liability company in which at least one member is a corporation." The notice must be given to all tenancies in effect before July 1, 2020 and must be included in all rental agreements in effect after July 1, 2020. If the landlord fails to do this, then your unit is covered by statewide eviction protections.
- **Owner-occupied duplexes.** This exemption applies only if the owner lived in the unit when the tenant moved in and continues to occupy the property as his or her principal residence. (CC § 1946.2(e)(6).)
- **Housing built within the previous 15 years.** For instance, tenants in a building built in 2010 would not be covered now but would be covered after 2025. (CC § 1946.2(e)(7).)
- **Transient and tourist hotel occupancy.** This exemption applies to hotels and motels with occupancies of less than 30 days. (CC § 1946.2(e)(1).) These types of hotels are generally reserved for tourist use, but some now have occupancies of more than 30 days. If that is the case, then you are covered by statewide eviction protections. Units in "residential hotels" or "SRO" units are generally covered by statewide eviction protections and are often covered by local rent ordinances. Note, a landlord cannot require a tenant of a residential hotel to move out before 30 days has expired if the purpose is to avoid being subject to landlord tenant laws. (CC § 1940.1)

- **Housing designated as low or moderate income housing if the landlord has an agreement with a governmental agency.** This exemption includes low and moderate income housing projects as well as government-sponsored housing subsidy or voucher programs, such as Section 8. (CC § 1946.2(e)(9))
- **Dormitories owned and operated by educational institutions.** (CC § 1946.2(e)(3))
- **Housing in nonprofit facilities such as nonprofit hospitals, elderly care facilities, and religious facilities.** (CC § 1946.2(e)(2))

The 30-, 60-, or 90-Day Notice Where Statewide Eviction Protections Apply

If none of the exemptions described above apply, then you are covered by statewide "just cause for eviction" protections. The advantages of these protections are:

1. The landlord can evict you only for one of the "just causes" for eviction listed in the law. (CC § 1946.2(b).)
The notice of termination must state the reason for the termination. (CC § 1946.2(a).)
2. When tenants are evicted through no fault of their own (as happens with an owner-move-in eviction), the landlord must offer some form of relocation reimbursement when giving the notice of termination. (CC § 1946.2(d).)

The "just causes" for eviction are broken down into two categories: "at-fault" and "no fault" (CC § 1946.2(b)(1) and (2).)

At-fault evictions include:

1. Failure to pay rent
2. Breach of a material term of the rental agreement
3. Maintaining or permitting a nuisance
4. Committing waste (usually property damage)
5. Failing to sign a new lease that is similar to the previous lease
6. Criminal activity by the tenant, including threatening the landlord or the landlord's agent
7. Subletting or assigning the premises without permission
8. Refusing to allow the owner to enter the property after receiving notice (see Chapter 5)
9. Using the premises for an unlawful purpose
10. Failing to vacate after the landlord has terminated the tenant's employment (as happens with a resident manager)
11. When the tenant gives a 30-day notice to the landlord that the tenant is vacating, and the tenant does not vacate.

No-fault evictions include:

1. The landlord intends to move in or have an immediate relative move in.
2. The landlord intends to withdraw the unit from the rental market.
3. The unit must be vacant in order to comply with a government order or an ordinance that requires that the tenant vacate.
4. The landlord intends to demolish or substantially remodel the property.

For both at-fault and no-fault evictions, the landlord must state the cause for eviction in the notice to vacate.

If the cause for eviction is for violation of a provision of the lease agreement (such as subletting), the landlord must first give the tenant a written notice of the breach and an opportunity to cure the breach. If the tenant does not cure after this notice expires, the landlord can give a unconditional three-day notice to quit. (CC § 1946.2(c).) This provision seems to apply to those situations such as subletting, some nuisances, some unlawful use (where a landlord would otherwise be allowed to use an unconditional three-day notice). In these instances, the legislature has provided an additional protection by giving the tenant an opportunity to cure the violation (such as subletting), if it can be done.

If the cause for eviction is a no-fault cause, the landlord must provide the relocation benefits specified under Section 1946(d). This assistance can be either 1) a direct payment of an amount equal to one month's rent, payable within 15 days of the service of the notice to vacate, or 2) a statement that the rent for the final month of the tenancy is waived.

The 30-, 60-, or 90-Day Notice in Rent Control Cities With "Just Cause" Requirements

Many local rent control ordinances limit the landlord's right to evict. (See Chapter 3 and the Rent Control Chart in Appendix A for more on rent control.) San Diego has its own "just cause eviction" ordinance, without rent control, for tenants who have lived in their rental units two years or more. The City of Glendale has "just cause eviction" requirements, also in the absence of rent control provisions. Like their state law counterpart, these ordinances require the landlord to have an allowed "just cause" or "good cause" reason to evict, and that a list of acceptable reasons is stated in the ordinance. It does not matter whether the tenant has a month-to-month tenancy or had a fixed-term lease that has expired. The list of specified "just causes" is unique for each city.

Here is a list of common "just cause" reasons:

- **Wrongdoing by the tenant—such as nonpayment of rent or creating a legal nuisance.** As discussed above, a three-day notice is typically used in this situation. Under the ordinances of some cities, the landlord must first notify the tenant of the alleged lease or rental agreement violations—for example, moving in too many people, damaging the premises, or making too much noise—and give the tenant a chance to correct it. In other types of situations—such as using the premises to sell illegal drugs—the landlord need not give the tenant the alternative of stopping the misbehavior.

- **Tenant refuses to sign a new lease or extension.** In cities with just cause eviction requirements, a landlord cannot evict merely because the tenant's lease has expired, unless the tenant refuses to sign a new lease with similar (and legal) terms at a legal rent.

- **Landlord needs to make major repairs or do large-scale remodeling on the premises.** Under the terms of many ordinances, however, a tenant has the right to move back in after the remodeling is completed, at the original rent plus an extra "pass-through" increase that allows the landlord to recover part of the cost of the improvements.

- **To enable the landlord or landlord's relative to live in the rental unit.** Most just cause ordinances allow landlords to evict in order to move in themselves or have certain close relatives move in, if the landlord has no other comparable vacant units.

- **"Ellis Act" Evictions—the landlord wants to permanently remove the building from residential rental use.** A state law called the Ellis Act (Gov't Code § 7060) allows landlords to get out of the residential rental business. This type of eviction subjects landlords to several requirements, one of which is that the tenant must receive a 120-day notice of termination. And, if the tenant is over 62 years of age or disabled, the landlord must give a year's notice.

Many "just cause" provisions have very detailed requirements. Some, for instance, require landlords to pay moving expenses, others provide for additional grace periods, and many have restrictions on evictions when an owner wants to move into a property. You are strongly encouraged to check with your local rental authorities and obtain a copy of the ordinance and applicable regulations (see Appendix A for contact information).

! **CAUTION**
Some landlords have abused the move-in provision by falsely telling the tenant that the landlord or a relative is going to move in. Later—after the tenant moves out—they rent the place out at a higher rent. If you move out for one of these reasons, be sure to periodically check to see if the landlord does what he stated in the termination notice. If he hasn't followed through, it's time to find a lawyer to discuss the possibility of filing a lawsuit.

You should continue to pay rent up to and including the last day of the 30-, 60-, or 90- day notice. Otherwise, the landlord can give you a three-day notice to pay rent or quit. Also, unless the lease describes part of your initial deposit as "last month's rent," you cannot apply your security deposit to rent. One strategy is to continue to pay rent and hope that the landlord accepts rent for beyond the termination date. This would give you a strong defense to any eviction.

Possible Defenses to a Termination Notice

When evaluating how to respond to a termination notice, the first thing you will want to know is, "With each of these possible responses, what are my chances of winning?" If you are covered by state or local "just cause" for eviction provisions, the reason for eviction should be stated by the landlord. Carefully read the provision in the law that applies to the claimed reason. This should help you evaluate the legitimacy of the landlord's stated reasons. Also, if you can, consult with a tenants' rights organization or a lawyer specializing in tenants' rights for further information. Here are some of the most typical defenses that arise in these cases:

- **Is the notice correct?** The three-day or the 30-, 60-, or 90-day notice is the foundation for the landlord's case and almost always the most critical part. Therefore evaluate whether the notice is correct in both form and substance. For instance, did the notice to quit state the correct address to the premises? Did the three-day notice to pay rent state the precise sum due? Was the address to which the rent should be delivered included in the notice to pay rent or quit? Did you pay the rent within the three days? Did you cure the breach of covenant within three days? Is the alleged breach trivial or was it substantial?

- **Does the reason for termination comply with "just cause" requirements?** If you are covered by statewide eviction protections or live in a jurisdiction that requires a just cause for eviction, determine whether the notice stated a valid reason for eviction and met all the requirements to evict. Sometimes the "just cause" reason has very detailed requirements. Again, you will want to look at the specific language of Civil Code Section 1946.2 or your local ordinance and the applicable rules and regulations to help you make this determination.

- **Is the notice retaliatory?** A landlord is not allowed to retaliate (get back at you) because you exercised a right that you have under the law. (CC § 1942.5.) For example, if the landlord is evicting you because you contacted the building inspector, reported bedbugs, demanded repairs, organized a tenant's union, or exercised some other legal right, you have a strong defense to the eviction. It is the tenant's burden, however, to prove that it is more likely than not that the landlord's reason (motive) for eviction is to retaliate.

- **Is the landlord discriminating?** It is unlawful for a landlord to discriminate because of race, religion, gender, sexual orientation, disability, age, or marital status. (See Gov't Code § 12955 and Chapter 4.) If you can prove that it is more likely than not that the landlord's dominant purpose for eviction is to discriminate, you have a strong defense to the eviction.

- **Has the landlord accepted rent for a period after the notice expired?** As mentioned just above, a landlord who accepts rent after the termination of the tenancy "waives" that termination. Thus, if you receive a 60-day notice you have to pay rent up to the 60th day, but if the landlord accepts rent for a period after the 60th day, he might have waived the right to termination. Likewise, if you are being evicted for nonpayment of rent, and pay the rent after the three days, the landlord who accepts the payment waives the right to declare your tenancy terminated. (*EDC Associates v. Gutierrez,* 153 Cal.App.3d 167 (1984).) Note that this is different from a scenario wherein you paid rent on the first of the month and on the tenth of the month the landlord gives a three-day notice to cure or quit (for instance, get rid of your dog to comply with a "no pets" clause in your lease). In this situation, the fact that you paid rent to the end of the month does not provide you with a defense (but you might have a "waiver and estoppel" argument, described below).

- **Waiver and estoppel.** Using the example above, sometimes a landlord (or building manager) will give you reason to believe that it's okay to have a dog even when the lease says otherwise. The landlord then accepts rent knowing that you have a dog. It would be unfair to evict under these circumstances. The argument is that the landlord has waived the right to accuse you of a breach and should be estopped (stopped) from proceeding with the eviction. This situation usually boils down to whether the landlord actually knew about the pet and then accepted rent, so it's important to have solid evidence that the landlord knew of the pet.

- **Did the landlord fail to provide habitable premises?** The landlord is obligated under the warranty of habitability to comply with building codes, housing codes, and health and safety codes. When the landlord's failure to comply is substantial, the landlord has "breached" (broken) this obligation, thereby excusing payment by the tenant. The duty to provide habitable housing begins when a landlord first rents the unit to you and applies at all times after that. (See the discussion of habitability in Chapters 6 and 7.) Failure to provide habitable premises can be used as a defense to nonpayment of rent cases. Under this defense you are essentially saying that the landlord is charging you full rent but did not provide the full package of housing services required. At trial, the jury will have to determine what the "reasonable rent" for the premises should have been given the conditions. The tenant will then be required to pay the reasonable rent as determined by the jury. If paid within five days of the judgment, the tenant will not have to move. (CCP § 1174.2.)

For more information about possible defenses, see in Chapter 15, "Filling out the Form Answer—Affirmative Defenses."

Your Options After a Three-Day or 30-, 60-, or 90-Day Notice Is Served

If you get a three-day, 30-day, 60-day, or 90-day notice, sit down and think things over. Don't worry—you won't be thrown out on the fourth, 31st, 61st, or 91st day, as the case may be. As we mentioned, the landlord must first sue to evict you, and you must be notified of the lawsuit. Only if you lose the lawsuit can you be evicted, and then only by the sheriff or marshal. Usually, it will take the landlord over a month to finish the lawsuit (longer if you contest it) and, if the landlord wins, get the sheriff or marshal to give you an eviction order.

You have several choices:

- **Comply with the notice**—for example, pay the rent, get rid of the dog, or simply move out. If the landlord is in the right and you are able to comply, this might be the best course. If you do comply, be sure to notify the landlord in writing of your compliance (for instance, send an email stating that you got rid of the dog or paid the rent). Likewise, if you received a 30-, 60-, or 90-day notice, you have the choice of complying by moving out. Deciding whether to move out will be influenced by the defenses that you might have if the case goes to court.
- **Negotiate a solution with the landlord**, either by yourself, through a neighborhood or city-sponsored mediation program, or through a lawyer. (See Chapter 18 for a discussion of mediation services.) It will cost the landlord time and money to file an eviction lawsuit, which gives the landlord some incentive to work out a fair deal with you.
- **Let the landlord file an eviction lawsuit.** The discussion above should help you decide your chance of winning. For some, staying might be their only realistic option. The eviction lawsuit will take time and give you a chance to save money to move. You will also have time to discuss settlement during the case. And, of course, if you are in the right, this could be the only way to defend your legal right to stay. You might also want to get some advice from a tenants' organization or an experienced tenants' lawyer.

If you decide to fight the eviction, you can represent yourself or hire a lawyer. If your lease or rental agreement requires the loser to pay the winner's attorney fees—and your chances of winning look pretty good—you may well want to do the latter.

If you decide to represent yourself, prepare carefully. The key is to do your homework—both on the law and on the facts. Get your witnesses, receipts, photos, and other evidence lined up, and learn the procedural rules set out in Chapter 15.

Will an Eviction Lawsuit Become a Matter of Public Record?

Most civil lawsuits are a matter of public record. With few exceptions, anyone can walk into the clerk's office and ask to see the case file. Eviction cases are one of those exceptions. A special law severely limits public access to the court files. (CCP § 1161.2.) The public has access to an unlawful detainer case file only when the landlord obtains a judgment against the tenant, or when there is a special court order (very rare), or if the case is an eviction of a former owner of a property that has been foreclosed on.

Stopping an Eviction by Filing for Bankruptcy

If you file for bankruptcy before the landlord files the eviction lawsuit, the landlord cannot legally file an eviction lawsuit unless he first goes to the Bankruptcy Court and asks for permission to proceed. If the landlord has started an eviction lawsuit but hasn't gotten a judgment for possession of the property (discussed in Chapter 15), the landlord must stop it once you file for bankruptcy, and can proceed only after getting permission from the Bankruptcy Court to go ahead. (11 U.S.C. § 362.) But don't get your hopes up—bankruptcy judges usually grant these requests, and it takes only a week or so if the landlord or the landlord's attorney acts quickly.

If you file for bankruptcy after the landlord has completed the eviction lawsuit and obtained a judgment for possession, but before the sheriff arrives, you are out of luck—the sheriff can go ahead and do his job. However, under very narrow circumstances, you might be able to stop an eviction based on nonpayment of rent when the landlord obtained a judgment before you declared bankruptcy. You'll be able to stop the eviction only if, within 30 days of filing bankruptcy, you (1) file

a paper with the Bankruptcy Court certifying that California has a law (CCP § 1179) allowing tenants to avoid eviction (called "relief from forfeiture") by paying unpaid rent (plus court costs and any attorney fees awarded the landlord); (2) deposit that sum with the Bankruptcy Court clerk, plus any rent due 30 days from the date you filed for bankruptcy; and (3) certify to the Bankruptcy Court that you have paid these amounts, serving the landlord (or landlord's attorney) with this certification. The documents must all be in proper legal form.

Landlords can sometimes avoid the automatic bankruptcy stay (proceed with an eviction without asking the court for permission), when the reason for the eviction is the tenant's alleged drug use or damage to the property. In these situations, the landlord files a certification to that effect with the Bankruptcy Court.

Some nonlawyer eviction defense organizations (primarily in the Los Angeles area) routinely help tenants file for bankruptcy as a means of buying a little more time to find new premises. While the extra time might seem like a minor miracle at the time, we recommend against filing for bankruptcy solely to stave off an eviction. It will hurt your credit rating and could cause you to lose property you wanted to hang on to. However, if other reasons justify filing for bankruptcy, stopping an eviction temporarily may be a beneficial side effect.

RESOURCE

For more information on bankruptcy, see *How to File for Chapter 7 Bankruptcy*, by Albin Renauer and Cara O'Neill (Nolo).

Your Rights If Your Building Is Foreclosed Upon

Banks and real estate companies are often very aggressive towards tenants after their rental has been foreclosed, often saying things that they know are untrue, in order to get the tenant to move out quickly. This section deals with the rights of a tenant whose building is foreclosed on, and the property in which you live is now owned by a bank, other lender, or other person or entity that has purchased the property at the foreclosure sale. The information in this section does *not* apply to owners who have suffered foreclosure. It applies only to *tenants* of landlords whose properties were foreclosed by their mortgage lender.

The Effect of Foreclosure

When an owner defaults on a mortgage, the mortgage holder, usually a bank, arranges for the property to be sold at a foreclosure sale. At such sales, the mortgage holder usually winds up owning the property, though sometimes a third-party investor outbids the mortgage holder and winds up with the property.

California tenants living in foreclosed buildings have essentially the same protections after the fore-closure proceedings as they did before—with only a few exceptions. Tenants on a month-to-month tenancy are entitled to a 90-day notice terminating the tenancy. (CCP § 1161b(a).) In addition, tenants who have leases may be able to assert their leasehold rights and remain until the end of their lease (see below). Finally, in cities where "just cause" for eviction provisions apply, tenants in foreclosed buildings have additional protections against eviction. (*Gross v. Superior Court,* 171 Cal.App.3d 265 (1985). CCP § 1161b(b).)

Statewide eviction controls may also be available, although they are likely weaker than local laws.

TIP

Even though you have a new landlord, that landlord has the same legal obligations that any other landlord has. For example, the new landlord must maintain the property and can't invade your right to privacy. If you live in a rent control jurisdiction, or are covered by statewide rent and eviction protections, the new owner cannot raise your rent beyond that allowed under the ordinance, and can't evict you for "any reason or no reason at all" if there is a "just cause" for eviction provision that applies.

What Happens When Your Lease Was in Place Before the Foreclosure Sale?

In years past, a foreclosure sale effectively wiped out almost all existing leases. However, this harsh result was changed in 2012 with the addition of Code of Civil Procedure Section 1161b(b). Now, if a lease was signed before the foreclosure sale, that lease will remain in effect, but new owners can give a 90-day notice if they can prove that any of the following situations exist:

- the property was bought at the foreclosure sale by a purchaser who intends to live on the property
- the tenant isn't the spouse, child, or parent of the owner
- the leasing transaction was conducted in an "arms' length" manner. An arm's length transaction is one where the parties do not have a close relationship (such as family or a very close friend), and
- the rent charged under the lease isn't "substantially below" fair market value, except, of course, for government-subsidized tenancies.

However, an existing lease may still be valid (no 90-day notice) if the following conditions are met:

- the lease was recorded in the County Recorder's Office, and
- the lease was recorded before the Deed of Trust (mortgage) that was the basis for the foreclosure was recorded.

This is an extremely rare situation.

If you receive notice that the property in which you live has been foreclosed (that is, a "trustee's sale" has been held), you should stop paying rent to the now-former owner and pay it to the new owner. If you don't know who that is, set aside your rent payment each month, so that you can pay it to the new owner once you find out who that is.

Under Civil Code Section 1962, any new owner—whether the person becomes owner by foreclosure or regular sale—must advise tenants, in writing, to whom, where, and how to pay the rent, within 15 days of taking ownership. Failure to do so means that any nonpayment of rent that accrued during such noncompliance can't be used as a basis for eviction—a defense the tenant would assert via the Answer (a topic discussed in Chapter 15). If you receive a three-day notice to pay rent or quit from the new owner, you might want to confirm with your county's Recorder's Office—usually located at the county seat—that the person or entity giving you the notice is truly the new owner.

Tenants who are covered by local and statewide rent and eviction protections are additionally protected from terminations at the hands of an acquiring bank or new owner. (*Gross v. Superior Court*, 171 Cal. App. 3d 265 (1985); CCP § 1161b(b)). These tenants can rely on the laws' list of allowable reasons for termination. Because a change of ownership, without more, does not justify a termination under the cities' lists of allowable reasons to evict or the state's, the fact that the change occurred through foreclosure will not justify a termination. However, a new owner who has a "just cause" to evict, such as an "owner move-in" intention, may do so, as long as the owner complies with the "just cause for eviction" protections.

Responding to Termination Notices After Foreclosure: Tenants With Leases

If the property you rent changes ownership due to a foreclosure, you might receive any one of several different kinds of termination notices (you may even receive two at once). Whether the notice is legally valid, and your proper response to the notice, will depend on a number of factors. You'll need to know, first, whether you have protections under a local or statewide rent control or "just cause" for eviction ordinance, or have additional protections under an existing lease agreement. It is often a good idea to notify the new landlord (or that person's attorney) of your status (for example, that you are a tenant, whether you have a lease and whether you are protected by state or local rent or eviction protections.

Remember, banks usually prefer to have their properties vacant so that they can sell them, but you are not obliged to move unless they follow the proper procedures for eviction.

Cash for Keys

To encourage tenants to leave quickly and save on the court costs associated with an eviction, banks offer tenants a cash payout in exchange for their rapid departure. Thinking that they have little choice, many tenants—even protected Section 8 and rent-control tenants—take the deal. To make matters worse, real estate agents who claim to be working for the banks try to pressure tenants to leave, implying such tenants have no rights. Do not be intimidated by real estate agents or banks or their attorneys. Know your rights and stand your ground, unless, of course, a financial offer to move quickly seems like a good deal. Keep in mind that it will cost the bank one to two thousand dollars to evict you and that the process, if you contest the case, could take well over a month.

Why a Three-Day and a 90-Day Notice?

Some banks send tenants both a three-day and a 90-day notice, particularly in the case of single-family properties. Here's why: When owners *who also live on the property* default, they can properly be told to move with a three-day notice. Many banks don't know, however, whether the residents are tenants or former owners. To cover each possibility, they send two notices. But you're a tenant, not an owner, so the three-day notice does not apply to you.

The Eviction Lawsuit

fter reading Chapter 14, you should have a clear idea of what leads up to an eviction lawsuit. This chapter gets into the details that will help you go to court and defend yourself (assuming you choose to fight the eviction). This chapter will also help you understand what your lawyer is doing, if you choose to hire one.

We concentrate on the basic and most commonly used tools suitable for tenants to use in defending against most straightforward eviction proceedings. The material set out here is by no means a complete summary of every defense or litigation device available to a tenant, but it will invaluable for many readers, even those with a complicated defense who end up hiring an attorney.

RESOURCE

Lawyers' eviction resources. You can supplement this information by consulting the *California Eviction Defense Manual*, and *California Landlord-Tenant Practice*, both of which are published by Continuing Education of the Bar (CEB) in Berkeley, California. The *California Eviction Defense Manual* is the source most often used by lawyers when defending unlawful detainer cases. Unlike many law books, it is not difficult to use. You should be able to find both books in your county law library. Be sure you consult the latest supplements to these books, which contain the most recent cases and statutes.

Key Eviction Rule

One very important rule cuts across all other rules in an eviction case: The landlord must strictly comply with all legal requirements. (*Vasey v. California Dance Co.,* 70 Cal.App.3d 742 (1977).) This is the price the landlord pays for a special, quick procedure, and reflects the seriousness of the matter, which seeks to deprive you of your home.

TIP

Time your settlement conversation carefully. Keep in mind the case can settle at any time, although it is usually not a good idea to introduce settlement too early in the proceedings—so you don't appear "too eager" to settle. Be prepared to stand up for yourself. Unfortunately, many lawyers are legal bullies and may try to push you around and intimidate you, but if you hold your ground you change the dynamic and they will eventually have to treat you more civilly. One way to introduce the subject of settlement would be during a discussion about some other issue (like scheduling a hearing or allowing entry to make a repair).

Where Eviction Lawsuits Are Filed

Landlords may not use small claims court to evict a tenant. Eviction lawsuits must be brought in superior court. (CCP §§ 86, 116.220.) More populous counties have "divisions" or "branches" of superior court. The eviction case filed by your landlord will normally be heard in the court or its division nearest the rental property.

An eviction lawsuit is technically called an "unlawful detainer" lawsuit. We use both terms interchangeably, but courts and lawyers almost always use the term "unlawful detainer."

The Complaint and Summons

The Summons is a one-page document that advises you that an unlawful detainer action has been filed against you, and that you are required to file a response within five days (do not count Saturdays, Sundays, or holidays). If you do not file a formal written response within the five days, a default will be entered against you. (CCP § 1167.) The Summons will have your name, your landlord's name, and the name, address, and telephone number of the attorney representing the landlord. It will also have the name and address of the court you will have to appear in. The Summons will also have the names of other tenants and known subtenants in the unit. Landlords often serve a separate form called a "Prejudgment Claim of Right to Possession" in case there are unknown occupants in the unit. (See "What if an Occupant Is Not Named in the Complaint?" below.)

The Complaint—Unlawful Detainer (or Complaint) is the paper the landlord files in court to get the case going. It states the basic facts that the landlord says justify eviction and asks the court to order you out and to enter a judgment against you for unpaid rent, court costs, and sometimes attorney fees.

Before you can be evicted, you must receive proper notice of an unlawful detainer suit against you by being named in the Complaint and served with that Complaint, as well as with a Summons— Unlawful Detainer—Eviction (or Summons). The Summons is a notice from the court telling you that you must file a written response (Answer, Demurrer, or Motion to Quash) with the court within five days or lose the lawsuit. The Summons also tells you whether you should give your response to the landlord's attorney or to the landlord. If the Summons and Complaint aren't served on you according to law, you can ask the court to dismiss the lawsuit as explained below.

Both the Complaint and Summons forms are official government forms published by the California Judicial Council.

How the Summons Must Be Served

The landlord cannot get sloppy about service of the Summons and Complaint. Whether or not you actually receive these documents, the landlord's failure to strictly abide by the rules governing their service means that the court has no authority (jurisdiction) to hear the case.

There are two allowable ways to serve a Summons and Complaint: personal service and substituted service. A third method (posting and mailing) requires judicial permission.

Personal Service: The landlord must first attempt personal service of the Summons and Complaint. Someone over the age of 18 who is not a named party to the lawsuit—someone other than the landlord— must personally hand you the papers. (CCP §§ 414.10 and 415.10.) Even if you don't accept the papers, service has properly been made as long as you are personally presented with them. It is a common practice, when people realize they are about to be served, to slam the door in the server's face. Forget it. The server can deposit the papers outside the door (after you slam it) and you will be considered served.

Substituted Service: If several unsuccessful attempts are made to personally serve you (three is the general rule), the server may make substituted service by:

- leaving a copy of the Summons and Complaint with a competent person in your house (this can be someone less than 18 years of age), or with a person over 18 at your business
- explaining the nature of the papers to the person with whom they are left, and
- mailing a copy of the papers to the address where the papers were left. (CCP § 415.20(b).)

"Posting and Mailing" or "Nail and Mail" Service: In limited situations, state law allows the landlord's process server to post copies of the Summons and Complaint on your front door and mail a second set of copies. (CCP § 415.45.) Before a landlord can use posting and mailing, the landlord must get written permission from a judge after showing that the process server made several unsuccessful attempts to serve the papers at reasonable times. If this method of service is used, your time to respond is extended from five to 15 days.

Shortly after the landlord or landlord's lawyer has filed the complaint, the clerk will mail you a "Notice to Defendant," informing you that an eviction case has been filed. The notice will also give you information about some organizations that provide information and assistance to tenants facing eviction. This is not a Summons and Complaint, but just information that is being provided by the court. If you haven't seen the Summons and Complaint and want to review it, you can go to court and ask to review it. Because these files are not available for public viewing (CCP § 1161.2), you must show the clerk of the court some form of identification. It would be helpful to also show the clerk the "Notice to Defendant" that you received.

Remember, each named defendant (tenant) must be served with a copy of the Summons and Complaint. You each start counting the five (or 15) days to respond separately, depending on when each defendant was served.

CAUTION

If you think you were not properly served with the Summons and Complaint, be sure to file a response within five calendar days, not counting Saturdays, Sundays, or holidays. You may contest the defective service by filing a Motion to Quash (discussed below), or you may choose to file some other response discussed below. In either event, you must respond within the five days.

Responding to the Summons

Your first response to the Summons can be one of three documents, each of which is discussed below:

- **Motion to Quash**—if the Summons was not properly served on you or if there was a defect in the Summons itself
- **Demurrer**—if the Complaint is not in proper technical form or does not properly allege the landlord's right to evict you, or
- **Answer**—if you want to deny statements in the Complaint or allege new facts.

Tenant Responses Are Not Mutually Exclusive

Responses are not mutually exclusive. So your response could be a Motion to Quash Service of Summons, then (if that were denied by a judge) a Demurrer. If the judge denied ("overruled") the Demurrer, your response could then be an Answer. Or you may simply file an Answer as your response in the first place, which is the most common response. This chapter will help you choose the appropriate response.

CAUTION

Always file a written response to the Complaint, even if you've moved out! Even if you have moved out, you should file a written response (usually an Answer) unless the landlord or landlord's attorney has assured you, preferably in writing, that the eviction will not proceed against you because you have moved out. Ideally, you'll want the landlord or his attorney to file a dismissal with the court, which will clearly end the case. If you move out but don't file a written response, and the landlord goes ahead and obtains a default judgment, you'll wind up having a judgment for rent that you perhaps do not owe, and for court costs. (You might also owe attorney fees, if your lease or rental agreement has a fees clause.)

Be sure to check your lease or rental agreement for an attorney fees clause even if you get the landlord to file a dismissal.

Timeline for Filing a Response

You have five days, not counting Saturdays, Sundays, and holidays, to file your written response. For instance, if you were served on a Thursday, Friday will be day one, Monday will be day two (unless it's a holiday), Tuesday, day three, Wednesday is day four, and Thursday is day five.

You have until the end of business on Thursday to file your response in court, otherwise the landlord's attorney can go in Friday morning and file a Request to Enter Default. The clerk will not accept your filing if you attempt to do so after the Request to Enter Default is filed with the clerk. (CCP § 1167.) The address of the clerk's office should be on the first page of the Summons. You should file your response in person, not by mail.

The timeline explained just above is the method for counting the time to respond to a Summons and Complaint. After you file your first response, the time for counting subsequent filings is different. It is five *calendar* days. If the last day falls on a Saturday, Sunday, or holiday, then the time to respond is the next business day. For instance, if you file a Motion to Quash or a Demurrer, and it is denied, then the court will order you to file a response with the court in five calendar days.

You have 15 days (not five) to file a response if substituted service or "posting and mailing" service was used. Again, Saturdays, Sundays, and holidays are not counted.

Fees to File a Response

If this is your first written response filed with the court, you will have to pay a filing fee. The amount depends on how many defendants there are who are filing. It will probably be around $370 per defendant. Call the court clerk (civil division) for information on filing fees in your county, or check online. If you win or the case is dismissed, you can ask for a judgment for your filing fee against the landlord as "costs."

If you are unable to pay the filing fees, you may apply to have them waived on the basis that your income is low, by filing a Request to Waive Court Fees form. If you receive certain governmental aid (SSI/SSP, CalWORKS, Food Stamps, and/or county general assistance), or if your gross monthly household income is under a certain level (as

stated on that form), you are entitled to have your fees waived if you file an application asking that they be waived. (The dollar amounts are raised approximately every six months, be sure to check for the current form.) If you don't receive such aid, and your income is higher than the maximum income listed on the form, the court does not have to waive your fees, but might still do so if you show hardship.

FORM

You'll find copies of the Request to Waive Court Fees and the Order on Court Fee Waiver in Appendix C, and the Nolo website includes download- able copies of these forms. (See Appendix B for the link to the forms in this book.) Judicial Council forms are also available at the court clerk's office.

These forms are straightforward and should be simple to fill in. If you fill these waiver forms out correctly—the clerk is required to assist you—and present them to the clerk, the clerk must file any other documents you present at the same time, without your having to pay the fee right then. (Gov't Code § 68634 (c).) Later, if the court denies your application, you'll have to pay the filing fee within ten days of being notified. If you don't pay up, the papers you filed will be "unfiled," and a default judgment will be entered against you.

TIP

Check the local practice. Because unlawful detainer actions go through the courts quickly, each court has its own way of dealing with them. For instance, in some courts special judges hear only eviction cases; in others, the presiding judge will decide which judge to send the case to on the morning of trial. Check to see how your court operates. Also, it is helpful to review any local Rules of Court. You can get these from the local court's website or ask the clerk for instructions on how to obtain them.

Timeline for Eviction

How long does the entire eviction process take? Of course, it varies from case to case. Every lawyer who has defended a lot of eviction cases has a story about how great lawyering brilliantly created a paper blizzard and staved off an eviction for many months. On the other hand, an eviction can occur in a blindingly short period of time if the landlord does everything right and you do nothing. Nevertheless, the time estimates we set out here (one to three months from when you were served with a Summons and Complaint) should prove broadly accurate, assuming the following facts:

- The Summons and Complaint are personally served on you.
- You contest the action by filing written responses with the court.
- All papers (after the Summons and Complaint) are served by mail, which is permitted (and is usual practice).
- The landlord (or landlord's attorney) stays on top of the case and files all papers as fast as possible.
- You are unable to make a settlement that allows you to stay or get extra time. (See "Negotiating a Settlement," below.)

Eviction might occur earlier if the landlord:

- had all papers personally served on you, rather than by mail, or
- wins a "summary judgment" and doesn't have to go to trial.

The timeline will be longer if the landlord lets time slip by between any of the procedural steps necessary to move an eviction case along.

It is rare that a landlord's case marches along without one snag or another, many of them caused either by the landlord's attorney's schedule, by courthouse delays, or delays in serving. Practically speaking, if you added two (and sometimes as many as four) weeks to the timeline, you would have a better picture of how long the typical contested eviction takes. On the other hand, if you fail to take one of the steps indicated in the timeline, or you lose on your Motion to Quash or Demurrer, you should deduct the appropriate number of days.

What If an Occupant Is Not Named in the Complaint?

If you are living in the property but are not named as a defendant in the Complaint, and the person named in the Complaint was not served with a document called a "Prejudgment Claim of Right to Possession," you should protect yourself against eviction for a while by filing a Claim of Right to Possession or a Response.

Here's how this process works: If, on filing the unlawful detainer lawsuit, the landlord believes that there are adults other than the tenant listed on the lease or rental agreement living in the property, and if the landlord does not know their names, the landlord can reach those known-but-unnamed occupants by having a sheriff, marshal, or registered process server serve a Prejudgment Claim of Right to Possession on the defendant and these other occupants of the property. This may be accomplished by personal service, by substitute service, or by posting and mailing. When this happens, any unnamed occupants must fill out the Prejudgment Claim of Right to Possession within ten days, to protect their rights. If an unnamed-but-served adult occupant doesn't do this or does not file a Response, the occupant will not be able to stop the eviction later on.

On the other hand, if the landlord does not take the step of serving a Prejudgment Claim of Right to Possession at the outset, a person who is not named in the judgment (and hence not named in the writ of possession) may stop the eviction. This is done by filing the Claim of Right to Possession at a very late stage—namely, when the sheriff or marshal posts the preevict notice. (See "After the Lawsuit— Eviction by the Sheriff or Marshal," below.)

FORM
You'll find a copy of the Prejudgment Claim of Right to Possession (as well as a regular Claim of Right to Possession form, discussed below) in Appendix C, and the Nolo website includes downloadable copies of these forms. (See Appendix B for the link to the forms in this book (it's also available at the court clerk's office).)

TIP
If you are being evicted for nonpayment of rent or for breach of covenant, one option is to offer early in the proceedings to pay the rent or to cure the breach. This way you can avoid the time and trouble of defending an eviction and your landlord can avoid further time and expenses. If the landlord refuses to agree, you might want to bring that fact up later in the proceedings if you lose and decide to file a Motion for Relief from Eviction (discussed later in this chapter).

Deciding How to Respond to the Complaint

As we have stated repeatedly, it is absolutely essential that you respond to the complaint within the five days. As a general rule, tenants facing eviction want to delay any eviction as long as possible and make it harder and more expensive for the landlord to evict them. But you might find that filing a Motion to Quash or Demurrer to be too complicated and time-consuming a task, or a Motion to Quash or Demurrer might not be applicable to your situation. Ultimately, as the case proceeds, you will have to file an Answer, which involves filling out a court-approved form and is relatively much easier. You may also choose to file an Answer even though you could have filed a Motion to Quash or Demurrer. Not filing a Motion to Quash or Demurrer will not prejudice the outcome of your case.

We will be discussing each of the three possible responses.

1. If you were not properly served with the Summons and Complaint, you might want to file a Motion to Quash. If you were not properly served but do not want to file a Motion to Quash, you may file a Demurrer (see below) or an Answer, but you may not later argue that you were improperly served.

2. If the Complaint has certain technical defects, then you could file a Demurrer. (See "The Demurrer," discussed below.) If you file an Answer instead of a Demurrer, you do not give up the right to raise the technical defect of the Complaint.

3. Sooner or later you will likely have to file an Answer. Fortunately, there is a court-approved Answer form that allows you to check boxes and fill in information about your claims. You can file this after being served with the Summons and Complaint, or after a Motion to Quash is denied or after a Demurrer is overruled.

TIP
It is a good idea to familiarize yourself with Rules of Court. Learning the rules is particularly important if you are going to file a Motion to Quash or Demurrer, or if you anticipate that your case will ultimately go to trial. You can find state rules of court online at www.courts.ca.gov/cms/rules/index.cfm?title=three. Rules relating to motion hearings start at Rule 3.1300, Motions to Quash are at Rule 3.1327, and Demurrers are at 3.320. They are, for the most part, brief and to the point. Some local courts also have their own sets of rules in addition to the state rules. Check the website of your local court.

The Motion to Quash

Once you become aware that the landlord has filed an unlawful detainer action against you, your first step is to decide whether the landlord has complied with the strict requirements for how the Summons must be served on you. If the landlord didn't follow the rules exactly, you are entitled to file a paper called a "Motion to Quash Service of Summons," asking the court to rule that service of the Summons was improper. (CCP §§ 418.10, 1167.4.) You can also file a Motion to Quash based on a defect in the Summons itself—for example, that it lists the wrong court or judicial district. If this ruling is in your favor, the landlord has to serve you with the Summons again. Often, they do this in the courthouse right after the judge has ruled in your favor.

When to File a Motion to Quash Service of Summons

If you file a Motion to Quash, make sure you have a valid reason. Courts frown on your filing motions for the sole purpose of delay.

Typical grounds for a tenant's Motion to Quash based on defective service are:

- You were not properly served with the Summons and Complaint. For instance, you found it on your doorstep when you got home, or they "substitute served" it on your 12-year-old daughter.
- The process server used substitute service without first attempting to serve you in person at your home or known place of business.
- The landlord himself served you.
- The papers were given to someone other than you, and they were not later mailed.

Be aware that after you file the Motion to Quash, the landlord may try again to serve you. If he does, then you will have five days from the date you are actually served to file another response (15 days if you are served by substitute service or posting and mailing).

Preparing the Motion to Quash

There are three parts to a Motion to Quash.

The Notice of Motion and Motion to Quash: This notifies the other side (the landlord or the landlord's attorney) that you are making the motion and have scheduled a court hearing on a certain day.

Memorandum of Points and Authorities: This is a short statement of the legal authority for your position.

Your Declaration: This is a written statement, made under penalty of perjury, stating the facts supporting your conclusion that service of the Summons was improper.

We do not have a downloadable Motion to Quash on the companion page for this book. You will need to prepare your own on legal paper, as explained below.

If you want to file a Motion to Quash, you must do so within your five-day period to respond.

Here are the basic steps for doing so:

Step 1: Print out (or make) several copies of the blank numbered legal paper with the Superior Court heading and the blank numbered legal paper included in this book. (You'll use different sheets for different parts of the Motion to Quash, as explained below.) You can also buy blank numbered legal paper at a stationery store. Most commonly used word processing programs, like Microsoft *Word*, allow you to generate such line-numbered documents.

FORM
You'll find copies of the blank numbered legal paper (with and without the Superior Court heading) in Appendix C, and the Nolo website includes downloadable copies of these forms. (See Appendix B for the link to the forms in this book.)

Step 2: Take a piece of the numbered legal paper with the Superior Court heading and put your name, address, and telephone number in the same location (and on approximately the same lines) as is shown in the sample. Don't go crazy about trying to line up your text exactly with the numbers. Just do the best you can. You'll use the legal paper with the Superior Court heading for the first page of your response and the legal paper without the Superior Court heading for subsequent pages.

Step 3: Put the county where you are being sued, the court division or branch, as applicable, and the case number in the spaces as indicated on the sample. Get this information from the Summons and Complaint that were served on you.

Step 4: Call the court clerk and ask when and in what department or division motions are heard. In large cities, this tends to be every morning. In less populous areas, motions may be heard only once or twice a week.

Sample Notice of Motion to Quash

1   TOM TENANT
    1234 Apartment St.
2   Berkeley, CA 94710
    510-123-4567
3

4   Defendant in Pro Per

5

6

7

8   SUPERIOR COURT OF THE STATE OF CALIFORNIA, COUNTY OF ALAMEDA

9   BERKELEY-ALBANY DIVISION/BRANCH

10   )
)
11 LENNY LANDLORD ,   )   Case No. S-0258
)
12   Plaintiff(s),   )   DEFENDANT'S NOTICE OF MOTION TO
)
13 v.   )   QUASH SERVICE OF SUMMONS; POINTS AND
)
14 TOM TENANT ,   )   AUTHORITIES; DEFENDANT'S DECLARATION
)
15   Defendant(s).   )   IN SUPPORT THEREOF
)

16

17   To: LENNY LANDLORD, plaintiff, and to LAURA LAWYER, his attorney;

18   PLEASE TAKE NOTICE THAT on _____①_____ , 20___ , at ___②___ in Department No.

19 __③__ of the above-entitled court, located at _____④_____ ,

20 defendant will appear specially pursuant to Code of Civil Procedure Section 418.10 and will move the court for an

21 order quashing the service of Summons herein on the ground(s) that the Summons and Complaint in this

22 case was not served in compliance with C.C.P. § 415 et. seq.

23   ////

24   ////

25   ////

26   ////

27

28

Notice of Motion to Quash   Page 1 of 2

Sample Notice of Motion to Quash (continued)

1   The motion shall be based upon this notice, the memorandum of points and authorities in support thereof,

2   the files and records of this case, *and the declaration of Tom Tenant, attached hereto.*

3   Dated: February 10 , 20xx   *Tom Tenant*
                                 TOM TENANT

4   Defendant in Pro Per

5

6   POINTS AND AUTHORITIES

7   I. DEFENDANT'S MOTION IS PROPERLY NOTICED.

8   Code of Civil Procedure Section 1167.4 specifies a 3-to-7-day period for noticing unlawful detainer motions

9   to quash. However, Rule 3.1327(a), California Rules of Court, requires motions to quash to be noticed "in

10   compliance with [C.C.P.] sections 1013 and 1167.4." Therefore, when the defendant serves the moving papers by

11   mail, five days' additional notice is required under section 1013, and the 3-to-7-day period for notice is extended

12   to an 8-to-12-day period.

13   II. DEFENDANT'S MOTION TO QUASH SHOULD BE GRANTED.

14   A defendant in an unlawful detainer action is entitled to file a Motion to Quash Service of Summons when

15   service has not been validly completed. Code of Civil Procedure Sec. 418.10.

16   In this action, plaintiff did not serve the Summons and Complaint in compliance with Code of Civil

17   Procedure Sec. 415 *et. seq.* Instead, the Summons and Complaint was found on defendant's doorstep.

18   To confer jurisdiction, a plaintiff must comply with C.C.P. § 415 *et. seq.* (*American Express v. Zara*, 199 Cal.

19   App. 4th 383, 391, 392 (2011).)

20   Because plaintiff did not properly serve the Summons and Complaint, this Motion should be granted.

21

22   Respectfully submitted,

23   *Tom Tenant*

24   TOM TENANT
                        Defendant in Pro Per

25

26

27

28

Declaration

DECLARATION

TOM TENANT declares and says:

1. I am a tenant at 1234 Apartment St., Berkeley, CA 94710.

2. On January 8, 20xx, I found a copy of the Summons and Complaint on my doorstep in front of my house.

3. At no time have I been personally served with a copy of the Summons and Complaint in this action.

4. At no time has a copy of the Summons and Complaint arrived in the mail, addressed to me.

5. I declare under penalty of perjury under the laws of the State of California that the foregoing is true and correct.

Dated: February , 20xx

Tom Tenant
_____
TOM TENANT
Defendant in Pro Per

Step 5: Once you find out which dates and times are available and which department hears motions, immediately fill in the blanks as follows:

(1) Pick a date that is no less than eight and no more than 12 days from the date you plan to file the motion. (CCP § 1167 specifies a three-to-seven-day period or window, but Rule 3.1327(a), Calif. Rules of Court, references CCP § 1013, which adds five more days, for an eight-to-12-day window, where the papers are mailed to the landlord or her attorney.)

(2) Fill in the time the court hears motions.

(3) Fill in the department where motions are heard.

(4) Fill in the address of the court.

Step 6: Fill in your grounds for filing a motion to quash and date and sign your motion as shown in the sample Notice of Motion to Quash, below.

Step 7: Prepare your Points and Authorities.

Skip a couple of lines after the last line of your Notice of Motion to Quash, type the words POINTS AND AUTHORITIES in capitals, and then begin typing your points and authorities. You can copy the first sentence directly from the sample. You also need to explain:

- what the landlord did wrong, and
- the specific statute the landlord violated.

If the Summons and Complaint weren't served by someone over 18 or if they were served by someone who was a party to the action, the landlord violated Code of Civil Procedure Section 414.10. If the server used substituted service without first unsuccessfully attempting personal service, the landlord violated Code of Civil Procedure Section 415.20 (b). If some other requirement for substituted service was missed, Section 415.20(b) was violated.

If the landlord erred for some other reason, you will need to find a legal basis for your conclusion and put it in the Points and Authorities. Talk to a tenants' group or lawyer, or research the law yourself (see Chapter 18 for advice), or consult the *California Eviction Defense Manual* (CEB), available in most law libraries.

Step 8: Prepare a Declaration.

Skip a couple of lines after the last line of your Points and Authorities, type the word DECLARATION in capitals, and type your statement, as shown in the sample. Number each paragraph. The judge will use your declaration in place of oral testimony as a basis for deciding whether to grant your motion. So use simple sentences, and don't argue. ("Just the facts, ma'am.") Review your information to make sure it accurately and clearly tells the court what the landlord did wrong. Sign and date the Declaration.

Note: The sample Notice of Motion to Quash, Points and Authorities, and Declaration shown above are based on the scenario that you were not personally served or properly substitute served. The papers will, of course, have to be modified appropriately if you bring your motion for a different reason.

Preparing the Proof of Service by First-Class Mail—Civil

Before you file your motion, you must prepare a Proof of Service by Mail, which tells the court that you have given notice to the landlord. Your motion must be served on the attorney for the landlord or the landlord if he does not have an attorney (usually by mail). The person serving the motion must be over 18 years old and not a party in your case. You can ask a friend or neighbor to mail the motion and to sign the form. You'll give this form to the clerk when you file the motion. The form you'll use is the Proof of Service by First-Class Mail—Civil. A sample is shown below.

 FORM

You'll find a copy of the Proof of Service by First-Class Mail in Appendix C, and the Nolo website includes a downloadable copy of this form. (If you use the Appendix C form, make several copies because you may need more later.) (See Appendix B for the link to the forms in this book on the Nolo website; this form should be available at the court clerk's office.)

Proof of Service By First-Class Mail

POS-030

ATTORNEY OR PARTY WITHOUT ATTORNEY *(Name, State Bar number, and address):*

TOM TENANT

1234 Apartment Street

Berkeley, CA 94710

TELEPHONE NO.: 510-123-4567

E-MAIL ADDRESS *(Optional):*   FAX NO. *(Optional):*

ATTORNEY FOR *(Name):* Defendant in Pro Per

FOR COURT USE ONLY

SUPERIOR COURT OF CALIFORNIA, COUNTY OF ALAMEDA

STREET ADDRESS: 2120 Martin Luther King Way

MAILING ADDRESS:

CITY AND ZIP CODE: Berkeley, CA 94704

BRANCH NAME: Berkeley-Albany

PETITIONER/PLAINTIFF: LENNY LANDLORD

RESPONDENT/DEFENDANT: TOM TENANT

PROOF OF SERVICE BY FIRST-CLASS MAIL—CIVIL

CASE NUMBER:
S-0258

(Do not use this Proof of Service to show service of a Summons and Complaint.)

1. I am over 18 years of age and **not a party to this action.** I am a resident of or employed in the county where the mailing took place.

2. My residence or business address is: 1345 Apartment St., Berkeley, CA 94710

3. On *(date):* June 15, 20xx   I mailed from *(city and state):*   Berkeley, California the following **documents** *(specify):*

   Defendant's Notice of Motion to Quash Service of Summons; Points and Authorities; Declaration in Support Thereof

   ☐ The documents are listed in the *Attachment to Proof of Service by First-Class Mail—Civil (Documents Served)* (form POS-030(D)).

4. I served the documents by enclosing them in an envelope and *(check one):*
   a. ☑ **depositing** the sealed envelope with the United States Postal Service with the postage fully prepaid.
   b. ☐ **placing** the envelope for collection and mailing following our ordinary business practices. I am readily familiar with this business's practice for collecting and processing correspondence for mailing. On the same day that correspondence is placed for collection and mailing, it is deposited in the ordinary course of business with the United States Postal Service in a sealed envelope with postage fully prepaid.

5. The envelope was addressed and mailed as follows:
   a. **Name** of person served: Lenny D. Landlord
   b. **Address** of person served: 123 Walnut St.

   Walnut Creek, CA 94596

   ☐ The name and address of each person to whom I mailed the documents is listed in the *Attachment to Proof of Service by First-Class Mail—Civil (Persons Served)* (POS-030(P)).

I declare under penalty of perjury under the laws of the State of California that the foregoing is true and correct.

Date: June 15, 20xx

Serena Server

(TYPE OR PRINT NAME OF PERSON COMPLETING THIS FORM)

▶ *Serena Server*

(SIGNATURE OF PERSON COMPLETING THIS FORM)

Form Approved for Optional Use
Judicial Council of California
POS-030 [New January 1, 2005]

PROOF OF SERVICE BY FIRST-CLASS MAIL—CIVIL
(Proof of Service)

Code of Civil Procedure, §§ 1013, 1013a
www.courtinfo.ca.gov

Follow these instructions to prepare the Proof of Service by First-Class Mail. (After your server has served the landlord, that person will finish it and sign it, but you can begin completing the proof of service now.) Note that the Judicial Council has also written a set of instructions, which you'll find in Appendix C, right after the Proof of Service by First-Class Mail form; these Judicial Council instructions are also on the Nolo website, along with a downloadable version of the form itself. (See Appendix B for the link.)

Top of the form: Put your name in the top box (after the words, "Attorney or Party Without an Attorney"). Add your address, phone number, and email and fax number (the latter two are optional). After "Attorney For (Name)" write "in pro per."

In the second box, enter the county and the name and address of the Superior Court, which will be the same as the information you entered on the papers that will be served.

Enter your name in the third box, under the line, "Respondent/Defendant." Add the landlord's name under "Petitioner/Plaintiff."

Leave the tall box ("For Court Use Only") on the right blank, but add the case number (again, it's on the papers being served) to the box at the lower right.

Item 1: This statement declares that the person serving the papers is over 18 years of age and either lives in or is employed in the county where the papers are being mailed. You don't need to add anything to this item.

Item 2: The server should print his or her home or business address.

Item 3: Provide the name of each document that the server will mail. Leave the date and "city and state" lines blank for now; your server will fill this information in after he or she actually places the documents in the mail.

Item 4: Your server will check either box a or box b, depending on how the server mailed the documents. Box a is for servers who personally deposit the envelope in a mailbox. Box b is for those who mail from their business, as long as the business has an established procedure for collecting mail and mailing it on the same day it's placed in their "out" box.

Item 5: Provide the name and address of the person to whom the server will mail the documents. If the documents are going to be mailed to more than one person, you'll need to use and attach another form, "Attachment to Proof of Service by First-Class Mail—Civil (Persons Served)." This form, POS-030(P), is in Appendix C (and available for download on the Nolo website; see Appendix B for the link), but not shown here. To fill it out, enter the name of the case at the top, as it appears on the Complaint, and the case number. Provide the names and addresses of any additional persons served.

At the bottom of the Proof of Service by First-Class Mail—Civil, after your server has mailed the documents, he or she will fill in the date he or she signed the form, print his or her name, and sign the document. Your server is now stating, under penalty of perjury, that the information provided on the form is true and correct.

How to Serve and File the Notice of Motion to Quash

After you have prepared your Notice of Motion to Quash, you must have a copy of it served on the landlord promptly, to give her enough time to respond before the hearing date. As a defendant, you cannot serve your own legal papers, but you can have a friend or relative do it. The server must be a person over 18 and not a party to the action—that is, not named in the Complaint as a plaintiff or defendant.

Step 1: Complete the document called Proof of Service by First-Class Mail—Civil, following the instructions above.

Step 2: Make three copies of your Notice of Motion to Quash, Points and Authorities, and Declaration, and the filled-in but unsigned Proof of Service by First-Class Mail—Civil. Refer to "Preparing the Proof of Service by First-Class Mail—Civil," above, to make sure that the Proof of Service is complete and correct (enter any missing information now). You'll file the original of the documents with the court clerk, one copy goes to the other side, one copy you keep, and the third copy is a "courtesy copy" that goes to the courtroom of the judge who will hear the motion.

Step 3: Attach a copy of the unsigned Proof of Service to each set of your motion papers.

Step 4: Have your server mail one set of copies (the motion papers and the Proof of Service) to the landlord's attorney (listed on the Summons) or the landlord if there is no attorney. The papers must be mailed on the day indicated on the Proof of Service.

Step 5: Now have your server fill in the blanks in the last paragraph of the Proof of Service and sign the document. Attach it to the original motion.

Step 6: Take the original motion papers and one set of copies to the court clerk. Give the original set of papers to the clerk, who will stamp (or have you stamp) your copies with a "filed" message. This is your proof that you filed the originals with the clerk. The clerk will ask you to pay the filing fee.

Step 7: Deliver a file-stamped copy of the papers to the courtroom of the judge who will hear the motion. Many courts require these "courtesy copies," but some don't. Check with the clerk when you file your papers.

Step 8: The clerk will note the date you indicated for the hearing on the Notice of Motion and enter it on the court calendar after you leave.

Step 9: Rule 3.1327, California Rules of Court, says that the landlord may oppose the motion orally, at the hearing, or file a written opposition and serve it on you one court day before the hearing.

Step 10: Judges sometimes make a tentative decision solely on the basis of the papers filed. If so, this tentative decision may be posted outside the courtroom on the date of the hearing. Some courts have specific telephone lines connected to voice mail that list tentative rulings. Increasingly, tentative rulings are posted on the court's own website. (See "Tentative Rulings on the Web," below, for instructions on how to access your court's website.) If the decision is for the landlord, some courts require you to call the landlord and/or the court the day before the hearing if you want to argue your side.

Step 11: The day of the hearing, go a little early and check with the clerk's office to make sure your case is on the calendar. If it isn't, find out why. If it is, go to the courtroom indicated.

Tentative Rulings on the Web

Your court may use its website to announce tentative rulings. To find your court's site, go first to the Judicial Council website at www.courts.ca.gov. Choose the Courts link at the top, then the Superior Courts link on the next page. Find your county on the alphabetical list of California counties. When you're at your county court's website, search for "tentative rulings."

CAUTION

Don't file by mail. Though it is legal to file papers by mail, we don't recommend it. The time limits are so tight in unlawful detainer cases that a postal foul-up or a mishandling in the clerk's office can cause you no end of grief.

The Court Hearing on a Motion to Quash

The evening before the hearing, you should sit down, relax, and go over the points stated in your motion papers to familiarize yourself with them. Judges are getting more and more used to people representing themselves in court, and generally treat self-represented people with courtesy and respect. Although they understand that you are not a lawyer, they expect parties representing themselves to be familiar with proper procedures. On the day of the hearing, dress conservatively, though you don't have to wear a business suit. Try to get to the courtroom a little early.

When your case is called, step forward. Some judges begin by asking questions, but others prefer that the person bringing the motion (you) talk first. In any case, don't start talking until the judge asks you to begin. Your argument should be straightforward and based on the facts and issues set forth in your declaration and motion papers and the landlord's responses to your papers.

Limit your presentation to the facts related to service of the Summons and Complaint. For example, discuss how the lawsuit came to your attention (for example, you found the papers on your doorstep when you came home). Don't state your opinion of the landlord, or argue the merits of your situation beyond what you have raised in your motion papers.

After the landlord or landlord's lawyer has had a chance to argue their side, you can respond. The judge will either rule on the motion or take the matter "under submission" and decide later.

If the judge denies the motion, you will have five calendar days to file your next response (counting Saturdays, Sundays, and holidays). If the fifth day falls on a Saturday, Sunday, or holiday, you will have the next business day to file a response. If you win the Motion to Quash, the landlord may have another Summons ready to serve on you right there, and you start all over again.

The Demurrer

Once the landlord has properly served you with a Summons and Complaint, you are entitled to file an Answer to the Complaint or a Demurrer. (CCP § 1170.) You must either answer or demur within five days from the date of service of the Summons and Complaint. Remember, you do not count Saturdays, Sundays, or holidays when computing the five days from service of the Summons and Complaint. However, if you filed a Motion to Quash and lost, you have five calendar days to file. If the fifth day falls on a Sunday or holiday, the last day for your response is extended to the next business day.

When you file a Demurrer, what you are really saying is, "Assuming, only for the purpose of argument, that everything the landlord says in the Complaint is true, it still doesn't provide legal justification for the court to order me evicted." For instance, you might say that the landlord did not allege that he served you with a notice to quit, or you could argue that the notice to quit attached to the complaint is somehow defective.

Note that when you file a Demurrer, you assume that the facts as stated in the Complaint are true, but only for the purpose of this particular hearing. You are not conceding the truth of anything in the Complaint beyond the hearing on Demurrer. Once the court rules on your Demurrer, you will still have a chance to file a written Answer, in which you may deny any factual allegations in the Complaint that you believe are false or don't actually know to be true, and where you may raise affirmative defenses. (The Answer is discussed below.)

When to File a Demurrer

Here are some common legal grounds on which you may properly demur to a Complaint:

- **The three-day notice wasn't in the alternative.** All three-day notices—including those based on nonpayment of rent—must be in the alternative, unless the landlord is alleging violation of a lease provision that is not curable within that time (Unconditional Three-Day Notice to Quit). For example, if you receive a Three-Day Notice to Quit because you have a dog (or failed to pay the rent) and the notice fails to say that you have the alternative of getting rid of the dog (or paying the rent) in three days, it is defective. (See the discussion of three-day notices under "Termination of Tenancy" in Chapter 14, for details on three-day notices.) (See *Turney v. Collins*, 48 Cal. App.2d 381, 392 (1949); *Horton-Howard v. Payton*, 44 Cal.App. 108, 112 (1919).)

- **The Three-Day Notice to Pay Rent or Quit failed to tell the tenant where, or during what days or hours, the rent could be paid.** If the notice omits this information, it's defective. (CCP § 1161(2).)

- **The Complaint was filed too soon.** The date the Complaint was filed will be stamped on the first page of the Complaint. Look at this date. If the three days or the 30, 60, or 90 days given by the notice did not expire before the date the Complaint was filed, you can demur. In the case of the Three-Day Notice to Pay Rent or Quit or the Three-Day Notice to Perform

Covenant or Quit, be sure that Saturdays, Sundays, and holidays were not counted in computing the three days. (See *LaManna v. Vognar*, 17 Cal.App.4th Supp. 1 (1993).)

- In jurisdictions that require a "just cause for eviction" (either under state "just cause for eviction" or local rent control jurisdictions—see Appendix A), the landlord's failure to comply with all the requirements of a particular "just cause" for eviction may be grounds for a Demurrer. Remember, it's the form of the landlord's allegation, not its substance, that matters. For instance, under state "just cause for eviction" and in many rent control jurisdictions, the landlord is supposed to state the grounds for eviction in the notice. If the notice attached to the complaint does not state any grounds, then you can demur. In the case of an eviction for "nuisance," a landlord is supposed to describe what the nuisance is. Again, if he fails to do so in the notice, you have a Demurrer. Suppose, however, that the landlord says you are dealing drugs (which is a nuisance) and it is not a true statement; that is something that the landlord would have to prove at trial, and you cannot file a Demurrer.

For additional affirmative defenses, consult the *California Eviction Defense Manual*, published by Continuing Education of the Bar.

Preparing the Demurrer

You need to prepare four documents to file a Demurrer:

- The Demurrer
- Notice of Hearing
- Memorandum of Points and Authorities, and
- Request for Judicial Notice (of the Complaint you are demurring to).

TIP

Unlike a Notice of Motion to Quash, don't use a Declaration to support your Demurrer. In a Demurrer, the only question is whether the allegations in the landlord's Complaint (assuming they are true only for the purpose of the hearing), are sufficient to state a case. Since that is purely a question of law, any facts you might submit by declaration would be irrelevant to your Demurrer.

FORM

You'll find copies of the Demurrer (and related forms, Points and Authorities in Support of Demurrer and Notice of Hearing on Demurrer, discussed below) in Appendix C, and the Nolo website includes downloadable copies of these forms. (See Appendix B for the link to the forms in this book.)

Filling Out the Demurrer

For instructions on how to complete the Demurrer, refer to Steps 1–3 for preparing the Motion to Quash set out above.

The list of legal grounds for a Demurrer are discussed in "When to File a Demurrer," above. For example:

If the first reason for filing applies to your situation, enter: "The three-day notice attached to the Complaint simply ordered me to vacate, without giving me the alternative of stopping any alleged breach of the rental agreement."

If the second reason for filing applies to you, enter: "The three-day notice failed to state the days/times/place where rent could be paid."

If the third ground fits your situation, enter: "The Complaint was filed prematurely, before the time set in the notice expired."

Sign and date the Demurrer.

Filling Out the Memorandum of Points and Authorities

The next step is to prepare a Points and Authorities in Support of Demurrer. There is a blank copy of this form in Appendix C and a downloadable copy on the Nolo website (See Appendic B for the link).

To complete the top portion of this form, refer to Steps 1–3 for preparing the Motion to Quash, above.

The next section (I. Defendant's Demurrer Is Properly Before the Court) is boilerplate language. You don't need to add anything to this.

Sample Demurrer

1 TOM TENANT
   1234 Apartment St.
2 Berkeley, CA 94710
   510-123-4567
3

4 Defendant in Pro Per

5

6

7

8   SUPERIOR COURT OF THE STATE OF CALIFORNIA, COUNTY OF ___ALAMEDA___

9   ___BERKELEY/ALBANY___ DIVISION/BRANCH

10
)
11 LENNY LANDLORD   ) Case No. ___5-0258___
    _____ ,)
12   ) DEMURRER OF
    _____ ,)
           Plaintiff(s),   )   TOM TENANT
13   ) _____
    v.   )
14   )
    TOM TENANT   )
    _____ ,)
15   ) TO THE COMPLAINT OF
    _____ ,)
16   Defendant(s).   )   LENNY LANDLORD
) _____
)

17   Defendant(s) demur to the Complaint on the following ground(s):

18 1. The three-day notice attached to the Complaint simply ordered me to vacate, without

19 giving me the alternative of curing any alleged breach of the rental agreement.

20 _____

21 2. _____

22 _____

23 _____

24 3. _____

25 _____

26 _____

27

28 Dated: ___February 20, 20xx___   *Tom Tenant*
                                                        Tom Tenant

---
                            Demurrer   Page 1 of 1

Sample Points and Authorities (Demurrer)

1   Tom Tenant
     1234 Apartment St.
2   Berkeley, CA 94710
     510-123-4567
3

4   Defendant in Pro Per

5

6

7

8   SUPERIOR COURT OF THE STATE OF CALIFORNIA, COUNTY OF __ALAMEDA__

9   _____BERKELEY/ALBANY_____   DIVISION/BRANCH

10

11   LENNY LANDLORD _____ ,)   Case No. __S-0258__

12   _____ ,)   POINTS AND AUTHORITIES

13   v.   )   IN SUPPORT OF DEMURRER

14   _____ ,)

15   TOM TENANT _____ ,)   (CCP § 430.10)

16   Defendant(s).   )

17

18   I. DEFENDANT'S DEMURRER IS PROPERLY BEFORE THE COURT

19   A defendant in an unlawful detainer action may demur. C.C.P. § 1170. See Hinman v. Wagnon, 172 Cal.

20   App.2d 24 (1959), where the court held that a demurrer was proper where the incorporated 3-day notice was

21   defective on its face. The court sustained a dismissal following sustaining the demurrer without leave to amend.

22   The periods for noticing hearing on a demurrer are not stated in the unlawful detainer statutes, so C.C.P.

23   Section 1177 incorporates the regular provisions of the Code of Civil Procedure, such as C.C.P. Section 1005

24   requiring that motions be noticed on 16 court days' notice, plus five calendar days for mailing. Rule 3.1320(c),

25   California Rules of Court, specifies that demurrers shall be heard in accordance with Section 1005.

26

27

28

Points and Authorities in Support of Demurrer   Page 1 of 2

Sample Points and Authorities (Demurrer) (continued)

1	II. ARGUMENT
2	The three-day notice attached to the complaint simply ordered me to vacate, without giving me the
3	alternative of curing any alleged breach of the rental agreement. *Turney v. Collins*, 48 Cal.App. 2d. 381,
4	392 (1949); *Horton-Howard v. Payton*, 44 Cal.App. 108, 112 (1919).
5	
6	
7	
8	
9	
10	
11	
12	
13	
14	
15	
16	
17	
18	
19	
20	
21	
22	
23	
24	
25	
26	
27	Dated: February 20, 20xx *Tom Tenant*
	Tom Tenant
28	

Notice of Hearing on Demurrer

1	TOM TENANT
2	1234 Apartment St.
	Berkeley, CA 94710
3	510-123-4567
4	Defendant in Pro Per
5	
6	
7	

8 SUPERIOR COURT OF THE STATE OF CALIFORNIA, COUNTY OF __ALAMEDA__

9 _____BERKELEY/ALBANY_____ DIVISION/BRANCH

10

11 LENNY LANDLORD _____ ,) Case No. _____S-0258_____

12 _____ ,)
        Plaintiff(s),   ) NOTICE OF HEARING ON DEMURRER OF

13 v.   ) TOM TENANT _____

14 TOM TENANT _____ ,)

15 _____ ,) TO THE COMPLAINT OF
        Defendant(s).   ) LENNY LANDLORD _____

16 _____)

17

18 To: _____

19 PLEASE TAKE NOTICE THAT on _____ , _____ , at

20 _____ in Department No. _____ of the above entitled court, located at _____

21 _____ ,

22 a hearing will be held on Defendant's demurrer to the Complaint, a copy of which is served with this notice.

23

24 Dated: __February 20, 20xx__   *Tom Tenant*
                               Tom Tenant

25

26

27

28

For the bottom portion of the Points and Authorities in Support of Demurrer (II. Argument), repeat each ground in the numbered paragraphs provided as you did at the start of the Demurrer. This time, however, you should follow each ground by an appropriate legal reference:

- For the first ground (three-day notice wasn't in the alternative), this is: *Turney v. Collins*, 48 Cal.App.2d 381, 392 (1949); *Horton-Howard v. Payton*, 44 Cal.App. 108, 112 (1919).)
- For the second ground (three-day notice failed to specify where or when the rent could be paid), put CCP § 1161(2).
- For the third ground (the Complaint was filed too soon), put *LaManna v. Vognar*, 17 Cal.App.4th Supp. 1 (1993).

(See the sample Points and Authorities with the Demurrer, above.)

Attach your Points and Authorities to your Demurrer.

Filling Out the Notice of Hearing on Demurrer

A blank form for the Notice of Hearing is in Appendix C and a downloadable copy is on the Nolo website (See Appendix B for the link).

A sample is included with the Demurrer shown below. Refer to the instructions for "Preparing the Motion to Quash," above. Follow them for the Notice of Hearing on Demurrer, with the following exceptions:

- Call the court clerk and ask when Demurrers (rather than motions) are heard by the court.
- Unless the court clerk says otherwise (some courts insist that Demurrers in unlawful detainer cases be heard on short notice), select a hearing date that is at least 16 court (not calendar) days—don't count Saturdays, Sundays, or holidays—after the date you plan to file your Demurrer, plus five calendar days (add them because the copy of the Demurrer and other papers will be mailed to the landlord or landlord's attorney).
- Some courts will require you to confer with the other side about picking a date for a

hearing on the Demurrer. Consult the local rules on this.

Request for Judicial Notice

Because a Demurrer attacks the complaint, many courts require that you file a copy of the complaint along with the Demurrer (even though it's already in the court file). This request puts the complaint that's been filed against you before the court at this hearing on your Demurrer. Whether or not it is required in your jurisdiction, it's a good idea to attach a copy so that the court will be able to easily look at the pleading that's the subject of the hearing.

Use the form Request for Judicial Notice included with the forms for this book (a sample is provided below). Then copy the complaint, along with any exhibits to the complaint, write "Exhibit A" across the top of the first page of the complaint, and attach these pages as Exhibit A to the Request for Judicial Notice. That's it!

Filing and Serving the Demurrer

After you have prepared your Demurrer, here's how to file and serve it.

Step 1: Complete the document included in this book called Proof of Service by First-Class Mail—Civil, following the instructions found in the discussion of Motion to Quash, above. The server must be a person over 18 and not a party to the action—that is, not named in the Complaint as a plaintiff or defendant. As a defendant, you cannot serve your own legal papers.

Step 2: Make three copies of your Demurrer papers (Notice of Hearing, Demurrer, Points and Authorities in Support of Demurrer, Request for Judicial Notice, and the Proof of Service). Print the server's name on the last line of both copies of the Proof of Service. You'll file the original of the documents with the court clerk, one copy goes to the other side, one copy you keep, and the third copy is a "courtesy copy" that goes to the courtroom of the judge who will hear the motion.

Sample Request for Judicial Notice

1 TOM TENANT
   1234 Apartment St.
2 Berkeley, CA 94710
   510-123-4567
3

4 Defendant in Pro Per

5

6

7

8   SUPERIOR COURT OF THE STATE OF CALIFORNIA, COUNTY OF ALAMEDA

9   BERKELEY/ALBANY   DIVISION/BRANCH

10   )
)
11 LENNY LANDLORD   ,) Case No. CGC-12-521271
)
12 _____ ,) REQUEST FOR JUDICIAL NOTICE
            Plaintiff(s),   )
13 v.   )
)
14 _____ ,)
)
15 TOM TENANT   ,)
            Defendant(s).   )
16   )

17

18   Defendant TOM TENANT hereby requests that the Court take judicial notice of the Complaint filed in this

19 action and attached hereto as Exhibit A, pursuant to California Evidence Code Section 452(d).

20   California Evidence Code Section 453 provides that the trial court shall take judicial notice of any matter

21 specified in Section 452 if a party requests it, provide each party has been given sufficient notice and the court

22 has been provided a copy. Defendant has complied with these requirements.

23

24

25

26 Dated: February 20, 20xx   Tom Tenant

27

28

Step 3: Attach one copy of the Proof of Service by First-Class Mail—Civil, to each set of copies of your Demurrer papers.

Step 4: Have your server mail one set of copies (your Demurrer papers and an unsigned Proof of Service) to the landlord's attorney (listed on the Summons) or the landlord if there is no attorney.

Step 5: Now have your server fill in the blanks in the last paragraph of the Proof of Service and sign it, stating that the mailing has occurred. Attach this original to your original Demurrer papers.

Step 6: Take the original Demurrer papers and two sets of copies to the court clerk. Give the original set of papers to the clerk, who will stamp (or have you stamp) your copies with a "filed" notation, in the upper-right corner. This is your proof that you filed the originals with the clerk.

Step 7: Deliver a file-stamped copy of the papers to the courtroom of the judge who will hear the motion. Many courts require these "courtesy copies," but some don't. Check with the clerk when you file your papers.

Step 8: The clerk will note the date you indicated for the hearing on the Demurrer and enter it on the court calendar.

If the landlord desires to respond to your Demurrer, he or she must file a response at least nine court days before the hearing. If you wish to make a written response to those papers, you must do so at least five court days before the hearing. (CCP § 1005.)

Step 9: Courts sometimes make a tentative decision solely on the basis of the papers filed. (See "Tentative Rulings on the Web," above.) If you want to argue your side even if the tentative decision is against you, some courts require you to call the landlord (or landlord's attorney) and say you're still going to argue.

Step 10: On the day of the hearing, check to see that your case is on the calendar. If it isn't, ask the clerk why and get it rescheduled.

CAUTION

Don't file by mail. Though it is legal to file papers by mail, we don't recommend it. The time limits are so tight in unlawful detainer cases that a postal foul-up or a mishandling in the clerk's office could result in your papers not being filed on time and a default being entered against you.

Sometimes a landlord (or landlord's attorney) will see your Demurrer and realize that the basis may well be valid. Then, rather than going to the hearing and risking a loss, the landlord will file an "amended complaint" and serve it on you— even before the Demurrer hearing. The amended complaint takes the place of the original complaint and starts the clock ticking again.

In this situation, you must respond to the amended complaint within five calendar days of when you were personally served, or ten days if the amended complaint was mailed to you. If the fifth day falls on a Saturday, Sunday, or holiday, you have until the close of the next business day to file your response with the court. When this happens, you cannot file a Motion to Quash the amended complaint because you have already submitted to the court's jurisdiction by filing a Demurrer attacking the first complaint. You can either file another Demurrer or an answer to the first amended complaint. You shouldn't worry about the hearing for the Demurrer to the original complaint. Since the landlord has filed an amended complaint, the court has no reason to hear the Demurrer, and it should be "taken off calendar."

At the Court Hearing

(See the discussion on "The Court Hearing on a Motion to Quash," above.)

The judge will do one of three things at the hearing:

- **Overrule (deny) the Demurrer.** This means that you've lost the motion, and you will have five days to file your Answer. A word of caution: Technically, you have to answer only after you receive a formal Notice of Ruling (usually prepared by opposing counsel), (you have five days if served personally, ten days if served by mail). However, this requirement of first receiving the formal notice has caused some confusion in some courts and clerks have inadvertently entered defaults, even though the formal Notice of Ruling was not given to the tenant. You should check with a local legal resource or the court clerk before relying on the date of the Notice of Ruling.
- **Sustain the Demurrer "without leave to amend."** This means you've won the motion and the landlord has to start over (usually by giving a new notice of termination).
- **Sustain the Demurrer "with leave to amend."** This gives the landlord an opportunity to file an "amended complaint." If you are served with an amended complaint, you have five days to respond (if served personally; ten days if it is mailed to you).

Procedures Other Than a Demurrer

Other motions may be appropriate at this stage of the proceedings. For instance, a "motion to strike" might be appropriate if the landlord's Complaint requests relief that is not justified by the allegations. For more on this, consult the *California Eviction Defense Manual,* published by Continuing Education of the Bar (CEB).

The Answer

The Answer is where you tell your version of what happened. You must file it with the court within five days of receiving the Summons and Complaint (15 days if substituted service was used), unless you file a Motion to Quash or Demurrer instead. If you miss the deadline, the landlord can take a default judgment against you. Defaults are discussed just below.

Even if you first file a Demurrer or Motion to Quash, you will have to file an Answer sooner or later, unless the landlord drops the case.

If your Demurrer is upheld by the court, the landlord will have to amend the Complaint. Then you can demur again, if you have grounds, or file an Answer. If, on the other hand, your Demurrer is overruled, you will have to file an Answer within five days after the date of the notice of the court order overruling the Demurrer. If the fifth day falls on a Saturday, Sunday, or holiday, you have until the next business day to file.

Filling Out the Form Answer

Fortunately, a form Answer has been developed by the California Judicial Council specifically for unlawful detainer cases (see the sample shown above). The form is straightforward and relatively easy to use.

FORM
You'll find copies of the Answer—Unlawful Detainer (and the related Attachment form discussed below) in Appendix C, and the Nolo website includes downloadable copies of these forms. (See Appendix B for the link to the forms in this book and details on how to access and use Judicial Council forms.) This form will change sometime in 2020 because of the new "just cause for eviction" provisions. Be sure to check the Judicial Council website for an updated form (see the instructions in Appendix B).

Answer—Unlawful Detainer

UD-105

ATTORNEY OR PARTY WITHOUT ATTORNEY		FOR COURT USE ONLY

ATTORNEY OR PARTY WITHOUT ATTORNEY   STATE BAR NUMBER:

NAME: TOM TENANT

FIRM NAME:

STREET ADDRESS: 1234 Apartment Street

CITY: Berkeley, CA 94710   STATE: ZIP CODE:

TELEPHONE NO.:   FAX NO.:

E-MAIL ADDRESS:

ATTORNEY FOR (name): Defendant in Pro Per

SUPERIOR COURT OF CALIFORNIA, COUNTY OF

STREET ADDRESS: Alameda County Superior Court

MAILING ADDRESS: 2000 Center St.

CITY AND ZIP CODE: Berkeley, CA 94704

BRANCH NAME: Berkeley—Albany Judicial Division

Plaintiff: LENNY LANDLORD

Defendant: TOM TENANT

FOR COURT USE ONLY

ANSWER—UNLAWFUL DETAINER	CASE NUMBER: S-0258

1. Defendant *(each defendant for whom this answer is filed must be named and must sign this answer unless his or her attorney signs):* TOM TENANT

   answers the complaint as follows:

2. ***Check ONLY ONE of the next two boxes:***

   a. [ ] Defendant generally denies each statement of the complaint. *(Do not check this box if the complaint demands more than $1,000.)*

   b. [✓] Defendant admits that all of the statements of the complaint are true EXCEPT

       (1) defendant claims the following statements of the complaint are false *(state paragraph numbers from the complaint or explain below or on form MC-025):* [✓] Explanation is on MC-025, titled as Attachment 2b(1).

           5.d., 6.a.(1), 7.a.(1), 8.a., 9, 10, and 11

       (2) defendant has no information or belief that the following statements of the complaint are true, so defendant denies them *(state paragraph numbers from the complaint or explain below or on form MC-025):*

           [ ] Explanation is on MC-025, titled as Attachment 2b(2).

3. AFFIRMATIVE DEFENSES (***NOTE:*** *For each box checked, you must state brief facts to support it in item 3l (page 2).)*

   a. [✓] *(Nonpayment of rent only)* Plaintiff has breached the warranty to provide habitable premises.

   b. [ ] *(Nonpayment of rent only)* Defendant made needed repairs and properly deducted the cost from the rent, and plaintiff did not give proper credit.

   c. [ ] *(Nonpayment of rent only)* On *(date):*   before the notice to pay or quit expired, defendant offered the rent due but plaintiff would not accept it.

   d. [ ] Plaintiff waived, changed, or canceled the notice to quit.

   e. [ ] Plaintiff served defendant with the notice to quit or filed the complaint to retaliate against defendant.

   f. [ ] By serving defendant with the notice to quit or filing the complaint, plaintiff is arbitrarily discriminating against the defendant in violation of the Constitution or the laws of the United States or California.

   g. [ ] Plaintiff's demand for possession violates the local rent control or eviction control ordinance of *(city or county, title of ordinance, and date of passage):*

       (Also, briefly state in item 3l the facts showing violation of the ordinance.)

   h. [ ] Plaintiff accepted rent from defendant to cover a period of time after the date the notice to quit expired.

   i. [ ] Plaintiff seeks to evict defendant based on an act against defendant or a member of defendant's household that constitutes domestic violence, sexual assault, stalking, human trafficking, or abuse of an elder or a dependent adult. *(This defense requires one of the following: (1) **a temporary restraining order, protective order, or police report** that is not more than 180 days old; OR (2) **a signed statement from a qualified third party** (e.g., a doctor, domestic violence or sexual assault counselor, human trafficking caseworker, or psychologist) concerning the injuries or abuse resulting from these acts.)*

Page 1 of 2

Form Approved for Optional Use
Judicial Council of California
UD-105 [Rev. September 1, 2019]   **ANSWER—UNLAWFUL DETAINER**   Civil Code, § 1940 et seq.;
Code of Civil Procedure, §§ 425.12, 1161 et seq.
www.courts.ca.gov

Answer—Unlawful Detainer (continued)

UD-105

CASE NUMBER: 5-0258

3. AFFIRMATIVE DEFENSES (cont'd.)

j. ☐ Plaintiff seeks to evict defendant based on defendant or another person calling the police or emergency assistance (e.g., ambulance) by or on behalf of a victim of abuse, a victim of crime, or an individual in an emergency when defendant or the other person believed that assistance was necessary.

k. ☑ Other affirmative defenses are stated in item 3*l*.

l. Facts supporting affirmative defenses checked above *(identify facts for each item by its letter below or on form MC-025)*:

☐ Description of facts is on MC-025, titled as Attachment 3*l*.

3.a. I did not pay rent because the landlord did not fix the broken heater in my apartment, despite my repeated requests.

4. OTHER STATEMENTS

a. ☐ Defendant vacated the premises on *(date)*:

b. ☐ The fair rental value of the premises alleged in the complaint is excessive *(explain below or on form MC-025)*:
☐ Explanation is on MC-025, titled as Attachment 4b.

c. ☐ Other *(specify below or on form MC-025 in attachment)*:
☐ Other statements are on MC-025, titled as Attachment 4c.

5. DEFENDANT REQUESTS

a. that plaintiff take nothing requested in the complaint.

b. costs incurred in this proceeding.

c. ☐ reasonable attorney fees.

d. ☑ that plaintiff be ordered to (1) make repairs and correct the conditions that constitute a breach of the warranty to provide habitable premises and (2) reduce the monthly rent to a reasonable rental value until the conditions are corrected.

e. ☐ Other *(specify below or on form MC-025)*:
☐ All other requests are stated on MC-025, titled as Attachment 5e.

6. Number of pages attached: ___1___

UNLAWFUL DETAINER ASSISTANT (Bus. & Prof. Code, §§ 6400-6415)

7. *(Must be completed in all cases.)* An **unlawful detainer assistant** ☐ did not ☐ did for compensation give advice or assistance with this form. *(If defendant has received any help or advice for pay from an unlawful detainer assistant, state)*:

a. assistant's name: b. telephone number:

c. street address, city, and zip code:

d. county of registration: e. registration number: f. expiration date:

(Each defendant for whom this answer is filed must be named in item 1 and must sign this answer unless his or her attorney signs.)

TOM TENANT
(TYPE OR PRINT NAME)

▶ *Tom Tenant*
(SIGNATURE OF DEFENDANT OR ATTORNEY)

▶
(SIGNATURE OF DEFENDANT OR ATTORNEY)
(TYPE OR PRINT NAME)

VERIFICATION

(Use a different verification form if the verification is by an attorney or for a corporation or partnership.)

I am the defendant in this proceeding and have read this answer. I declare under penalty of perjury under the laws of the State of California that the foregoing is true and correct. Date:

TOM TENANT
(TYPE OR PRINT NAME)

Tom Tenant
(SIGNATURE OF DEFENDANT)

UD-105 [Rev. September 1, 2019]   **ANSWER—UNLAWFUL DETAINER**   Page 2 of 2

Top of the Form: This is self-explanatory. Put your name in both the top box—"Attorney or Party Without Attorney"—and the one marked "Defendant." Put your landlord's name under Plaintiff. You will find the name and address of the court and the case number on the Complaint.

Item 1: Fill in your name under Defendant.

Item 2: If the Complaint expressly asks for less than $1,000 in rent, check Box a. If it asks for more than $1,000, check Box b.

If you checked Box b (as our sample Answer does), you have a little more work to do before going to Item 3. Follow these directions and you should have no trouble.

Carefully read the Complaint, paragraph by paragraph. As you do, take the following actions for each paragraph:

1. If you agree with *everything* in a paragraph of the Complaint, go on to the next one.

2. If you disagree with *any* statement in a paragraph, enter the paragraph number in the space on the Answer form after 2b(1). You may very well disagree with more than one paragraph. If so, enter the numbers of all such paragraphs. If you don't have enough space to list all the paragraphs, check the box labeled "Explanation is on MC-025, titled as Attachment 2b(1)," and use the Attachment form included in Appendix C and on the Nolo website. (A sample of this attachment form is not included in this chapter.) Clearly label each attachment with the number of the paragraph on the printed form Answer to which it refers. Each attachment should be on one side of the Attachment form and should be stapled to the Answer.

3. If you don't have enough information to agree or disagree with a statement in a paragraph, enter the paragraph number in the space on the Answer form labeled 2b(2). If you need more room, check the box labeled "Explanation is on MC-025, titled as Attachment 2b(2)," and prepare an attachment page as described above.

Do a careful job of reading each paragraph of the Complaint. The court will accept as true any of the landlord's statements in any paragraph that isn't listed on your Answer form. For example, suppose a landlord's Complaint alleges, in Paragraphs 7.a or 8.a, that the tenant was served with a three-day notice to pay rent or quit on January 7th. If the tenant doesn't list "7.a or 8.a" as one of the denied paragraphs in Item 2.a(2) of the Answer, the tenant has admitted that he or she was served the notice. At trial, the judge will not permit the tenant to say otherwise. Any paragraph that isn't listed after Box 2.b(1) or 2.b(2) will be accepted as true by the court.

Therefore you will want to deny paragraph 7c: "all facts stated in the notice are true" and, if you are covered by local rent control you would want to deny paragraph 14: "plaintiff has met all applicable requirements of the ordinance."

If you are raising the defense of breach of implied warranty of habitability, you will want to deny paragraphs 7, 10, and 11.

Item 3. Affirmative Defenses. An affirmative defense consists of new facts that constitute a legal excuse or justification. For example, the fact that you did not pay the landlord the rent is justified by the additional fact, or affirmative defense, that he failed, despite your request, to fix a leaky roof, overflowing toilet, or nonworking heating system. The Answer lists common affirmative defenses; check any that you plan to raise if your eviction goes to trial.

Here's another example. Suppose the landlord seeks to evict you because you didn't pay your full rent. If your defense is that you didn't pay the rent because you properly used the repair and deduct remedy to address a serious problem, as discussed in Chapter 6, it is based on different facts from those found in the Complaint and is therefore an affirmative defense—in this case, Item 3.b.

Another example is an eviction that was supposedly based on "just cause"—such as a landlord in a rent control city evicting a tenant on the grounds that the owner needs to make major repairs. If this eviction was made in bad faith—for example, the tenant checked with the city and found out that the landlord had not taken out the necessary building permits—the tenant would have an affirmative defense to the eviction. In this case, the tenant should check Item 3.g and list the name of this city's rent control or just cause eviction ordinance and the date of its enactment (see the Rent Control Chart in Appendix A for this information). Be sure you also deny the allegations of Paragraph 14.

Likewise, under statewide "just cause" eviction protections, a landlord must plead and prove the "just cause" for eviction. The notice must also state the cause for eviction. If the landlord has not complied, or if you think that the landlord is not going to do what he or she intended to do, then you should so state.

In Item 3.l, state the facts on which you base your affirmative defense. Briefly state the factual basis for your defense. You do not have to set forth all the evidence to prove your case; a brief statement will do. If your statement fits in the space under 3.k, fine. However, even if you try to be brief, the room provided might not be enough. If you need more space, check the box next to "Description of facts is on MC-025, titled as Attachment 3k." Then take a sheet of 8½" x 11" paper, label it "Attachment to Item 3.k of Answer" at the top, and explain the facts regarding each affirmative defense.

Affirmative Defenses in Rent Control Situations: If your rental is covered by state or local rent control, it is possible that you have been charged more rent than the law allows. (See Chapter 3.) If this is the case, the landlord's claim that you failed to pay rent can be defeated on the ground that the rent demanded in the three-day notice was higher than it should have been. Although this defense is technically raised by a simple denial in Item 2 of the Answer, it is also a good idea to describe your position in an affirmative defense—in this case, Item 3.g.

State law says that landlords in rent control cities that require registration of rents (Berkeley, Santa Monica, East Palo Alto, Los Angeles, and West Hollywood) can't be penalized for good faith mistakes in the amount of rent they charge. (CC § 1947.7.) Landlords may argue that the statute also protects them from having a three-day notice thrown out because it demanded the wrong rent. Your response should be that dismissal of a Complaint because of a deficient three-day notice is not one of the penalties covered by the statute.

If you receive a 30- or 60-day notice of eviction because the landlord or the landlord's relative plans (in good faith) to move in (reside) in the unit (a "just cause" for eviction in many rent control cities), do a little checking before you decide to leave. To evaluate your chances for this type of eviction, review the local ordinance providing for "just cause" eviction. Many ordinances have detailed requirements. For example, some jurisdictions require landlords to pay moving expenses, or that the landlord has to live in the building in order to move a relative in, or that the landlord has to inform the tenant if any other units owned by the landlord are vacant.

If the landlord says he is moving in himself, find out where he lives now. If he lives in a fancy neighborhood and you live in a not-so-fancy one, it would seem very unusual for him to really plan to move in. If your rent is among the lowest rents in the building, the landlord may want you out pretty badly, because he can make the greatest profit by evicting you and charging a higher rent to a new tenant. In either case, see if he owns other vacant apartments he could move into instead. If he does, most ordinances require that he occupy one of these.

If a landlord claims that a relative is moving in, try to find out if the relative really exists, and if it would make sense for the relative to want to live there. For example, if the landlord's daughter is going to college in another city, it is not likely that she would want to move into your place in the middle of the semester.

If you do move out because the landlord says that she or a relative is moving in, go back and check up on whether the person moved in and, if so, how long he or she stayed. If it turns out that this was merely a scheme to take advantage of vacancy decontrol, you might be able to file a profitable lawsuit.

Here are some brief examples of affirmative defenses, with references to sections in this book where these issues are discussed in greater detail.

Item 3.a. Breach of Warranty of Habitability: If you are being evicted for nonpayment of rent and the landlord had reason to know that there are deficiencies in your apartment affecting its habitability, you should check Box 3.a and put the details in 3.k and any attachments. (See Chapter 6.)

Sample Statement of Details

> On December 25, 20xx, I notified my landlord (the plaintiff in this action) that the heating unit in my apartment was broken and asked that it be fixed. This was not done. Or, On March 19, 20xx, I notified my landlord that the roof was seriously leaking in three places. The roof has never been fixed.

Item 3.b. Use of Repair and Deduct Remedy: If you used the repair and deduct remedy, and the landlord failed to give you credit in the three-day notice for the amount you deducted from your rent (see Chapter 6), check this box and put the details in 3.k.

Item 3.c. Landlord's Refusal to Accept Rent: If you tried to pay the rent during the time allowed you by a three-day notice but the landlord refused to accept it, check this box. If you tried to pay the rent after the three days (but before the lawsuit was filed) and the notice did not mention "forfeiture" of your tenancy, check this box. (See the discussion of three-day notices in Chapter 14.)

Item 3.d. Cancellation of Notice: Sometimes, after a three-day or 30-, 60-, or 90-day notice is served, the landlord (or the landlord's agent) says something to indicate that he didn't mean to give you the notice, or that he has reconsidered evicting you, that you can have more time, or something else inconsistent with the notice. This also applies where the landlord has accepted all or part of the rent demanded in a three-day notice. If this happens, he may have implicitly waived or canceled the notice, so check Item 3.d.

Sample Statement of Details

> After I received the notice, Plaintiff's resident manager told me that she had served the notice on me only to scare me, and as long as I paid by the end of the month, no eviction lawsuit would be filed.

Item 3.e. Retaliatory Eviction: Retaliatory eviction is a very common defense. Tenants are protected on the following fronts:

- **Habitability.** Civil Code Section 1942.5(a) prohibits a landlord from evicting, increasing rent, or decreasing services within 180 days after the tenant has reported a habitability defect to the landlord (including reporting an infestation of bedbugs), or to an appropriate governmental agency; or after commencing an arbitration or judicial proceeding against the landlord regarding habitability defects.

- **Inspections and awards concerning habitability.** Additionally, a landlord may not retaliate within 180 days of an inspection by a governmental agency, a judgment entered against the landlord, or an arbitration award for the tenant regarding habitability defects.

- **Immigration status.** Landlords are not allowed to report or threaten to report the tenant or persons known to the tenant to immigration authorities. (CC § 1942.5(c).)

- **Organizing or participating in a tenants' association.** Civil Code Section 1942.5(d) prohibits a landlord from evicting, increasing rent, or threatening to do so if the landlord's purpose is to retaliate against the tenant because the tenant has organized or participated in a tenants' association.

- **Lawfully exercising *any* legal right.** Tenants are protected if they have lawfully exercised *any* right under the law. In one case, a tenant defended an eviction claiming that the landlord was retaliating because she told police that the landlord had sexually molested her child. The court stated that Section 1942.5(c) should be interpreted broadly, and said that the tenant could use that accusation to defend against an eviction. (*Barela v. Superior Court,* 30 Cal.3d 244 (1981).) "Any right under the law" most likely includes any right provided by the Constitution, a state law, or a local law, including a local rent control ordinance. Section 1942.5(e) makes it illegal for a landlord to contact immigration authorities (or threaten to do so) in retaliation for any of the above actions.

It's important to understand that these anti-retaliatory protections do not prevent a landlord from terminating and evicting, if necessary, following a tenant's exercise of any of the legal rights set forth above. The question for a judge will be whether the landlord's dominant motive in taking the negative act was retaliatory, or based on a valid business reason. The landlord's Notice to Quit should give the landlord's good faith reason behind the Notice; the court will decide whether to believe it. (CC § 1942.5(g).)

If a landlord violates any of the above sections the tenant may use the landlord's acts as a defense to an eviction, and as a basis for fighting a rent increase or reduction in services. It may also be used as a basis for suing the landlord. Under Section 1942.5(h), a tenant may sue for actual damages suffered, punitive damages of no less than $100 or more than $2,000 for each retaliatory act, plus reasonable attorney fees (if you win).

The remedies described here are in addition to rights under court decisions or other statutory laws. For instance, laws against discrimination often prohibit retaliation. Some local rent control laws also have provisions that forbid retaliation. (CC § 1942.5(j).)

If you believe that your landlord is illegally retaliating against you, check Item 3.e and put the details in 3.k.

Sample Statement of Details

> After Plaintiff twice refused to respond to our request that he fix the toilet, we complained to the city health department. Forty-five days later, we received a 30-day termination notice. We believe that we are being evicted in retaliation for our complaint to the health department.

Item 3.f. Discrimination: The landlord may not evict you because of your race, religion, sex, sexual preference, or job; because you have children; or for any reason based on your personal characteristic or trait. (See Chapter 4.)

Sample Statement of Details

> Plaintiff served me with the 30-day notice because he doesn't want African American people living in his rental units.

Item 3.g. "Just Cause for Eviction" Ordinances: If you live in a city with a rent control ordinance that requires "just cause for eviction" or if the TPA applies to you, and you dispute the "just cause" alleged in the Complaint, simply deny that allegation of the Complaint (by putting the paragraph number in Item 2.b(1)). We also recommend that you check Item 3.g. (See Chapter 3 and "Termination of Tenancy" in Chapter 14.)

Sample Statements of Details

> The rent control ordinance of the City of Santa Monica says that a three-day notice must tell me of my right to call the rent board for advice. The notice served on me by Plaintiff did not say this, so it is invalid.

> The rent control ordinance of the City of San Francisco requires that the 30-day notice state a "just cause" to evict. The 30-day notice served on me by the landlord did not do this.

> Landlord has sued to evict me because she wants her mother to live in the unit. This is not a "just cause" to evict because under the rent control ordinance of the City of San Francisco, landlord must first establish that there are no other vacant units that her mother can live in. In fact, at the time she served me with the 30-day notice, she had two equivalent vacancies.

Item 3.h. Acceptance of Rent Beyond Notice Period: If the landlord served a 30-, 60-, or 90-day notice and then accepted rent covering a period beyond the 30, 60, or 90 days, he has implicitly withdrawn the notice, so check this box. (*EDC Associates v. Gutierrez,* 158 Cal.App.3d 167 (1984).) This also applies if the landlord has subsequently accepted any of the rent demanded in a three-day notice.

Item 3.i. Domestic Violence Protection: If you are a victim of domestic violence, sexual assault, stalking, human trafficking, or abuse of an elder or a dependent adult, and the landlord gives you a 30-, 60-, or 90-day notice to move because of the behavior of the perpetrator, the law protects you from being evicted for that reason. (You still have to pay the full rent, however, in the case where you've had an abusive now-former partner move out.) You'll have to provide a temporary restraining order, protective order, or police report that is not more than 180 days old, or a signed statement from a qualified party (such as a doctor or counselor) concerning injuries from these acts.

Item 3.j. The landlord cannot evict you based on you or someone else calling the police or other emergency assistance for a victim of abuse, a victim of a crime, or an individual in an emergency, as long as you or the other person thought that call was necessary.

Item 3.k. Other Affirmative Defenses: Sometimes landlords orally allow tenants to get behind on their rent or to make certain repairs to their premises in exchange for free rent, or they make other agreements on which the tenant relies because of a good relationship with the landlord. Then, when a falling-out occurs, the landlord will attempt an eviction on the basis of a particular tenant default and deny that any oral agreement was made. In such a case, you have an affirmative defense based on the agreement and should check this box and place the details on 3.k.

Here are some examples of other affirmative defenses you would detail in Item 3.k:

Not a Material Breach of Covenant. For a landlord to evict for violation of a lease provision, that provision must be a "material" one. (*Keating v. Preston,* 42 Cal.App.3d 110 (1940), *Boston LLC v. Juarez,* 245 Cal.App.4th 75 (2016).) The question of whether a term is "material" is a question of fact for the jury. For this defense, you might say something like, "The breach of lease alleged in the complaint was not a material breach."

Waiver of Lease Provision. Some lease provisions are not strictly enforced by the landlord. For instance, a lease might prohibit pets, but the landlord might have implicitly or explicitly said that it's okay for the tenant to get a dog. In this way, the landlord has "waived" the prohibition on pets and is therefore "estopped" (forbidden) from enforcing that provision. The law recognizes "equitable" (fairness) defenses such as this. (*Howard J. White, Inc. v. Varian Assoc.,* 178 Cal. App.2d 348 (1960), *Salton Community Services District v. Southard,* 256 Cal.App.2d 526 (1967). Your defense in this situation might look like this: "The landlord, by word and conduct led me to reasonably believe that I could have a dog and thereby waived that provision of the lease agreement."

Landlord's Bad Faith. A landlord who prevents your performance of a lease agreement cannot then later turn around and sue you for non-performance. (*Underwood v. Corsino,* 133 Cal. App.4th 132 (2005), (landlord refused rent payment within the three-day period). *Bawa v. Terhune,* 33 Cal.App.5th Supp 1 (2019). (landlord's failure to accept check one penny short gives rise to defense against eviction).

Frequent Requests for Police or Emergency Assistance. Under a new state law, a landlord cannot evict you for making frequent calls for police or emergency assistance. (CC § 1946.8, CCP § 1161.3). These situations arise most often in instances of domestic violence, or when an occupant has a physical or mental condition that requires frequent emergency help.

Eviction following Foreclosure. As explained in "Your Rights If Your Building Is Foreclosed Upon" in Chapter 14, banks or third-party foreclosure-sale buyers must generally honor existing leases, and must in any event give 90 days' notice of termination where allowed in the case of a buyer who wants to live in the property, or to terminate a month-to-month tenancy. If the new owner has brought an unlawful detainer case against you and failed to comply with the law, you should check this box and place the details on 3.k, starting with, "Plaintiff has failed to comply with the federal Protecting Tenants at Foreclosure Act of 2009" and state Code of Civil Procedure Section 1161b. (b), as follows: Then state the specifics, including what type of tenancy you had and why any notice provided was incorrect.

Landlord Hasn't Complied With Civil Code Section 1962. As discussed in Chapter 14, a landlord may not demand rent in a three-day notice for any period exceeding 15 days from the landlord's failure to advise you in writing of the name and address of the person authorized to collect rents, and the normal days and hours that rent will be accepted. If you have not received this sort of notice, and didn't pay your rent because of truly not knowing where or how to pay it, you may assert this defense.

Landlord's Failure to Provide Advance Notice Regarding Tenant's Abandoned Property

A 30-, 60-, or 90-day notice must include language about the disposition of any property you leave behind after vacating. (See "Belongings You Leave Behind" in Chapter 12.) That said, we believe a termination notice without the necessary language regarding abandoned property is not necessarily defective on that account.

Item 4. Other Statements

Item 4.a: Tenant has moved out: If you have moved out of the unit and have turned it over to the landlord, it is important that you check this box. At this point, the lawsuit against you is no longer one for unlawful detainer, and the case is (or should be) converted to a normal civil action. (CC §§ 1951.2, 1952.3.) The landlord should be required to either dismiss the action or amend the complaint to ask for rent (including post-termination daily "holdover rent"), as well as other damages he thinks you caused (such as property damage).

The tenant can then file an answer to this amended complaint and, if applicable, file a cross-complaint for affirmative relief (like asking to collect overpaid rent and for the return of your security deposit). If the landlord has not amended the Complaint to reflect the new nature of the lawsuit, you should also raise this in the "other statements" part of your answer.

Item 4.b: Although the landlord may not accept rent after the expiration of the notice to quit, the court will award the landlord the fair market rental value of the premises for the time between the expiration of the notice and the day the judgment is entered. This is normally computed by dividing the total rent amount by 30 to arrive at a daily rental, and then multiplying this amount by the number of days. If you believe that the "fair rental value" stated in the Complaint is too high, check this box. Then explain any habitability problems on the premises, any change in the neighborhood that might have affected rental value, or any other reason you think the landlord's estimate is excessive. If the action against you is based on nonpayment of rent, and you are defending the lawsuit on the basis that the landlord breached the implied warranty to provide habitable premises, you should have checked Box 3.a and explained why the premises are not worth what the landlord says they are. In this case, simply type "See item 3.a" in this space.

Item 4.c: This box gives you a chance to say anything relevant and not covered by the other boxes.

Although it is not required, it might be helpful to mention that eviction would result in an extreme hardship and that, should you not prevail at trial, you are entitled to "Relief from Forfeiture" (see "Stopping an Eviction," later in this chapter). You could write something like: "Eviction would result in an extreme hardship to myself and my family. In the event judgment is entered for plaintiff, defendants seek relief from forfeiture under Code of Civil Procedure Section 1179."

Item 5. Defendant Requests

Item 5.a: This item is self-explanatory. You don't want the court to meet any of the landlord's requests made in the Complaint, such as past due rent for damages. You indicate your specific requests for costs in the rest of Item 5. If your affirmative defense was the landlord's breach of the warranty of habitability (Item 3.a) or you believe the "fair rental value" stated in the Complaint is excessive, check Item 5.d. If you are going to hire an attorney, check Item 5.c, "reasonable attorney fees." You are entitled to reasonable attorney fees if you win with a court judgment and your rental agreement or lease provides for landlord's attorney fees. Obviously, you cannot get attorney fees if you did not have an attorney. If you believe you are entitled to some other remedy, provide details in Item 5.e.

Item 6. Attachments: If you have prepared any attachments, check the box here and list the total number of pages attached.

Item 7: If an unlawful detainer assistant helped you prepare your Answer form, you must provide the requested information.

Signing and Verifying Your Answer

Here are the rules:
- Unless you have an attorney, the Answer must be signed by all of the named defendants who are answering.
- The verification at the bottom of the Answer (the statement under penalty of perjury that the statements in the Answer are true) need be signed only by any one defendant.

Filing and Serving Your Answer

After you've prepared your Answer, here's how to file and serve it.

Step 1: Complete the document called Proof of Service by First Class Mail—Civil, following the instructions found in the section "Preparing the Motion to Quash," above. As explained in that section, you will find a blank form in Appendix C and a downloadable version on the Nolo website (see Appendix B for the link). Make several copies before using the Proof of Service, as you may need more later. The server must be a person over 18 and not a party to the action—that is, not named in the Complaint as a plaintiff or defendant. As a defendant, you cannot serve your own legal papers.

Step 2: Make two copies of your Answer and the unsigned but filled-in Proof of Service by Mail. Print the server's name on the last line of both copies of the Proof of Service.

Step 3: Attach one copy of the Proof of Service to each copy of your Answer.

Step 4: Have your server mail one copy of the Answer and attached unsigned Proof of Service to the landlord's attorney (listed on the Summons), or the landlord if there is no attorney. The papers must be mailed on the day indicated on the Proof of Service.

Step 5: Now have your server fill in the blanks in the last paragraph of the Proof of Service and sign it, stating that the mailing has occurred. Attach this original to your original Answer.

Step 6: Take the original Answer and Proof of Service and a copy to the court clerk. (It is possible to file papers by mail, but this is not advised. A postal service or clerk's office foul-up could cause grave problems given the short time limits in these kinds of cases.) Give the original set of papers to the clerk, who will stamp (or have you stamp) your copy package with a "filed" notation in the upper right-hand corner. This is your proof that you filed the originals with the clerk.

> **CAUTION**
>
> **Make sure your Answer is filed within five days of the day the Complaint was served (or your Motion to Quash or Demurrer was overruled).** To compute the five days, see "Timeline for Filing a Response" above. If you miss this deadline, you may find yourself having to dig yourself out from under a default judgment obtained by the landlord. (See "The Complaint and Summons," above, for how to compute the five-day period.)

> **CAUTION**
>
> **Don't file by mail.** Though it is legal to file papers by mail, we don't recommend it. The time limits are so tight in unlawful detainer cases that a postal foul-up or a mishandling in the clerk's office could result in your papers not being filed on time and a default being entered against you.

> **TIP**
>
> **If you forgot to put in a defense, or if you become aware that you have another potential defense, you may file a First Amended Answer.** You should be able to file this as a matter of right within 10 days of filing your original Answer. After the 10 days, you must ask permission from the court to file an Amended Answer.

Trial Setting and Demanding a Jury

It makes sense to file a Demand for Jury trial at your earliest opportunity—usually when you file your Answer. (CCP § 1171 guarantees the right to a jury trial.) You have nothing to lose (you can change your mind later and "waive" the jury). After you've filed your Answer, the landlord will file a Request to Set Case for Trial. The court will schedule the case as a jury trial and, in many jurisdictions, will automatically set a date for a pretrial settlement conference.

You will have to pay one day of jury fees at least five days before the trial date—unless you request a waiver of additional costs and the court waives the requirement. (CCP § 631(c)(1).) If you later decide that you want a judge to decide your case, you can give up your right to a jury trial up to the time the case is assigned to a judge for trial. (You won't get your initial fees back, but if you win, you can claim them as a cost of the lawsuit. (CCP § 631.))

The Trial

After you file your Answer, the landlord may ask the court clerk to set the case for trial by filing a "Request to Set Case for Trial" with the court clerk. Having received this memo from the landlord, the clerk is supposed to set the trial for a time within 20 days of the landlord filing his request. (CCP § 1170.5(a).) You may file a motion to have this date extended ("continued"), and it might be granted if you can show the judge that, for example, a key witness (such as you) must be out of town that day.

Sample Demand for Jury Trial

1 TOM TENANT
   1234 Apartment St.
2 Berkeley, CA 94710
   510-123-4567
3

4 Defendant in Pro Per

5

6

7

8   SUPERIOR COURT OF THE STATE OF CALIFORNIA, COUNTY OF ___ALAMEDA___

9   ___BERKELEY/ALBANY___   DIVISION/BRANCH

10   )
    LENNY LANDLORD_____,)   Case No. ____5-0258_____
11   )
    _____,)
12   Plaintiff(s),   )   DEMAND FOR JURY TRIAL
)
13 v.   )
)
14 TOM TENANT_____,)
)
15 _____,)
              Defendant(s).   )
16   )

17

18   To the clerk of the above-entitled court:

19   Defendant(s) hereby demand a jury trial in this action.

20

21

22 Dated: ___February 20, 20xx___   *Tom Tenant*_____

23   Tom Tenant

24

25

26

27

28

Consult the *California Eviction Defense Manual* (CEB), which is available at law libraries, for how to file and serve a Motion to Continue.

Requesting a jury trial often prompts the judge to try to get you and the landlord to settle the case before trial, which can be helpful to you. In the experience of most landlord-tenant lawyers, 12 ordinary people tend to be more sympathetic to tenants than one crusty old (or even young) judge. If, however, you will be representing yourself at trial, you might be better off having a judge decide the case. Judge trials are much more simple and informal than jury trials, which are usually too complicated for most non-lawyers to comfortably handle by themselves.

A sample Demand for Jury Trial form is shown above.

FORM

You'll find a copy of the Demand for Jury Trial form in Appendix C, and the Nolo website includes a downloadable copy of this form. (See Appendix B for the link to the forms in this book.)

Here are instructions for completing, filing, and serving the Demand for Jury Trial.

CAUTION

Jury trials aren't free. If you request a jury trial, you will have to post about $150 with the court to pay for the jurors for one day of trial. If you win, you can recover these fees from the landlord. If the landlord posted the jury fees and wins, the landlord can recover these from you. You must pay the fee at least five days before trial, or you will lose the right to a jury trial. (CCP § 631(b).) (If you cannot afford the fee, you can ask the court to waive it by filling out a fee waiver form called "Request to Waive Additional Court Fees and Costs" (Judicial Council form FW-0021). Go to the Judicial Council website (www.courts.ca.gov/forms.htm) to download the form. You cannot use the Request to Waive Court Fees form that you used to file your Answer; you must use a different form to have jury fees waived.

Step 1: Complete the document called Proof of Service by First-Class Mail, following the instructions under "Preparing a Motion to Quash," above. You will find a blank form in Appendix C and a downloadable version on the Nolo website; if you don't have access to a computer, make several copies before using this form, as you may need more later. The server must be a person over 18 and not a party to the action—that is, not named in the Complaint as a plaintiff or defendant. As a defendant, you cannot serve your own legal papers.

Step 2: Make copies of Demand for Jury Trial and Proof of Service forms.

Step 3: Attach a copy of the unsigned Proof of Service to a copy of the Demand for Jury Trial.

Step 4: Have your server mail one copy package to the landlord or the landlord's attorney, then fill in the last paragraph of the original Proof of Service and sign it.

Step 5: File the original Demand and original signed Proof of Service with the court. Have the court clerk stamp the second copy package for your files.

"Peremptory Challenge" of a Judge

Whether or not you have a jury, the judge you get will could have a significant impact on the outcome. If you believe that the judge in your case might not treat you fairly, you can "challenge" the judge and ask that he or she be removed from the case. This must be done as soon as is practical, and before the judge makes any ruling in your case! Furthermore, this can be done only one time.

If you learn before trial which judge will hear the case, and you have reason to believe that this judge will not be fair to you, you may file a motion to disqualify the judge. (CCP § 170.6.) This is called a "peremptory challenge" and is described in the *California Eviction Defense Manual* (CEB). Ask other tenants, tenant lawyers, or others with experience in this courthouse, about which judges have a reputation for being hard on tenants.

File the motion at least five days before trial, together with a statement that you believe the judge will be prejudiced against you. You need not prove that the judge is prejudiced or even state detailed reasons for your belief—the disqualification is automatic. You may do this only once in any case. If you do it, you cannot be sure which judge will replace the one you disqualified—the next one might even be worse! So don't use your challenge lightly.

If you do not know before trial who your judge will be, be prepared to use your challenge on the morning of trial if you find out that you have been assigned to a judge who would be bad for tenants. Again, you only have one challenge, so get an idea beforehand how the various judges stack up in your particular court.

Getting ready for trial involves preparation, learning the procedure, and understanding how to present evidence. Many law books cover these subjects and it is often complicated. The CEB *Eviction Defense Manual* has some information and forms related to trial procedure and evidence. CEB also has a publication called *Civil Procedure During Trial*, which gives great detail on both procedure and rules of evidence.

On the morning of trial, judges will often try to make one last attempt at getting the case settled. They may send you to a separate judge or commissioner for this purpose. Once attempts at settlement have failed, you will be sent to the courtroom of the judge who will conduct the trial. If it is a jury trial, the judge will usually have a pretrial meeting to discuss how the trial will proceed, discuss how jury selection will take place (if you have a jury), and talk about some of the special rules of that particular judge (such as what times court will be in session, if exhibits should be exchanged, and so on). The judge may also hear motions about the case. For instance, there are motions to exclude certain documents, witnesses, or testimony.

Before the trial, carefully organize your witnesses, documents, and photographs; and any other evidence you think is important. Ask yourself what it would take to convince a neutral person that you are right, and then organize that evidence for the judge.

At trial, be courteous and respectful to everyone. The purpose of a trial is to resolve disputes in a civilized manner; it's not a forum for yelling, sarcasm, and the like. Address yourself to the judge and the witnesses only, not the other party or the opposing attorney. It's advantageous to be forceful and to stand up for your rights, and a serious mistake to be rude or unnecessarily hostile. The most important thing is to present your side of the case clearly and with as few complications as possible. Try not to be repetitive. If you confuse, bore, or annoy the judge, you lessen your chance of winning.

TIP

Watch and learn. If you are worried about representing yourself, watch several contested unlawful detainer trials before your court date. You'll learn what to do and, equally important, what to avoid.

Trial Before a Jury

The first part of a jury trial will be to select a jury. Here you get to ask the potential jurors questions about who they are ("Are you a tenant? Have you or someone close to you ever been evicted?"). Sample questions, called "voir dire" are available in the CEB *Eviction Defense Manual.* You will be allowed to exclude a certain number of potential jurors simply because you don't think they will be on your side. Usually, 12 jurors are ultimately chosen. To win a trial, either side has to get the votes of nine of the 12 jurors. If the landlord (or you) can only get eight, then you have a "hung jury."

Opening statements

After the jury has been picked, each side will be allowed to make an opening statement. First the landlord tells the jury about his case, then you get to tell the jury about yours. During the opening statement, each side can talk about the evidence (documents and testimony) that will be presented. This is not the time when you actually argue the case. For instance, you could say "the evidence will show that Lenny Landlord was told about the roof leaking on several occasions, both orally in writing. The evidence will further show that he refused to fix it. I called the building inspector who then issued a violation notice. The evidence will also show that Lenny Landlord issued his Notice of Termination of Tenancy a few weeks after he received the notice." These are all facts that you intend to present to the jury during the trial. You cannot argue the case at this point, however, by saying something like: "Lenny Landlord is a slumlord who is retaliating against me." Stick to the facts; the argument will come later.

Presenting the Case

The landlord gets to present his case first. This will include testimony from the landlord and from others, as well as presenting documents. The landlord (and you) must present "admissible evidence." This is evidence that is relevant to the case, and presented in a proper form. For instance, a witness can testify only about what he personally saw or heard. He can't guess or speculate or provide an opinion. You can object if the landlord tries to elicit such testimony or, if the testimony is already given, ask that it be stricken. Again, more information about presenting evidence is available from the CEB *Eviction Defense Manual* and CEB *Civil Procedure During Trial* manuals.

After the landlord presents his case, you get to present yours. This is where careful preparation really pays off. Have your witnesses and documents organized in an order that makes sense, and to the extent possible, follows the logic of your case. Then it's just a matter of presenting it. Your landlord might object to some of your evidence (if only to make you nervous), so be prepared to defend how the evidence is relevant and presented properly.

After you present your defense the landlord has the option of presenting additional evidence, but only to rebut your evidence. You would then be allowed to rebut the evidence the landlord presents in his rebuttal.

Arguments

After the landlord and you have presented the evidence, the landlord will be allowed to give a closing argument, which discusses the evidence and why the jury should vote to evict you. Next comes your closing argument, where you try to prove just the opposite. Because the landlord has the burden of proof in eviction cases, he will be allowed to make a rebuttal argument.

The judge will then instruct the jury about points of law related to the case. You can request that the judge give specific instructions to the jury. Sample Jury Instructions are available in the CEB *Eviction Defense Manual*. After instruction, the jury will deliberate and render its verdict. Once a verdict is rendered, judgment will be entered according to the verdict.

Trial Before a Judge (a "Court Trial")

Court trials proceed much the same way as jury trials, except that there is no jury selection, jury instruction, or jury deliberation. The judge will hear opening arguments, presentation of evidence, and closing arguments. After closing arguments, the judge can issue a decision right then, or can take the matter "under submission" and decide later. If the case takes more than eight hours, you can request that the judge prepare a written "Statement of Decision" explaining his ruling. (See CCP § 632 and California Rule of Court 3.1590 for more information.) Making the written request may give you several extra days in the event you lose the case.

Setting Aside a Default Judgment

If you miss the deadline for responding to the landlord's Complaint, the landlord may ask the court for a default judgment against you. That means you lose without a trial and the landlord has the legal right to evict you. If this happens, you may file a motion asking the court to set aside the default judgment. If the motion is granted, you may then file your Answer and have your trial.

To persuade the judge to grant your motion to set aside a default, you must show all of the following:

- That you have a pretty good excuse (such as illness) for your failure to respond to the Summons in five days. "I didn't know how to respond, and it took me a few days to get hold of a copy of *California Tenants' Rights*" might work, but don't count on it.
- That you did not unnecessarily delay too long in filing your motion to set aside the default. There is no set period of time for which a delay is or is not excusable. It depends on the facts of each case.
- That you have a defense to the lawsuit.

In addition, be sure to ask for a stay (postponement) of the eviction until the court rules on your motion to set aside the default.

Moving to set aside a default requires a lot of paperwork. More importantly, you have to act very quickly. The sheriff will be knocking at your door very soon, if he hasn't already. Don't wait until the last minute! We recommend that you try to get a lawyer or tenants' rights advocate to help you with it. If you still want to do it yourself, the necessary forms and procedures are contained in the *California Eviction Defense Manual,* published by Continuing Education of the Bar (CEB), and available in most county law libraries.

Discovery: Learning About the Landlord's Case

"Discovery" is the process of finding out what evidence the other side has before the trial begins, so you can prepare your own case to meet it. Discovery is not used in most cases, but landlords are beginning to use it more and more, often to intimidate tenants representing themselves. Discovery is conducted in two basic ways.

One is to question the other party face to face in a proceeding called a deposition (discussed below).

The second is to send the other party a written document that specifies what is being sought. This document typically consists of:

- questions (interrogatories)
- a request that certain documents be produced for inspection
- a request that certain facts be admitted as true, or
- all of the above.

You or the landlord can make any of these requests following the instructions below. The law provides a set period of time within which a party must respond to discovery requests. The response must be given within five days, or within ten days if the request was served on you by mail. (CCP §§ 1013, 2030.260(a), 2031.260, 2033.250.)

TIP

You can begin the discovery process at any time after you are lawfully served with the Summons and Complaint. (However, if you are contesting service—by filing a Motion to Quash—then you have to wait until after the hearing before initiating discovery.) The sooner you start discovery, the better. Landlords or their attorneys often "stonewall" discovery by objecting, giving evasive answers, or not answering at all. You may need the time to ask the court to "compel" the landlord to comply with the request.

Request for Inspection

Use a Request to Inspect to make the other side let you see and copy any documents or other things before trial. You may want to see copies of leases, building inspector's reports, or checks.

The landlord must respond to your request within five days. (CCP § 2031.260.) Add five days to each of these periods if you mailed the request for inspection to the landlord (or to the landlord's attorney), instead of personally serving them. (CCP § 1013.) If the landlord refuses to respond adequately to your discovery request within that time, you may file a motion to compel and ask the court to impose sanctions on the landlord, which include paying your costs or preventing the landlord from using certain evidence. (CCP § 2031.310.)

Be sure to describe what you're asking for with clarity. For example, you might write, "All documents related to the defendant's tenancy at the subject premises." Or, "All documents supporting the contention that you have a good reason to evict any defendant in this action."

Take a look at our sample Request for Inspection form, shown below.

FORM

You'll find a copy of the Request to Inspect (official name, Request to Inspect and for Production of Documents) in Appendix C, and the Nolo website includes a downloadable copy of this form. (See Appendix B for the link to the forms in this book.)

You'll need to fill in your name, address, and telephone number; the county where you are being sued; the court district and the case documents you are requesting; and where and when you want to see and copy these documents.

After you've prepared your Request to Inspect, you must file and serve it.

Step 1: Make one copy of your Request to Inspect.

Step 2: Complete the document called Proof of Service by First-Class Mail, following the instructions included in "Preparing the Motion to Quash," above.

FORM

You will find a blank Proof of Service by Mail form in Appendix C and a downloadable copy on the Nolo website. (See Appendix B for the link to the forms in this book.) If you don't have access to a computer, make several copies of the Proof of Service form before using it, as you may need more later.

The server must be a person over 18 and not a party to the action—that is, not named in the Complaint as a plaintiff or defendant. As a defendant, you cannot serve your own legal papers.

Step 3: Make a copy of the Proof of Service by Mail, print your server's name on the last line of the copy, and attach it to the copy of your Request to Inspect.

Step 4: Have your server place these papers in the mail with first-class postage attached.

Step 5: Now have your server fill in the blanks in the last paragraph of the Proof of Service and sign it.

Step 6: Keep the originals of your Proof of Service by Mail and Request to Inspect in your records. You need not file these papers with the court clerk unless a dispute arises over your request.

Interrogatories

The discovery devices most often used in unlawful detainer cases are written interrogatories. These are questions you pose that the other side must answer. Of course, the other side may pose their own set of questions to you, too. You can use a set of Form Interrogatories designed for eviction cases. (See CCP §§ 2030.010–2030.410.)

FORM

You'll find a copy of the Form Interrogatories —Unlawful Detainer in Appendix C, and the Nolo website includes a downloadable copy of this form. (See Appendix B for the link to the forms in this book.)

Sample Request for Inspection

1	TOM TENANT
	1234 Apartment St.
2	Berkeley, CA 94710
	510-123-4567
3	
4	Defendant in Pro Per
5	
6	
7	
8	SUPERIOR COURT OF THE STATE OF CALIFORNIA, COUNTY OF ___ALAMEDA___
9	_____BERKELEY/ALBANY_____ DIVISION/BRANCH
10	
	LENNY LANDLORD _____ ,) Case No. ____S-0258____
11	)
	_____ ,)
12	Plaintiff(s),) REQUEST TO INSPECT AND FOR
13	v.) PRODUCTION OF DOCUMENTS
14	TOM TENANT _____ ,)
15	) (Code of Civil Procedure Sec. 2031.101–2031.510)
	_____ ,)
16	Defendant(s).)
17	
18	To: _____ , Plaintiff,
19	and _____ , Plaintiff's attorney:
20	Defendant requests that you produce and permit the copying of the following documents: _____
21	[describe documents] _____ .
22	Defendant requests that you produce these documents at the following address: ___[your address
23	or any other location]_____ , at the following date and time: ___[within 5 days, plus 5 days,
24	if this request is served by mail]___ .
25	
26	Dated: _____ **Tom Tenant** _____
	Tom Tenant
27	
28	

Here is how to use the interrogatories:

- **Read the interrogatories.** If any is relevant to the issues in your case, check off the number of that interrogatory in the proper box of the "Form Interrogatories—Unlawful Detainer."
- **Do not simply check off every box in the Form Interrogatories.** If you do, the landlord may take you to court and get sanctions against you (usually a fine) based on the claim that you are using the interrogatories for purposes of harassment and delay. Make sure that the interrogatory pertains to some claim by the landlord or denial or affirmative defense you raised in your Answer—and that the landlord's answer might help you know what to expect at trial.
- **The Judicial Council Form Interrogatories provided in this book include instructions; here are additional ones:**

Step 1: Complete the document called Proof of Service by First-Class Mail—Civil, following the instructions in "Preparing the Motion to Quash," above. You will find a blank form in Appendix C, and a downloadable version on the Nolo website (see Appendix B for the link); if you do not have access to a computer, make several copies before using the proof of service form, as you may need more later. The server must be a person over 18 and not a party to the action—that is, not named in the Complaint as a plaintiff or defendant. As a defendant, you cannot serve your own legal papers.

Step 2: Make one copy of your Interrogatories and the Proof of Service by First-Class Mail. Fill in the server's name on the last line of the copy of the Proof of Service.

Step 3: Attach the copy of the Proof of Service to the copy of your Interrogatories.

Step 4: Have your server mail the copy package (the Interrogatories and the Proof of Service) to the landlord's attorney (listed on the Summons) or the landlord, if there is no attorney. The package must be mailed on the day indicated on the Proof of Service. You may also include a full set of the Interrogatories themselves if you wish.

Step 5: Now have your server fill in the blanks in the last paragraph of the Proof of Service and sign it. Attach this original to your original Interrogatories. Place these documents in your file. You don't have to file them with the court unless a dispute arises.

The landlord or landlord's attorney must respond to your interrogatories within five days. (CCP § 2030.260(a)), plus five days if you served them by mail. If the landlord (or landlord's attorney) refuses to respond adequately within that time, you may ask the court to impose sanctions on the other side. (CCP §§ 2030.290–030.300.)

The Deposition

Depositions are oral statements made under oath. The other party must sit down with you in your lawyer's office or another site and answer questions. You must arrange (and pay for) a court reporter to take down the questions and answers. The transcript can be used against the person if he or she tries to change his or her story at trial.

Explaining how to set up and conduct a deposition is beyond the scope of this book. More to the point is what happens if the landlord's attorney serves a notice of deposition on you, telling you to appear somewhere at a certain time for a deposition. All you have to do is appear and answer the questions. However, you may be tricked into giving an answer that later comes back to haunt you. For this reason, if possible, it is often a good idea to have a lawyer there to help you avoid the traps set by the landlord's attorney.

 RESOURCE

For more information on how to prepare for a deposition and how to give one, see *Nolo's Deposition Handbook*, by Paul Bergman and Albert Moore (Nolo). See www.nolo.com for a sample chapter and complete table of contents for this book.

Sample Settlement of Unlawful Detainer Action

SETTLEMENT AGREEMENT

1. __Tom Tenant_____ ("tenant")

resides at the following premises: ___1234 Apartment Street, Berkeley, CA 94710_____

_____ ("premises").

2. __Lenny Landlord_____ ("landlord")

is the owner of the premises.

3. On __January 8_____, 20_XX_ landlord caused a Summons and Complaint

in unlawful detainer to be served on tenant. The complaint was filed in the Superior Court for the County of

__Alameda_____, __Berkeley–Albany_____ District, and carries

the following civil number: ___S-0258_____ .

4. Landlord and tenant agree that tenant shall vacate the premises on or before __March 1_____,

20_XX_ . In exchange for this agreement, and upon full performance by tenant, landlord agrees to file a

voluntary dismissal with prejudice of the Complaint specified in clause #3.

5. Also in exchange for tenant's agreement to vacate the premises on or before the date specified in clause

#4, landlord agrees to:

(Choose one or more of the following)

☑ Forgive all past due rent

☐ Forgive past due rent in the following amount: $_____

☐ Pay the tenant $_____ to cover tenant's moving expenses, new deposit requirements, and

other incidentals related to the tenant moving out.

6. Any sum specified in clause #5 to be paid by the landlord shall be paid as follows:

(Choose one or more of the following)

☑ Upon tenant surrendering the keys to the premises

☐ Upon the signing of this agreement

☐ $_____ upon the signing of this agreement and $_____ upon

tenant surrendering the keys

☐ in the following manner:

Settlement Agreement   Page 1 of 2

Sample Settlement of Unlawful Detainer Action (continued)

1

2

3

4

5

6

7

8

9

10

11

12

13

14

15

16

17

18

19

20

21

22

23

24

25

26

27

28

7. The tenant's security deposit being held by landlord shall be handled as follows:

☐ restored in full to the tenant upon surrender of the keys

☑ treated according to law

☐ other: _____

_____

8. Subject to the terms and conditions set forth in this agreement, tenant and landlord agree to waive and release all claims, rights and causes of action against the other arising out of tenant's occupancy of the premises. This waiver extends to each party hereto, their agents, employees, successors, and assigns.

9. That this settlement agreement shall not be construed as reflecting on the merits of the dispute.

10. Landlord agrees not to not make any negative representations to any credit reporting agency or to any other person or entity seeking information about the tenant's tenancy at the premises.

11. Time is of the essence in this agreement. If tenant fails to timely vacate the premises in accordance with this agreement, landlord may, upon 24 hours notice, apply for an ex parte judgment for possession of the premises.

12. This agreement was executed on ____January_____ , 20 _XX_ at

__Berkeley, California_____ .

Signed: ___*Tom Tenant*_____
           Tom Tenant

Signed: ___*Lenny Landlord*_____
           Lenny Landlord

The Request to Admit

You can find out just what you and the landlord agree and disagree about by requesting the landlord to admit certain statements that you believe to be true. If they are admitted, it saves you the trouble of having to prove them in court. If, on the other hand, the landlord denies a statement, and you later prove it to be true, the landlord can be required to reimburse you for the cost of the proof. We don't provide you the forms for this discovery device, but if you are interested in using it, consult *California Civil Discovery Practice,* published by Continuing Education of the Bar (CEB) and available in most law libraries.

Negotiating a Settlement

At any point in a dispute, you may negotiate a settlement with the landlord. The keys to any settlement are (1) that each side has something the other wants, and (2) that each side is willing to talk to the other in a reasonable manner.

The landlord usually wants you to get out, pay back rent, or both. The owner wants minimum expense and hassle. You have the power to cause the landlord expense and trouble by your use of the defenses that you have, as well as procedural tools described in this chapter. Plus, there is the possibility that you could win the case. Therefore, the landlord might be willing (reluctantly) to give you more time to get out, reduce the claim for back rent, and/or pay you additional sums of money; or allow you to stay under certain conditions. Both sides benefit from a settlement because they avoid the expense and uncertainty of a trial.

Of course, depending on the facts of your situation, you might instead want to hang tough, go to trial, and win everything. But you always run the risk of losing. The landlord is often in the same boat. What this amounts to is that, commonly, it could be in both of your interests to lessen your risks by negotiating a settlement both of you can live with.

EXAMPLE: When Tom fails to pay his rent of $1,000 on May 1, his landlord, Lenny, serves a three-day notice on him, and when the three days expire without Tom paying the rent, Lenny sues Tom for an eviction order and a judgment for the $1,000. Tom's Answer says that Lenny breached the implied warranty of habitability by not getting rid of cockroaches. Lenny tells Tom that at trial Lenny will try to prove that the cockroaches were caused by Tom's poor housekeeping. Lenny thinks he will win the trial, and Tom thinks that he will win. Each of them is sensible enough to know, however, that they might lose—and that it is certain that a trial will take up a lot of time and energy (and maybe some costs and attorney fees). So they get together and hammer out a settlement agreement: Tom agrees to get out by August 1, and Lenny agrees to drop his lawsuit and any claim for back rent and to pay Tom his security deposit back within a week. Another possible settlement could involve Tom agreeing to pay the full back rent, remaining in the rental, and Lenny and Tom splitting the cost of a professional pest service.

Here are a few pointers about negotiation:

- It is common for the tenant to get extra time to move and receive forgiveness of past rent (or some of it) plus, in some instances, get extra money sometimes characterized as "moving expenses." Sometimes tenants bargain for even some financial help with a new security deposit, as a condition of moving out without a court fight.

- Another framework is to "pay and stay." Under this scenario, the tenant pays the back rent (or cures the breach) and gets to stay in the unit. Sometimes a landlord will demand that the tenant also pay his court costs for having to bring the eviction case. Where the tenant owes a lot of back rent, a payment plan can be arranged so that the tenant pays in installments. If the tenant doesn't pay on time, the agreement could allow the landlord to get a judgment for possession without a trial.

- Similar to the above is a probation-like scenario. Let's say the tenant is accused of disturbing the neighbors and causing a nuisance. Under the agreement, the tenant could agree to behave and if the tenant disturbs the neighbors again (for instance, within the next six months), the landlord could get a judgment for possession without a trial.

- Be courteous, but don't be weak. If you have a good defense, let the landlord know that you have the resources and evidence to fight and win if the landlord won't agree to a reasonable settlement.

- If you are in a rent control city and your defense is that the landlord breached rent control rules, consult the staff at your local rent board. They may be able to help.

- Many courts have trained volunteer mediators who help self-represented parties try to work out settlements on the eve of trial. Be open to this type of mediation, as it can be very helpful. Before trial, you can avail yourself of a local neighborhood mediation service, perhaps for a small fee. Do an Internet search using the name of the city or county in which the property is located, and the word "mediation." (See "Mediation" in Chapter 18 for more on the subject.)

- Put the settlement agreement in writing. If you can (and you may not be able to), try to avoid agreeing to a "stipulated judgment," which enables the landlord to get you out very quickly if he thinks you are not abiding by the settlement agreement. Also, credit reporting agencies get records of judgments, so a stipulated judgment may hurt your credit rating.

- If your lease or rental agreement has an attorney fees clause, you'll want to avoid having to pay the landlord's fees (and court costs), which may be considerable even though the case hasn't proceeded very far. Include a statement in your settlement agreement that there is no "prevailing party" and that neither side owes the other for fees and costs.

A sample Settlement Agreement where a tenant agrees to leave is shown above; it may be used with appropriate modification.

FORM
You'll find a copy of the Settlement Agreement in Appendix C, and the Nolo website includes a downloadable copy of this form that you can edit to fit your particular situation. (See Appendix B for the link to the forms in this book.)

Summary Judgment

Although the landlord is entitled to a trial date within three weeks after you file your Answer, landlords don't have to wait that long to obtain a judgment if they can convince the court that there is no substantial disagreement over the facts. For instance, if you both agree that you have been conducting a mail order business from your apartment, but disagree as to whether this is a breach of the lease, which limits the use of the premises to residential use, the court can decide the case without holding a full trial. This speedy procedure is termed a "summary judgment."

If the landlord files a Motion for Summary Judgment (few do so anymore, because the filing fee for this type of motion is over $500), you will be served with the Notice of Motion and an accompanying Declaration setting out the landlord's version of the facts. These motions often include a Separate Statement of Undisputed Facts. Under Code of Civil Procedure Sections 1170.7 and 1013, and Rule 3.1351(a), Cal. Rules of Court, the landlord must personally serve the motion papers on you no later than five days in advance of the hearing, or ten days if they're served by mail. If you do not contest the motion, the landlord will be able to obtain a judgment against you. To contest the motion, you should file and serve a statement of your own, called a "Declaration in Opposition to Motion for Summary Judgment," setting forth your version of the facts. Your statement must respond specifically to the facts that the landlord set forth in his declaration and in his statement of undisputed facts. If there are documents that support your case, you should attach them to your declaration, saying something like, "Attached as Exhibit A is a copy of an email I received from my landlord, stating that I could have a dog." You should also state facts that support the affirmative defenses that you raised in your answer. If your landlord's statements are not disputed and you are unable to provide evidence of a viable affirmative defense, the judge will likely rule against you.

You can support your statement with declarations (from you or others), or references to other documents such as the Complaint. If your statement contradicts the landlord's facts in important particulars, and the difference in facts is important to the case, the judge should deny the motion and require the landlord to proceed to trial.

Refer to the instructions for completing the Declaration accompanying the Motion to Quash for the required format. If the landlord or landlord's attorney personally serves the motion on you, you're entitled to only five days' notice. This does not allow you much time to respond. Though the law does not say how soon before the hearing your opposing declaration needs to be filed, get it filed as soon as you can. Filing it the day before court, or worse, bringing it with you to court on the day of the hearing, may result in your losing the case. Serve it according to the method described for serving the Answer. For additional information, consult the *California Eviction Defense Manual*, published by Continuing Education of the Bar (CEB), available in most law libraries.

Although technically you can oppose the motion orally, we advise against it. California Rule of Court 3.1351(b) does provide, "Any opposition to the motion and any reply to an opposition may be made orally at the time of hearing." In theory, this means that you should be able to go to the hearing and ask the judge to place you under oath to refute any statement made in the landlord's written declaration. However, oral testimony is usually not taken at motion hearings. In order to protect your rights, we strongly recommend that you file a written declaration under penalty of perjury, and serve it on the other party (or their attorney), at least the day before the hearing, as allowed under subdivision (c) of this rule. Be sure to deliver a courtesy copy to the courtroom that will hear the motion. We say this because this rule is fairly new, some judges will not be acquainted with it, and they may be strongly inclined to rule against you if you simply show up without filing a written opposition. Remember, you must personally or otherwise serve your opposition papers on the landlord or his attorney in time to be received at least one court day before the hearing.

If you defeat the landlord's Motion for Summary Judgment, you get to go to trial to defend your case. If you lose, the landlord will be able to get a judgment.

The Judgment

If you win at trial, the landlord cannot evict you, and you can get a judgment for your court costs—mainly your filing fee and jury fees, if you paid them. If your lease or rental agreement provides for attorney fees for the prevailing party—or just for the landlord—you can recover them, too, if you hired an attorney. (CCP § 1717.) You will have to pay all or part of the back rent, though.

If the landlord wins, the judgment will award possession of the premises. It may also award money for unpaid rent (if the action was based on nonpayment of rent), daily rent after the date the tenancy was terminated, costs, and attorney fees (if attorney fees are provided for in the lease or rental agreement). If you do not pay up, the landlord may file the appropriate forms with the court in order to garnish your wages and bank accounts.

If you asserted a habitability defense in your Answer, and the judge or jury finds the landlord substantially breached the habitability requirements, you will be required to pay into the court, within five days, the amount the judge or jury determines is the reasonable rental value of the premises (in their "untenantable state") up to the time of the trial. If you pay that amount, then you win and you get to stay. If you don't make the payment on time, you will not be the "prevailing party" for purposes of awarding attorney fees and costs, and the court must award possession of the property to the landlord. (CCP § 1174.2.) The landlord may then try to collect the money part of the judgment—including court costs and applicable attorney fees—and the court must award possession of the property to the landlord. For this reason, it's very important to pay any reduced rent the judge ordered you to pay. Not doing so can convert a partial win into a big loss—snatching defeat from the jaws of victory.

If you do make your payment on time and you are the "prevailing party," the court can order the landlord to make repairs and to charge only the reasonable rental value of the premises until the repairs are made. The court can maintain continuing supervision over the landlord until the repairs are completed. (CCP § 1174.2.)

If you lose the case, the landlord will get a judgment for money as well as possession of the premises. The landlord will then get a writ of execution and deliver it to the Sheriff's Department. After a few days, sometimes weeks, the sheriff will post a Notice to Vacate on your front door (or hand it to you). The Notice will say that the sheriff will come out in five days to physically remove you—although the sheriff often takes longer.

Stopping an Eviction

Even if you lose an eviction lawsuit, the judge may give you "relief from forfeiture" of your tenancy—that is, save you from eviction if you can show hardship. For example, suppose you were temporarily out of work and fell behind in your rent, but you now have a job and can pay all the back rent. Furthermore, your children go to a neighborhood school and there is no alternative housing in the area that will allow them to continue at that school. The judge might stop the eviction. (CCP §§ 1179 and 1174(c), provided you pay the back rent.)

You can file an Application for Relief from Forfeiture at any time after judgment is entered, but before you are evicted. Your motion should be personally served with five days' advance notice of the hearing date. File the motion as soon as possible, so it can be heard before eviction by the sheriff. If you find yourself short of time, you will want to seek a Stay of Eviction. (See below, "Postponing an Eviction.")

To persuade the judge to do this, you will probably have to show two things:

- that the eviction would cause a severe hardship on you or your family—for example, because your kids are in school, or you cannot find other housing, or you would have to move away from your job, or you are elderly or handicapped, and
- that you are willing and able to pay both the money you owe the landlord (for back rent and costs and fees, if there is a costs and fees clause in your lease or rental agreement), and the rent in the future.

How do judges determine whether the hardship is severe enough to grant relief? The mere fact that you have to move is not enough without other aggravating factors. The court will likely balance the hardship you will suffer if you are evicted against the prejudice to the landlord if the relief is granted. In doing so, the court looks at all the underlying facts, including the nature of the action (the reason for the eviction), whether the tenant's actions were willful or in bad faith, and whether the landlord's actions were in good or bad faith. (*Thrifty Oil v. Batarse,* 174 Cal.App.3d 770 (1985).)

If you win the motion, be sure to have the judge sign the Order Granting Relief from Eviction (see Appendix B) and personally deliver a copy of the Order to the Sheriff's Department.

Sample Application for Stay of Eviction

```
 1   TOM TENANT
     1234 Apartment St.
 2   Berkeley, CA 94710
     510-123-4567
 3

 4   Defendant in Pro Per

 5

 6

 7

 8           SUPERIOR COURT OF THE STATE OF CALIFORNIA, COUNTY OF  ALAMEDA

 9                    BERKELEY/ALBANY      DIVISION/BRANCH

10                                         )
     LENNY LANDLORD                      , )   Case No.     5-0258
11                                         )
     _____    , )
12            Plaintiff(s),                )   APPLICATION AND DECLARATION
                                           )
13   v.                                    )   FOR STAY OF EVICTION
                                           )
14   TOM TENANT                          , )
                                           )
15   _____    , )
              Defendant(s).               )
16                                         )

17

18      Defendant(s) _____

19   _____ hereby apply

20   for stay of execution from any writ of restitution or possession in this case, for the following period of time:

21   _____.

22      Such a stay is appropriate in this case for the following reason(s): _____

23   _____

24   _____.

25      I declare under penalty of perjury that the above statements are true and correct to the best of my knowledge.

26

27   Dated:     February 20, 20xx              Tom Tenant
                                               _____
28                                             Tom Tenant
```

Application and Declaration for Stay of Eviction   Page 1 of 1

FORM
You will find a blank Application and Declaration for Relief From Eviction form, a Notice of Motion and Points and Authorities for Relief Form Eviction, plus an Order Granting Stay of Eviction, in Appendix C and downloadable versions on the Nolo website (see Appendix B for the link). Samples are not included in this chapter.

Here are the instructions for completing these forms.

Step 1: Fill in the blank Application and Declaration for Relief From Eviction form, using the guidelines mentioned above.

Step 2: Complete the document called Proof of Service by Mail (see the instructions in "Preparing the Motion to Quash," above). You will find a blank form in Appendix C and a downloadable version on the Nolo website (see Appendix B for the link); if you don't have access to a computer, make several copies before using this form, as you may need more later. The server must be a person over 18 and not a party to the action—that is, not named in the Complaint as a plaintiff or defendant. As a defendant, you cannot serve your own legal papers.

Step 3: Make copies of the Application and Declaration for Relief From Eviction and Proof of Service forms.

Step 4: Attach a copy of the unsigned Proof of Service to a copy of the Application and Declaration for Relief From Eviction.

Step 5: Have your server mail one copy package to the landlord or his attorney, then fill in the last paragraph of the original Proof of Service and sign it.

Step 6: File the original Application and Declaration for Relief From Eviction, the proposed Order (the judge will complete it), and the original signed Proof of Service with the court. Have the court clerk stamp the second copy package for your files.

How a Tenant's Bankruptcy Affects Evictions

Whether a not a landlord can legally evict a tenant who is filing for bankruptcy depends on when you file to do so. (For details, see "Stopping an Eviction by Filing for Bankruptcy" in Chapter 14.)

Postponing an Eviction

Many courts will agree to postpone (stay) the eviction for a limited time, for a good reason—for example, to give you more time to find another place. If you need time to find another place, explain how difficult it is to locate available housing in your city and ask for a stay of about 30 days. In some cases, if you file an appeal, the court will stay the eviction while the appeal is pending in court. File an application for a stay as soon as possible after you receive notice of the judgment.

If you seek a stay during an appeal, you must show the court that (1) you will suffer "extreme hardship" if you are evicted, and (2) that the landlord will not be hurt by the stay. The judge will condition the stay on your paying rent into court as it comes due. The court may also impose other conditions on the stay. If the trial court denies a stay during appeal, you may ask the appellate court to grant a stay. (CCP § 1176.) You will probably need a lawyer's help to accomplish this.

If you decide to appeal your case, you will naturally hope for a stay while the case makes its way through the appeals process. Judges seldom grant stays pending appeal, so you should not count on one being granted in your case. Experience shows that judges are most likely to grant stays pending an appeal when the basis for the appeal is a claim that the judge or jury somehow erred in applying the law. If you do apply for a stay, be sure to give the court the reasons why you are appealing and explain how the judge or jury made a mistake concerning the law.

Notice of Appeal and Notice to Prepare Clerk's Transcript

1   TOM TENANT
    1234 Apartment St.
2   Berkeley, CA 94710
    510-123-4567
3

4   Defendant in Pro Per

5

6

7

8   SUPERIOR COURT OF THE STATE OF CALIFORNIA, COUNTY OF __ALAMEDA__

9   _____BERKELEY/ALBANY_____ DIVISION/BRANCH

10 LENNY LANDLORD_____,)   Case No. ____5-0258_____
)
11 _____,)
              Plaintiff(s),   )   NOTICE OF APPEAL AND NOTICE
12   )
)   TO PREPARE CLERK'S TRANSCRIPT
13 v.   )
)
14 TOM TENANT_____,)
)
15 _____,)
             Defendant(s).   )
16 _____)

17   Defendant(s) _____

18 _____ hereby appeal to the Appellate Department

19 of the Superior Court.

20   Defendant(s) hereby request that a Clerk's Transcript be prepared, and that this transcript include all documents

21 filed in this action and all minute orders and other rulings and judgments issued by the court in this action.

22

23 Dated: _____   *Tom Tenant*_____
                                            Tom Tenant
24

25

26

27

28

You will find a sample Application and Declaration for Stay of Eviction above.

FORM

You'll find a copy of the Application and Declaration for Stay of Eviction form plus Order Granting Stay of Eviction in Appendix C, and the Nolo website includes a downloadable copy of this form. (See Appendix B for the link to the forms in this book.)

Here are the instructions for completing them.

Step 1: Complete the document called Proof of Service by First-Class Mail, following the instructions found in "Preparing the Motion to Quash," above. You will find a blank form in Appendix C and a downloadable version on the Nolo website; if you don't have access to a computer, make several copies before using this form, as you may need more later. The server must be a person over 18 and not a party to the action—that is, not named in the Complaint as a plaintiff or defendant. As a defendant, you cannot serve your own legal papers.

Step 2: Make copies of the Application and Declaration for Stay of Eviction and Proof of Service forms.

Step 3: Attach a copy of the unsigned Proof of Service to a copy of the Application for Relief From Eviction.

Step 4: Have your server mail one copy package to the landlord or the landlord's attorney, then fill in the last paragraph of the original Proof of Service and sign it.

Step 5: File the original Application and Declaration for Stay of Eviction, the proposed Order (the judge will complete it) and the original signed Proof of Service with the court. Have the court clerk stamp the second copy package for your files.

If the court grants your Request for Stay of Eviction, be sure to have the judge sign the Order Granting Stay of Eviction (see Appendix B) and personally deliver a copy of the Order to the Sheriff's Department.

Appeal From an Eviction

To appeal a court's eviction order, you must file a paper called "Notice of Appeal and Notice to Prepare Clerk's Transcripts" with the clerk of the court. You must file it within 30 days of receiving notice that judgment was entered against you. The appeal is to the Appellate Division of the Superior Court.

On appeal, you may argue only issues of law, not fact. This means that you may argue that the trial court erred by ruling that, for example, there can be no breach of the implied warranty of habitability if the lease says that the tenant waives his rights under this doctrine—an issue of law. But you may not argue that the judge was wrong in believing the landlord's testimony rather than yours, because that is an issue of fact. After you file your Notice of Appeal, the Appellate Division will tell you when your brief (the document in which you argue points of law) must be filed in that court.

Appeals are pretty technical, and we recommend that you get a lawyer if possible.

CAUTION

Filing a Notice of Appeal does not automatically stop the sheriff or marshal from carrying out an eviction. To do that, you must seek a stay of the eviction from the trial court judge, as discussed in the preceding section. If you plan to appeal and feel you have a good argument that the trial court misinterpreted the law, include these facts in your application for the stay.

You will find a sample Notice of Appeal form above.

FORM

You'll find a copy of the Notice to Appeal and Notice to Prepare Clerk's Transcript in Appendix C, and the Nolo website includes a downloadable copy of this form. (See Appendix B for the link to the forms in this book.)

Here are the instructions for completing the Notice of Appeal:

Step 1: Complete the document called Proof of Service by First-Class Mail, following the instructions found in "Preparing the Motion to Quash," above. You will find a blank form in Appendix C and a downloadable version on the Nolo website (see Appendix B for the link); if you don't have access to a computer, make several copies before using this form, as you may need more later. The server must be a person over 18 and not a party to the action—that is, not named in the Complaint as a plaintiff or defendant. As a defendant, you cannot serve your own legal papers.

Step 2: Make copies of the Notice of Appeal and Proof of Service forms.

Step 3: Attach a copy of the unsigned Proof of Service to a copy of the Notice of Appeal.

Step 4: Have your server mail one copy package to the landlord or the landlord's attorney, then fill in the last paragraph of the original Proof of Service and sign it.

Step 5: File the original Notice of Appeal and original signed Proof of Service with the court. Have the court clerk stamp the second copy package for your files.

After the Lawsuit—Eviction by the Sheriff or Marshal

If the landlord wins the eviction case in court (or by default, because you never responded in writing to the landlord's lawsuit within the time allowed), the judge will sign a "writ of possession." The landlord will give this writ to the sheriff's or marshal's department and pay a fee, which will be added to the judgment against you. A deputy sheriff will serve the writ on you, along with an Order to Vacate that requires you to vacate within five days. It might take the sheriff a few days to serve you with the Order to Vacate. Some sheriffs serve these Orders only on certain days of the week.

If you are served with the Order and are not out in five days, the sheriff or marshal will return and

physically evict you and your family. That official is not allowed to throw your belongings out with you. Neither is the landlord, who must store them. (You may have to pay storage fees to get them back. See Chapter 12.)

If you are served with a five-day notice to vacate by the sheriff, it's time to move. It is much better to manage your own moving than be thrown out by the sheriff.

What if you occupied the premises on or before the date the eviction action was filed, but you are not named in the writ of possession or were not served with a Prejudgment Claim of Right to Possession (discussed above under "What If an Occupant Is Not Named in the Complaint?" above)? If you're in this situation, you have not been formally given the opportunity to appear and defend your right to stay. You might be able to do so at this point by filing a form called a "Claim of Right to Possession and Notice of Hearing" after the sheriff serves the writ of possession on you or other tenants. (CCP § 1174.3.) The sheriff or marshal who serves the writ of possession is required by statute to serve a copy of this form at the same time. We have included a sample below.

 FORM

You'll find a copy of the Claim of Right to Possession and Notice of Hearing in Appendix C, and the Nolo website includes a downloadable copy of this form. (See Appendix B for the link to the forms in this book.)

The sheriff should have filled in the case number on the front of the form.

Here's how to make a claim:

Step 1: Fill out the Claim of Right to Possession and Notice of Hearing form.

Step 2: Give the form to the sheriff or marshal. Submitting the Claim form will stop the eviction. You can give the sheriff the form any time until and including when the sheriff comes back to evict you. You do not have to take it to the sheriff's office, although you may; you can just hand it to the sheriff.

Claim of Right to Possession and Notice of Hearing

CP10

CLAIMANT OR CLAIMANT'S ATTORNEY (Name and Address): TELEPHONE NO.:	FOR COURT USE ONLY

ATTORNEY FOR (Name):

NAME OF COURT:
STREET ADDRESS:
MAILING ADDRESS:
CITY AND ZIP CODE:
BRANCH NAME:

CASE NUMBER:

Plaintiff:

Defendant:

CLAIM OF RIGHT TO POSSESSION AND NOTICE OF HEARING	(For levying officer use only) Completed form was received on Date: _____ Time: _____ By: _____

Complete this form only if ALL of these statements are true:
1. You are NOT named in the accompanying form called *Writ of Possession*.
2. You occupied the premises on or before the date the unlawful detainer (eviction) action was filed. *(The date is in the accompanying Writ of Possession.)*
3. You still occupy the premises.
4. A *Prejudgment Claim of Right to Possession* form was NOT served with the *Summons and Complaint*, OR this eviction results from a foreclosure.

NOTICE: If you are being evicted because of foreclosure, you have additional rights and should seek legal assistance immediately.

I DECLARE THE FOLLOWING UNDER PENALTY OF PERJURY:
1. My name is *(specify):*
2. I reside at *(street address, unit no., city and ZIP code):*
3. The address of "the premises" subject to this claim is *(address):*

[ ] Check here if this property was foreclosed on.

4. On *(insert date):* , the owner, landlord, or the landlord's authorized agent filed a complaint to recover possession of the premises. *(This date is in the accompanying Writ of Possession.)*
5. I occupied the premises on the date the complaint was filed *(the date in item 4)*. I have continued to occupy the premises ever since.
6. I was at least 18 years of age on the date the complaint was filed *(the date in item 4)*.
7. I claim a right to possession of the premises because I occupied the premises on the date the complaint was filed *(the date in item 4)*.
8. I was not named in the *Writ of Possession*.
9. I understand that if I make this claim of possession, a court hearing will be held to decide whether my claim will be granted.
10. *(Filing fee)* To obtain a court hearing on my claim, I understand that after I present this form to the levying officer I must go to the court and pay a filing fee of $ or file with the court *"Application for Waiver of Court Fees and Costs."* I understand that if I don't pay the filing fee or file the form for waiver of court fees within 2 court days, the court will immediately deny my claim.
11. *(Immediate court hearing unless you deposit 15 days' rent)* To obtain a court hearing on my claim, I understand I must also present a copy of this completed complaint form or a receipt from the levying officer. I also understand the date of my hearing will be set immediately if I do not deliver to the court an amount equal to 15 days' rent.

(Continued on reverse)

CP10 [Rev. July 1, 2017]   **CLAIM OF RIGHT TO POSSESSION AND NOTICE OF HEARING**   Code of Civil Procedure, §§ 715.010, 715.020, 1174.3

Claim of Right to Possession and Notice of Hearing (continued)

CP10

Plaintiff:	CASE NUMBER:
Defendant:	

12. I am filing my claim in the following manner *(check the box that shows how you are filing your claim. Note that you must deliver to the court a copy of the claim form or a levying officer's receipt)*:

   a. ☐ I presented this claim form to the sheriff, marshal, or other levying officer, AND within two court days I shall deliver to the court the following: (1) a copy of this completed claim form or a receipt, (2) the court filing fee or form for proceeding in forma pauperis, and (3) an amount equal to 15 days' rent; or

   b. ☐ I presented this claim form to the sheriff, marshal, or other levying officer, AND within two court days I shall deliver to the court (1) a copy of this completed claim form or a receipt, and (2) the court filing fee or form for proceeding in forma pauperis.

IMPORTANT: Do not take a copy of this claim form to the court unless you have first given the form to the sheriff, marshal, or other levying officer.

(To be completed by the court)

Date of hearing:	Time:	Dept. or Div.:	Room:
Address of court:			

NOTICE: If you fail to appear at this hearing you will be evicted without further hearing.

13. **Rental agreement.** I have *(check all that apply to you)*:

   a. ☐ an oral rental agreement with the landlord.
   b. ☐ a written rental agreement with the landlord.
   c. ☐ an oral rental agreement with a person other than the landlord.
   d. ☐ a written rental agreement with a person other than the landlord.
   e. ☐ a rental agreement with the former owner who lost the property through foreclosure.
   f. ☐ other *(explain):*

I declare under penalty of perjury under the laws of the State of California that the foregoing is true and correct.

WARNING: Perjury is a felony punishable by imprisonment in the state prison.

Date:

▶

_____
(TYPE OR PRINT NAME)

_____
(SIGNATURE OF CLAIMANT)

NOTICE: If your claim to possession is found to be valid, the unlawful detainer action against you will be determined at trial. At trial, you may be found liable for rent, costs, and, in some cases, treble damages.

— NOTICE TO OCCUPANTS —

YOU MUST ACT AT ONCE if all the following are true:

1. **You are NOT named, in the accompanying form called Writ of Possession;**
2. **You occupied the premises on or before the date the unlawful detainer (eviction) action was filed**; *and*
3. **You still occupy the premises.**
4. **A Prejudgment Claim of Right to Possession form was NOT served with the Summons and Complaint, OR you are being evicted due to foreclosure.**
   You can complete and SUBMIT THIS CLAIM FORM
   (1) Before the date of eviction at the sheriff's or marshal's office located at *(address):*

   (2) OR at the premises at the time of the eviction. *(Give this form to the officer who comes to evict you.)*

If you do not complete and submit this form (and pay a filing fee or file the form for proceeding in forma pauperis if you cannot pay the fee), YOU WILL BE EVICTED along with the parties named in the writ.

After this form is properly filed, A HEARING WILL BE HELD to decide your claim. If you do not appear at the hearing, you will be evicted without a further hearing.

CP10 [Rev. July 1, 2017]   **CLAIM OF RIGHT TO POSSESSION AND NOTICE OF HEARING**   Page two

Step 3: Send the court the filing fee (or a form requesting waiver of the fee) within two court days, as explained on the Claim of Right to Possession and Notice of Hearing form. If you submit 15 days' rent with your filing fee, the hearing will be held within five to 15 days. If you don't submit 15 days' rent with your filing fee, the hearing will be held in five days. (See sample letter to court, below.)

When the court holds its hearing, it will determine the validity of your claim. You have the burden to show that you were lawfully residing in the unit at the time the summons and complaint were filed, and that you were not served with a Prejudgment Claim of Right to Possession. (See Code of Civil Procedure Section 415.46 to see if Prejudgment Claim of Right to Possession Form was properly served and if the process server met all of the requirements.) If the court rules in your favor, the Complaint will be deemed to have been served on you at the hearing, and you will be able to respond to it in any of the ways discussed above. If the court rules against you, it will order the sheriff to proceed with the eviction.

RESOURCE

Landlords' eviction resource. If you want a clear understanding of evictions from the landlord's point of view, including all the forms and procedures landlords must follow to evict (from preparing the Complaint and Summons to collecting a money judgment), see *The California Landlord's Law Book: Evictions*, by Nils Rosenquest (Nolo).

Sample Letter to Court Regarding Claim of Right to Possession

(Date)

Superior Court of California
County of _____ ,
_____ Judicial Division/Branch

Re: Unlawful Detainer Action, Case No. _____

Enclosed is a check for $_____ as payment of the fee for filing a Claim of Right to Possession. I filed a Claim of Right to Possession to the premises at

_____
_____ on _____ ,
20____ , by giving the Claim to the sheriff/marshal of _____ County.

I have also enclosed a check for $_____ , an amount equal to 15 days' rent of the premises.

Sincerely,

Tom Tenant

Tom Tenant

Renters' Insurance

Renters' insurance policies are designed to protect tenants from losses caused by fire, criminal activity, and for a little extra, flood and earthquake. Buying renters' insurance is a good idea, because you have a lot to lose if there's an event like the ones mentioned above. For instance, a serious fire can be devastating—you lose your home, your belongings, and your life is disrupted. Insurance will pay, up to a certain amount ("policy limits") the replacement cost of your belongings, cost of a hotel and, depending on the policy, other out-of-pocket losses.

Renters' insurance can also provide protection against claims made against the tenant. For example, let's say you or someone in your household leaves the house, but has inadvertently left a pot of rice cooking. A fire ensues and causes damage to your landlord's property or another tenant's property. You would be liable, but insurance should help pay the cost.

Renters' insurance policies are surprisingly inexpensive, $150 to $300 per year depending on where you live, how much insurance coverage you want, and the types of coverage you've purchased.

Renters' insurance is a package of several types of insurance designed to cover tenants for more than one risk. Each insurance company's package will be slightly different—types of coverage offered, the dollar amounts specified for coverage, and the deductible will vary. There is nothing we can tell you here that will substitute for your shopping around and comparing policies and prices. It's a good idea to talk to friends and see if they are happy with their insurance.

The average renters' policy covers you against losses to your belongings occurring as a result of fire and theft, up to the amount stated on the face of the policy, which is often $15,000 or $25,000. As thefts have become more common, most policies have included deductible amounts of $500, or even $1,000. This means that if your apartment is burglarized, you collect from the insurance company only for the amount of your loss over and above the deductible amount.

Compensation for lost property will differ, depending on whether the policy will pay for the "replacement cost" of the item (that is, the current cost of replacing the item you lost), or the "fair market value" or "actual cash value" of the item (that is, what the item cost minus depreciation). If you can get it, it is better to get replacement cost—although the insurance may cost you a little more.

Many renters' policies completely exclude certain property from theft coverage, including cash, credit cards, and pets. Others limit the amount of cash covered to $100, jewelry and furs to $500. The value of home computers and equipment may be included as part of the contents coverage amount, or they may be separately scheduled on the policy. If you live in a flood- or earthquake-prone area, you'll have to pay extra for coverage. Earthquake policies, for example, typically run from $2 to $4 for each $1,000 of coverage, with a deductible of 10% to 15% of total coverage. Make sure your policy covers what you think it does. If it doesn't, check out the policies of other companies. As a general rule, you can get whatever coverage you want if you are willing to pay for it.

If you do take out insurance on valuable items, you should inventory them: Note down their values and take photos or make videotapes. Include the estimated value of each item. If you can, back it up with information on the model number and date of purchase. Keep the inventory and photos at work or some place other than your apartment, so that if there is a disaster, your inventory won't suffer the same fate as your belongings.

In addition to fire and theft coverage, most renters' policies give you (and your family living with you) personal liability coverage to an amount stated in the policy ($100,000 is typical). This means that if you injure someone (for example, you accidentally hit a guest on the head with a golf ball), a guest is injured through your negligence on the rental property that you occupy (for example, he slips on a broken front step), or you damage his belongings (for example, your garden hose floods the neighbor's cactus garden), you are covered. There are a lot of exclusions to personal liability coverage. Any damage you do with a motor vehicle, with a boat, or through your business won't be covered.

CAUTION

Your landlord's homeowners' insurance won't cover you. Even if you live in a duplex with your landlord and the landlord has a homeowners' policy, this policy won't protect your belongings if there is a fire or theft. Of course, if you suffer a loss as a result of your landlord's negligence, you may have a valid claim against her. Most landlords have insurance specifically to protect against this sort of risk.

If you have a loss, be sure your insurance company treats you fairly. If the company won't pay you a fair amount, consider taking the dispute to small claims court if it is for $10,000 or less. If the loss is a major one, you might consider seeing a lawyer, but agree to pay the lawyer only a percentage of what he or she can recover over and above what the insurance company offers you without the lawyer's help.

Finding Earthquake Insurance Can Be Difficult

The occurrence and risk of earthquakes in California has made it increasingly difficult and expensive for tenants to obtain renters' insurance. Insurance Code Section 10083 requires insurance companies to offer earthquake coverage with every homeowners' policy (renters' insurance is considered a form of homeowners' insurance), but most large companies are limiting the number of policies and type of coverage they issue as a result of the 1994 Northridge earthquake, which cost the insurance industry billions of dollars. Smaller companies are, however, continuing to offer policies, sometimes only for specified, earthquake-safe buildings. Independent brokers are usually the best sources for available and affordable policies.

Many landlords insert a clause into their leases or rental agreements requiring that the tenant purchase renters' insurance. This is legal under California law. The landlord's motive for requiring insurance is threefold:

- If the tenant's property is damaged in any way that is not the landlord's legal responsibility and the damage is covered by the renters' policy, the landlord won't have to rely on his or her own insurance policy.
- Anyone who suffers a personal injury on the property in a situation where the tenant is at fault is less likely to also sue the landlord.
- A number of landlords believe that tenants who are willing to buy insurance are more responsible than other tenants.

Landlords who are serious about requiring their tenants to obtain insurance often write lease clauses that state that failure to obtain and maintain a policy is grounds for eviction. One court has stated that a tenant's failure to get renters' insurance is *not* grounds for eviction. (*Boston v. Juarez*, 245 Cal.App.4th 75 (2016).) Nevertheless, you're well-advised to obtain insurance:

- It is relatively inexpensive, and the cost of replacing your "stuff" is surprisingly high.
- If there is a fire or flood that was not the fault of the landlord, you still recover for your losses.
- If you (or a cotenant or subtenant) are at fault for fire or some other accident, you are protected against lawsuits that are filed against you.

What to Look for in an Insurance Policy

If you are shopping for renters' insurance, you'll find it helpful to understand the policy provisions and some of the basic terms used. You should be clear about what you want when talking with the insurance broker or agent. Be sure to review the policy they give you so that you understand what you have bought. You can ask to add to or amend the policy if you want more insurance.

The first page or two of the policy will consist of what is often referred to as a "Declarations Page." It provides a basic description of the policy you are considering. It should have your name, the address of the premises covered, and the type of insurance ("Renters' Insurance"). You'll find other specialized terms that you should pay attention to:

Policy Period. This is the period of time that you are covered for (usually a one-year period). If your policy period is March 1, 2020 to February 28, 2021, then you would be covered for any "occurrence" during that period. For example, if there was a fire

on February 1, 2021, your losses due to the fire would be covered, but if it occurred in April 2021, you would be out of luck unless you had renewed your policy.

Premium. This is the amount you pay for the insurance.

Coverages/Endorsements. Here you'll find a general description of the type of coverages that you are purchasing and the limits of those coverages. For example: "Personal Property—$25,000" would mean that your personal property is insured up to $25,000 in losses. If, under a section called "Liability," it says "Personal Property—$25,000," that would be the maximum value of the property of others in case you are at fault for its loss or destruction. Under Liability, if it says "Bodily Injury," followed by a dollar amount, that would refer to the most the company would pay out to cover injury caused to others as a result of your negligence.

Deductible. This amount is what you have to pay before the insurance company pays anything. For instance, if you have $1,000 worth of property stolen and your "deductible" is $500, the insurance company would have to pay only $500.

After the Declarations Page is a lengthy document that contains the policy provisions. It looks intimidating, but we can break it down to four general categories (not necessarily in this order):

- **Definitions.** This section includes definitions of all the specialized terms contained in the policy.
- **Coverages.** This part includes a description of who is covered by the policy, the address of the property, the types of incidents (such as fire) that the policy covers, and the types of coverage (like personal property, loss of use, and personal liability). When reading this, you might have to refer back to the definitions part for terms such as "loss of use," "personal liability," and so on.

- **Obligations of an insured.** This describes what you are supposed to do in case of an incident. It usually involves requirements that you promptly report the incident and cooperate with respect to the claims process, as well as any investigation the insurer wants to undertake.

- **Exclusions.** These are types of incidents or injuries that the policy will not insure. For instance, the policy will not insure you if you start a fire, or if the fire is due to war or domestic terrorism. Mold and other toxic substances are also commonly excluded from these policies as well.

If you are unsure about some of the language of the policy, call your agent or broker. They receive a commission for placing your policy and an additional commission each time you renew, so it is good business for them to retain good customer relations.

RESOURCE

More information on renters' insurance. Check out the Insurance Information Institute website at www.iii.org, which includes useful articles including a renters' insurance checklist and advice on doing a home inventory.

Condominium Conversion

Converting buildings from rental properties into condominiums was unusual several years ago. Now, however, high demand for housing—specially in urban areas—and greater profitability for landlords and developers have led to a condominium boom. What, exactly is a "condominium conversion"? It's a change in the legal description of a building so that each individual unit in the building is a separate property that can be bought and sold independently. Condominium unit owners pay their own taxes, insurance, and mortgage payments. Building-wide matters like maintaining common areas are left up to a condominium owners' association. Condominium occupants are usually owner-occupants, but some owners choose to rent out their units.

Because the conversion to condominiums often displaces tenants, many cities have enacted condominium conversion ordinances that, in addition to state law, create protections for the tenant, the current owner of the building, and any future owners of individual units.

Condominium ownership as an abstract idea can make great sense. People have a basic need to own their own spaces, and with the high cost of land and construction, condominiums are often the only way this need can find expression. But many tenants of existing rental properties are unable or unwilling to pay large sums of money to purchase their units.

Here is a little story about what this could mean to you.

One day the mail carrier delivers an identical letter to all the tenants in a multiunit building. The owner, it seems, has decided to convert the building from rental units to condominiums. Once the conversion is completed, all of the tenants will have to decide whether they want to buy the unit or eventually move out. (Laws in some cities provide the option of lifetime leases for existing tenants.) Everyone will either have to buy their apartments and a share of the common space (such as halls and grounds) or move out. Those

with leases might have to leave when they run out, and those with month-to-month tenancies under a written rental agreement might have to leave in 30, 60, or 90 days. The letter concludes politely that the owners hope that they have caused no inconvenience and are sure that many tenants will welcome this opportunity to buy their units at the rock bottom price of $850,000 each.

Is there anything tenants can do if they want neither to move nor to buy their units? Yes.

Legal Protection for Tenants

Converting rental units to a condominium constitutes a "subdivision" under California law. This means that the property lines will change so that each unit becomes a separate property. The project must comply with the statewide Subdivision Map Act, and the landowner must apply for and receive approval of a "plan," or project, from the county agency in charge of reviewing the applications. (Gov't. Code § 66427.1.) In addition, many cities have enacted their own ordinances, which impose additional requirements. If you live in a city that has additional protections, it is worth your while to learn more about your legal rights when your building is being converted. Contact your local rent control board or city government for further information. (You can find contact information for rent control cities in Appendix A.)

Statewide Application Process

A landowner who wishes to convert rental property to condominiums, or who intends to demolish existing rental property and replace it with new condos, must follow the procedures outlined in the Subdivision Map Act (if a local ordinance applies, the procedures outlined there must be followed, too). The state law specifies that the landowner must:

- apply for tentative tract map approval with the county or, if there is a local ordinance, with the city.

- participate in the public hearing held by the planning agency, which will recommend approval or disapproval of the project. The agency can also attach conditions to its approval. These conditions can include certain concessions to tenants who are living in the building.
- receive a public report from the State Department of Real Estate (for conversions of five or more units). The public report is completed only after the landowner has complied with all the conditions of the tentative tract map issued by the planning agency. At this point, the application process ends.

The landowner or tenant may appeal the decision to the agency's governing body (the board of supervisors or the city council, if there is a local ordinance involved).

Required Notices

According to state law, tenants who will be evicted because of a planned condo conversion must be given notice of all the steps outlined above. These notice periods are as follows:

- Sixty days before the filing of a tentative tract map application, you must be told of the owner's intent to convert. (Gov't. Code §§ 66427.1(a), 7060.4(b).)
- Ten days' notice that an application to the Department of Real Estate for a public report will be or has been submitted, that the tenant can inspect the public report, and that the time for the tenant to purchase the property will begin to run once the final public report is issued. The owner must notify the tenant within five days of receiving the public report. (Gov't. Code § 66427.1(a)(2)(B)(C).)
- Ten days after the county or city approves the final map, you must be told of its approval. (Gov't. Code § 66427.1(a)(2)(D).)

- Notice of intent to convert must be given 180 days before termination of any tenancy. (Gov't. Code § 66427.1(a)(2)(E)).) (Keep in mind that you might have defenses under local rent control laws—see Chapters 14, 15, and Appendix A.)
- Ten days before *any* hearing regarding the proposed conversion, you must be informed of the hearing, where you have the right to appear and speak. (Gov't. Code §§ 66451.3, 65090, and 65091.) This is where you will have an opportunity to request additional concessions if you have not been able to negotiate successfully with your landlord beforehand.

Local ordinances may impose stricter notice requirements.

The Tenants' Right to Purchase

Once the final report has been issued by the State Department of Real Estate, you will have a 90-day exclusive right to purchase the property. The owner is required to provide written notice of this right. (Gov't. Code § 66427.1(a)(2)(F).)

The selling price and terms must be as good as or better than those that will be initially offered to the public at large.

Renting After Conversion Has Been Approved

Landlords who have received condo conversion approval will typically continue to rent the units in the building during the time that it takes to sell all the units. Tenants who have been residents since before the approval are, of course, aware of the tenuousness of their position and should have the benefit of the 90 days' right to purchase when their unit is put up for sale (see the discussion above). But what about the tenant who begins a tenancy *after* the final conversion approval?

Where the landlord owns a total of five units in the condominium project, and the tenant moves in after the final approval of the project, certain state protections apply. (Gov't. Code § 66459.) If you enter into a lease or rental agreement *after* the final approval of a subdivision map for that property, and if the project consists of five or more units, your landlord must include a clause in the lease that reads (in bold, 14-point type) as follows:

> **THE UNIT YOU MAY RENT HAS BEEN APPROVED FOR SALE TO THE PUBLIC AS A CONDOMINIUM PROJECT, COMMUNITY APARTMENT PROJECT OR STOCK COOPERATIVE PROJECT (WHICHEVER APPLIES). THE RENTAL UNIT MAY BE SOLD TO THE PUBLIC AND, IF IT IS OFFERED FOR SALE, YOUR LEASE MAY BE TERMINATED. YOU WILL BE NOTIFIED AT LEAST 90 DAYS PRIOR TO ANY OFFERING TO SELL. IF YOU STILL LAWFULLY RESIDE IN THE UNIT, YOU WILL BE GIVEN A RIGHT OF FIRST REFUSAL TO PURCHASE THE UNIT.**

Conversions That Don't Comply With Proper Notice to the Tenants

A landowner's failure to abide by the notice requirements imposed by state law will not necessarily defeat his bid to have his conversion project approved by the county agency reviewing the project. State law provides that a tentative or final map may not be disapproved solely because the tenants were not given the full amount of notice. There must be other reasons for disapproval besides the lack of notice to the tenants. (Gov't. Code § 66451.4.) You might have a case against the landlord if you can prove that the failure to give you notice caused you damage (or will cause you damage). In this situation, you should consult with a qualified attorney.

As a further precaution, the landlord is not even allowed to refer to his property as an "apartment" in a lease or rental agreement once the final approval for his conversion project has come through. (Gov't. Code § 66459(b).) Landlords with at least five units in the building must also provide the 90-day right to purchase described above. (Gov't. Code § 66459(c).

Unfortunately, the landlord's failure to comply will not invalidate a sale. (Gov't. Code § 66459(e).) However, the tenant will have a right to reimbursement of up to $1,100 of the actual cost to move, plus $1,100 of the first month's rent in the unit the tenant moves into. (Gov't. Code § 66459(f).)

Your Right to Relocation Assistance After Conversion

Except for the above situation, state law does not require the landlord to assist tenants with moving costs or finding new housing, but many local ordinances do. These ordinances typically provide for assistance to elderly, disabled, or low-income tenants, and to families with minor children. Some ordinances direct the landlord to offer lifetime leases to elderly tenants. Often, moving costs must be covered by the landlord; check your local code to find out whether you qualify for assistance.

Changing the Law

Tenants can also band together to get the local government to pass an ordinance allowing condominium conversions only if a number of conditions have been met. A good condominium conversion ordinance should require most, if not all, of the following conditions, before a conversion can take place:

- Fifty percent of the current tenants approve of the conversion.

- All tenants over 65 or disabled are allowed to continue as tenants for life if they wish.
- No conversions are allowed where the landlord has evicted large groups of tenants or greatly raised rents to get rid of tenants just before the conversion.
- No conversions of any kind are allowed when the rental vacancy rate in a city is below 5%, unless new rental units are being built at least fast enough to replace those converted.
- Special scrutiny is given to conversion of units rented to people with low and moderate incomes, to see that the units are priced at a level that the existing tenants can afford.
- The landlord provides adequate relocation assistance.

To stop a proposed condominium conversion, it is essential that tenants act together and that they create political alliances with sympathetic groups in the city. You will want to start by checking out your landlord carefully. Look for facts about the landlord that would tend to make local government agencies unsympathetic to the conversion. Among the best are the following:

- The landlord is from out of town and has recently bought your building (and perhaps others) as a speculation.
- The landlord has a long history of violating housing codes and generally is known as a bad landlord.
- The landlord raised rents excessively, terminated tenancies for no reason, and did other things to clear out the building before the conversion was announced.
- The building is occupied by many older people (or others on fixed incomes) who have no place to go, and the landlord has made little or no effort to either allow them to stay on at terms they can afford or find them a decent place to live.
- The landlord is making an excellent return on his money as rental units, and conversion to condominiums would result in huge profits.

Lawyers, Legal Research, and Mediation

Most of the time, you'll be able to learn of your rights, and hopefully communicate them to your landlord and enforce them, without the need to look at the law itself or consult an attorney. But sometimes you'll need to do one or both—for example, you may want to make sure that the steps you're taking to withhold rent are the current, legally required steps; and you may want to consult with an attorney before taking on your landlord by yourself in an eviction lawsuit. This chapter gives you some suggestions on how to find and understand the law (statutes and cases), and how to find a good lawyer. If gentle persuasion fails and you appear headed for a formal conflict with your lawyer, you may want to first try mediation, an efficient, low-cost alternative to court (you can do this with or without a lawyer). This chapter gives you the information you need on that score, too.

RESOURCE
Advice on small claims court. If your legal issue involves a small claims court dispute over security deposits, see Chapter 13; if it involves drug houses in your neighborhood, check out the discussion in Chapter 11 on small claims court lawsuits involving groups of tenants and neighbors.

Lawyers

This book is not designed to replace an attorney. It is meant to give you a clear understanding of your rights and obligations, and help you decide whether you need a lawyer.

Lawyers, like most of the rest of us, are in business to make money. Most charge from $200 to $400 an hour. In some cases, lawyers will charge a "flat fee"; in others, a "contingency fee" might be appropriate. We will talk about those later in this chapter. Clearly, when you have a dispute with your landlord that involves a few hundred dollars, it does not make good sense to pay someone as much (or more) than that to try to vindicate your

position. In addition, if your lease has an "attorney fees" clause, there is the danger that you will lose and end up paying both your landlord and your attorney, too.

When Do You Need a Lawyer?

There is no simple answer to the question of when you need a lawyer. This is because there are many possible areas of dispute between landlord and tenant, and many levels of tenant ability to deal with problems. In addition, representation can range from a single consultation session, to negotiation, to a full blown lawsuit. Throughout this book, we suggest times when the advice or other services of an attorney would be useful, but here are a few general pointers:

- If you believe that you have been discriminated against in a significant way, especially if there are others who have suffered a similar experience, consider seeing an attorney (but read about discrimination in Chapter 4 first).
- Attorneys will sometimes agree to sue a landlord (such as for discrimination or habitability violations) on a "contingency fee" basis. That is, rather than charge you out-of-pocket, the attorney will take a percentage of the amount you win from a lawsuit. Under these arrangements, you do not have to pay the attorney if you lose the case.
- If you believe you've been abused in other ways, such as an illegal eviction, severe habitability problems, being injured on the premises, harassment, or invasion of privacy, you might want to consult with an attorney. Again, attorneys might consider a contingency fee arrangement as explained above.
- If your landlord sues you for a lot of money, or if you suffer a significant physical or emotional injury because of action or inaction by the landlord or manager, see an attorney.
- If you have any problem that you can't understand or solve by reading this book, you should do some legal research yourself or get some professional advice.

- If you're being evicted and have concluded that you may have trouble conducting your defense, consider at least consulting with an attorney.

What Lawyers Can Do for You

There are three basic ways a lawyer can help with the problems a tenant commonly faces.

Consultation and Advice

The lawyer can listen to the details of your situation, analyze it for you, and advise you on your position and best plan of action. Ideally, the lawyer will give you more than just conclusions—an attorney can educate you about your whole situation and tell you all the various alternatives available. Then you can make your own choices. Or, you may just want a lawyer to look over the papers you have prepared, to be sure they are correct. This kind of service is the least expensive, as it involves only an office call and a little time. Find out the fee before you go in.

Negotiation

The lawyer has special talents, knowledge, and experience that will help you negotiate with the landlord. In case of serious problems, a lawyer can probably do this more successfully than you, especially if you are at odds with the landlord, or if your landlord has an attorney. Without spending much time, the attorney can often accomplish a lot through a letter or phone call. Receiving a message on an attorney's letterhead is, in itself, often very sobering to a landlord. Also, if bad turns to worse, a lawyer can convincingly threaten legal action. You can then decide at a later time whether to actually pursue it.

Lawsuits

In some instances, your case may merit going into court with a lawsuit. Having your lawyer go into court can be expensive and is only rarely warranted. However, in cases where the lawyer believes a recovery is possible, a case can be taken on a contingency fee basis, as discussed above. If the landlord sues you first, it is more likely that you will end up in court, and very likely that you will need a lawyer's help.

Finding a Lawyer

Finding a lawyer who charges reasonable prices and who you feel can be trusted is not always an easy task. There is always the danger that by just picking a name out of the telephone book you may get someone unsympathetic (perhaps an attorney who specializes in representing landlords) or an attorney who will charge too much. Here are some suggestions.

Legal Aid

If you are very poor, you may qualify for free help from your Legal Aid (often called Legal Services) office. Check your phone directory or search online for their location, or ask your Superior Court Clerk. Legal Aid personnel may not be able to represent tenants in court, but may offer self-help materials.

Tenants' Rights Organizations

In a number of California communities, tenants have gotten together and established tenants advocacy organizations. Many of these groups provide free or low-cost tenant counseling, provided by paralegals, and sometimes by volunteer lawyers. Counseling involves helping tenants understand their rights and sometimes extends to helping them prepare paperwork necessary to file or defend a lawsuit. Local bar associations also sometimes provide clinics for low-income tenants.

"Tenants Together" is a nonprofit, statewide tenants' rights organization (www.tenantstogether. org) that educates, organizes, and advocates on behalf of tenants in California. Tenants Together works on a day-to-day basis with other housing organizations and tenant attorneys, and promotes pro-tenant efforts on a state and local level. Their website provides a wide array of useful information.

Personal Referrals

If you're looking for a lawyer on your own, this is the best approach. If you know someone who has consulted a lawyer on a landlord-tenant matter and was pleased with the lawyer, call that lawyer first.

Prepaid Legal Plans

Many unions, employers, private companies, and consumer groups now offer membership in prepaid legal plans.

The services provided by the plans vary widely. Some give legal services at reduced fees; some offer free advice. If a plan offers extensive free advice, your initial membership fee may be worth the consultation you receive, even if you use it only once. Most plans have renewal fees; it's common to join a plan for a specific service and then not renew.

There's no guarantee that the lawyers available through these plans are any good. Check out the plan, and if possible its lawyers, in advance. And when using any of these prepaid plans, remember this: The lawyer is typically paid very little by the prepaid plan for dealing with you. Some lawyers sign up in the hope they can talk you into buying extra services not covered by your monthly premium. The best plans are those that do not permit the consulting lawyers to "self-refer." This means that the person you're talking to cannot attempt to persuade you to become his or her client.

Private Law Clinics

To market their services, some law firms advertise on TV, over the Internet, and on radio, offering low initial consultation fees. This generally means that a basic consultation is cheap (often less than $100), but anything after that isn't. If you consult a law clinic, the trick is to quickly extract what information you need and to resist any attempt to make you think you need further services.

Lawyer Referral Panels

Most county bar associations maintain lawyer referral services. Usually, you can get a referral to an attorney who specializes in landlord-tenant law, and an initial consultation for free or for a low fee. But some of the panels don't really screen the listed attorneys, and some of the attorneys participating may not have much experience or ability. If you contact an attorney this way, be sure to ask about experience with tenant problems, and make sure the lawyer is sympathetic to tenants' rights.

Yellow Pages or the Internet

The Yellow Pages has an extensive listing of attorneys and sublistings by specialty. Look for "Tenant Rights," "Landlord Tenant" and "Real Estate" areas of practice. If you have Internet access, even better. Try "Tenant Rights attorneys in [your city]." Beware, though, in both the Yellow Pages and online, advertising is paid for and prominent advertising does not necessarily mean that an attorney is the best in that area.

Shop around by calling different law offices and stating your problem. Ask to talk to a lawyer personally; if the law firm won't allow it, this should give you an idea of how accessible the lawyer is. Ask some specific questions. Do you get clear, concise answers? If not, try someone else. If the lawyer says little except to suggest that he handle the problem (with a substantial fee, of course), watch out. You are talking with someone who either doesn't know the answer and won't admit it (common), or someone who pulls rank on the basis of professional standing. Don't be a passive client or deal with a lawyer who wants you to be one.

Keep in mind that lawyers learn mostly from experience and special training, not from law school. Because you're already well informed (you've read this book), you should be in a good position to evaluate a lawyer's preparedness to handle your problem.

Remember, lawyers whose offices and lifestyles are reasonably simple are more likely to help you for less money than lawyers who feel naked unless wearing a $2,000 suit. You should be able to find an attorney willing to represent you for either a flat rate or an hourly rate of between $200 and $400, depending on where the lawyer's office is located (big city lawyers tend to be pricier) and how complex your case is.

Nolo's Lawyer Directories

You'll find a wealth of lawyers who advertise on Nolo.com and our associated websites.

Nolo's Lawyer Directory. Nolo has an easy-to-use online directory of lawyers, organized by location and area of expertise. You can find the directory and its comprehensive profiles at www.nolo.com/lawyers.

Lawyers.com. At Lawyers.com you'll find a user-friendly search tool that allows you to tailor results by area of law and geography. You can also search for attorneys by name. Attorney profiles prominently display contact information, list topics of expertise, and show ratings—by both clients and other legal professionals.

Martindale.com. Martindale.com allows you to search not only by practice area and location, but also by criteria, such as by law school. Whether you look for lawyers by name or expertise, you'll find listings with detailed background information, peer and client ratings, and even profile visibility.

Keep in mind that these online resources are simply modern versions of the Yellow Pages: The listed lawyers have paid to have their names show up on the relevant pages.

RESOURCE

For advice on hiring and working with lawyers, including what to ask a prospective attorney, see www.nolo.com/lawyers/tips.html.

Typing Services and Unlawful Detainer Assistants

What if you don't want to hire a lawyer but don't want to do all your legal paperwork yourself? There's a middle ground. A number of businesses, known as "legal typing services," "legal document preparers,"

"unlawful detainer assistants," or "independent paralegals," assist people doing their own legal work in filling out the forms. Most typing services concentrate on family law or bankruptcy, but some handle landlord-tenant matters, too.

These services aren't lawyers. They can't give legal advice and can't represent you in court—only lawyers can. You must decide what steps to take in your case, and the information to put in any needed forms. Such services can, however:

- provide written instructions and legal information you need to handle your own case
- provide the appropriate forms, and
- prepare your papers so they'll be accepted by the court.

Unlawful detainer assistants and similar services commonly charge far less than attorneys, because their customers do much of the work and make the basic decisions. Also, these services handle only routine cases.

If you're looking for this type of service, go online and search for "legal document preparation [your county]." For example, a search for "legal document preparation San Francisco" resulted in four hits, and more outside the county. Or, check classified sections of newspapers under Referral Services, usually immediately following Attorneys. Also check the Internet or Yellow Pages under "Eviction Services" or "Paralegals." A local Legal Aid office may provide a reference, as will the occasional court clerk. Many offices have display ads in local throwaway papers like the *Classified Flea Market*.

Occasionally, these types of services have taken money from a customer and then failed to deliver the services as promised. As with any other business rip-off, you, as a consumer, can sue in small claims or regular court, and report the matter to your local district attorney's consumer fraud division. But legal remedies are often ineffective. The best precaution is to select a reliable document preparation service at the beginning. As with finding a lawyer, a recommendation from a satisfied customer is best. Also, as a general matter, the longer such a service has been in business, the better.

Paralegals who handle eviction matters, whether for the tenant or landlord, must be registered and bonded as an "unlawful detainer assistant." (B&P §§ 6400–6415.) If the service isn't registered, don't use it. The court forms that an eviction service prepares, such as the Answer (discussed in Chapter 15), require you to state under penalty of perjury whether an "unlawful detainer assistant" helped you. If you hired an unlawful detainer assistant, you must give the eviction service's name, address, and registration number on the form.

Legal Research

We don't have space here to show you how to do your own legal research in anything approaching a comprehensive fashion. *Legal Research: How to Find & Understand the Law,* by the Editors of Nolo (Nolo), is an excellent resource if you wish to learn basic legal research skills, something we highly recommend. For free information on the subject, see the Laws and Legal Research section of www. nolo.com.

Our goal in this section is only to tell you how to find the basic laws that control your residential tenancy. In addition, we show you how to locate the important judicial decisions (most of which are mentioned in this book) that interpret these laws.

TIP

Keep up-to-date on landlord-tenant law so that you know your rights and can avoid legal problems. Check this book's companion page on the Nolo website at www.nolo.com. (Appendix B includes a link to this companion page.)

State Laws

Landlord-tenant laws and legal procedure are principally contained in two parts of California law—the Civil Code (CC) and the Code of Civil Procedure (CCP), both of which are available online at all law libraries and most public libraries. The Civil Code is divided into numerous sections, dealing generally with people's legal rights and responsibilities to each other. Most of California's substantive residential landlord-tenant law is contained in Sections 1940 through 1991 of this code, with laws governing minimum building standards, payment of rent, change and termination of tenancy, privacy, and security deposits, to name a few. The Code of Civil Procedure is a set of laws that tells how people enforce legal rights in civil lawsuits. Eviction lawsuit procedures are contained in Sections 1161 through 1179 of the Code of Civil Procedure. Also of interest are the small claims court procedures mentioned in Sections 116.110 through 116.950.

 RESOURCE

Where to read state statutes themselves (and check pending legislation). See the website maintained by the Legislative Council at www.leginfo. legislature.ca.gov. For advice on finding a law, statute, code section, or case, see the Laws and Legal Research section on the Nolo site, www.nolo.com/legal-research. You may also find it useful to go to the reference desk at your public library for help; many have good law collections. If your county maintains a law library that's open to the public (often in a courthouse, state-funded law school, or a state capital building), you can get help there, too, from law librarians.

In this book, we make frequent references to statutes found in sources like the California Code of Civil Procedure and California Civil Code. We use standard abbreviations like CCP and CC to make future references to these sources easier. For your convenience, there is a list of standard abbreviations used in this book located on the last page of the "Your Legal Companion," at the beginning of this book.

Examples of Case Citations

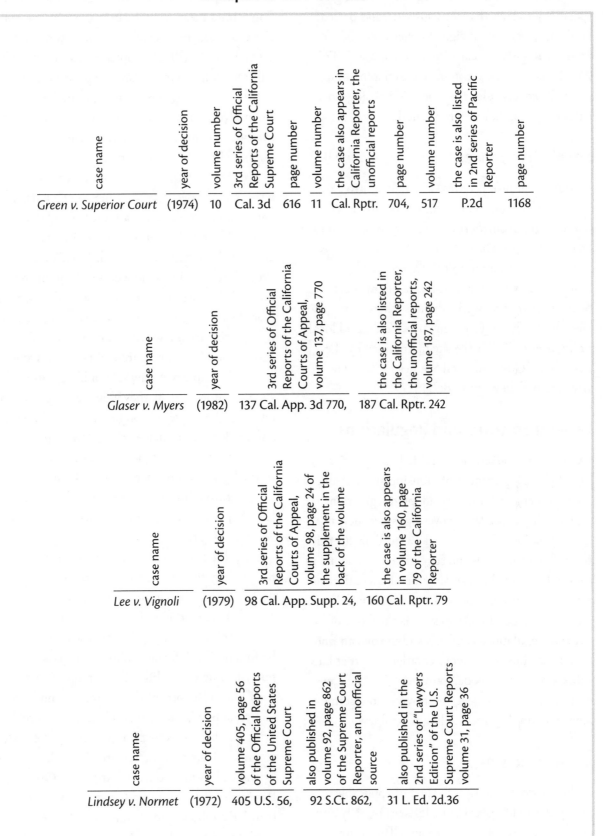

If you want to check out regulations that give specificity to laws that the legislature has passed (and the governor has signed), check out the Code of Regulations at http://ccr.oal.ca.gov. Title 25, Housing and Community Development, for example, covers rules that apply to housing, such as rules regarding hot water in rental.

Local Ordinances

If your rental unit is covered by rent control, and/or just cause for eviction protection, be sure to check out local rent control rules (see Appendix A and the chart in Chapter 3).

Even if your rental unit is not covered by rent control, you should be aware of any local ordinances that may affect you, such as your city's health and safety standards. You'll find local ordinances online at the site maintained by the Institute of Governmental Studies in Berkeley, at www.igs.berkeley.edu/node/11317.

Federal Statutes and Regulations

Congress has passed laws, and federal agencies such as the U.S. Department of Housing and Urban Development (HUD) have adopted regulations that amplify those laws, covering issues such as discrimination. We refer to relevant federal agencies throughout this book and suggest you contact them for publications that explain federal laws affecting tenants. If you want to check out a specific federal regulation, a good place to start is the Code of Federal Regulations (C.F.R.), which you can find at the U.S. House of Representatives Internet Law Library at http://uscode.house.gov. (See the Laws and Legal Research section on www.nolo.com for advice on finding and reading federal law.)

Court Decisions

Although codes contain the text of applicable laws passed each year by the legislature, they don't contain the text of any of the appellate court decisions that determine what those laws mean. Sometimes these cases are extremely important. For example, the case of *Green v. Superior Court*, 40 Cal.3d 616 (1974) adopted a "common law" rule allowing tenants in substandard housing to withhold rent—without paying to make repairs themselves. To gain access to the printed reports of important court decisions, you have to go to a law library, either "real" or "virtual."

The best way to learn of the existence of written court decisions that interpret a particular law is to first look in an "annotated code." An annotated code is a set of volumes of a particular code, such as the Civil Code or Code of Civil Procedure mentioned above, that contains not only all the laws (as do the regular codes), but also a brief summary of many of the court decisions interpreting each law. These annotated codes can be found in some public libraries and any county law library or law school library in the state. (Unfortunately, they aren't available for free online.) They have comprehensive indexes by topic, and are kept up to date each year with paperback supplements ("pocket parts") located in a pocket in the back cover of each volume. Don't forget to look through these pocket parts for the latest law changes or case decisions since the hardcover volume was printed.

Each brief summary of a court decision is followed by the title of the case, the year of the decision, and the "citation." The citation is a sort of shorthand identification for the set of books, volume, and page where the case can be found. The "official" volumes of cases are published by the California Supreme Court as the Official Reports of the California Supreme Court (abbreviated "Cal.," "Cal.2d," "Cal.3d," or "Cal.4th," respectively, representing the first, second, third, and fourth "series" of volumes) and by the California Courts of Appeal as Official Reports of the California Courts of Appeal (similarly abbreviated "Cal.App.," "Cal.App.2d," "Cal.App.3d," and "Cal.App.4th"). The same cases are also published in "unofficial volumes" by the West Publishing Company. These are California Reporter (abbreviated "Cal.Rptr." and "Cal. Rptr.2d") and Pacific Reporter (abbreviated "P." or "P.2d," respectively, for the first and second series). The case is the same whether you read it in the official or unofficial reporter.

Above are examples of case citations which should take some of the mystery out of legal research. If, in the course of your research, you still have questions, again we recommend *Legal Research: How to Find & Understand the Law,* by The Editors of Nolo (Nolo).

Where to Find Statutes, Ordinances, and Cases

Every California county maintains a law library that is open to the public. All have the California statutes (including annotated versions), written court opinions, and expert commentary. You can find and read any statute or case we've referred to at the law library by looking it up according to its citation. For most of you, the fastest and most convenient way to read codes is on the Internet, as explained above.

Instead, you may want to start your research with a good background resource. We mention several of these (The *California Eviction Defense Manual,* for example) throughout the book. Another good resource, usually kept behind the desk at the reference counter of most libraries, is a loose-leaf two-volume set published by The Rutter Group entitled *Landlord-Tenant (The Rutter Group California Practice Guide).*

Mediation and Arbitration

Mediation and arbitration are alternatives to court—more involved than a settlement, but not as complex as litigation. The terms "mediation" and "arbitration" are commonly confused.

Arbitration is a process where a third party hears the case and comes to a determination as to who is right and who is wrong, and whether any damages should be awarded. In "binding arbitration" the determination by the arbitrator is final and not appealable. In "non-binding arbitration" the decision may be appealed or the matter brought to court for determination. Rental agreements that require the parties to arbitrate their disputes (rather than go to court) are invalid and not enforceable. (CC § 1953(a)(4); *Jaramillo v. JH Real Estate Partners, Inc.,* 111 Cal.App.4th 394 (2003).

One example of an arbitration that is enforceable is the proceedings before a rent control board. For instance, if a tenant wants to protest an illegal rent increase, the tenant would have to file a petition for arbitration with the rent board. Both the landlord and the tenant will appear before an administrative law judge (ALJ) and make their case. The ALJ will then make their decision. (See Chapter 3 section, "Rent Control Board Hearings").

Mediation involves using a neutral third party to help the disputants resolve their dispute. The mediator does not make decisions or judgments, but merely tries to help the parties come to an agreement. You will not be forced to make an agreement if you don't want to. You'll often get more practical results in mediation than you would get in a court of law. That's because a court is somewhat limited in the kinds of orders it can hand down. For instance, suppose you and your upstairs neighbor are having a dispute regarding noise from the neighbor's unit. In court, you could seek money damages against the neighbor and maybe the landlord, but that might not solve the problem. In a mediation, anything goes. The participants could agree to "quiet hours," the neighbor might promise to place carpeting on the floor, you could switch apartments, or do whatever else that would resolve the dispute.

The mediator normally has no power to impose a solution if the parties can't agree. Generally, mediation works well in situations where the parties want to settle their disputes in order to work together in the future. In a landlord-tenant context, mediation can be extremely helpful in a number of areas, such as disputes about noise, drug use in the building, the necessity for repairs, a tenant's decision to withhold rent because defects have not been repaired, rent increases, privacy, and many more. Many tenants and especially groups of tenants with a list of grievances find that mediating disputes with a landlord is a better approach to problem solving than is withholding rent, filing a lawsuit, and so on.

Mediators do not impose a decision on the parties, but use their skills to facilitate a compromise. Mediation is most effective when procedures are established in advance. Typically, the tenant or landlord with a problem contacts some respected neutral organization, such as a city or county landlord-tenant mediation project (not every area has one, but many do); the American Arbitration Association (www.adr.org); or a neighborhood dispute resolution center, such as San Francisco's Community Board program, and arranges for this group to mediate a landlord-tenant dispute. There are a great number of mediation programs in California, and if you ask your District Attorney's office or county clerk, you should find one.

At the mediation session, each side gets to state their position. Just doing this often cools people off considerably and frequently results in a compromise. If the dispute is not taken care of easily, however, the mediator may suggest several ways to resolve the problem, or may even keep everyone talking long enough to realize that the problem goes deeper than the one being mediated. For example, a landlord who thinks she runs a tight ship may learn that the real problem from the tenant's point of view is that her manager is lazy and slow to make repairs. This, of course, may lead to the further discovery that the manager is angry at several tenants for letting their kids pull up his tulips.

Because mediation lets both sides air their grievances, it often works well to improve the climate of stormy landlord-tenant relationships. And if it doesn't, you haven't lost much, especially if you make sure mediation occurs promptly and you use it only in situations where your landlord has some arguably legitimate position. If mediation fails, you can still fight it out in court.

Small claims court judges often use mediation as a required first step. Parties are required to attend a mediation session and to attempt to settle their differences before the case will be heard in court.

Rent Control and Eviction Protection Laws

Statewide and Local Rent Control and Eviction Protection

State Law

The following chart summarizes the major features of California's statewide rent control and eviction protection law, the Tenant Protection Act of 2019 ("TPA").

State of California Tenant Protection Act of 2019 (AB 1482)

Name of Legislation
(AB 1482)
California Civil Code
Division 3. Obligations
Part 4. Obligations Arising from Particular
  Transactions
Title 5. Hiring
Chapter 2. Hiring of Real Property
Tenant Protection Act of 2019

1946.2 Just Cause
1947.12. Cap on rent increases
1947.13 Assisted and Affordable Housing

Effective Dates
Effective 1/1/20 and scheduled to expire on 1/1/30.

Note: AB 1482 is preempted by more protective local rent control ordinances, and ordinances requiring just cause that were 1); adopted on or before 9/1/19, or 2); adopted or amended after that date and with *more protective* "just cause" provisions than AB 1482.

Exemptions
Apartments built within 15 years of the current date are exempt ("rolling" exemption), along with hotels and related short-term housing, medical facilities, dormitories, and religious, extended, or residential care facilities. Duplexes are exempt where the owner occupies one unit as a principal place of residence at the start of the tenancy, and continues to do so.

Single family homes are exempt where 1) the owner is a "natural person" rather than an institutional investor like a corporation, real estate investment trust, or LLC with at least one corporate member; or 2) the owner maintains a principal residence in the unit and shares a bathroom or kitchen with the tenant, or 3) owner-occupied homes where the owner rents two or less units (granny flats, ADUs).

Caution: Beginning 7/1/20, landlords of exempt properties must provide both existing and new tenants with specific written notice of the exemptions. (CC § 1946.2.)

Administration
No state agency is responsible for enforcement. Tenant must file a lawsuit to enforce rights.

Cap on Rent Increases
Annual rent increases are limited to the lesser of 5% plus the metropolitan area Consumer Price Index, or 10% of the total of the lowest gross rental rate charged at any time during the 12 months prior to the effective date of the increase.

Starting 1/1/20 the base rent for calculating increases will be the rent in effect as of 3/15/19. Rent may be increased only twice over any 12-month period. (CC § 1947.12.)

"Just Cause" Required for Eviction?
Yes, once the tenant has continuously/lawfully occupied the unit for 12+ months. If additional tenant(s) are added *before the existing tenant has occupied for 24 months*, then *all* tenants must have occupied the unit for 12+ months, or *one or more* tenants for 24+ months. (CC§ 1946.2(a)).

Other

Tenants subjected to a no-fault eviction are entitled to either relocation assistance or a rent waiver equal to one month's rent. (CC § 1946.2.)

For a curable lease violation (tenant at fault, see below), the owner must first give the tenant notice and an opportunity to cure pursuant to California Code of Civil Procedure Section 1161(3) (i.e., three-day notice to cure or quit). A three-day notice to quit without an opportunity to cure may then be served to terminate the tenancy. For a no-fault termination, tenant must be informed of the right to relocation assistance or rent waiver.

Reasons Allowed for Just Cause Evictions—Tenant at Fault (CC § 1946.2(a)	Additional Local Notice Requirements and Limitations
Failure to pay rent.	
Breach of the lease.	Breach as described in Cal. Civ. Proc. § 1161(3), including violation of a provision of the lease after being issued a written notice to correct the violation.
Maintaining, committing, or permitting nuisance.	Tenant commits or maintains a public nuisance as described in Cal. Civ. Proc. § 1161(4), Cal Civ. Code § 3482.8 (dog/cockfighting), 3485(c) (guns & ammo), or 3486(c) (drugs).
Committing waste.	See Cal Civ. Code § 1161(4).
Tenant refuses to renew.	A written lease terminates on or after January 1, 2020, and following a written request tenant refuses to execute a renewal of similar duration and terms. Refusal to renew can include tenant's failure to agree to a clause allowing for landlord move-in. Cal Civ. Code § 1161(2)(A)(ii).
Criminal activity.	Tenant engages in criminal activity on the property, including common areas, or criminal activity or threats, as defined in Penal Code § 422(a) (death or great bodily injury to another person), on or off the property, directed at owner or owner's agent.
Assigning or subletting in violation of lease.	Assigning or subletting the premises in violation of the lease, per Cal Civ. Code § 1161(4).
Tenant refuses to allow landlord reasonable access to the unit.	Tenant's refusal to allow access as authorized by Cal Civ. Code §§ 1101.5, 1954, and 1946.2; and Cal. Health and Safety Code §§ 13113.7 and 17926.1.
Using premises for unlawful purpose.	Unlawful purpose as described in Cal Civ. Proc. § 1161(4), i.e., Cal. Civ. Code §§ 3482.8 (dog/cockfighting), 3485(c) (guns & ammo), and 3486(c) (drugs).
Terminated employee refuses to vacate.	Tenant is landlord's employee, agent, or licensee who refuses to vacate following termination. (Cal. Civ. Code § 1161(1)).
Hold-over tenant.	Tenant fails to deliver possession after providing written notice pursuant to Cal. Civ. Code § 1946 of tenant's intention to terminate the lease; or tenant's written offer to surrender is accepted in writing by the landlord, but tenant fails to deliver. (Cal Civ. Proc. § 1161(5)).

Reasons Allowed for Just Cause Evictions—No Fault	Additional Local Notice Requirements and Limitations
Owner move-in by owner or owner's spouse, domestic partner, children, grandchildren, parents, or grandparents.	For leases entered into on or after 7/1/20, move-ins are available only if the tenant agrees in writing, or if a lease provision specifically allows termination for owner move-ins. Adding a provision to a renewal which allows termination for owner move-in constitutes a "similar provision" for the purposes of refusing to renew a lease.
Withdrawal of property from the rental market.	
Landlord must evict tenant to comply with a local ordinance or an order from a court or government agency.	Eviction must be necessary to comply with (I) a government agency or court order relating to habitability that requires vacating the property; (II) a government agency or court order to vacate the property; or (III) a local ordinance that requires vacating the property. If a government agency or court determines tenant is at fault for triggering the order/need to vacate under Clause (I), the tenant is not entitled to relocation assistance.
Intent to demolish or to substantially remodel the property.	"Substantially remodel" means the replacement or substantial modification requiring a permit, or abatement of hazardous materials that requires the tenant to vacate for at least 30 days. Cosmetic improvements alone that can be performed safely without vacating, don't qualify as substantial rehabilitation.

Local Law

As this book went to press, cities (and counties) in California with existing rent control and/ or eviction protection ordinances were busy modifying those ordinances. Cities without those ordinances were busy adding them. To access an updated chart of local ordinances, go to the companion page (www.nolo.com/back-of-book/ CTEN.html).

Understanding the Law

We recommend that you always check the law or ordinance itself before making decisions that involve the laws. In case you are (understandably) intimidated at the prospect of deciphering the TPA or your city's ordinance, here are a few hints about reading and understanding rent control ordinances.

Almost all rent control laws begin with a statement of purpose, followed by definitions of terms used in the ordinance. If such terms as "rental unit" and "landlord" aren't defined specifically enough to tell you who and what is covered by the ordinance, another section dealing with applicability of the ordinance usually follows. After that, the ordinance usually sets out the structure and rules of the rent board and will say whether landlords must register their properties with the board. Your ordinance probably then has a section entitled something like "Annual Increases" or "General Rent Ceiling."

Following the rent sections should be a section on "Individual Adjustments" or "Hardship Adjustments." This section tells landlords how to get an increase over and above any general across-the-board increase. Finally, any requirement that landlords show "just cause" for eviction should be found under a section entitled "Just (or Good) Cause for Eviction." It will contain a list of the permissible reasons for eviction, along with any extra requirements for eviction notices, and prohibit evictions for any other reason.

If you have received a rent hike or termination notice (or eviction papers—a Summons and Complaint), you'll want to know whether the landlord has followed the rules. Specifically:

- **Registration requirements.** If the landlord is required to register the unit with the rent board but didn't, you might be able to win an eviction lawsuit.
- **Rent increase restrictions.** Read the individual adjustments section to see if the landlord must apply to the rent board for increases over a certain amount. If so, make sure any rent increases were properly applied for and legal.
- **Special notice requirements.** Check both the general and individual rent adjustment sections, as well as any regulations adopted by the rent board, for special notice requirements for rent increase notices.
- **Just cause requirements.** This is crucial; a landlord can evict only for one of the permissible reasons, and must comply with any additional notice requirements. If a landlord wants to evict tenants in order to demolish the building or simply go out of business, the landlord may do so under the Ellis Act (Gov't. Code §§ 7060–7060.7), even if this reason isn't listed in the ordinance.

Finding the TPA and Municipal Codes and Rent Control Ordinances Online

If you live in a city that has rent control and/or eviction protection, you should have a current version of the city's rent control law. You can usually obtain a paper copy from the administrative agency that oversees the workings of the ordinance. It's quicker and safer, however, to read the material online, where updates should appear. Most cities have posted their ordinances. Use the Rent Control Chart, which provides detailed, city-by-city analyses, as a guide to your own reading of the law. Keep in mind that ordinances often change and their meaning evolves as rent boards issue regulations and make decisions, so check the site often for updates.

You can also access many cities' municipal codes at the following sites: www.municode.com/library/ca, and https://igs.berkeley.edu/library/california-local-government-documents/codes-and-charters.

If you want to read the text of the TPA, follow these instructions:

- Go to the website of the California legislature, leginfo.legislature.ca.gov.
- In the "Quick Bill Search" field, enter "AB 1482." You'll get the entire text of the law.

How to Use the Downloadable Forms on the Nolo Website

This book comes with eforms that you can access online at **www.nolo.com/back-of-book/CTEN.html** To use the files, your computer must have specific software programs installed. Here is a list of types of files provided by this book, as well as the software programs you'll need to access them.

- **RTF.** You can open, edit, save, and print these form files with most word processing programs such as Microsoft *Word*, Windows *WordPad*, and recent versions of *WordPerfect*.

- **PDF.** You can view these files with Adobe *Reader*, free software from www.adobe.com. Judicial Council PDFs are fillable using your computer.

Editing RTFs

Here are some general instructions about editing RTF forms in your word processing program. Refer to the book's instructions and sample agreements for help about what should go in each blank.

- **Underlines.** Underlines indicate where to enter information. After filling in the needed text, delete the underline. In most word processing programs you can do this by highlighting the underlined portion and typing CTRL-U.

- **Bracketed and italicized text.** Bracketed and italicized text indicates instructions. Be sure to remove all instructional text before you finalize your document.

- **Optional text.** Optional text gives you the choice to include or exclude text. Delete any optional text you don't want to use. Renumber numbered items, if necessary.

- **Alternative text.** Alternative text gives you the choice between two or more text options. Delete those options you don't want to use. Renumber numbered items, if necessary.

- **Signature lines.** Signature lines should appear on a page with at least some text from the document itself.

Every word processing program uses different commands to open, format, save, and print documents, so refer to your software's help documents for help using your program. Nolo cannot provide technical support for questions about how to use your computer or your software.

> (!) CAUTION
> **In accordance with U.S. copyright laws, the forms provided by this book are for your personal use only.**

List of Forms Available on the Nolo Website

To download any of the files listed on the following pages go to:
www.nolo.com/back-of-book/CTEN.html

The following files are in rtf format:

Form Name	File Name
Landlord-Tenant Checklist	Checklist.rtf
Fixed-Term Residential Lease	FixedLease.rtf
Month-to-Month Residential Rental Agreement	RentalAgreement.rtf
Notice to Repair	NoticetoRepair.rtf
Notice of Rent Withholding	RentWithholding.rtf
Agreement Regarding Tenant Alterations to Rental Unit	Alteration.rtf
Indemnification of Landlord	Indemnification.rtf
Blank Numbered Legal Paper	BlankLegal.rtf
Blank Numbered Legal Paper With Superior Court Heading	LegalSuperior.rtf
Demurrer	Demurrer.rtf
Points and Authorities in Support of Demurrer	Points.rtf
Notice of Hearing on Demurrer	NoticeofHearing.rtf
Request for Judicial Notice	RequestNotice.rtf
Request to Inspect and for Production of Documents	RequestInspect.rtf

Form Name	File Name
Settlement Agreement	Settlement.rtf
Demand for Jury Trial	DemandJury.rtf
Application and Declaration for Relief From Eviction	AppEviction.rtf
Order Granting Relief From Eviction	OrderReliefEviction.rtf
Application and Declaration for Stay of Eviction	StayEviction.rtf
Notice of Motion and Points and Authorities for Relief from Eviction	NoticeReliefEviction.rtf
Order Granting Stay of Eviction	OrderEviction.rtf
Notice of Appeal and Notice to Prepare Clerk's Transcript	ClerkTranscript.rtf

The following files are in pdf format:

Form Name	File Name
Bed Bug Information Sheet	BedBug.pdf
Declaration of Small Estate	SmallEstate.pdf
Request to Waive Court Fees (a Judicial Council form)	fw001.pdf
Order on Court Fee Waiver (Superior Court) (a Judicial Council form)	fw003.pdf
Prejudgment Claim of Right to Possession (a Judicial Council form)	cp105.pdf
Proof of Service by First-Class Mail—Civil (a Judicial Council form)	pos030.pdf
Attachment to Proof of Service by First-Class Mail—Civil (Persons Served) (a Judicial Council form)	pos030p.pdf
Answer–Unlawful Detainer (a Judicial Council form)	ud105.pdf
Attachment	mc025.pdf
Form Interrogatories–Unlawful Detainer (a Judicial Council form)	disc003.pdf
Claim of Right to Possession and Notice of Hearing (a Judicial Council form)	cp10.pdf

The following files are sample forms and letters in pdf format:

Form Name	File Name
Landlord-Tenant Agreement Regarding Tenant's Credit Information	CreditInfo.pdf
Sample Addendum to Lease or Rental Agreement	SampleAddendum.pdf
Sample Agreement Between Roommates	Roommates.pdf
Sample Letter or Email When a New Roommate Moves In	NewRoommate.pdf
Sample Letter or Email When One Tenant Moves Out and the Other Remains (Lease)	MoveOutLease.pdf
Sample Letter or Email When One Tenant Moves Out and the Other Remains (Rental Agreement)	MoveOutRenAgree.pdf
Sample Agreement for Partial Rent Payments	PartialPayments.pdf
Sample Letter or Email When Landlord Violates Privacy	ViolatesPrivacy.pdf
Sample Request for Repair or Maintenance	RepairRequest.pdf
Sample Letter or Email of Understanding Regarding Repairs	UnderstandRepairs.pdf
Sample Letter or Email Telling the Landlord You Intend to Withhold the Rent	WithholdRent.pdf
Sample Letter or Email Telling the Landlord You Intend to Repair and Deduct	RepairDeduct.pdf
Sample Letter or Email Asking for Minor Repairs	MinorRepairs.pdf
Sample Letter or Email Requesting Permission to Do a Minor Repair	PermissionRepair.pdf
Sample Letter or Email to Landlord Regarding Tenant Injury	TenantInjury.pdf

Form Name	File Name
Sample Letter or Email Regarding Deteriorating Asbestos	Asbestos.pdf
Sample Letter or Email Requesting Reimbursement for Temporary Housing	TempHousing.pdf
Sample Letter or Email Regarding Lead Test Results	LeadTest.pdf
Sample Letter or Email Asking for Check of CO Detector	CODetector.pdf
Sample Letter or Email Alerting the Landlord to Dangerous Conditions	DangerousCond.pdf
Sample Sublease Agreement	Sublease.pdf
Sample Agreement Regarding Cancellation of Lease	LeaseCancel.pdf
Sample Letter or Email to Landlord Suggesting Potential Tenants	PotentialTenants.pdf
Sample Letter or Email Demanding Security Deposit	SecDeposit.pdf
Sample Letter or Email Requesting Landlord to Apply Deposit to Last Month's Rent	LastMonthRent.pdf

Using California Judicial Council Government Forms

The Nolo website includes several government forms that were created by the Judicial Council, California's official forms publisher. The list of forms at the beginning of this appendix notes the ten or so forms that are Judicial Council forms. These forms are in Adobe Acrobat PDF format, so to use them, you need Adobe *Reader* installed on your computer (available free at www.adobe.com).

In addition to being available on the Nolo website, the Judicial Council forms are available at www.courts.ca.gov/forms.htm. To find a specific Judicial Council form on the Council's website, just search for the name of the form and the form number. The Judicial Council forms will have the words "Judicial Council of California" in the bottom left-hand corner of the form and revision date, and will have a form number in the upper right; for example, the Answer—Unlawful Detainer is Judicial Council form UD-105.

You might find it easiest to complete a Judicial Council form on the Council's website. (Because the Judicial Council revises forms from time to time, you can make sure you have the most current form available.) If you want to download a form from the Judicial Council site that you will complete online, consult the useful information on filling out one of the official court forms in the "Using Judicial Council forms" section at www.courts.ca.gov/selfhelp-forms.htm.

Some of you might prefer to download the relevant forms (Nolo or Judicial Council forms), complete them online, and then print. If you're old school and prefer to use a typewriter, you may type in the required information in any of the forms in this book. Courts are required to accept forms that are filled in by hand.

Forms

Form	Discussed in Chapter
Landlord-Tenant Checklist	Chapter 1
Fixed-Term Residential Lease	Chapter 1
Month-to-Month Residential Rental Agreement	Chapter 1
Notice to Repair	Chapter 6
Notice of Rent Withholding	Chapter 6
Agreement Regarding Tenant Alterations to Rental Unit	Chapter 8
Indemnification of Landlord	Chapter 12
Declaration Re Small Estate of Less Than $150,000	Chapter 12
Request to Waive Court Fees (a Judicial Council form)	Chapter 15
Order on Court Fee Waiver (Superior Court) (a Judicial Council form)	Chapter 15
Prejudgment Claim of Right to Possession (a Judicial Council form)	Chapter 15
Blank Numbered Legal Paper	Chapter 15
Blank Numbered Legal Paper With Superior Court Heading	Chapter 15
Proof of Service by First-Class Mail—Civil (a Judicial Council form)	Chapter 15
Attachment to Proof of Service by First-Class Mail—Civil (Persons Served) (a Judicial Council form)	Chapter 15
Demurrer	Chapter 15
Points and Authorities in Support of Demurrer	Chapter 15
Notice of Hearing on Demurrer	Chapter 15
Request for Judicial Notice	Chapter 15
Answer—Unlawful Detainer (a Judicial Council form)	Chapter 15
Attachment	Chapter 15
Request to Inspect and for Production of Documents	Chapter 15
Form Interrogatories—Unlawful Detainer (a Judicial Council form)	Chapter 15
Settlement Agreement	Chapter 15
Demand for Jury Trial	Chapter 15
Application and Declaration for Relief From Eviction	Chapter 15
Notice of Motion and Points and Authorities for Relief From Eviction	Chapter 15
Order Granting Relief From Eviction	Chapter 15
Application and Declaration for Stay of Eviction	Chapter 15
Order Granting Stay of Eviction	Chapter 15
Notice of Appeal and Notice to Prepare Clerk's Transcript	Chapter 15
Claim of Right to Possession and Notice of Hearing (a Judicial Council form)	Chapter 15

Landlord/Tenant Checklist
General Condition of Rental Unit and Premises

Street Address _____ Unit Number _____ City _____

	Condition on Arrival	Condition on Initial Move-Out Inspection	Condition on Departure	Actual or Estimated Cost of Cleaning, Repair/Replacement
Living Room				
Floors & Floor Coverings				
Drapes & Window Coverings				
Walls & Ceilings				
Light Fixtures				
Windows, Screens, & Doors				
Front Door & Locks				
Smoke Detector				
Fireplace				
Other				
Kitchen				
Floors & Floor Coverings				
Walls & Ceilings				
Light Fixtures				
Cabinets				
Counters				
Stove/Oven				
Refrigerator				
Dishwasher				
Garbage Disposal				
Sink & Plumbing				
Smoke Detector				
Other				

	Condition on Arrival	Condition on Initial Move-Out Inspection	Condition on Departure	Actual or Estimated Cost of Cleaning, Repair/Replacement
Dining Room				
Floors & Floor Coverings				
Walls & Ceilings				
Light Fixtures				
Windows, Screens, & Doors				
Smoke Detector				
Other				
Bathroom				
Floors & Floor Coverings				
Walls & Ceilings				
Windows, Screens, & Doors				
Light Fixtures				
Bathtub/Shower				
Sinks & Counters				
Toilet				
Other				
Other				
Bedroom				
Floors & Floor Coverings				
Windows, Screens, & Doors				
Walls & Ceilings				
Light Fixtures				
Smoke Detector				
Other				
Other				
Other				

	Condition on Arrival	Condition on Initial Move-Out Inspection	Condition on Departure	Actual or Estimated Cost of Cleaning, Repair/Replacement
Other Areas				
Heating System				
Air-Conditioning				
Lawn/Garden				
Stairs & Hallway				
Patio, Terrace, Deck, etc.				
Basement				
Parking Area				
Other				
Other				
Other				
Other				
Other				

☐ Tenants acknowledge that all smoke detectors were tested in their presence and found to be in working order, and that the testing procedure was explained to them. Tenants agree to promptly notify Landlord in writing should any smoke detector appear to be malfunctioning or inoperable. Tenants will not refuse Landlord access for the purpose of inspecting, maintaining, repairing, or installing legally required smoke detectors.

Notes: _____

_____

_____

_____

_____

_____

_____

_____

Furnished Property

	Condition on Arrival	Condition on Initial Move-Out Inspection	Condition on Departure	Actual or Estimated Cost of Cleaning, Repair/Replacement
Living Room				
Coffee Table				
End Tables				
Lamps				
Chairs				
Sofa				
Other				
Other				
Kitchen				
Broiler Pan				
Ice Trays				
Other				
Other				
Dining Room				
Chairs				
Stools				
Table				
Other				
Other				
Bathroom				
Mirrors				
Shower Curtain				
Hamper				
Other				

	Condition on Arrival	Condition on Initial Move-Out Inspection	Condition on Departure	Actual or Estimated Cost of Cleaning, Repair/Replacement
Bedroom				
Beds (single)				
Beds (double)				
Chairs				
Chests				
Dressing Tables				
Lamps				
Mirrors				
Night Tables				
Other				
Other				
Other Area				
Bookcases				
Desks				
Pictures				
Other				
Other				

Use this space to provide any additional explanation:

Landlord/Tenant Checklist completed on moving in on _____, 20 ____ .

_____ and _____
Landlord/Manager   Tenant

_____
                                          Tenant

_____
                                          Tenant

Landlord/Tenant Checklist completed at Initial Move-Out Inspection on _____, 20 ____ .

_____ and _____
Landlord/Manager   Tenant

_____
                                          Tenant

_____
                                          Tenant

Landlord/Tenant Checklist completed on moving out on _____, 20 ____ .

_____ and _____
Landlord/Manager   Tenant

_____
                                          Tenant

_____
                                          Tenant

Fixed-Term Residential Lease

1. **Identification of Landlord and Tenants.** This Agreement is made and entered into on _____ , 20_____ , between _____ ("Tenants") and _____ ("Landlord"). Each Tenant is jointly and severally liable for the payment of rent and performance of all other terms of this Agreement.

2. **Identification of Premises and Occupants.** Subject to the terms and conditions set forth in this Agreement, Landlord rents to Tenants, and Tenants rent from Landlord, for residential purposes only, the premises located at _____ _____ , California ("the premises"). The premises will be occupied by the undersigned Tenants and the following minor children: _____ _____ _____ .

3. **Limits on Use and Occupancy.** The premises are to be used only as a private residence for Tenants and any minors listed in Clause 2 of this Agreement, and for no other purpose without Landlord's prior written consent. Occupancy by guests for more than ten days in any six-month period is prohibited without Landlord's written consent and will be considered a breach of this Agreement.

4. **Defining the Term of the Tenancy.** The term of the rental will begin on _____ , 20____ and will expire on _____ , 20_____ . Should Tenants vacate before expiration of the term, Tenants will be liable for the balance of the rent for the remainder of the term, less any rent Landlord collects or could have collected from a replacement tenant by reasonably attempting to rerent. Tenants who vacate before expiration of the term are also responsible for Landlord's costs of advertising for a replacement tenant.

5. **Amount and Schedule for the Payment of Rent.** Tenants will pay to Landlord a monthly rent of $ _____ , payable in advance on the _____ day of each month, except when that day falls on a weekend or legal holiday, in which case rent is due on the next business day. Rent will be paid to _____ _____ at _____ _____ , or at such other place as Landlord may designate.

   ☐ a. The form of payment will be   ☐ cash   ☐ personal check   ☐ certified funds or money order

            ☐ credit card   ☐ bank debit   ☐ automatic credit card debit

   ☐ b. [*Check if rent will be accepted personally, not by mail.*] Rent is accepted during the following days and hours: _____ _____

   ☐ c. [*Check if rent will be paid by electronic funds transfer.*] Rent may be paid by electronic funds transfer to account number _____ in the name of _____ at _____ (*institution*), _____ (*branch*), a financial institution located at _____ (*bank address*), and can be reached at _____ (*telephone number*).

   ☐ d. [*Prorated rent.*] On signing this agreement, Tenants will pay to Landlord for the period of _____ , 20____ , through _____ , 20____ , the sum of $ _____ as rent, payable in advance.

6. **Late Charges.** Because Landlord and Tenants agree that actual damages for late rent payments are very difficult or impossible to determine, Landlord and Tenants agree to the following stated late charge as liquidated damages. Tenants will pay Landlord a late charge if Tenants fail to pay the rent in full within _____ days after the date it is due. The late charge will be $ _____ , plus $ _____ for each additional day that the rent continues to be unpaid. The total late charge for any one month will not exceed $ _____ . Landlord does not waive the right to insist on payment of the rent in full on the date it is due.

7. **Returned Check and Other Bank Charges.** In the event any check offered by Tenants to Landlord in payment of rent or any other amount due under this Agreement is returned for lack of sufficient funds, a "stop payment," or any other reason, Tenants will pay Landlord a returned check charge as follows: $25 for the first returned check, and $35 for subsequent returned checks.

8. **Amount and Payment of Deposits.** On signing this Agreement, Tenants will pay to Landlord the sum of $_____ as a security deposit. Tenants may not, without Landlord's prior written consent, apply this security deposit to the last month's rent or to any other sum due under this Agreement. Within three weeks after Tenants have vacated the premises, Landlord will furnish Tenants with an itemized written statement of the reasons for, and the dollar amount of, any of the security deposit retained by the Landlord, receipts for work done or items purchased, if available, along with a check for any deposit balance. Under Section 1950.5 of the California Civil Code, Landlord may withhold only that portion of Tenants' security deposit necessary to: (1) remedy any default by Tenants in the payment of rent; (2) repair damages to the premises exclusive of ordinary wear and tear; (3) clean the premises if necessary to restore it to the same level of cleanliness it was in at the beginning of the tenancy; and (4) remedy any default by tenants, under this Agreement, to restore, replace, or return any of Landlord's personal property mentioned in this Agreement, including but not limited to the property referred to in Clause 11.

    Landlord will pay Tenants interest on all security deposits as follows:

    ☐ a. Per state law, no interest payments are required.

    ☐ b. Local law requires that interest be paid or credited, or Landlord has decided voluntarily to do so, which will occur as follows: _____
    _____
    _____ .

9. **Utilities.** Tenants will be responsible for payment of all utility charges, except for the following, which shall be paid by Landlord:

    _____
    _____ .

    ☐ Tenants' gas or electric meter serves area(s) outside of their premises, and there are not separate gas and electric meters for Tenants' unit and the area(s) outside their unit. Tenants and Landlord agree as follows: _____
    _____
    _____ .

10. **Prohibition of Assignment and Subletting.** Tenants will not sublet any part of the premises or assign this Agreement without the prior written consent of Landlord.

    ☐ a. Tenants shall not sublet or rent any part of the Premises for short-term stays of any duration, including but not limited to vacation rentals.

    ☐ b. Short-stay rentals are prohibited except as authorized by law. Any short-stay rental is expressly conditioned upon the tenants' following all regulations, laws, and other requirements as a condition to offering a short-stay rental. Failure to follow all laws, ordinances, regulations, and other requirements, including any registration requirement, will be deemed a material, noncurable breach of this Agreement and will furnish cause for termination.

11. **Condition of the Premises.** Tenants agree to: (1) keep the premises clean and sanitary and in good repair and, upon termination of the tenancy, to return the premises to Landlord in a condition identical to that which existed when Tenants took occupancy, except for ordinary wear and tear; (2) immediately notify Landlord of any defects or dangerous conditions in and about the premises of which they become aware; and (3) reimburse Landlord, on demand by Landlord, for the cost of any repairs to the premises, including Landlord's personal property therein, damaged by Tenants or their guests or invitees through misuse or neglect.

Tenants acknowledge that they have examined the premises, including appliances, fixtures, carpets, drapes, and paint, and have found them to be in good, safe, and clean condition and repair, except as noted here: _____

_____

_____

_____

_____ .

12. **Possession of the Premises.** If, after signing this Agreement, Tenants fail to take possession of the premises, they will be responsible for paying rent and complying with all other terms of this Agreement. In the event Landlord is unable to deliver possession of the premises to Tenants for any reason not within Landlord's control, including, but not limited to, failure of prior occupants to vacate or partial or complete destruction of the premises, Tenants will have the right to terminate this Agreement. In such event, Landlord's liability to Tenants will be limited to the return of all sums previously paid by Tenants to Landlord.

13. **Pets.** No animal may be kept on the premises without Landlord's prior written consent, except animals needed by tenants who have a disability, as that term is understood by law, and: _____

_____ , under the following conditions:

_____ .

14. **Landlord's Access for Inspection and Emergency.** Landlord or Landlord's agents may enter the premises, with or without Tenant's presence, to make necessary or agreed repairs, alterations, decorations, or improvements; to supply necessary or agreed services; to inspect for waterbed violations; to show the premises to prospective or actual buyers, mortgagees, tenants, workers, or contractors; to conduct an initial move-out inspection as provided by California Civil Code Section 1950.5(f); and pursuant to court order or agreement with Tenant. Landlord will give Tenant reasonable notice of intent to enter (at least 24 hours' notice) and will enter only during regular business hours. When entry is for the purpose of an initial move-out inspection, the notice period will be 48 hours. Notices will include the purpose, date, and approximate time of the intended entry. Landlord may enter without notice and at any time in case of emergency or when Tenant has abandoned or surrendered the premises.

15. **Extended Absences by Tenants.** Tenants agree to notify Landlord in the event that they will be away from the premises for _____ consecutive days or more. During such absence, Landlord may enter the premises at times reasonably necessary to maintain the property and inspect for damage and needed repairs.

16. **Prohibitions Against Violating Laws and Causing Disturbances.** Tenants are entitled to quiet enjoyment of the premises. Tenants and their guests or invitees will not use the premises or adjacent areas in such a way as to: (1) violate any law or ordinance, including laws prohibiting the use, possession, or sale of illegal drugs; (2) commit waste or nuisance; or (3) annoy, disturb, inconvenience, or interfere with the quiet enjoyment and peace and quiet of any other tenant or nearby resident.

17. **Repairs and Alterations**

    a. Tenants will not, without Landlord's prior written consent, alter, rekey, or install any locks to the premises or install or alter any burglar alarm system. Tenants will provide Landlord with a key or keys capable of unlocking all such rekeyed or new locks as well as instructions on how to disarm any altered or new burglar alarm system.

    b. Except as provided by law or as authorized by the prior written consent of Landlord, Tenants will not make any repairs or alterations to the premises. Landlord will not unreasonably withhold consent for such repairs, but will not authorize repairs that require advanced skill or workmanship or that would be dangerous to undertake. Landlord will not authorize repairs unless such repairs are likely to return the item or element of the rental to its predamaged state of usefulness and attractiveness.

18. **Damage to the Premises.** In the event the premises are partially or totally damaged or destroyed by fire or other cause, the following will apply:

a. If the premises are totally damaged and destroyed, Landlord will have the option to: (1) repair such damage and restore the premises, with this Agreement continuing in full force and effect, except that Tenants' rent will be abated while repairs are being made; or (2) give written notice to Tenants terminating this Agreement at any time within thirty (30) days after such damage, and specifying the termination date; in the event that Landlord gives such notice, this Agreement will expire and all of Tenants' rights pursuant to this Agreement will cease.

b. Landlord will have the option to determine that the premises are only partially damaged by fire or other cause. In that event, Landlord will attempt to repair such damage and restore the premises within thirty (30) days after such damage. If only part of the premises cannot be used, Tenants must pay rent only for the usable part, to be determined solely by Landlord. If Landlord is unable to complete repairs within thirty (30) days, this Agreement will expire and all of Tenants' rights pursuant to this Agreement will terminate at the option of either party.

c. In the event that Tenants, or their guests or invitees, in any way caused or contributed to the damage of the premises, Landlord will have the right to terminate this Agreement at any time, and Tenants will be responsible for all losses, including, but not limited to, damage and repair costs as well as loss of rental income.

d. Landlord will not be required to repair or replace any property brought onto the premises by Tenants.

19. **Tenants' Financial Responsibility and Renters' Insurance.** Tenants agree to accept financial responsibility for any loss or damage to personal property belonging to Tenants and their guests and invitees caused by theft, fire, or any other cause. Landlord assumes no liability for any such loss. Landlord recommends that Tenants obtain a renters' insurance policy from a recognized insurance firm to cover Tenants' liability, personal property damage, and damage to the premises.

20. **Waterbeds.** No waterbed or other item of water-filled furniture may be kept on the premises without Landlord's written consent.

☐ Landlord grants Tenants permission to keep water-filled furniture on the premises. Attachment _____ : Agreement Regarding Use of Waterbed is attached to and incorporated into this Agreement by reference.

21. **Tenant Rules and Regulations**

☐ Tenant acknowledges receipt of, and has read a copy of, Landlord's rules and regulations, which are attached to and incorporated into this agreement by reference (Attachment _____). Tenant understands that serious or repeated violations of the rules may be grounds for termination. Landlord may change the rules and regulations without notice.

22. **Payment of Attorney Fees in a Lawsuit.** In any action or legal proceeding to enforce any part of this Agreement, the prevailing party ☐ will not / ☐ will recover reasonable attorney fees and court costs.

23. **Authority to Receive Legal Papers.** Any person managing the premises, the Landlord, and anyone designated by the Landlord are authorized to accept service of process and receive other notices and demands, which may be delivered to:

☐ a. the manager, at the following address and telephone number: _____
_____
_____

☐ b. the Landlord, at the following address and telephone number: _____
_____
_____

☐ c. the following: _____
_____
_____
_____
_____

24. **Cash-Only Rent.** Tenants will pay rent in the form specified above in Clause 5a. Tenants understand that if Tenants pay rent with a check that is not honored due to insufficient funds, or with a money order or cashier's check whose issuer has been instructed to stop payment, Landlord has the legal right to demand that rent be paid only in cash for up to three months after Tenants have received proper notice. (CC § 1947.3.) In that event, Landlord will give Tenants the legally required notice, and Tenants agree to abide by this change in the terms of this tenancy.

25. **Additional Provisions**

☐ a. None

☐ b. Additional provisions are as follows: _____

_____

_____ .

26. **State Database Disclosure.** Notice: Pursuant to Section 290.46 of the Penal Code, information about specified registered sex offenders is made available to the public via an Internet website maintained by the Department of Justice at www.meganslaw.ca.gov. Depending on an offender's criminal history, this information will include either the address at which the offender resides or the community of residence and ZIP Code in which he or she resides.

27. **Lead-Based Paint and Other Disclosures.** Tenant acknowledges that Landlord has made the following disclosures regarding the premises:

☐ Disclosure of Information on Lead-Based Paint and/or Lead-Based Paint Hazards

☐ Other disclosures: _____

_____

_____ .

28. **Grounds for Termination of Tenancy.** The failure of Tenants or Tenants' guests or invitees to comply with any term of this Agreement, or the misrepresentation of any material fact on Tenants' Rental Application, is grounds for termination of the tenancy, with appropriate notice to Tenants and procedures as required by law.

29. **Entire Agreement.** This document constitutes the entire Agreement between the parties, and no promises or representations, other than those contained here and those implied by law, have been made by Landlord or Tenants. Any modifications to this Agreement must be in writing signed by Landlord and Tenants.

_____   _____
Landlord/Manager   Date

_____
Landlord/Manager's Street Address, City, State, & Zip

_____

_____   _____
Tenant   Date

_____   _____
Tenant   Date

_____   _____
Tenant   Date

Month-to-Month Residential Rental Agreement

1. **Identification of Landlord and Tenants.** This Agreement is made and entered into on _____ , 20_____ , between _____ ("Tenants") and _____ ("Landlord"). Each Tenant is jointly and severally liable for the payment of rent and performance of all other terms of this Agreement.

2. **Identification of Premises and Occupants.** Subject to the terms and conditions set forth in this Agreement, Landlord rents to Tenants, and Tenants rent from Landlord, for residential purposes only, the premises located at _____ , California ("the premises"). The premises will be occupied by the undersigned Tenants and the following minor children: _____ _____ _____ .

3. **Limits on Use and Occupancy.** The premises are to be used only as a private residence for Tenants and any minors listed in Clause 2 of this Agreement, and for no other purpose without Landlord's prior written consent. Occupancy by guests for more than ten days in any six-month period is prohibited without Landlord's written consent and will be considered a breach of this Agreement.

4. **Defining the Term of the Tenancy.** The rental will begin on _____ , 20_____ , and will continue on a month-to-month basis. This tenancy may be terminated by Landlord or Tenants and may be modified by Landlord, by giving 30 days' written notice to the other, or 60 days' notice by Landlord to Tenant, in accordance with Civil Code Section 827 or 1946.1 (subject to any local rent control ordinances that may apply).

5. **Amount and Schedule for the Payment of Rent.** Tenants will pay to Landlord a monthly rent of $ _____ , payable in advance on the _____ day of each month, except when that day falls on a weekend or legal holiday, in which case rent is due on the next business day. Rent will be paid to _____ _____ at _____ _____ , or at such other place as Landlord may designate.

   ☐ a. The form of payment will be   ☐ cash   ☐ personal check   ☐ certified funds or money order
   ☐ credit card   ☐ bank debit   ☐ automatic credit card debit

   ☐ b. [*Check if rent will be accepted personally, not by mail.*] Rent is accepted during the following days and hours: _____ _____

   ☐ c. [*Check if rent will be paid by electronic funds transfer.*] Rent may be paid by electronic funds transfer to account number _____ in the name of _____ at _____ (*institution*), _____ (*branch*), a financial institution located at _____ (*bank address*), and and can reached at _____ (*telephone number*).

   ☐ d. [*Prorated rent.*] On signing this agreement, Tenants will pay to Landlord for the period of _____ , 20_____ , through _____ , 20_____ , the sum of $ _____ as rent, payable in advance.

6. **Late Charges.** Because Landlord and Tenants agree that actual damages for late rent payments are very difficult or impossible to determine, Landlord and Tenants agree to the following stated late charge as liquidated damages. Tenants will pay Landlord a late charge if Tenants fail to pay the rent in full within _____ days after the date it is due. The late charge will be $ _____ , plus $ _____ for each additional day that the rent continues to be unpaid. The total late charge for any one month will not exceed $ _____ . Landlord does not waive the right to insist on payment of the rent in full on the date it is due.

7. **Returned Check and Other Bank Charges.** In the event any check offered by Tenants to Landlord in payment of rent or any other amount due under this Agreement is returned for lack of sufficient funds, a "stop payment," or any other reason, Tenants will pay Landlord a returned check charge as follows: $25 for the first returned check, and $35 for subsequent returned checks.

8. **Amount and Payment of Deposits.** On signing this Agreement, Tenants will pay to Landlord the sum of $_____ as a security deposit. Tenants may not, without Landlord's prior written consent, apply this security deposit to the last month's rent or to any other sum due under this Agreement. Within three weeks after Tenants have vacated the premises, Landlord will furnish Tenants with an itemized written statement of the reasons for, and the dollar amount of, any of the security deposit retained by the Landlord, along with a check for any deposit balance. Under Section 1950.5 of the California Civil Code, Landlord may withhold only that portion of Tenants' security deposit necessary to: (1) remedy any default by Tenants in the payment of rent; (2) repair damages to the premises exclusive of ordinary wear and tear; (3) clean the premises if necessary to restore it to the same level of cleanliness it was in at the beginning of the tenancy; and (4) remedy any default by tenants, under this Agreement, to restore, replace, or return any of Landlord's personal property mentioned in this Agreement, including but not limited to the property referred to in Clause 11.

   Landlord will pay Tenants interest on all security deposits as follows:

   ☐ a. Per state law, no interest payments are required.

   ☐ b. Local law requires that interest be paid or credited, which will occur as follows: _____
   _____
   _____ .

9. **Utilities.** Tenants will be responsible for payment of all utility charges, except for the following, which shall be paid by Landlord: _____
   _____
   _____ .

   ☐ Tenants' gas or electric meter serves area(s) outside of their premises, and there are not separate gas and electric meters for Tenants' unit and the area(s) outside their unit. Tenants and Landlord agree as follows: _____
   _____
   _____ .

10. **Prohibition of Assignment and Subletting.** Tenants will not sublet any part of the premises or assign this Agreement without the prior written consent of Landlord. Neither shall Tenants sublet or rent any part of the premises for short-term stays of any duration, including but not limited to vacation rentals.

11. **Condition of the Premises.** Tenants agree to: (1) keep the premises clean and sanitary and in good repair and, upon termination of the tenancy, to return the premises to Landlord in a condition identical to that which existed when Tenants took occupancy, except for ordinary wear and tear; (2) immediately notify Landlord of any defects or dangerous conditions in and about the premises of which they become aware; and (3) reimburse Landlord, on demand by Landlord, for the cost of any repairs to the premises, including Landlord's personal property therein, damaged by Tenants or their guests or invitees through misuse or neglect.

   Tenants acknowledge that they have examined the premises, including appliances, fixtures, carpets, drapes, and paint, and have found them to be in good, safe, and clean condition and repair, except as noted here: _____
   _____
   _____
   _____
   _____
   _____
   _____ .

12. **Possession of the Premises.** If, after signing this Agreement, Tenants fail to take possession of the premises, they will be responsible for paying rent and complying with all other terms of this Agreement. In the event Landlord is unable to deliver possession of the premises to Tenants for any reason not within Landlord's control, including, but not limited to, failure of prior occupants to vacate or partial or complete destruction of the premises, Tenants will have the right to terminate this Agreement. In such event, Landlord's liability to Tenants will be limited to the return of all sums previously paid by Tenants to Landlord.

13. **Pets.** No animal may be kept on the premises without Landlord's prior written consent, except animals needed by tenants who have a disability, as that term is understood by law, and: _____ , _____ under the following conditions: _____ .

14. **Landlord's Access for Inspection and Emergency.** Landlord or Landlord's agents may enter the premises, with or without Tenant's presence, to make necessary or agreed repairs, alterations, decorations, or improvements; to supply necessary or agreed services; to inspect for waterbed violations; to show the premises to prospective or actual buyers, mortgagees, tenants, workers, or contractors; to conduct an initial move-out inspection as provided by California Civil Code Section 1950.5(f); and pursuant to court order or agreement with Tenant. Landlord will give Tenant reasonable notice of intent to enter (at least 24 hours' notice) and will enter only during regular business hours. When entry is for the purpose of an initial move-out inspection, the notice period will be 48 hours. Notices will include the purpose, date, and approximate time of the intended entry. Landlord may enter without notice and at any time in case of emergency or when Tenant has abandoned or surrendered the premises.

15. **Extended Absences by Tenants.** Tenants agree to notify Landlord in the event that they will be away from the premises for _____ consecutive days or more. During such absence, Landlord may enter the premises at times reasonably necessary to maintain the property and inspect for damage and needed repairs.

16. **Prohibitions Against Violating Laws and Causing Disturbances.** Tenants are entitled to quiet enjoyment of the premises. Tenants and their guests or invitees will not use the premises or adjacent areas in such a way as to: (1) violate any law or ordinance, including laws prohibiting the use, possession, or sale of illegal drugs; (2) commit waste or nuisance; or (3) annoy, disturb, inconvenience, or interfere with the quiet enjoyment and peace and quiet of any other tenant or nearby resident.

17. **Repairs and Alterations**

    a. Tenants will not, without Landlord's prior written consent, alter, rekey, or install any locks to the premises or install or alter any burglar alarm system. Tenants will provide Landlord with a key or keys capable of unlocking all such rekeyed or new locks as well as instructions on how to disarm any altered or new burglar alarm system.

    b. Except as provided by law or as authorized by the prior written consent of Landlord, Tenants will not make any repairs or alterations to the premises. Landlord will not unreasonably withhold consent for such repairs, but will not authorize repairs that require advanced skill or workmanship or that would be dangerous to undertake. Landlord will not authorize repairs unless such repairs are likely to return the item or element of the rental to its predamaged state of usefulness and attractiveness.

18. **Damage to the Premises.** In the event the premises are partially or totally damaged or destroyed by fire or other cause, the following will apply:

    a. If the premises are totally damaged and destroyed, Landlord will have the option to: (1) repair such damage and restore the premises, with this Agreement continuing in full force and effect, except that Tenants' rent will be abated while repairs are being made; or (2) give written notice to Tenants terminating this Agreement at any time within thirty (30) days after such damage, and specifying the termination date; in the event that Landlord gives such notice, this Agreement will expire and all of Tenants' rights pursuant to this Agreement will cease.

    b. Landlord will have the option to determine that the premises are only partially damaged by fire or other cause. In that event, Landlord will attempt to repair such damage and restore the premises within thirty (30) days after such damage. If only part of the premises cannot be used, Tenants must pay rent only for the usable part, to be determined solely by Landlord. If Landlord is unable to complete repairs within thirty (30) days, this Agreement will expire and all of Tenants' rights pursuant to this Agreement will terminate at the option of either party.

c. In the event that Tenants, or their guests or invitees, in any way caused or contributed to the damage of the premises, Landlord will have the right to terminate this Agreement at any time, and Tenants will be responsible for all losses, including, but not limited to, damage and repair costs as well as loss of rental income.

d. Landlord will not be required to repair or replace any property brought onto the premises by Tenants.

19. **Tenants' Financial Responsibility and Renters' Insurance.** Tenants agree to accept financial responsibility for any loss or damage to personal property belonging to Tenants and their guests and invitees caused by theft, fire, or any other cause. Landlord assumes no liability for any such loss. Landlord recommends that Tenants obtain a renters' insurance policy from a recognized insurance firm to cover Tenants' liability, personal property damage, and damage to the premises.

20. **Waterbeds.** No waterbed or other item of water-filled furniture may be kept on the premises without Landlord's written consent.

☐ Landlord grants Tenants permission to keep water-filled furniture on the premises. Attachment _____ : Agreement Regarding Use of Waterbed is attached to and incorporated into this Agreement by reference.

21. **Tenant Rules and Regulations**

☐ Tenant acknowledges receipt of, and has read a copy of, Landlord's rules and regulations, which are attached to and incorporated into this agreement by reference (Attachment _____). Tenant understands that serious or repeated violations of the rules may be grounds for termination. Landlord may change the rules and regulations without notice.

22. **Payment of Attorney Fees in a Lawsuit.** In any action or legal proceeding to enforce any part of this Agreement, the prevailing party ☐ will not / ☐ will recover reasonable attorney fees and court costs.

23. **Authority to Receive Legal Papers.** Any person managing the premises, the Landlord, and anyone designated by the Landlord are authorized to accept service of process and receive other notices and demands, which may be delivered to:

☐ a. the manager, at the following address and telephone number: _____
_____
_____

☐ b. the Landlord, at the following address and telephone number: _____
_____
_____
_____

☐ c. the following: _____
_____
_____
_____

24. **Cash-Only Rent.** Tenants will pay rent in the form specified above in Clause 5a. Tenants understand that if Tenants pay rent with a check that is not honored due to insufficient funds, or with a money order or cashier's check whose issuer has been instructed to stop payment, Landlord has the legal right to demand that rent be paid only in cash for up to three months after Tenants have received proper notice. (CC § 1947.3.) In that event, Landlord will give Tenants the legally required notice, and Tenants agree to abide by this change in the terms of this tenancy.

25. **Additional Provisions**

☐ a. None

☐ b. Additional provisions are as follows: _____
_____
_____
_____ .

26. **State Database Disclosure.** Notice: Pursuant to Section 290.46 of the Penal Code, information about specified registered sex offenders is made available to the public via an Internet website maintained by the Department of Justice at www.meganslaw.ca.gov. Depending on an offender's criminal history, this information will include either the address at which the offender resides or the community of residence and ZIP Code in which he or she resides.

27. **Lead-Based Paint and Other Disclosures.** Tenant acknowledges that Landlord has made the following disclosures regarding the premises:

☐ Disclosure of Information on Lead-Based Paint and/or Lead-Based Paint Hazards

☐ Other disclosures: _____

_____

_____ .

28. **Grounds for Termination of Tenancy.** The failure of Tenants or Tenants' guests or invitees to comply with any term of this Agreement, or the misrepresentation of any material fact on Tenants' Rental Application, is grounds for termination of the tenancy, with appropriate notice to Tenants and procedures as required by law.

29. **Entire Agreement.** This document constitutes the entire Agreement between the parties, and no promises or representations, other than those contained here and those implied by law, have been made by Landlord or Tenants. Any modifications to this Agreement must be in writing signed by Landlord and Tenants.

_____   _____
Landlord/Manager   Date

_____
Landlord/Manager's Street Address, City, State, & Zip

_____   _____
Tenant   Date

_____   _____
Tenant   Date

_____   _____
Tenant   Date

Notice to Repair

To _____ ,

Landlord of the premises located at _____

_____ .

    NOTICE IS HEREBY GIVEN that unless certain defects on the premises are repaired within a reasonable time, the undersigned tenant shall exercise any and all rights accruing to him or her pursuant to law, including those granted by California Civil Code Sections 1941–1942.

    The defects are the following: _____

_____

_____

_____

_____

_____

_____

_____

_____

_____ .

_____   _____

Signature of Tenant   Date

Notice of Rent Withholding

To _____ ,

Landlord of the premises located at _____

_____ .

   NOTICE IS HEREBY GIVEN that because of your failure to comply with your implied warranty of habitability by refusing to repair defects on the premises, as previously demanded of you, the undersigned tenant has elected to withhold this month's rent in accordance with California law. Rent payments will be resumed in the future, as they become due, only after said defects have been properly repaired.

_____   _____

Signature of Tenant   Date

Authority: *Green v. Superior Court*, 10 Cal.3d 616 (1974).

Agreement Regarding Tenant Alterations to Rental Unit

_____ (Landlord)

and _____ (Tenant)

agree as follows:

1. Tenant may make the following alterations to the rental unit at: _____
   _____ .

2. Tenant will accomplish the work described in Paragraph 1 by using the following materials and procedures: _____
   _____
   _____ .

3. Tenant will do only the work outlined in Paragraph 1 using only the materials and procedures outlined in Paragraph 2.

4. The alterations carried out by Tenant (check either a or b):
   ☐ a. will become Landlord's property and are not to be removed by Tenant during or at the end of the tenancy
   ☐ b. will be considered Tenant's personal property, and as such may be removed by Tenant at any time up to the end of the tenancy. Tenant promises to return the premises to their original condition upon removing the improvement.

5. Landlord will reimburse Tenant only for the costs checked below:
   ☐ the cost of materials listed in Paragraph 2
   ☐ labor costs at the rate of $ _____ per hour for work done in a workmanlike manner acceptable to Landlord up to _____ hours.

6. After receiving appropriate documentation of the cost of materials and labor, Landlord shall make any payment called for under Paragraph 5 by:
   ☐ lump sum payment, within _____ days of receiving documentation of costs, or
   ☐ by reducing Tenant's rent by $ _____ per month for the number of months necessary to cover the total amounts under the terms of this agreement.

7. If under Paragraph 4 of this contract the alterations are Tenant's personal property, Tenant must return the premises to their original condition upon removing the alterations. If Tenant fails to do this, Landlord will deduct the cost to restore the premises to their original condition from Tenant's security deposit. If the security deposit is insufficient to cover the costs of restoration, Landlord may take legal action, if necessary, to collect the balance.

8. If Tenant fails to remove an improvement that is his or her personal property on or before the end of the tenancy, it will be considered the property of Landlord, who may choose to keep the improvement (with no financial liability to Tenant), or remove it and charge Tenant for the costs of removal and restoration. Landlord may deduct any costs of removal and restoration from Tenant's security deposit. If the security deposit is insufficient to cover the costs of removal and restoration, Landlord may take legal action, if necessary, to collect the balance.

9. If Tenant removes an item that is Landlord's property, Tenant will owe Landlord the fair market value of the item removed plus any costs incurred by Landlord to restore the premises to their original condition.

10. If Landlord and Tenant are involved in any legal proceeding arising out of this agreement, the prevailing party shall recover reasonable attorney fees, court costs, and any costs reasonably necessary to collect a judgment.

_____   _____
Signature of Landlord   Date

_____   _____
Signature of Tenant   Date

Indemnification of Landlord

This indemnification agreement is between _____, Landlord/Manager of the rental property at _____ and _____ [*Visitor*]. This agreement concerns Visitor's access to the Rental Premises rented by _____ [*Deceased Tenant*].

No executor or administrator has been appointed to represent the estate of Deceased Tenant. Visitor is Deceased Tenant's _____ (for example, daughter, friend), and is taking responsibility, in the absence of a court-appointed personal representative, to gather and dispose of Deceased Tenant's property according to California law.

[*Check if applicable*]

☐ Visitor is Deceased Tenant's executor.

Visitor accepts responsibility for any liability to Deceased Tenant's estate or third parties resulting from Visitor's removal of property from the Rental Premises.

In the event of any third-party claim, demand, suit, action, or proceeding [Claim] against Landlord based upon Visitor's removal or use of property, Landlord will have the right to select counsel to defend itself. If the third-party claim results in an enforceable judgment or is settled, Visitor will indemnify and hold harmless Landlord and any successors or assigns. Visitor will cooperate fully in the defense of any such Claim. Landlord may settle any such Claim against it or waive any appeal of any judgment of a trial court or arbitrator against it. If a Claim is successfully defended, Visitor's indemnity will be limited to fifty percent (50%) of the cost of defense.

_____   _____
Visitor's signature   Date

_____
Print name

_____   _____
Landlord or Manager's signature   Date

_____
Print name

Visitor's contact information: Home

_____   _____
Street   City, state, zip

_____   _____
Phone   Cell

Visitor's contact information: Work

_____   _____
Street   City, state, zip

_____   _____
Phone   Cell

Other ID (such as a driver's license): _____

DECLARATION RE SMALL ESTATE OF LESS THAN $150,000
CALIFORNIA PROBATE CODE SECTIONS 13100-13115

I, _____ , state as follows:

1. _____ (name of decedent), died on

_____ (date of death) in _____ (place of death).

2. At least 40 days have elapsed since the death of the decedent, as shown in a certified copy of the decedent's death certificate, attached to this declaration.

3. ☐ No proceeding is now being or has been conducted in California for administration of the decedent's estate. **OR** ☐ The decedent's Personal Representative has consented in writing to the payment, transfer, or delivery to me of the property described in this declaration.

4. The current gross fair market value of the decedent's real and personal property in California, excluding the property described in Probate Code Section 13050, does not exceed $150,000.

5. The following property is to be paid, transferred or delivered to me according to Probate Code Section 13100: [*describe the property to be transferred*]

_____

_____

_____

6. The successor(s) of the decedent, as defined in California Probate Code Section 13006, is/are:

_____

_____

_____

7. I am:

☐ the successor(s) of the decedent (as defined in Section 13006 of the California Probate Code) with respect to the decedent's interest in the described property. **OR** ☐ authorized under Section 13051 of the California Probate Code to act on behalf of the successor of the decedent (as defined in Section 13006 of the California Probate Code) with respect to the decedent's interest in the described property.

8. No other person has a superior right to the interest of the decedent in the described property.

9. I request that the above-described property be paid, delivered or transferred to me.

I declare under penalty of perjury under the laws of the State of California that the foregoing is true and correct.

Date _____ Sign Name _____ Print Name _____

Date _____ Sign Name _____ Print Name _____

Clerk stamps date here when form is filed.

If you are getting public benefits, are a low-income person, or do not have enough income to pay for your household's basic needs and your court fees, you may use this form to ask the court to waive your court fees. The court may order you to answer questions about your finances. If the court waives the fees, you may still have to pay later if:

- You cannot give the court proof of your eligibility,
- Your financial situation improves during this case, or
- You settle your civil case for **$10,000** or more. The trial court that waives your fees will have a lien on any such settlement in the amount of the waived fees and costs. The court may also charge you any collection costs.

Fill in court name and street address:

Superior Court of California, County of

(1) **Your Information** *(person asking the court to waive the fees):*
Name: _____
Street or mailing address: _____
City: _____ State: ____ Zip: _____
Phone: _____

Fill in case number and name:

Case Number:

(2) **Your Job,** if you have one *(job title):* _____
Name of employer: _____
Employer's address: _____

Case Name:

(3) **Your Lawyer,** if you have one *(name, firm or affiliation, address, phone number, and State Bar number):*
_____
_____

a. The lawyer has agreed to advance all or a portion of your fees or costs *(check one):* Yes ☐ No ☐
b. *(If yes, your lawyer must sign here)* Lawyer's signature: _____
  If your lawyer is not providing legal-aid type services based on your low income, you may have to go to a hearing to explain why you are asking the court to waive the fees.

(4) **What court's fees or costs are you asking to be waived?**
☐ Superior Court (See *Information Sheet on Waiver of Superior Court Fees and Costs* (form FW-001-INFO).)
☐ Supreme Court, Court of Appeal, or Appellate Division of Superior Court (See *Information Sheet on Waiver of Appellate Court Fees* (form APP-015/FW-015-INFO).)

(5) **Why are you asking the court to waive your court fees?**
a. ☐ I receive *(check all that apply; see form FW-001-INFO for definitions):* ☐ Food Stamps ☐ Supp. Sec. Inc.
  ☐ SSP ☐ Medi-Cal ☐ County Relief/Gen. Assist. ☐ IHSS ☐ CalWORKS or Tribal TANF ☐ CAPI
b. ☐ My gross monthly household income (before deductions for taxes) is less than the amount listed below. *(If you check 5b, you must fill out 7, 8, and 9 on page 2 of this form.)*

Family Size	Family Income	Family Size	Family Income	Family Size	Family Income	
1	$1,301.05	3	$2,221.88	5	$3,142.71	*If more than 6 people at home, add $460.42 for each extra person.*
2	$1,761.46	4	$2,682.30	6	$3,603.13	

c. ☐ I do not have enough income to pay for my household's basic needs *and* the court fees. I ask the court to:
  *(check one and you **must** fill out page 2):*
  ☐ waive all court fees and costs ☐ waive some of the court fees
  ☐ let me make payments over time

(6) ☐ Check here if you asked the court to waive your court fees for this case in the last six months.
  (If your previous request is reasonably available, please attach it to this form and check here:) ☐

I declare under penalty of perjury under the laws of the State of California that the information I have provided on this form and all attachments is true and correct.

Date: _____ ▶

_____   _____
Print your name here   *Sign here*

Judicial Council of California, *www.courts.ca.gov*
Revised March 15, 2019, Mandatory Form
Government Code, § 68633
Cal. Rules of Court, rules 3.51, 8.26, and 8.818

Request to Waive Court Fees

FW-001, Page 1 of 2 →

Your name: _____

Case Number: _____

*If you checked 5a on page 1, do not fill out below. If you checked 5b, fill out questions 7, 8, and 9 only. If you checked 5c, you **must** fill out this entire page. If you need more space, attach form MC-025 or attach a sheet of paper and write Financial Information and your name and case number at the top.*

(7) ☐ Check here if your income changes a lot from month to month. If it does, complete the form based on your average income for the past 12 months.

(8) Your Gross Monthly Income

a. List the source and amount of *any* income you get each month, including: wages or other income from work before deductions, spousal/child support, retirement, social security, disability, unemployment, military basic allowance for quarters (BAQ), veterans payments, dividends, interest, trust income, annuities, net business or rental income, reimbursement for job-related expenses, gambling or lottery winnings, etc.

(1) _____ $_____
(2) _____ $_____
(3) _____ $_____
(4) _____ $_____

b. **Your total monthly income:** $_____

(9) Household Income

a. List the income of all other persons living in your home who depend in whole or in part on you for support, or on whom you depend in whole or in part for support.

Name	Age	Relationship	Gross Monthly Income
(1) _____	___	_____	$_____
(2) _____	___	_____	$_____
(3) _____	___	_____	$_____
(4) _____	___	_____	$_____

b. **Total monthly income of persons above:** $_____

Total monthly income *and* household income *(8b plus 9b):* $_____

To list any other facts you want the court to know, such as unusual medical expenses, etc., attach form MC-025 or attach a sheet of paper and write Financial Information and your name and case number at the top.

Check here if you attach another page. ☐

***Important!* If your financial situation or ability to pay court fees improves, you must notify the court within five days on form FW-010.**

(10) Your Money and Property

a. Cash $_____

b. All financial accounts (List bank name and amount):
(1) _____ $_____
(2) _____ $_____
(3) _____ $_____

c. Cars, boats, and other vehicles

Make / Year	Fair Market Value	How Much You Still Owe
(1) _____	$_____	$_____
(2) _____	$_____	$_____
(3) _____	$_____	$_____

d. Real estate

Address	Fair Market Value	How Much You Still Owe
(1) _____	$_____	$_____
(2) _____	$_____	$_____

e. Other personal property (jewelry, furniture, furs, stocks, bonds, etc.):

Describe	Fair Market Value	How Much You Still Owe
(1) _____	$_____	$_____
(2) _____	$_____	$_____

(11) Your Monthly Deductions and Expenses

a. List any payroll deductions and the monthly amount below:
(1) _____ $_____
(2) _____ $_____
(3) _____ $_____
(4) _____ $_____

b. Rent or house payment & maintenance $_____
c. Food and household supplies $_____
d. Utilities and telephone $_____
e. Clothing $_____
f. Laundry and cleaning $_____
g. Medical and dental expenses $_____
h. Insurance (life, health, accident, etc.) $_____
i. School, child care $_____
j. Child, spousal support (another marriage) $_____
k. Transportation, gas, auto repair and insurance $_____
l. Installment payments *(list each below):*
Paid to:
(1) _____ $_____
(2) _____ $_____
(3) _____ $_____

m. Wages/earnings withheld by court order $_____
n. Any other monthly expenses *(list each below).*

Paid to:	How Much?
(1) _____	$_____
(2) _____	$_____
(3) _____	$_____

Total monthly expenses *(add 11a –11n above):* $_____

FW-003

Order on Court Fee Waiver
(Superior Court)

(1) Person who asked the court to waive court fees:

Name: _____

Street or mailing address: _____

City: _____ State: _____ Zip: _____

(2) Lawyer, if person in (1) has one *(name, firm name, address, phone number, e-mail, and State Bar number):*

_____

_____

_____

_____

_____

_____

Fill in court name and street address:

Superior Court of California, County of

Fill in case number and name:

Case Number:

Case Name:

(3) A request to waive court fees was filed on *(date):* _____

☐ The court made a previous fee waiver order in this case on *(date):*

_____

Read this form carefully. All checked boxes ☑ are court orders.

Notice: The court may order you to answer questions about your finances and later order you to pay back the waived fees. If this happens and you do not pay, the court can make you pay the fees and also charge you collection fees. If there is a change in your financial circumstances during this case that increases your ability to pay fees and costs, you must notify the trial court within five days. (Use form FW-010.) If you win your case, the trial court may order the other side to pay the fees. If you settle your civil case for **$10,000** or more, the trial court will have a lien on the settlement in the amount of the waived fees. The trial court may not dismiss the case until the lien is paid.

(4) After reviewing your: ☐ *Request to Waive Court Fees* ☐ *Request to Waive Additional Court Fees*
the court makes the following orders:

a. ☐ The court **grant**s your request, as follows:

(1) ☐ **Fee Waiver.** The court grants your request and waives your court fees and costs listed below. *(Cal. Rules of Court, rules 3.55 and 8.818.)* You do not have to pay the court fees for the following:

- Filing papers in superior court
- Making copies and certifying copies
- Sheriff's fee to give notice
- Court fee for phone hearing
- Giving notice and certificates
- Sending papers to another court department
- Reporter's fee for attendance at hearing or trial, if the court is not electronically recording the proceeding and you request that the court provide an official reporter
- Assessment for court investigations under Probate Code section 1513, 1826, or 1851
- Preparing, certifying, copying, and sending the clerk's transcript on appeal
- Holding in trust the deposit for a reporter's transcript on appeal under rule 8.130 or 8.834
- Making a transcript or copy of an official electronic recording under rule 8.835

(2) ☐ **Additional Fee Waiver.** The court grants your request and waives your additional superior court fees and costs that are checked below. *(Cal. Rules of Court, rule 3.56.)* You do not have to pay for the checked items.

☐ Jury fees and expenses
☐ Fees for court-appointed experts
☐ Other *(specify):* _____
☐ Fees for a peace officer to testify in court
☐ Court-appointed interpreter fees for a witness

Judicial Council of California, *www.courts.ca.gov*
Revised September 1, 2019, Mandatory Form
Government Code, § 68634(e)
Cal. Rules of Court, rule 3.52

Order on Court Fee Waiver (Superior Court)

b. ☐ The court **denies** your fee waiver request because:

> **Warning!** If you miss the deadline below, the court cannot process your request for hearing or the court papers you filed with your original request. If the papers were a notice of appeal, the appeal may be dismissed.

(1) Your request is incomplete. You have **10 days** after the clerk gives notice of this Order (see date of service ☐ on next page) to:

- Pay your fees and costs, or
- File a new revised request that includes the incomplete items listed:
    ☐ Below   ☐ On Attachment 4b(1)

_____
_____
_____
_____

(2) ☐ The information you provided on the request shows that you are not eligible for the fee waiver you requested for the reasons stated: ☐ Below   ☐ On Attachment 4b(2)

_____
_____
_____
_____
_____

The court has enclosed a blank *Request for Hearing About Court Fee Waiver Order (Superior Court)* (form FW-006). You have **10 days** after the clerk gives notice of this order (see date of service below) to:
- Pay your fees and costs in full or the amount listed in c below, or
- Ask for a hearing in order to show the court more information. *(Use form FW-006 to request hearing.)*

c. (1) ☐ The court needs more information to decide whether to grant your request. You must go to court on the date on page 3. The hearing will be about the questions regarding your eligibility that are stated:
    ☐ Below   ☐ On Attachment 4c(1)

_____
_____
_____
_____

(2) ☐ Bring the items of proof to support your request, if reasonably available, that are listed:
    ☐ Below   ☐ On Attachment 4c(2)

_____
_____
_____
_____
_____
_____
_____
_____

This is a Court Order.

b. ☐ The court **denies** your fee waiver request because:

> **Warning!** If you miss the deadline below, the court cannot process your request for hearing or the court papers you filed with your original request. If the papers were a notice of appeal, the appeal may be dismissed.

(1) Your request is incomplete. You have **10 days** after the clerk gives notice of this Order (see date of service ☐ on next page) to:

- Pay your fees and costs, or
- File a new revised request that includes the incomplete items listed:
  ☐ Below   ☐ On Attachment 4b(1)

_____

_____

_____

_____

(2) ☐ The information you provided on the request shows that you are not eligible for the fee waiver you requested for the reasons stated: ☐ Below   ☐ On Attachment 4b(2)

_____

_____

_____

_____

_____

The court has enclosed a blank *Request for Hearing About Court Fee Waiver Order (Superior Court)* (form FW-006). You have **10 days** after the clerk gives notice of this order (see date of service below) to:

- Pay your fees and costs in full or the amount listed in c below, or
- Ask for a hearing in order to show the court more information. *(Use form FW-006 to request hearing.)*

c. (1) ☐ The court needs more information to decide whether to grant your request. You must go to court on the date on page 3. The hearing will be about the questions regarding your eligibility that are stated:
☐ Below   ☐ On Attachment 4c(1)

_____

_____

_____

_____

(2) ☐ Bring the items of proof to support your request, if reasonably available, that are listed:
☐ Below   ☐ On Attachment 4c(2)

_____

_____

_____

_____

_____

_____

This is a Court Order.

Your name: _____

Case Number: _____

<table>
<tr><td rowspan="2">**Hearing Date**</td><td>→ Date: _____ Time: _____</td><td rowspan="2">Name and address of court if different from above:
_____
_____</td></tr>
<tr><td>Dept.: _____ Room: _____</td></tr>
</table>

Name and address of court if different from above:

_____

_____

_____

_____

Warning! If item c(1) is checked, and you do not go to court on your hearing date, the judge will deny your request to waive court fees, and you will have 10 days to pay your fees. If you miss that deadline, the court cannot process the court papers you filed with your request. If the papers were a notice of appeal, the appeal may be dismissed.

Date: _____

Signature of (check one):   ☐ *Judicial Officer*   ☐ *Clerk, Deputy*

Request for Accommodations

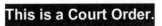

Assistive listening systems, computer-assisted real-time captioning, or sign language interpreter services are available if you ask at least five days before the hearing. Contact the clerk's office for *Request for Accommodations by Persons With Disabilities and Response* (form MC-410). (Civ. Code, § 54.8.)

Clerk's Certificate of Service

I certify that I am not involved in this case and *(check one):*

☐ I handed a copy of this Order to the party and attorney, if any, listed in ① and ②, at the court, on the date below.

☐ This order was mailed first class, postage paid, to the party and attorney, if any, at the addresses listed in ① and ②, from *(city):* _____, California, on the date below.

   ☐ A certificate of mailing is attached.

Date: _____

Clerk, by _____ , Deputy

Name: _____

This is a Court Order.

NOTICE: EVERYONE WHO LIVES IN THIS RENTAL UNIT MAY BE EVICTED BY COURT ORDER. READ THIS FORM IF YOU LIVE HERE AND IF YOUR NAME IS NOT ON THE ATTACHED SUMMONS AND COMPLAINT.

1. If you live here and you do not complete and submit this form, you may be evicted without further hearing by the court along with the persons named in the Summons and Complaint.
2. You must file this form within 10 days of the date of service listed in the box on the right hand side of this form.
   Exception: If you are a tenant being evicted after your landlord lost the property to foreclosure, the 10-day deadline does not apply to you and you may file this form at any time before judgment is entered.
3. If you file this form, your claim will be determined in the eviction action against the persons named in the complaint.
4. If you do not file this form, you may be evicted without further hearing.
5. If you are a tenant being evicted due to foreclosure, you have additional rights and should seek legal advice immediately.

CLAIMANT OR CLAIMANT'S ATTORNEY (*Name and Address*): TELEPHONE NO.:	*FOR COURT USE ONLY*
ATTORNEY FOR (*Name*):	
NAME OF COURT:	
STREET ADDRESS:	
MAILING ADDRESS:	
CITY AND ZIP CODE:	
BRANCH NAME:	
Plaintiff:	
Defendant:	

PREJUDGMENT CLAIM OF RIGHT TO POSSESSION	CASE NUMBER:
Complete this form only if ALL of these statements are true: 1. **You are NOT named in the accompanying Summons and Complaint.** 2. **You occupied the subject premises on or before the date the unlawful detainer (eviction) complaint was filed. (The date is in the accompanying Summons and Complaint.)** 3. **You still occupy the subject premises.**	*(To be completed by the process server)* DATE OF SERVICE: *(Date that form is served or delivered, posted, and mailed by the officer or process server)*

I DECLARE THE FOLLOWING UNDER PENALTY OF PERJURY:

1. My name is *(specify):*
2. I reside at *(street address, unit no., city and ZIP code):*
3. The address of "the premises" subject to this claim is *(address):*
4. On *(insert date):*   , the landlord or the landlord's authorized agent filed a complaint to recover possession of the premises. *(This date is in the accompanying Summons and Complaint.)*
5. I occupied the premises on the date the complaint was filed *(the date in item 4)*. I have continued to occupy the premises ever since.
6. I was at least 18 years of age on the date the complaint was filed *(the date in item 4)*.
7. I claim a right to possession of the premises because I occupied the premises on the date the complaint was filed *(the date in item 4)*.
8. I was not named in the Summons and Complaint.
9. I understand that if I make this claim of possession, I will be added as a defendant to the unlawful detainer (eviction) action.
10. *(Filing fee)* I understand that I must go to the court and pay a filing fee of $ or file with the court an "Application for Waiver of Court Fees and Costs." I understand that if I don't pay the filing fee or file the form for waiver of court fees, I will not be entitled to make a claim of right to possession.

(Continued on reverse)

CP10.5 [Rev. June 15, 2015]   **PREJUDGMENT CLAIM OF RIGHT**   Code of Civil Procedure, §§ 415.46,
                                      TO POSSESSION   715.010, 715.020, 1174.25

11. If my landlord lost this property to foreclosure, I understand that I can file this form at any time before judgment is entered, and that I have additional rights and should seek legal advice.

12. I understand that I will have *five days* (excluding court holidays) to file a response to the Summons and Complaint after I file this Prejudgment Claim of Right to Possession form.

> **NOTICE: If you fail to file this claim, you may be evicted without further hearing.**

13. **Rental agreement.** I have *(check all that apply to you):*

    a. ☐ an oral or written rental agreement with the landlord.

    b. ☐ an oral or written rental agreement with a person other than the landlord.

    c. ☐ an oral or written rental agreement with the former owner who lost the property to foreclosure.

    d. ☐ other *(explain):*

I declare under penalty of perjury under the laws of the State of California that the foregoing is true and correct.

> **WARNING: Perjury is a felony punishable by imprisonment in the state prison.**

Date:

_____ ▶ _____
(TYPE OR PRINT NAME)   (SIGNATURE OF CLAIMANT)

> **NOTICE:** If you file this claim to possession, the unlawful detainer action against you will be determined at trial. At trial, you may be found liable for rent, costs, and, in some cases, treble damages.

— NOTICE TO OCCUPANTS —

YOU MUST ACT AT ONCE if all the following are true:
1. **You are NOT named in the accompanying Summons and Complaint.**
2. **You occupied the premises on or before the date the unlawful detainer (eviction) complaint was filed.**
3. **You still occupy the premises.**

You can complete and SUBMIT THIS CLAIM FORM WITHIN 10 DAYS from the date of service (on the form) at the court where the unlawful detainer (eviction) complaint was filed. If you are a tenant and your landlord lost the property you occupy through foreclosure, this 10-day deadline does not apply to you. You may file this form at any time before judgment is entered. You should seek legal advice immediately.

If you do not complete and submit this form (and pay a filing fee or file a fee waiver form if you cannot pay the fee), YOU WILL BE EVICTED.

After this form is properly filed, you will be added as a defendant in the unlawful detainer (eviction) action and your right to occupy the premises will be decided by the court. *If you do not file this claim, you may be evicted without a hearing.*

1

2

3

4

5

6

7

8

9

10

11

12

13

14

15

16

17

18

19

20

21

22

23

24

25

26

27

28

1

2

3

4   Defendant in Pro Per

5

6

7

8   SUPERIOR COURT OF THE STATE OF CALIFORNIA, COUNTY OF _____

9   _____ DIVISION/BRANCH

10   )
)
11   _____ ,)   Case No._____
)
12   _____   ,)
              Plaintiff(s),   )
13   v.   )
)
14   _____ ,)
)
15   _____ ,)
              Defendant(s).   )
16   _____)

17

18

19

20

21

22

23

24

25

26

27

28   Dated: _____   _____

ATTORNEY OR PARTY WITHOUT ATTORNEY *(Name, State Bar number, and address):*

FOR COURT USE ONLY

TELEPHONE NO.:

E-MAIL ADDRESS *(Optional):*   FAX NO. *(Optional):*

ATTORNEY FOR *(Name):*

SUPERIOR COURT OF CALIFORNIA, COUNTY OF

STREET ADDRESS:

MAILING ADDRESS:

CITY AND ZIP CODE:

BRANCH NAME:

PETITIONER/PLAINTIFF:

RESPONDENT/DEFENDANT:

PROOF OF SERVICE BY FIRST-CLASS MAIL—CIVIL	CASE NUMBER:

(Do not use this Proof of Service to show service of a Summons and Complaint.)

1. I am over 18 years of age and **not a party to this action.** I am a resident of or employed in the county where the mailing took place.

2. My residence or business address is:

3. On *(date):*   I mailed from *(city and state):*
   the following **documents** *(specify):*

   ☐ The documents are listed in the *Attachment to Proof of Service by First-Class Mail—Civil (Documents Served)* (form POS-030(D)).

4. I served the documents by enclosing them in an envelope and *(check one):*
   a. ☐ **depositing** the sealed envelope with the United States Postal Service with the postage fully prepaid.
   b. ☐ **placing** the envelope for collection and mailing following our ordinary business practices. I am readily familiar with this business's practice for collecting and processing correspondence for mailing. On the same day that correspondence is placed for collection and mailing, it is deposited in the ordinary course of business with the United States Postal Service in a sealed envelope with postage fully prepaid.

5. The envelope was addressed and mailed as follows:
   a. **Name** of person served:
   b. **Address** of person served:

   ☐ The name and address of each person to whom I mailed the documents is listed in the *Attachment to Proof of Service by First-Class Mail—Civil (Persons Served)* (POS-030(P)).

I declare under penalty of perjury under the laws of the State of California that the foregoing is true and correct.

Date:

▶

_____
(TYPE OR PRINT NAME OF PERSON COMPLETING THIS FORM)

_____
(SIGNATURE OF PERSON COMPLETING THIS FORM)

PROOF OF SERVICE BY FIRST-CLASS MAIL—CIVIL
(Proof of Service)

INFORMATION SHEET FOR PROOF OF SERVICE BY FIRST-CLASS MAIL—CIVIL

(This information sheet is not part of the Proof of Service and does not need to be copied, served, or filed.)

NOTE: This form should **not** be used for proof of service of a summons and complaint. For that purpose, use *Proof of Service of Summons* (form POS-010).

Use these instructions to complete the *Proof of Service by First-Class Mail—Civil* (form POS-030).

A person over 18 years of age must serve the documents. There are two main ways to serve documents: (1) by personal delivery and (2) by mail. Certain documents must be personally served. You must determine whether personal service is required for a document. Use the *Proof of Personal Service–Civil* (form POS-020) if the documents were personally served.

The person who served the documents by mail must complete a proof of service form for the documents served. **You cannot serve documents if you are a party to the action.**

INSTRUCTIONS FOR THE PERSON WHO SERVED THE DOCUMENTS

The proof of service should be printed or typed. If you have Internet access, a fillable version of the Proof of Service form is available at *www.courtinfo.ca.gov/forms*.

Complete the top section of the proof of service form as follows:

First box, left side: In this box print the name, address, and telephone number of the person *for* whom you served the documents.

Second box, left side: Print the name of the county in which the legal action is filed and the court's address in this box. The address for the court should be the same as on the documents that you served.

Third box, left side: Print the names of the Petitioner/Plaintiff and Respondent/Defendant in this box. Use the same names as are on the documents that you served.

First box, top of form, right side: Leave this box blank for the court's use.

Second box, right side: Print the case number in this box. The case number should be the same as the case number on the documents that you served.

Complete items 1–5 as follows:

1. You are stating that you are over the age of 18 and that you are not a party to this action. You are also stating that you either live in or are employed in the county where the mailing took place.

2. Print your home or business address.

3. Provide the date and place of the mailing and list the name of each document that you mailed. If you need more space to list the documents, check the box in item 3, complete the *Attachment to Proof of Service by First-Class Mail—Civil (Documents Served)* (form POS-030(D)), and attach it to form POS-030.

4. For item 4:

     Check box a if you personally put the documents in the regular U.S. mail.
     Check box b if you put the documents in the mail at your place of business.

5. Provide the name and address of each person to whom you mailed the documents. If you mailed the documents to more than one person, check the box in item 5, complete the *Attachment to Proof of Service by First-Class Mail—Civil (Persons Served)* (form POS-030(P)), and attach it to form POS-030.

At the bottom, fill in the date on which you signed the form, print your name, and sign the form. By signing, you are stating under penalty of perjury that all the information you have provided on form POS-030 is true and correct.

PROOF OF SERVICE BY FIRST CLASS MAIL—CIVIL
(Proof of Service)

SHORT TITLE:

CASE NUMBER:

ATTACHMENT TO PROOF OF SERVICE BY FIRST-CLASS MAIL—CIVIL (PERSONS SERVED)

(This Attachment is for use with form POS-030)

NAME AND ADDRESS OF EACH PERSON SERVED BY MAIL:

<u>Name of Person Served</u>   Address *(number, street, city, and zip code)*

Form Approved for Optional Use
Judicial Council of California
POS-030(P) [New January 1, 2005]

**ATTACHMENT TO PROOF OF SERVICE BY FIRST-CLASS MAIL—CIVIL
(PERSONS SERVED)**
(Proof of Service)

Page ____ of ____

1

2

3

4   Defendant in Pro Per

5

6

7

8   SUPERIOR COURT OF THE STATE OF CALIFORNIA, COUNTY OF _____

9   _____ DIVISION/BRANCH

10   )
)
     _____ ,)   Case No. _____
11   )
     _____ ,)   DEMURRER OF
12   Plaintiff(s),   )
)   _____
13   v.   )
)
14   _____ ,)
)   TO THE COMPLAINT OF
15   _____ ,)
            Defendant(s).   )   _____
16   _____)

17

18   Defendant(s) demur to the Complaint on the following ground(s):

19   1. _____

20   _____

21   _____

22   2. _____

23   _____

24   _____

25   3. _____

26   _____

27   _____

28   Dated: _____   _____

```
 1

 2

 3

 4    Defendant in Pro Per

 5

 6

 7

 8        SUPERIOR COURT OF THE STATE OF CALIFORNIA, COUNTY OF _____

 9        _____ DIVISION/BRANCH

10                                                    )
                                                      )
      _____ , )    Case No._____
11                                                    )
      _____ , )
12              Plaintiff(s),                   )    POINTS AND AUTHORITIES
                                                )
13    v.                                        )    IN SUPPORT OF DEMURRER
                                                )
14    _____ , )
                                                )    (CCP § 430.10)
15    _____ , )
                Defendant(s).                   )
16                                                    )
```

I. DEFENDANT'S DEMURRER IS PROPERLY BEFORE THE COURT

A defendant in an unlawful detainer action may demur. C.C.P. § 1170. Although dicta in Delta Imports v. Municipal Court, 146 Cal.App.3d 1033 (1983), suggests that a motion to quash is the remedy where a complaint fails to state a cause of action in unlawful detainer, Delta did not overrule prior cases. See Hinman v. Wagnon, 172 Cal.App.2d 24 (1959), where the court held that a demurrer was proper where the incorporated 3-day notice was defective on its face. The court sustained a dismissal following sustaining the demurrer without leave to amend.

The periods for noticing hearing on a demurrer are not stated in the unlawful detainer statutes, so Code of Civil Procedure Section 1177 incorporates the regular provisions of the Code of Civil Procedure, such as Code of Civil Procedure 1005 requiring that motions be noticed on 16 court days' notice, plus five calendar days for mailing. Rule 3.1320(c), California Rules of Court, specifies that demurrers shall be heard in accordance with Section 1005.

1 //////

2 <center>II. ARGUMENT</center>

3

4

5

6

7

8

9

10

11

12

13

14

15

16

17

18

19

20

21

22

23

24

25

26

27

28 Dated: _____   _____

1

2

3

4   Defendant in Pro Per

5

6

7

8   SUPERIOR COURT OF THE STATE OF CALIFORNIA, COUNTY OF _____

9   _____ DIVISION/BRANCH

10   )
)
     _____ ,)   Case No. _____
11   )
     _____ ,)
12   Plaintiff(s),   )   NOTICE OF HEARING ON DEMURRER OF
)
13   v.   )   _____
)
14   _____ ,)
)   TO THE COMPLAINT OF
15   _____ ,)
                Defendant(s).   )   _____
16   _____)

17

18   To: _____

19   PLEASE TAKE NOTICE THAT on _____ , _____ , at

20   _____ in Department No. _____ of the above entitled court, located at _____

21   _____ ,

22   a hearing will be held on Defendant's demurrer to the Complaint, a copy of which is served with this notice.

23

24

25

26   Dated: _____   _____

27

28

1

2

3

4   Defendant in Pro Per

5

6

7

8   SUPERIOR COURT OF THE STATE OF CALIFORNIA, COUNTY OF _____

9   _____ DIVISION/BRANCH

10   )
)
     _____,)   Case No. _____
11   )
     _____,)
12   Plaintiff(s),   )   REQUEST FOR JUDICIAL NOTICE
)
13   v.   )
)
14   _____,)
)
15   _____,)
            Defendant(s).   )
16   _____)

17

18   Defendant _____ hereby requests that the Court take judicial notice of the Complaint

19   filed in this action and attached hereto as Exhibit A, pursuant to California Evidence Code Section 452(d).

20

21   California Evidence Code Section 453 provides that the trial court shall take judicial notice of any matter

22   specified in Section 452 if a party requests it, provide each party has been given sufficient notice and the court has

23   been provided a copy. Defendant has complied with these requirements.

24

25

26   Dated: _____   _____
                                         Defendant In Pro Per
27

28

1
2
3
4
5
6
7
8
9
10
11
12
13
14
15
16
17
18
19
20
21
22
23
24
25
26
27
28

		FOR COURT USE ONLY
ATTORNEY OR PARTY WITHOUT ATTORNEY STATE BAR NUMBER: NAME: FIRM NAME: STREET ADDRESS: CITY: STATE: ZIP CODE: TELEPHONE NO.: FAX NO.: E-MAIL ADDRESS: ATTORNEY FOR (*name*):		

SUPERIOR COURT OF CALIFORNIA, COUNTY OF
   STREET ADDRESS:
   MAILING ADDRESS:
   CITY AND ZIP CODE:
   BRANCH NAME:

      Plaintiff:
     Defendant:

ANSWER—UNLAWFUL DETAINER	CASE NUMBER:

1. Defendant (*each defendant for whom this answer is filed must be named and must sign this answer unless his or her attorney signs*):

   answers the complaint as follows:

2. **Check ONLY ONE of the next two boxes:**

   a. ☐ Defendant generally denies each statement of the complaint. (*Do not check this box if the complaint demands more than $1,000.*)

   b. ☐ Defendant admits that all of the statements of the complaint are true EXCEPT

     (1) defendant claims the following statements of the complaint are false (*state paragraph numbers from the complaint or explain below or on form MC-025*): ☐ Explanation is on MC-025, titled as Attachment 2b(1).

     (2) defendant has no information or belief that the following statements of the complaint are true, so defendant denies them (*state paragraph numbers from the complaint or explain below or on form MC-025*):
       ☐ Explanation is on MC-025, titled as Attachment 2b(2).

3. AFFIRMATIVE DEFENSES (**NOTE:** *For each box checked, you must state brief facts to support it in item 3l (page 2).*)

   a. ☐ (*Nonpayment of rent only*) Plaintiff has breached the warranty to provide habitable premises.

   b. ☐ (*Nonpayment of rent only*) Defendant made needed repairs and properly deducted the cost from the rent, and plaintiff did not give proper credit.

   c. ☐ (*Nonpayment of rent only*) On (*date*): before the notice to pay or quit expired, defendant offered the rent due but plaintiff would not accept it.

   d. ☐ Plaintiff waived, changed, or canceled the notice to quit.

   e. ☐ Plaintiff served defendant with the notice to quit or filed the complaint to retaliate against defendant.

   f. ☐ By serving defendant with the notice to quit or filing the complaint, plaintiff is arbitrarily discriminating against the defendant in violation of the Constitution or the laws of the United States or California.

   g. ☐ Plaintiff's demand for possession violates the local rent control or eviction control ordinance of (*city or county, title of ordinance, and date of passage*):
     (*Also, briefly state in item 3l the facts showing violation of the ordinance.*)

   h. ☐ Plaintiff accepted rent from defendant to cover a period of time after the date the notice to quit expired.

   i. ☐ Plaintiff seeks to evict defendant based on an act against defendant or a member of defendant's household that constitutes domestic violence, sexual assault, stalking, human trafficking, or abuse of an elder or a dependent adult. (*This defense requires one of the following: (1) **a temporary restraining order, protective order, or police report** that is not more than 180 days old; OR (2) **a signed statement from a qualified third party** (e.g., a doctor, domestic violence or sexual assault counselor, human trafficking caseworker, or psychologist) concerning the injuries or abuse resulting from these acts.*)

Page 1 of 2

3. AFFIRMATIVE DEFENSES (cont'd.)

  j. ☐ Plaintiff seeks to evict defendant based on defendant or another person calling the police or emergency assistance (e.g., ambulance) by or on behalf of a victim of abuse, a victim of crime, or an individual in an emergency when defendant or the other person believed that assistance was necessary.

  k. ☐ Other affirmative defenses are stated in item 3*l*.

  l. Facts supporting affirmative defenses checked above *(identify facts for each item by its letter below or on form MC-025)*:

      ☐ Description of facts is on MC-025, titled as Attachment 3*l*.

4. OTHER STATEMENTS

  a. ☐ Defendant vacated the premises on *(date)*:

  b. ☐ The fair rental value of the premises alleged in the complaint is excessive *(explain below or on form MC-025)*:

      ☐ Explanation is on MC-025, titled as Attachment 4b.

  c. ☐ Other *(specify below or on form MC-025 in attachment)*:

      ☐ Other statements are on MC-025, titled as Attachment 4c.

5. DEFENDANT REQUESTS

  a. that plaintiff take nothing requested in the complaint.

  b. costs incurred in this proceeding.

  c. ☐ reasonable attorney fees.

  d. ☐ that plaintiff be ordered to (1) make repairs and correct the conditions that constitute a breach of the warranty to provide habitable premises and (2) reduce the monthly rent to a reasonable rental value until the conditions are corrected.

  e. ☐ Other *(specify below or on form MC-025)*:

      ☐ All other requests are stated on MC-025, titled as Attachment 5e.

6. Number of pages attached: _____

UNLAWFUL DETAINER ASSISTANT (Bus. & Prof. Code, §§ 6400-6415)

7. *(Must be completed in all cases.)* An **unlawful detainer assistant** ☐ did not ☐ did for compensation give advice or assistance with this form. *(If defendant has received **any** help or advice for pay from an unlawful detainer assistant, state)*:

  a. assistant's name: b. telephone number:

  c. street address, city, and zip code:

  d. county of registration: e. registration number: f. expiration date:

(Each defendant for whom this answer is filed must be named in item 1 and must sign this answer unless his or her attorney signs.)

▶ _____

_____ (SIGNATURE OF DEFENDANT OR ATTORNEY)
(TYPE OR PRINT NAME)

▶ _____

_____ (SIGNATURE OF DEFENDANT OR ATTORNEY)
(TYPE OR PRINT NAME)

VERIFICATION

(Use a different verification form if the verification is by an attorney or for a corporation or partnership.)

I am the defendant in this proceeding and have read this answer. I declare under penalty of perjury under the laws of the State of California that the foregoing is true and correct. Date:

_____   _____
(TYPE OR PRINT NAME)   (SIGNATURE OF DEFENDANT)

ANSWER—UNLAWFUL DETAINER

SHORT TITLE:

CASE NUMBER:

ATTACHMENT *(Number):* _____

(This Attachment may be used with any Judicial Council form.)

(If the item that this Attachment concerns is made under penalty of perjury, all statements in this Attachment are made under penalty of perjury.)

Page _____ **of** _____

(Add pages as required)

Form Approved for Optional Use
Judicial Council of California
MC-025 [Rev. July 1, 2009]

ATTACHMENT
to Judicial Council Form

www.courtinfo.ca.gov

4 Defendant in Pro Per

8 SUPERIOR COURT OF THE STATE OF CALIFORNIA, COUNTY OF _____

9 _____ DIVISION/BRANCH

10)
) Case No._____
11 _____,)
)
   _____,)
12 Plaintiff(s),) REQUEST TO INSPECT AND FOR
)
13 v.) PRODUCTION OF DOCUMENTS
)
14 _____,)
)
15 _____,)
   Defendant(s).) (Code of Civil Procedure Sec. 2031.101–2031.510)
16 _____)

17

18 To: _____ , Plaintiff,

19 and _____ , Plaintiff's attorney:

20 Defendant requests that you produce and permit the copying of the following documents: _____

21 _____ .

22 Defendant requests that you produce these documents at the following address: _____

23 _____ , at the following date and time: _____

24 _____ .

25

26 Dated: _____   _____

ATTORNEY OR PARTY WITHOUT ATTORNEY *(Name, State Bar number, and address):*

ATTORNEY FOR *(Name):*

SUPERIOR COURT OF CALIFORNIA, COUNTY OF:

SHORT TITLE:

UNLAWFUL DETAINER ASSISTANT

(Check one box): An unlawful detainer assistant ☐ did ☐ did not for compensation give advice or assistance with this form. *(If one did, state the following):*

ASSISTANT'S NAME:

ADDRESS:

TEL. NO.:

COUNTY OF REGISTRATION:

REGISTRATION NO.:

EXPIRES *(DATE):*

FORM INTERROGATORIES—UNLAWFUL DETAINER

Asking Party:

Answering Party:

Set No.:

CASE NUMBER:

Sec. 1. Instructions to All Parties

(a) These are general instructions. For time limitations, requirements for service on other parties, and other details, see Code of Civil Procedure sections 2030.010-2030.410 and the cases construing those sections.

(b) These interrogatories do not change existing law relating to interrogatories nor do they affect an answering party's right to assert any privilege or objection.

Sec. 2. Instructions to the Asking Party

(a) These interrogatories are designed for optional use in unlawful detainer proceedings.

(b) There are restrictions that generally limit the number of interrogatories that may be asked and the form and use of the interrogatories. For details, read Code of Civil Procedure sections 2030.030–2030.070.

(c) In determining whether to use these or any interrogatories, you should be aware that abuse can be punished by sanctions, including fines and attorney fees. See Code of Civil Procedure section 128.7.

(d) Check the box next to each interrogatory that you want the answering party to answer. Use care in choosing those interrogatories that are applicable to the case.

(e) Additional interrogatories may be attached.

Sec. 3. Instructions to the Answering Party

(a) An answer or other appropriate response must be given to each interrogatory checked by the asking party. Failure to respond to these interrogatories properly can be punished by sanctions, including contempt proceedings, fine, attorneys fees, and the loss of your case. See Code of Civil Procedure sections 128.7 and 2030.300.

(b) As a general rule, within five days after you are served with these interrogatories, you must serve your responses on the asking party and serve copies of your responses on all other parties to the action who have appeared. See Code of Civil Procedure sections 2030.260–2030.270 for details.

(c) Each answer must be as complete and straightforward as the information reasonably available to you permits. If an interrogatory cannot be answered completely, answer it to the extent possible.

(d) If you do not have enough personal knowledge to fully answer an interrogatory, say so, but make a reasonable and good faith effort to get the information by asking other persons or organizations, unless the information is equally available to the asking party.

(e) Whenever an interrogatory may be answered by referring to a document, the document may be attached as an exhibit to the response and referred to in the response. If the document has more than one page, refer to the page and section where the answer to the interrogatory can be found.

(f) Whenever an address and telephone number for the same person are requested in more than one interrogatory, you are required to furnish them in answering only the first interrogatory asking for that information.

(g) Your answers to these interrogatories must be verified, dated, and signed. You may wish to use the following form *at the end of your answers:*

I declare under penalty of perjury under the laws of the State of California that the foregoing answers are true and correct.

_____   _____
(DATE)   (SIGNATURE)

Sec. 4. Definitions

Words in **BOLDFACE CAPITALS** in these interrogatories are defined as follows:

(a) **PERSON** includes a natural person, firm, association, organization, partnership, business, trust, corporation, or public entity.

(b) **PLAINTIFF** includes any **PERSON** who seeks recovery of the **RENTAL UNIT** whether acting as an individual or on someone else's behalf and includes all such **PERSONS** if more than one.

Form Approved for Optional Use
Judicial Council of California
DISC-003/UD-106 [Rev. January 1, 2014]

FORM INTERROGATORIES–UNLAWFUL DETAINER

Code of Civil Procedure,
§§ 2030.010-2030.410, 2033.710
www.courts.ca.gov

(c) **LANDLORD** includes any **PERSON** who offered the **RENTAL UNIT** for rent and any **PERSON** on whose behalf the **RENTAL UNIT** was offered for rent and their successors in interest. **LANDLORD** includes all **PERSONS** who managed the **PROPERTY** while defendant was in possession.

(d) **RENTAL UNIT** is the premises **PLAINTIFF** seeks to recover.

(e) **PROPERTY** is the building or parcel (including common areas) of which the **RENTAL UNIT** is a part. (For example, if **PLAINTIFF** is seeking to recover possession of apartment number 12 of a 20-unit building, the building is the **PROPERTY** and apartment 12 is the **RENTAL UNIT**. If **PLAINTIFF** seeks possession of cottage number 3 in a five-cottage court or complex, the court or complex is the **PROPERTY** and cottage 3 is the **RENTAL UNIT**.)

(f) **DOCUMENT** means a writing, as defined in Evidence Code section 250, and includes the original or a copy of handwriting, typewriting, printing, photostating, photographing, electronically stored information, and every other means of recording upon any tangible thing and form of communicating or representation, including letters, words, pictures, sounds, or symbols, or combinations of them.

(g) **NOTICE TO QUIT** includes the original or copy of any notice mentioned in Code of Civil Procedure section 1161 or Civil Code section 1946, including a 3-day notice to pay rent and quit the **RENTAL UNIT**, a 3-day notice to perform conditions or covenants or quit, a 3-day notice to quit, and a 30-day notice of termination.

(h) **ADDRESS** means the street address, including the city, state, and zip code.

Sec. 5. Interrogatories

The following interrogatories have been approved by the Judicial Council under section 2033.710 of the Code of Civil Procedure for use in unlawful detainer proceedings:

CONTENTS

70.0 General
71.0 Notice
72.0 Service
73.0 Malicious Holding Over
74.0 Rent Control and Eviction Control
75.0 Breach of Warranty to Provide Habitable
    Premises
76.0 Waiver, Change, Withdrawal, or Cancellation
    of Notice to Quit
77.0 Retaliation and Arbitrary Discrimination
78.0 Nonperformance of the Rental Agreement
    by Landlord
79.0 Offer of Rent by Defendant
80.0 Deduction from Rent for Necessary Repairs
81.0 Fair Market Rental Value

70.0 General

[Either party may ask any applicable question in this section.]

☐ 70.1 State the name, **ADDRESS**, telephone number, and relationship to you of each **PERSON** who prepared or assisted in the preparation of the responses to these interrogatories. (Do not identify anyone who simply typed or reproduced the responses.)

☐ 70.2 Is **PLAINTIFF** an owner of the **RENTAL UNIT**? If so, state:
(a) the nature and percentage of ownership interest;
(b) the date **PLAINTIFF** first acquired this ownership interest.

☐ 70.3 Does **PLAINTIFF** share ownership or lack ownership? If so, state the name, the **ADDRESS**, and the nature and percentage of ownership interest of each owner.

☐ 70.4 Does **PLAINTIFF** claim the right to possession other than as an owner of the **RENTAL UNIT**? If so, state the basis of the claim.

☐ 70.5 Has **PLAINTIFF'S** interest in the **RENTAL UNIT** changed since acquisition? If so, state the nature and dates of each change.

☐ 70.6 Are there other rental units on the **PROPERTY**? If so, state how many.

☐ 70.7 During the 12 months before this proceeding was filed, did **PLAINTIFF** possess a permit or certificate of occupancy for the **RENTAL UNIT**? If so, for each state:
(a) the name and **ADDRESS** of each **PERSON** named on the permit or certificate;
(b) the dates of issuance and expiration;
(c) the permit or certificate number

☐ 70.8 Has a last month's rent, security deposit, cleaning fee, rental agency fee, credit check fee, key deposit, or any other deposit been paid on the **RENTAL UNIT**? If so, for each item state:
(a) the purpose of the payment;
(b) the date paid;
(c) the amount;
(d) the form of payment;
(e) the name of the **PERSON** paying;
(f) the name of the **PERSON** to whom it was paid;
(g) any **DOCUMENT** which evidences payment and the name, **ADDRESS**, and telephone number of each **PERSON** who has the **DOCUMENT**;
(h) any adjustments or deductions including facts.

☐ 70.9 State the date defendant first took possession of the **RENTAL UNIT**.

☐ 70.10 State the date and all the terms of any rental agreement between defendant and the **PERSON** who rented to defendant.

☐ 70.11 For each agreement alleged in the pleadings:
(a) identify all **DOCUMENTS** that are part of the agreement and for each state the name, **ADDRESS**, and telephone number of each **PERSON** who has the **DOCUMENT**;
(b) state each part of the agreement not in writing, the name, **ADDRESS**, and telephone number of each **PERSON** agreeing to that provision, and the date that part of the agreement was made;
(c) identify all **DOCUMENTS** that evidence each part of the agreement not in writing and for each state the name, **ADDRESS**, and telephone number of each **PERSON** who has the **DOCUMENT**;
(d) identify all **DOCUMENTS** that are part of each modification to the agreement, and for each state

the name, **ADDRESS**, and telephone number of each **PERSON** who has the **DOCUMENT** (see also §71.5);

(e) state each modification not in writing, the date, and the name, **ADDRESS**, and telephone number of the **PERSON** agreeing to the modification, and the date the modification was made (see also §71.5).

(f) identify all **DOCUMENTS** that evidence each modification of the agreement not in writing and for each state the name, **ADDRESS**, and telephone number of each **PERSON** who has the **DOCUMENT** (see also §71.5).

70.12 Has any **PERSON** acting on the **PLAINTIFF'S** behalf been responsible for any aspect of managing or maintaining the **RENTAL UNIT** or **PROPERTY**? If so, for each **PERSON** state:
(a) the name, **ADDRESS**, and telephone number;
(b) the dates the **PERSON** managed or maintained the **RENTAL UNIT** or **PROPERTY**;
(c) the **PERSON'S** responsibilities.

70.13 For each **PERSON** who occupies any part of the **RENTAL UNIT** (except occupants named in the complaint and occupants' children under 17) state:
(a) the name, **ADDRESS**, telephone number, and birthdate;
(b) the inclusive dates of occupancy;
(c) a description of the portion of the **RENTAL UNIT** occupied;
(d) the amount paid, the term for which it was paid, and the person to whom it was paid;
(e) the nature of the use of the **RENTAL UNIT**;
(f) the name, **ADDRESS**, and telephone number of the person who authorized occupancy;
(g) how occupancy was authorized, including failure of the **LANDLORD** or **PLAINTIFF** to protest after discovering the occupancy.

70.14 Have you or anyone acting on your behalf obtained any **DOCUMENT** concerning the tenancy between any occupant of the **RENTAL UNIT** and any **PERSON** with an ownership interest or managerial responsibility for the **RENTAL UNIT**? If so, for each **DOCUMENT** state:

(a) the name, **ADDRESS**, and telephone number of each individual from whom the **DOCUMENT** was obtained;
(b) the name, **ADDRESS**, and telephone number of each individual who obtained the **DOCUMENT**;
(c) the date the **DOCUMENT** was obtained;
(d) the name, **ADDRESS**, and telephone number of each **PERSON** who has the **DOCUMENT** (original or copy).

71.0 Notice

[If a defense is based on allegations that the 3-day notice or 30- day NOTICE TO QUIT is defective in form or content, then either party may ask any applicable question in this section.]

71.1 Was the **NOTICE TO QUIT** on which **PLAINTIFF** bases this proceeding attached to the complaint? If not, state the contents of this notice.

71.2 State all reasons that the **NOTICE TO QUIT** was served and for each reason:
(a) state all facts supporting **PLAINTIFF'S** decision to terminate defendant's tenancy;

(b) state the names, **ADDRESSES**, and telephone numbers of all **PERSONS** who have knowledge of the facts;
(c) identify all **DOCUMENTS** that support the facts and state the name, **ADDRESS**, and telephone number of each **PERSON** who has each **DOCUMENT**.

71.3 List all rent payments and rent credits made or claimed by or on behalf of defendant beginning 12 months before the **NOTICE TO QUIT** was served. For each payment or credit state:
(a) the amount;
(b) the date received;
(c) the form in which any payment was made;
(d) the services performed or other basis for which a credit is claimed;
(e) the period covered;
(f) the name of each **PERSON** making the payment or earning the credit;
(g) the identity of all **DOCUMENTS** evidencing the payment or credit and for each state the name, **ADDRESS**, and telephone number of each **PERSON** who has the **DOCUMENT**.

71.4 Did defendant ever fail to pay the rent on time? If so, for each late payment state:
(a) the date;
(b) the amount of any late charge;
(c) the identity of all **DOCUMENTS** recording the payment and for each state the name, **ADDRESS**, and telephone number of each **PERSON** who has the **DOCUMENT**.

71.5 Since the beginning of defendant's tenancy, has **PLAINTIFF** ever raised the rent? If so, for each rent increase state:
(a) the date the increase became effective;
(b) the amount;
(c) the reasons for the rent increase;
(d) how and when defendant was notified of the increase;
(e) the identity of all **DOCUMENTS** evidencing the increase and for each state the name, **ADDRESS**, and telephone number of each **PERSON** who has the **DOCUMENT**.

[See also section 70.11 (d) - (f).]

71.6 During the 12 months before the **NOTICE TO QUIT** was served was there a period during which there was no permit or certificate of occupancy for the **RENTAL UNIT**? If so, for each period state:
(a) the inclusive dates;
(b) the reasons.

71.7 Has any **PERSON** ever reported any nuisance or disturbance at or destruction of the **RENTAL UNIT** or **PROPERTY** caused by defendant or other occupant of the **RENTAL UNIT** or their guests? If so, for each report state;
(a) a description of the disturbance or destruction;
(b) the date of the report;
(c) the name of the **PERSON** who reported;
(d) the name of the **PERSON** to whom the report was made;
(e) what action was taken as a result of the report;
(f) the identity of all **DOCUMENTS** evidencing the report and for each state the name, **ADDRESS**, and telephone number of each **PERSON** who has each **DOCUMENT**.

71.8 Does the complaint allege violation of a term of a rental agreement or lease (other than nonpayment of rent)? If so, for each covenant:
(a) identify the covenant breached;
(b) state the facts supporting the allegation of a breach;
(c) state the names, **ADDRESSES,** and telephone numbers of all **PERSONS** who have knowledge of the facts;
(d) identify all **DOCUMENTS** that support the facts and state the name, **ADDRESS,** and telephone number of each **PERSON** who has each **DOCUMENT.**

71.9 Does the complaint allege that the defendant has been using the **RENTAL UNIT** for an illegal purpose? If so, for each purpose:
(a) identify the illegal purpose;
(b) state the facts supporting the allegations of illegal use;
(c) state the names, **ADDRESSES,** and telephone numbers of all **PERSONS** who have knowledge of the facts;
(d) identify all **DOCUMENTS** that support the facts and state the name, **ADDRESS,** and telephone number of each **PERSON** who has each **DOCUMENT.**

[Additional interrogatories on this subject may be found in sections 75.0, 78.0, 79.0, and 80.0.]

72.0 Service

[If a defense is based on allegations that the NOTICE TO QUIT was defectively served, then either party may ask any applicable question in this section.]

72.1 Does defendant contend (or base a defense or make any allegations) that the **NOTICE TO QUIT** was defectively served? If the answer is "no", do not answer interrogatories 72.2 through 72.3.

72.2 Does **PLAINTIFF** contend that the **NOTICE TO QUIT** referred to in the complaint was served? If so, state:
(a) the kind of notice;
(b) the date and time of service;
(c) the manner of service;
(d) the name and **ADDRESS** of the person who served it:
(e) a description of any **DOCUMENT** or conversation between defendant and the person who served the notice.

72.3 Did any person receive the **NOTICE TO QUIT** referred to in the complaint? If so, for each copy of each notice state:
(a) the name of the person who received it;
(b) the kind of notice;
(c) how it was delivered;
(d) the date received;
(e) where it was delivered;
(f) the identity of all **DOCUMENTS** evidencing the notice and for each state the name, **ADDRESS,** and telephone number of each **PERSON** who has the **DOCUMENT.**

73.0 Malicious Holding Over
[If a defendant denies allegations that defendant's continued possession is malicious, then either party may ask any applicable question in this section. Additional questions in section 75.0 may also be applicable.]

73.1 If any rent called for by the rental agreement is unpaid, state the reasons and the facts upon which the reasons are based.

73.2 Has defendant made attempts to secure other premises since the service of the **NOTICE TO QUIT** or since the service of the summons and complaint? If so, for each attempt:
(a) state all facts indicating the attempt to secure other premises;
(b) state the names, **ADDRESSES,** and telephone numbers of all **PERSONS** who have knowledge of the facts;
(c) identify all **DOCUMENTS** that support the facts and state the name, **ADDRESS,** and telephone number of each **PERSON** who has each **DOCUMENT.**

73.3 State the facts upon which **PLAINTIFF** bases the allegation of malice.

74.0 Rent Control and Eviction Control

74.1 Is there an ordinance or other local law in this jurisdiction which limits the right to evict tenants? If your answer is no, you need not answer sections 74.2 through 74.6.

74.2 For the ordinance or other local law limiting the right to evict tenants, state:
(a) the title or number of the law;
(b) the locality.

74.3 Do you contend that the **RENTAL UNIT** is exempt from the eviction provisions of the ordinance or other local law identified in section 74.2? If so, state the facts upon which you base your contention.

74.4 Is this proceeding based on allegations of a need to recover the **RENTAL UNIT** for use of the **LANDLORD** or the landlord's relative? If so, for each intended occupant state:
(a) the name;
(b) the residence **ADDRESSES** from three years ago to the present;
(c) the relationship to the **LANDLORD;**
(d) all the intended occupant's reasons for occupancy;
(e) all rental units on the **PROPERTY** that were vacated within 60 days before and after the date the **NOTICE TO QUIT** was served.

74.5 Is the proceeding based on an allegation that the **LANDLORD** wishes to remove the **RENTAL UNIT** from residential use temporarily or permanently (for example, to rehabilitate, demolish, renovate, or convert)? If so, state:
(a) each reason for removing the **RENTAL UNIT** from residential use;
(b) what physical changes and renovation will be made to the **RENTAL UNIT;**
(c) the date the work is to begin and end;
(d) the number, date, and type of each permit for the change or work;

(e) the identity of each **DOCUMENT** evidencing the intended activity (for example, blueprints, plans, applications for financing, construction contracts) and the name, **ADDRESS**, and telephone number of each PERSON who has each **DOCUMENT**.

[ ] 74.6 Is the proceeding based on any ground other than those stated in sections 74.4 and 74.5? If so, for each:
(a) state each fact supporting or opposing the ground;
(b) state the names, **ADDRESSES**, and telephone numbers of all **PERSONS** who have knowledge of the facts;
(c) identify all **DOCUMENTS** evidencing the facts and state the name, **ADDRESS**, and telephone number of each **PERSON** who has each **DOCUMENT**.

75.0 Breach of Warranty to Provide Habitable Premises

[If plaintiff alleges nonpayment of rent and defendant bases his defense on allegations of implied or express breach of warranty to provide habitable residential premises, then either party may ask any applicable question in this section.]

[ ] 75.1 Do you know of any conditions in violation of state or local building codes, housing codes, or health codes, conditions of dilapidation, or other conditions in need of repair in the **RENTAL UNIT** or on the **PROPERTY** that affected the **RENTAL UNIT** at any time defendant has been in possession? If so, state:
(a) the type of condition;
(b) the kind of corrections or repairs needed;
(c) how and when you learned of these conditions;
(d) how these conditions were caused;
(e) the name, **ADDRESS**, and telephone number of each **PERSON** who has caused these conditions.

[ ] 75.2 Have any corrections, repairs, or improvements been made to the **RENTAL UNIT** since the **RENTAL UNIT** was rented to defendant? If so, for each correction, repair, or improvement state:
(a) a description giving the nature and location;
(b) the date;
(c) the name, **ADDRESS**, and telephone number of each **PERSON** who made the repairs or improvements;
(d) the cost;
(e) the identity of any **DOCUMENT** evidencing the repairs or improvements;
(f) if a building permit was issued, state the issuing agencies and the permit number of your copy.

[ ] 75.3 Did defendant or any other **PERSON** during 36 months before the **NOTICE TO QUIT** was served or during defendant's possession of the **RENTAL UNIT** notify the **LANDLORD** or his agent or employee about the condition of the **RENTAL UNIT** or **PROPERTY**? If so, for each written or oral notice state:
(a) the substance;
(b) who made it;
(c) when and how it was made;
(d) the name and **ADDRESS** of each **PERSON** to whom it was made;
(e) the name and **ADDRESS** of each person who knows about it;
(f) the identity of each **DOCUMENT** evidencing the notice and the name, **ADDRESS**, and telephone number of each **PERSON** who has it;

(g) the response made to the notice;
(h) the efforts made to correct the conditions;
(i) whether the **PERSON** who gave notice was an occupant of the **PROPERTY** at the time of the complaint.

[ ] 75.4 During the period beginning 36 months before the **NOTICE TO QUIT** was served to the present, was the **RENTAL UNIT** or **PROPERTY** (including other rental units) inspected for dilapidations or defective conditions by a representative of any governmental agency? If so, for each inspection state:
(a) the date;
(b) the reason;
(c) the name of the governmental agency;
(d) the name, **ADDRESS**, and telephone number of each inspector;
(e) the identity of each **DOCUMENT** evidencing each inspection and the name, **ADDRESS**, and telephone number of each **PERSON** who has it.

[ ] 75.5 During the period beginning 36 months before the **NOTICE TO QUIT** was served to the present, did **PLAINTIFF** or **LANDLORD** receive a notice or other communication regarding the condition of the **RENTAL UNIT** or **PROPERTY** (including other rental units) from a governmental agency? If so, for each notice or communication state:
(a) the date received;
(b) the identity of all parties;
(c) the substance of the notice or communication;
(d) the identity of each **DOCUMENT** evidencing the notice or communication and the name, **ADDRESS**, and telephone number of each **PERSON** who has it.

[ ] 75.6 Was there any corrective action taken in response to the inspection or notice or communication identified in sections 75.4 and 75.5? If so, for each:
(a) identify the notice or communication;
(b) identify the condition;
(c) describe the corrective action;
(d) identify each **DOCUMENT** evidencing the corrective action and the name, **ADDRESS**, and telephone number of each **PERSON** who has it.

[ ] 75.7 Has the **PROPERTY** been appraised for sale or loan during the period beginning 36 months before the **NOTICE TO QUIT** was served to the present? If so, for each appraisal state:
(a) the date;
(b) the name, **ADDRESS**, and telephone number of the appraiser;
(c) the purpose of the appraisal;
(d) the identity of each **DOCUMENT** evidencing the appraisal and the name, **ADDRESS**, and telephone number of each **PERSON** who has it.

[ ] 75.8 Was any condition requiring repair or correction at the **PROPERTY** or **RENTAL UNIT** caused by defendent or other occupant of the **RENTAL UNIT** or their guests? If so, state:
(a) the type and location of condition;
(b) the kind of corrections or repairs needed;
(c) how and when you learned of these conditions;
(d) how and when these conditions were caused;
(e) the name, **ADDRESS**, and telephone number of each **PERSON** who caused these conditions;

(f) the identity of each **DOCUMENT** evidencing the repair (or correction) and the name, **ADDRESS**, and telephone number of each **PERSON** who has it.

[See also section 71.0 for additional questions.]

76.0 Waiver, Change, Withdrawal, or Cancellation of Notice to Quit

[If a defense is based on waiver, change, withdrawal, or cancellation of the **NOTICE TO QUIT,** *then either party may ask any applicable question in this section.]*

☐ 76.1 Did the **PLAINTIFF or LANDLORD** or anyone acting on his or her behalf do anything which is alleged to have been a waiver, change, withdrawal, or cancellation of the **NOTICE TO QUIT**? If so:
(a) state the facts supporting this allegation;
(b) state the names, **ADDRESSES**, and telephone numbers of all **PERSONS** who have knowledge of these facts;
(c) identify each **DOCUMENT** that supports the facts and state the name, **ADDRESS**, and telephone number of each **PERSON** who has it.

☐ 76.2 Did the **PLAINTIFF** or **LANDLORD** accept rent **which covered a period after the date for vacating the RENTAL UNIT** as specified in the **NOTICE TO QUIT**? If so:
(a) state the facts;
(b) state the names, **ADDRESSES,** and telephone numbers of all **PERSONS** who have knowledge of the facts;
(c) identify each **DOCUMENT** that supports the facts and state the name, **ADDRESS**, and telephone number of each **PERSON** who has it.

77.0 Retaliation and Arbitrary Discrimination

[If a defense is based on retaliation or arbitrary discrimination, then either party may ask any applicable question in this section.]

☐ 77.1 State all reasons that the **NOTICE TO QUIT** was served or that defendant's tenancy was not renewed and for each reason:
(a) state all facts supporting **PLAINTIFF'S** decision to terminate or not renew defendant's tenancy;
(b) state the names, **ADDRESSES**, and telephone numbers of all **PERSONS** who have knowledge of the facts;
(c) identify all **DOCUMENTS** that support the facts and state the name, **ADDRESS**, and telephone number of each **PERSON** who has it.

78.0 Nonperformance of the Rental Agreement by Landlord

[If a defense is based on nonperformance of the rental agreement by the **LANDLORD** *or someone acting on the* **LANDLORD'S** *behalf, then either party may ask any applicable question in this section.]*

☐ 78.1 Did the **LANDLORD** or anyone acting on the **LANDLORD'S** behalf agree to make repairs, alterations, or improvements at any time or provide services to the **PROPERTY** or **RENTAL UNIT**? If so, for each agreement state:
(a) the substance of the agreement;

(b) when it was made;
(c) whether it was written or oral;
(d) by whom and to whom;
(e) the name and **ADDRESS** of each person who knows about it;
(f) whether all promised repairs, alterations, or improvements were completed or services provided;
(g) the reasons for any failure to perform;
(h) the identity of each **DOCUMENT** evidencing the agreement or promise and the name, **ADDRESS**, and telephone number of each **PERSON** who has it.

☐ 78.2 Has **PLAINTIFF** or **LANDLORD** or any resident of the **PROPERTY** ever committed disturbances or interfered with the quiet enjoyment of the **RENTAL UNIT** (including, for example, noise, acts which threaten the loss of title to the property or loss of financing, etc.)? If so, for each disturbance or interference, state:
(a) a description of each act;
(b) the date of each act;
(c) the name, **ADDRESS,** and telephone number of each **PERSON** who acted;
(d) the name, **ADDRESS,** and telephone number of each **PERSON** who witnessed each act and any **DOCUMENTS** evidencing the person's knowledge;
(e) what action was taken by the **PLAINTIFF** or **LANDLORD** to end or lessen the disturbance or interference.

79.0 Offer of Rent by Defendant

[If a defense is based on an offer of rent by a defendant which was refused, then either party may ask any applicable question in this section.]

☐ 79.1 Has defendant or anyone acting on the defendant's behalf offered any payments to **PLAINTIFF** which **PLAINTIFF** refused to accept? If so, for each offer state:
(a) the amount;
(b) the date;
(c) purpose of offer;
(d) the manner of the offer;
(e) the identity of the person making the offer;
(f) the identity of the person refusing the offer;
(g) the date of the refusal;
(h) the reasons for the refusal.

80.0 Deduction from Rent for Necessary Repairs

[If a defense to payment of rent or damages is based on claim of retaliatory eviction, then either party may ask any applicable question in this section. Additional questions in section 75.0 may also be applicable.]

☐ 80.1 Does defendant claim to have deducted from rent any amount which was withheld to make repairs after communication to the **LANDLORD** of the need for the repairs? If the answer is "no", do not answer interrogatories 80.2 through 80.6.

☐ 80.2 For each condition in need of repair for which a deduction was made, state:
(a) the nature of the condition;
(b) the location;
(c) the date the condition was discovered by defendant;
(d) the date the condition was first known by **LANDLORD** or **PLAINTIFF**;

(f) the identity of each **DOCUMENT** evidencing the repair (or correction) and the name, **ADDRESS**, and telephone number of each **PERSON** who has it.

[See also section 71.0 for additional questions.]

76.0 Waiver, Change, Withdrawal, or Cancellation of Notice to Quit

[If a defense is based on waiver, change, withdrawal, or cancellation of the **NOTICE TO QUIT,** *then either party may ask any applicable question in this section.]*

☐ 76.1 Did the **PLAINTIFF or LANDLORD** or anyone acting on his or her behalf do anything which is alleged to have been a waiver, change, withdrawal, or cancellation of the **NOTICE TO QUIT**? If so:
(a) state the facts supporting this allegation;
(b) state the names, **ADDRESSES**, and telephone numbers of all **PERSONS** who have knowledge of these facts;
(c) identify each **DOCUMENT** that supports the facts and state the name, **ADDRESS**, and telephone number of each **PERSON** who has it.

☐ 76.2 Did the **PLAINTIFF** or **LANDLORD** accept rent **which covered a period after the date for vacating the RENTAL UNIT** as specified in the **NOTICE TO QUIT**? If so:
(a) state the facts;
(b) state the names, **ADDRESSES,** and telephone numbers of all **PERSONS** who have knowledge of the facts;
(c) identify each **DOCUMENT** that supports the facts and state the name, **ADDRESS**, and telephone number of each **PERSON** who has it.

77.0 Retaliation and Arbitrary Discrimination

[If a defense is based on retaliation or arbitrary discrimination, then either party may ask any applicable question in this section.]

☐ 77.1 State all reasons that the **NOTICE TO QUIT** was served or that defendant's tenancy was not renewed and for each reason:
(a) state all facts supporting **PLAINTIFF'S** decision to terminate or not renew defendant's tenancy;
(b) state the names, **ADDRESSES**, and telephone numbers of all **PERSONS** who have knowledge of the facts;
(c) identify all **DOCUMENTS** that support the facts and state the name, **ADDRESS**, and telephone number of each **PERSON** who has it.

78.0 Nonperformance of the Rental Agreement by Landlord

[If a defense is based on nonperformance of the rental agreement by the **LANDLORD** *or someone acting on the* **LANDLORD'S** *behalf, then either party may ask any applicable question in this section.]*

☐ 78.1 Did the **LANDLORD** or anyone acting on the **LANDLORD'S** behalf agree to make repairs, alterations, or improvements at any time or provide services to the **PROPERTY** or **RENTAL UNIT**? If so, for each agreement state:
(a) the substance of the agreement;

(b) when it was made;
(c) whether it was written or oral;
(d) by whom and to whom;
(e) the name and **ADDRESS** of each person who knows about it;
(f) whether all promised repairs, alterations, or improvements were completed or services provided;
(g) the reasons for any failure to perform;
(h) the identity of each **DOCUMENT** evidencing the agreement or promise and the name, **ADDRESS**, and telephone number of each **PERSON** who has it.

☐ 78.2 Has **PLAINTIFF** or **LANDLORD** or any resident of the **PROPERTY** ever committed disturbances or interfered with the quiet enjoyment of the **RENTAL UNIT** (including, for example, noise, acts which threaten the loss of title to the property or loss of financing, etc.)? If so, for each disturbance or interference, state:
(a) a description of each act;
(b) the date of each act;
(c) the name, **ADDRESS,** and telephone number of each **PERSON** who acted;
(d) the name, **ADDRESS,** and telephone number of each **PERSON** who witnessed each act and any **DOCUMENTS** evidencing the person's knowledge;
(e) what action was taken by the **PLAINTIFF** or **LANDLORD** to end or lessen the disturbance or interference.

79.0 Offer of Rent by Defendant

[If a defense is based on an offer of rent by a defendant which was refused, then either party may ask any applicable question in this section.]

☐ 79.1 Has defendant or anyone acting on the defendant's behalf offered any payments to **PLAINTIFF** which **PLAINTIFF** refused to accept? If so, for each offer state:
(a) the amount;
(b) the date;
(c) purpose of offer;
(d) the manner of the offer;
(e) the identity of the person making the offer;
(f) the identity of the person refusing the offer;
(g) the date of the refusal;
(h) the reasons for the refusal.

80.0 Deduction from Rent for Necessary Repairs

[If a defense to payment of rent or damages is based on claim of retaliatory eviction, then either party may ask any applicable question in this section. Additional questions in section 75.0 may also be applicable.]

☐ 80.1 Does defendant claim to have deducted from rent any amount which was withheld to make repairs after communication to the **LANDLORD** of the need for the repairs? If the answer is "no", do not answer interrogatories 80.2 through 80.6.

☐ 80.2 For each condition in need of repair for which a deduction was made, state:
(a) the nature of the condition;
(b) the location;
(c) the date the condition was discovered by defendant;
(d) the date the condition was first known by **LANDLORD** or **PLAINTIFF**;

(e) the dates and methods of each notice to the **LANDLORD** or **PLAINTIFF** of the condition;
(f) the response or action taken by the **LANDLORD** or **PLAINTIFF** to each notification;
(g) the cost to remedy the condition and how the cost was determined;
(h) the identity of any bids obtained for the repairs and any **DOCUMENTS** evidencing the bids.

☐ 80.3 Did **LANDLORD** or **PLAINTIFF** fail to respond within a reasonable time after receiving a communication of a need for repair? If so, for each communication state:
(a) the date it was made;
(b) how it was made;
(c) the response and date;
(d) why the delay was unreasonable.

☐ 80.4 Was there an insufficient period specified or actually allowed between the time of notification and the time repairs were begun by defendant to allow **LANDLORD** or **PLAINTIFF** to make the repairs? If so, state all facts on which the claim of insufficiency is based.

☐ 80.5 Does **PLAINTIFF** contend that any of the items for which rent deductions were taken were not allowable under law? If so, for each item state all reasons and facts on which you base your contention.

☐ 80.6 Has defendant vacated or does defendant anticipate vacating the **RENTAL UNIT** because repairs were requested and not made within a reasonable time? If so, state all facts on which defendant justifies having vacated the RENTAL UNIT or anticipates vacating the rental unit.

81.0 Fair Market Rental Value

*[If defendant denies **PLAINTIFF** allegation on the fair market rental value of the **RENTAL UNIT**, then either party may ask any applicable question in this section. If defendant claims that the fair market rental value is less because of a breach of warranty to provide habitable premises, then either party may also ask any applicable question in section 75.0.]*

☐ 81.1 Do you have an opinion on the fair market rental value of the **RENTAL UNIT**? If so, state:
(a) the substance of your opinion;
(b) the factors upon which the fair market rental value is based;
(c) the method used to calculate the fair market rental value.

☐ 81.2 Has any other **PERSON** ever expressed to you an opinion on the fair market rental value of the **RENTAL UNIT**? If so, for each **PERSON**:
(a) state the name, **ADDRESS**, and telephone number;
(b) state the substance of the **PERSON'S** opinion;
(c) describe the conversation or identify all **DOCUMENTS** in which the **PERSON** expressed an opinion and state the name, **ADDRESS**, and telephone number of each **PERSON** who has each **DOCUMENT**.

☐ 81.3 Do you know of any current violations of state or local building codes, housing codes, or health codes, conditions of delapidation or other conditions in need of repair in the **RENTAL UNIT** or common areas that have affected the **RENTAL UNIT** at any time defendant has been in possession? If so, state:
(a) the conditions in need of repair;
(b) the kind of repairs needed;
(c) the name, ADDRESS, and telephone number of each PERSON who caused these conditions.

SETTLEMENT AGREEMENT

1. _____ ("tenant")

resides at the following premises: _____

_____ ("premises").

2. _____ ("landlord")

is the owner of the premises.

3. On _____ , 20_____ landlord caused a Summons and Complaint

in unlawful detainer to be served on tenant. The complaint was filed in the Superior Court for the County of

_____ , _____ District, and carries

the following civil number:_____ .

4. Landlord and tenant agree that tenant shall vacate the premises on or before _____ ,

20_____ . In exchange for this agreement, and upon full performance by tenant, landlord agrees to file a voluntary

dismissal with prejudice of the Complaint specified in clause #3.

5. Also in exchange for tenant's agreement to vacate the premises on or before the date specified in clause #4,

landlord agrees to:

(Choose one or more of the following)

☐ Forgive all past due rent

☐ Forgive past due rent in the following amount: $_____

☐ Pay the tenant $_____ to cover tenant's moving expenses, new deposit requirements, and

other incidentals related to the tenant moving out.

6. Any sum specified in clause #5 to be paid by the landlord shall be paid as follows:

(Choose one or more of the following)

☐ Upon tenant surrendering the keys to the premises

☐ Upon the signing of this agreement

☐ $_____ upon the signing of this agreement and $_____ upon tenant

surrendering the keys

☐ in the following manner: _____

7. The tenant's security deposit being held by landlord shall be handled as follows:

☐ restored in full to the tenant upon surrender of the keys

☐ treated according to law

☐ other: _____

_____

8. Subject to the terms and conditions set forth in this agreement, tenant and landlord agree to waive and release all claims, rights, and causes of action against the other arising out of tenant's occupancy of the premises. This waiver extends to each party hereto, their agents, employees, successors, and assigns.

9. That this settlement agreement shall not be construed as reflecting on the merits of the dispute.

10. Landlord agrees not to make any negative representations to any credit reporting agency or to any other person or entity seeking information about the tenant's tenancy at the premises.

11. Time is of the essence in this agreement. If tenant fails to timely vacate the premises in accordance with this agreement, landlord may, upon 24 hours' notice, apply for an ex parte judgment for possession of the premises.

12. This agreement was executed on _____, _____ at _____.

Signed: _____

_____

Signed: _____

_____

```
 1
 2
 3
 4    Defendant in Pro Per
 5
 6
 7
 8    SUPERIOR COURT OF THE STATE OF CALIFORNIA, COUNTY OF _____
 9    _____ DIVISION/BRANCH
10                                              )
                                                )
11    _____ , )      Case No._____
                                                )
12    _____ , )
              Plaintiff(s),               )      DEMAND FOR JURY TRIAL
                                          )
13    v.                                  )
                                          )
14    _____ , )
                                          )
15    _____ , )
              Defendant(s).               )
16    _____ )
17
18        To the clerk of the above-entitled court:
19        Defendant(s) hereby demand a jury trial in this action.
20
21    Dated: _____    _____
22
23
24
25
26
27
28
```

1

2

3 Defendant in Pro Per

4

5

6

7 SUPERIOR COURT OF THE STATE OF CALIFORNIA, COUNTY OF _____

8 _____ DIVISION/BRANCH

9   )
) Case No._____
10 _____ ,)
)
11 _____ ,)
              Plaintiff(s),   ) APPLICATION AND DECLARATION
)
12 v.   ) FOR RELIEF FROM EVICTION
)
13 _____ ,)
)
14 _____ ,)
              Defendant(s).   ) (Code of Civil Procedure Secs. 1174(c), 1179)
15 _____)

16

17   Defendant(s) _____

18 _____ ,

19 hereby apply for relief from eviction, after judgment for plaintiff in this action.

20   If Defendants are evicted, they will suffer undue hardship in the following way(s): _____

21 _____

22 _____ .

23   Plaintiff will not be substantially prejudiced if relief is granted.

24   Defendants are willing and able to pay all money they presently owe to Plaintiff, as a condition to this

25 application being granted. Defendants are also willing and able to pay the rent as it comes due in the future.

26   I declare under penalty of perjury under the laws of the State of California that the above statements are true

27 and correct.

28   Dated: _____   _____

1

2

3

4 Defendant in Pro Per

5

6

7 SUPERIOR COURT OF THE STATE OF CALIFORNIA, COUNTY OF _____

8 _____ DIVISION/BRANCH

9

)
10 _____ ,) Case No._____
)
11 _____ ,)
           Plaintiff(s),   ) NOTICE OF MOTION AND POINTS
)
12   v.   ) AND AUTHORITIES FOR
)
13 _____ ,) RELIEF FROM EVICTION
)
14 _____ ,)
           Defendant(s).   ) (Code of Civil Procedure Sec. 1179)
)
15 _____)

16

17 TO PLAINTIFF AND ITS ATTORNEYS OF RECORD:

18   NOTICE IS HEREBY GIVEN that on _____ or as soon thereafter as may be heard in

19 the Law and Motion department of the above entitled court located at _____ ,

20 Courtroom _____, Defendant _____ will move the court for an order relieving

21 it from the forfeiture of its ten-year lease, said forfeiture resulting from a failure to pay one month's rent within the

22 three days requested in the Three-Day Notice to Pay Rent or Quit. In exchange for such relief, Defendant will make full

23 compensation to Plaintiff. This motion is brought under Code of Civil Procedure § 1179 on the grounds that Defendant

24 will suffer extreme hardship should the requested relief not be granted.

25

26

27

28

1   This motion will be based on this Notice of Motion, the Memorandum of Points and Authorities attached

2   hereto, the Declarations of _____ , and on all other such oral and documentary

3   evidence and argument as may be presented at the hearing on said motion.

4   Dated: _____   _____

5   Defendant In Pro Per

6

7   MEMORANDUM OF POINTS AND AUTHORITIES

8   Defendant is seeking relief from forfeiture under Code of Civil Procedure Section 1179.

9   This section reads as follows:

10   The court may relieve a tenant against a forfeiture of a lease or rental agreement, whether

11   written or oral, and whether or not the tenancy has terminated, and restore him or her to his or

        her former estate or tenancy, in case of hardship, as provided in Section 1174. The court has the

12   discretion to relieve any person against forfeiture on its own motion.

13   An application for relief against forfeiture may be made at any time prior to restoration of the

14   premises to the landlord. The application may be made by a tenant or subtenant, or a mortgagee

        of the term, or any person interested in the continuance of the term. It must be made upon

15   petition, setting forth the facts upon which the relief is sought, and be verified by the applicant.

16   Notice of the application, with a copy of the petition, must be served at least five days prior

        to the hearing on the plaintiff in the judgment, who may appear and contest the application.

17   Alternatively, a person appearing without an attorney may make the application orally, if the

18   plaintiff either is present and has an opportunity to contest the application, or has been given ex

19   parte notice of the hearing and the purpose of the oral application. In no case shall the application

        or motion be granted except on condition that full payment of rent due, or full performance of

20   conditions or covenants stipulated, so far as the same is practicable, be made.

21

22 This Statute is specific to unlawful detainer actions and vests the court with equitable power to relieve a tenant

23 from forfeiture and restore him or her to his or her former estate or tenancy; so long as court imposes statutory

24 conditions, full payment of rent due. *Gill Petroleum, Inc. v. Hayer*, 137 Cal.App.4th 826, 832, 833 (2006). In

25 considering this relief, courts will balance the hardship to the tenant against the prejudice (if any) to the landlord

26 if relief is granted. In doing so, the court looks at all the underlying facts, including the nature of the underlying

27 reasons for eviction, whether or not the tenant's actions were willful, or in bad faith, and whether the landlord's

28 actions were in good or bad faith. *Thrifty Oil v. Batarse*, 174 Cal.App.3d 770 (1985).

1 In this case, _____ ,

2 _____ ,

3 _____ ,

4 _____ ,

5 _____ ,

6 _____ ,

7 _____ ,

8 _____ ,

9 _____ ,

10 _____ ,

11 _____ ,

12 _____ ,

13 Defendant will suffer extreme hardship because _____ ,

14 _____ ,

15 _____ ,

16 Defendant is willing to pay all the rent that is due to the plaintiff.

17   Plaintiff will not be substantially prejudiced if the relief requested is granted.

18

19 Dated: _____   _____

20   Defendant In Pro Per

21

22

23

24

25

26

27

28

```
 1   Name:
     Address:
 2
     Phone:
 3

 4   Defendant in Pro Per

 5

 6

 7

 8        SUPERIOR COURT OF THE STATE OF CALIFORNIA, COUNTY OF _____

 9        _____ DIVISION/BRANCH

10                                                    )
                                                      )
     _____ , )   Case No._____
11                                                    )
     _____ , )
12              Plaintiff(s),                         )   ORDER GRANTING RELIEF
                                                      )
13   v.                                               )   FROM EVICTION
                                                      )
14   _____ , )
                                                      )
15   _____ , )
                Defendant(s).                         )
16   _____ )

17

18        Defendant's motion for Relief From Eviction came on for hearing in Department _____ of the

19   above-entitled Court on _____ , _____ , said defendant appearing in

20   pro per and Plaintiff(s) appearing by _____ .

21   The matter having been argued and submitted,

22        IT IS HEREBY ORDERED that Defendant's Application for Relief From Eviction is granted at the following date

23   and time: _____ .

24

25   Dated: _____        _____
                                             Judge of the Superior Court
26

27

28
```

1

2

3

4   Defendant in Pro Per

5

6

7

8   SUPERIOR COURT OF THE STATE OF CALIFORNIA, COUNTY OF _____

9   _____ DIVISION/BRANCH

10   )
)
11   _____ ,)   Case No._____
)
12   _____ ,)
              Plaintiff(s),   )   APPLICATION AND DECLARATION
)
13   v.   )   FOR STAY OF EVICTION
)
14   _____ ,)
)
15   _____ ,)
              Defendant(s).   )
16   _____)

17

18   Defendant(s) _____

19   _____ hereby apply

20   for stay of execution from any writ of restitution or possession in this case, for the following period of time:

21   _____ .

22   Such a stay is appropriate in this case for the following reason(s): _____

23   _____

24   _____ .

25   I declare under penalty of perjury under the laws of the State of California that the above statements are true

26   and correct.

27

28   Dated: _____

1   Name:
       Address:

2

       Phone:

3

4   Defendant in Pro Per

5

6

7

8   SUPERIOR COURT OF THE STATE OF CALIFORNIA, COUNTY OF _____

9   _____ DIVISION/BRANCH

10   )

11   _____ ,)   Case No._____
)

12   _____ ,)
          Plaintiff(s),   )   ORDER GRANTING STAY OF EVICTION

13   v.   )

14   _____ ,)

15   _____ ,)
          Defendant(s).   )

16   _____)

17

18   Defendant's motion for Stay of Eviction came on for hearing in Department _____ of the above-

19   entitled Court on _____ , _____ , said defendant appearing in pro per

20   and Plaintiff(s) appearing by_____ .

21   The matter having been argued and submitted,

22   IT IS HEREBY ORDERED that Defendant's Application for Stay of Eviction is granted.

23

24   Dated: _____   _____

25   Judge of the Superior Court

26

27

28

Defendant in Pro Per

SUPERIOR COURT OF THE STATE OF CALIFORNIA, COUNTY OF _____

_____ DIVISION/BRANCH

_____,)	Case No._____
_____,)	
Plaintiff(s),)	NOTICE OF APPEAL AND NOTICE
v.)	TO PREPARE CLERK'S TRANSCRIPT
_____,)	
_____,)	
Defendant(s).)	
_____)	

Defendant(s) _____

_____ hereby appeal to the Appellate Department

of the Superior Court.

Defendant(s) hereby request that a Clerk's Transcript be prepared, and that this transcript include all

documents filed in this action and all minute orders and other rulings and judgments issued by the court in this

action.

Dated: _____   _____

CLAIMANT OR CLAIMANT'S ATTORNEY *(Name and Address)*: TELEPHONE NO.:	*FOR COURT USE ONLY*

ATTORNEY FOR *(Name)*:

NAME OF COURT:

  STREET ADDRESS:

  MAILING ADDRESS:

CITY AND ZIP CODE:

   BRANCH NAME:

    CASE NUMBER:

  Plaintiff:

Defendant:

(For levying officer use only)

Completed form was received on

Date: _____ Time: _____

By: _____

CLAIM OF RIGHT TO POSSESSION
AND NOTICE OF HEARING

Complete this form only if ALL of these statements are true:

1. You are NOT named in the accompanying form called *Writ of Possession.*
2. You occupied the premises on or before the date the unlawful detainer (eviction) action was filed. *(The date is in the accompanying Writ of Possession.)*
3. You still occupy the premises.
4. A *Prejudgment Claim of Right to Possession* form was NOT served with the *Summons and Complaint,* OR this eviction results from a foreclosure.

NOTICE: If you are being evicted because of foreclosure, you have additional rights and should seek legal assistance immediately.

I DECLARE THE FOLLOWING UNDER PENALTY OF PERJURY:

1. My name is *(specify):*

2. I reside at *(street address, unit no., city and ZIP code):*

3. The address of "the premises" subject to this claim is *(address):*

☐   Check here if this property was foreclosed on.

4. On *(insert date):*   , the owner, landlord, or the landlord's authorized agent filed a complaint to recover possession of the premises. *(This date is in the accompanying Writ of Possession.)*

5. I occupied the premises on the date the complaint was filed *(the date in item 4).* I have continued to occupy the premises ever since.

6. I was at least 18 years of age on the date the complaint was filed *(the date in item 4).*

7. I claim a right to possession of the premises because I occupied the premises on the date the complaint was filed *(the date in item 4).*

8. I was not named in the *Writ of Possession.*

9. I understand that if I make this claim of possession, a court hearing will be held to decide whether my claim will be granted.

10. *(Filing fee)* To obtain a court hearing on my claim, I understand that after I present this form to the levying officer I must go to the court and pay a filing fee of $ or file with the court *"Application for Waiver of Court Fees and Costs."* I understand that if I don't pay the filing fee or file the form for waiver of court fees within 2 court days, the court will immediately deny my claim.

11. *(Immediate court hearing unless you deposit 15 days' rent)* To obtain a court hearing on my claim, I understand I must also present a copy of this completed complaint form or a receipt from the levying officer. I also understand the date of my hearing will be set immediately if I do not deliver to the court an amount equal to 15 days' rent.

(Continued on reverse)

       CLAIM OF RIGHT TO POSSESSION
AND NOTICE OF HEARING   Code of Civil Procedure, §§ 715.010, 715.020, 1174.3

Plaintiff:	CASE NUMBER:
Defendant:	

12. I am filing my claim in the following manner *(check the box that shows how you are filing your claim. Note that you must deliver to the court a copy of the claim form or a levying officer's receipt):*

a. ☐ I presented this claim form to the sheriff, marshal, or other levying officer, AND within two court days I shall deliver to the court the following: (1) a copy of this completed claim form or a receipt, (2) the court filing fee or form for proceeding in forma pauperis, and (3) an amount equal to 15 days' rent; or

b. ☐ I presented this claim form to the sheriff, marshal, or other levying officer, AND within two court days I shall deliver to the court (1) a copy of this completed claim form or a receipt, and (2) the court filing fee or form for proceeding in forma pauperis.

IMPORTANT: Do not take a copy of this claim form to the court unless you have first given the form to the sheriff, marshal, or other levying officer.

(To be completed by the court)

Date of hearing:	Time:	Dept. or Div.:	Room:
Address of court:			

NOTICE: If you fail to appear at this hearing you will be evicted without further hearing.

13. **Rental agreement.** I have *(check all that apply to you)*:

a. ☐ an oral rental agreement with the landlord.

b. ☐ a written rental agreement with the landlord.

c. ☐ an oral rental agreement with a person other than the landlord.

d. ☐ a written rental agreement with a person other than the landlord.

e. ☐ a rental agreement with the former owner who lost the property through foreclosure.

f. ☐ other *(explain):*

I declare under penalty of perjury under the laws of the State of California that the foregoing is true and correct.

WARNING: Perjury is a felony punishable by imprisonment in the state prison.

Date:

▶

_____   _____
(TYPE OR PRINT NAME)   (SIGNATURE OF CLAIMANT)

NOTICE: If your claim to possession is found to be valid, the unlawful detainer action against you will be determined at trial. At trial, you may be found liable for rent, costs, and, in some cases, treble damages.

— NOTICE TO OCCUPANTS —

YOU MUST ACT AT ONCE if all the following are true:

1. **You are NOT named, in the accompanying form called Writ of Possession;**

2. **You occupied the premises on or before the date the unlawful detainer (eviction) action was filed;** *and*

3. **You still occupy the premises.**

4. **A Prejudgment Claim of Right to Possession form was NOT served with the Summons and Complaint, OR you are being evicted due to foreclosure.**

   You can complete and SUBMIT THIS CLAIM FORM

   (1) Before the date of eviction at the sheriff's or marshal's office located at *(address):*

   (2) OR at the premises at the time of the eviction. *(Give this form to the officer who comes to evict you.)*

If you do not complete and submit this form (and pay a filing fee or file the form for proceeding in forma pauperis if you cannot pay the fee), YOU WILL BE EVICTED along with the parties named in the writ.

After this form is properly filed, A HEARING WILL BE HELD to decide your claim. If you do not appear at the hearing, you will be evicted without a further hearing.

CLAIM OF RIGHT TO POSSESSION
AND NOTICE OF HEARING

Index

R

NOLO *Save 15%* off your next order

Register your Nolo purchase, and we'll send you a **coupon for 15% off** your next Nolo.com order!

Nolo.com/customer-support/productregistration

On Nolo.com you'll also find:

Books & Software
Nolo publishes hundreds of great books and software programs for consumers and business owners. Order a copy, or download an ebook version instantly, at Nolo.com.

Online Forms
You can quickly and easily make a will or living trust, form an LLC or corporation, apply for a provisional patent, or make hundreds of other forms—online.

Free Legal Information
Thousands of articles answer common questions about everyday legal issues, including wills, bankruptcy, small business formation, divorce, patents, employment, and much more.

Plain-English Legal Dictionary
Stumped by jargon? Look it up in America's most up-to-date source for definitions of legal terms, free at Nolo.com.

Lawyer Directory
Nolo's consumer-friendly lawyer directory provides in-depth profiles of lawyers all over America. You'll find information you need to choose the right lawyer.